A SELECTION OF CASES

UNDER THE

INTERSTATE COMMERCE ACT

EDITED BY

FELIX FRANKFURTER

BYRNE PROFESSOR OF ADMINISTRATIVE LAW IN HARVARD UNIVERSITY

> In the law we only occasionally can reach an absolutely final and quantitative determination, because the worth of the competing social ends which respectively solicit a judgment for the plaintiff or the defendant cannot be reduced to number and accurately fixed. The worth, that is, the intensity of the competing desires, varies with the various ideals of the time, and, if the desires were constant, we could not get beyond a relative decision that one was greater and one was less. But it is of the essence of improvement that we should be as accurate as we can.
>
> MR. JUSTICE HOLMES.

SECOND EDITION

CAMBRIDGE
HARVARD UNIVERSITY PRESS
1922

THE PLIMPTON PRESS
NORWOOD · MASS · U · S · A

NOTE TO SECOND EDITION

According to authoritative estimates the volume of interstate traffic in the United States is about three-fourths of the whole. This means that three-quarters of the country's transportation business, — not to mention other vast interstate utilities, such as the telegraph, the express service, the pipe lines, — are subject to the control of governmental regulation. Ample *a priori* justification would thus exist for systematic study, according to proved methods of legal education, of that body of law through which this governmental control is exercised. Such justification has been confirmed by eight years of experience, at the Harvard Law School and elsewhere throughout the country, in including in their curricula the body of law consisting of the successive Interstate Commerce Acts and their interpretative enforcement by the Interstate Commerce Commission and Courts, to which the Railroad Labor Board has now been added.

Many modifications and additions to this body of law — adjudications involving old legislation, and new legislation which extends the scope as well as the details of Federal regulation — have called for this revision of the original selection of cases. The new edition follows the original outline because the basic elements of the body of law under consideration, as seen in 1914, have not been fundamentally altered in the interval. The successive Acts regulating Interstate Commerce have for a period of thirty-five years — barring the brief intermission of Federal Railroad Administration, born of the War and only shortly surviving it — followed a coherent and progressive evolution. With all its changes and extensions, the Transportation Act of 1920 is only the last in a series of consistently developing statutes. The major lines of chief concern to lawyers — the jurisdiction and procedure of the Interstate Commerce Commission, the legal relation between Commission and Courts — are substantially maintained. Some of the chief issues raised by the new Act have already received judicial settlement. Questions still open, or that will be opened from time to time, will, it may be confidently suggested, find their answers through, and as a part of, a coherent body of living law.

I am greatly obliged to Professor Homer B. Vanderblue of the School of Commerce, Northwestern University, for generous help in suggesting rate cases before the Interstate Commerce Commission (Chap. III, *infra*) found especially useful by him.

It needs hardly to be added that in the use of this collection of cases an indispensable complement is the compilation of the Interstate Commerce Acts, published by the Government.

F. F.

HARVARD LAW SCHOOL,
September, 1922.

NOTE TO FIRST EDITION

THE original Interstate Commerce Act has now been on the statute books for twenty-eight years. Since then, by successive amendments, the scope of the Act has been greatly extended, both as to the kinds of the utilities affected and as to the extent of the regulation of their business. As a result, the vast and increasing volume of utility enterprise which transcends the confines of a single state, (and even intrastate business which is inseparably connected with or affects interstate commerce), is now governed by a single act and is primarily enforced by a single tribunal. The real scope and meaning of the Act must be sought in a mass of decisions through which there is gradually emerging a body of principles. The intrinsic importance of the subject, the part it plays, and the greater part it is likely to play, in the work of the modern lawyer, calls for the training of men equipped to participate in its enforcement as lawyers, administrators, and judges. In other words, the subject calls for organized, systematic study as one of the most vital branches of the law. Such study is the more imperative now that the Interstate Commerce Act and the experience of its enforcement have, *mutatis mutandis,* served as the basis for the far-reaching regulation of interstate industrial business embodied in the Federal Trade Commission Act of September 26, 1914, as well as for the regulation of state utilities, through the more recent state utility commission statutes. The present selection of cases has been prepared for use in the Harvard Law School.

The generous co-operation of Mr. Max Lowenthal of the New York Bar has made this collection possible at this time.

F. F.

CAMBRIDGE, January, 1915

TABLE OF CONTENTS

CHAPTER PAGE

I. SCOPE OF COMMERCE REGULATED BY THE ACT 1
1. *Kinds of Carriers* 1
2. *Kinds of Commerce* 23
3. *"Railroad" and "Transportation"* 160

II. DUTIES OF CARRIER UNDER THE ACT 212
1. *Services to be Rendered* 212
2. *Equality of Service* 259
3. *Maintenance of Competition* 322

III. FUNCTIONS OF THE INTERSTATE COMMERCE COMMISSION IN THE ENFORCEMENT OF THE ACT 340
1. *Constitutionality* 340
2. *Powers and Duties* 344

IV. FUNCTION OF COURTS IN THE ENFORCEMENT OF THE ACT . . . 635
1. *Primary Jurisdiction of the Commission* 635
2. *Judicial Review* 660
3. *Proceedings for Enforcement* 723

APPENDIX 761

LIST OF CASES

PAGE

Arlington Heights Fruit Exchange *v.* Southern Pacific Co. (22 I. C. C. 149, 1911) .. 430
Armour Packing Co. *v.* United States (209 U. S. 56, 1908) .. 101
Atchison, Topeka & Santa Fe Ry. Co. *v.* United States (232 U. S. 199, 1914) 181
Atchison, Topeka & Santa Fe Railway Co. *v.* Harold (241 U. S. 371, 1916) 34

Bluefield Shippers Association *v.* N. & W. Ry. Co. (22 I. C. C. 519, 1912) 441
Brotherhood of Locomotive Engineers *et al.* *v.* Eastern Railroad & Power Co. *et al.* (Decision No. 33, 1 Dec. U. S. R. R. Labor Board, 53, 1920) 6
Burnham, Hanna, Munger Drygoods Co. *v.* Chicago, Rock Island & Pacific Co. (14 I. C. C. 299, 1908) 372

Chicago Junction Ry. Co. *v.* United States (226 U. S. 286, 1912) 113
Chicago, Milwaukee & St. Paul R. R. Co. *v.* McCall-Dinsmore Co. (253 U. S. 97, 1920) 661
Class and Commodity Rates to Salt Lake City (32 I. C. C. 551, 1915) 388
Consolidated Classification Cases (54 I. C. C. 1, 1919) .. 344
Crane Iron Works *v.* United States (Interstate Commerce Commission *et al.* Interveners) (209 Fed. Rep. 238, 1912) 134
Cudahy Packing Co. *v.* Grand Trunk Western Ry. Co. (215 Fed. Rep. 93, 1914) 315
Cudahy Packing Co. *v.* United States (209 U. S. 56, 1908) .. 101

PAGE

Director General of Railroads *et al.* *v.* The Viscose Co. (254 U. S. 498, 1921) 656

Ellis *v.* Interstate Commerce Commission (237 U. S. 434, 1915) 738
Erie Ry. Co. *v.* Shuart *et al.* (250 U. S. 465, 1919) 167

Florida East Coast Ry. Co. *v.* United States (234 U. S. 267, 1914) 681

Galveston, Harrisburg & San Antonio Ry. Co. *v.* Woodbury *et al.* (254 U. S. 357, 1920) 104
Georgia, Florida & Alabama Ry. Co. *v.* Blish Milling Co. (241 U. S. 190, 1916) 225
Great Northern Ry. Co. *v.* Merchants Elevator Co. (259 U. S., 1922) 783

Houston, East and West Texas Railway Co. *v.* United States (234 U. S. 342, 1914) 69

Illinois Central Ry. Co. *v.* Railroad Commission of Louisiana (236 U. S. 157, 1915) ... 160
Illinois Central Ry. Co. *v.* State Public Utilities Commission of Illinois *et al.* (245 U. S. 493, 1918) 81
Increased Rates (58 I. C. C. 220, 1920) 515
In re Investigation of Advances in Rates, etc. (20 I. C. C. 307, 1911) 470
Intermountain Rate Cases (234 U. S. 476, 1914) 576
Interstate Commerce Commission *v.* Baird (194 U. S. 25, 1904) 723

PAGE

Interstate Commerce Commission v. Louisville & Nashville Ry. Co. (227 U. S. 88, 1913). 663
Interstate Commerce Commission v. Illinois Central Ry. Co. (215 U. S. 452, 1910) .. 660
Interstate Commerce Commission v. Brimson (154 U. S. 447, 1894) 340
Interstate Commerce Commission v. Baltimore & Ohio Ry. Co. (145 U. S. 263, 1892) ... 297
Interstate Commerce Commission v. Chesapeake & Ohio Ry. Co. (200 U. S. 361, 1906) 280
Interstate Commerce Commission v. Alabama Midland Ry. Co. (168 U. S. 144, 1897) 264
Interstate Commerce Commission v. Illinois Central Ry. Co. (215 U. S. 452, 1910) ... 189
Interstate Commerce Commission v. Diffenbaugh (222 U. S. 42, 1911) 173
Interstate Commerce Commission v. U. S. of America *ex rel.* Humboldt Steamship Co. (224 U. S. 474, 1912) 106
Interstate Commerce Commission v. Goodrich Transit Co. (224 U. S. 194, 1912) 90

Knapp v. Lake Shore & Michigan Southern Ry. Co. (197 U. S. 536, 1905) 729

Lehigh Coal & Navigation Co. v. United States (250 U. S. 566, 1919) 753
Lehigh Valley Ry. Co. v. United States (213 U. S. 444, 1917). 179
Louisville & Nashville Ry. Co. v. Ohio Valley Tie Co. (242 U. S. 288, 1915) 741
Louisiana and Pine Bluff Ry. Co. v. United States (257 U. S., 1921) 707
Louisville & Nashville Ry. Co. *et al.* v. United States *et al.* (242 U. S. 60, 1916) 212

Morris & Co. v. United States (209 U. S. 56, 1908) 101
Murfreesboro Board of Trade v. Louisville & Nashville Ry. Co. (55 I. C. C. 648, 1919) .. 461

PAGE

New York Central & Hudson River Ry. Co. v. Board of Chosen Freeholders of the County of Hudson (227 U. S. 248, 1913) 204
New York, New Haven and Hartford Ry. Co. v. Interstate Commerce Commission (200 U. S. 361, 1906) 280
North Iowa Traffic Association v. Director General (58 I.C.C. 491, 1920) 363
Norfolk and Western Ry. Co. v. Dixie Tobacco Co. (228 U. S. 593, 1913) 223
Northern Pacific Ry. Co. v. Solum (247 U. S. 477, 1918). 248

Omaha & Council Bluffs Street Railway v. Interstate Commerce Commission (230 U. S. 324, 1913) 1

Pennsylvania Railroad Co. v. Clark Brothers Coal Mining Co. (238 U. S. 456, 1915) ... 23
Pennsylvania Ry. Co. v. Steinman Coal Mining Co. (242 U. S. 298, 1916) 653
Pennsylvania Ry. Co. v. Sonman Shaft Coal Co. (242 U. S. 120, 1916) 648
Proctor & Gamble Co. v. U. S. of America, Interstate Commerce Commission, Cincinnati, Hamilton & Dayton Ry. Co. *et al.* (255 U. S. 282, 1912 709
Pere Marquette Ry. Co. v. J. F. French & Co. (254 U. S. 538, 1921) 252
Pittsburgh, Cincinnati, Chicago & St. Louis Ry. Co. v. Fink (250 U. S. 577, 1919) 306

Railroad Commission of Nevada v. Southern Pacific Co. (19 I. C. C. 238, 1910) 409
Railroad Commission of Wisconsin *et al.* v. Chicago Burlington & Quincy Ry. Co. (257 U. S., 1922) 761

Seaboard Air Line Ry. Co. *et al.* v. United States *et al.* (254 U. S. 57, 1920) 703

PAGE

Seaboard Air Line Ry. Co. *et al.* *v.* United States *et al.* (254 U. S., 57, 1920) 271

Shanks *v.* Delaware, Lackawanna and Western Railroad Co. (239 U. S. 556, 1916) .. 31

South Bend Chamber of Commerce *v.* Director General (57 I. C. C. 215, 1920) 356

Southern Pacific Terminal Co. *v.* Interstate Commerce Commission and Young (219 U. S. 498, 1911) 141

Southern Pacific Co. *v.* Interstate Commerce Commission (200 U. S. 536, 1906) 242

Southern Pacific Co. *v.* Interstate Commerce Commission (200 U. S. 536, 1906) 322

Southern Pacific Co. *et al.* *v.* Darnell-Taenzer Lumber Co. *et al.* (245 U. S. 531, 1918) .. 744

Spiller *v.* Atchison, Topeka & Santa Fe Ry. Co. *et al.* (253 U. S. 117, 1920) 671

State of New York and Charles D. Newton, personally and as Attorney General of the State of New York, Appellants *v.* The U. S. and Edgar E. Clark, *et al.* (25 U. S., 1922). 773

Swift & Co. *v.* Hocking Valley Ry. Co. (243 U. S. 281, 1917) 198

Swift & Co. *v.* United States (209 U. S. 56, 1908) 101

Tap Line Cases (234 U. S., 1914) 122

Texas & Pacific Ry. Co. *v.* Abilene Cotton Oil Co. (204 U. S. 426, 1907) 635

Texas and Pacific Ry. Co. *v.* United States (234 U. S. 342, 1914) 69

Texas Common Point Case (26 I. C. C. 528, 1913) 397

The Los Angeles Switching Case (234 U. S. 294, 1914) 693

The Central Rd. Co. of New Jersey *et al.* *v.* The United States *et al.* (257 U. S., 1921) 275

The Fifteen per cent Case (45 I. C. C. 303, 1917) 485

The Minnesota Rate Cases (230 U. S. 352, 1913) 39

PAGE

The Pipe Line Cases (234 U. S. 548, 1914) 18

The State of Texas, Appellant, *v.* Eastern Texas Ry. Co., *et al.* The State of Texas *et al.*, Appellants *v.* The United States (258 U. S., 1922) 777

The Vicksburg, Shreveport & Pacific Ry. Co. *et al.* *v.* Anderson-Tully Co. (256 U. S. 408, 1921) 746

United States *v.* Adams Express Co. (229 U. S. 381, 1913) ... 139

United States of America, upon the Application of the Attorney General *v.* Union Stockyard Co. of Chicago (226 U. S. 286, 1912) 295

United States *v.* Brooklyn Eastern District Terminal (249 U. S. 296, 1919) 153

United States *v.* Delaware, Lackawanna & Western Ry. Co. (238 U. S. 516, 1915) ... 326

United States *v.* Erie Ry. Co. (236 U. S. 259, 1915) 318

United States *v.* Northern Pacific Ry. Co. (242 U. S. 190, 1916) 750

United States at the Relation of Kansas City Southern Ry. Co. *v.* Interstate Commerce Commission (252 U. S. 178, 1920) 732

U. S. of America *v.* Union Stock Yard & Transit Co. of Chicago (226 U. S. 286, 1912) 113

United States *v.* White Star Line (224 U. S. 194, 1912) .. 90

Vandalia Ry. Co. *v.* United States (226 Fed. 713, 1915). 309

Wells Fargo & Co. *v.* Taylor (254 U. S. 175, 1920) 13

Western Transit Co. *v.* A. C. Leslie & Co., Limited (242 U. S. 448, 1917) 230

Western Transit Co. *v.* Leslie Co. (242 U. S. 448, 1917) ... 163

Western Union Tel. Co., Petitioner, *v.* Esteve Brothers & Co. (256 U. S., 1921) 234

PAGE

Whitaker-Glessner Co. *v.* Baltimore & Ohio R. R. Co. (63 I. C. C. 47, 1921) 562

White *v.* United States (167 U. S. 512, 1897) 259

William Wylie Beall *v.* Wheeling Traction Co. (63 I. C. C. 220, 1921) 557

Young *v.* Interstate Commerce Commission *et al.* (219 U. S. 498, 1911) 141

A SELECTION OF CASES

UNDER THE

INTERSTATE COMMERCE ACT

The Congress shall have Power . . . .

[3] To regulate Commerce with foreign Nations, and among the several States, and with the Indian Tribes; . . . .

. . . . — And

[18] To make all Laws which shall be necessary and proper for carrying into execution the foregoing Powers. . . . .

ARTICLE I, SECTION 8, of the Constitution of the United States.

CHAPTER I

SCOPE OF THE COMMERCE REGULATED BY THE ACT

1. KINDS OF "CARRIERS"

OMAHA & COUNCIL BLUFFS STREET RAILWAY *v.* INTERSTATE COMMERCE COMMISSION

230 U. S. 324 (1913)

MR. JUSTICE LAMAR delivered the opinion of the court.

The Omaha & Council Bluffs Railway & Bridge Company was chartered as a Street Railroad Company under the laws of Iowa. It owned street car lines in Council Bluffs and, in 1887, was authorized by Congress to construct a bridge across the Missouri River and to operate thereon "steam, cable and street cars." (March 3, 1887, 24 Stat. 501, c. 356.) The Omaha & Council Bluffs Railway, chartered as a Street Railroad under the laws of Nebraska, owned the street car lines in Omaha and its suburbs, South Omaha, Benson, Dundee and Florence. This street railroad had no right of eminent domain and was not authorized to haul freight, being limited by its charter to carrying passengers only. By lease it acquired the bridge and car lines in Council Bluffs which thereafter it operated as part of its system. Complaint having been made that certain interstate fares were unreasonable, a hearing was had before the Commerce

Commission, which, on November 27, 1909 (17 I. C. C. 239), ordered a reduction in the rate between Council Bluffs, Iowa, and points beyond the Loop, in Omaha, Nebraska. The two companies, lessor and lessee, thereupon filed a bill in the United States Circuit Court for the District of Nebraska to enjoin the order. The case was heard before three Circuit Judges, who (179 Fed. Rep. 243) granted a temporary injunction.

The case was transferred to the Commerce Court, which, on October 5, 1911, dismissed the bill, 191 Fed. Rep. 40.

On the argument of the appeal in this court, the sole question discussed was whether the provisions of the Commerce Act as to railroads applied to street railroads, the appellant relying, among other things, on the fact that during the discussion in the Senate the author of the bill and Chairman of the Senate Committee to which it had been referred, said (17 Cong. Rec. Pt. IV, p. 3472) "that the Bill is not intended to affect the stage coach, the *street railway*, the telegraph lines, the canal boat, or the vessel employed in the inland or coasting trade, even though they may be engaged in interstate commerce, because it is not deemed necessary or practicable to cover such a multitude of subjects." After quoting § 1 [1] and this statement and construing it in the light of the broad scope of the act, the Commerce Court held that the meaning of the statute could not be determined from statements used in debate. We concur in that view. The act must be interpreted by its own terms, and we must look to it as a whole, in order to determine whether it applies to Street Railroads, carrying passengers between cities divided by a state line.

The statute in terms applies to carriers engaged in the transportation of passengers or property by railroad.

But, in 1887, that word had no fixed and accurate meaning, for there was then, as now, a conflict in the decisions of the state courts as to whether street railroads were embraced within the provisions of a statute giving rights or imposing burdens on railroads. The appellants cite decisions from twelve States holding that in a statute the word "railroad" does not mean "street railroad." The defense cite decisions to the contrary from an equal number of States. The present record discloses a similar disagreement in Federal tribunals. For not only did the Commerce Court and the Circuit Court differ, but it appears that the members of the Commission were divided on the subject

[1] The text of Section 1 of the Interstate Commerce Act set forth in the official report is here omitted. — Ed.

when this case was decided and also when the question was first raised in *Willson* v. *Rock Creek Ry. Co.*, 7 I. C. C. 83.

This conflict is not so great as at first blush would appear. For all recognize that while there is similarity between railroads and street railroads, there is also a difference. Some courts, emphasizing the similarity, hold that in statutes the word "Railroad" includes Street Railroad, unless the contrary is required by the context. Others, emphasizing the dissimilarity, hold that "Railroad" does not include Street Railroad unless required by the context, since, as tersely put by the Court of Appeals of Kentucky, "a street railroad, in a technical and popular sense, is as different from an ordinary railroad as a street is from a road." *Louisville & Portland R. R. Co.* v. *Louisville City Ry. Co.*, 2 Duvall, 175.

But all the decisions hold that the meaning of the word is to be determined by construing the statute as a whole. If the scope of the act is such as to show that both classes of companies were within the legislative contemplation, then the word "Railroad" will include Street Railroad. On the other hand, if the act was aimed at Railroads proper, then Street Railroads are excluded from the provisions of the statute. Applying this universally accepted rule of construing this word, it is to be noted that ordinary railroads are constructed on the companies' own property. The tracks extend from town to town and are usually connected with other railroads, which themselves are further connected with others, so that freight may be shipped, without breaking bulk, across the continent. Such railroads are channels of interstate commerce. Street Railroads, on the other hand, are local, are laid in streets as aids to street traffic, and for the use of a single community, even though that community be divided by state lines, or under different municipal control. When these street railroads carry passengers across a state line they are, of course, engaged in interstate commerce, but not the commerce which Congress had in mind when legislating in 1887. Street railroads transport passengers from street to street, from ward to ward, from city to suburbs, but the commerce to which Congress referred was that carried on by railroads engaged in hauling passengers or freight "between States," "between States and Territories," "between the United States and foreign countries." The act referred to Railroads which were required to post their schedules — not at street corners where passengers board street cars, but in "*every depot, station or office where passengers or freight are received for transportation.*" The railroads referred to in the act were not those having separate, distinct and local street lines, but those of whom it was required that they should make joint rates and reasonable facilities for interchange of traffic with connecting lines, so that freight might be easily and expeditiously moved in interstate commerce.

Every provision of the statute is applicable to railroads. Only a few of its requirements are applicable to street railroads which did not do the business Congress had in contemplation and had not engaged in the pooling, rebating and discrimination which the statute was intended to prohibit. This was recognized in *Willson* v. *Rock Creek Ry. Co.*, 7 I. C. C. 83, where, although it was held that the statute applied to a street railroad between Washington, D. C., and a point in Maryland, the Commission nevertheless said (7 I. C. C. 88): "It may be conceded that this class of railroads was not specifically within the contemplation of the framers of that law, for the evils which it was intended to remedy would, in the nature of the case, but rarely arise in the management of such roads in their dealing with the public."

Street railroads not being guilty of the mischief sought to be corrected, the remedial provisions of the statute not being applicable to them, commands upon every railroad "subject to the act" being such that they could not be obeyed by street railroads because of the nature of their business and character and location of their tracks, it is evident that the case is within that large line of authorities which hold that under such a statute the word "railroad" cannot be construed to include street railroad.

But it is said that since 1887, when the act was passed, a new type of interurban railroad has been developed which, with electricity as a motive power, uses larger cars and runs through the country from town to town, enabling the carrier to haul passengers, freight, express and the mail for long distances at high speed. We are not dealing with such a case, but with a company chartered as a street railroad, doing a street railroad business and hauling no freight. The case was heard on demurrer, with the opinion of the Commission treated as a part of the record. It indicates that at some points the line is on private property, but where this is and to how great an extent does not appear. Indeed, the record does not show that electricity was used as a motive power, though, in the light of modern methods, that may possibly be assumed. But it affirmatively appears that the company was chartered as a street railroad, and hauls no freight and is doing only a business appropriate to a street railroad. So that whatever the motive power or the size or speed of the cars is immaterial. In any event, there were "street cars" referred to in the act of Congress authorizing the construction of the Bridge from Council Bluffs to Omaha (24 Stat. 501). The company used such cars and did a street passenger business only. It laid its tracks in crowded thoroughfares of those cities and their suburbs and it is manifest that Congress did not intend that these tracks should be connected with Railroads for hauling freight cars and long trains through and along the streets of Omaha and Council Bluffs.

It is contended, however, that the amendment of June 18, 1910, 36 Stat. 539, 553, c. 309, shows that Congress considered that street railroads were under the jurisdiction of the Commission inasmuch as it then provided that "the Commission shall not establish any through route, classification or rate between street electric passenger railways not engaged in . . . transporting freight . . . and railroads of a different character." It is contended on the other hand that in that statute Congress distinctly recognized that a street electric road was "a different character of railroad," and apprehending that the broad language of the amendment of 1910 might be construed to take in street railroads, this provision was inserted out of abundant caution to prevent that result, as in the case of establishing routes wholly by water, which certainly were not within the terms of the original Act.

This section of the act of 1910, however, having been passed after the order was made by the Commission, Nov. 27, 1909, is not before us for construction and, manifestly, cannot be given a retrospective operation, though the Government insists that it should be given a prospective operation and in its brief contends that "even if the Commission's order was without lawful authority at the time it was made (Nov. 27, 1909) the amendment of 1910 either ratified it altogether, or, at least, validated it for the future," and, therefore, it was contended "that the judgment should be affirmed, or if not affirmed as rendered, should be modified to set aside the order only in its operation prior to June 18, 1910," on which day the amendment as to electric street passenger cars became effective. *Mattingly* v. *District of Columbia*, 97 U. S. 687; *Lowrey* v. *Hawaii*, 206 U. S. 206; *B. & O. R. R.* v. *I. C. C.*, 221 U. S. 612, are cited to show that Congress might ratify what had not been originally commanded. The first two decisions relate to transactions of a nature entirely different from that here involved; and, in the *Baltimore & Ohio Case*, which was more like this on its facts, the parties pending the suit stipulated that the order should apply only to the future, and it was said that the "question of the authority of the Commission at the time the order was made has become a moot one" (621). There was no such stipulation here, and there being nothing to show that Congress attempted an express ratification, and it being open whether the amendment was intended to confer a jurisdiction not previously given, the motion of the Government to make the order of November 27, 1909, effective from June 18, 1910, cannot prevail.

The decree of the Commerce Court is reversed and that of the three Circuit Judges made permanent. *Reversed.*

MR. JUSTICE PITNEY did not hear the argument and took no part in the decision of this case.

BROTHERHOOD OF LOCOMOTIVE ENGINEERS ET AL. *v.* SPOKANE & EASTERN RAILROAD & POWER CO., ET AL.

Decision No. 33, 1 Dec. U. S. R. R. Labor Board, 53 (1920)

Representatives of employees on the electric railways named herein have brought before the Labor Board for consideration and determination disputes between these railways and certain of their employees. All the organizations which are petitioners do not have a dispute with every respondent railway, but each petitioner has a dispute with one or more of the respondents, and each respondent has a dispute with one or more of the petitioners. The railway representatives having questioned the Labor Board's jurisdiction, this decision is upon that question solely.

The ground upon which jurisdiction is questioned is that these railways are interurban electric railways not operating as a part of a general steam railroad system of transportation, and that they are therefore excepted from section 300 of the Transportation Act, 1920, subsection 1 of which is as follows:

(1) The term "carrier" includes any express company, sleeping-car company, and any carrier by railroad, subject to the Interstate Commerce Act, except a street, interurban, or suburban electric railway not operating as a part of a general steam railroad system of transportation.

It is clear that Congress intended to exclude certain kinds of transportation facilities from the jurisdiction of the Labor Board. So far as the railways here in question are concerned, if they either are not interurbans or are operated as a part of a general steam railroad system of transportation, then they are not excluded and remain within the Labor Board's jurisdiction.

The 11 railways divide themselves, roughly speaking, into two groups. In one are the Hudson & Manhattan Railroad, the New York, Westchester & Boston Railway, and the Denver and Interurban Railroad, which do almost exclusively a passenger business. In the other group are the eight remaining railways, which, in addition to a passenger service, do a more or less extensive freight interchange business with steam trunk lines, carry mail and express, and, in general, perform the same public service as steam lines. In each group are roads which operate equipment jointly with steam trunk lines. They range in size of road operation from the Lackawanna & Wyoming Valley Railroad, with 20 miles of road, to the Pacific Electric Railway Co., with 600 miles. Several are interstate in their operation.

While no two railroads are exactly alike, they are generally similar as to method of operation and character of employment, except for the Hudson & Manhattan Railroad, whose equipment and operation are similar to that of the Interborough and the Brooklyn Rapid Transit Cos. of New York. There are also certain other features characterizing one or more of the railways which, being emphasized by the petitioners to prove that particular railways are within the jurisdiction of the Labor Board, deserve careful consideration. Such consideration will obviate the necessity of presenting in detail the facts about each railway. The points to consider are as follows:

(1) That this or that railway is physically an interstate property.

(2) That it performs the principal functions of a steam railroad.

(3) That its charter permits it to operate either by steam or by electricity.

(4) That it has at some time in the past operated by steam.

(5) That to a certain extent it operates jointly with a steam trunk line certain equipment and makes certain joint use of track.

(6) That its stock is entirely or partially owned by a steam trunk line.

(7) That it does a considerable interstate business.

(8) That it has received a freight increase from the Interstate Commerce Commission under Ex Parte 74.

Noting the further fact that none of the respondents is under the same operating management as any general steam railroad system as hereinafter defined, what bearing do the above-described characteristics have on the question whether any of these railways is an interurban and whether it is operating as a part of a general steam railroad system of transportation?

(1) The interurban status of an electric railway is not affected by the fact that it operates between states.

See *Spokane & Inland Empire Railroad Co.* v. *United States* (241 U. S., 244), in which the court says:

> The railroad company operated a street railway system in Spokane and several interurban electric lines, one of which existed from Spokane to Coeur d'Alene, Idaho, a distance of about 40 miles. . . . In addition to its passenger trains, the interurban line also operated freight trains.

(2) The fact that an electric railway performs the functions of a steam railroad is characteristic of a large number of so-called interurban railways and is not regarded by the courts as bearing upon the roads' interurban status. See *Sandquist* v. *Fort Dodge, Des Moines & Southern Railroad* (159 Iowa, 194), in which the court says:

> The defendant is an interurban railroad operating a line of road for the carriage of passengers and freight between the cities of Des Moines and Fort Dodge, run by means of electricity.

(The distance between Des Moines and Fort Dodge is 85 miles, and the service rendered, except for minor details, is primarily that which a steam road would perform.)

(3) That the road is chartered so that either steam or electricity may be used as a motive power has no practical bearing on the status of the road. The important thing is the actual nature of its operation.

(4) Similarly, the past history of the railway can not be considered as important as its present actual operation. To hold otherwise would raise a number of awkward questions.

For instance, the Washington & Old Dominion Railway and the Piedmont & Northern Railway are doing the same kind of business as the Spokane & Inland Empire Railroad Co. and the Fort Dodge, Des Moines & Southern Railroad, both of which are recognized interurbans. How can it be fairly said that the

Washington & Old Dominion Railway and the Piedmont & Northern Railway are not interurbans merely because one once ran by steam and the other may now run by steam if it so elects? How long must a road have operated by steam to prevent it subsequently becoming an interurban when the motive power changes to electricity; or, having once been operated by steam, how long must it operate by electricity before it may become an interurban? Does the fact that a road once operated by steam prevent it from ever becoming an interurban?

(5) The joint use of equipment and trackage is not regarded in the case of the Pacific Electric Railway Co. as disqualifying it from being an interurban. See decision 1961 of the California Railroad Commission, which, speaking of the Pacific Electric Railway Co., says:

> Applicant operates a large suburban and interurban railway system in southern California, and its financial condition has heretofore been investigated on several occasions when applications were made for the issuance of securities.

(6) Neither does the above decision consider important the fact that the Southern Pacific Co. owns the stock of the Pacific Electric Railway Co. and that certain of the officers of these two companies are the same persons, or that certain equipment is operated jointly with the Southern Pacific Co.

(7) The amount of interstate freight business is immaterial on the question whether or not an electric railway is an interurban. (See *Sandquist* v. *Fort Dodge, Des Moines & Southern Railroad* cited above.) The interstate freight business of the Fort Dodge, Des Moines & Southern Railroad amounts to approximately 80 per cent of its total business.

This feature of interchange of freight, however, raises a further question: It is argued that such interchange, which is sometimes accompanied by interstate passenger traffic, brings the railroad within the definition "part of a general steam railroad system of transportation," thus raising the questions: (1) What is a general steam railroad system of transportation? (2) What constitutes operating as a part of a system?

The word "system" as used throughout the Transportation Act, 1920, means a system similar to the Pennsylvania System, Baltimore & Ohio Railroad System, Southern Pacific Co. (Pacific System), etc. The word "System" is used, in other words, in customary railroad parlance. (See also the opinion of the court in *Hines* v. *Dahn*, 267 Fed., 105, where the Illinois Central

Railroad is referred to as a system within the Federal Control Act.) Such roads and others doing a general railroad business with country-wide connections are general steam railroad systems within the meaning of the act.

It is to be noted, also, that the act specifically says "a" system of transportation, which can not be interpreted to mean "the" systems of transportation in the United States or a group of systems.

Operating as a part of a system means, as a practical matter, operating as an integral part of that system and under a unified control. If there is a physical connection and a common control and the lines are used together as one general system, the definition of the act would cover and include such a road. But when there is separate control and management, mere contiguity at points of connection, or even some common officials, would not be a decisive test. If a road is under such separate control that its officials can manage its own business, make its own contracts, and regulate its own affairs, then it is not a part of another.

The idea that engaging in a large interstate freight business, in the course of which it interchanges cars with several steam trunk lines, brings a railway within the term "operating as a part of a general steam railroad system of transportation" is negatived by the phraseology of various sections of the Transportation Act, 1920.

Interurban electric railways are excluded from the provisions of the act under three heads:

(*a*) In all matters pertaining to Federal control, namely, section 204–A, "reimbursement for deficits," and section 209–A, "guarantee to carriers," the exclusion covers an "interurban electric railway which has as its principal source of operating revenue urban, suburban, or interurban passenger traffic, or sale of power, heat and light, or both."

(*b*) In section 1, subsection 22, forbidding extension and further construction without authority from the Interstate Commerce Commission; in section 20–A, requiring the assent of the Interstate Commerce Commission to the issuance of securities; and in section 300, giving the Labor Board jurisdiction, the exception is "a street, interurban, or suburban electric railway not operating as a part of a general steam railroad system of transportation."

(*c*) In section 15–A, dealing with rates, are excluded "interurban electric railways, unless operated as a part of a general steam railroad system of transportation or engaged in the general transportation of freight."

The contention that interchange of freight makes an electric line part of those trunk lines with which it interchanges assumes that section 300 includes by inference exactly what section 15–A specifically states, namely, "or engaged in the general transportation of freight." If that is what section 300 means, then the use of the words "or engaged in the general transportation of freight" as used in section 15–A is surplusage. As matter of fundamental legal construction such an assumption is unsound.

On the other hand, Congress must be assumed to have spoken with discrimination. The purpose here of differentiating in the phraseology of the two sections was to differentiate in the meaning. Had Congress meant to describe the same kind of railways in these two sections, it would have described them in similar terms.

The Labor Board is not bound by interpretations of the Interstate Commerce Commission. Nevertheless, it should give careful thought to such interpretations where the Labor Board itself is interpreting identical language.

For example, section 20–A, above quoted, includes interurban railways in exactly the same language as section 300. Under section 20–A the Interstate Commerce Commission has not thought itself warranted in assuming jurisdiction over the issuance of securities by interurban roads, some of those here in question. In other words, the Interstate Commerce Commission does not regard engaging "in the general transportation of freight" as equivalent to "operating as a part of a general steam railroad system of transportation." And again, directly interpreting section 300 with regard to the nominations of members of the Labor Board, the Interstate Commerce Commission excluded from participation in such nominations both interurban electric railways and the most important organization of employees engaged in operating these railways.

(8) The railways have received a freight increase from the Interstate Commerce Commission. They have not received a passenger increase. The reason they have received the former and not the latter is that the freight business done by interurban roads is sufficiently general to give Congress jurisdiction over the matter. Passenger traffic, on the other hand, is so local that Congress can not properly regulate it. Therefore, such rates are left to the State commissions.

Apart from the significant exclusion of the Labor Board from jurisdiction over railways engaged in the freight business, it is obvious as a practical matter that the granting by the Labor Board of a wage increase, without corresponding authority to the Interstate Commerce Commission to raise rates, would result in serious complications. The Labor Board and the Interstate Commerce Commission were clearly intended to be interdependent in this matter. Such intention would be nullified if the Labor Board assumed jurisdiction where the Interstate Commerce Commission was without it.

And so it does not seem to the Labor Board that any or all of the eight factors above discussed materially affect the question of jurisdiction. It remains to say a word regarding the matter of statutory construction and the purpose of Congress.

In construing section 300 of the Transportation Act, 1920, in reference to the railways before the Labor Board, it is well to bear in mind the settled rules of construction and interpretation. Whether an act be remedial or not, it is to be strictly construed as to the classes of people, citizens, parties, and subjects included, and none are to be included by any intendment not expressed in the terms used.

The intention of Congress becomes material only in case of an ambiguity in the language of the act. While such an ambiguity does not exist here it nevertheless is not inappropriate to consider what the intention of Congress was.

It is plain that Congress has dealt in discriminating language with interurban electric railways throughout the Interstate Commerce Act and the Transportation Act, 1920, and has consistently treated them differently from steam lines. Congress has done this because there is a material difference, generally speaking, between steam and electric roads in the matter of equipment, nature of service, and standards of employment. With a few exceptions, one service is general, the other is local. The difficulty is that a few electric railways have developed far beyond the original idea of an interurban. They have now come to rival many steam lines in service and size. And still the definition of what is an interurban has likewise broadened, not only by popular conception, but by legal, statutory, and executive decree, so that the Pacific Electric Railway Co., operating upward of 600 miles of road; the Fort Dodge, Des Moines and Southern Railroad, owning 2,400 box and coal cars; and the Spokane & Inland Empire Railroad Co., crossing State lines and operating passenger and freight trains, are all judicially labeled "interurban." It is difficult, if not impossible, to get away from this definition.

All the respondents are electrically operated. Some have been judicially determined to be interurban; the remainder either are so similar in character that they can not be successfully differentiated or are otherwise clearly excluded by the words of the act. Neither are the respondents operating as a part of any general steam railroad systems of transportation. Therefore the Labor Board must decide that it has no jurisdiction over any of these respondents, and it herewith dismisses the applications of the petitioners for further hearing.

WELLS FARGO & COMPANY *v.* TAYLOR

254 U. S. 175 (1920)

MR. JUSTICE VAN DEVANTER delivered the opinion of the court.

Oscar G. Taylor, an express messenger of Wells Fargo & Company, a common carrier by express, received substantial personal injuries through the derailment of an express car in which he was working, and which was part of a passenger train moving over the railroad of the St. Louis and San Francisco Railroad Company in the State of Mississippi, — the derailment resulting from negligence on the part of the railroad company and its employees. To recover for these injuries Taylor brought an action against the railroad company in the Circuit Court of Monroe County, Mississippi, and obtained a judgment for $4,000, which was affirmed by the Supreme Court of the State without an opinion. See 58 So. 485.

In his declaration in that case Taylor explained and justified his presence on the train and in the express car by alleging that he was then in the employ of the express company as its messenger and in the course of that employment was in charge of express matter which the railroad company was transporting for the express company, that this transportation was in pursuance of a contract between the two companies, and that under the contract the express car was furnished by the railroad company and he, as the express company's messenger, was permitted to accompany the express matter carried therein.

While the declaration said nothing more about the nature or terms of that contract, it is important here to have them in mind. The contract shows that it was intended to, and did, cover all express business on and over the railroad company's road, both within and without the State of Mississippi, for a specified period, including the day when Taylor was injured. It gave to the express company the exclusive privilege of conducting an express business on and over the railroad and obligated the railroad company to refrain from conducting an express business. There were provisions whereby the railroad company agreed, (*a*) to transport by suitable cars, to be provided by it and attached to its passenger trains, all express matter of the express company and the messengers accompanying the same, (*b*) to light and warm the cars and equip them with necessary conveniences, and (*c*) to permit portions of its station houses to be used by the express company for the reception, safekeeping and delivery of express matter. And there were other provisions whereby the express company agreed, (*a*) to make stated payments — usually a percentage of the gross earnings — for the facilities furnished and service rendered by the railroad company, (*b*) to assume all risks, losses, and damages to its own property, express matter and valuable packages transported under the contract, (*c*) to assume all risk and damage to its agents and employees while engaged in its business on the trains or property of the railroad company, and (*d*) to indemnify and hold harmless the railroad company in respect of all claims for damages suffered by such agents and employees while so engaged.

There was also a contract between Taylor and the express company, spoken of as a messenger's agreement, wherein, — following a recital that he had full knowledge of the service required and the conditions on which the railroad company would permit messengers to accompany express matter on its trains, and that with such knowledge he was desirous of becoming a messenger of the express company, — it was stipulated, as a term or condition of his employment, that neither the express company nor the railroad company should under any circumstances or in any case be liable for any injury which he might receive while on the railroad company's trains as such messenger, whether caused by negligence of the railroad company or otherwise, and that he would assume all and every risk incident to such employment, from whatever cause arising.

Promptly after Taylor sued the railroad company in the Circuit Court of Monroe County, and before the case was brought to trial, the express company presented to that court in that cause a petition wherein it set out the contracts just described and asked to be made a party defendant. To this the railroad company assented, but Taylor evidently objected and the petition was denied. The railroad company by its answer and evidence sought to avail itself of the stipulation in the messenger's agreement, in connection with those in the other contract, but the court ruled against it and Taylor obtained the judgment before mentioned.

What has been recited will conduce to a right understanding of another suit the decree in which we are now to review.

The suit is in equity and was brought by the express company against Taylor in the District Court of the United States for the Northern District of Mississippi. The federal jurisdiction rests on diversity of citizenship, — the express company being a corporation and citizen of Colorado, and Taylor a citizen of Mississippi residing in the Northern District. The bill, with a supplement and amendment, proceeds on the theory that, in suing the railroad company and obtaining a judgment against it, which as between that company and the express company must be paid by the latter as stipulated in their contract, Taylor not only violated the messenger's agreement, but perpetrated a legal fraud on the express company; that the judgment is therefore one which in equity and good conscience he has no right to enforce; that if he be permitted to enforce it the express company will be without any effective remedy in that he has no property which can be reached by legal process (a fact which is both alleged and proved); and that the express company, which was not a party to that case, and has not been in any wise negligent or at fault, is in equity and good conscience entitled to have the messenger's agreement respected and to demand that the claims embraced in the inequitable judgment be relinquished and the enforcement of the judgment enjoined. The prayer conforms to that theory and is in substance that Taylor be required specifically to perform and carry out the messenger's agreement, to execute a sufficient release of all claims on account of the injuries received, and to abstain from enforcing the judgment. General relief also is prayed.

Taylor challenged the bill by a demurrer, which was overruled, and after a hearing in due course the express company prevailed. On appeal to the Circuit Court of Appeals that decree was reversed and the suit remanded because in that court's opinion the bill did not show that Taylor was not in the employ of the railroad company or that he was solely in the employ of the express company. 220 Fed. 796. After the mandate was received, Taylor, conceiving that the decision of the Circuit Court of Appeals fully disposed of the merits and was final, requested the District Court to enter a decree dismissing the bill, and the express company requested leave to amend the bill by correcting the defect pointed out by the Circuit Court of Appeals. Taylor's request was denied and that of the express company was granted. The bill was accordingly amended so as to show that Taylor was not in the employ of the railroad company, but was on the train solely in virtue of his employment by the express company, and that in his declaration in the action against the railroad company he did not claim or allege any employment by that company, but, on the contrary, claimed and alleged that it permitted him to be on the train because he was accompanying the express matter as the express company's employee. Taylor then filed a new answer, and on a further hearing a decree for the express company was entered. By it the District Court found that the allegations of the bill, with its supplement and amendment, were all true; declared that the institution of the action against the railroad company and its prosecution to judgment constituted a violation of the messenger's agreement and a legal fraud on the express company; directed Taylor to carry out and perform the messenger's agreement and to execute, within a fixed time, an appropriate instrument releasing the express company and the railroad company from all claims for damages on account of his injuries, and enjoined him from collecting or attempting to collect the judgment against the railroad company. On a further appeal to the Circuit Court of Appeals that decree was reversed with directions to dismiss the bill. 249 Fed. 109. A writ of certiorari was then granted by this court.

On the second appeal the Circuit Court of Appeals put its decision entirely on the ground that the express company was a "common carrier by railroad" within the meaning of the Employers' Liability Act of April 22, 1908, c. 149, 35 Stat. 65, and therefore under § 5 of the act the messenger's agreement was void. Taylor advanced that and other grounds in asking a reversal, but the court did not discuss the other grounds. All are pressed on our attention, and we take them up in what seems the natural order.[1]

3. Does the Employers' Liability Act affect the validity of the messenger's agreement?

The act provides that "every common carrier by railroad" shall be liable in damages for the injury or death of any of its

[1] The first two grounds, dealing with jurisdictional issues, are omitted. — Ed.

employees occurring while it is engaged and he is employed in interstate commerce and resulting in whole or in part from the negligence of any of its officers, agents or employees, or from any defect or insufficiency, due to its negligence, "in its cars, engines, appliances, machinery, track, roadbed," etc.; and in § 5 it declares that any contract whereby a common carrier exempts itself from "any liability created by this act" shall to that extent be void.

In his declaration in the state court Taylor did not claim that he was in the employ of the railroad company, and his judgment was not obtained on that theory. Here it is shown with certainty that he was not in that company's employ. True he urges that the contract between the two companies shows a co-proprietorship or sort of partnership between them which made him an employee of both; but the contract discloses no basis for the claim or for distinguishing his case from that of the Pullman porter recently before us. *Robinson* v. *Baltimore & Ohio R. R. Co.*, 237 U. S. 84. Here the businesses of the companies concerned were quite as distinct in point of control and otherwise as they were there. That here the railroad company provided the express car is not material, for it is measurably equalized by other differences. In both cases the railroad company provided the motive power and the train operatives. The messenger here, like the porter there, was on the train as an employee, not of the railroad company, but of another by whom he was employed, directed and paid, and at whose will he was to continue in service or be discharged.

As respects the express company, it appears not merely that Taylor was in its employ, but also that the injuries were received while it was engaged and he was employed in interstate commerce; and so the question is presented whether the act embraces a common carrier by express which neither owns nor operates a railroad, but uses and pays for railroad transportation in the manner before shown. The District Court answered the question in the negative and the Circuit Court of Appeals in the affirmative. A negative answer also has been given in a like situation by the Court of Errors and Appeals of New Jersey, *Higgins* v. *Erie R. R. Co.*, 89 N. J. L. 629; and a recent decision by the Supreme Court of Minnesota makes persuasively for that view. *State ex rel.* v. *District Court*, 142 Minn. 410.

In our opinion the words "common carrier by railroad," as used in the act, mean one who operates a railroad as a means of carrying for the public, — that is to say, a railroad company acting as a common carrier. This view not only is in accord with the ordinary acceptation of the words, but is enforced by the mention of cars, engines, track, roadbed and other property pertaining to a going railroad (see *Southern Pacific Company* v. *Jensen*, 244 U. S. 205, 212–213); by the obvious reference in the latter part of §§ 3 and 4 to statutes requiring engines and cars to be equipped with automatic couplers, standard drawbars and other appliances intended to promote the safety of railroad employees (see *San Antonio & Aransas Pass Ry. Co.* v. *Wagner*, 241 U. S. 476, 484); by the use of similar words in closely related acts which apply only to carriers operating railroads, c. 196, 27 Stat. 531; c. 225, 35 Stat. 476; c. 208, 36 Stat. 350, and by the fact that similar words in the original Interstate Commerce Act had been construed as including carriers operating railroads but not express companies doing business as here shown. 1 I. C. C. 349; *United States* v. *Morseman*, 42 Fed. 448; *Southern Indiana Express Co.* v. *United States Express Co.*, 88 Fed. 659, 662; s. c. 92 Fed. 1022. And see *American Express Co.* v. *United States*, 212 U. S. 522, 531, 534.

As Taylor was not an employee of the railroad company and the express company was not within the Employers' Liability Act, it follows that the act has no bearing on the liability of either company or on the validity of the messenger's agreement. . . .

It follows that the decree of the District Court was right and that the Circuit Court of Appeals erred in reversing it.

Decree reversed.

THE PIPE LINE CASES [1]

234 U. S. 548 (1914)

Mr. Justice Holmes delivered the opinion of the court.

By the act of Congress of June 29, 1906, c. 3591, 34 Stat. 584, the Act to Regulate Commerce was amended so that the first section reads in part as follows: "That the provisions of this

[1] Docket title of these cases: No. 481. United States *v.* Ohio Oil Company. No. 482. United States *v.* Standard Oil Company. No. 483. United States *v.* Standard Oil Company of Louisiana. No. 506. United States *v.* Prairie Oil & Gas Company. No. 507. United States *v.* Uncle Sam Oil Company. No. 508. United States *v.* Benson, doing business under the Partnership Name of Tide Water Pipe Company, Limited.

Act shall apply to any corporation or any person or persons engaged in the transportation of oil or other commodity, except water and except natural or artificial gas, by means of pipe lines, or partly by pipe lines and partly by railroad, or partly by pipe lines and partly by water, who shall be considered and held to be common carriers within the meaning and purpose of this Act." Thereafter the Interstate Commerce Commission issued an order requiring the appellees among others, being parties in control of pipe lines, to file with the Commission, schedules of their rates and charges for the transportation of oil. 24 I. C. C. 1. The appellees thereupon brought suit in the Commerce Court to set aside and annul the order, and a preliminary injunction was issued by that court, on the broad ground that the statute applies to every pipe line that crosses a state boundary and that thus construed it is unconstitutional. 204 Fed. Rep. 798. The United States, the Interstate Commerce Commission and other intervening respondents appealed.

The circumstances in which the amendment was passed are known to every one. The Standard Oil Company, a New Jersey corporation, owned the stock of the New York Transit Company, a pipe line made a common carrier by the laws of New York, and of the National Transit Company, a Pennsylvania corporation of like character, and by these it connected the Appalachian oil field with its refineries in the east. It owned nearly all the stock of the Ohio Oil Company, which connected the Lima-Indiana field with its system; and the National Transit Company, controlled by it, owned nearly all the stock of the Prairie Oil and Gas Company, which ran from the Mid-Continent field in Oklahoma and Kansas and the Caddo field in Louisiana to Indiana and connected with the previously mentioned lines. It also was largely interested in the Tide Water Pipe Company, Limited, which connected with the Appalachian and other fields and pursued the methods of the Standard Oil Company about to be described. By the before mentioned and subordinate lines the Standard Oil Company had made itself master of the only practicable oil transportation between the oil fields east of California and the Atlantic Ocean and carried much the greater part of the oil between those points. Before the recent dissolution the New York and Pennsylvania Companies had extended their lines into New Jersey and Maryland to the refineries and the laws of those States did not require them to be common carriers. To meet the present amendment the Standard Oil Company took a conveyance of the New Jersey and Maryland lines, and the common carrier lines now end at insignificant places where there are neither market nor appliances except those of the Standard Oil, by which it would seem that the whole transport of the carriers' lines is received. There is what seems to be merely a formal breach of continuity when the carriers' pipes stop. The change is not material to our view of the case.

Availing itself of its monopoly of the means of transportation the Standard Oil Company refused through its subordinates to carry any oil unless the same was sold to it or to them and through them to it on terms more or less dictated by itself. In this way it made itself master of the fields without the necessity of owning them and carried across half the continent a great subject of international commerce coming from many owners but, by the duress of which the Standard Oil Company was master, carrying it all as its own. The main question is whether the act does and constitutionally can apply to the several constituents that then had been united into a single line.

Taking up first the construction of the statute, we think it plain that it was intended to reach the combination of pipe lines that we have described. The provisions of the act are to apply to any person engaged in the transportation of oil by means of pipe lines. The words 'who shall be considered and held to be common carriers within the meaning and purpose of this act' obviously are not intended to cut down the generality of the previous declaration to the meaning that only those shall be held common carriers within the act who were common carriers in a technical sense, but an injunction that those in control of pipe lines and engaged in the transportation of oil shall be dealt with as such. If the Standard Oil Company and its coöperating companies were not so engaged no one was. It not only would be a sacrifice of fact to form but would empty the act if the carriage to the seaboard of nearly all the oil east of California, were held not to be transportation within its meaning, because by the exercise of their power the carriers imposed as a condition to the carriage a sale to themselves. As applied to them, while the amendment does not compel them to continue in operation it does require them not to continue except as common carriers. That is the plain meaning as has been held with regard to other statutes similarly framed. *Atlantic Coast Line R. R. Co.* v. *Riverside Mills*, 219 U. S. 186, 195, 203. Its evident purpose was to bring within its scope pipe lines that although not technically common carriers yet were carrying all oil offered, if only the offerers would sell at their price.

The only matter requiring much consideration is the constitutionality of the act. That the transportation is commerce among the States we think clear. That conception cannot be made wholly dependent upon technical questions of title, and the fact that the oils transported belonged to the owner of the pipe line is not conclusive against the transportation being such commerce. *Rearick* v. *Pennsylvania,* 203 U. S. 507, 512. See *Texas & New Orleans R. R. Co.* v. *Sabine Tram Co.,* 227 U. S. 111. The situation that we have described would make it illusory to deny the title of commerce to such transportation, beginning in purchase and ending in sale, for the same reasons that make it transportation within the act.

The control of Congress over commerce among the States cannot be made a means of exercising powers not entrusted to it by the Constitution, but it may require those who are common carriers in substance to become so in form. So far as the statute contemplates future pipe lines and prescribes the conditions upon which they may be established there can be no doubt that it is valid. So the objection is narrowed to the fact that it applies to lines already engaged in transportation. But, as we already have intimated, those lines that we are considering are common carriers now in everything but form. They carry everybody's oil to a market, although they compel outsiders to sell it before taking it into their pipes. The answer to their objection is not that they may give up the business, but that, as applied to them, the statute practically means no more than they must give up requiring a sale to themselves before carrying the oil that they now receive. The whole case is that the appellees if they carry must do it in a way that they do not like. There is no taking and it does not become necessary to consider how far Congress could subject them to pecuniary loss without compensation in order to accomplish the end in view. *Hoke* v. *United States,* 227 U. S. 308, 323. *Lottery Case,* 188 U. S. 321, 357.

These considerations seem to us sufficient to dispose of the cases of the Standard Oil Company, the Ohio Oil Company, the Prairie Oil and Gas Company and the Tide Water Pipe Company, Limited. The Standard Oil Company of Louisiana was incorporated since the passage of the amendment, and before the beginning of this suit to break up the monopoly of the New Jersey Standard Oil Company. It buys a large part of its oil from the Prairie

Oil and Gas Company, which buys it at the wells in the Mid-Continent field and transfers the title to the Louisiana Company in that State. Its case also is covered by what we have said.

There remains to be considered only the Uncle Sam Oil Company. This company has a refinery in Kansas and oil wells in Oklahoma, with a pipe line connecting the two which it has used for the sole purpose of conducting oil from its own wells to its own refinery. It would be a perversion of language, considering the sense in which it is used in the statute, to say that a man was engaged in the transportation of water whenever he pumped a pail of water from his well to his house. So as to oil. When, as in this case, a company is simply drawing oil from its own wells across a state line to its own refinery for its own use, and that is all, we do not regard it as falling within the description of the act, the transportation being merely an incident to use at the end. In that case the decree will be affirmed. In the others the decree will be reversed. *No.* 507, *Decree affirmed.*

Nos. 481, 482, 483, 506 *and* 508, *Decrees reversed.*

THE CHIEF JUSTICE concurring.

Agreeing in every particular with the conclusions of the court and with its reasoning except as to one special subject, my concurrence as to that matter because of its importance is separately stated. The matter to which I refer is the exclusion of the Uncle Sam Oil Company from the operation of the act. The view which leads the court to exclude it is that the company was not engaged in transportation under the statute, a conclusion to which I do not assent. The facts are these: That company owns wells in one State from which it has pipe lines to its refinery in another State, and pumps its own oil through such pipe lines to its refinery and the product of course when reduced at the refinery passes into the markets of consumption. It seems to me that the business thus carried on is transportation in interstate commerce within the statute. But despite this I think the company is not embraced by the statute because it would be impossible to make the statute applicable to it without violating the due process clause of the Fifth Amendment, since to apply it would necessarily amount to a taking of the property of the company without compensation. It is shown beyond question that the company buys no oil and by the methods which have been mentioned simply carries its own product to its own refinery; in other words, it is engaged in a purely private business. Under these conditions in my opinion there is no power under the Constitution without the exercise of the right of eminent domain to convert without its consent the private business of the company into a public one.

Of course this view has no application to the other companies which the court holds are subject to the act because as pointed out the principal ones were chartered as common carriers and they all either directly or as a necessary result of their association were engaged in buying oil and shipping it through their pipes; in other words, were doing in reality a common carrier business, disguised, it may be, in form, but not changed in substance. Under these conditions I do not see how it would be possible to avoid the conclusion which the court has reached without declaring that the shadow and not the substance was the criterion to be resorted to for the purpose of determining the validity of the exercise of legislative power.

MR. JUSTICE MCKENNA, dissenting.[1]

---

2. KINDS OF COMMERCE

PENNSYLVANIA RAILROAD COMPANY *v.* CLARK BROTHERS COAL MINING COMPANY

238 U. S. 456 (1915)

MR. JUSTICE HUGHES delivered the opinion of the court.

This suit was brought in January, 1912, by the Clark Brothers Coal Mining Company (defendant in error) in the Court of Common Pleas of Clearfield County, Pennsylvania, to recover damages for inadequate and unjustly discriminatory car service and supply. The complaint related to the action of the defendant company with respect to cars required for the transportation of coal from the plaintiff's mines known as Falcon, Nos. 2, 3, and 4, in Clearfield County, and Falcon, Nos. 5 and 6, in Indiana County, Pennsylvania, between October, 1905, and April 30, 1907. A statute of Pennsylvania [Act of June 4, 1883, P. L. 72, 4 Purd. 3906; see Const. (Pa.) 1873, Art. 17] prohibits undue or unreasonable discrimination by any common carrier 'in charges for or in facilities for the transportation of freight within this State or coming from or going to any other State,' and provides that the carrier guilty of unjust discrimination shall be liable 'for damages treble the amount of injury suffered.'

[1] The dissenting opinion is omitted. — ED.

On behalf of the defendant (plaintiff in error) the jurisdiction of the court to entertain the action was challenged upon the ground that with respect to car distribution the defendant was subject to the Act to Regulate Commerce, and that the claim of the plaintiff was cognizable only by the Interstate Commerce Commission or by the courts of the United States. It was urged further that in a proceeding before the Interstate Commerce Commission, which had been instituted by the plaintiff against the defendant prior to the beginning of this action, the Commission had found that the method of car distribution practiced by the defendant with respect to the plaintiff's mines known as Falcon, Nos. 2, 3, and 4, was unjustly discriminatory, and that the Commission had made an award of damages accordingly; and that by reason of this proceeding and the action of the Commission the plaintiff was precluded from maintaining the present action so far as it related to the alleged loss sustained with respect to the mines last described.

The trial court overruled these contentions of the defendant. The jury, finding discrimination, assessed the damage at $41,481 and trebled the amount, making $124,443. Motions in arrest of judgment and for a new trial and for judgment *non obstante veredicto*, upon the grounds above stated (and others) were denied. Judgment for the total amount of the verdict was entered and was affirmed by the Supreme Court of the State, 241 Pa. St. 515. And this writ of error has been sued out.

It clearly appeared that the proceeding before the Interstate Commerce Commission as to the mines Falcon, Nos. 2, 3, and 4, embraced substantially the same claim as that litigated in this action. As the trial judge said: "It" (the plaintiff) "did get an award of damages for what we understand to be practically the same subject-matter." That proceeding was instituted by the plaintiff in June, 1907. Its petition, among other things, alleged that it had been, and was, 'engaged in mining and shipping coal to points and places of delivery and to the coal markets beyond the State of Pennsylvania,' and that it had during all the period mentioned, to wit, 'from the fifteenth day of October, 1905, to the date of the filing of this complaint,' orders for coal to be mined and shipped 'beyond the lines of said State.' It complained of the rating of its mines by the defendant and also of unjust and unreasonable discrimination against it in the daily distribution of cars 'for the transportation of its coal into the interstate markets'; that it had suffered "great loss and damage in its business 'as a producer, shipper and seller of bituminous coal' in the interstate coal trade, and that such damage amounted in the aggregate to $36,401.12. It prayed for hearing, for an ascertainment of the damages which it had sustained in its interstate business by reason of unreasonable preferences given to its competitors as alleged, and for a determination of the proper basis of car distribution to be observed. After hearing, the Commission made its report on March 7, 1910. 19 I. C. C. 392. On the same day, the Commission rendered its decision in *Hillsdale Coal & Coke Co.* v. *Penna. R. R.* (19 I. C. C. 356), involving similar questions as to the method practiced by the defendant in distributing 'its available coal car equipment.' Upon this point, the Commission there said:

"Under a rule announced by it on February 1, 1903, the defendant seems to have charged all railroad cars, regardless of ownership, and private cars not owned by the operator loading them, against the distributive share of each mine, but it treated its own fuel cars as a special allotment in addition to the distributive share. On March 28, 1905, a notice was sent to shippers of bituminous coal from mines on the lines of the defendant advising them that thereafter all railroad cars, regardless of ownership, and all private cars not owned by the operator loading them, should be considered as cars available for distribution, except its own company fuel cars and fuel cars sent upon its lines by foreign companies and specially consigned to particular mines.

"On January 1, 1906, the defendant divided all cars into two classes which it designated as 'assigned' and 'unassigned' cars. In the former class were its own fuel cars, foreign railway fuel cars, and individual or private cars loaded by their owners or assigned by their owners to particular mines. The rule then made effective and still in force provides that the capacity in tons of any 'assigned' cars shall be deducted from the rated capacity in tons of the particular mine receiving such cars, and that the remainder is to be regarded as the rated capacity of the mine in the distribution of all 'unassigned' or system cars." *Id.*, p. 362.

After illustrating the operation of this system and the advantage in distribution thus given to mines having assigned cars (*Id.*, pp. 363, 364), the Commission concluded:

"Upon all the facts shown of record the Commission therefore finds that throughout the period of the action the system upon which the defendant distributed its available coal-car equipment, including system fuel cars, foreign railway fuel cars, and individual or private cars, has subjected the complainant to an undue and an unlawful discrimination."

In the case of the plaintiff's petition, the Commission held that so far as the rating of its mines was concerned 'there was no substantial basis for any finding of discrimination.' But, in the matter of car distribution, unjust discrimination was found. The Commission said (19 I. C. C. 394–6):

"There are a number of mines on the Moshannon branch of the defendant that are owned by other operators, but in this connection it will suffice to mention only the six mines operated by or for the Berwind-White Coal Mining Company, one of which, known as Eureka No. 27, immediately adjoins the complainant's Falcon No. 2. The same 'D' coal vein is worked in these two mines. The quality of the coal is therefore the same and it is claimed that the capacities of the two mines were substantially the same at the period involved in the first of these two complaints. . . . .

"But neither Falcon No. 2 nor the mines of the complainant, the Clark Brothers Coal & Mining Company, was placed on an equal footing with the mines of the Berwind-White Coal Mining Company in the matter of the distribution of the defendant's available coal-car equipment during the period of the actions. . . . .

"It is established with reasonable clearness on the record that the Berwind-White mines during the years 1906 and 1907, as well as to a period immediately preceding those dates, were daily in receipt of coal cars in large numbers and were therefore kept in operation almost continuously while the complainants received an inadequate supply and were not able, therefore, to run their mines to the best advantage. This difference is largely explained by the fact that the Berwind-White Coal Mining Company owned a large number of private cars and also enjoyed contracts for supplying the defendant and its connection with coal. Under the rules of defendant, fully explained in *Hillsdale Coal & Coke Co.* v. *P. R. R. Co.*, *ante*, the ownership of such private cars and the enjoyment of these contracts resulted in the special allotment to the mines of that company of these so-called assigned cars. For the reasons explained at some length in that case those rules operated as an undue discrimination against these complainants, and we so find. But for the present and for the reasons there explained we shall limit our order to a finding that in the several respects here mentioned the defendant was guilty of a discrimination against these complainants, leaving for determination after further argument the question of the extent to which the complainants may have been damaged thereby."

Order was entered accordingly condemning the defendant's rule and practice of distribution (as stated) as a violation of § 3 of the Act to Regulate Commerce, requiring the defendant to desist from that practice, and reserving the question of damages for further consideration. Subsequently, in April, 1911, this question was submitted, and it was determined on March 11, 1912. 23 I. C. C. 191. The Commission then made its report as follows: "We now find that the damages sustained by this claimant as result thereof" (the discrimination found) "amounted to $31,127.96, and that it is entitled to an award of reparation in that sum, with interest from June 25, 1907."

The Commission set forth its primary findings of fact upon which this ultimate finding was based, showing its calculations with respect to shipments, selling prices, cost of production, and profits, during the times in question. It found the number of tons, in case of each of the mines, actually shipped and the amount which would have been shipped and sold, with a proper car supply, for 'interstate destinations,' that is, for points without the State of Pennsylvania.

This action was brought after the first report of the Commission, and while the question of damages was under its consideration. The trial judge in charging the jury described the system of car distribution in use, and the practice of the defendant prior to and after January 1, 1906. Referring to the rule promulgated on that date, it was recognized that it in effect gave a distinct advantage to the mine having 'assigned cars' over one that did not have them, but the jury were instructed that 'for the purposes of this case,' it might 'be considered that it was a fair rule of distribution.' The subject committed to them was thus stated in the concluding portion of the instructions: "In considering the damages, therefore, in case you find discrimination, you must first ascertain what would have been, under all the circumstances testified to, a fair rating of the plaintiff's mines in both regions. Second, if after having such fair rating a comparison with the alleged preferred shippers would entitle it to an increased number of cars and what that increased number of cars would be, and if the evidence at the same time shows that the preferred shipper received day by day and month by month throughout the period of the action, an excess over its proper *pro rata* share, the plaintiff would be entitled to recover at your hands a verdict for what you may find its fair share of such excess of cars amounted to in tons, estimated just as we have laid down the rule with respect to the method of calculating. Now then, if you allow for discrimination, then you may disregard all question as to inadequacy or insufficiency of car supply, because you cannot allow for both. For discrimination, after you have made an estimate of the amount of damages and found a definite sum as compensation for the injuries which it sustained, that would be single damages, and if you find that there was discrimination, as claimed by the plaintiff's counsel then you can go to the question as to whether there shall be treble damages under the Act of 1883. . . . . If you find discrimination, therefore, and you arrive at or estimate the amount of single damages which you believe the plaintiff has sustained by reason of such undue and unreasonable discriminatory acts practiced against it, it is for you to say whether or not that amount should be trebled, that is, multiplied by three." The jury, as we have said, did find discrimination, and trebled the damages.

In considering the right of the plaintiff to maintain this action, despite the proceeding before the Commission, an initial question is presented as to the nature of the commerce involved. It appeared, as stated by the state court, that practically all the coal mined by the plaintiff was sold f. o. b. cars at the mines. About ninety-five or ninety-eight per cent. was sold in this way. Hence, it is said, it is "not subject to Interstate Commerce regulation."

We do not understand that it is questioned that a very large part of the damages recovered in this action pertain to coal which with a fair method of car distribution would have been shipped from the mines to purchasers in other States. There is no controversy as to the course of business. The plaintiff sold to persons within and without the State of Pennsylvania. The coal was loaded on cars to be transported to various points of destination not only in Pennsylvania but in other States. The transportation to other States absolutely depended upon a proper supply of cars, and it is manifest that unjust discrimination against the plaintiff in car distribution would improperly obstruct the freedom of such transportation, in which the plaintiff had a direct interest. And the question presented is whether unjust discrimination of this character is a subject which falls without the scope of the jurisdiction conferred upon the Interstate Commerce Commission, that is, whether there is an absence of such jurisdiction merely because the plaintiff sold its product, which was to be transported to other States, f. o. b. at its mines.

This question must be answered in the negative. In determining whether commerce is interstate or intrastate, regard must be had to its essential character. Mere billing, or the place at which title passes, is not determinative. If the actual movement is interstate, the power of Congress attaches to it and the provisions of the Act to Regulate Commerce, enacted for the purpose of preventing and redressing unjust discrimination by interstate carriers, whether in rates or facilities, apply. *Rearick* v. *Pennsylvania*, 203 U. S. 507, 512; *So. Pac. Terminal Co.* v. *Inter. Comm. Comm.*, 219 U. S. 498, 526, 527; *Ohio R. R. Comm.* v. *Worthington*, 225 U. S. 101, 108, 110; *Savage* v. *Jones*, 225 U. S. 501, 520; *Texas & N. O. R. R.* v. *Sabine Tram Co.*, 227 U. S. 111, 127; *Louisiana R. R. Comm.* v. *Tex. & Pac. Ry.*, 229 U. S. 336; *Ill. Cent. R. R.* v. *Louisiana R. R. Comm.*, 236 U. S. 157, 163. Thus, in the case of *Southern Pacific Terminal Co.* v. *Interstate Commerce Commission*, *supra*, cotton seed cake which had been purchased by one Young at various places in Texas was shipped to him at the port of Galveston, where it was prepared for export. The court sustained the jurisdiction of the Interstate Commerce Commission with respect to the transportation to Galveston, although between Texas points, it being an incident to the export movement, and held that the special privileges given by the Terminal Company to Young on the wharf were undue preferences. As the commodity was destined for export it made no difference, said the court, 'that the shipments of the products were not made on through bills of lading or whether their initial points were Galveston or some other points in Texas.' In *Ohio Railroad Commission* v. *Worthington*, *supra*, it appeared that the State Commission had established a rate on what was called 'lake cargo coal' transported from a coal field in eastern Ohio to ports in the same State on Lake Erie for carriage thence by lake vessels to other States. Ordinarily, the shipper had the coal transported 'upon bills of lading to himself, or to another for himself,' at Huron, Ohio. The rate covered the transportation to Huron and the placing of the coal on the vessels and trimming it for its interstate journey. In view of the proved nature of the movement, the court held that the action of the State Commission was an attempt directly to regulate interstate commerce and the enforcement of the order of the State Commission was enjoined. Again, in *Savage* v. *Jones*, 225 U. S. 501, 520, the complainant was a manufacturer in Minnesota and sold his commodity to purchasers in Indiana, the delivery being f. o. b. cars at Minneapolis for transportation to Indiana in the original unbroken packages, the freight being paid by the purchasers. Referring to an objection similar to the one here urged, the court said: "In answer, it must again be said that 'commerce among the States is not a technical legal conception, but a practical one, drawn from the course of business.' *Swift & Co.* v. *United States,* 196 U. S. 375, 398; *Rearick* v. *Pennsylvania,* 203 U. S. 507, 512. It clearly appears from the bill that the complainant was engaged in dealing with purchasers in another State. His product manufactured in Minnesota was, in pursuance of his contracts of sale, to be delivered to carriers for transportation to the purchasers in Indiana. This was interstate commerce in the freedom of which from any unconstitutional burden the complainant had a direct interest." In *Texas & N. O. R. R. Co.* v. *Sabine Tram Co.,* 227 U. S. 111, 127, it was found that the Powell Company bought lumber for export to different ports in Europe through the ports of Sabine and Port Arthur, both in Texas. To fill its export contracts, it purchased of the Sabine Tram Company a large amount of lumber, which according to the seller's option was delivered f. o. b. cars at Sabine, Texas. There were separate bills of lading for delivery at Sabine to the Sabine Tram Company. Upon arrival at Sabine, the lumber was carried a short distance beyond the station to the dock where it was unloaded from cars into water of the slip ready for loading upon ships. The Sabine Tram Company had no connection with the further carriage. The railroad company collected, over protest, the rates fixed by tariffs filed with the Interstate Commerce Commission, and the Sabine Tram Company brought suit to recover the difference between the amount thus paid and the amount which would have been payable at the rate fixed by the State Commission. The court held that the rate fixed by the Interstate Commerce Commission was applicable as the lumber was destined for export and that, as the movement was one actually in the course of transportation to a foreign destination, the form of the billing to Sabine, and the transactions there, were not determinative.

Thus, in varying circumstances, the same principle has been applied in these cases and in the others cited; and that principle is that the jurisdiction of the Commission is determined by the essential character of the commerce in question. In the present case, to repeat, it appears that for the purpose of filling contracts with purchasers in other States, coal is delivered f. o. b. at the mines for transportation to such purchasers. The movement thus initiated is an interstate movement and the facilities required are facilities of interstate commerce. A very large part of what in fact is the interstate commerce of the country is conducted upon this basis and the arrangements that are made between seller and purchaser with respect to the place of taking title to the commodity, or as to the payment of freight, where the actual movement is interstate, does not affect either the power of Congress or the jurisdiction of the Commission which Congress has established. . . . .

SHANKS *v.* DELAWARE, LACKAWANNA AND WESTERN RAILROAD COMPANY

239 U. S. 556 (1916)

MR. JUSTICE VAN DEVANTER delivered the opinion of the court.

Shanks sued the Railroad Company for damages resulting from personal injuries suffered through its negligence while he was in its employ, and rested his right to recover upon the Employers' Liability Act of Congress. His injuries were received in New Jersey and his action was brought in the Supreme Court of New York. He prevailed at the trial, but in the Appellate Division the judgment was reversed with a direction that his complaint be dismissed without prejudice to any remedy he might have under the law of New Jersey, and this was affirmed by the Court of Appeals, the ground of the appellate rulings being that at the time of the injury he was not employed in interstate commerce. 163 App. Div. 565; 214 N. Y. 413. To obtain a review of the judgment of the Court of Appeals he sued out this writ of error, which was directed to the Supreme Court because the record was then in its possession. See *Atherton* v. *Fowler*, 91 U. S. 143; *Wurts* v. *Hoagland*, 105 U. S. 701; *Sioux Remedy Co.* v. *Cope*, 235 U. S. 197.

In so far as its words are material here, the Employers' Liability Act declares that "every common carrier by railroad while engaging in commerce between any of the several States . . . . shall be liable in damages to any person suffering injury while he is employed by such carrier in such commerce," if the injury results in whole or in part from the negligence of the carrier or of any of its officers, agents or employés. Thus it is essential to a right of recovery under the act not only that the carrier be engaged in interstate commerce at the time of the injury but also that the person suffering the injury be then employed by the carrier in such commerce. And so it results where the carrier is also engaged in intrastate commerce or in what is not commerce at all, that one who while employed therein by the carrier suffers injury through its negligence, or that of some of its officers, agents or employés, must look for redress to the laws of the State wherein the injury occurs, save where it results from the violation of some Federal statute, such as the Safety Appliance Acts.

The facts in the present case are these: The Railroad Company was engaged in both interstate and intrastate transportation and was conducting an extensive machine shop for repairing parts of locomotives used in such transportation. While employed in this shop Shanks was injured through the negligence of the company. Usually his work consisted in repairing certain parts of locomotives, but on the day of the injury he was engaged solely in taking down and putting into a new location an overhead counter-shaft — a heavy shop fixture — through which power was communicated to some of the machinery used in the repair work.

The question for decision is, was Shanks at the time of the injury employed in interstate commerce within the meaning of the Employers' Liability Act? What his employment was on other occasions is immaterial, for, as before indicated, the act refers to the service being rendered when the injury was suffered.

Having in mind the nature and usual course of the business to which the act relates and the evident purpose of Congress in adopting the act, we think it speaks of interstate commerce, not in a technical legal sense, but in a practical one better suited to the occasion (see *Swift & Co.* v. *United States*, 196 U. S. 375, 398), and that the true test of employment in such commerce in the sense intended is, was the employé at the time of the injury engaged in interstate transportation or in work so closely related to it as to be practically a part of it.

Applying this test, we have held that the requisite employment in interstate commerce exists where a car repairer is replacing a drawbar in a car then in use in such commerce, *Walsh* v. *New York, New Haven & Hartford R. R.*, 223 U. S. 1; where a fireman is walking ahead of and piloting through several switches a locomotive which is to be attached to an interstate train and to assist in moving the same up a grade, *Norfolk & Western Ry.* v. *Earnest*, 229 U. S. 114; where a workman about to repair a bridge regularly used in interstate transportation is carrying from a tool car to the bridge a sack of bolts needed in his work, *Pederson* v. *Del., Lack. & West. R. R.*, 229 U. S. 146; where a clerk is on his way through a railroad yard to meet an inbound interstate freight train and to mark the cars so the switching crew will know what to do with them when breaking up the train, *St. Louis, San Francisco & Texas Ry.* v. *Seale*, 229 U. S. 156; where a fireman, having prepared his engine for a trip in interstate commerce, and being about to start on his run, is walking across adjacent tracks on an errand consistent with his duties, *North Carolina R. R.* v. *Zachary*, 232 U. S. 248; and where a brakeman on a train carrying several cars of interstate and two of intrastate freight is assisting in securely placing the latter on a side track at an intermediate station to the end that they may not run back on the main track and that the train may proceed on its journey with the interstate freight, *New York Central R. R.* v. *Carr*, 238 U. S. 260.

Without departing from this test, we also have held that the requisite employment in interstate commerce does not exist where a member of a switching crew, whose general work extends to both interstate and intrastate traffic, is engaged in hauling a train or drag of cars, all loaded with intrastate freight, from one part of a city to another, *Ill. Cent. R. R.* v. *Behrens*, 233 U. S. 473, and where an employé in a colliery operated by a railroad company is mining coal intended to be used in the company's locomotives moving in interstate commerce, *Del., Lack. & West. R. R.* v. *Yurkonis*, 238 U. S. 439. In neither instance could the service indicated be said to be interstate transportation or so closely related to it as to be practically a part of it.

Coming to apply the test to the case in hand, it is plain that Shanks was not employed in interstate transportation, or in repairing or keeping in usable condition a roadbed, bridge, engine, car or other instrument then in use in such transportation. What he was doing was altering the location of a fixture in a machine shop. The connection between the fixture and interstate transportation was remote at best, for the only function of the fixture was to communicate power to machinery used in repairing parts of engines some of which were used in such transportation. This, we think, demonstrates that the work in which Shanks was engaged, like that of the coal miner in the *Yurkonis Case*, was too remote from interstate transportation to be practically a part of it, and therefore that he was not employed in interstate commerce within the meaning of the Employers' Liability Act.

Judgment affirmed.

ATCHISON, TOPEKA & SANTA FE RAILWAY COMPANY *v.* HAROLD

241 U. S. 371 (1916)

MR. CHIEF JUSTICE WHITE delivered the opinion of the court.

We are of the opinion that a motion to dismiss is without merit but the reasons which lead us to that conclusion will be more clearly appreciated after we have made a statement of the case. Until that is done we hence postpone the subject.

J. Bell & Son, having sold a carload of bulk corn to the C. V. Fisher Grain Company residing and doing business at Kansas City, Missouri, on September 21, 1910, shipped the same from Yanka, Nebraska, over the Union Pacific Railroad. The bill of lading identified the car as L. W. No. 33791 containing 100,420 pounds of corn, and the same was consigned to Topeka, Kansas, to the order of the consignors (Bell & Son) with a direction, however, in the bill of lading to "notify C. V. Fisher Grain Company, care of Santa Fe for shipment." A draft for the purchase price of the corn was mailed to Kansas City, Missouri, accompanied with the bill of lading endorsed over to the order of the Fisher Grain Company and on the presentation of this draft to the Grain Company at Kansas City, Missouri, while the car was yet in transit it paid the same and became the possessor and owner of the bill of lading. On September 24 the Grain Company surrendered to an agent of the Santa Fe at Kansas City, Missouri, the Yanka bill of lading which it had thus acquired and took in exchange for it another bill consigning the identical car to their own order at Elk Falls, Kansas, a place on the Santa Fe road, with a direction, however, to notify at Elk Falls the Nevling Elevator Company. This bill of lading was dated the same day as the original bill for which it was exchanged, that is, September 21, although it was in fact only signed and issued on the twenty-fourth of that month; and although on its face it treated the car as being at Kansas City, in reality the car was in transit from Yanka, not having yet reached Topeka.

Harold, the defendant in error, a grain dealer at Wichita, Kansas, who had sold on September 15 a carload of corn to Shoe & Jackson at Elk Falls to be shipped or delivered in a stated number of days, bought the carload of corn described by the bill of lading issued at Kansas City, and, paying a draft for the purchase price drawn by Fisher Grain Company with the bill annexed, he became the owner of the bill and directed that delivery of the corn be made to Shoe & Jackson. The car from Yanka had then not yet been delivered to the Santa Fe at Topeka, having reached that point only on September 28, on which day it was offered to the Santa Fe for carriage and delivery at Elk Falls. Finding that the car was in bad order the delivery was declined and the car turned back to the Union Pacific. That road discovering that the damage was such that the car could not be repaired while it was loaded, sent it to an elevator, transferred the grain to another car, S. P. No. 85721, and turned that car over to the Santa Fe. The new car, however, did not contain the exact quantity of grain originally shipped from Yanka as one of the defects in the old car was a leaky door and several hundred pounds of the corn had been lost in transit. The car was promptly carried by the Santa Fe to Elk Falls and offered for delivery, but as the period for the fulfillment by Harold of his contract with Shoe & Jackson had elapsed and there had been a decline in the market price of corn, the latter refused to take the car. Thereupon this suit against the Santa Fe was commenced by Harold to recover the loss which he had suffered by the alleged unreasonable delay in delivery at Elk Falls consisting of three items: First, the difference between the price at which the corn had been contracted to be sold to Shoe & Jackson and the market price at the date the car was offered for delivery; Second, the amount of the freight paid on the corn which had been lost; and Third, a reasonable attorney's fee which it was alleged a statute of the State of Kansas authorized to be recovered in case of delay of a carrier in the delivery of grain.

In its defense the company alleged the shipment over the Union Pacific from Yanka, averred that the corn was received by it at Topeka in order to complete the transportation to Elk Falls, and charged that by a condition of the bill of lading issued at Kansas City as the delay had been wholly caused by the Union Pacific, there was no liability on the part of the Santa Fe, and that besides that company was not liable because of a failure to give a notice of claim in compliance with a condition which was also contained in the Kansas City bill of lading. There was judgment in the trial court for the plaintiff and the judgment of the court below affirming such action is the one now under review.

The court after referring to the bill of lading sued on (the one issued at Kansas City), and after stating that "the shipment intended to be described in the bill of lading originated at Yanka, Nebraska, on the Union Pacific Railway," proceeded to state the facts which we have recapitulated and which had been admitted in evidence without objection. In substance conceding that if the facts stated were made the test of the rights of the parties the judgment under review was wrong because there had been as a matter of fact no unreasonable delay in delivering the corn by the Santa Fe, it was held that the judgment rendered was right since the plaintiff below as the purchaser of a bill of lading for value had a right to rely upon the face of the bill, to treat the corn as having been received by the carrier at Kansas City on the date the bill of lading was issued, and therefore to recover for the unreasonable delay in delivery which necessarily would result from excluding from view the facts concerning the movement of the corn from Yanka, Nebraska, and the date of its delivery at Topeka to the Santa Fe. The essence of the opinion, 93 Kansas, 456, was aptly summed up in the syllabus which preceded it drawn by the court which is as follows:

"1. The rule which invests the innocent holder of a bill of lading with rights not available to the shipper, declared in *Savings Bank* v. *A., T. & Santa Fe R. R.*, 20 Kansas, 519; *Railway Co.* v. *Hutchings*, 78 Kansas, 758, 99 Pac. Rep. 230; and *Hutchings* v. *Railway Co.*, 84 Kansas, 479, 114 Pac. Rep. 1079, is followed in a case where the plaintiff purchased corn described in a bill of lading, and paid the shipper's draft attached to the bill in the usual course of business."

In addition the allowance of the attorney's fees under the Kansas statute was upheld on the ground that the statute was within the legitimate police power of the State to enact and not repugnant to the state or Federal Constitution.

The motion to dismiss referred to at the outset is based on the ground that the action of the court involved no question of interstate but purely one of intrastate commerce. But this disregards the fact that the bill of lading which was sued upon was an interstate commerce bill covering a shipment from Kansas City, Missouri, to Elk Falls, Kansas. True it is urged that that bill of lading is not the test of whether there is jurisdiction because it was shown that in reality the shipment was an intrastate one from Topeka, Kansas, to Elk Falls in that State. But this assumes that although the judgment rests upon the conception that the previous movement of the corn from Yanka could not be considered as against the plaintiff because he was an innocent third holder of the bill of lading issued at Kansas City, nevertheless for the purpose of determining whether jurisdiction exists the facts as to the shipment from Yanka must be treated as relevant. Leaving aside however, this contradiction and considering the facts as to the movement of the grain from its inception, we are of opinion that from that point of view it was clearly established that the grain moved in a continuous interstate commerce shipment from the date of its departure from Yanka to the termination of the transit at Elk Falls and that the delivery of the car to the Santa Fe at Topeka for further movement was therefore not a new and distinct shipment in intrastate commerce. We reach this conclusion in view of the place of business of the Fisher Grain Company (Kansas City, Missouri), of the fact that there was no person at Topeka to whom the grain was consigned, of the endorsement of the bill of lading to the Fisher Grain Company and the annexing to it of a draft drawn on that company at Kansas City for the purchase price, and because the order on the face of the bill of lading to "notify C. V. Fisher Grain Company, care of Santa Fe for shipment" made it apparent that it was not contemplated that the interstate shipment should terminate at Topeka, but that the car should move on as the result of such direction as might be given while it was in transit by the Fisher Grain Company at Kansas City, Missouri. . . . .

That the local rule applied by the court below was in direct conflict with the general commercial law on the subject as repeatedly settled by this court, is plain. *Shaw* v. *Railroad Co.*, 101 U. S. 557; *Pollard* v. *Vinton*, 105 U. S. 7; *Iron Mountain Ry.* v. *Knight*, 122 U. S. 79; *Friedlander* v. *Tex. & Pac. Ry.*, 130 U. S. 416; *Mo. Pac. Ry.* v. *McFadden*, 154 U. S. 155; *The Carlos F. Roses*, 177 U. S. 655, 665.

Nothing could better point out the irreconcilable conflict between the local doctrine applied by the court below and the general law as illustrated in the cases cited than does the following statement in the opinion in the *Roses Case* last cited (p. 665):

"A pledgee to whom a bill of lading is given as security gets the legal title to the goods and the right of possession only if such is the intention of the parties, and that intention is open to explanation. Inquiry into the transaction in which the bill originated is not precluded because it came into the hands of persons who may have innocently paid value for it."

Whether in the absence of legislation by Congress the attributing to an interstate bill of lading of the exceptional and local characteristic applied by the court below in conflict with the general commercial rule constituted a direct burden on interstate commerce and was therefore void need not now be considered. This is so because irrespective of that question and indeed without stopping to consider the general provisions of the Act to Regulate Commerce it is not disputable that what is known as the Carmack Amendment to the Act to Regulate Commerce (act of June 29, 1906, c. 3591, § 7, 34 Stat. 593) was an assertion of the power of Congress over the subject of interstate shipments, the duty to issue bills of lading and the responsibilities thereunder, which in the nature of things excluded state action. *Adams Express Co.* v. *Croninger*, 226 U. S. 491, 505–506; *Mo., Kan. & Tex. Ry.* v. *Harriman Bros.*, 227 U. S. 657, 671–672; *Boston & Maine R. R.* v. *Hooker*, 233 U. S. 97, 110; *Atchison, Topeka & Santa Fe Ry.* v. *Robinson*, 233 U. S. 173, 180; *Cleveland & St. Louis Ry.* v. *Dettlebach*, 239 U. S. 588; *Georgia, Florida & Alabama Ry.* v. *Blish Milling Co.*, *ante* [240 U. S.], p. 190.

Indeed in the argument it is frankly conceded that as the subject of a carrier's liability for loss or damage to goods moving in interstate commerce under a bill of lading is embraced by the Carmack Amendment, state legislation on that subject has been excluded. It is insisted, however, that this does not exclude liability for error in the bill of lading purporting to cover an interstate shipment because "Congress has legislated relative to the one, but not relative to the other." But this ignores the view expressly pointed out in the previous decision dealing with the Carmack Amendment that its prime object was to bring about a uniform rule of responsibility as to interstate commerce and interstate commerce bills of lading, — a purpose which would be wholly frustrated if the proposition relied upon were upheld. The principal subject of responsibility embraced by the act of Congress carried with it necessarily the incidents thereto. See the subject aptly and clearly illustrated by *St. Louis & San Francisco R. R.* v. *Woodruff Mills*, 105 Mississippi, 214, where a statute of the State of Mississippi accomplishing the very result applied by the court below was decided to be no longer applicable to interstate commerce because of the taking possession by Congress of the field by virtue of the amendment referred to.

As it follows from what we have said that the court below erred in applying the local law to the interstate commerce shipment under consideration, its judgment must be reversed and the case remanded for further proceedings not inconsistent with this opinion. *And it was so ordered.*

THE MINNESOTA RATE CASES

230 U. S. 352 (1913) [1]

These suits were brought in the Circuit Court of the United States for the district of Minnesota by stockholders of the Northern Pacific Railway Company, the Great Northern Railway Company, and the Minneapolis and St. Louis Railroad Company to restrain the enforcement of two orders of the Railroad and Warehouse Commission of the State of Minnesota and two acts of the legislature of that State prescribing maximum charges for transportation of freight in that State and a maximum rate of two cents a mile for passengers. The rates related to traffic exclusively between points in the State. It was contended, however, that as applied to cities on the State's boundaries or to places within competitive districts crossed by the state line, the railways disturbed the relation previously existing between interstate and intrastate rates, thus imposing a direct burden on interstate commerce and creating discriminations as against localities in other states. The rates were also assailed as confiscatory. The jurisdiction of the Circuit Court was sustained in *Ex parte Young*, 209 U. S. 123, where it was also held that the penal provisions of the acts, operating to preclude a fair opportunity to test their validity, were unconstitutional on their face. The Circuit Court then referred the suits to a special master, who took the evidence and made an elaborate report sustaining the complainant's contentions. His findings were confirmed by the court and decrees were entered accordingly, adjudging the acts and orders (with the exception, in the case of the Minneapolis and St. Louis Railroad Company, of the order of May 3, 1907) to be void and permanently enjoining the enforcement of the prescribed rates, freight and passenger, and their adoption or maintenance by the railroad companies. 184 Fed. Rep. 765.

From these decrees, the Attorney-General of the State and the members of the Railroad and Warehouse Commission prosecute these appeals.

Mr. Justice Hughes delivered the opinion of the court. . . .

The situation is not peculiar to Minnesota. The same question

[1] A brief statement of the facts has been framed based upon that in the opinion of the court. — Ed.

[2] Only so much of the opinion as deals with the effect of the acts and orders on interstate commerce is here reprinted. — Ed.

has been presented by the appeals, now before the court, which involve the validity of intrastate tariffs fixed by Missouri, Arkansas, Kentucky and Oregon. Differences in particular facts appear, but they cannot be regarded as controlling. A scheme of state rates framed to avoid discrimination between localities within the State, and to provide an harmonious system for intrastate transportation throughout the State, naturally would embrace those places within the State which are on or near the State's boundaries; and, when these are included in a general reduction of intrastate rates, there is, of course, a change in the relation of rates as theretofore existing to points adjacent to, but across, the state line. Kansas City, Kansas, and Kansas City, Missouri; East St. Louis, Illinois, and St. Louis, Missouri; Omaha, Nebraska, and Council Bluffs, Iowa; Cincinnati, Ohio, and Covington and Newport, Kentucky; and many other places throughout the country which might be mentioned, present substantially the same conditions as those here appearing with respect to localities on the boundaries of Minnesota. It is also a matter of common knowledge that competition takes but little account of state lines and in every part of the land competitive districts embrace points in different States.

With appreciation of the gravity of the controversy, the Railroad Commissioners of eight States[1] have filed their brief as *amici curiæ*, in support of the appeals, stating that, if the doctrine of the court below were accepted, the regulation by the States of rates for intrastate transportation would be practically destroyed. They say that "there is practically no movement of traffic between two towns within a State that does not come into competition with some interstate haul," and that "if the disturbance of the existing relation between competitive state and interstate rates is the correct criterion, no reduction can be made in state rates without interfering with interstate commerce." The Governors of three States, pursuant to a resolution of a conference of the Governors of all the States, have also presented, by leave of the court, their argument in defense of the position taken by Minnesota. They do not seek "to belittle the effect of the action of Minnesota on the business between the places" named in the findings, but they are convinced that if the principle announced by the Circuit Court is upheld, it can be made to apply by a showing of similar facts in virtually every State. Insist-

[1] Nebraska, Iowa, Kansas, South Dakota, North Dakota, Oklahoma, Missouri and Texas.

ing that, under their reserved power, "the right of the States to regulate their own commerce is as clear and broad as that of Congress to regulate interstate commerce," they assail the decision below, not upon the ground that it incorrectly sets forth conditions in Minnesota and adjoining States, but for what they consider to be "its plain disregard of the provisions of the Federal Constitution, which establish the relations between the Nation and the States." "The operation of these provisions," they maintain, "was not made to depend on geography or convenience or competition. They cannot apply in one State and not in another, according to circumstances as they may be found by the courts, because they are vital principles which constitute the very structure of our dual form of government."

The controversy thus arises from opposing conceptions of the fundamental law, and of the scope and effect of Federal legislation, rather than from differences with respect to the salient facts.

For the purpose of the present inquiry, the rates fixed by the State must be assumed to be reasonable rates so far as intrastate traffic is concerned; that is, they must be taken to be rates which the State, in the exercise of its legislative judgment, could constitutionally fix for intrastate transportation separately considered. If the state rates are not of this character — a question to be dealt with later — they cannot be sustained in any event; but, assuming them to be otherwise valid, the decree below, with respect to the present branch of the case, rests upon two grounds: (1) That the action of the State imposes a direct burden upon interstate commerce; and (2) that it is in conflict with the provisions of the Act to Regulate Commerce.

These grounds are distinct. If a state enactment imposes a *direct burden* upon interstate commerce, it must fall regardless of Federal legislation. The point of such an objection is not that Congress has acted, but that the State has directly restrained that which in the absence of Federal regulation should be free. If the acts of Minnesota constitute a direct burden upon interstate commerce, they would be invalid without regard to the exercise of Federal authority touching the interstate rates said to be affected. On the other hand, if the State, in the absence of Federal legislation, would have had the power to prescribe the rates here assailed, the question remains whether its action is void as being repugnant to the statute which Congress has enacted.

Prior to the passage of the Act to Regulate Commerce, carriers fixed their interstate rates free from the actual exertion of Federal control; and under that act, as it stood until the amendment of June 29, 1906, 34 Stat. 584, c. 3591, the Interstate Commerce Commission had no power to prescribe interstate rates. *Interstate Commerce Commission* v. *C., N. O. & T. P. Ry. Co.*, 167 U. S. 479, 511. The States, however, had long exercised the power to establish maximum rates for intrastate transportation. Was this power, apart from Federal action, subject to the limitation that the State could not fix intrastate rates, reasonable as such, generally throughout the State, but only as to such places and in such circumstances that the interstate business of the carriers would not be thereby affected? That is, was the State debarred from fixing reasonable rates on traffic, wholly internal, as to all state points so situated that as a practical consequence the carriers would have to reduce the rates they had made to competing points without the State, in order to maintain the volume of their interstate business or to continue the parity of rates or the relation between rates as it had previously existed? Was the State, in prescribing a general tariff of reasonable intrastate rates otherwise within its authority bound not to go below a minimum standard established by the interstate rates made by the carriers within competitive districts? If the state power, independently of Federal legislation, is thus limited, the inquiry need proceed no further. Otherwise it must be determined whether Congress has so acted as to create such a restriction upon the state authority theretofore existing.

(1) The general principles governing the exercise of state authority when interstate commerce is affected are well established. The power of Congress to regulate commerce among the several States is supreme and plenary. It is "complete in itself, may be exercised to its utmost extent, and acknowledges no limitations other than are prescribed in the Constitution." *Gibbons* v. *Ogden*, 9 Wheat. 1, 196. The conviction of its necessity sprang from the disastrous experiences under the Confederation when the States vied in discriminatory measures against each other. In order to end these evils, the grant in the Constitution conferred upon Congress an authority at all times adequate to secure the freedom of interstate commercial intercourse from state control and to provide effective regulation of that intercourse as the national interest may demand. The words "among the several States" distinguish between the commerce which con-

cerns more States than one and that commerce which is confined within one State and does not affect other States. "The genius and character of the whole government," said Chief Justice Marshall, "seem to be, that its action is to be applied to all the external concerns of the nation, and to those internal concerns which affect the States generally; but not to those which are completely within a particular State, which do not affect other States, and with which it is not necessary to interfere, for the purpose of executing some of the general powers of the government. The completely internal commerce of a State, then, may be considered as reserved for the State itself." (*Id.*, p. 195.) This reservation to the States manifestly is only of that authority which is consistent with and not opposed to the grant to Congress. There is no room in our scheme of government for the assertion of state power in hostility to the authorized exercise of Federal power. The authority of Congress extends to every part of interstate commerce, and to every instrumentality or agency by which it is carried on; and the full control by Congress of the subjects committed to its regulation is not to be denied or thwarted by the commingling of interstate and intrastate operations. This is not to say that the Nation may deal with the internal concerns of the State, as such, but that the execution by Congress of its constitutional power to regulate interstate commerce is not limited by the fact that intrastate transactions may have become so interwoven therewith that the effective government of the former incidentally controls the latter. This conclusion necessarily results from the supremacy of the national power within its appointed sphere. *McCulloch* v. *Maryland*, 4 Wheat. 316, 405, 426; *The Daniel Ball*, 10 Wall. 557, 565; *Smith* v. *Alabama*, 124 U. S. 465, 473; *Baltimore & Ohio R. R. Co.* v. *Interstate Commerce Commission*, 221 U. S. 612, 618, 619; *Southern Railway Co.* v. *United States*, 222 U. S. 20, 26, 27; *Mondou* v. *N. Y., N. H. & H. R. R. Co.*, 223 U. S. 1, 47, 54, 55.

The grant in the Constitution of its own force, that is, without action by Congress, established the essential immunity of interstate commercial intercourse from the direct control of the States with respect to those subjects embraced within the grant which are of such a nature as to demand that, if regulated at all, their regulation should be prescribed by a single authority. It has repeatedly been declared by this court that as to those subjects which require a general system or uniformity of regulation the power of Congress is exclusive. In other matters, admitting of diversity of treatment according to the special requirements of local conditions, the States may act within their respective jurisdictions until Congress sees fit to act; and, when Congress does act, the exercise of its authority overrides all conflicting state legislation. *Cooley* v. *Board of Wardens*, 12 How. 299, 319; *Ex parte McNiel*, 13 Wall. 236, 240; *Welton* v. *Missouri*, 91 U. S. 275, 280; *County of Mobile* v. *Kimball*, 102 U. S. 691, 697; *Gloucester Ferry Co.* v. *Pennsylvania*, 114 U. S. 196, 204; *Bowman* v. *Chicago &c. Railway Co.*, 125 U. S. 465, 481, 485; *Gulf, Colorado & Santa Fe Ry. Co.* v. *Hefley*, 158 U. S. 98, 103, 104; *Northern Pacific Ry. Co.* v. *Washington*, 222 U. S. 370, 378; *Southern Ry. Co.* v. *Reid*, 222 U. S. 424, 436.

The principle, which determines this classification, underlies the doctrine that the States cannot under any guise impose direct burdens upon interstate commerce. For this is but to hold that the States are not permitted directly to regulate or restrain that which from its nature should be under the control of the one authority and be free from restriction save as it is governed in the manner that the national legislature constitutionally ordains.

Thus, the States cannot tax interstate commerce, either by laying the tax upon the business which constitutes such commerce or the privilege of engaging in it, or upon the receipts, as such, derived from it (*State Freight Tax Case*, 15 Wall. 232; *Robbins* v. *Shelby Taxing District*, 120 U. S. 489; *Philadelphia & Southern Mail S. S. Co.* v. *Pennsylvania*, 122 U. S. 325; *Leloup* v. *Mobile*, 127 U. S. 640; *McCall* v. *California*, 136 U. S. 104; *Brennan* v. *Titusville*, 153 U. S. 289; *Galveston, Harrisburg & San Antonio Railway Co.* v. *Texas*, 210 U. S. 217; *Western Union Telegraph Co.* v. *Kansas*, 216 U. S. 1; *Pullman Co.* v. *Kansas*, 216 U. S. 1, 56; *Meyer* v. *Wells, Fargo & Co.*, 223 U. S. 298; *Crenshaw* v. *Arkansas*, 227 U. S. 389); or upon persons or property in transit in interstate commerce (*Passenger Cases*, 7 How. 283; *Crandall* v. *Nevada*, 6 Wall. 35; *State Freight Tax Case*, *supra*, p. 281; *Coe* v. *Errol*, 116 U. S. 517; *Kelley* v. *Rhoads*, 188 U. S. 1; *Bacon* v. *Illinois*, 227 U. S. 504).

They have no power to prohibit interstate trade in legitimate articles of commerce (*Bowman* v. *Chicago &c. Railway Co.*, *supra;* *Leisy* v. *Hardin*, 135 U. S. 100; *Vance* v. *Vandercook Co.* (No. 1), 170 U. S. 438; *Schollenberger* v. *Pennsylvania*, 171 U. S. 1; *Oklahoma* v. *Kansas Natural Gas Co.*, 221 U. S. 229; *L. & N. R. R. Co.* v. *Cook Brewing Co.*, 223 U. S. 70); or to discriminate against the products of other States (*Ward* v. *Maryland*, 12 Wall. 418;

Welton v. *Missouri, supra; Hannibal & St. J. R. R. Co.* v. *Husen,* 95 U. S. 465; *Guy* v. *Baltimore,* 100 U. S. 434; *Walling* v. *Michigan,* 116 U. S. 446; *Minnesota* v. *Barber,* 136 U. S. 313; *Brimmer* v. *Rebman,* 138 U. S. 78; *Darnell* v. *Memphis,* 208 U. S. 113); or to exclude from the limits of the State corporations or others engaged in interstate commerce or to fetter by conditions their right to carry it on (*Crutcher* v. *Kentucky,* 141 U. S. 47; *Western Union Telegraph Co.* v. *Kansas, supra; Pullman Co.* v. *Kansas, supra; International Text Book Co.* v. *Pigg,* 217 U. S. 91; *Buck Stove Co.* v. *Vickers,* 226 U. S. 205); or to prescribe the rates to be charged for transportation from one State to another, or to subject the operations of carriers in the course of such transportation to requirements that are unreasonable or pass beyond the bounds of suitable local protection (*Wabash &c. Railway Co.* v. *Illinois,* 118 U. S. 557, 577; *Covington &c. Bridge Co.* v. *Kentucky,* 154 U. S. 204; *Louisville & Nashville R. R. Co.* v. *Eubank,* 184 U. S. 27; *Hanley* v. *Kansas City Southern Ry. Co.,* 187 U. S. 617; *R. R. Commission of Ohio* v. *Worthington,* 225 U. S. 101; *Texas & N. O. R. R. Co.* v. *Sabine Tram Co.,* 227 U. S. 111; *Hall* v. *DeCuir,* 95 U. S. 485, 488; *Cleveland, C., C. & St. L. Railway Co.* v. *Illinois,* 177 U. S. 514; *Houston & T. C. R. R. Co.* v. *Mayes,* 210 U. S. 321; *McNeill* v. *Southern Railway Co.,* 202 U. S. 543; *Mississippi R. R. Commission* v. *Illinois Cent. R. R. Co.,* 203 U. S. 335; *Atlantic Coast Line* v. *Wharton,* 207 U. S. 328; *St. Louis Southwestern Ry. Co.* v. *Arkansas,* 217 U. S. 136; *Herndon* v. *C., R. I. & Pac. R. R. Co.,* 218 U. S. 135; *Yazoo &c. R. R. Co.* v. *Greenwood Grocery Co.,* 227 U. S. 1).

But within these limitations there necessarily remains to the States, until Congress acts, a wide range for the permissible exercise of power appropriate to their territorial jurisdiction although interstate commerce may be affected. It extends to those matters of a local nature as to which it is impossible to derive from the constitutional grant an intention that they should go uncontrolled pending Federal intervention. Thus, there are certain subjects having the most obvious and direct relation to interstate commerce, which nevertheless, with the acquiescence of Congress, have been controlled by state legislation from the foundation of the Government because of the necessity that they should not remain unregulated and that their regulation should be adapted to varying local exigencies; hence, the absence of regulation by Congress in such matters has not imported that there should be no restriction but rather that the States should continue to supply the needed rules until Congress should decide to supersede them. Further, it is competent for a State to govern its internal commerce, to provide local improvements, to create and regulate local facilities, to adopt protective measures of a reasonable character in the interest of the health, safety, morals and welfare of its people, although interstate commerce may incidentally or indirectly be involved. Our system of government is a practical adjustment by which the National authority as conferred by the Constitution is maintained in its full scope without unnecessary loss of local efficiency. Where the subject is peculiarly one of local concern, and from its nature belongs to the class with which the State appropriately deals in making reasonable provision for local needs, it cannot be regarded as left to the unrestrained will of individuals because Congress has not acted, although it may have such a relation to interstate commerce as to be within the reach of the Federal power. In such case, Congress must be the judge of the necessity of Federal action. Its paramount authority always enables it to intervene at its discretion for the complete and effective government of that which has been committed to its care, and, for this purpose and to this extent, in response to a conviction of national need, to displace local laws by substituting laws of its own. The successful working of our constitutional system has thus been made possible.

The leading illustrations may be noted. Immediately upon the adoption of the Constitution, Congress recognized the propriety of local action with respect to pilotage, in view of the local necessities of navigation. Act of August 7, 1789, c. 9, § 4; 1 Stat. 53, 54; *Cooley* v. *Board of Wardens, supra.* It was sixty years before provision for Federal license of pilots was made (act of August 30, 1852, c. 106; 10 Stat. 61), and even then port pilots were not included. *Pacific Mail Steamship Co.* v. *Joliffe,* 2 Wall. 450, 459. And while Congress has full power over the subject and to a certain extent has prescribed rules, it is still in a large measure subject to the regulation of the States. *Anderson* v. *Pacific Coast S. S. Co.,* 225 U. S. 187.

A State is entitled to protect its coasts, to improve its harbors, bays and streams, and to construct dams and bridges across navigable rivers within its limits, unless there is conflict with some act of Congress. Plainly, in the case of dams and bridges, interference with the accustomed right of navigation may result. But this exercise of the important power to provide local improvements has not been regarded as constituting such a direct burden upon intercourse or interchange of traffic as to be repugnant to the Federal authority in its dormant state. *Willson* v. *Blackbird Creek Marsh Co.*, 2 Pet. 245; *Gilman* v. *Philadelphia*, 3 Wall. 713; *Pound* v. *Turck*, 95 U. S. 459; *County of Mobile* v. *Kimball, supra; Escanaba Co.* v. *Chicago*, 107 U. S. 678; *Cardwell* v. *American Bridge Co.*, 113 U. S. 205; *Huse* v. *Glover*, 119 U. S. 543, 547; *Willamette Bridge Co.* v. *Hatch*, 125 U. S. 1; *Lake Shore & Michigan C. Ry. Co.* v. *Ohio*, 165 U. S. 365; *Cummings* v. *Chicago*, 188 U. S. 410; *Manigault* v. *Springs*, 199 U. S. 473. Thus, in *Gilman* v. *Philadelphia, supra*, the complainants were the owners of a valuable wharf and dock property in the Schuylkill River and sought to prevent the construction of a bridge which had been authorized by the legislature of Pennsylvania to connect East and West Philadelphia. It appeared that the bridge would prevent the passage of vessels having masts which had formerly navigated the river up to the complainants' wharf, and would largely reduce the income from the property. The court affirmed the dismissal of the bill upon the ground that in the absence of legislation by Congress the State was acting within its authority. "The States have always exercised this power," said the court (*id.*, p. 729), "and from the nature and objects of the two systems of government they must always continue to exercise it, subject, however, in all cases, to the paramount authority of Congress, whenever the power of the States shall be exerted within the sphere of the commercial power which belongs to the Nation." Again, in *Escanaba Co.* v. *Chicago, supra*, the question related to the power of the City of Chicago, acting under the authority of the State, to regulate the closing of draws in the bridges over the Chicago River. The court said: "The Chicago River and its branches must . . . . be deemed navigable waters of the United States, over which Congress under its commercial power may exercise control to the extent necessary to protect, preserve, and improve their free navigation. But the States have full power to regulate within their limits matters of internal police, including in that general designation, whatever will promote the peace, comfort, convenience, and prosperity of their people. This power embraces the construction of roads, canals, and bridges, and the establishment of ferries, and it can generally be exercised more wisely by the States than by a distant authority. . . . . When its (the State's) power is exercised, so as to unnecessarily obstruct the navigation of the river or its branches, Congress may interfere and remove the obstruction. . . . But until Congress acts on the subject, the power of the State over bridges across its navigable streams is plenary." (*Id.*, p. 683.)

While the State may not impose a duty on tonnage (*Steamship Co.* v. *Portwardens*, 6 Wall. 31; *State Tonnage Tax Cases*, 12 Wall. 204, 212; *Cannon* v. *New Orleans*, 12 Wall. 577), it may regulate wharfage charges and exact tolls for the use of artificial facilities provided under its authority. The subject is one under state control, where Congress has not acted, although the payment is required of those engaged in interstate or foreign commerce. *Keokuk Packet Co.* v. *Keokuk*, 95 U. S. 80; *Cincinnati &c. Packet Co.* v. *Catlettsburg*, 105 U. S. 559; *Parkersburg & O. R. Transportation Co.* v. *Parkersburg*, 107 U. S. 691; *Huse* v. *Glover*, *supra*, *Ouachita Packet Co.* v. *Aiken*, 121 U. S. 444; *Sands* v. *Manistee River Improvement Co.*, 123 U. S. 288, 295. In *Transportation Co.* v. *Parkersburg*, *supra*, the court had before it an ordinance of that city prescribing rates of wharfage on vessels discharging or receiving freight at public landings belonging to the city. A transportation company having steamers plying between Pittsburg and Cincinnati complained that the wharfage charge was exorbitant. The court held that the reasonableness of the charge, it being simply one for wharfage, was to be determined by the state law. "The regulation of wharves belongs *prima facie*, and in the first instance, to the States, and would only be assumed by Congress when its exercise by the States is incompatible with the interests of commerce." (*Id.*, p. 703.) Again, in *Ouachita Packet Co.* v. *Aiken*, *supra*, where the owners of steamboats engaged in interstate commerce on the Mississippi River complained of wharfage rates at New Orleans as unreasonable and excessive, and in effect "a direct duty, or burden, upon commerce," the court, overruling the contention, held that the case was "clearly within the principles of the former decisions of this court, which affirm the right of a State, in the absence of regulation by Congress, to establish, manage and carry on works and improvements of a local character, though necessarily more or less affecting interstate and foreign commerce." (*Id.*, p. 447.)

Quarantine regulations are essential measures of protection which the States are free to adopt when they do not come into conflict with Federal action. In view of the need of conforming such measures to local conditions, Congress from the beginning has been content to leave the matter for the most part, notwithstanding its vast importance, to the States and has repeatedly acquiesced in the enforcement of state laws. (Acts of February

25, 1799, c. XII, 1 Stat. 619, R. S., § 4797; Act of April 29, 1878, c. 66, 20 Stat. 37; Act of February 15, 1893, c. 114, 27 Stat. 449.) Such laws undoubtedly operate upon interstate and foreign commerce. They could not be effective otherwise. They cannot, of course, be made the cover for discriminations and arbitrary enactments having no reasonable relation to health (*Hannibal & St. J. Railroad Co.* v. *Husen*, 95 U. S. 465, 472, 473); but the power of the State to take steps to prevent the introduction or spread of disease, although interstate and foreign commerce are involved (subject to the paramount authority of Congress if it decides to assume control), is beyond question. *Morgan's &c. S. S. Co.* v. *Louisiana*, 118 U. S. 455; *Missouri, Kansas & Texas Ry. Co.* v. *Haber*, 169 U. S. 613; *Louisiana* v. *Texas*, 176 U. S. 1; *Rasmussen* v. *Idaho*, 181 U. S. 198; *Compagnie Francaise &c.* v. *Board of Health*, 186 U. S. 380; *Reid* v. *Colorado*, 187 U. S. 137, 138; *Asbell* v. *Kansas*, 209 U. S. 251. In *Compagnie Francaise &c.* v. *Board of Health*, *supra*, the court had before it the quarantine law of Louisiana which, among other things, provided the State Board of Health might "in its discretion, prohibit the introduction into any infected portions of the State, persons acclimated, or unacclimated or said to be immune, when in its judgment the introduction of such persons would add to or increase the prevalence of the disease." The Supreme Court of the State, interpreting the statute, held that it empowered the Board to exclude healthy persons from a locality infested with a contagious or infectious disease, whether they came from without or within the State. It was objected that this provision was too broad and that the former decisions of the court were based upon the right of the States to exclude diseased persons and things which were not legitimate subjects of commerce. The court sustained the law, saying, with respect to this argument: "But it must be at once observed that this erroneously states the doctrine as concluded by the decisions of this court previously referred to, since the proposition ignores the fact that those cases expressly and unequivocally hold that the health and quarantine laws of the several States are not repugnant to the Constitution of the United States, although they affect foreign and domestic commerce, as in many cases they necessarily must do in order to be efficacious, because until Congress has acted under the authority conferred upon it by the Constitution, such state health and quarantine laws producing such effect on legitimate interstate commerce are not in conflict with the Constitution. True is it that, in some of the cases relied on in the argument, it was held that a state law absolutely prohibiting the introduction, under all circumstances, of objects actually affected with disease, was valid because such objects were not legitimate commerce. But this implies no limitation on the power to regulate by health laws the subjects of legitimate commerce. In other words, the power exists until Congress has acted, to incidentally regulate by health and quarantine laws, even although interstate and foreign commerce is affected, and the power to absolutely prohibit additionally obtains where the thing prohibited is not commerce, and hence not embraced in either interstate or foreign commerce." (*Id.*, p. 391.)

State inspection laws and statutes designed to safeguard the inhabitants of a State from fraud and imposition are valid when reasonable in their requirements and not in conflict with Federal rules, although they may affect interstate commerce in their relation to articles prepared for export or by including incidentally those brought into the State and held for sale in the original imported packages. *Gibbons* v. *Ogden*, *supra*, p. 203; *Turner* v. *Maryland*, 107 U. S. 38; *Plumley* v. *Massachusetts*, 155 U. S. 461; *Patapsco Guana Co.* v. *North Carolina*, 171 U. S. 345, 357, 358; *Savage* v. *Jones*, 225 U. S. 501. And for the protection of its game and the preservation of a valuable food supply, the State may penalize the possession of game during the closed season whether obtained within the State or brought from abroad. *Silz* v. *Hesterberg*, 211 U. S. 31.

Interstate carriers, in the absence of Federal statute providing a different rule, are answerable according to the law of the State for nonfeasance or misfeasance within its limits. *Chicago, Milwaukee &c. Ry. Co.* v. *Solan*, 169 U. S. 133, 137; *Pennsylvania R. R. Co.* v. *Hughes*, 191 U. S. 477, 491; *Martin* v. *Pittsburg & Lake Erie R. R. Co.*, 203 U. S. 284, 294; *Southern Pacific Co.* v. *Schuyler*, 227 U. S. 601, 613. Until the enactment by Congress of the act of April 22, 1908, c. 149, 35 Stat. 65, the laws of the States determined the liability of interstate carriers by railroad for injuries received by their employés while engaged in interstate commerce, and this was because Congress, although empowered to regulate the subject, had not acted thereon. In some States the so-called fellow-servant rule obtained; in others, it had been abrogated; and it remained for Congress, in this respect and in other matters specified in the statute, to establish a uniform rule. *Mondou* v. *N. Y., N. H. & H. R. R. Co.*, *supra;*

Michigan Central R. R. Co. v. *Vreeland*, 227 U. S. 59, 66, 67. So, where Congress has not intervened, state statutes providing damages for wrongful death may be enforced not only against land carriers but also against the owners of vessels engaged in interstate commerce where the wrong occurs within the jurisdiction of the State. *Sherlock* v. *Alling*, 93 U. S. 99, 103. See *American Steamboat Co.* v. *Chase*, 16 Wall. 522; *The Hamilton*, 207 U. S. 398. And, until Congress legislated on the matter, liability for loss of property, on interstate as well as intrastate shipments, was subject to state regulation. Some States allowed an exemption by contract from all or a part of the common law liability; others allowed no exemption. These differences in the applicable laws created inequalities with respect to interstate transportation, but each State exercised the power inherent in its territorial jurisdiction, and the remedy for the resulting diversity lay with Congress, which was free to substitute its own regulations; and this was done in the recent amendment of § 20 of the Act to Regulate Commerce. Act of June 29, 1906, c. 3591, 34 Stat. 584; *Adams Express Co.* v. *Croninger*, 226 U. S. 491, 500. It is within the competency of a State to create and enforce liens upon vessels for supplies furnished under contracts not maritime in their nature, and it is no valid objection that the state law may obstruct the prosecution of a voyage of an interstate character. *The Winnebago*, 205 U. S. 354. It may also create liens for damages to property on land occasioned by negligence of vessels. *Johnson* v. *Chicago &c. Elevator Co.*, 119 U. S. 388; *Martin* v. *West*, 222 U. S. 191. Cars employed in interstate commerce may be seized by attachment under state law, in order to compel the payment of debts. *Davis* v. *C., C., C. & St. L. Ry. Co.*, 217 U. S. 157. And the legislation of the States, safeguarding life and property and promoting comfort and convenience within its jurisdiction, may extend incidentally to the operations of the carrier in the conduct of interstate business, provided it does not subject that business to unreasonable demands and is not opposed to Federal legislation. *Smith* v. *Alabama*, 124 U. S. 465; *Hennington* v. *Georgia*, 163 U. S. 299; *N. Y., N. H. & H. R. R. Co.* v. *New York*, 165 U. S. 628; *Lake Shore & M. S. Ry. Co.* v. *Ohio*, 173 U. S. 285; *Missouri Pacific Ry. Co.* v. *Larabee Mills*, 211 U. S. 612; *Missouri Pacific Ry. Co.* v. *Kansas*, 216 U. S. 262. It has also been held that the State has the power to forbid the consolidation of state railroad corporations with competing lines although both may be interstate carriers and the prohibition may have a far-reaching effect upon interstate commerce. *Pearsall* v. *Great Northern Ry. Co.*, 161 U. S. 646, 677; *Louisville & Nashville R. R. Co.* v. *Kentucky*, 161 U. S. 677, 701, 702. See *Northern Securities Co.* v. *United States*, 193 U. S. 197, 317, 348, 382.

Again, it is manifest that when the legislation of the State is limited to internal commerce to such degree that it does not include even incidentally the subjects of interstate commerce, it is not rendered invalid because it may affect the latter commerce indirectly. In the intimacy of commercial relations, much that is done in the superintendence of local matters may have an indirect bearing upon interstate commerce. The development of local resources and the extension of local facilities may have a very important effect upon communities less favored and to an appreciable degree alter the course of trade. The freedom of local trade may stimulate interstate commerce, while restrictive measures within the police power of the State enacted exclusively with respect to internal business, as distinguished from interstate traffic, may in their reflex or indirect influence diminish the latter and reduce the volume of articles transported into or out of the State. It was an objection of this sort that was urged and overruled in *Kidd* v. *Pearson*, 128 U. S. 1, to the law of Iowa prohibiting the manufacture and sale of liquor within the State, save for limited purposes. See also *Geer* v. *Connecticut*, 161 U. S. 519, 534; *Austin* v. *Tennessee*, 179 U. S. 343; *Capital City Dairy Co.* v. *Ohio*, 183 U. S. 238, 245; *Missouri Pacific Ry. Co.* v. *Kansas*, *supra*. When, however, the State in dealing with its internal commerce undertakes to regulate instrumentalities which are also used in interstate commerce, its action is necessarily subject to the exercise by Congress of its authority to control such instrumentalities so far as may be necessary for the purpose of enabling it to discharge its constitutional function. *Southern Railway Co.* v. *United States, supra; Baltimore & Ohio Railroad Co.* v. *Interstate Commerce Commission, supra.*

Within the state power, then, in the words of Chief Justice Marshall is, "that immense mass of legislation, which embraces everything within the territory of a State, not surrendered to a general government: all which can be most advantageously exercised by the States themselves. Inspection laws, quarantine laws, health laws of every description, as well as laws for regulating the internal commerce of a State, and those which respect turnpike roads, ferries, &c., are component parts of this mass.

No direct general power over these objects is granted to Congress: and, consequently, they remain subject to state legislation. If the legislative power of the Union can reach them, it must be for national purposes; it must be where the power is expressly given for a special purpose, or is clearly incidental to some power which is expressly given." *Gibbons* v. *Ogden*, *supra*, pp. 203, 304.

And, wherever as to such matters, under these established principles, Congress may be entitled to act, by virtue of its power to secure the complete government of interstate commerce, the state power nevertheless continues until Congress does act and by its valid interposition limits the exercise of the local authority.

(2) These principles apply to the authority of the State to prescribe reasonable maximum rates for intrastate transportation.

State regulation of railroad rates began with railroad transportation. The railroads where chartered by the States and from the outset, in many charters, maximum rates for freight or passengers, or both were prescribed.[1] Frequently — and this became the more general practice — the board of directors was permitted to fix charges in its discretion, an authority which in numerous instances was made subject to a limitation upon the amount of net earnings.[2] In several States maximum rates were also established, or the power to alter rates was expressly reserved, by general laws.[3] In 1853, the State of New York fixed the maximum fare for way passengers on the railroads forming the line of New York Central at two cents a mile (Laws of 1853, c. 76, § 7) and this rate extending to Buffalo and Suspension Bridge, on the bound-

[1] E. g. Maryland, Laws of 1826, c. CXXIII, § 18; 1830, c. 117, §§ 2, 3; 1834, c. 281, § 3: Massachusetts, Laws of 1829, c. XXVI, § 6; 1830, c. XCIII, § 10: New York, Laws of 1828, c. 21, § 11; c. 238, § 11; 1831, c. 83, § 10; 1836, c. 242, § 9: Virginia, Laws of 1830–1831, c. CXIX, § 19; c. CXXI, § 18; 1835–1836, c. 121, § 24: Ohio, Laws of 1833–1834, p. 203, § 19, p. 396, § 9: North Carolina, Laws of 1836–1837, c. XL, § 30.

[2] Connecticut, 1832, II Resolves and Private Laws (1789–1836), p. 992: Indiana, Laws of 1832, c. CXLVI, §§ 23, 24: Florida, Laws of 1848, c. 244, § 11: New York, Laws of 1828, c. 304, § 13; 1832, c. 162, §§ 12, 17: Massachusetts, Laws of 1833, c. CXVIII, § 4: Virginia, Laws of 1839, c. 110, § 5: Wisconsin, Laws of 1847, p. 72, § 15; 1851, c. 262, § 7.

[3] Illinois, Laws of 1849, p. 15, §§ 21, 32: Massachusetts, Laws of 1845, c. 191, § 2; 1860, c. 201, § 2: New York, Laws of 1850, c. 140, § 33: California, Laws of 1850, c. 128, § 77; 1861, c. DXXXII, § 51: Iowa, Code of 1873, § 1305; Laws of 1874, c. 68, §§ 1–5: Report of Industrial Commission, 1901, Vol. IX, pp. 903–905, 911–915.

ary of the State, has continued to the present day (Cons. Laws, N. Y., 1910, c. 49, § 57). As a rule the restrictions imposed by the early legislation were far from onerous, but they are significant in the assertion of the right of control. More potent than these provisions, in the actual effect upon railroads tariffs, was the state canal. It is a matter of common knowledge that the traffic on the trunk lines from the Atlantic seaboard to the west was developed in competition with the Erie Canal, built, maintained and regulated by the State of New York to promote its commerce.

The authority of the State to limit by legislation the charges of common carriers within its borders was not confined to the power to impose limitations in connection with grants of corporate privileges. In view of the nature of their business, they were held subject to legislative control as to the amount of their charges unless they were protected by their contract with the State. This was decided in *Chicago, Burlington & Quincy R. R. Co.* v. *Iowa*, 94 U. S. 155; *Peik* v. *Chicago & Northwestern Railway Co.*, 94 U. S. 164; *Winona & St. Peter R. R. Co.* v. *Blake*, 94 U. S. 180, and other cases, following *Munn* v. *Illinois*, 94 U. S. 113. The question was presented by acts of the legislatures of Illinois, Iowa, Wisconsin and Minnesota, passed in the years 1871 and 1874 in response to a general movement for a reduction of rates. The section of the country in which the demand arose was to a large degree homogeneous and one in which the flow of commerce was only slightly concerned with state lines. But resort was had to the States for relief. In the *Munn Case*, the court had before it the statute of Illinois governing the grain warehouses in Chicago. Through these elevators, located with the river harbor on the one side and the railway tracks on the other, it was necessary according to the course of trade for the product of seven or eight States of the West to pass on its way to the States on the Atlantic coast. In addition to the denial of any legislative authority to limit charges it was urged that the act was repugnant to the exclusive power of Congress to regulate interstate commerce. The court answered that the business was carried on exclusively within the limits of the State of Illinois, that its regulation was a thing of domestic concern and that "certainly, until Congress acts in reference to their interstate relations, the State may exercise all the powers of government over them, even though in so doing it may indirectly operate upon commerce outside its immediate jurisdiction." In the decision of the railroad cases, above cited, the same opinion was expressed. The language of the court, however, went further than to sustain the state law with respect to rates for purely intrastate carriage. Thus, the act of Wisconsin covered traffic which started within the State and was destined to points outside, and this was treated as being within the state power (*Peik* v. *Chicago & Northwestern Railway Co.*, 94 U. S. 164, 177, 178), a view which was later repudiated. *Wabash, St. L. & P. Railway Co.* v. *Illinois*, 118 U. S. 557.

It became a frequent practice for the States to create commissions, as agencies of state supervision and regulation, and in many instances the rate-making power was conferred upon these bodies. A summary of such legislation is given in *Interstate Commerce Commission* v. *Chicago, N. O. & T. P. Ry. Co.*, 167 U. S. 479, 495, 496. One of these state laws, that of Mississippi, passed in 1884, came under review in *Stone* v. *Farmers Loan & Trust Co.*, 116 U. S. 307. The suit was brought to enjoin the Railroad Commission from enforcing the statute against the Mobile and Ohio Railroad Company. It had been incorporated in the States of Alabama, Mississippi, Tennessee and Kentucky, for the purpose of constructing a railroad from Mobile to some point near the mouth of the Ohio River where it would connect with another railroad, thus forming a continuous line of interstate communication between the Gulf of Mexico and the Great Lakes. The Commission as yet had not acted. Sustaining the state power to fix rates upon traffic wholly internal, the court directed the dismissal of the bill. The State, said the court, (p. 334) "may, beyond all question, by the settled rule of decision in this court, regulate freights and fares for business done exclusively within the State, and it would seem to be a matter of domestic concern to prevent the company from discriminating against persons and places in Mississippi." In the same case, it was declared that the power of regulation was not a power to confiscate; and that under pretense of regulating fares and freights, the States could not "require a railroad corporation to carry persons or property without reward," or do that which in law amounted "to a taking of private property for public use without just compensation, or without due process of law." (*Id.*, p. 331.)

In *Wabash, St. L. & P. Railway Co.* v. *Illinois*, *supra*, it was finally determined that the authority of the State did not extend to the regulation of charges for interstate transportation. There the state statute was aimed at discrimination. It was said to have been violated by the railroad company in the case of shipments from points within Illinois to the city of New York. The state court had construed the statute to be binding as to that part of the interstate haul which was within the State although inoperative beyond the boundary. So applied, this court held the act to be invalid.

But no doubt was entertained of the State's authority to regulate rates for transportation that was wholly intrastate. And, in illustrating the extent of state power (*id.*, p. 564), the court selected transportation across the State from Cairo to Chicago and from Chicago to Alton, all boundary points constituting important centers of commerce — the one on Lake Michigan, and the others at the confluence of the Mississippi and Ohio rivers, and of the Mississippi and Missouri rivers, respectively. After reviewing decisions holding state laws to be ineffective which imposed a direct burden upon interstate commerce, including the cases of the *State Freight Tax*, 15 Wall. 232; *Hall* v. *DeCuir*, 95 U. S. 485; *Gloucester Ferry Co.* v. *Pennsylvania*, 114 U. S. 196; *Pickard* v. *Pullman Southern Car Co.*, 117 U. S. 24, the court emphasized the distinction with respect to the operation of the statute upon domestic transactions saying: "Of the justice or propriety of the principle which lies at the foundation of the Illinois statute it is not the province of this court to speak. As restricted to a transportation which begins and ends within the limits of the State it may be very just and equitable, and it certainly is the province of the state legislature to determine that question." (*Id.*, p. 577.)

The doctrine was thus fully established that the State could not prescribe interstate rates but could fix reasonable intrastate rates throughout its territory. The extension of railroad facilities has been accompanied at every step by the assertion of this authority on the part of the States and its invariable recognition by this court. It has never been doubted that the State could, if it saw fit, build its own highways, canals and railroads. (*Railroad Company* v. *Maryland*, 21 Wall. 456, 470, 471.) It could build railroads traversing the entire State and thus join its border cities and commercial centers by new highways of internal intercourse to be always available upon reasonable terms. Such provision for local traffic might indeed alter relative advantages in competition, and, by virtue of economic forces, those engaged in interstate trade and transportation might find it necessary to make readjustments extending from market to market through a wide sphere of influence; but such action of the State would not for that reason be regarded as creating a direct restraint upon interstate commerce and as thus transcending the state power. Similarly, the authority of the State to prescribe what shall be reasonable charges of common carriers for intrastate transportation, unless it be limited by the exertion of the constitutional power of Congress, is state-wide. As a power appropriate to the territorial jurisdiction of the State, it is not confined to a part of the State, but extends throughout the State — to its cities adjacent to its boundaries as well as to those in the interior of the State. To say that this power exists, but that it may be exercised only in prescribing rates that are on an equal or higher basis than those that are fixed by the carrier for interstate transportation, is to maintain the power in name while denying it in fact. It is to assert that the exercise of the legislative judgment in determining what shall be the carrier's charge for the intrastate service is itself subject to the carrier's will. But this state-wide authority controls the carrier and is not controlled by it; and the idea that the power of the State to fix reasonable rates for its internal traffic is limited by the mere action of the carrier in laying an interstate rate to places across the State's border, is foreign to our jurisprudence.

If this authority of the State be restricted, it must be by virtue of the paramount power of Congress over interstate commerce and its instruments; and, in view of the nature of the subject, a limitation may not be implied because of a dormant Federal power, that is, one which has not been exerted, but can only be found in the actual exercise of Federal control in such measure as to exclude this action by the State which otherwise would clearly be within its province.

(3) When Congress, in the year 1887, enacted the Act to Regulate Commerce (24 Stat. 379, c. 104), it was acquainted with the course of the development of railroad transportation and with the exercise by the States of the rate-making power. An elaborate report had been made to the Senate by a committee authorized to investigate the subject of railroad regulation in which the nature and extent of state legislation, including the commission plan, were fully reviewed (Senate Report 46, submitted January 6, 1886, 49th Congress, 1st session). And it was the fact that beyond the bounds of state control there lay a vast field of unregulated activity in the conduct of interstate transportation which was found to be the chief cause of the demand for Federal action.

Congress carefully defined the scope of its regulation, and expressly provided that it was not to extend to purely intrastate traffic. In the first section of the Act to Regulate Commerce there was inserted the following proviso:

"*Provided, however,* That the provisions of this act shall not apply to the transportation of passengers or property, or to the receiving, delivering, storage, or handling of property, wholly within one State, and not shipped to or from a foreign country from or to any State or Territory as aforesaid."

When in the year 1906 (act of June 29, 1906, c. 3591, 34 Stat. 584), Congress amended the act so as to confer upon the Federal commission power to prescribe maximum interstate rates, the proviso in section one was reënacted. Again, in 1910, when the act was extended to embrace telegraph, telephone and cable companies engaged in interstate business, the proviso was once more reënacted, with an additional clause so as to exclude intrastate messages from the operation of the statute. Act of June 18, 1910, c. 309, 36 Stat. 539, 545. The proviso in its present form reads:

"*Provided, however,* That the provisions of this Act shall not apply to the transportation of passengers or property, or to the receiving, delivering, storage, or handling of property wholly within one State and not shipped to or from a foreign country from or to any State or Territory as aforesaid, nor shall they apply to the transmission of messages by telephone, telegraph, or cable wholly within one State and not transmitted to or from a foreign country from or to any State or Territory as aforesaid."

There was thus excluded from the provisions of the act that transportation which was "wholly within one State," with the specified qualification where its subject was going to or coming from a foreign country.

It is urged, however, that the words of the proviso are susceptible of a construction which would permit the provisions of section three of the act, prohibiting carriers from giving an undue or unreasonable preference or advantage to any locality, to apply to unreasonable discriminations between localities in different States, as well when arising from an intrastate rate as compared with an interstate rate as when due to interstate rates exclusively. If it be assumed that the statute should be so construed, and it is not necessary now to decide the point, it would inevitably follow that the controlling principle governing the enforcement of the act should be applied to such cases as might thereby be brought within its purview; and the question whether the carrier, in such a case, was giving an undue or unreasonable preference or advantage to one locality as against another, or subjecting any locality to an undue or unreasonable prejudice or disadvantage, would be primarily for the investigation and determination of the Interstate Commerce Commission and not for the courts. The dominating purpose of the statute was to secure conformity to the prescribed standards through the examination and appreciation of the complex facts of transportation by the body created for that purpose; and, as this court has repeatedly held, it would be destructive of the system of regulation defined by the statute if the court without the preliminary action of the Commission were to undertake to pass upon the administrative questions which the statute has primarily confided to it. *Texas & Pacific Ry. Co.* v. *Abilene Cotton Oil Co.*, 204 U. S. 426; *Baltimore & Ohio R. R. Co.* v. *Pitcairn Coal Co.*, 215 U. S. 481; *Robinson* v. *Baltimore & Ohio R. R. Co.*, 222 U. S. 506; *United States* v. *Pacific & Arctic Co.*, 228 U. S. 87. In the present case, there has been no finding by the Interstate Commerce Commission of unjust discrimination violative of the act; and no action of that body is before us for review.

The question we have now before us, essentially, is whether after the passage of the Interstate Commerce Act, and its amendment, the State continued to possess the state-wide authority which it formerly enjoyed to prescribe reasonable rates for its exclusively internal traffic. That, as it plainly appears, was the nature of the action taken by Minnesota, and the attack, however phrased, upon the rates here involved as an interference with interstate commerce, is in substance a denial of that authority.

Having regard to the terms of the Federal statute, the familiar range of state action at the time it was enacted, the continued exercise of state authority in the same manner and to the same extent after its enactment, and the decisions of this court recognizing and upholding this authority, we find no foundation for the proposition that the Act to Regulate Commerce contemplated interference therewith.

Congress did not undertake to say that the intrastate rates of interstate carriers should be reasonable or to invest its administrative agency with authority to determine their reasonableness. Neither by the original act nor by its amendment, did Congress seek to establish a unified control over interstate and intrastate rates; it did not set up a standard for intrastate rates, or prescribe, or authorize the Commission to prescribe, either maximum or minimum rates for intrastate traffic. It cannot be supposed that

Congress sought to accomplish by indirection that which it expressly disclaimed, or attempted to override the accustomed authority of the States without the provision of a substitute. On the contrary, the fixing of reasonable rates for intrastate transportation was left where it had been found; that is, with the States and the agencies created by the States to deal with that subject. *Missouri Pacific Ry. Co.* v. *Larabee Mills*, 211 U. S. 612, 620, 621.

How clear was the purpose not to occupy the field thus left to the exercise of state power is shown by the clause uniformly inserted in the numerous acts passed by Congress to authorize the construction of railways across the Indian Territory. This clause, while fixing a maximum passenger rate, made the laws of an adjoining State (in some cases Arkansas, in others Texas, and in others Kansas) applicable to the freight rates to be charged within the Territory; and while the right to regulate rates on the authorized line of railroad was reserved to Congress until a state government should be established, it was expressly provided that, when established, the State should be entitled to fix rates for intrastate transportation — the right remaining with Congress to prescribe rates for such transportation as should be interstate. Within a month after the Act to Regulate Commerce was enacted, two acts were passed by Congress for this purpose with respect to railways extending across the Territory from the Texas to the Kansas boundary. The provision — in both cases in identical language — save that the one referred to the laws of Texas and the other to the laws of Kansas — was as follows (act of Feb. 24, 1887, c. 254, § 4, 24 Stat. 420; act of March 2, 1887, c. 319, § 4, *id.*, 447):

"Sec. 4. That said railroad company shall not charge the inhabitants of said Territory a greater rate of freight than the rate authorized by the laws of the State of Texas for services or transportation of the same kind: *Provided*, That passenger rates on said railway shall not exceed three cents per mile. Congress hereby reserves the right to regulate the charges for freight and passengers on said railway, and messages on said telegraph and telephone lines, *until a State government or governments shall exist in said Territory within the limits of which said railway, or a part thereof, shall be located; and then such State government or governments shall be authorized to fix and regulate the cost of transportation of persons and freights within their respective limits by said railway;* but Congress expressly reserves the right to fix and regulate at all times the cost of such transportation by said railway or said company whenever such transportation shall extend from one State into another, or shall extend into more than one State: *Provided, however,* That the rate of such transportation of passengers, local or inter-State, shall not exceed the rate above expressed: *And provided further,* That said railway company shall carry the mail at such prices as Congress may by law provide; and until such rate is fixed by law the Postmaster-General may fix the rate of compensation."

The same provision is found in similar statutes passed in almost every year from 1884 to 1902 and relating to lines intended to serve as highways of interstate communication.[1] When Oklahoma became a State, the laws of other States which were referred to in these various acts ceased to be operative within its limits, and by virtue of its Statehood and with the direct sanction of Congress, it became authorized to prescribe reasonable maximum rates for intrastate transportation throughout its extent. *Oklahoma* v. *A., T. & S. F. Ry. Co.,* 220 U. S. 277, 285; *Oklahoma* v. *C., R. I. & Pac. Ry. Co.,* 220 U. S. 302, 306.

The decisions of this court since the passage of the Act to Regulate Commerce have uniformly recognized that it was competent for the State to fix such rates, applicable throughout

[1] Referring to Laws of Texas: Acts of July 4, 1884, c. 177, § 4, 23 Stat. 69, 70; July 1, 1886, c. 601, § 4, 24 Stat. 117, 119; Feb. 18, 1888, c. 13, § 4, 25 Stat. 35, 37; May, 14, 1888, c. 248, § 4, 25 Stat. 140, 142; May 30, 1888, c. 337, § 4, 25 Stat. 162, 163; June 26, 1888, c. 494, § 4, 25 Stat. 205, 207; Oct. 1, 1890, c. 1248, § 4, 26 Stat. 632, 634; July 30, 1892, c. 329, § 4, 27 Stat. 336, 338; Mar. 1, 1893, c. 188, § 4, 27 Stat. 524, 525; Aug. 4, 1894, c. 215, § 4, 28 Stat. 229, 230; Mar. 23, 1898, c. 87, § 4, 30 Stat. 341, 342.

Referring to Laws of Kansas: Acts of July 4, 1884, c. 179, § 4, 23 Stat. 73, 74; June 21, 1890, c. 479, § 4, 26 Stat. 170, 171; June 30, 1890, c. 638, § 4, 26 Stat. 184, 185; Sept. 26, 1890, c. 947, § 4, 26 Stat. 485, 487; Feb. 27, 1893, c. 171, § 4, 27 Stat. 492, 493; Mar. 18, 1896, c. 60, § 4, 29 Stat. 69, 70; Mar. 30, 1896, c. 82, § 4, 29 Stat. 80, 82.

Referring to Laws of Arkansas: Acts of June 1, 1886, c. 395, § 4, 24 Stat. 73, 74; July 6, 1886, c. 744, § 4, 24 Stat. 124, 125; Feb. 18, 1888, c. 13, § 4, 25 Stat. 35, 37; May 30, 1888, c. 337, § 4, 25 Stat. 162, 163; Feb. 26, 1889, c. 280, § 4, 25 Stat. 745, 746; Feb. 24, 1891, c. 288, § 4, 26 Stat. 783, 785; Mar. 3, 1891, c. 535, § 4, 26 Stat. 844, 846; Feb. 24, 1896, c. 30, § 6, 29 Stat. 13, 15; Mar. 2, 1896, c. 38, § 4, 29 Stat. 40, 41; Apr. 6, 1896, c. 93, § 4, 29 Stat. 86, 88; Jan. 29, 1897, c. 108, § 4, 29 Stat. 502, 504; Mar. 30, 1898, c. 104, § 5, 30 Stat. 347, 349; Jan. 28, 1899, c. 65, § 5, 30 Stat. 806, 808; Feb. 4, 1899, c. 88, § 6, 30 Stat. 816, 818; Mar. 3, 1899, c. 453, § 6, 30 Stat. 1368, 1370.

Referring to Laws of Territory of Oklahoma: Act of Feb. 28, 1902, c. 124, § 4, 32 Stat. 43, 45.

its territory. If it be said that in the contests that have been waged over state laws during the past twenty-five years, the question of interference with interstate commerce by the establishment of state-wide rates for intrastate traffic has seldom been raised, this fact itself attests the common conception of the scope of state authority. And the decisions recognizing and defining the state power wholly refute the contention that the making of such rates either constitutes a direct burden upon interstate commerce or is repugnant to the Federal statute.

In *Dow* v. *Beidelman*, 125 U. S. 680, the statute of Arkansas, enacted in April, 1887 (April 4, 1887, Acts 1887, p. 227), which established three cents a mile as the maximum fare for carrying passengers within the State on railroads over seventy-five miles in length, was sustained against the objection of the owners of the Memphis and Little Rock Railroad who attacked the act as confiscatory and arbitrary in its classification. The same statute was again upheld in *St. Louis & San Francisco Railway Co.* v. *Gill*, 156 U. S. 649. In *Chicago &c. Railway Co.* v. *Minnesota*, 134 U. S. 418, the statute of that State (March 7, 1887, Gen. Laws 1887, c. 10) creating a commission with power to prescribe intrastate rates was adjudged to be invalid, but this was upon the ground that the act as construed by the state court made the rates published by the commission final and conclusive and precluded any judicial inquiry whether they were reasonable. In *Chicago &c. Railway Co.* v. *Wellman*, 143 U. S. 339, the act of the legislature of Michigan (June 28, 1889, Pub. Laws 1889, p. 282) fixing the maximum fare for passengers within the State at two cents a mile in the case of companies whose gross earnings exceeded three thousand dollars a mile was unsuccessfully assailed as confiscatory and no contention was advanced that such an act operating throughout the State was an unwarrantable interference with interstate commerce.

In *Reagan* v. *Farmers Loan & Trust Co.*, 154 U. S. 362, the trustee of a railroad mortgage attacked the statute of Texas (April 3, 1891, Gen. Laws 1891, c. 51, p. 55) which established a railroad commission with authority to regulate tariffs, and the order of the commission providing a schedule of classified rates for the transportation of goods within the State. The challenge was of the tariff as a whole and the inquiry was whether the body of rates was unreasonable and such as to work a practical destruction of rights of property. Viewed in this aspect, the court, upon the allegations admitted by demurrer, held the action of the commission to be beyond its constitutional power and affirmed the decree of the Circuit Court enjoining the rates. The decree, however, was reversed so far as it restrained the commission from discharging the duties imposed by the statute and from proceeding to prescribe reasonable rates and regulations. A further question was presented in *Reagan* v. *Mercantile Trust Company*, 154 T. S. 413, in respect to the same statute and order as applied to the Texas and Pacific Railway Company which had been organized under the laws of the United States (March 3, 1871, 16 Stat. 573, c. 122) and operated its road not only within that State but also for several hundred miles outside. It was insisted that this company was "not subject to the control of the State, even as to rates for transportation wholly within the State," the argument being that it was not within the state power to limit the Federal franchise to collect tolls. But the court held that the act of Congress did not go to the extent asserted but left the company, as to its intrastate business, subject to state authority.

The effect of intrastate rates upon interstate rates was urged in *Smyth* v. *Ames*, 169 U. S. 466, and in the cases decided therewith. These suits were brought by stockholders of the Union Pacific Railway Company, the Chicago and Northwestern Railroad Company and the Chicago, Burlington and Quincy Railroad Company, to enjoin the enforcement of the act of the legislature of Nebraska passed in 1893 (April 12, 1893, Acts 1893, c. 24). This was a comprehensive statute classifying the freight transported from any point in Nebraska to any other point in that State and prescribing tables of maximum rates. The companies affected were interstate carriers engaged in a vast commerce only a small portion of which was wholly local to the State. On the eastern boundary lay Omaha, a city of large importance in interstate trade, situated on the Missouri river with Council Bluffs, in the State of Iowa, directly opposite. The point was distinctly made in the Circuit Court that the statute interfered with interstate commerce because, first, it established a classification of freights different from that which prevailed west of Chicago, and second, by reducing local rates it necessarily reduced rates on interstate business. Mr. Justice Brewer, who tried the cases, overruled these objections holding that neither the convenience of the carriers nor the consequences of competition with respect to interstate rates could be pleaded "in restraint of the otherwise undeniable power of the State." *Ames* v. *Union Pacific Railway*

Co., 64 Fed. Rep. 165, 171, 172. Having disposed of this contention, the court considered the question of the reasonableness of the rates and reached the conclusion that they were invalid because they amounted to a deprivation of the carriers' rights of property. On appeal to this court the counsel for the appellees directed attention to the conditions of transportation in Nebraska. It was argued that the local traffic was carried over the same tracks, in the same trains and often in the same cars with the interstate traffic; that to separate the cost of carrying the one sort of traffic from that of the other was a "manifest impossibility"; and that it was a necessary consequence of existing conditions that, if Nebraska controlled the local rates, it at the same time controlled the interstate rates. But this contention was not sustained and the affirmance of the decree was placed upon the distinct ground that the rates were confiscatory. It was ruled that the reasonableness of intrastate rates was to be determined by considering the intrastate business separately. In answer to the suggestion that the conditions of business might have changed for the better since the decrees, the court called attention to the proviso in the decrees intended to meet such a case, adding that if the Circuit Court found that conditions were such as to permit the application of the state rates without depriving the carriers of just compensation it would "be its duty to discharge the injunction" and to make whatever order was necessary "to remove any obstruction placed by the decrees in these cases in the way of the enforcement of the statute." (*Id.*, p. 550; see *Smyth* v. *Ames*, 171 U. S. 361, 365.)

In that one of the *Smyth Cases* which was brought by the stockholders of the Union Pacific Railway Company not only was the case presented of a trunk line crossing the State with a relatively small proportion of business local to Nebraska, but the company had been formed by a consolidation of several companies by authority of Congress, one of them being the Union Pacific Railroad Company, incorporated by the act of July 1, 1862, c. 120, 12 Stat. 489. By this act (§ 18, *id.*, 497), it was expressly provided that Congress might reduce the rates of fare if unreasonable and might fix the same by law whenever the net earnings of the entire road and telegraph should exceed a certain amount. But this language, while showing that Congress intended to reserve the power to prevent unreasonable exactions, was not deemed to be equivalent to a declaration that the States through which the road might be constructed should not regulate rates for intrastate transportation. The court said: "It cannot be doubted that the making of rates for transportation by railroad corporations along public highways, between points wholly within the limits of a State, is a subject primarily within the control of that State. . . . . Congress not having exerted this power, we do not think that the national character of the corporation constructing the Union Pacific Railroad stands in the way of a State prescribing rates for transporting property on that road wholly between points within its territory. Until Congress, in the exercise either of the power specifically reserved by the eighteenth section of the act of 1862 or its power under the general reservation made of authority to add to, alter, amend or repeal that act, prescribes rates to be charged by the railroad company, it remains with the States through which the road passes to fix rates for transportation beginning and ending within their respective limits." (169 U. S., pp. 521, 522.) It is plain that had the intrastate rates, established by the comprehensive statute of Nebraska, not been found to be confiscatory they would have been sustained in their application to all intrastate traffic notwithstanding the reserved power of Congress over the Union Pacific line and despite the argument based upon the interdependence of interstate and intrastate rates.

The cases of *Louisville & Nashville Railroad Co.* v. *Kentucky*, 183 U. S. 503, and *Louisville & Nashville Railroad Co.* v. *Eubank*, 184 U. S. 27, concerned the validity of the long and short haul provision of the constitution of Kentucky adopted in 1891. In the first case, violation was charged with respect to the transportation of coal from Altamont to Lebanon, an intermediate station, as compared with charges for transportation from Altamont to Elizabethtown and Louisville, all places being within Kentucky. The difference in rate was justified by the company on the ground that at Louisville the coal hauled from Altamont came into competition with that brought down the Ohio River and at Elizabethtown with western Kentucky coal brought there by the Illinois Central Railroad. The contention that the state provision operated as an interference with interstate commerce was presented and overruled, the court saying: "It is plain that the provision in question does not in terms embrace the case of interstate traffic. It is restricted in its regulation to those who own or operate a railroad within the State, and the long and short distances mentioned are evidently distances upon the railroad line within the State. The particular case before us is one involving only the transportation of coal from one point in the State of Kentucky to another by a corporation of that State. It may be that the enforcement of the state regulation forbidding discrimination in rates in the case of articles of a like kind carried for different distances over the same line may somewhat affect commerce generally; but we have frequently held that such a result is too remote and indirect to be regarded as an interference with interstate commerce; that the interference with the commercial power of the general government to be unlawful must be direct, and not the merely incidental effect of enforcing the police powers of a State." (183 U. S., pp. 518, 519.) In the *Eubank Case*, which had been argued before the first case was decided, it appeared that the state court had construed the same provision of the Kentucky constitution as embracing a long haul from a place outside to one within the State (Nashville and Louisville) and a shorter haul on the same line and in the same direction between points within the State. The court held that, so construed, the provision was invalid as being a regulation of interstate commerce because it linked the interstate rate to the rate for the shorter haul and thus the interstate charge was directly controlled by the state law. (184 U. S., pp. 41, 43.) The authority of the former decision upholding the state law, as applied to places all of which were within the State, was in no way impaired and the court fully recognized the power of the State to prescribe maximum charges for intrastate traffic although carried over an interstate road to points on the state line. (*Id.*, pp. 33, 42.)

The case of *Minneapolis & St. Louis Railroad Co.* v. *Minnesota*, 186 U. S. 257, involved shipments of hard coal in carload lots from Duluth, Minnesota, to points in the southern and western portions of that State. The Railroad and Warehouse Commission of Minnesota, in 1899, prescribed a joint rate to be observed by the St. Paul and Duluth Railroad Company, the Minneapolis and St. Louis Railroad Company and other carriers. The state court directed the issue of a writ of mandamus to compel compliance with the order. It was objected that the act under which the order was made was unconstitutional so far as it assumed to establish joint through rates over the lines of independent connecting railroads and to divide joint earnings, and that the tariff as fixed was not compensatory. This court affirmed the judgment. In *Alabama & Vicksburg Railroad Co.* v. *Mississippi Railroad Commission*, 203 U. S. 496, the company made what it called a "rebilling rate" on grain shipped from Vicksburg to Meridian, Mississippi, which was applicable only in case of shipments received at Vicksburg over the Shreveport line. It gave, however, to such shippers an option for a specified time to send other grain from Vicksburg instead, and thus it was in fact a local rate. To end this discrimination, the state commission, in 1903, fixed the same rate for all grain products shipped from Vicksburg to Meridian. It was urged that the effect of the order would be to force the plaintiff to enter into joint through interstate tariffs and divisions with all lines reaching Vicksburg by rail or river whether it desired such arrangements or not. The court sustained the order holding that it was competent for the State to enforce equality as to local transportation, and that this equality could not be defeated "in respect to any local shipments by arrangements made with or to favor outside companies."

In *Northern Pacific Railway Co.* v. *North Dakota*, 216 U. S. 579, the Attorney General of North Dakota charged the company with continuous violation of a law fixing rates for the carriage of coal within the State (North Dakota, Laws of 1907, c. 51) and asked for an injunction. It appears by the record that in its return to the rule to show cause in the state court, the company alleged that the statute was void because repugnant to the commerce clause and also that the rate fixed thereby was confiscatory. In support of the last contention the return set forth that the maximum rates for carrying coal which the company was allowed to charge under the act in question, were greatly lower than the rates for similar service fixed by Minnesota for that State (reference being made to c. 322 of the Laws of 1907, the commodity rate act now in question) and those fixed by the Railroad Commissions of Illinois and Iowa, respectively; and that the conditions existing in North Dakota made it impossible to transport coal at a less rate than in the States named. The contention that the act violated the interstate commerce clause was said by the Supreme Court of the State to be based upon the assumption that state regulation of local rates on interstate lines amounted to an interference with interstate commerce. In view of the decisions of this court, the last question was not considered open to debate. *State* v. *Northern Pacific Railway Co.*, 19 N. Dak. 45, 56. This ruling was not challenged by the argument for the plaintiff in error here, and the question as to interference with interstate commerce was treated as removed from the case by the holding of the state court that the rates applied only to transportation within the State. (216 U. S., p. 580.)

To suppose, however, from a review of these decisions, that the exercise of this acknowledged power of the State may be permitted to create an irreconcilable conflict with the authority of the Nation, or that through an equipoise of powers an effective control of interstate commerce is rendered impossible, is to overlook the dominant operation of the Constitution which, creating a Nation, equipped it with an authority, supreme and plenary, to control National commerce and to prevent that control, exercised in the wisdom of Congress, from being obstructed or destroyed by any opposing action. But, as we said at the outset, our system of government is a practical adjustment by which the National authority as conferred by the Constitution is maintained in its full scope without unnecessary loss of local efficiency. It thus clearly appears that, under the established principles governing state action, the State of Minnesota did not transcend the limits of its authority in prescribing the rates here involved, assuming them to be reasonable intrastate rates. It exercised an authority appropriate to its territorial jurisdiction and not opposed to any action thus far taken by Congress.

The interblending of operations in the conduct of interstate and local business by interstate carriers is strongly pressed upon our attention. It is urged that the same right-of-way, terminals, rails, bridges, and stations are provided for both classes of traffic; that the proportion of each sort of business varies from year to year and, indeed, from day to day; that no division of the plant, no apportionment of it between interstate and local traffic, can be made to-day, which will hold to-morrow; that terminals, facilities and connections in one State aid the carrier's entire business and are an element of value with respect to the whole property and the business in other States; that securities are issued against the entire line of the carrier and cannot be divided by States; that tariffs should be made with a view to all the traffic of the road and should be fair as between through and short-haul business; and that, in substance, no regulation of rates can be just, which does not take into consideration the whole field of the carrier's operations, irrespective of state lines. The force of these contentions is emphasized in these cases, and in others of like nature, by the extreme difficulty and intricacy of the calculations which must be made in the effort to establish a segregation of intrastate business for the purpose of determining the return to which the carrier is properly entitled therefrom.

But these considerations are for the practical judgment of Congress in determining the extent of the regulation necessary under existing conditions of transportation to conserve and promote the interests of interstate commerce. If the situation has become such, by reason of the interblending of the interstate and intrastate operations of interstate carriers, that adequate regulation of their interstate rates cannot be maintained without imposing requirements with respect to their intrastate rates which substantially affect the former, it is for Congress to determine, within the limits of its constitutional authority over interstate commerce and its instruments the measure of the regulation it should supply. It is the function of this court to interpret and apply the law already enacted, but not under the guise of construction to provide a more comprehensive scheme of regulation than Congress has decided upon. Nor, in the absence of Federal action, may we deny effect to the laws of the State enacted within the field which it is entitled to occupy until its authority is limited through the exertion by Congress of its paramount constitutional power.

. . . .

HOUSTON, EAST AND WEST TEXAS RAILWAY COMPANY *v.* UNITED STATES

TEXAS AND PACIFIC RAILWAY COMPANY *v.* UNITED STATES

234 U. S. 342 (1914)

Mr. Justice Hughes delivered the opinion of the court.

These suits were brought in the Commerce Court by the Houston, East & West Texas Railway Company, and the Houston & Shreveport Railroad Company, and by the Texas & Pacific Railway Company, respectively, to set aside an order of the Interstate Commerce Commission, dated March 11, 1912, upon the ground that it exceeded the Commission's authority. Other railroad companies [1] intervened in support of the petitions, and the Interstate Commerce Commission and the Railroad Commission of Louisiana intervened in opposition. The petitions were dismissed. 205 Fed. Rep. 380.

[1] The Missouri, Kansas & Texas Railway Company of Texas, the St. Louis Southwestern Railway Company, and the St. Louis Southwestern Railway Company of Texas.

The order of the Interstate Commerce Commission was made in a proceeding initiated in March, 1911, by the Railroad Commission of Louisiana. The complaint was that the appellants, and other interstate carriers, maintained unreasonable rates from Shreveport, Louisiana, to various points in Texas, and, further, that these carriers in the adjustment of rates over their respective lines unjustly discriminated in favor of traffic within the State of Texas and against similar traffic between Louisiana and Texas. The carriers filed answers; numerous pleas of intervention by shippers and commercial bodies were allowed; testimony was taken and arguments were heard.

The gravamen of the complaint, said the Interstate Commerce Commission, was that the carriers made rates out of Dallas and other Texas points into eastern Texas which were much lower than those which they extended into Texas from Shreveport. The situation may be briefly described: Shreveport, Louisiana, is about 40 miles from the Texas state line, and 231 miles from Houston, Texas, on the line of the Houston, East & West Texas and Houston & Shreveport Companies (which are affiliated in interest); it is 189 miles from Dallas, Texas, on the line of the Texas & Pacific. Shreveport competes with both cities for the trade of the intervening territory. The rates on these lines from Dallas and Houston, respectively, eastward to intermediate points in Texas were much less, according to distance, than from Shreveport westward to the same points. It is undisputed that the difference was substantial and injuriously affected the commerce of Shreveport. It appeared, for example, that a rate of 60 cents carried first class traffic a distance of 160 miles to the eastward from Dallas, while the same rate would carry the same class of traffic only 55 miles into Texas from Shreveport. The first class rate from Houston to Lufkin, Texas, 118.2 miles, was 50 cents per 100 pounds, while the rate from Shreveport to the same point, 112.5 miles, was 69 cents. The rate on wagons from Dallas to Marshall, Texas, 147.7 miles, was 36.8 cents, and from Shreveport to Marshall, 42 miles, 56 cents. The rate on furniture from Dallas to Longview, Texas, 124 miles, was 24.8 cents, and that from Shreveport to Longview, 65.7 miles, was 35 cents. These instances of differences in rates are merely illustrative; they serve to indicate the character of the rate adjustment.

The Interstate Commerce Commission found that the interstate class rates out of Shreveport to named Texas points were unreasonable, and it established maximum class rates for this traffic. These rates, we understand, were substantially the same as the class rates fixed by the Railroad Commission of Texas, and charged by the carriers, for transportation for similar distances in that State. The Interstate Commerce Commission also found that the carriers maintained "higher rates from Shreveport to points in Texas" than were in force "from cities in Texas to such points under substantially similar conditions and circumstances," and that thereby "an unlawful and undue preference and advantage" was given to the Texas cities and a "discrimination" that was "undue and unlawful" was effected against Shreveport. In order to correct this discrimination, the carriers were directed to desist from charging higher rates for the transportation of any commodity from Shreveport to Dallas and Houston, respectively, and intermediate points, than were contemporaneously charged for the carriage of such commodity from Dallas and Houston toward Shreveport for equal distances, as the Commission found that relation of rates to be reasonable. 23 I. C .C. 31, 46–48.

The order in question is set forth in the margin.[1] The report states that under this order it will be the duty of the companies

[1] "This case being at issue upon complaint and answers on file, and having been duly heard and submitted by the parties, and full investigation of the matters and things involved having been had, and the Commission having, on the date hereof, made and filed a report containing its findings of fact and conclusions thereon, which said report is hereby referred to and made a part hereof:

"It is ordered, That defendants The Texas & Pacific Railway Company, The Houston, East & West Texas Railway Company, and Houston & Shreveport Railroad Company be, and they are hereby, notified and required to cease and desist, on or before the 1st day of May, 1912, and for a period of not less than two years thereafter abstain, from exacting their present class rates for the transportation of traffic from Shreveport, La., to the points in Texas hereinafter mentioned on their respective lines, as the Commission in said report finds such rates to be unjust and unreasonable.

"It is further ordered, That defendant The Texas & Pacific Railway Company be, and it is hereby, notified and required to establish and put in force, on or before the 1st day of May, 1912, and maintain in force thereafter during a period of not less than two years, and apply to the transportation of traffic from Shreveport, La., to the below-named points in Texas, class rates which shall not exceed the following, in cents per 100 pounds, which rates are found by the Commission in its report to be reasonable, to wit: (rates inserted).

"It is further ordered, That defendants The Houston, East & West Texas Railway Company and Houston & Shreveport Railroad Company be, and they are hereby, notified and required to establish and put in force, on or before the 1st day of May, 1912, and maintain in force thereafter during a period of not less than two years, and apply to the transportation of traffic "to duly and justly equalize the terms and conditions" upon which they will extend "transportation to traffic of a similar character moving into Texas from Shreveport with that moving wholly within Texas," but that, in effecting such equalization, the class scale rates as prescribed shall not be exceeded.

In their petition in the Commerce Court, the appellants assailed the order in its entirety, but subsequently they withdrew their opposition to the fixing of maximum class rates and these rates were put in force by the carriers in May, 1912.

The attack was continued upon that portion of the order which prohibited the charge of higher rates for carrying articles from Shreveport into Texas than those charged for eastward traffic from Dallas and Houston, respectively, for equal distances. There are, it appears, commodity rates fixed by the Railroad Commission of Texas for intrastate hauls, which are substantially

---

from Shreveport, La., to the below-named points in Texas, class rates which shall not exceed the following, in cents per 100 pounds, which rates are found by the Commission in its report to be reasonable, to wit: (rates inserted).

"It is further ordered, That defendant The Texas & Pacific Railway Company be, and it is hereby, notified and required to cease and desist, on or before the 1st day of May, 1912, and for a period of not less than two years thereafter abstain, from exacting any higher rates for the transportation of any article from Shreveport, La., to Dallas, Tex., and points on its line intermediate thereto, than are contemporaneously exacted for the transportation of such article from Dallas, Tex., toward said Shreveport for an equal distance, as said relation of rates has been found by the Commission in said report to be reasonable.

"It is further ordered, That defendants The Houston, East & West Texas Railway Company and Houston & Shreveport Railroad Company be, and they are hereby, notified and required to cease and desist, on or before the 1st day of May, 1912, and for a period of not less than two years thereafter abstain, from exacting any higher rates for the transportation of any article from Shreveport, La., to Houston, Tex., and points on its line intermediate thereto, than are contemporaneously exacted for the transportation of such article from Houston, Tex., toward said Shreveport for an equal distance, as said relation of rates has been found by the Commission in said report to be reasonable.

"And it is further ordered, That said defendants be, and they are hereby, notified and required to establish and put in force, on or before the 1st day of May, 1912, and maintain in force thereafter during a period of not less than two years, substantially similar practices respecting the concentration of interstate cotton at Shreveport, La., to those which are contemporaneously observed by said defendants respecting the concentration of cotton within the state of Texas, provided the practices adopted shall be justifiable under the act to regulate commerce and applicable fairly under like conditions elsewhere on the lines of such defendants."

less than the class, or standard, rates prescribed by that Commission; and thus the commodity rates charged by the carriers from Dallas and Houston eastward to Texas points are less than the rates which they demand for the transportation of the same articles for like distances from Shreveport into Texas. The present controversy relates to these commodity rates.

The point of the objection to the order is that, as the discrimination found by the Commission to be unjust arises out of the relation of intrastate rates, maintained under state authority, to interstate rates that have been upheld as reasonable, its correction was beyond the Commission's power. Manifestly the order might be complied with, and the discrimination avoided, either by reducing the interstate rates from Shreveport to the level of the competing intrastate rates, or by raising these intrastate rates to the level of the interstate rates, or by such reduction in the one case and increase in the other as would result in equality. But it is urged that, so far as the interstate rates were sustained by the Commission as reasonable, the Commission was without authority to compel their reduction in order to equalize them with the lower intrastate rates. The holding of the Commerce Court was that the order relieved the appellants from further obligation to observe the intrastate rates and that they were at liberty to comply with the Commission's requirements by increasing these rates sufficiently to remove the forbidden discrimination. The validity of the order in this aspect is challenged upon two grounds:

(1) That Congress is impotent to control the intrastate charges of an interstate carrier even to the extent necessary to prevent injurious discrimination against interstate traffic; and

(2) That, if it be assumed that Congress has this power, still it has not been exercised, and hence the action of the Commission exceeded the limits of the authority which has been conferred upon it.

First. It is unnecessary to repeat what has frequently been said by this court with respect to the complete and paramount character of the power confided to Congress to regulate commerce among the several States. It is of the essence of this power that, where it exists, it dominates. Interstate trade was not left to be destroyed or impeded by the rivalries of local governments. The purpose was to make impossible the recurrence of the evils which had overwhelmed the Confederation and to provide the necessary basis of national unity by insuring 'uniformity of regulation against conflicting and discriminating state legislation.' By virtue of the comprehensive terms of the grant, the authority of Congress is at all times adequate to meet the varying exigencies that arise and to protect the national interest by securing the freedom of interstate commercial intercourse from local control. *Gibbons* v. *Ogden*, 9 Wheat. 1, 196, 224; *Brown* v. *Maryland*, 12 Wheat. 419, 446; *County of Mobile* v. *Kimball*, 102 U. S. 691, 696, 697; *Smith* v. *Alabama*, 124 U. S. 45, 473; *Second Employers' Liability Cases*, 223 U. S. 1, 47, 53, 54; *Minnesota Rate Cases*, 230 U. S. 352, 398, 399.

Congress is empowered to regulate, — that is, to provide the law for the government of interstate commerce; to enact 'all appropriate legislation' for its 'protection and advancement' (*The Daniel Ball*, 10 Wall. 557, 564); to adopt measures 'to promote its growth and insure its safety' (*County of Mobile* v. *Kimball, supra*); 'to foster, protect, control and restrain' (*Second Employers' Liability Cases, supra*). Its authority, extending to these interstate carriers as instruments of interstate commerce, necessarily embraces the right to control their operation in all matters having such a close and substantial relation to interstate traffic that the control is essential or appropriate to the security of that traffic, to the efficiency of the interstate service, and to the maintenance of conditions under which interstate commerce may be conducted upon fair terms and without molestation or hindrance. As it is competent for Congress to legislate to these ends, unquestionably it may seek their attainment by requiring that the agencies of interstate commerce shall not be used in such manner as to cripple, retard or destroy it. The fact that carriers are instruments of intrastate commerce, as well as of interstate commerce, does not derogate from the complete and paramount authority of Congress over the latter or preclude the Federal power from being exerted to prevent the intrastate operations of such carriers from being made a means of injury to that which has been confided to Federal care. Wherever the interstate and intrastate transactions of carriers are so related that the government of the one involves the control of the other, it is Congress, and not the State, that is entitled to prescribe the final and dominant rule, for otherwise Congress would be denied the exercise of its constitutional authority and the State, and not the Nation, would be supreme within the national field. *Baltimore & Ohio Railroad Co.* v. *Interstate Commerce Commission*, 221 U. S. 612, 618; *Southern Railway Co.* v. *United States*, 222 U. S. 20, 26, 27; *Second Employers' Liability Cases, supra*, pp. 48, 51; *Interstate Commerce*

Commission v. *Goodrich Transit Co.*, 224 U. S. 194, 205, 213; *Minnesota Rate Cases, supra,* p. 431; *Illinois Central Railroad Co.* v. *Behrens,* 233 U. S. 473.

In *Baltimore & Ohio Railroad Co.* v. *Interstate Commerce Commission, supra,* the argument against the validity of the Hours of Service Act (March 4, 1907, c. 2939, 34 Stat. 1415) involved the consideration that the interstate and intrastate transactions of the carriers were so interwoven that it was utterly impracticable for them to divide their employés so that those who were engaged in interstate commerce should be confined to that commerce exclusively. Employés dealing with the movement of trains were employed in both sorts of commerce; but the court held that this fact did not preclude the exercise of Federal power. As Congress could limit the hours of labor of those engaged in interstate transportation, it necessarily followed that its will could not be frustrated by prolonging the period of service through other requirements of the carriers or by the commingling of duties relating to interstate and intrastate operations. Again, in *Southern Railway Co.* v. *United States, supra,* the question was presented whether the amendment to the Safety Appliance Act (March 2, 1903, c. 976, 32 Stat. 943) was within the power of Congress in view of the fact that the statute was not confined to vehicles that were used in interstate traffic but also embraced those used in intrastate traffic. The court answered affirmatively, because there was such a close relation between the two classes of traffic moving over the same railroad as to make it certain that the safety of the interstate traffic, and of those employed in its movement, would be promoted in a real and substantial sense by applying the requirements of the act to both classes of vehicles. So, in the *Second Employers' Liability Cases, supra,* it was insisted that while Congress had the authority to regulate the liability of a carrier for injuries sustained by one employé through the negligence of another, where all were engaged in interstate commerce, that power did not embrace instances where the negligent employé was engaged in intrastate commerce. The court said that this was a mistaken theory, as the causal negligence when operating injuriously upon an employé engaged in interstate commerce had the same effect with respect to that commerce as if the negligent employé were also engaged therein. The decision in *Employers' Liability Cases,* 207 U. S. 463, is not opposed, for the statute there in question (June 11, 1906, c. 3073, 34 Stat. 232) sought to regulate the liability of interstate carriers for injuries to any employé even though his employment had no connection whatever with interstate commerce. (See *Illinois Central R. R. Co.* v. *Behrens, supra.*)

While these decisions sustaining the Federal power relate to measures adopted in the interest of the safety of persons and property, they illustrate the principle that Congress in the exercise of its paramount power may prevent the common instrumentalities of interstate and intrastate commercial intercourse from being used in their intrastate operations to the injury of interstate commerce. This is not to say that Congress possesses the authority to regulate the internal commerce of a State, as such, but that it does possess the power to foster and protect interstate commerce, and to take all measures necessary or appropriate to that end, although intrastate transactions of interstate carriers may thereby be controlled.

This principle is applicable here. We find no reason to doubt that Congress is entitled to keep the highways of interstate communication open to interstate traffic upon fair and equal terms. That an unjust discrimination in the rates of a common carrier, by which one person or locality is unduly favored as against another under substantially similar conditions of traffic, constitutes an evil is undeniable; and where this evil consists in the action of an interstate carrier in unreasonably discriminating against interstate traffic over its line, the authority of Congress to prevent it is equally clear. It is immaterial, so far as the protecting power of Congress is concerned, that the discrimination arises from intrastate rates as compared with interstate rates. The use of the instrument of interstate commerce in a discriminatory manner so as to inflict injury upon that commerce, or some part thereof, furnishes abundant ground for Federal intervention. Nor can the attempted exercise of state authority alter the matter, where Congress has acted, for a State may not authorize the carrier to do that which Congress is entitled to forbid and has forbidden.

It is also to be noted — as the Government has well said in its argument in support of the Commission's order — that the power to deal with the relation between the two kinds of rates, as a relation, lies exclusively with Congress. It is manifest that the State cannot fix the relation of the carrier's interstate and intrastate charges without directly interfering with the former, unless it simply follows the standard set by Federal authority. This question was presented with respect to the long and short haul provision of the Kentucky constitution, adopted in 1891, which the court had before it in *Louisville & Nashville R. R. Co.* v. *Eubank*, 184 U. S. 27. The state court had construed this provision as embracing a long haul, from a place outside to one within the State, and a shorter haul on the same line and in the same direction between points within the State. This court held that, so construed, the provision was invalid as being a regulation of interstate commerce because 'it linked the interstate rate to the rate for the shorter haul and thus the interstate charge was directly controlled by the state law.' See 230 U. S. pp. 428, 429. It is for Congress to supply the needed correction where the relation between intrastate and interstate rates presents the evil to be corrected, and this it may do completely by reason of its control over the interstate carrier in all matters having such a close and substantial relation to interstate commerce that it is necessary or appropriate to exercise the control for the effective government of that commerce.

It is also clear that, in removing the injurious discriminations against interstate traffic arising from the relation of intrastate to interstate rates, Congress is not bound to reduce the latter below what it may deem to be a proper standard fair to the carrier and to the public. Otherwise, it could prevent the injury to interstate commerce only by the sacrifice of its judgment as to interstate rates. Congress is entitled to maintain its own standard as to these rates and to forbid any discriminatory action by interstate carriers which will obstruct the freedom of movement of interstate traffic over their lines in accordance with the terms it establishes.

Having this power, Congress could provide for its execution through the aid of a subordinate body; and we conclude that the order of the Commission now in question cannot be held invalid upon the ground that it exceeded the authority which Congress could lawfully confer.

Second. The remaining question is with regard to the scope of the power which Congress has granted to the Commission.

Section three of the Act to Regulate Commerce provides (February 4, 1887, c. 104, 24 Stat. 379, 380):

"Sec. 3. That it shall be unlawful for any common carrier subject to the provisions of this act to make or give any undue or unreasonable preference or advantage to any particular person, company, firm, corporation, or locality, or any particular description of traffic, in any respect whatsoever, or to subject any particular person, company, firm, corporation, or locality, or any particular description of traffic, to any undue or unreasonable prejudice or disadvantage in any respect whatsoever."

This language is certainly sweeping enough to embrace all the discriminations of the sort described which it was within the power of Congress to condemn. There is no exception or qualification with respect to an unreasonable discrimination against interstate traffic produced by the relation of intrastate to interstate rates as maintained by the carrier. It is apparent from the legislative history of the act that the evil of discrimination was the principal thing aimed at, and there is no basis for the contention that Congress intended to exempt any discriminatory action or practice of interstate carriers affecting interstate commerce which it had authority to reach. The purpose of the measure was thus emphatically stated in the elaborate report of the Senate Committee on Interstate Commerce which accompanied it: "The provisions of the bill are based upon the theory that the paramount evil chargeable against the operation of the transportation system of the United States as now conducted is unjust discrimination between persons, places, commodities, or particular descriptions of traffic. The underlying purpose and aim of the measure is the prevention of these discriminations . . . ." (Senate Report No. 46, 49th Cong., 1st Sess., p. 215.)

The opposing argument rests upon the proviso in the first section of the act which in its original form was as follows: "*Provided, however*, that the provisions of this act shall not apply to the transportation of passengers or property, or to the receiving, delivering, storage, or handling of property, wholly within one State, and not shipped to or from a foreign country from or to any State or Territory as aforesaid." When the act was amended so as to confer upon the Commission the authority to prescribe maximum interstate rates, this proviso was reënacted; and when the act was extended to include telegraph, telephone, and cable companies engaged in interstate business, an additional clause was inserted so as to exclude intrastate messages. See acts of June 29, 1906, c. 3591, 34 Stat. 584; June 18, 1910, c. 309, 36 Stat. 539, 545.

Congress thus defined the scope of its regulation and provided that it was not to extend to purely intrastate traffic. It did not undertake to authorize the Commission to prescribe intrastate rates and thus to establish a unified control by the exercise of the rate-making power over both descriptions of traffic. Undoubtedly — in the absence of a finding by the Commission of unjust discrimination — intrastate rates were left to be fixed by the carrier and subject to the authority of the States or of the agencies created by the States. This was the question recently decided by this court in the *Minnesota Rate Cases, supra.* There, the State of Minnesota had established reasonable rates for intrastate transportation throughout the State and it was contended that, by reason of the passage of the Act to Regulate Commerce, the State could no longer exercise the state-wide authority for this purpose which it had formerly enjoyed; and the court was asked to hold that an entire scheme of intrastate rates, otherwise validly established, was null and void because of its effect upon interstate rates. There had been no finding by the Interstate Commerce Commission of any unjust discrimination. The present question, however, was reserved, the court saying (230 U. S. p. 419): "It is urged, however, that the words of the proviso" (referring to the proviso above-mentioned) "are susceptible of a construction which would permit the provisions of section three of the act, prohibiting carriers from giving an undue or unreasonable preference or advantage to any locality, to apply to unreasonable discriminations between localities in different States, as well when arising from an intrastate rate as compared with an interstate rate as when due to interstate rates exclusively. If it be assumed that the statute should be so construed, and it is not necessary now to decide the point, it would inevitably follow that the controlling principle governing the enforcement of the act should be applied to such cases as might thereby be brought within its purview; and the question whether the carrier, in such a case, was giving an undue or unreasonable preference or advantage to one locality as against another, or subjecting any locality to an undue or unreasonable prejudice or disadvantage, would be primarily for the investigation and determination of the Interstate Commerce Commission and not for the courts."

Here, the Commission expressly found that unjust discrimination existed under substantially similar conditions of transportation and the inquiry is whether the Commission had power to correct it. We are of the opinion that the limitation of the proviso in section one does not apply to a case of this sort. The Commission was dealing with the relation of rates injuriously affecting, through an unreasonable discrimination, traffic that was interstate. The question was thus not simply one of transportation that was 'wholly within one State.' These words of the proviso have appropriate reference to exclusively intrastate traffic, separately considered; to the regulation of domestic commerce, as such. The powers conferred by the act are not thereby limited where interstate commerce itself is involved. This is plainly the case when the Commission finds that unjust discrimination against interstate trade arises from the relation of intrastate to interstate rates as maintained by a carrier subject to the act. Such a matter is one with which Congress alone is competent to deal, and, in view of the aim of the act and the comprehensive terms of the provisions against unjust discrimination, there is no ground for holding that the authority of Congress was unexercised and that the subject was thus left without governmental regulation. It is urged that the practical construction of the statute has been the other way. But, in assailing the order, the appellants ask us to override the construction which has been given to the statute by the authority charged with its execution, and it cannot be said that the earlier action of the Commission was of such a controlling character as to preclude it from giving effect to the law. The Commission, having before it a plain case of unreasonable discrimination on the part of interstate carriers against interstate trade, carefully examined the question of its authority and decided that it had the power to make this remedial order. The Commerce Court sustained the authority of the Commission and it is clear that we should not reverse the decree unless the law has been misapplied. This we cannot say; on the contrary, we are convinced that the authority of the Commission was adequate.

The further objection is made that the prohibition of section three is directed against unjust discrimination or undue preference only when it arises from the voluntary act of the carrier and does not relate to acts which are the result of conditions wholly beyond its control. *East Tennessee &c. Rwy. Co.* v. *Interstate Commerce Commission*, 181 U. S. 1, 18. The reference is not to any inherent lack of control arising out of traffic conditions, but to the requirements of the local authorities which are assumed to be binding upon the carriers. The contention is thus merely a repetition in another form of the argument that the Commission exceeded its power; for it would not be contended that local rules could nullify the lawful exercise of Federal authority. In the view that the Commission was entitled to make the order, there is no longer compulsion upon the carriers by virtue of any inconsistent local requirement. We are not unmindful of the gravity of the question that is presented when state and Federal views conflict. But it was recognized at the beginning that the Nation could not prosper if interstate and foreign trade were governed by many masters, and, where the interests of the freedom of interstate commerce are involved, the judgment of Congress and of the agencies it lawfully establishes must control.

In conclusion: Reading the order in the light of the report of the Commission, it does not appear that the Commission attempted to require the carriers to reduce their interstate rates out of Shreveport below what was found to be a reasonable charge for that service. So far as these interstate rates conformed to what was found to be reasonable by the Commission, the carriers are entitled to maintain them, and they are free to comply with the order by so adjusting the other rates, to which the order relates, as to remove the forbidden discrimination. But this result they are required to accomplish.

The decree of the Commerce Court is affirmed in each case.

Affirmed.

MR. JUSTICE LURTON and MR. JUSTICE PITNEY dissent.

ILLINOIS CENTRAL RAILROAD COMPANY *v.* STATE PUBLIC UTILITIES COMMISSION OF ILLINOIS ET AL.

STATE PUBLIC UTILITIES COMMISSION OF ILLINOIS ET AL, *v.* UNITED STATES ET AL.

245 U. S. 493 (1918)

These cross appeals present a controversy over the validity, scope and effect of an order of the Interstate Commerce Commission dealing with discrimination found to result from a disparity in interstate and intrastate passenger rates. The facts and proceedings to be considered are these: The Mississippi River forms the boundary between the States of Missouri and Iowa on the west and the State of Illinois on the east. East St. Louis, in southwestern Illinois, is directly across the river from St. Louis, Missouri, and Hamilton, in western Illinois, is directly across the river from Keokuk, Iowa. At both places the river is spanned by railroad bridges whereby the lines of railroad on one side are connected with those on the other. For some years prior to December 1, 1914, interstate passenger rates between St. Louis and Keokuk on the one hand and points in Illinois on the other were on a substantial parity with intrastate rates between East St. Louis and Hamilton, respectively, and points in Illinois. All were on a basis of 2 cents per mile, save that the rates to and from St. Louis and Keokuk included a bridge toll over the river. All other rates between points in Illinois were also on the same basis, any intrastate rate in excess of 2 cents per mile being prohibited by a statute of that State. On December 1, 1914, the rates between St. Louis and Keokuk, respectively, and points in Illinois were increased by the carriers to $2\frac{1}{2}$ cents per mile, plus bridge tolls, the parity theretofore existing being thereby broken. Following this increase the Business Men's League of St. Louis, a corporate body of that city engaged in fostering its interests, filed with the Interstate Commerce Commission a petition against the carriers charging that the rates between St. Louis and points in Illinois were unreasonable in themselves, and, in connection with the lower intrastate rates, worked an unreasonable discrimination against St. Louis and in favor of Illinois cities, particularly East St. Louis and Chicago, and a like discrimination against interstate passenger traffic to and from St. Louis and in favor of intrastate passenger traffic to and from East St. Louis and Chicago. An association representing interests in Keokuk, Iowa, intervened and urged that any relief granted with respect to St. Louis be extended to Keokuk, so the former would not have an undue advantage over the latter. The State of Illinois, the Public Utilities Commission of that State, an association representing interests in Chicago and another association representing interests in East St. Louis, also intervened and opposed any action contemplating or requiring an increase in intrastate rates. After a hearing, in which all the parties and intervenors participated, the Interstate Commerce Commission filed a report (41 I. C. C. 13) finding that the existing bridge tolls at St. Louis and Keokuk were unobjectionable, that rates between either of those cities and points in Illinois were reasonable when not in excess of 2.4 cents per mile, plus bridge tolls, and that the service, equipment and accommodations provided for intrastate passengers to and from East St. Louis, Hamilton, and Chicago, were the same as those provided for interstate passengers to and from St. Louis and

Keokuk. In that report the Commission also found that the contemporaneous maintenance between East St. Louis [1] and Hamilton,[2] respectively, and other points in Illinois, of rates on a lower basis than those maintained via the same routes between St. Louis and Keokuk, respectively, and the same points in Illinois, bridge tolls excepted, gave an undue preference to East St. Louis and Hamilton and to intrastate passenger traffic to and from the latter points, and subjected St. Louis and Keokuk and interstate passenger traffic to and from those cities to an unreasonable disadvantage; that the existing disparity in interstate and intrastate rates worked an unjust discrimination against St. Louis and in favor of Chicago in so far as the rates between St. Louis and points in Illinois approximately equidistant from those cities exceeded, by more than the bridge toll, the rates between Chicago and the same points; that the disparity worked a like discrimination against Keokuk and in favor of Chicago; and that the existence on the reasonably direct lines of the carriers in the territory between Chicago on the one hand and St. Louis and Keokuk on the other of intrastate rates on a lower basis per mile than the rates between that territory and St. Louis and Keokuk, bridge tolls excepted, operated to subject interstate traffic to an unreasonable disadvantage.

The Commission then made an order intended to result in the installation of rates not exceeding 2.4 cents per mile between St. Louis and Keokuk, respectively, and points in Illinois and to remove the discrimination shown in the report; but shortly thereafter the Commission recalled that order and filed a supplemental report (41 I. C. C. 503) indicating that lawful interstate rates between St. Louis and Keokuk on the one hand and Illinois points on the other could be defeated by the use of two tickets, one purchased at the interstate rate for a part of the journey and the other at the lower intrastate rate for the remainder, and therefore that the order should be so framed as to cover the rates between the intermediate points. In this connection it was said that the discrimination against interstate traffic resulting from the lower intrastate rates "would not be removed merely by an increase in the intrastate fares to and from the east bank points," and that "any contemporaneous adjustments of fares between

[1] The report similarly speaks of other towns across the river from St. Louis, East St. Louis being here mentioned as representative of all.

[2] The report refers to a plurality of points opposite Keokuk, but it suffices here to mention Hamilton.

St. Louis or Keokuk and Illinois points, and generally within Illinois, which would permit the defeat of the St. Louis, Keokuk, East St. Louis, or any other east side city fares by methods such as described above, and which would thereby permit the continuance of the undue prejudice which we have found is suffered by St. Louis and Keokuk, and continue to burden interstate commerce," would not comply with the order about to be entered. An order was then made, which is copied in the margin. [1]

In obedience to that order the carriers — of whom there were 29 — took the requisite steps to establish and put in force inter-

[1] The order is dated October 17, 1916, and, omitting the caption, reads as follows:

"*It appearing*, That on July 12, 1916, the Commission entered its report and order in this proceeding, and on the date hereof a supplemental report, which reports are hereby referred to and made a part hereof:

"*It is ordered*, That the said order of July 12, 1916, be, and it is hereby, vacated, and that the following be substituted therefor:

"*It is further ordered*, That the above-named defendants, according as they participate in the transportation, be, and they are hereby, notified and required to cease and desist, on or before January 15, 1917, and thereafter to abstain, from publishing, demanding, or collecting passenger fares between St. Louis, Mo., and points in Illinois upon a basis higher than 2.4 cents per mile, bridge tolls excepted, which basis was found reasonable in said report, or higher than the fares contemporaneously exacted for the transportation of passengers between East St. Louis, Ill., and the same Illinois points, by more than a reasonable bridge toll; or fares constructed upon a higher basis per mile, bridge tolls excepted, than fares contemporaneously maintained between Illinois points intermediate between St. Louis, Mo., and points in Illinois, as such fares have been found in said report to be unlawfully discriminatory.

"*It is further ordered*, That the above defendants, according as they participate in the transportation, be, and they are hereby, notified and required to cease and desist, on or before January 15, 1917, and thereafter to abstain, from publishing, demanding, or collecting fares for the transportation of passengers between St. Louis, Mo., and points in Illinois, the basis of which per mile, bridge tolls excepted, is higher than the basis per mile for fares contemporaneously maintained between Chicago and the same Illinois points, as such fares have been found in said report to be unlawfully discriminatory.

"*It is further ordered*, That the above-named defendants, according as they participate in the transportation, be, and they are hereby, notified and required to cease and desist, on or before January 15, 1917, and thereafter to abstain, from publishing, demanding, or collecting passenger fares between Keokuk, Iowa, and points in Illinois upon a basis higher than 2.4 cents per mile, bridge tolls excepted, which basis was found reasonable in said report, or higher per mile than the fares contemporaneously exacted for the transportation of passengers between Illinois points directly opposite to Keokuk and the same Illinois points, by more than a reasonable bridge toll; or fares

state rates on a basis of 2.4 cents per mile between St. Louis and Keokuk, respectively, and points in Illinois, and those rates became effective. Then, believing the order required all intrastate rates in Illinois to be on a level with those interstate rates, bridge tolls excepted, the carriers proceeded to establish and put in force new rates between all points in that State on a basis of 2.4 cents per mile. This met with opposition on the part of the state authorities and the carriers severally brought suits against them,

---

constructed upon a higher basis per mile, bridge tolls excepted, than fares contemporaneously maintained between Illinois points intermediate between Keokuk, Iowa, and points in Illinois, as such fares have been found in said report to be unlawfully discriminatory.

"*It is further ordered,* That the above-named defendants, according as they participate in the transportation, be, and they are hereby, notified and required to cease and desist, on or before January 15, 1917, and thereafter to abstain, from publishing, demanding, or collecting fares for the transportation of passengers between Keokuk, Iowa, and points in Illinois, the basis of which per mile, bridge tolls excepted, is higher than the basis per mile for fares contemporaneously maintained between Chicago and the same Illinois points, as such fares have been found in said report to be unlawfully discriminatory.

"*It is further ordered,* That the above-named defendants, according as they participate in the transportation, be, and they are hereby, notified and required to establish and put in force on or before January 15, 1917, upon notice to this Commission and to the general public by not less than 30 days' filing and posting in the manner prescribed in section 6 of the act to regulate commerce, and thereafter to maintain and apply to the transportation of passengers between St. Louis and points in Illinois fares upon a basis not in excess of the fares between East St. Louis, Ill., and the same points by more than a reasonable bridge toll; nor upon a higher basis per mile, bridge tolls excepted, than fares contemporaneously maintained between Illinois points intermediate between St. Louis and points in Illinois, as such fares have been found in said report to be unlawfully discriminatory.

"*It is further ordered,* That the above-named defendants, according as they participate in the transportation, be, and they are hereby, notified and required to establish and put in force on or before January 15, 1917, upon notice to this Commission and to the general public by not less than 30 days' filing and posting in the manner prescribed in section 6 of the act to regulate commerce, and thereafter to maintain and apply to the transportation of passengers between St. Louis, Mo., and points in Illinois fares, the basis of which per mile, bridge tolls excepted, is not higher than the basis per mile for fares contemporaneously maintained between Chicago and those same Illinois points.

"*It is further ordered,* That the above-named defendants, according as they participate in the transportation, be, and they are hereby, notified and required to establish and put in force on or before January 15, 1917, upon notice to this Commission and to the general public by not less than 30 days' filing in the District Court for the Northern District of Illinois, to enjoin them from interfering, by civil or criminal proceedings, or otherwise, with the establishment and maintenance of such intrastate rates under the Commission's order. The suits were consolidated and the present appeals are from decrees dismissing the bills for want of equity and dismissing cross bills of the state authorities for want of jurisdiction. . . .

MR. JUSTICE VAN DEVANTER, after making the foregoing statement, delivered the opinion of the court. . . .

Whether the suits by the carriers were rightly dismissed on the merits is the principal question, and its solution turns on the power of the Commission to deal with discrimination arising out of a disparity in interstate and intrastate rates, and on the scope and effect of the order made.

---

and posting in the manner prescribed in section 6 of the act to regulate commerce, and thereafter to maintain and apply to the transportation of passengers between Keokuk, Iowa, and points in Illinois fares upon a basis not in excess of 2.4 cents per mile, bridge tolls excepted, which basis has been found reasonable in the said report, nor in excess per mile of the fares between points in Illinois directly opposite to Keokuk and the same points by more than a reasonable bridge toll; nor upon a higher basis per mile, bridge tolls excepted, than fares contemporaneously effective between Illinois points intermediate between Keokuk, Iowa, and points in Illinois.

"*It is further ordered*, That the above-named defendants, according as they participate in the transportation, be, and they are hereby, notified and required to establish and put in force on or before January 15, 1917, upon notice to this Commission and to the general public by not less than 30 days' filing and posting in the manner prescribed in section 6 of the act to regulate commerce, and thereafter to maintain and apply to the transportation of passengers between Keokuk, Iowa, and points in Illinois fares, the basis of which per mile, bridge tolls excepted, is not higher than the basis per mile for fares contemporaneously maintained between Chicago and those same Illinois points.

"*It is further ordered*, That said defendants, according as they participate in the transportation, be, and they are hereby, notified and required to cease and desist, on or before January 15, 1917, and thereafter to abstain, from the undue preferences and the undue and unreasonable prejudices and disadvantages found in said report to result from the contemporaneous maintenance between Illinois points of passenger fares, which fares, in combination with other fares required or permitted by this order, would produce the discrimination against interstate commerce and the undue preferences in favor of intrastate commerce condemned in the report of the Commission.

"*And it is further ordered*, That this order shall continue in force for a period of not less then two years from the date when it shall take effect."

In their answers the state authorities took the position that in so far as the order purports to authorize or require a removal of the discrimination found to exist by a change in intrastate rates it is in excess of any power that has been or can be conferred on the Commission, and therefore neither relieves the carriers from full compliance with the state rate law nor prevents that law from being fully enforced against them. If the premise were sound the conclusion doubtless would follow, for where the Commission makes an order which it has no power to make the order is necessarily void, not merely voidable. But that the premise is not sound is settled by the *Shreveport Case* (*Houston, East & West Texas Ry. Co.* v. *United States*), 234 U. S. 342. Upon full consideration it there was held:

1. Under the commerce clause of the Constitution Congress has ample power to prevent the common instrumentalities of interstate and intrastate commerce, such as the railroads, from being used in their intrastate operations in such manner as to affect injuriously traffic which is interstate.

2. Where unjust discrimination against interstate commerce arises out of the relation of intrastate to interstate rates this power may be exerted to remove the discrimination, and this whether the intrastate rates are maintained under a local statute or by the voluntary act of the carrier.

3. In correcting such discrimination Congress is not restricted to an adjustment or reduction of the interstate rates, but may prescribe a reasonable standard to which they shall conform and require the carrier to adjust the intrastate rates in such way as to remove the discrimination; for where the interstate and intrastate transactions of carriers are so related that the effective regulation of one involves control of the other, it is Congress, and not the State, that is entitled to prescribe the dominant rule.

4. It is admissible for Congress to provide for the execution of this power through a subordinate body such as the Interstate Commerce Commission, and this it has done by the Act to Regulate Commerce.

5. Where in the exercise of its delegated authority the Commission not only finds that a disparity in the two classes of rates is resulting in unjust discrimination against interstate commerce but also determines what are reasonable rates for the interstate traffic, and then directs the removal of the discrimination, the carrier not only is entitled to put in force the interstate rates

found reasonable but is free to remove the forbidden discrimination by bringing the intrastate rates to the same level.

Upon further consideration that decision was approved and followed in *American Express Co.* v. *Caldwell*, 244 U. S. 617.

The parties differ widely about the scope of the order. The carriers assert that it covers every intrastate passenger rate in Illinois, is addressed to the removal of discrimination found to be state-wide, and gives ample authority for increasing all rates between points in Illinois from 2 cents to 2.4 cents per mile. On the other hand, the state authorities assert that it is not state-wide and that the extent to which it is intended to affect the state-made rates is so indefinitely and vaguely stated as to make it inoperative and of no effect as to them. Of course, the Commission could adjust the remedy to the evil and make the order as broad as the wrongful discrimination; and not improbably it would intend to go that far and no farther. But the extent of the discrimination found and of the remedy applied must be gathered from the reports and order of the Commission, for they constitute the only authoritative evidence of its action. The reports show that the only discrimination found relates to the passenger traffic between Illinois and two cities outside that State — St. Louis and Keokuk. There is no finding that this traffic extends in appreciable volume to all sections of Illinois. As to some sections its volume may be very large and as to others almost or quite negligible. At best the reports leave the matter uncertain. Obviously this traffic is only a small part of the interstate passenger traffic moving over the railroads in Illinois, and yet the finding is merely that there was discrimination against this part. Had the Commission regarded the discrimination as state-wide it is but reasonable to believe that it would have said so in its findings. And had it intended to require or authorize a state-wide readjustment of the intrastate rates it doubtless would have given direct expression to that purpose, which easily could have been done in a few lines. But neither in any part nor as a whole does the order plainly manifest such a purpose. In harmony with the reports it deals with the intrastate rates in so far only as they result in discrimination against interstate traffic to and from St. Louis and Keokuk. Its most comprehensive paragraph — the next to the last — declares that the carriers must "abstain from the undue preferences and the undue and unreasonable prejudices and disadvantages found in said report to result from the contemporaneous maintenance between Illinois points of passenger fares, which fares, in combination with other fares required or permitted by this order, would produce the discrimination against interstate commerce and the undue preferences in favor of intrastate commerce condemned in the report of the Commission." But even here the general terms are so far restrained by the reference to the reports as to show that nothing more is intended than to command the removal of the discrimination to which the traffic to and from St. Louis and Keokuk is subjected. Besides, this paragraph evidently proceeds upon the theory that some of the intrastate rates are not affected by the other paragraphs, and ought not to be disturbed save where their use in connection with rates sanctioned by the order will be productive of the discrimination which it is intended to correct.

But while the order shows that it is not intended to require or authorize a readjustment of all the intrastate rates, the description of those to which it applies is at best indefinite. There may be less uncertainty in some parts of the order than in others, but when each is read in the light of the rest and all in the light of the reports it is apparent that none has a certain or definite field of operation. The uncertainty arises out of a failure to designate with appropriate precision the territory or points to and from which the intrastate rates must or may be readjusted, and this omission accords with the absence from the reports of any finding showing definitely the territory or points where those rates operate prejudicially against the interstate traffic which the order is intended to protect.

To be effective in respect of intrastate rates established and maintained under state authority an order of the Commission of the kind now under consideration must have a definite field of operation and not leave the territory or points to which it applies uncertain. Upon this point we said in *American Express Co.* v. *Caldwell, supra,* p. 625:

"Where a proceeding to remove unjust discrimination presents solely the question whether the carrier has improperly exercised its authority to initiate rates, the Commission may legally order, in general terms, the removal of the discrimination shown, leaving upon the carrier the burden of determining also the points to and from which rates must be changed, in order to effect a removal of the discrimination. But where, as here, there is a conflict between the federal and the state authorities, the Commission's order cannot serve as a justification for disregarding a regulation or order issued under state authority, unless, and except so far as, it is definite as to the territory or points to which it applies. For the power of the Commission is dominant only to the extent that the exercise is found by it to be necessary to remove the existing discrimination against interstate traffic."

In construing federal statutes enacted under the power conferred by the commerce clause of the Constitution the rule is that it should never be held that Congress intends to supersede or suspend the exercise of the reserved powers of a State, even where that may be done, unless, and except so far as, its purpose to do so is clearly manifested. *Reid* v. *Colorado*, 187 U. S. 137, 148; *Cummings* v. *Chicago*, 188 U. S. 410, 430; *Savage* v. *Jones*, 225 U. S. 501; *Missouri, Kansas & Texas Ry. Co.* v. *Harris*, 234 U. S. 412, 419. This being true of an act of Congress, it is obvious that an order of a subordinate agency, such as the Commission, should not be given precedence over a state rate statute otherwise valid, unless, and except so far as, it conforms to a high standard of certainty.

We conclude that the uncertainty in this order is such as to render it inoperative and of no effect as to the intrastate rates, established and maintained under a law of the State, and therefore that the suits by the carriers were rightly dismissed on the merits.

Decrees affirmed.

INTERSTATE COMMERCE COMMISSION *v.* GOODRICH TRANSIT COMPANY

INTERSTATE COMMERCE COMMISSION *v.* SAME

UNITED STATES *v.* WHITE STAR LINE

UNITED STATES *v.* SAME

224 U. S. 194 (1912)

MR. JUSTICE DAY delivered the opinion of the court.

The appellees in these four cases are corporations organized under state laws and engaged in the carriage of passengers and freight by water upon the Great Lakes. They filed bills in the United States Circuit Court for the Northern District of Illinois to enjoin the enforcement of certain orders of the Interstate Commerce Commission. The cases were afterwards transferred to the United States Commerce Court.

The orders of the Commission complained of comprise: First, an order prescribing the method of accounts and bookkeeping as to the operating expenses of the carriers and a similar order as to bookkeeping concerning the operating revenues of the carriers; and, second, an order requiring a report of the carriers respecting their corporate organization, financial condition, etc.

The Government of the United States intervened and filed an answer in each case, but the cases were practically heard on demurrer, as the record discloses, and therefore the allegations of the bills well pleaded must be deemed to be true. The bills contain many conclusions, and argumentative deductions as to the effect of the orders upon the carriers, which, under the rules of pleading, are not considered as admitted. *United States* v. *Ames*, 99 U. S. 35, 45.

The pertinent averments necessary to a decision of the cases, as we view them, show that the carriers are corporations organized under the laws of certain States of the Union; that they carry passengers and freight upon the Great Lakes between ports in different States, which they designate as their port-to-port interstate business; that they carry passengers and freight wholly within a State, which they designate as their port-to-port intrastate business; and that they also carry passengers and property in interstate commerce under joint tariffs in connection with certain railroad carriers of the United States with whom they have agreed upon joint through rates, which they designate as their joint rail and water business. As to the Goodrich Transit Company, it is averred that eighty per cent of its gross revenue is derived from its port-to-port interstate and intrastate business, and less than twenty per cent of its gross earnings is derived from its joint rail and water business. A like averment is made with respect to the White Star Line, except that it is said that in its business the revenue derived from joint rail and water traffic, as aforesaid, is less than one per cent of its entire revenue.

It is averred that the bookkeeping and accounting methods required by the orders of the Commission differ from those prescribed and now kept by the companies; that the orders of the Commission make no difference between the intrastate port-to-port business and the interstate port-to-port business and the joint rail and water business; and that the orders entered by the Commission prohibit the companies from keeping any accounts, records or memoranda other than those prescribed by the Commission in such orders.

In the White Star Line cases the bills contain an additional averment that that company operates two amusement parks, one at Tashmoo and one at Sugar Island, both in the State of Michigan, and in connection therewith owns, operates and derives revenue from lunch stands, merry-go-rounds, bowling alleys, bath houses, etc., and collects admission fees from people entering the parks. It complains that its business concerning said parks is included within the accounting methods prescribed by the Commission.

As to the report called for by the order of the Commission, it is averred that such report was not required because of any complaint filed against the corporations for the violation of the Act to Regulate Commerce; that there is no statute requiring the report to be kept secret, and, if it is made public, the affairs of the companies will be thrown open to inspection to their injury; that a large number of the inquiries contained in the order of the Commission relate to details of the companies' business solely intrastate, or that which is from port to port; and that the report is not limited to the joint rail and water business of complainants.

There are also averments that the orders were unconstitutional, because the Commission, in undertaking to put in force such requirements, exceeded its authority in so far as the power was asserted to examine into the affairs of the companies not relating to their joint rail and water business, and having reference, as it was alleged, to their domestic business or interstate business not within the terms of the act.

The Commerce Court enjoined the execution of the orders (190 Fed. Rep. 943), declaring that (p. 966):

"It [the Commission] acted within its authority when it made an order calling for reports of all business done by the petitioners under through bills of lading where the transportation was partly by railroad from one State to another, or from one place in the United States to Canada, an adjacent foreign country; and it was within its power when it prescribed the system of accounts and the uniform method of keeping accounts for such interstate business, and so far as the orders call for information confined to such traffic, or directly related thereto, and so far as the orders prescribe uniform systems of bookkeeping and accounting for such traffic and such as is directly related thereto, they must be sustained. But, in so far as the reports called for and the accounting rules prescribed extend beyond such interstate business of the carriers, or include matters of intrastate traffic accounts and affairs and concerns exclusively, they become invasions of the rights of the carriers, and to the extent of such invasions are unlawful."

The court held that the orders concerning the report and auditing would be lawful respecting the interstate business done by the carriers in connection with railroads, as provided by the act, but, in requiring a report concerning the other business of the companies and prescribing bookkeeping methods therefor, the Commission exceeded its authority, and the court granted the prayers of the petitioners for the orders of injunction, ordered a recast of the form of report in conformity with its opinion and remanded the cases to the Commission for that purpose.

Whether this order of the Commerce Court was correct or not primarily depends upon the construction of the Interstate Commerce Act and the extent to which, in the respect involved in these cases, the carriers herein interested are within the terms of the law. The terms of the act of Congress, as amended June 29, 1906, 34 Stat. 584, c. 3591, and in force at the time when these orders were made, are plain and simple, and, we think, not difficult to comprehend. They are: "The provisions of this act [to regulate commerce] shall apply to . . . . any common carrier or carriers engaged in the transportation of passengers or property wholly by railroad (or partly by railroad and partly by water when both are used under a common control; management, or arrangement for a continuous carriage or shipment), from one State or Territory of the United States, or the District of Columbia, to any other State or Territory of the United States, etc." The proviso, at the end of the section, that its terms shall not apply to the transportation of passengers or property wholly within one State was inserted for the purpose of showing the congressional purpose not to undertake to regulate a commerce wholly domestic. The first section makes the act apply alike to common carriers engaged in the transportation of passengers or property wholly by railroad or partly by railroad and partly by water under an arrangement for a continuous carriage or shipment. It is conceded that the carriers filing the bills in these cases were common carriers engaged in the transportation of passengers and property partly by railroad and partly by water under a joint arrangement for a continuous carriage or shipment. Such common carriers are declared to be subject to the provisions of the act in precisely the same terms as those which comprehend the other companies named in the act. Carriers partly by railroad and partly by water under a common arrangement for a continuous carriage or shipment are as specifically within the terms of the act as any other carrier named therein. It may be that certain provisions of the act are in their nature applicable to some carriers and not to others; but we are only concerned to inquire in this case whether the carriers thus broadly brought within the terms of the act by § 1 thereof are subject to the provisions of the statute by the authority of which the Commission undertook to require the system of accounting and the report as to the organization and business of the corporations, and whether, if within the terms of the act, the orders are constitutionally made.

Certain it is that, when engaged in carrying on traffic under joint rates with railroads, filed with the Commission, the carriers are bound to deal upon like terms with all shippers who seek to avail themselves of such joint rates, and are subject to the general requirements of the act preventing and punishing the giving of rebates, the making of unjust discriminations, the showing of favoritism and other practices denounced in the various sections of the act. They are undoubtedly subject to the provisions of § 12 of the act, which permits the Commission to inquire into the management of the business of all common carriers subject to the act and to keep itself informed as to the manner and method in which the same is conducted, with the right to obtain from such common carriers the full and complete information necessary to enable the Commission to carry out the objects for which it was created. The joint rates established are subject to revision by the Commission under § 15 of the act. We must remember, also, in this connection, that under § 21 of the act the Commission is required to make a report each year to the Congress containing such information and data as may be considered of value in the determination of questions connected with the regulation of commerce, together with such recommendations as to additional legislation as the Commission may see fit to make.

As to annual reports, the power conferred in § 20 of the act extends to all common carriers subject to the provisions of the act. The Commission is vested with authority to prescribe the manner in which such reports shall be made and to require specific answers to all questions as to which the Commission may need information. The report required in these cases was declared to be needed to enable the Commission to procure full information of the scope and character of the business of carriers by water within the jurisdiction of the Commission and of the extent of their operations, such as would enable the Commission to determine the form for annual report which would best give the information required by the Commission, and at the same time conform as nearly as may be to the accounting systems of carriers by water.

The form of report adopted by the Commission requires a showing as to the corporate organization of each carrier by water subject to the act, the companies owned by it and the parties or companies controlling it; as to the financial condition of the carrier, the cost of its real property and equipment, its capital stock and other stock and securities owned by it, together with all special funds and current assets and liabilities, as well as its funded indebtedness, with collateral security covering same; and as to finances with respect to the operations of the carrier for the current year, giving the revenue of the company and its source, whether from transportation, and what kind, or from outside operations, and all expenses, detailed, with a statement as to the net income or deficit from the various sources, and the report contains a profit and loss account and a general balance sheet. The report further requires certain statistical information, as follows: The routes of the carrier and their mileage; a general description of the equipment owned, leased or chartered by the carrier; the amount of traffic, both passenger and freight, and mileage and revenue statistics, together with a separation of freight into the quantity of the various products transported, showing also whether originating on the carrier's line or received from a connecting line; and a general description of any separate business carried on by the carrier. But such report is no broader than the annual report of such carriers, as prescribed by the act, for § 20 provides that:

"Such annual reports shall show in detail the amount of capital stock issued, the amounts paid therefor, and the manner of payment for the same; the dividends paid, the surplus fund, if any, and the number of stockholders; the funded and floating debts and the interest paid thereon; the cost and value of the carrier's property, franchises, and equipments; the number of employés and the salaries paid each class; the accidents to passengers, employés, and other persons, and the causes thereof; the amounts expended for improvements each year, how expended, and the character of such improvements; the earnings and receipts from each branch of business and from all sources; the operating and other expenses; the balances of profit and loss; and a complete exhibit of the financial operations of the carrier each year, including an annual balance sheet. Such reports shall also contain such information in relation to rates or regulations concerning fares or freights, or agreements, arrangements, or contracts affecting the same as the Commission may require."

As to the accounts, the statute permits the Commission, in its discretion, for the purpose of enabling it the better to carry out the purposes of the act, to prescribe a period of time within which such common carriers shall have a uniform system of accounts and the manner in which such accounts shall be kept. The Commission may, the statute further provides, in its discretion, prescribe the forms of all accounts, records and memoranda to be kept by the common carriers, to which accounts the Commission shall have access. And the act makes it unlawful for the carriers to keep any accounts, records or memoranda other than those prescribed by the Commission.

We think this section contains ample authority for the Commission to require a system of accounting as provided in its orders and a report in the form shown to have been required by the order of the Commission. It is true that the accounts required to be kept are general in their nature and embrace business other than such as is necessary to the discharge of the duties required in carrying passengers and freight in interstate commerce by joint arrangement between the railroad and the water carrier, but the Commission is charged under the law with the supervision of such rates as to their reasonableness and with the general duty of making reports to Congress which might require a knowledge of the business of the carrier beyond that which is strictly of the character mentioned. If the Commission is to successfully perform its duties in respect to reasonable rates, undue discriminations and favoritism, it must be informed as to the business of the carriers by a system of accounting which will not permit the possible concealment of forbidden practices in accounts which it is not permitted to see and concerning which it can require no information. It is a mistake to suppose that the requiring of information concerning the business methods of such corporations, as shown in their accounts, is a regulation of business not within the jurisdiction of the Commission, as seems to be argued for the complainants. The object of requiring such accounts to be kept in a uniform way and to be open to the inspection of the Commission is not to enable it to regulate the affairs of the corporations not within its jurisdiction, but to be informed concerning the business methods of the corporations subject to the act that it may properly regulate such matters as are really within its jurisdiction. Further, the requiring of information concerning a business is not regulation of that business. The necessity of keeping such accounts has been developed in the reports of the Commission and has been the subject of great consideration. It caused the employment of those skilled in such matters, and has resulted in the adoption of a general form of accounting which will enable the Commission to examine into the affairs of the corporations, with a view to discharging its duties of regulation concerning them.

There is nothing in the case of *Harriman* v. *Interstate Commerce Commission,* 211 U. S. 407, contrary to the conclusion herein announced. That case dealt with the authority of the Commission to compel the attendance and testimony of witnesses in cases where complaints had not been made. The extent to which the Commission might require systems of accounting and reports of corporations subject to the act was expressly left open in the opinion of the court. 211 U. S. pp. 421, 422.

The necessity of such accounts is emphasized under the English practice, and accounts and reports are required in great detail under the laws of that country.

In the report of the committee appointed by the Board of Trade under the Railway Regulation Acts to make inquiries with respect to the form and scope of the accounts and statistical returns rendered by railway companies the omission of the former law to make provision for any prescribed and uniform system of accounts is pointed out, and it is said:

"It is obviously of the first importance, from the point of view of comparison between the different railway companies, that there should be uniformity of practice among all the companies with regard to the keeping of accounts and statistics; that is to say, that every heading, both in the accounts and in the statistics, should bear precisely the same meaning in the case of all railways — should, in effect, be standardized."

The Railway Companies (Accounts and Returns) Act, December 16, 1911, 1 and 2 Geo. 5, c. 34, — to amend the laws with respect to accounts and returns of railway companies — contains requirements as to financial accounts and statistical returns which call for a uniform system of accounting, showing the organization and workings of the companies in great detail, together with statistical returns as to their business, subdivided so as to include all the operations of the companies as carriers and in all other enterprises in which they may engage.

The learned Commerce Court was of the opinion that the Commission might require accounts and reports, so far as the business of the water carriers with reference to joint rates by rail and water under a common arrangement was concerned, and remanded the cases to the Commission for revision of their orders upon that basis. But it is argued for the Commission, and it seems to us with great force, that it would be impracticable to make such separation in any system of accounting. It is a matter of general knowledge, of which we may take judicial notice, that traffic of all kinds is conducted upon the same ship and passage. A boat may leave a lake port carrying passengers and freight destined for ports within the State and for ports beyond the State, and as a part of the freight for carriage embrace some carried under the terms of joint arrangements made with connecting railroad carriers. How would it be practicable to separate the items of expense entailed in the carriage of these various classes? It is done upon one boat, with one set of officers and crew, and must, in the nature of things, be under one general bill of expense — at least it would seem impracticable to separate it into its items so as to show the expense of that which it is contended is alone within the terms of the act, as construed by the carriers.

We think the act should be given a practical construction, and one which will enable the Commission to perform the duties required of it by Congress, and, conceding for this purpose that the regulating power of the Commission is limited so far as rates are concerned to joint rates of the character named in § 1, it is still essential that to enable the Commission to perform its required duties, even with respect to such rates, and to make reports to Congress of the business of carriers subject to the terms of the act, it should be informed as to the matters contained in the report. Congress, in § 20, has authorized the Commission to inquire as to the business which the carrier does and to require the keeping of uniform accounts, in order that the Commission may know just how the business is carried on, with a view to regulating that which is confessedly within its power.

It is contended that this construction of the statute enables the Commission not only to regulate the interstate business, but as well the wholly intrastate business of the complaining corporations, and is, therefore, beyond the power of Congress. Such cases are cited and relied upon by complainants as the *Employers'*

Liability Cases, 207 U. S. 463, and *Illinois Central R. R. Co.* v. *McKendree*, 203 U. S. 514. In those cases acts of Congress and orders of executive departments were held void because they undertook to regulate matters wholly intrastate, as distinguished from those matters of an interstate character and within the legislative power of Congress. And what we have already said as to the character of these orders is enough to indicate that in our opinion they are not regulations of intrastate commerce.

Furthermore, it is said that such construction of § 20 makes it an unlawful delegation of legislative power to the Commission. We cannot agree to this contention. The Congress may not delegate its purely legislative power to a commission, but, having laid down the general rules of action under which a commission shall proceed, it may require of that commission the application of such rules to particular situations and the investigation of facts, with a view to making orders in a particular matter within the rules laid down by the Congress. This rule has been frequently stated and illustrated in recent cases in this court, and needs no amplification here. *Buttfield* v. *Stranahan*, 192 U. S. 470; *Union Bridge Co.* v. *United States*, 204 U. S. 384; *United States* v. *Grimaud*, 220 U. S. 506.

In § 20 Congress has authorized the Commission to require annual reports. The act itself prescribes in detail what those reports shall contain. The Commission is permitted, in its discretion, to require a uniform system of accounting, and to prohibit other methods of accounting than those which the Commission may prescribe. In other words, Congress has laid down general rules for the guidance of the Commission, leaving to it merely the carrying out of details in the exercise of the power so conferred. This, we think, is not a delegation of legislative authority.

And it is argued that Congress has no visitorial power over state corporations. We need not reassert the ample power which the Constitution has been construed to confer upon Congress in the regulation of interstate commerce, declared in the many cases in this court, from *Gibbons* v. *Ogden*, 9 Wheaton, 1, to its most recent deliverances. In *Hale* v. *Henkel*, 201 U. S. 43, 75, while general visitorial power over state corporations was not asserted to be within the power of Congress, it was nevertheless declared as to interstate commerce that the General Government had, in the vindication of its own laws, the same power it would possess if the corporation had been created by act of Congress.

As to one of the corporations it is said that its business includes not only the carriage of passengers and freight, but that it owns and operates in connection therewith certain amusement parks. The report in controversy, as to business other than commerce, requires a general description of such outside operations, and also a statement of the income from and the expenses of the same. As we have said, if the Commission is to be informed of the business of the corporation, so far as its bookkeeping and reports are concerned, it must have full knowledge and full disclosures thereof, in order that it may ascertain whether forbidden practices and discriminations are concealed, even unintentionally, in certain accounts and whether charges of expense are made against one part of a business which ought to be made against another.

Bookkeeping, it is said, is not interstate commerce. True, it is not. But bookkeeping may and ought to show how a business which, in part at least, is interstate commerce, is carried on, in order that the Commission, charged with the duty of making reasonable rates and prohibiting unfair and unreasonable ones, may know the nature and extent of the business of the corporation, the cost of its interstate transactions and otherwise to inform itself so as to enable it to properly regulate the matters which are within its authority.

We think the uniform system of accounting prescribed and the report called for are such as it is within the power of the Commission to require under § 20 of the act. Nor do the requirements exceed the constitutional authority of Congress to pass such a law. It therefore follows that the Commerce Court erred in granting the injunctions and in remanding the cases to the Commission with instructions to recast its orders.

Judgments reversed.

ARMOUR PACKING COMPANY *v.* UNITED STATES

SWIFT AND COMPANY *v.* SAME

MORRIS AND COMPANY *v.* SAME

CUDAHY PACKING COMPANY *v.* SAME

209 U. S. 56 (1908)

MR. JUSTICE DAY delivered the opinion of the court.

These cases are here upon writs of certiorari to the United States Circuit Court of Appeals for the Eighth Circuit. By stipulation there was a single petition for certiorari and the cases in the Circuit Court of Appeals were considered together on the record in the *Armour Packing Company case*, and, as it is conceded in the brief of the learned counsel for the petitioners that the differences in the cases are unsubstantial, the same course may be followed here.

Each of the petitioners was convicted in the District Court of the United States, Western District of Missouri, for violation of the so-called Elkins Act of February 19, 1903, chap. 708, 32 Stat. 847, in obtaining from the Chicago, Burlington and Quincy Railway Company an unlawful concession of 12 cents per 100 pounds from the published and filed rate on that portion of the route between the Mississippi River and New York for transportation upon a shipment made August 17, 1905, for carriage by rail of certain packing house products from Kansas City, Kansas, to New York for export. Upon writs of error from the Circuit Court of Appeals of the Eighth Circuit the sentences of conviction were affirmed. 153 Fed. Rep. 1. . . . .

It is further contended by petitioners that the statutes have no application to a shipment on a through bill of lading from an interior point in the United States to a foreign port. It is alleged that the Elkins law refers to the original Interstate Commerce Act, and that its terms do not include such shipments. Analyzing the first section of the act (24 Stat. 379), it is said that it applies to the following kinds of commerce: (*a*) interstate commerce; (*b*) commerce between the United States and an *adjacent* foreign country; (*c*) commerce between places in the United States passing through a foreign country; (*d*) commerce from the United States to a foreign country, only while being transported to a point of transshipment; (*e*) commerce from a foreign country to points in the United States, but only while being carried from port of entry either in the United States or an adjacent foreign country. And, it is contended, that § 6, as amended (25 Stat. 855), does not require the filing of through export tariffs.

The purpose of Congress to embrace the whole field of interstate commerce is made apparent by the exclusion only of wholly domestic commerce in the last clause of section one of the original act of 1887, and in the declaration of the scope and purpose of the act declared in its title. *Texas & Pacific Ry. Co.* v. *Interstate Commerce Commission,* 162 U. S. 197, 211. There is no attempt in the language of the act to exempt such foreign commerce as is carried on a through bill of lading; on the contrary, the act in terms applies to the transportation of property shipped from any place in the United States to a foreign country and carried from such place to a port of transshipment.

What reasonable ground is there for supposing that Congress intended to exercise no control over such commerce if it happens to be billed through to the foreign port? Such construction would place such important commerce shipped in the United States to a port for transshipment abroad wholly outside the restrictions of the law, and enable shippers to withdraw such commerce from the regulations enforced against other interstate commerce by the expedient of a through bill of lading. Take the present case. The through rate is obtained by adding the ocean rate to the inland rate. There is no contractual relation between the railroad carrier and the ocean carrier. The ocean rate is uncertain and variable, depending upon time of sailing and available space. The accommodation for ocean shipment was obtained by the shipper and by it made known to the inland carrier. We think the language of the statute, read in the light of the manifest purpose of its passage, shows the intent of Congress to bring interstate commerce within the control of the provisions of the law up to the time of ocean shipment. This construction is reinforced by the broad provisions of § 6 of the act as to publishing schedules, showing rates, fares and charges, and filing the same with the Interstate Commerce Commission. That such rates, notwithstanding through bills of lading, were subject to the provisions of the act, was held, upon full consideration, and rightfully, as we think, by the Interstate Commerce Commission. *Re Tariffs* v. *Export and Import Traffic,* 10 I. C. C. Rep. 55.

It is contended that the act, as construed by the Circuit Court of Appeals, makes it conflict with Art. I, § 9, par. 5, of the Constitution, which provides: "No tax or duty shall be laid on articles exported from any State. No preference shall be given by any regulation of commerce or revenue to the ports of one State over those of another; nor shall vessels bound to or from one State be obliged to enter, clear or pay duties in another."

The petitioner contends that to permit a statute to have such application to articles intended for foreign export is to place a burden on the exercise of this right, because before the shipper can lawfully send his goods abroad and before the carrier can lawfully accept them there must be a compliance with the established rate on file with the Interstate Commerce Commission. This rate is subject only to be changed as provided by law; and this can be done without notice to the exporter and regardless of his power to comply with the legal rate and meet the competition at the seaport and the conditions of foreign markets. These things, it is said, place a distinct burden upon export trade, and therefore come within the constitutional prohibition. But it is to be observed that the Constitution provides for a burden only by the way of taxation or duty, and unless the alleged interference amounts to such taxation or duty it does not come within the constitutional prohibition. *Cornell* v. *Coyne,* 192 U. S. 418.

The regulations of interstate commerce provided by the statute now under consideration are within the acknowledged power of Congress under the interstate commerce clause of the Constitution. There is no attempt to levy duties on goods to be exported, and the mere incidental effect in the legal regulation of interstate commerce upon such exportations does not come within this constitutional prohibition.

Nor do we think there is any more force in the contention that this legislation amounts to a preference of ports of one State over those of another within the meaning of the constitutional provision under consideration. This provision was intended to prevent legislation intended to give and having the effect of giving preference to the ports of one State over those of another State. It may be true that the regulation of interstate commerce by rail has the effect to give an advantage to commerce wholly by water and to ports which can be reached by means of inland navigation, but these are natural advantages and are not created by statutory law. The fact that regulation, within the acknowledged power of Congress to enact, may affect the ports of one State more than those of another cannot be construed as a violation of this constitutional provision. *South Carolina* v. *Georgia,* 93 U. S. 4, 13; *Pennsylvania* v. *Wheeling & Belmont Bridge Company,* 18 How. 421, 433. . . . .

GALVESTON, HARRISBURG & SAN ANTONIO RAILWAY COMPANY *v.* WOODBURY *et al.*

254 U. S. 357 (1920)

MR. JUSTICE BRANDEIS delivered the opinion of the court.

On March 14, 1917, Mrs. Woodbury took the Galveston, Harrisburg & San Antonio Railway at San Antonio, Texas, for El Paso, Texas, and checked her trunk, which she took with her. It was lost and she sued the company in a state district court for the value of trunk and contents, which the jury found to be $500. Mrs. Woodbury was traveling on a coupon ticket purchased at Timmins, Ontario, from a Canadian railroad, entitling her to travel over it and connecting lines, from Timmins to El Paso and return, apparently with stop-over privileges. When the trunk was lost she was on her journey out. She was not told when she purchased her ticket or when she checked her trunk that there was any limitation upon the amount of the carrier's liability. It did not appear whether the ticket purchased contained notice of any such limitation, nor did it appear what was the law of Canada in this respect. The company insisted that Mrs. Woodbury was on an interstate journey; and that under the Act to Regulate Commerce, February 4, 1887, c. 104, 24 Stat. 379, as amended it was not liable for more than $100; since it had duly filed with the Interstate Commerce Commission and published a tariff limiting liability to that amount unless the passenger declared a higher value and paid excess charges, which Mrs. Woodbury had not done. She insisted that here transportation was not subject to the Act to Regulate Commerce, because it began in a foreign country; and that the liability was governed by the law of Canada, which should in the absence of evidence be assumed to be like the law of Texas, the forum; and that by the law of Texas the limitation of liability was invalid. The trial court held that she was entitled to recover only $100, and entered judgment for that amount. This judgment was reversed by the Court of Civil Appeals, which entered judgment for Mrs. Woodbury in the sum of $500. 209 S. W. Rep. 432. The case came here on writ of certiorari, 250 U. S. 637. The only question before us is the amount of damages recoverable.

If Mrs. Woodbury's journey had started in New York instead of across the border in Canada, the provision in the published tariff would clearly have limited the liability of the carrier to

$100. For her journey would have been interstate although the particular stage of it on which the trunk was lost lay wholly within the State of Texas. Compare *Texas and New Orleans Railroad Co.* v. *Sabine Tramway Co.*, 227 U. S. 111. And the Carmack Amendment under which carriers may limit liability by published tariff applies to the baggage of a passenger carried in interstate commerce, *Boston & Maine Railroad Co.* v. *Hooker*, 233 U. S. 97; although it does not deal with liability for personal injuries suffered by the passenger. *Chicago, Rock Island & Pacific Railway Co.* v. *Maucher*, 248 U. S. 359. The subsequent legislation, the Cummins Amendment, Act of March 4, 1915, c. 176, 38 Stat. 1196, as amended by the Act of August 9, 1916, c. 301, 39 Stat. 441, has not altered the rule regarding liability for baggage.

But counsel for Mrs. Woodbury insists that solely because her journey originated in Canada the provisions of the Act to Regulate Commerce do not apply. The contention is that § 1 of the Act of 1887 does not apply to the transportation of passengers from a foreign country to a point in the United States. To this there are two answers. The first is that the transportation here in question is not that of a passenger but of property. *Boston & Maine Railroad Co.* v. *Hooker*, *supra.* The second is that the Act does apply to the transportation of both passengers and property from an *adjacent* foreign country, such as Canada. Section one declares that the Act applies to "any common carrier . . . . engaged in the transportation of passengers or property. . . . from any place in the United States to an adjacent foreign country." A carrier engaged in transportation by rail *to* an adjacent foreign country is, at least ordinarily, engaged in transportation also *from* that country to the United States. The test of the application of the act is not the direction of the movement, but the nature of the transportation as determined by the field of the carriers' operation. This is the construction placed upon the act by the Interstate Commerce Commission, *International Paper Co.* v. *D. & H. Co.*, 33 I. C. C. 270, 273, citing *T. & P. Ry. Co.* v. *I. C. C.*, 162 U. S. 197. It is in harmony with that placed upon the words of § 1 of the Harter Act, February 13, 1893, c. 105, 27 Stat. 445, "any vessel transporting merchandise or property from or between ports of the United States and foreign ports," which in *Knott* v. *Botany Mills*, 179 U. S. 69, 75, were construed to include vessels bringing cargoes from foreign ports to the United States. There is a later clause in § 1 which deals specifically with the transportation of property to or from foreign countries; but cases arising under that clause are not applicable here. That clause applies where the foreign country is *not* adjacent to the United States. The cases which hold that the Act does not govern shipments from a foreign country in bond through the United States to another place in a foreign country, whether adjacent or not, are also not in point. Compare *United States* v. *Philadelphia & Reading Ry. Co.*, 188 Fed. 484; *In the Matter of Bills of Lading*, 52 I. C. C. 671, 726–729; *M. Canales* v. *Galveston, Harrisburg & San Antonio Railway Co.*, 37 I. C. C. 573.

Since the transportation here in question was subject to the Act to Regulate Commerce, both carrier and passenger were bound by the provisions of the published tariffs. As these limited the recovery for baggage carried to $100, in the absence of a declaration of higher value and the payment of an excess charge, and as no such declaration was made and excess charge paid, that sum only was recoverable.

Reversed.

INTERSTATE COMMERCE COMMISSION *v.* UNITED STATES OF AMERICA *EX REL.* HUMBOLDT STEAMSHIP COMPANY

224 U. S. 474 (1912)

MR. JUSTICE MCKENNA delivered the opinion of court.

The ultimate question in the case is whether Alaska is a Territory of the United States within the meaning of the Interstate Commerce Act as amended.

The Interstate Commerce Commission resolved the question in the negative and dismissed the petition of the Humboldt Steamship Company, the relator, which alleged violations of the act by the White Pass & Yukon Railway Company, operating in Alaska, applying its decision in *Matter of Jurisdiction Over Rail and Water Carriers Operating in Alaska*, 19 I. C. C. Rep. 81.

The steamship company instituted an action in the Supreme Court of the District of Columbia praying for a mandamus against the Commission to require it to take jurisdiction and proceed as required by the act and grant the relief for which the steamship company had petitioned, hereinafter specifically mentioned. The proceeding was dismissed. The court expressed the view that the Commission had "ample authority to assume jurisdiction over common carriers in Alaska, the same as in any other Territory, and over those carriers operating between the State of Washington and Alaska, and between Alaska and Canada, and if they took jurisdiction no one could successfully question their right to do so." The court, however, held that it had no power "to require the Interstate Commerce Commission to act contrary to its own judgment in a matter wherein, after investigation, it had reached a conclusion, honestly and fairly, which might be contrary to the conclusion which the court would reach."

The Court of Appeals, to which court the case was taken by the steamship company, entertained the same view of the Interstate Commerce Act as that expressed by the Supreme Court, but took a different view of the power of the courts to compel action upon the part of the Commission, and reversed the judgment of the Supreme Court and remanded the cause, "with directions to issue a peremptory writ of mandamus directed to the Interstate Commerce Commission requiring it to take jurisdiction of said cause and proceed therein as by law required." To this ruling the Interstate Commerce Commission prosecutes this writ of error.

The proceedings before the Commission were instituted by the steamship company filing a petition (No. 2578) against the White Pass & Yukon Route, consisting of the Pacific & Arctic Railway & Navigation Company, British Columbia-Yukon Railway Company, British-Yukon Railway Company, and British-Yukon Navigation Company, to require said companies to file with the Commission, in the form prescribed by the Act to Regulate Commerce, and to print and keep open for public inspection, schedules showing their rates and charges for transportation of passengers and property between points in Alaska and points in the Dominion of Canada and other places; to establish through routes and joint rates in conjunction with the petitioner between certain named places in Alaska and Seattle, in the State of Washington; to afford all reasonable, proper and equal facilities for the interchange of traffic between their respective lines; and to cease and desist from preventing by sundry devices the carriage of freights from being continuous from place of shipment to place of destination when such freight is originated or in any wise handled by the Humboldt Steamship Company.

The companies proceeded against filed answers. There were intervening companies on both sides of the controversy.

A hearing was assigned and had in October, 1909, and subsequently, July 6, 1910, the Commission decided that it was "without jurisdiction to make the order sought by complainant," resting its ruling upon the authority of its decision in *Matter of Jurisdiction Over Rail and Water Carriers Operating in Alaska, supra.*

Section 1 of the Interstate Commerce Act provides that the provisions of the act "shall apply to any . . . . common carrier or carriers engaged in the transportation of passengers or property wholly by railroad (or partly by railroad and partly by water when both are used under a common control, management, or arrangement for a continuous carriage or shipment), from one State or Territory of the United States, or the District of Columbia, to any other State or Territory of the United States, or the District of Columbia, or from one place in a Territory to another place in the same Territory, ... or from any place in the United States through a foreign country to any other place in the United States. . . . ." 34 Stat. 584.

The pivotal words are: "From one State or Territory of the United States . . . . to any other State or Territory, ... or from one place in a Territory to another place in the same Territory," "Territory" being the especially significant word.

If we may venture to reduce to a single proposition an elaborate discussion of elements and considerations, we may say that the Commission gave to the word "territory" the signification of "organized territory," the chief and determining feature of which is a local legislature as distinguished from a territory having a more rudimentary and less autonomous form of government which it considered Alaska possessed.

To this signification and distinction the arguments of counsel are addressed, and much of the reasoning of the lower courts. That field, however, has been traversed by cases in this court, and it need not again be passed over. We may accept and apply the conclusions which have been reached and expressed.

In the case of *Steamer Coquitlam* v. *United States,* 163 U. S. 346, the relation of the courts of Alaska to the Federal judicial system and the applicability of certain statutes concerning the same were decided, after a review of those statutes and those defining the status of Alaska.

By the fifteenth section of the act of March 3, 1891, creating the Circuit Court of Appeals, it is provided that the Circuit Court of Appeals, in cases in which the judgments of the Circuit Courts of Appeal are made final by this act, shall have "the same appellate jurisdiction, by writ of error or appeal, to review the judgments, orders, and decrees of the supreme courts of the several Territories as by this act they may have to review the judgments, orders, and decrees of the district courts and circuit courts; and for that purpose the several Territories shall, by orders of the supreme court, to be made from time to time, be assigned to particular circuits." 26 Stat. 826, 830, c. 517.

In execution of the duty imposed by that section, this court, by an order promulgated May 11, 1891, assigned Alaska to the Ninth Judicial Circuit.

Subsequent to this order the United States brought a suit in admiralty in the District Court of Alaska for the forfeiture of the steamer Coquitlam because of an alleged violation of the revenue laws. A decree was rendered for the United States and an appeal was prosecuted to the Circuit Court of Appeals for the Ninth Circuit. The United States disputed the jurisdiction of the court on the grounds: (1) that the District Court of Alaska was not a district court within the meaning of the sixth section of the Circuit Court of Appeals Act; and (2) that the District Court of Alaska was not a Supreme Court of a Territory within the meaning of that act and the order of this court assigning Alaska to the Ninth Circuit.

The court certified the questions to this court. We answered the first in the negative and the second in the affirmative. We said, through Mr. Justice Harlan, that the Circuit Court of Appeals Act was necessarily interpreted by this court as conferring appellate jurisdiction upon the Circuit Court of Appeals when by the "order of May 11, 1891, 139 U. S. 707, Alaska was assigned to the Ninth Circuit." And it was further said (p. 352): "Alaska is one of the Territories of the United States. It was so designated in that order and has always been so regarded. And the court established by the act of 1884 (providing for a civil government for Alaska) is the court of last resort within the limits of that Territory. . . . No reason can be suggested why a Territory of the United States, in which the court of last resort is called a Supreme Court, should be assigned to some circuit established by Congress that does not apply with full force to the Territory of Alaska, in which the court of last resort is designated as the District Court of Alaska. The title of the territorial court is not so material as its character."

The case needs no comment. It clearly defines the relation of Alaska to the rest of the United States. It was not a description of a definite area of land or "landed possession," but of a political unit, governing and being governed as such.

This view is reinforced by other cases. In *Binns* v. *United States*, 194 U. S. 486, 490, 491, we said, through Mr. Justice Brewer, that we had held in *Steamer Coquitlam* v. *United States* that "Alaska is one of the Territories of the United States." And also: "Nor can it be doubted that it is an organized Territory, for the act of May 17, 1884, 23 Stat. 24, entitled 'An act providing a civil government for Alaska,' provided: That the territory ceded to the United States by Russia by the treaty of March thirtieth, eighteen hundred and sixty-seven, and known as Alaska, shall constitute a civil and judicial district, the government of which shall be organized and administered as hereinafter provided."

In *Binns* v. *United States* the fact of a local legislature, or indeed any special form of government, was not considered as necessarily a feature of an organized Territory. "It must be remembered," it was said, "that Congress in the government of the Territories as well as of the District of Columbia, has plenary power, save as controlled by the provisions of the Constitution, that the form of government it shall establish is not prescribed, and may not necessarily be the same in all the Territories." There is much more in that case which might be quoted as establishing that the status of Alaska is that of an organized Territory. See also *Rassmussen* v. *United States*, 197 U. S. 516.

It is contended further by the Commission that railways were first authorized to be constructed in Alaska by the act passed May 14, 1898, 30 Stat. 409, c. 299, and that § 2 of the act provided as follows:

"That all charges for the transportation of freight and passengers on railroads in the District of Alaska shall be printed and posted as required by section six of an Act to regulate commerce as amended on March second, eighteen hundred and eighty-nine, and such rates shall be subject to revision and modification by the Secretary of the Interior."

The argument is that this provision brings into force § 6 of the Interstate Commerce Act, and that, it is said, "under familiar rules of construction, excludes the application of every other section in the act," and that, besides, the provision that the rates on the Alaskan railroads should be subject to revision and modification by the Secretary of the Interior "negatived the jurisdiction of the Interstate Commerce Commission, even if Alaska was apprehended to be within section 1 of the Interstate Commerce Act."

These contentions do not seem to have been made in either the Supreme Court of the District or in the Court of Appeals. It was referred to very briefly as a circumstance to be considered in a majority report of the Interstate Commerce Commission in the ruling case, and more at length in the minority report. In the latter report important circumstances were pointed out. The Interstate Commerce law preceded that which gave authority to the Secretary of the Interior to revise and modify railroad rates, and the authority was confined to that special exercise, and, so far, it may be said to have amended the Interstate Commerce Act. At that time it had been held in the *Maximum Rate Cases* (162 U. S. 184; 167 U. S. 479, and 168 U. S. 144), that Congress had not conferred upon the Interstate Commerce Commission the legislative power to prescribe rates, either maximum, minimum or absolute. The power to prescribe a rate was conferred by the amendment of June 29, 1906, and that amendment extended the provisions of the act for the first time to intraterritorial commerce. The amendment made the act completely comprehensive of the whole subject and entirely superseded the minor authority which had been conferred upon the Secretary of the Interior. As said by the minority of the Commission: "There is no suggestion of doubt that the ends of justice require as much the application of the same principle and regulation in Alaska as in New Mexico or Arizona." The two latter at the time this was said were Territories.

It is next contended by the Commission that "mandamus is not a proper proceeding to correct an error of law like that alleged in the petition."

The general principle which controls the issue of a writ of mandamus is familiar. It can be issued to direct the performance of a ministerial act, but not to control discretion. It may be directed against a tribunal or one who acts in a judicial capacity to require it or him to proceed, the manner of doing so being left to its or his discretion. It is true there may be a jurisdiction to determine the possession of jurisdiction. *Ex parte Harding,* 219 U. S. 363. But the full doctrine of that case cannot be extended to administrative officers. The Interstate Commerce Commission is purely an administrative body. It is true it may exercise and must exercise *quasi* judicial duties, but its functions are defined and, in the main, explicitly directed by the act creating it. It may act of its own motion in certain instances — it may be petitioned to move by those having rights under the act. It may exercise judgment and discretion, and, it may be, cannot be controlled in either. But if it absolutely refused to act, deny its power, from a misunderstanding of the law, it cannot be said to exercise discretion. Give it that latitude and yet give it the power to nullify its most essential duties, and how would its non-action be reviewed? The answer of the Commission is, by "a reversal by the tribunal of appeal." And such a tribunal, it is intimated, is the United States Commerce Court.

But the proposition is plainly without merit, even although it be conceded, for the sake of argument, that the Commerce Court is by law vested with the exclusive power to review any and every act of the Commission taken in the exertion of the authority conferred upon it by statute; that is, to exclusively review, not only affirmative orders of the Commission granting relief, but also the action of that body in refusing to award relief on the ground that an applicant was not entitled to relief. This is so because the action of the Commission refusing to entertain a petition on the ground that its subject-matter was not within the scope of the powers conferred upon it, would not be embraced within the hypothetical concessions thus made. A like view disposes of the cases relied upon in which it was decided that certain departmental orders were not susceptible of being reviewed by mandamus. We do not propose to review the cases, as we consider them to be plainly inapposite to the subject in hand.

In the case at bar the Commission refused to proceed at all, though the law required it to do so; and to so do as required — that is, to take jurisdiction, not in what manner to exercise it — is the effect of the decree of the Court of Appeals, the order of the court being that a peremptory writ of mandamus be issued directing the Commission "to take jurisdiction of said cause and proceed therein as by law required." In other words, to proceed to the merits of the controversy, at which point the Commission stopped because it was "constrained to hold," as it said, "upon authority of the decision recently announced in *In the Matter of Jurisdiction Over Rail and Water Carriers Operating in Alaska*, 19 I. C. C. Rep. 81, that the Commission is without jurisdiction to make the order sought by complainant," the steamship company.

Judgment Affirmed.

UNITED STATES OF AMERICA, UPON THE APPLICATION OF THE ATTORNEY GENERAL, AT THE REQUEST OF THE INTERSTATE COMMERCE COMMISSION, *v.* UNION STOCK YARD & TRANSIT COMPANY OF CHICAGO

CHICAGO JUNCTION RAILWAY COMPANY *v.* UNITED STATES

226 U. S. 286 (1912)

MR. JUSTICE DAY delivered the opinion of the court.

These are appeals from a decree entered by the Commerce Court in an action begun by the United States on the application of the Attorney General at the request of the Interstate Commerce Commission against the Union Stock Yard and Transit Company of Chicago, an Illinois corporation (hereinafter called the "Stock Yard Company"), the Chicago Junction Railway Company, an Illinois corporation (hereinafter called the "Junction Company"), and the Chicago Junction Railways and Union Stock Yards Company, a New Jersey corporation (hereinafter called the "Investment Company"), and David Pfælzer, Abe Pfælzer and Jones L. Pfælzer, a copartnership doing business under the firm name and style of Louis Pfælzer & Sons. The bill sought to enjoin violations of §§ 2, 6 and 20 of the Interstate Commerce Act, as amended 24 Stat. 379, c. 104; 34 Stat. 584; 36 Stat. 539, c. 309 and of § 1 of the Elkins Law as amended 34 Stat. 584, c. 3591. Its prayer was that an injunction should issue to restrain the Stock Yard Company and the Junction Company from further engaging in interstate commerce until they had filed tariffs as required by § 6 of the act and to restrain the performance of a certain contract with the Pfælzers, and that the Stock Yard Company and the Junction Company be required to file the statements and reports provided by § 20 of the act. The Commerce Court held that neither the Stock Yard Company nor the Investment Company was a common carrier, and that it had no jurisdiction to determine whether the contract would amount to an unlawful discrimination or advantage, or rebate, and dismissed the bill as to the Stock Yard Company and the Investment Company and as to the Pfælzers. As to the Junction Company, it held that it was a common carrier subject to the Interstate Commerce Act and obliged to file its tariffs as required by the statute.

It further held that, since there was no allegation in the bill that the Interstate Commerce Commission had by general or special order required the Stock Yard Company or the Junction Company to file statements and reports under § 20, it could not issue mandamus to make such statements and reports. 192 Fed. Rep. 330.

The Government appealed from the dismissal of the bill as to the Stock Yard Company, the Investment Company and the Pfælzers, which is case No. 621. It, however, makes no contention against the holding of the Commerce Court as to the construction of § 20. The Junction Company appealed from the decision of the Commerce Court as to it, which appeal is case No. 622.

The correctness of the decision and decree of the Commerce Court is submitted upon facts which are practically undisputed. The Stock Yard Company was incorporated under a special act of the legislature of Illinois, February 13, 1865; Laws 1865, v. 2, p. 678, which authorized it to locate, construct and maintain near the southerly limits of the City of Chicago:

" . . . . All the necessary yards, inclosures, buildings, structures, and railway lines, tracks, switches, and turn-outs, aqueducts, for the reception, safe-keeping, feeding, and watering, and for the weighing, delivery, and transfer of cattle and live stock of every description, and also dead and undressed animals that may be at or passing through or near the city of Chicago, and for the accommodation of the business of a general union stock yard for cattle and live stock, including the erection and establishment of one or more hotel buildings, and the right to use the same; . . . . to make advances of money upon such cattle and live stock, for freight or other purposes, as may become expedient. . . . ."

The charter further provided:

"That said company shall construct a railway, with one or more tracks, as may be expedient, from the grounds which may be selected for its said yards, so as to connect, outside of the city of Chicago, the same with the tracks of all the railroads which terminate in Chicago, the lines of which enter the city on the south between the lake shore and the southwest corner of said city, ... and to make connections with such suitable sidetracks, switches, and connections as to enable all of the trains running upon said railroads easily and conveniently to approach the grounds selected for said yards, and may make such arrangements or contracts with such railroad companies, or either of them, for the use of any part or portion of the track or tracks of such company or companies which now is or hereafter may be constructed, for the purposes aforesaid, as may be agreed upon between the parties; . . . . and to transport and allow to be transported thereon between said railroads and cattle yards, all cattle and live stock and persons accompanying the same to and from said yards, and may also transport and allow to be transported between the railroads entering said city, ... freight and property of every kind as well as stock and cattle. . . . ."

After its creation it acquired real estate, constructed and operated stock yards, with a stock market, built a hotel for the accommodation of its patrons, and constructed in the stock yards district about 300 miles of railroad track consisting of main lines connecting with the trunk lines entering Chicago and a large number of switches to the various industries which had been established adjacent to such tracks.

Prior to December 15, 1897, the Stock Yard Company carried on the stock yards and railroad business, and, although it had regular charges for the services it performed, it filed no tariffs with the Interstate Commerce Commission and concurred in none. On December 15, 1897, the Stock Yard Company leased all of its railroad tracks and equipment for a term of fifty years to a corporation known as the Chicago and Indiana State Line Company (hereinafter called the "State Line Company"), retaining for itself the loading and unloading platforms and facilities used in connection with its stock yards business. This lease covered all its railroad and railroad tracks, switches, etc.; roundhouse, repair shops, machine shops, coal chutes, etc., then in existence or theretofore used by the Stock Yard Company in connection with its railroad; and all and singular the equipment and the telegraph lines, instruments and appurtenances owned or possessed by the Stock Yard Company and used by it in conducting its railroad business. By the terms of the lease the State Line Company was given the right in the future to maintain and operate upon the lands of the Stock Yard Company additional side tracks and switch tracks and other appurtenances necessary to reach industrial plants.

Afterwards the State Line Company consolidated with the Chicago, Hammond & Western Railroad Company, and the consolidated company became known as the Chicago Junction Railway Company (defendant herein) and, in addition to the railroad leased from the Stock Yard Company, operated a belt line around the City of Chicago. In November, 1907, the Junction Company sold the belt line to the East Chicago Belt Railroad Company, retaining the tracks which had been leased by the Stock Yard Company. The equipment operated by the Junction Company, consisting of locomotives and rolling stock, is owned by the Stock Yard Company, but the Junction Company employs its own engineers and crews.

The tracks of the Junction Company are frequently used by the trunk lines to connect the eastern and western systems and to deliver shipments originating without the State to the platforms of the Stock Yard Company, for which service they pay the Junction Company a trackage charge of a fixed sum per car. Large numbers of carload lots of dead freight from points without the State are placed on the receiving tracks of the Junction Company bearing transfer cards showing the destination of the cars, and the Junction Company delivers the cars either to the consignee, if situated on its tracks, or to the receiving track of the forwarding carrier. It is paid by the trunk lines a fixed charge for this service, which the latter absorb. The Junction Company upon the order of the trunk lines places cars for loading by shippers in the stock yards district and after they are loaded hauls them to the receiving tracks of the trunk lines, and it receives from the trunk lines a fixed amount for this service, which is absorbed by the latter. Less than carload lot freight is delivered at the freight depot known as the Union Freight Station and placed in cars by the Junction Company which transports them to the receiving tracks of trunk lines, and for this service the trunk lines pay the Junction Company five cents per hundred weight. Sometimes such freight is hauled from the industries in the stock yards district to the Union Freight Station by the Junction Company and distributed in the cars. The Junction Company receipts for the less than carload lot freight in the name of the trunk lines, such receipts being exchangeable for bills of lading at the office of the trunk lines, and all charges paid to the Junction Company are receipted for in the name of the trunk lines and remitted to them. The Junction Company has an arrangement with the Baltimore & Ohio Railroad Company whereby it performs a like service for such company as to the less than carload lot freight brought by it to the Union Freight Station and destined to points beyond the State. Shipments of horses are transported by the trunk lines to the loading platforms of the Stock Yard Company and there picked up by the Junction Company and hauled to the unloading chutes for horses, and the Junction Company receives, besides the trackage charge, a certain amount per car for this service. A large part of the service thus performed by the Junction Company is in connection with interstate shipments. The Junction Company does not issue any bills of lading with respect to any kind of freight.

After leasing its railroad property to the Junction Company, the Stock Yard Company continued to operate its stock yard facilities for loading and unloading cattle and other live stock bound for and coming from points outside the State, and to feed and water live stock in transit over the lines of trunk line carriers, and also to feed, bed and water live stock shipped to consignees doing business in the stock yards district.

The employés of trunk lines bringing live stock to the stock yards turn over the waybills accompanying such shipments, with what are called "live stock stubs" attached, to the employés of the Stock Yard Company, who use the waybills in unloading and counting the stock, and the waybills and stubs are then sent to the auditor of the Stock Yard Company (being also the auditor of the Junction Company) who retains the stubs and forwards the waybills to the local agents of the trunk lines. The Stock Yard Company advances the charges on such shipments to the trunk lines and collects from the consignees, usually commission men doing business at the stock yards, the moneys it has so advanced for their accommodation.

The Junction Company publishes tariffs showing the charges which it exacts for its services, such tariffs being in general circulation in Chicago, especially about the stock yards district, but they were not filed with the Interstate Commerce Commission. Prior to 1907, the Junction Company, while owning railroad facilities in Indiana, had filed tariffs with the Interstate Commerce Commission, but upon the sale of such properties cancelled the tariffs. It was the belief of the Government and of the Junction Company that all tariffs and concurrences had been cancelled, but it is shown by a stipulation which the parties have filed that since the isuses were made up it has been discovered that one particular concurrence through inadvertence was not cancelled.

The Investment Company is a holding company and owns over ninety per cent. of the shares of the Stock Yard Company and practically all of the shares of the Junction Company.

As to the contract with the Pfælzers: They were members of a copartnership (since incorporated) engaged in the slaughtering business, their plant being located in the vicinity of the tracks operated by the Junction Company and the cattle pens of the Stock Yard Company. They purchased cattle from time to time outside the City of Chicago and in States other than Illinois and shipped them to the partnership at the stock yards, where they were handled as hereinbefore stated for delivery to the consignee. The freight charges on such business averaged for the five years prior to the filing of the Pfælzers' answer about $2,800 annually. The amount of freight consigned to the Pfælzers tends to increase the business of the Stock Yard Company and the Junction Company and therefore the revenue of each.

In 1906 the Department of Agriculture required the Pfælzers to make changes in their plant; in 1908 it directed them to erect a new plant, and in 1909 they were notified that the Government would deny to them further inspection of the products of their plant. They then proposed to locate in Kansas City, Missouri, but upon negotiation with the Stock Yard Company made the contract under consideration here. This contract provided that upon the erection by the Pfælzers of a modern slaughtering, packing and canning plant adjacent to the stock yards in Chicago, costing a certain sum and having a required capacity, the Stock Yard Company would pay them $50,000, and the Pfælzers agreed that all live stock slaughtered or canned by them within a radius of 200 miles would either be purchased at such stock yards or pass through and use them, the customary yardage, tolls and charges to be paid thereon, or that the Pfælzers would pay full tolls and charges on live stock the same as if it had been sent to the stock yards for sale and had there been bought by them; and that for fifteen years they would conduct all their slaughtering, packing and canning business at such plant and not interest themselves directly or indirectly in any other plant or in any other stock yards. The Investment Company guaranteed the performance of the contract by the Stock Yard Company.

It is stated in the answer of the Stock Yard Company and stands admitted in the case that there are other competitive stock yards in the United States which have built up their business in competition with it by offering and giving inducements, either in the shape of land or money, to packing houses and other industries to locate at or near their yards.

From this statement it is apparent that the Stock Yard Company was organized for the purpose of maintaining a stock yard, with the usual facilities of such yards as to loading and unloading and caring for freight, and it was authorized to and did own and operate a railroad system, transporting cars to and from trunk lines in the course of their transportation from beyond the State and to points outside of the State. This service, so far as the railroad and its operation is concerned, is now performed by the Junction Company. The Stock Yard Company still continues to perform the customary stock yard operations, but by means of the lease to the Junction Company it has divested itself of the operation of the railroad system which it was authorized by its charter to construct and operate and which for many years before the lease it did in fact operate. The Stock Yard Company, under the lease, still gets, however, two-thirds of the profits received by the Junction Company for performing the service in connection with the railroad transportation. This joint service now takes the place of the single service formerly rendered by the Stock Yard Company. The stock of both these companies is held in common ownership by the Investment Company, and it appears that the Investment Company guarantees the contracts, or at least some of them, of the Stock Yard Company.

In view of this continuity of operation, the manner of compensation and the performance of services in connection with interstate transportation by railroads such as are described, are the Stock Yard Company and the Junction Company subject to the terms of the Act to Regulate Commerce and bound to conform to its requirements?

The Interstate Commerce Act, as amended by the Hepburn Act, 34 Stat. 584, c. 3591, § 1, applies to common carriers engaged in the transportation of persons or property from State to State wholly by railroad, and the term railroad is defined to include "all switches, spurs, tracks, and terminal facilities of every kind used or necessary in the transportation of the persons or property designated herein, and also all freight depots, yards, and grounds used or necessary in the transportation or delivery of any of said property"; and transportation is defined to include "cars and other vehicles and all instrumentalities and facilities of shipment or carriage, irrespective of ownership or of any contract, express or implied, for the use thereof and all services in connection with the receipt, delivery, elevation, and transfer in transit, ventilation, refrigeration or icing, storage, and handling of property transported."

That the service is performed wholly in one State can make no difference if it is a part of interstate carriage. "The transportation of live stock," said this court in *Covington Stock-Yards Co.* v. *Keith*, 139 U. S. 128, 136, in treating of the duties of commons carriers, irrespective of the Act to Regulate Commerce, "begins with their delivery to the carrier to be loaded upon its cars, and ends only after the stock is unloaded and delivered, or offered to be delivered, to the consignee." In this connection see *Coe* v. *Errol*, 116 U. S. 517; *Southern Pacific Terminal Co.* v. *Interstate Commerce Commission*, 219 U. S. 498.

The fact that the performance of the service is distributed among different corporations having common ownership in a holding company which controls an interstate system was held in *Southern Pacific Terminal Co.* v. *Interstate Commerce Commission, supra,* to make no difference, where the service to be performed was a part of the carriage of freight by railroad in interstate commerce. Nor does it make any difference that neither the Junction Company nor the Stock Yard Company issues through bills of lading. It is the character of the service rendered, not the manner in which goods are billed, which determines the interstate character of the service. *Southern Pacific Terminal Co.* v. *Interstate Commerce Commission, supra; Ohio R. R. Comm.* v. *Worthington*, 225 U. S. 101.

Together, these companies, as to freight which is being carried in interstate commerce, engage in transportation within the meaning of the act and perform services as a railroad when they take the freight delivered at the stock yards, load it upon cars and transport it for a substantial distance upon its journey in interstate commerce, under a through rate and bill furnished by the trunk line carrier, or receive it while it is still in progress in interstate commerce upon a through rate which includes the terminal services rendered by the two companies, and complete its delivery to the consignee. They are common carriers because they are made such by the terms of their charters, hold themselves out as such and constantly act in that capacity, and because they are so treated by the great railroad systems which use them. In *Union Stock Yards Co.* v. *United States*, 169 Fed. Rep. 404, Mr. Justice Van Devanter (while a Circuit Judge), speaking for the Court of Appeals, said (406):

"Its [the Stock Yards Company's] operations . . . . include the maintenance and use of railroad tracks and locomotives, the employment of a corps of operatives in that connection, and the carriage for hire over its tracks of all live stock destined to or from the sheds or pens, which, in effect, are the depot of the railroad companies for the delivery and receipt of shipments of live stock at South Omaha. The carriage of these shipments from the transfer track to the sheds or pens and vice versa is no less a part of their transit between their points of origin and destination than is their carriage over any other portion of the route. True, there is a temporary stoppage of the loaded cars at the transfer track, but that is merely incidental, and does not break the continuity of the transit any more than does the usual transfer of such cars from one carrier to another at a connecting point. And it is of little significance that the stock-yards company does not hold itself out as ready or willing generally to carry live stock for the public, for all the railroad companies at South Omaha do so hold themselves out, and it stands ready and willing to conduct, and actually does conduct, for hire a part of the transportation of every live stock shipment which they accept for carriage to or from that point, including such shipments as are interstate."

We think that these companies, because of the character of the service rendered by them, their joint operation and division of profits and their common ownership by a holding company, are to be deemed a railroad within the terms of the act of Congress to regulate commerce, and the services which they perform are included in the definition of transportation as defined in that act. It is the manifest purpose of the act to include interstate railroad carriers, and by its terms the act excludes transportation wholly within a State. In view of this purpose and so construing the act as to give it force and effect, we think the Stock Yard Company did not exempt itself from the operation of the law by leasing its railroad and equipment to the Junction Company, for it still receives two-thirds of the profits of that company and both companies are under a common stock ownership with its consequent control. We therefore think the Commerce Court was right in holding that the Junction Company should file its rates with the Interstate Commerce Commission and that it should also have held the Stock Yard Company subject to the provisions of the Interstate Commerce Acts.[1] . . . .

[1] The remainder of the opinion dealing with the legality of the Pfælzer contracts is printed p. *infra.*, — Ed.

TAP LINE CASES [1]

234 U. S. (1914)

THESE are all appeals from decrees of the United States Commerce Court (209 Fed. Rep. 244), annulling orders of the Interstate Commerce Commission refusing in whole or in part to compel certain common carriers which had filed schedules cancelling former schedules covering through routes and joint rates with the Louisiana & Pacific Railway Company, the Woodworth & Louisiana Central Railway Company, the Mansfield Railway & Transportation Company and the Victoria, Fisher & Western Railroad Company, appellees, hereinafter referred to as tap lines, to establish or reëstablish through routes and joint rates and to grant allowances and divisions to the tap lines.

The Commission, after an extensive investigation of the tap lines in the lumber regions, particularly in the States of Arkansas, Missouri, Louisiana and Texas, on April 23, and May 14, 1912, filed its report and supplemental report (23 I. C. C. 277, 549). The report deals at some length with the manner in which logs and lumber are moved in that territory and the practices attending such traffic. The Commission found the identification of the road with the industry, the necessity of incorporation to secure divisions and allowances, the great amount in the aggregate paid by the trunk lines to the tap lines, and the resulting discrimination, the fact that allowances were dependent upon the bargain the tap lines might exact from the trunk lines for a proportion of their traffic and not upon the amount of service rendered, and the fact that most of the lumber mills were near public carriers and that the tap lines would not be kept in operation if the mills were removed. General principles for determining the character of carriers were set forth, and the conclusion stated that the real

[1] Docket titles of the Tap Line Cases are: No. 829. *United States and Interstate Commerce Commission* v. *Louisiana & Pacific Railway Co.;* No. 830. *Atchison, Topeka & Santa Fe Railway Co.* v. *Louisiana & Pacific Railway Co.;* No. 831. *United States and Interstate Commerce Commission* v. *Woodworth & Louisiana Central Railway Co.;* No. 832. *Atchison, Topeka & Santa Fe Railway Co.* v. *Woodworth & Louisiana Central Railway Co.;* No. 833. *United States and Interstate Commerce Commission* v. *Mansfield Railway & Transportation Co.;* No. 834. *Atchison, Topeka and Santa Fe Railway Co.* v. *Mansfield Railway & Transportation Co.;* No. 835. *United States and Interstate Commerce Commission* v. *Victoria, Fisher & Western Railroad Co.*; No. 836. *Atchison, Topeka & Santa Fe Railway Co.* v. *Victoria, Fisher & Western Railroad Co.*

relation of a tap line was a question to be decided upon the facts in each case.

The Commission entered upon a particular examination of the various lines under investigation, among others, the appellees in these appeals. It found:

The Louisiana & Pacific Railway Company, controlled by the R. A. Long interests, owning a controlling interest in the Hudson River Lumber Company, the King-Ryder Lumber Company, Longville Lumber Company and the Calcasieu Long Leaf Lumber Company, consists of the following tracks, all of which were originally constructed as private logging roads: (1) a track from De Ridder Junction, Louisiana (all of the lines involved in these cases are within that State), to Bundicks, a distance of eight miles. The mill of the Hudson River Lumber Company in whose interest this track is operated is located at De Ridder within a few hundred feet of the trunk lines; Bundicks is apparently a logging camp with a company store. (2) A track from Lilly Junction to Walla, about seven and one-half miles, the latter being a point in the woods where the King-Ryder Lumber Company has a commissary and where is located a small independent yellow-pine mill, owned by the Bundick Creek Lumber Company. The mill of the King-Ryder Company is at Bon Ami, a town of 2,000, located on the Lake Charles & Northern Railroad Company a short distance from and connected by it with Lilly Junction. (3) A track of two miles at Longville, a town of 2,000 people, where the Longville Lumber Company has its mill and a store, and where also are several independent stores. (4) A track of nine miles from Fayette to Camp Curtis, a place of 200 population, where the Calcasieu Long Leaf Lumber Company has a store, its mill being at Lake Charles. (5) A track of one mile from Bridge Junction to Lake Charles station. The towns De Ridder, Bon Ami, Lilly Junction, Longville, Fayette and Lake Charles are connected by The Lake Charles & Northern Railroad, a Southern Pacific Railway Company line, originally built by the Long interests as a part of the Louisiana & Pacific, and sold to the Lake Charles & Northern with the reservation of trackage rights advantageous to the Louisiana & Pacific. By means of this arrangement the Louisiana & Pacific connects with the Kansas City Southern and the Santa Fe at De Ridder, with the Frisco at Fulton (a station south of Fayette) and with the Southern Pacific, Iron Mountain and Kansas City Southern at Lake Charles. Its equipment consists of 22 locomotives, 6 cabooses, 41 freight cars and 270 logging cars, and a private car used by its officers, who are connected with the lumber companies, in traveling around the country. The lumber companies have many miles of unincorporated logging tracks connecting with the Louisiana & Pacific at various points. There are a number of other stations on the line, among them Bannister, where the Brown Lumber Company owns a small independent mill.

The operation is this: The lumber companies load the logs and switch them over the logging spurs to connection with the tap line which hauls them to the mill, an average distance of 30 miles, for which no charge is made. The tap line switches the carloads of lumber from the mill at Lake Charles, a distance of three-quarters of a mile, to the Southern Pacific; at De Ridder only a few hundred feet to the trunk lines; from the Lake Charles mill to the Frisco a distance of 18 miles; from the Bon Ami mill to the Southern Pacific at Lake Charles a distance of 40 miles, and from the Longville mill to the Southern Pacific at Lake Charles a distance of 24 miles, — the average haul for the controlling companies being nearly 20 miles. By written agreement 50% of the lumber must be routed over the Frisco and 40% over the Southern Pacific, but this is not always done. 243,122 tons of lumber, as against 8,819 tons of merchandise were shipped in 1910, 98% of the whole tonnage being supplied by the controlling interests. The passenger receipts for 1910 were $473.77. A logging train runs daily on each branch and there is one "mixed" train, loaded chiefly with logs and lumber, between Lake Charles and De Ridder. The allowances paid by the trunk lines range from 1½ to 5½c per 100 pounds out of their earnings under the group-lumber rate. The operating revenue for the year ending June 30, 1910, was $220,985.94, with operating expenses of $145,433.69, and there was an accumulated surplus of $73,581.07 on that date.

The Commission found that no charge was made for hauling the logs to the mills by the tap line and that for the short switching service allowances were made as above stated, and concluded that it regarded the whole arrangement as indefensible and unlawful, and saw no ground upon which any allowance might lawfully be made.

The Woodworth & Louisiana Central Railway Company and the Rapides Lumber Company, situated at Woodworth, are identical in interest. The mill is near the Iron Mountain which has a spur track to the mill, and the tap line has a standard gauge track from the mill to La Moria, about six miles, where it connects with the Southern Pacific Railway, Texas & Pacific Railway and

Chicago, Rock Island & Pacific Railway, and a narrow gauge track in the other direction for 18 miles whence spur tracks go into the timber. The equipment consists of 1 standard gauge locomotive, 5 narrow gauge locomotives and 2 standard and 9 narrow gauge cars. The steel in the logging spurs and 4 of the narrow gauge locomotives used by the lumber company on the spurs are owned by the tap line and leased to the lumber company; while the right of way for the narrow gauge track is leased from the lumber company.

The tap line hauls the logs from its terminus to the mill without charge, where they are dumped by the trainmen into the mill pond. The carloads of lumber are switched by the tap line from the planing mill to the place where they are taken by the Iron Mountain, about 25 feet. About 95% of the lumber goes through La Moria, being switched there by the tap line; the allowances from the Iron Mountain out of through rates being from 1½ to 5½c per 100 pounds, while from the trunk lines at La Moria from 2 to 5½c. There are no joint rates except on lumber. For the year ending June 30, 1910, there was 40,707 tons of freight handled for the lumber company and 2,100 tons of outside traffic. It has no passenger business. Its operations for that year showed a deficit, but there was a surplus from previous years of nearly $10,000. It files annual reports with the Commission.

The Mansfield Railway & Transportation Company and the Frost-Johnson Lumber Company are identical in interest. The tap line extends from Mansfield to a logging camp in the woods known as Hunter, a distance of about 16 miles and the line which was originally incorporated by the citizens of Mansfield in 1881 consisting of 2 miles of track from the town to a connection with the Texas & Pacific at Mansfield Junction. Later the Mansfield Company acquired the two-mile track and equipment, and the interests controlling it purchased a large amount of timber lands near Mansfield at a point called Oak Hill where a mill was built, and spur tracks were laid into the timber, which were later turned over to the Mansfield Company, with the free privilege reserved to the Lumber Company to operate logging trains between the timber and the mill, which operation is performed by a subsidiary company. The purchase price did not reflect the value of the reservation. There are about 25 miles of unincorporated logging tracks. The tap line also has a connection with the Kansas City Southern. It owns a locomotive, a passenger coach and a box car.

The service performed by the tap line is switching cars between the mill and the Kansas City Southern about three-fourths of a mile, although the mill is within 300 feet of the Kansas City Southern and was formerly connected by a spur track which was abandoned and taken up, and to the Texas & Pacific, a distance of two and one-half miles. The tap line bears the expense of maintaining its tracks extending into the woods.

No other yellow-pine mills are served by the tap line, but there is a hardwood mill adjacent to the Frost-Johnson mill, obtaining a substantial portion of its logs from the latter company or subsidiaries, the price including delivery at the hardwood mill, the logs being hauled by the logging company under its trackage right. Some logs are also obtained from the Texas & Pacific, for the switching of which the hardwood mill pays the tap line $2.50 a car or less. The tap line maintains joint rates on hardwood as well as yellow-pine.

Practically no traffic other than that in which the Lumber Company is interested moves over the track from Mansfield to Hunter, but a good deal of outside traffic moves over the original two miles from Mansfield to Mansfield Junction. 16,539 tons of miscellaneous freight was handled during the year ending June 30, 1910, most of which passed over the Mansfield Junction branch, and much of which was for the controlling interests or their employés; while during the same time 28,596 tons of lumber were handled, 91.4 per cent. of which was supplied by the Lumber Company. A daily train is operated by the tap line in each direction on regular schedule, handling passengers, mail and express; but in 1910 the passenger revenues were only $1,209.76, while its freight revenues were $25,617.19.

The Commission noticed the abandonment of the 300 foot spur track and then the payment of an allowance of 1 to 4c per 100 pounds, and held that it was a mere manipulation of the situation in order to establish an unlawful relation; and also held that since the tap line crosses the right of way of the Texas & Pacific within a short distance, the allowance of a like amount by the Texas & Pacific for switching from the mill to Mansfield and down to the junction was unlawful.

The Victoria, Fisher & Western Railroad Company and the Louisiana Long Leaf Lumber Company have the same stockholders and officers. The tap line extends from Victoria, where it connects with the Texas & Pacific, to Fisher, where it crosses the Kansas City Southern Railway, and then extends to Cain, in all about 31 miles. A part of the track was built some time ago and was acquired by the Lumber Company in 1900. In 1902 the Railroad Company was incorporated and its stock exchanged as a stock dividend for the line. There are about 25 miles of logging spurs and sidetracks. The equipment consists of 5 locomotives, 4 cabooses, 3 box cars, 1 flat car and 105 logging cars. It does not operate any trains on regular schedule. There are two mills owned by the Lumber Company, one about a mile from the junction with the Texas & Pacific and the other about half a mile from the tracks of the Kansas City Southern.

The tap line hauls the logs from the forest to the mill, charging $1.50 per 1,000 feet, which is supposed to cover only the service performed on the logging spurs and not the haul over the main track. The greater part of the lumber from Fisher is turned over to the Kansas City Southern, involving a one-half mile switch by the tap line, and from Victoria is moved by the tap line one mile to the Texas & Pacific; a small amount of the lumber from each mill is taken by the tap line to the more distant trunk line, but the same divisions are paid. The allowances range from ¾ to 4c per 100 pounds, and the joint rates are the same as the rates published from adjacent mills on the trunk lines, except traffic moving to Texas, for which 1¼c per 100 pounds is added to the junction-point rate. No passengers are carried, and of 316,676 tons of freight for the year 1910, over 99% was furnished by the proprietary company. And the accumulated surplus at the end of June, 1910, was $13,509.17.

The Commission held that the tap line could not participate as a common carrier in joint rates on the products of the proprietary company, but said that the lumber rate of the trunk lines applied from the adjacent mills and that they might make a reasonable allowance for switching.

The Commission made an order in such matter on May 14, 1912, which it amended on October 30, 1912. The amended order, so far as these appeals are concerned, provided:

"The Commission upon the record finds in the case of the .... Woodworth & Louisiana Central Railway Company; Mansfield Railway & Transportation Company; Louisiana & Pacific Railway Company; Victoria, Fisher & Western Railroad Company; that the tracks and equipment with respect to the industry of the several proprietary companies are plant facilities, and that the service performed therewith for the respective proprietary lumber companies in moving logs to their respective mills and performed therewith in moving the products of the mills to the trunk lines is not a service of transportation by a common carrier railroad but is a plant service by a plant facility; and that any allowances or divisions out of the rate on account thereof are unlawful and result in undue and unreasonable preferences and unjust discriminations, as found in the said reports," and it ordered that the trunk lines should cease and for two years abstain from making any such allowances to the tap lines named.

The Commission further ordered that if the trunk lines failed by a time stated, to reëstablish the through routes and joint rates in effect on April 30, 1912, on traffic other than the products of the mills of certain proprietary companies, among others, the appellees herein, it would upon proper petition enter an order requiring the establishment of such routes and rates or enter upon an inquiry with respect thereto, and further provided that all divisions of joint rates should be submitted to the Commission for approval.

The appellees thereupon by their several petitions filed in the United States Commerce Court sought to have the order of the Commission, so far as applicable to them, enjoined and annulled. The Interstate Commerce Commission, the Atchison, Topeka and Santa Fe Railway Company, the Gulf, Colorado and Santa Fe Railway Company and the Railroad Commission of Louisiana intervened. The Commerce Court said that the question was whether the Commission had acted arbitrarily and on improper considerations in determining under what circumstances a common carrier tap line would be deemed to be performing a mere plant service for a proprietary company, and held that as the service rendered to the proprietary and non-proprietary mills by the tap lines was the same, and as it was held to be a transportation service by an interstate common carrier as to the non-proprietary mills, it must be held to be a similar service as to the proprietary mills, and concluded that the Commission was without power to prohibit the making of joint rates by the trunk lines and the tap lines and the payment of some division of such rates to the tap lines for their services in hauling logs to and lumber from the proprietary mills, and annulled the order of the Commission in this respect and so far as it applied to the appellees.

The United States and the Interstate Commerce Commission, and the Atchison, Topeka & Santa Fe Railway Company and the Gulf, Colorado and Santa Fe Railway Company entered separate appeals from the decrees of the Commerce Court in the four cases instituted by the appellees.

Mr. Justice Day, after making the foregoing statement, delivered the opinion of the court.

A preliminary objection is made to the jurisdiction of the Commerce Court in that the order of the Commission is not reviewable because merely of a negative character. The Commerce Court examined this question and in view of the amend order of October 30, 1912, reached the conclusion that the order was affirmative in its nature and of a character permitting of review by proper proceedings in that court under the act giving it jurisdiction in such cases. We find no reason to differ with this conclusion and are of opinion that the Commerce Court had jurisdiction in the case.

It is further insisted upon the authority of *Procter & Gamble Co.* v. *United States*, 225 U. S. 282, and other cases in this court which have followed that decision, that in the present cases the decision rests upon conclusions of the Commission as to matters of fact only, which are within the sole jurisdiction of that body and not reviewable in the courts. But we shall consider the case upon the findings of fact preceding this opinion, which are identical with those made by the Commission, and test the conclusions reached as matters of law, giving proper consideration to matters of fact which are not in dispute.

The final decree of the Commerce Court vacated and set aside the portion of the Commission's order reading as follows:

"That the tracks and equipment with respect to the industry of the several proprietary companies are plant facilities, and that the service performed therewith for the respective proprietary lumber companies in moving logs to their respective mills and performed therewith in moving the products of the mills to the trunk lines is not a service of transportation by a common carrier railroad, but is a plant service by a plant facility; and that any allowances or divisions out of the rate on account thereof are unlawful and result in undue and unreasonable preferences and unjust discriminations, as found in the said reports;

"3. It is Ordered, That the principal defendants [trunk lines, naming them], be, and they are hereby notified and required to cease and desist, and for a period of two years hereafter, or until otherwise ordered, to abstain from making any such allowances to any of the above named parties to the record in respect of any such above described service."

The question now before this court is the correctness of this decree.

A perusal of the findings and orders of the Commission makes it apparent that the grounds of decision upon which it proceeded were two, first, that these roads were mere plant facilities, second, that they were not common carriers as to proprietary traffic. The Commission held that before incorporation they were plant facilities and that after incorporation they remained such. What the Commission means by plant facilities may be gathered from a consideration of some of its decisions. In *General Electric Co.* v. *N. Y. C. & H. R. R. R.*, 14 I. C. C. 237, a network of interior switching tracks constructed to meet the necessities of the business were held to be mere plant facilities. The same principle was applied to the internal trackage of large industrial plants in *Solvay Process Company* v. *Delaware, Lackawanna & Western R. R. Co.*, 14 I. C. C. 246. These systems of internal trackage were not common carriers, and, however extensive, were intended to and did furnish service for the plants which owned and operated them. But a common carrier performing service as such, regulated and operated under competent authority, as observed by Commissioner Prouty in *Kaul Lumber Co.* v. *Central of Georgia Railway Co.*, 20 I. C. C. 450, 456, is no longer a mere appendage of a mill "but a public institution." It thus becomes apparent that the real question in these cases is the true character of the roads here involved. Are they plant facilities merely or common carriers with rights and obligations as such?

It is insisted that these roads are not carriers because the most of their traffic is in their own logs and lumber and that only a small part of the traffic carried is the property of others. But this conclusion loses sight of the principle that the extent to which a railroad is in fact used, does not determine the fact whether it is or is not a common carrier. It is the right of the public to use the road's facilities and to demand service of it rather than the extent of its business which is the real criterion determinative of its character. This principle has been frequently recognized in the decisions of the courts. We need not cite the many state cases in which it has been so held, in view of the fact that the same principle was laid down in the late case of *Union Lime Co.* v. *Chicago & N. W. Ry. Co.*, 233 U. S. 211. In that case the Supreme Court of Wisconsin sustained the extension of a spur track to reach the quarries and lime kilns of a single company as a public use authorizing the exercise of the right of eminent domain, and this court affirmed the judgment. Dealing with the contention that the Wisconsin statute was invalid because it authorized action appropriating property upon the exigency of a private business, this court said (p. 221):

"A spur may, at the outset, lead only to a single industry or establishment; it may be constructed to furnish an outlet for the products of a particular plant; its cost may be defrayed by those in special need of its service at the time. But none the less, by virtue of the conditions under which it is provided, the spur may constitute at all times a part of the transportation facilities of the carrier which are operated under the obligations of public service and are subject to the regulation of public authority. As was said by this court in *Hairston* v. *Danville & Western Rwy. Co.*, *supra* (p. 608) [208 U. S. 598]: 'The uses for which the track was desired are not the less public because the motive which dictated its location over this particular land was to reach a private industry, or because the proprietors of that industry contributed in any way to the cost.' There is a clear distinction between spurs which are owned and operated by a common carrier as a part of its system and under its public obligation and merely private sidings. See *De Camp* v. *Hibernia R. R. Co.*, 47 N. J. Law, 43; *Chicago &c. R. R. Co.* v. *Porter*, 43 Minnesota, 527; *Ulmer* v. *Lime Rock R. R. Co.*, 98 Maine, 579; *Railway Company* v. *Petty*, 57 Arkansas, 359; *Dietrich* v. *Murdock*, 42 Missouri, 279; *Bedford Quarries Co.* v. *Chicago &c. R. R. Co.*, 175 Indiana, 303."

The Commission has recognized this principle as applicable to tap lines, for in the *Central Yellow Pine Association* v. *The Vicksburg, Shreveport & Pacific R. R. Co.*, 10 I. C. C. 193, 199, it said:

"While these logging roads are almost or quite without exception mill propositions at the outset, built exclusively for the purpose of transporting logs to the mill, they soon reach a point where they engage in other business to a greater or less extent. As the length of the road increases, as the lumber is taken off and other operations obtain a foothold along the line, various commodities besides lumber are transported, and this business gradually develops until in several cases what was at first a logging road pure and simple has become a common carrier of miscellaneous freight and passengers. Almost all these lines, even where they are run as private enterprises, do more or less outside transportation, and it would be difficult to draw any line of demarkation between the logging road as such and the logging road which has become a general carrier of freight."

This representation it is contended by the Attorney General of Louisiana, who appears here in behalf of the Louisiana Railroad Commission, intervenor, is aptly descriptive of the growth and development of railroads in that State.

Furthermore, these roads are common carriers when tried by the test of organization for that purpose under competent legislation of the State. They are so treated by the public authorities of the State, who insist in this case that they are such and submit in oral discussion and printed briefs cogent arguments to justify that conclusion. They are engaged in carrying for hire the goods of those who see fit to employ them. They are authorized to exercise the right of eminent domain by the State of their incorporation. They were treated and dealt with as common carriers by connecting systems of other carriers, a circumstance to be noticed in determining their true character. *United States* v. *Union Stock Yard & Transit Co.*, 226 U. S. 286. They are engaged in transportation as that term is defined in the Commerce Act and described in decisions of this court. *Coe* v. *Errol*, 116 U. S. 517; *Covington Stock Yds. Co.* v. *Keith*, 139 U. S. 128; *Southern Pac. Term. Co.* v. *Interstate Com. Comm.*, 219 U. S. 498; *United States* v. *Union Stock Yard Co.*, *supra*.

Applying the principles which we have stated as determinative of the character of these roads and without repeating the facts concerning them, they would seem to fill all the requirements of common carriers so employed, unless the grounds upon which they were determined not to be such by the Commission are adequate to that end. The Commission itself as to all shippers other than those controlled by the so-called proprietary companies, treated them as common carriers, for it has ordered the trunk lines to reëstablish through routes and joint rates as to such traffic. But says the Government, and it insists that this fact alone might well control the decision, the roads are owned by the persons who also own the timber and mills which they principally serve.

This fact is not shown to be inconsistent with the laws of the State in which they are organized and operated. On the contrary the public authorities of that State are here insisting that these companies are common carriers. Congress has not made it illegal for roads thus owned to operate in interstate commerce. While Congress in enacting the Commodities Clause amending § 1 of the Act to Regulate Commerce (June 29, 1906, c. 3591, 34 Stat. 584) sought to divorce transportation from production and manufacture and to make transportation a business of and by itself unallied with manufacture and production in which a carrier was itself interested, the debates, which may be resorted to for the purpose of ascertaining the situation which prompted this legislation, show that the situation in some of the States as to the logging industry and transportation was sharply brought to the attention of Congress and led to the exemption from the Commodities Clause of timber and the manufactured products thereof, thus indicating the intention to permit a railroad to haul such lumber and products although it owned them itself. And that Congress had the constitutional power to enact such exemption was held in *United States* v. *Delaware & Hudson Co.*, 213 U. S. 366, 416–7. This declaration of public policy which is now part of the Commerce Act cannot be ignored in interpreting the power and authority of the Commission under the act. The discussion resulting in the action of Congress shows that railroads built and owned by the same persons who own the timber were regarded as essential to the development of the timber regions in the Southwest and the necessity of such roads was dwelt upon and set forth with ample illustration by Commissioner Prouty in his concurring opinion in this case.

As we have said, the Commission by its order herein required the trunk lines to reëstablish through routes and joint rates as to property to be transported by others than the proprietary owners over the tap lines. This order would of itself create a discrimination against proprietary owners, for lumber products are carried from this territory upon blanket rates applicable to all within its limits. It follows that independent owners would get this blanket rate for the entire haul of their products while proprietary owners would pay the same rate plus the cost of getting to the trunk line over the tap line. The Commission, by the effect of its order, recognizes that railroads organized and operated as these tap lines are, if owned by others than those who own the timber and mills, would be entitled to be treated as common carriers and to participate in joint rates with other carriers. We think the Commission exceeded its authority when it condemned these roads as a mere attempt to evade the law and to secure rebates and preferences for themselves.

. . . .

Affirmed.

CRANE IRON WORKS *v.* UNITED STATES (INTERSTATE COMMERCE COMMISSION *ET AL.* INTERVENERS)

UNITED STATES COMMERCE COURT

209 Fed. Rep. 238 (1912)

KNAPP, *Presiding Judge:*

The petitioner in this case, the Crane Iron Works, instituted proceedings before the Interstate Commerce Commission against the Central Railroad Company of New Jersey and the Crane Railroad Company to procure an order requiring the defendant railroads to establish through routes and joint rates on certain commodities between points on the Crane Railroad and points in the State of New Jersey on the lines of the Central Railroad; and also for reparation on account of previous shipments. After full hearing the Commission made a report (17 I. C. C. Rep., 514) to the effect that petitioner was not entitled to the relief sought, and thereupon entered an order dismissing the proceedings.

Thereafter this suit was brought to set aside and annul the Commission's order of dismissal on grounds which will be hereafter stated. The United States filed a motion to dismiss on the ground that the petition did not state a cause of action, and a like motion to dismiss was filed by the Commission which had intervened. On these motions the case has been argued and submitted.

There had been a previous application to the Commission for the same purpose by the Crane Railroad Company, which the Commission also dismissed, as appears by its report and order therein (15 I. C. C. Rep., 248). Both reports are attached to and made a part of the petition now before us, and from these reports and the petition itself the following facts appear:

The petitioner is a corporation organized under the laws of Pennsylvania and located in the borough of Catasauqua, in that State. It was incorporated about the year 1895 for the purpose of acquiring the plant and property of the Crane Iron Company, which had for many years carried on the business denoted by its name. At that time the plant consisted of three blast furnaces, together with appurtenant buildings, storage bins, etc., and a private railroad connected with the works. It does not appear when this railroad was constructed or when it was extended to connect with exchange tracks of the Central Railroad and other long-line carriers; but it does appear to have been in use for the purposes of the iron plant for more than thirty years.

In the operation of this plant it is necessary to transport loaded cars received by rail to various points within the limits of the plant for unloading, to transport cars which have been loaded with its product from various points within the plant to the line of railway by which they are taken to destination, and also to some extent necessary to move cars from point to point within the plant itself. For these purposes the iron works long ago laid down rails extending from a connection with the Central Railroad to the various points within its plant where cars were to be placed. The line of the Central Railroad extends through the premises of the iron works and the point where the two railroads connect is now and always has been upon the iron works' land. The iron works also provided the necessary locomotives for operating the various tracks which it had built to accommodate the needs of its plant. In actual operation loaded cars destined for the iron works were placed by the Central Railroad upon a track known as the exchange track, from which they were taken by the locomotives of the iron works and hauled to the required point within its plant. When cars were loaded for movement out they were taken by the same locomotives and placed upon the exchange track, where the Central Railroad received and transported them to destination. These locomotives were also used for moving cars from point to point within the plant as might be desired.

For this service the petitioner has never received and, until the organization of the Crane Railroad, had never claimed that it should receive compensation from the Central Railroad. Indeed, it seems to have been assumed that these tracks and engines were a necessary part of the plant of the iron works whose business could not be properly carried on without them.

In process of time a few other industries, perhaps half a dozen, were located in close proximity to the premises of the iron works, though not upon its land, and these industries were so situated that loaded cars could be transported between the tracks of the Central Railroad and the industry only over the rails of the Crane Iron Works. For the purpose of serving these industries, the Crane Iron Works extended its rails beyond its own land to these several plants. Cars for these industries were placed upon the same track with those intended for the iron works and taken by the locomotives of the iron works over the rails of that company to the several industries. For this service the iron works made a charge to the industry which seems to have been usually two dollars a car. The different railroads bringing these cars to Catasauqua, including the Central Railroad, paid to the iron works towards defraying this charge at first five cents and subsequently six cents per ton. This condition seems to have continued for many years, during which time, as above stated, the iron works neither claimed nor received any compensation for handling its own freight.

Under the statutes of Pennsylvania a private railroad cannot connect with a public railroad except for handling the business of the owners of the private railroad, and the iron works was advised that it had no lawful right to perform this switching service for the other industries. Accordingly, in 1905, the Crane Railroad Company was incorporated, and the tracks and other property used by the iron works in connection with its railroad were conveyed to the Crane Railroad Company, together with a strip of land ten feet wide wherever its rails were laid upon the land of the iron works and also whatever rights of way it might have in reaching the other industries in question. The capital stock of both the Crane Iron Works and the Crane Railroad Company is owned by the Empire Iron & Steel Company, and the management of the Crane Railroad Company after the incorporation continued in the same manner as before, although the operating accounts of the two companies were kept entirely separate.

Although the Crane Railroad Company was organized in 1905 it did not begin business on its own account until the following year, since which time it has charged both to the other industries and to the Crane Iron Works two dollars per car for this switching service, and it is insisted that the various railroads entering Catasauqua should absorb this switching charge. The Central Railroad has declined to make any allowance on account of cars handled for the Crane Iron Works, but has made an allowance of six cents per ton on traffic consigned to or from the other industries.

The principal contention of petitioner appears to be that the Crane Railroad Company is a common carrier subject to the provisions of the act to regulate commerce and the jurisdiction of the Commission; that this was conclusively established by the evidence before the Commission; that the Commission, in failing to find the fact accordingly and leaving it undetermined, committed an error of law; that as such common carrier the Crane Railroad Company is legally entitled to compensation for the transportation service which it is alleged to perform for petitioner; and that therefore it was error of law for the Commission to refuse the relief which the petitioner sought to secure. Incidentally, and in support of the main contention, it is further claimed that the dismissal order was erroneous because the undisputed evidence established as matter of law unjust discrimination on the part of the Central Railroad of New Jersey, in that it pays the Crane Railroad, out of the tariff charge which it collects, for transporting cars to and from the other industries located on the tracks of the Crane Railroad, but refuses to pay anything for transporting cars to or from the Crane Iron Works.

The Crane Railroad Company is organized under the railroad law of Pennsylvania; which, among other things, declares that all railroads so organized shall be common carriers. In that State it has undoubtedly the legal status of a common carrier, with such privileges and obligations as pertain to railroad corporations in Pennsylvania. It is not necessary to discuss whether the Crane Railroad is in fact a common carrier within the meaning of that term as used in the act to regulate commerce, because we shall assume for the purposes of this case that it is a common carrier subject to the act, and the matters in dispute will be decided on that assumption. . . . .

But the dismissal order in question rests upon another basis, which will be briefly considered. Upon all the circumstances connected with the location, construction, and operation of the Crane Railroad, the Commission found as an ultimate fact that, as to the Crane Iron Works, it was a mere plant facility, performing services which the iron works should perform for itself if it desired such services, and that the Central Railroad was under no obligation to pay the Crane Railroad for the switching service which it performs for the iron works and, indeed, could not lawfully do so. We see no reason to doubt the correctness of this conclusion. The Commission had previously pointed out the distinction between those operations which constitute a plant facility and the legitimate services of a common carrier (*General Electric Company* v. *N. Y. C. & H. R. R. R. Co. et al.*, 14 I. C. C. Rep., 237; *Solvay Process Company* v. *D., L. & W. R. R. Co.*, 14 I. C. C. Rep., 246), and the observations made in these illustrative cases seem to us to express a sound and wholesome principle. That there was substantial evidence to sustain the finding of the Commission as to the character of the services rendered is not open to reasonable question, and, this being so, the conclusion must be accepted accordingly.

But the argument is earnestly pressed that such a relation can not as matter of law be predicted of an incorporated railroad which is declared to be a common carrier by the fundamental law of the State of its creation. In other words, it is insisted that the Crane Railroad, being in law a common carrier and performing the functions of a common carrier, can not be a plant facility of the Crane Iron Works, but must be regarded as a common carrier for the Crane Iron Works, and entitled as a matter of legal right to a just share of the transportation charge which the Central Railroad makes and collects for carrying the traffic of the iron works; and on this theory it is argued that the finding and conclusion of the Commission involve an error of law which this court should correct.

We are constrained to reject this contention. Whether the Crane Railroad is a plant facility as to the Crane Iron Works or a common carrier of the traffic of that concern must be held to be a question of fact which is not affected by the circumstance of incorporation. We understand it to be admitted that the operations of this railroad when it was owned and operated by the iron works were the operations of a plant facility. It is contended, however, when the railroad was separately incorporated and passed from the ownership of the iron works, that its relation to the latter and the legal character of its services became immediately changed. That is to say, the mere fact of the separation of ownership and the transfer of the title and control of the railroad property to a new corporation, although there was not the slightest change in what was actually done, operated in legal effect to transform a plant facility into a common carrier and to impose obligations on the Central Railroad, as to the traffic of the iron works, which it could not theretofore have been required to assume. We can not believe that any such result was accomplished. The rights and duties of the Central Railroad respecting the iron works could not thus be altered. If its obligations as a common carrier were fully discharged and its tariff rate earned by delivering cars to and taking them from the exchange tracks before the iron works parted with its railroad, its rights and duties respecting that concern were neither increased nor diminished by the creation of the Crane Railroad. The services rendered to the iron works continuing to be precisely the same in point of fact, this railroad continued to be utilized as the facility of the iron works' plant in the same way after as before incorporation.

Nor do we perceive any serious objection to regarding a given agency as a plant facility of a particular shipper, although a common carrier as to other shippers. Whether considered from the standpoint of law or of practical administration, it seems reasonable to hold, as the Commission virtually held in this case, that a railroad of the kind in question may have this dual character and perform services for one concern which are not the services of a common carrier, but which that concern is bound to provide for itself, notwithstanding it occupies the relation of a common carrier to other concerns and the public generally. Concededly, the work which the Crane Railroad does in moving cars between different points in the iron works' plant has none of the incidents of common carriage, and why may not the same thing be affirmed of the work it does in switching cars for the iron works to and from the exchange track with the Central Railroad, even if the work it does for the other industries makes it as to them or the shippers of Catasauqua a common carrier? . . . .

Upon the whole case we are of opinion that no error of law was committed by the Commission in denying the petitioner's application. It follows that *the motions to dismiss the petition should be granted, and it will be so ordered.*

UNITED STATES *v.* ADAMS EXPRESS COMPANY

229 U. S. 381 (1913)

MR. JUSTICE HOLMES delivered the opinion of the court.

This is an indictment, under the Act to Regulate Commerce, of the Adams Express Company, by that name, alleging it to be 'a joint stock association, organized and existing under and by virtue of the common law of the State of New York.' . . . .

The indictment alleges that the Adams Express Company had filed with the Interstate Commerce Commission its schedules of rates and charges, specifies what those charges were in certain cases, and sets forth in different counts instances in which the company demanded and received sums in excess of its schedule rates for the parcels carried — in short, disobeyed the act of February 4, 1887, c. 104, § 6, 24 Stat. 379, 380. By § 10 (amended by act of June 18, 1910, c. 309, § 10, 36 Stat. 539, 549), any common carrier subject to the provisions of the act, wilfully doing this is guilty of a misdemeanor and liable to a fine.

The objection to applying § 10 to the defendant has been indicated. It is confirmed in argument by the citation of many cases in which such companies are treated as simple partnerships, including those in which this court has declined to extend the legal fiction applied in determining jurisdiction over corporations so as to cover them. *Chapman* v. *Barney*, 129 U. S. 677. *Great Southern Fireproof Hotel Co.* v. *Jones*, 177 U. S. 449, 454, 456. *Thomas* v. *Board of Trustees*, 195 U. S. 207. But the argument is met by the plain words of the statute as it now stands. For by § 1 of the original act of 1887, as amended by the act of June 29, 1906, c. 3591, 34 Stat. 584, "The term 'common carrier' as used in this act shall include express companies and sleeping car companies." And thus the liability of common carriers created by § 10 stands as if it read that express companies violating § 6 should be guilty of a misdemeanor and liable to fine.

It has been notorious for many years that some of the great express companies are organized as joint stock associations, and the reason for the amendment hardly could be seen unless it was intended to bring those associations under the act. As suggested in the argument for the Government, no one, certainly not the defendant, seems to have doubted that the statute now imposes upon them the duty to file schedules of rates. *American Express Co.* v. *United States*, 212 U. S. 522, 531. (The American Express Company is a joint stock association.) But if it imposes upon them the duties under the words common carrier as interpreted, it is reasonable to suppose that the same words are intended to impose upon them the penalty inflicted on common carriers in case those duties are not performed. It is true that a doubt was raised by the wording of § 10 in the original act, whether corporations were indictable under it. This doubt was met by the act of February 19, 1903, c. 708, § 1, 32 Stat. 847. We do not perceive that any inference can be drawn from this source in favor of a construction of the later amendment other than that we deem the natural one.

The power of Congress hardly is denied. The constitutionality of the statute as against corporations is established, *New York Central & Hudson River R. R. Co.* v. *United States*, 212 U. S. 481,

492, and no reason is suggested why Congress has not equal power to charge the partnership assets with a liability and to personify the company so far as to collect a fine by a proceeding against it by the company name. That is what we believe that Congress intended to do. It is to be observed that the structure of the company under the laws of New York is such that a judgment against it binds only the joint property, *National Bank* v. *Van Derwerker*, 74 N. Y. 234, and that it has other characteristics of separate being. *Westcott* v. *Fargo*, 61 N. U. 542. *Matter of Jones*, 172 N. Y. 575. *Hibbs* v. *Brown*, 190 N. Y. 167. Indeed, Article VIII of the constitution of the State after providing that the term corporations as there used shall be construed to include all joint stock companies, &c., having any of the powers or privileges of corporations not possessed by individuals or partnerships, as these companies do, *Matter of Jones*, 172 N. Y. 575, 579, goes on to declare that all corporations may sue and be sued 'in like cases as natural persons.' We do not refer to the law of New York in order to argue that by itself it would suffice to make applicable the principle of *Liverpool & London Life & Fire Ins. Co.* v. *Oliver*, 10 Wall. 566. We refer to it simply to show the semi-corporate standing that these companies already had locally as well as in the popular mind, and thus that the action of Congress was natural and to be expected, if we take its words to mean all that by construction they import.

Judgment reversed.

SOUTHERN PACIFIC TERMINAL COMPANY *v.* INTERSTATE COMMERCE COMMISSION AND YOUNG

YOUNG *v.* INTERSTATE COMMERCE COMMISSION *ET AL.*

219 U. S. 498 (1911)

THIS is a bill in equity to enjoin an order of the Interstate Commerce Commission requiring appellants to cease and desist, on or before the first day of September, 1908 (subsequently postponed to November 15, 1908), and for a period of not less than two years thereafter, from granting and giving undue preferences and advantages to one E. H. Young, a shipper of cotton seed products at the port of Galveston, Texas, through failure to exact from him payment of wharfage charges for handling cotton seed cake and meal over the wharves, docks and piers of appellants, while at the same time exacting such charges from other shippers of cotton seed cake and meal, and from giving and allowing him or any other person whomsoever, for his exclusive use, space on the wharves of appellants at Galveston for use in the storage and handling of cotton seed cake and meal, while contemporaneously refusing and denying similar privileges to other shippers under substantially similar circumstances and conditions.

Young was not a formal party before the Interstate Commerce Commission. However, he was made a respondent in this suit, and filed an answer and cross bill. The Commission demurred to both bill and cross bill, and, the demurrer being overruled, answered.

On final hearing the case was submitted upon an agreed statement of facts, and both bills were dismissed.

The most important facts we set out below and in the opinion. We refer to the report of the Interstate Commerce Commission for further details.

The Republic of Mexico conveyed to one Menard the property upon which the wharves of the Terminal Company are situated. Menard conveyed the property to the president and directors of the Galveston City Company, who conveyed it to Collis P. Huntington for the sum of $200,000, and it is recited in the deed to him that it "is made upon the further Express Covenant and condition as follows: . . . . when through and by means of such acts of Congress, act of the legislature, and ordinance and conveyance from the city of Galveston, if any, as may be required for the purpose, ... the right has been secured to the said Collis P. Huntington, or his heirs or assigns, to construct piers, as he or they may from time to time determine, ... then and in that event the said Collis P. Huntington, his heirs or assigns, will within six months thereof commence the construction of terminal facilities upon the property . . . . for the use of what are commonly called the Southern Pacific Railroad and Steamship Systems."

The city of Galveston, on the fourth of February, 1899, passed an ordinance which recited the conditions of Huntington's purchase to be as above stated, and that it was greatly to the interest of the city that the work contemplated by him should be performed, and that for the proper utility of the property no streets should be opened through or across it, and it was ordained that streets, avenues or alleys, if any, theretofore opened, laid out or in any manner designated upon the property be perpetually abandoned, discontinued and closed. And Huntington, his heirs and assigns, were granted the right perpetually to construct and maintain piers as he or they might from time to time determine, "and to maintain upon the property terminal facilities for the use of what are commonly called the Southern Pacific Railroad and Steamship Systems, their successors or assigns." It was provided that if Huntington should "charge wharfage for the use of such piers and other facilities upon said property, except so far as wharf service" might be covered by the freight rate, all such wharfage should be subject to the regulation of the railroad commission of Texas. And it was recited that it was greatly for the public interest that the property "should be developed for shipping and transportation purposes, and that the shipping facilities of the port of Galveston should be thereby improved and enlarged in order to better accommodate the commerce of the port and State. . . . ."

The ordinance was ratified by an act of the legislature approved May 1, 1899. The act set out the ordinance in full and relinquished to Huntington the title and claim of the State to the property upon the conditions expressed in the ordinance and, in addition to subjecting the wharfage charges to regulation by the railroad commission, required an annual report to that body. And it was provided "that the system of railroad tracks" which might be constructed by Huntington on the property should connect with the track of any railroad company which might be built to the property, at a place designated; and, further, that there should be no consolidation of the property, or the stock or franchise of any corporation which might own or control the same, with the Galveston Wharf Company or any other wharf company by which the "wharf or other terminal charges should be fixed," and that "no charter formed for the use, operation and management of the property" should be granted without containing the section providing as above.

Huntington performed the conditions expressed in the conveyance and in the ordinance and the act of the legislature.

The Southern Pacific Terminal Company is a Texas corporation, organized in 1901 to construct and maintain wharves and docks for the accommodation of all kinds of vessels, "and to avail of, use and enjoy the properties, rights, privileges and franchises granted and described and referred to in the act of the legislature of the State of Texas of May 1, 1899, ratifying the ordinance of the city of Galveston, and to construct and maintain upon the property terminal facilities for the use of what are commonly called the Southern Pacific Railroad and Steamship Systems."

At the time of the incorporation of the Terminal Company the following were commonly referred to as the Southern Pacific Railroad and Steamship Systems: the line of steamships owned by the Southern Pacific Company, running from New York to Galveston and New Orleans, and also running from and between the latter city and Havana; Morgan's Louisiana and Texas Railroad and Steamship Company; the Louisiana Western Railroad, which leads from New Orleans to the Sabine River; the Texas and New Orleans Railroad, leading from that river to the city of Houston; the Galveston, Harrisburg and San Antonio Railway, and the railroads in which the Southern Pacific Company owns stock, extending from the connection of the latter in El Paso at the Rio Grande River to San Francisco. Each of the railways was incorporated as a separate and distinct railway and has its own officers and board of directors, but the Southern Pacific Company owns ninety-nine per cent of their stock and the same per cent of the stock of the Terminal Company. The two latter companies have the same president, and the Galveston, Harrisburg and San Antonio Railway Company and the Terminal Company have the same general manager.

Import and export traffic passing through Galveston passes over the wharves of the Terminal Company, and the only track facilities for such traffic are those owned by the Terminal Company on its own lands. And the Galveston, Harrisburg and San Antonio Railway is the only railway having physical connection with the tracks of the Terminal Company, and it does all of the switching to and from the tracks of the Terminal Company, charging $1.75 per car. The latter company receives a trackage charge of 50 cents per car.

The Terminal Company owns no cars or locomotives and issues no bills of lading. It owns no stock in any of the railroads or corporations in which the Southern Pacific owns stock. It carries on a wharfage business and publishes a schedule of charges for such business, which, however, is not filed with the Interstate Commerce Commission, its charge being twenty cents per ton on cotton seed meal and cake passing over its docks, and is shown as wharfage charge in the tariffs of the Galveston, Harrisburg and San Antonio Railway Company and all other railways entering Galveston. Such tariffs do not show that any exception is made as to the docks occupied by E. H. Young as hereinafter shown, but as a fact the wharfage charge is not imposed by the Terminal Company on the cotton seed meal and cake handled over the dock of E. H. Young other than as the same may be included in the general lease or contract price fixed as hereinafter indicated.

The Terminal Company was a party to numerous circulars issued by the Southern Pacific Companies, known as the "Sunset Route," so termed, principally for advertising purposes. The circular of May 24, 1907, shows terminal charges (other than storage and switching). At the port of Galveston the circulars show a charge of one cent per 100 pounds on cotton seed cake and meal.

The Terminal Company has on its property two piers, known as pier "A" and pier "B," and has erected on them all facilities for handling imported and exported freight, and all freight which may come to or pass over its wharves, and it has abundant land under water upon which to erect other piers if they should become necessary.

It charges a fixed wharfage for all freight passing over its piers to or from vessels berthed thereat. The Galveston Wharf Company affords similar public wharfage facilities at the port of Galveston, having a number of piers. If the facilities of the Galveston Wharf Company should be destroyed those of the Terminal Company would become inadequate for handling the import and export and coastwise business. Ships to and from foreign ports, and coastwise ships other than those of the Southern Pacific Company, berth at piers "A" and "B," and there receive and deliver freight, and at these piers the Terminal Company carries on its general wharfage business.

In the building of pier "B" it was necessary to dredge a slip west of it, where ships could berth, and in order that the soil, through the action of storm and wave, should not drift into the slip, a bulkhead was built. To the westward of the slip the lands of the Terminal Company were lying idle and useless, they not being needed by it, and in pursuance of negotiations with Young the company proceeded to construct a pier, known as pier "C," for the use of Young, and to erect thereon a warehouse, shed and platform for his use, the original construction and subsequent enlargement of which cost the company about $65,000. At this time the pier is 300 feet wide at its widest part and about 1,400 feet in length.

The negotiations terminated in a lease under which Young is

to pay the Terminal Company a yearly rental of $15,000, payable monthly from the first day of November, 1906. And he agrees that he will route all shipments of cotton seed and cotton seed products purchased or shipped by him "over the lines of said Terminal Company and its connections, according to the instructions of said Terminal Company from time to time," and that he will insist upon and enforce such routing, except where the enforcement will prevent him from purchasing such products or from obtaining shipments which will be ready to move immediately and for which cars cannot be procured for the routing required. It is provided, however, that Young shall not be bound by these provisions if the rates be not equal to or lower than those of other competing lines or the service be not as adequate, but notice is to be given of such lower rates and service and an option to meet them.

The business of Young is that of a merchant and manufacturer, engaged in buying, selling and converting cotton seed cake and meal for his own account. He took possession of pier "C" and the improvements erected thereon by the Terminal Company under his contract with the latter company, paying the price stipulated in the contract, and has placed thereon cake, sacking and grinding machines, representing an investment of $50,000. Young's business consists in buying cotton seed cake in the interior, shipping it to himself by carloads at pier "C," there grinding it into meal, sacking it and loading it into steamships berthed at pier "C" for export.

All cotton seed meal cake passing over piers "A" and "B" pays a wharfage of 20 cents per short ton. Young pays no wharfage or storage charge other than as the same may be included in the rental of $15,000 per year. If any exporter handles cotton seed meal or cake over pier "C" the wharfage of 20 cents per ton is paid by him to Young.

Young has certain advantages by reason of his contract with the Terminal Company, which are enumerated in the agreed statement of facts and the result of which is stated as follows: "He makes a sum equal to 30 or 40 cents per ton more than he would receive if he handled his export product under methods in existence before he established his plant on pier 'C' and adopted the method of business he follows. This 30 to 40 cents per ton is in addition to the ordinary buying and selling profit." He at times pays more for cotton seed cake than his competitors can afford to pay, and at times he can undersell them in European markets, and since he commenced business some of the exporters who were engaged in business when he commenced have ceased exporting. A comparison of his business with that of all other exporters of cotton seed cake shows that from September 1, 1906, to September 1, 1907, he exported 105,000 tons of cotton seed cake and about the same amount of cotton seed meal; they, 50,000 tons of both products.

"Some of the cotton seed cake producers at interior mills in the State complain that Young is able to dominate the Texas market, and that his method of conducting business at Galveston enables him to command the foreign trade and may become a detriment to the cotton seed cake and meal industry, in that Young might acquire a monopoly. Others entertain a contrary opinion. They all agree that if there was a general establishment of plants in Galveston, so that a monopoly could not be acquired, it would be of great benefit to the cotton seed industry.

. . . .

"On the present constructed docks of the Galveston Wharf Company and the Terminal Company, with the structures as now located thereon, there is not space enough to furnish all exporters doing business at Galveston with space for erecting machinery and handling export business in the same manner as is done by Young."

This proceeding was instituted September 11, 1907, by Carl Eichenberg, an exporter of cotton seed and its products from the port of Galveston, by filing his complaint or petition before the Interstate Commerce Commission against the Southern Pacific Company and the Terminal Company, complaining that the companies, by the arrangement with Young, were violating § 3 of the act to regulate commerce, by giving him an undue and unreasonable preference and advantage over his competitors.

By order of the Commission the Galveston, Harrisburg and San Antonio Railway Company and other railroad companies entering Galveston were made parties defendant.

Answers were filed and full hearing was had by the Commission, which on June 24, 1908, made its report and order.

No rehearing was asked by defendant before the Interstate Commerce Commission. Young was not made a party to the proceedings before the Commission, but he appeared and testified as a witness for the Terminal Company, and his counsel was present at the hearing when the testimony was taken and engaged in the examination of witnesses. Young was also present when the case was argued and submitted.

MR. JUSTICE MCKENNA, after stating the facts as above, delivered the opinion of the court. . . . .

Four errors are assigned in the action of the Circuit Court in dismissing the bill of complaint. (1) The Interstate Commerce Commission had no jurisdiction over the Terminal Company, it not being a common carrier, and therefore not subject to the act to regulate commerce.[1] (2) The Commission had no power or authority to declare the lease to Young illegal. (3) The lease does not constitute an unlawful or undue preference or advantage within the meaning of the act to regulate commerce. (4) The Commission by its order assumed to control intrastate and foreign commerce, not subject to the act to regulate commerce.

Two facts are prominent in the case, that the piers of the Terminal Company are facilities of import and export traffic at the port of Galveston and that the arrangement of the Terminal Company with Young has enabled him to largely and rapidly increase his business until his exports of cotton seed products are more than twice those of all other competitors, that he derives therefrom 30 to 40 cents per ton over the ordinary buying and selling profit, and that some who were his competitors have ceased to export. A direct advantage to Young is manifest. A direct detriment to other exporters is equally manifest.

The situation challenges attention. Appellants find in it nothing but the natural and legal result of the sagacity which could see an opportunity for profit and the enterprise which could avail of it. It was the simple matter on the part of Young, it is contended, of bringing his business to the ship's side and cutting out intervening expenses. And it is said that the Terminal Company had an equally lawful inducement. It had an idle property, it is contended, over which it had absolute control and which it turned to use and profit by the arrangement with Young. And this, it is insisted, was a simple exercise of ownership. If the elements of the controversy are correctly stated, the justification may be considered as made out.

Appellants make much of their title and, assuming it to be absolute, assert the right to an unrestrained use of the property. But the assertion overlooks or underestimates the condition expressed in the deed to Huntington, that from his estate to the

[1] Only the part of the opinion relating to this point is printed here. — Ed.

Terminal Company, in the ordinance of the city of Galveston, and in the act of the legislature of the State of Texas. The condition expressed in all of them was that terminal facilities should be constructed upon the property for the use of the Southern Pacific Railroad and Steamship Systems. The act of the legislature declared that the property "should be developed for shipping and transportation purposes, and that the shipping facilities at the port of Galveston should be thereby improved and enlarged in order to better accommodate the commerce of the port and of the State." And wharfage charges, except so far as they should be covered by the freight rates, should be subject to regulation by the railroad commission of the State.

It is clear, therefore, that it was the purpose of the ordinance and of the act confirming it to secure shipping facilities for the city, open to public use, and necessarily so, for the property was to be the terminal of a railroad and steamship system. It may be, as it is contended, that there was no necessity for the ordinance, "except for the purpose of a valid relinquishment of the municipal right, often asserted by it, of opening streets through the bay front property and constructing wharves thereon." The relinquishment was treated as valuable and Huntington pledged the property to a public use as a consideration for it. And, as we have said, such use was also a condition expressed in the act of the legislature. It was not discharged by the expenditure of $150,000 and the erection of wharves by Huntington, as seems to be the contention.

The case has no likeness whatever to *Louisville &c. R. R. Co.* v. *West Coast Co.*, 198 U. S. 483. In the latter case there was no discrimination against the West Coast Company by the railroad company or a preference given to any person. The West Coast Company had the same privilege of using the wharves of the railroad company as other shippers were given. It asserted other privileges. It asserted the privilege of using the wharf for the purpose of transferring goods into vessels which it might arrange to take them; in other words, not into the vessels of the railroad company or into those with which it had traffic agreements. And we said, through Mr. Justice Peckham, "In brief, the fact seems to be that the only complaint of the plaintiff (West Coast Company) is that the defendant (the railroad company) will not permit competing vessels to make use of its wharf for the purpose of such competition."

It is true that there was a contention that the wharf was a public one, but the contention was based only on the fact that the wharf was built at the foot of a public street by authority from the city of Pensacola and the State of Florida. That fact alone was not considered sufficient to support the contention. And it was said, "The city or State authorities in granting the right to erect such facilities might, of course, have attached such conditions as they thought wise, but in their absence neither the public nor this plaintiff, as the owner of goods, would have the right, on this state of facts, to go to the wharf with vessels for the purpose of continuing transportation of goods in competition with defendant." It is true, it was said, that the railroad company never became a common carrier as to the wharf, in the sense that it was bound to accord to the public or to the West Coast Company the right to use it upon payment of compensation. But it was added that the railroad company would be bound to carry the West Coast Company's goods on the rails which led to the wharf, for the same purpose and upon the same terms that it did for others, viz., in order that it might itself, or through others it had contracted with, forward the goods beyond its own line. And it was further said that the West Coast Company demanded more than this; it demanded that the railroad company should carry its goods in order that it might itself forward them by vessels of its own selection, and that the railroad company should surrender possession of enough of its wharf to enable the other company to do so.

Nor is *Weems Steamboat Company* v. *People's Company*, 214 U. S. 344, applicable to the pending controversy. The contest there was between two independent lines of steamboats, the one claiming a right to use the wharves of the other, on the ground that the wharves had been dedicated to the public. The fact was found adversely to the contention, and the claim of right to the use of the wharves denied. A review of the reasoning of the court is unnecessary. There is great difference between competing carriers claiming the right to use the facilities of one another and the patrons of the same carrier contending for equality of treatment. In stating this we assume that the wharves in the pending case are the instruments of a common carrier. This is, however, denied, and it is asserted that the Terminal Company is purely a wharfage company, and "has no power under its charter to act as a common carrier." The contention is based on a partial view of the conditions. The Terminal Company was incorporated to execute the purposes expressed in the act of the legislature of the State of Texas, that is, to construct terminal facilities for the Southern Pacific Railroad and Steamship Systems, and to accommodate the export and import traffic at Galveston; and, necessarily, as instrumentalities of such traffic, wharves and piers are as essential as steamships and railroads, and are, in fact, as they were intended to be by the charter of their authorization, parts of a system. The only track facilities for movement of cars to or from the ships, from or to the tracks of the Southern Pacific Railways, are on the Terminal Company's lands, and are owned by it. To these tracks the Galveston, Harrisburg and San Antonio Railway switches cars for other railroads, charging $1.75 per car, and the Terminal Company receives a trackage charge of 50 cents per car. It is true that the Terminal Company does a wharfage business and publishes a schedule of its charges, which, while not filed with the Interstate Commerce Commission, shows a charge of 20 cents a ton on cotton seed cake and meal, and this appears as a wharfage charge in the tariffs of the Galveston, Harrisburg and San Antonio Railway Company and other railways entering the city of Galveston. And, besides, the Terminal Company was a party to numerous circulars issued by the Southern Pacific Railway Company, and that effective May 23, 1905, was filed with the Interstate Commerce Commission. These circulars gave terminal charges at the port of Galveston. The charge on cotton seed meal and cake was given at 1 cent per 100 pounds. Shipments on through bills of lading include in the freight rate the wharfage charge.

Another and important fact is the control of the properties by the Southern Pacific Company through stock ownership. There is a separation of the companies if we regard only their charters; there is a union of them if we regard their control and operation through the Southern Pacific Company. This control and operation are the important facts to shippers. It is of no consequence that by mere charter declaration the Terminal Company is a wharfage company or the Southern Pacific a holding company. Verbal declarations cannot alter the facts. The control and operation of the Southern Pacific Company of the railroads and the Terminal Company have united them into a system of which all are necessary parts, the Terminal Company as well as the railroad companies. As said by the Interstate Commerce Commission, "the Terminal Company was organized to furnish terminal facilities for the system at the port of Galveston," and it is further said that "through shipments on the railroad lines from and to points in different States of the Union pass and repass over the docks of the Terminal Company. It forms a link in this chain of transportation. It is necessary to complete the avenue through which move shipments over these lines owned by a single corporation." And this unity of the railroad's lines and the terminal facilities is recognized in the lease to Young. By it he agrees to route all of his shipments over "the lines of the Terminal Company and its connections, according to the instructions of said Terminal Company from time to time." And provision is made against the possibility of other lines bidding for the traffic by lower rates. In such event he must give notice to the Terminal Company and give it "the option of meeting such proposed rates," and if the company "elects to do so," then he "shall not divert such shipments, but shall abide by the provisions" of his agreement. And surely a system so constituted and used as an instrument of interstate commerce may not escape regulation as such because one of its constituents is a wharfage company and its dominating power a holding company. As well said by the Interstate Commerce Commission, "a corporation such as this Terminal Company, which has 'competing lines,' should not be permitted to defeat the jurisdiction of this Commission by showing that it is not in fact owned by any railroad company. . . . The Terminal Company is part and parcel of the system engaged in the transportation of commerce, and to the extent that such commerce is interstate the Commission has jurisdiction to supervise and control it within statutory limits. To hold otherwise would in effect permit carriers generally, through the organization of separate corporations, to exempt all of their terminals from our regulating authority."

The reasoning of the Commission is justified by the statute. It includes in the term "railroad" "all bridges and ferries used or operated in connection with any railroad, and also all the road in use by any corporation operating a railroad, whether owned or operated under a contract, agreement, or lease, and shall also include all switches, spurs, tracks, and terminal facilities of every kind used or necessary in the transportation of the persons or property designated herein, and also all freight depots, yards, and grounds used or necessary in the transportation or delivery of any of said property."

The property of the Terminal Company is "necessary in the transportation or delivery" of the interstate and foreign freight transported by the lines of the Southern Pacific system. It is the only terminal for freight moving over the lines of such system, the rails of one of those lines, the Galveston, Harrisburg and San Antonio Railway Company, connecting with tracks upon the docks of the Terminal Company. That the latter collects a trackage charge from the former and it a switching charge from the Terminal Company are, to quote the Commission, "but incidents of the separate corporations."

In opposition to these views appellants urge the legal individuality of the different railroads and the Terminal Company and cite cases which establish, it is contended, that stock ownership simply or through a holding company does not identify them. We are not concerned to combat the proposition. The record does not present a case of stock ownership merely or of a holding company which was content to hold. It presents a case, as we have already said, of one actively managing and uniting the railroads and the Terminal Company into an organized system. And it is with the system that the law must deal, not with its elements. Such elements may, indeed, be regarded from some standpoints as legal entities; may have, in a sense, separate corporate operation; but they are directed by the same paramount and combining power and made single by it. In all transactions it is treated as single. In the ordinance of the city of Galveston, in the act of 1899, of the legislature of the State, and in public circulars and in the lease of Young, it is the system which is dealt with and not its separate links. And, we have seen, the terminal facilities which the Terminal Company was authorized to maintain were for the system, not for the corporate elements considered separately. . . . .

Decree affirmed.

UNITED STATES v. BROOKLYN EASTERN DISTRICT TERMINAL

249 U. S. 296 (1919)

Mr. Justice Brandeis delivered the opinion of the court.

The Hours of Service Act (March 4, 1907, c. 2939, 34 Stat. 1415) [1] prohibits any common carrier by railroad engaged in interstate

[1] Act of March 4, 1907, c. 2939, 34 Stat. 1415.

"That the provisions of this Act shall apply to any common carrier or carriers, their officers, agents, and employees, engaged in the transportation of passengers or propery by railroad . . . . from one State . . . . to any other State. . . . . The term 'railroad' as used in this Act shall include all

commerce from requiring or permitting an employee to remain on duty for a longer period than sixteen consecutive hours. For alleged violation of this provision, proceedings were brought against the Brooklyn Eastern District Terminal in the District Court of the United States for the Eastern District of New York. The defendant contended that it was not a common carrier; that it was not engaged in interstate commerce by railroad; and that its employees were not "connected with the movement of any train." Upon facts which were agreed the trial court entered judgment for the Government. The Circuit Court of Appeals reversed the judgment on the ground that, while the Terminal was engaged in interstate commerce and the employment in question was connected with the movement of trains, it was not a common carrier. 239 Fed. Rep. 287. The case comes here on writ of certiorari (243 U. S. 647); and the substantial question before us is whether the Terminal is within the scope of the Hours of Service Act, as being a common carrier. The essential facts are these:

1. The Terminal is a navigation corporation with an authorized capital stock of one hundred thousand dollars ($100,000), incorporated under § 10 of Article III of the transportation corporations law of the State of New York, which reads as follows:

"Seven or more persons may become a corporation, for the purpose of building for their own use, equipping, furnishing, fitting, purchasing, chartering, navigating or owning steam, sail or other boats, ships, vessels or other property to be used in any lawful business, trade, commerce or navigation upon the ocean, or any seas, sounds, lakes, rivers, canals or other waterways, and for the carriage, transportation or storing of lading, freight, mails, property or passengers thereon."

In its certificate of incorporation, the corporate powers and purposes of the defendant are stated as follows:

"The purposes for which it is formed are to build for its own use, equip, furnish, fit, purchase, charter, navigate, and own steam, sail, and other boats, ships, vessels, and other property,

---

bridges and ferries used or operated in connection with any railroad, and also all the road in use by any common carrier operating a railroad, whether owned or operated under a contract, agreement, or lease; and the term 'employees' as used in this Act shall be held to mean persons actually engaged in or connected with the movement of any train.

"Sec. 2. That it shall be unlawful for any common carrier, its officers or agents, subject to this Act to require or permit any employee subject to this Act to be or remain on duty for a longer period than sixteen consecutive hours . . . ."

to be used in the business of carrying, transporting, storing, and lading merchandise in New York Harbor and the waters adjacent thereto and connected therewith and the territory bordering thereon."

2. The Terminal operates a union freight station at Brooklyn under individual contracts with ten interstate railroads and several steamship companies. From the railroads it receives both carload and less-than-carload freight and transports the same from their termini to its Brooklyn docks. There, the cars containing such freight are hauled from the car floats by its locomotives and placed for unloading either on its team tracks or at its freight houses. The Terminal receives likewise from shippers both carload and less-than-carload outgoing freight originating at Brooklyn and consigned to points upon the various railroads with which it has contracts. The cars carrying this outgoing freight are then switched and loaded by its locomotives upon its floats and transported by its tugs to the docks of the several railroads.

3. For its services in handling freight as above set forth the Terminal is paid not by the shipper or consignee, but by the railroad or steamship company upon whose account the transportation service is performed, at the rate of 3 cents per 100 pounds of freight moving to or from points east of the western termini of said railroads, and 4 1-5 cents per 100 pounds on freight moving to or from points beyond such termini. Upon prepaid shipments from shippers not on the credit lists of the railroads it collects from the shipper at Brooklyn the money and charges for the transportation of such freight from that point to its final destination; and also collects from the consignee at Brooklyn the charges for the transportation of such freight from its point of origin to that place, when such charges have not been prepaid. The freight moneys and charges so received by the defendant from shippers or consignees are accounted for and paid over by it without deduction to the railroads or steamship lines upon whose account they are collected.

4. The Terminal does not hold itself out as a common carrier; nor does it file with the Interstate Commerce Commission any tariffs or concurrences with tariffs, or copies of the contracts with the common carriers by whom it is paid for the transportation of freight, as heretofore set forth. The terminal at Brooklyn is designated by such railroads and rail and water lines, in the tariffs filed by them with the Interstate Commerce Commission, as one of their receiving and delivering stations for freight in the Port

of New York; and through bills of lading to such terminal as such station are issued by them on freight to be delivered there. For all freight originating at Brooklyn bills of lading of the railroad or steamship line to which the freight is to be delivered are there issued to the shipper by one of the defendant's employees, who is duly authorized to issue such bills of lading by the railroad or steamship line by which the freight is to be transported to its final destination or destinations after the same is delivered to such railroad or steamship line by defendant.

5. The tracks of the Terminal which extend from its float bridges to several warehouses, coal pockets, platforms, and team tracks have an aggregate length of 8 1-3 miles. One track connecting its several dock and delivery tracks which is kept clear for operating its switching engines is about one mile in length. The length of haul effected by its locomotives in moving cars between its float bridges and warehouses, platforms, pockets, and team tracks varies from a few yards to nearly a mile. The number of cars so hauled as part of a movement varies from a single car to eight cars. As an incident to such movement its locomotives hauling cars cross a public street in Brooklyn.

6. Defendant owns or hires no cars itself, and no cars, except the ones heretofore mentioned, are ever moved over its tracks. For the use of such cars defendant pays no charges; and except by the switching service heretofore described, it transports freight only by water. It handles interstate and intrastate freight indiscriminately, the larger part being interstate. It transports no passengers.

7. In connection with the movement of one or more cars between the floats and the loading tracks, warehouses, and team or delivery tracks, defendant employs four to eight switching crews during the day and two at night, each crew consisting of a conductor, engineer and two or more brakemen.

The Hours of Service Act declares (in the first section) that, "The term 'railroad' as used in this Act shall include all bridges and ferries used or operated in connection with any railroad, and also all the road in use by any common carrier operating a railroad, whether owned or operated under a contract, agreement, or lease." Hence, neither the character of the Terminal's railroad nor its independent ownership excludes it from the scope of the act. But the Terminal contends that it is not subject to the provisions of the statute, since it is not incorporated as a common carrier and does not hold itself out as such; does not file tariffs;

and does not undertake to transport property for all who may apply to have their goods transported; but merely transports as agent such freight as is delivered to it by or for those carriers, and those only, with whom it has elected to make special contracts; and that, under these contracts it performs for the railroads, and not for the public, a part of the whole carriage which they, as common carriers, have undertaken with the shipper to perform.

We need not undertake a definition of the term "common carrier" for all purposes. Nor are we concerned with questions of corporate power or of duties to shippers, which frequently compel nice distinctions between public and private carriers. We have merely to determine whether Congress, in declaring the Hours of Service Act applicable "to any common carrier or carriers, their officers, agents, and employees, engaged in the transportation of passengers or property by railroad," made its prohibitions applicable to the Terminal and its employees engaged in the operations here involved. The answer to that question does not depend upon whether its charter declares it to be a common carrier, nor upon whether the State of incorporation considers it such; but upon what it does. *Terminal Taxicab Co.* v. *District of Columbia,* 241 U. S. 252, 254.

The relation of the Terminal to the several railroads is substantially the same as that of the terminal considered in *United States* v. *Baltimore & Ohio R. R. Co.,* 225 U. S. 306; 231 U. S. 274, 288. The transportation performed by the railroads begins and ends at the Terminal. Its docks and warehouses are public freight stations of the railroads. These with its car floats, even if not under common ownership or management, are used as an integral part of each railroad line, like the stockyards in *United States* v. *Union Stock Yard Co.,* 226 U. S. 286, and the wharfage facilities in *Southern Pacific Terminal Co.* v. *Interstate Commerce Commission,* 219 U. S. 498. They are clearly unlike private plant facilities. Compare *Tap Line Cases,* 234 U. S. 1, 25. The services rendered by the Terminal are public in their nature; and of a kind ordinarily performed by a common carrier. If these terminal operations were conducted directly by any, or jointly by all, of the ten railroad companies with which the Terminal has contracts, the operations would clearly be within the scope of the Hours of Service Law. The evils sought to be remedied exist equally, whether the terminal operations are conducted by the railroad companies themselves or by the Terminal as their agent; and whether the

Terminal acts only as such agent for railroads or undertakes in addition to transport on its own account goods for shippers. The precise question presented is, therefore, whether the fact that the Terminal conducts these operations, not as an integral part of a single railroad system but wholly as an agent for one or several, exempts the railroad companies, because they are not the employer and exempts the Terminal, because it is not a common carrier; thus making inapplicable a provision regarding the physical operation of the property devised for the protection of employees and the public.

One who transports property from place to place over a definite route as agent for a common carrier may, under conceivable circumstances, be a private carrier. But what is there in the facts above recited to endow the Terminal with that character? The service which it performs is distinctly public in character; — that is, conveying between Brooklyn and points on any of the ten interstate carriers and their connections all property that is offered. The fact that the railroad of the Terminal is short does not prevent it from being a common carrier, *United States* v. *Sioux City Stock Yards Co.*, 162 Fed. Rep. 556; nor does the fact that the thing which it undertakes to carry is contained only in cars furnished by the railroad companies with which it has contracts. Railroads, whose only service is hauling cars for other railroads, have been held liable as common carriers under the Safety Appliance Acts, *Union Stockyards Co. of Omaha* v. *United States*, 169 Fed. Rep. 404; *Belt Railway Co. of Chicago* v. *United States*, 168 Fed. Rep. 542; and under the Twenty-Eight Hour Law, *United States* v. *Sioux City Stock Yards Co.*, *supra.* [1]

What the Terminal contracts to transport, however, is not primarily cars, but their contents. Its compensation is measured not by the weight, size, or character of the car, but by the weight and the origin or destination of the goods carried therein. These goods the Terminal must, under its contracts with the railroad companies, receive and carry at the rates specified for all who offer them, as fully as the railroad companies do at their other stations. The incidental services performed by the Terminal in respect to these goods are also the same as those performed by the railroad companies at their other stations. For all freight originating at Brooklyn, it issues through bills of lading to destination. Upon prepaid shipments originating there,

[1] Compare also *McNamara* v. *Washington Terminal Co.*, 37 App. D. C. 384, 394, *et seq.*; *State* v. *Union Stock Yards Co.*, 81 Nebraska, 67.

it collects from the sh ppers the charges for transportation from Brooklyn to final destination; except where shippers are on the credit lists of the railroad companies. Upon goods arriving over its line at Brooklyn, it collects from the consignees the charges from point of origin, unless these were prepaid. As the Terminal receives both from railroad companies and from shippers also less-than-carload freight, it doubtless performs the loading and unloading, as is done at other railroad stations; and for freight delivered at Brooklyn takes appropriate receipts. In no respect, therefore, does the service actually performed by the Terminal for or in respect to shippers differ from that performed by the railroad companies at their other stations. True, the service is performed by the Terminal under contracts with the railroad companies as agent for them and not on its own account. But a common carrier does not cease to be such merely because the services which it renders to the public are performed as agent for another. The relation of connecting carriers with the initial carrier is frequently that of agent. See *Bank of Kentucky* v. *Adams Express Co.*, 93 U. S. 174. The relation of agency may preclude contractual obligations to the shippers, but it cannot change the obligations of the carrier concerning the physical operation of the railroad under the Hours of Service Act, which as this court has said, must be liberally construed to secure the safety of employees and the public. *Atchison, Topeka & Santa Fe Ry. Co.* v. *United States*, 244 U. S. 336.

It is now admitted that the Terminal is engaged in interstate commerce; and it is clear that at least "switching crews" engaged in moving at one time a locomotive with seven or eight cars between the docks and the warehouses or team tracks, a distance of nearly a mile, are engaged in the movement of a "train." The decisions under the Safety Appliance Acts depend upon the particular context in which the word "train" there occurs, and are not here applicable. Compare *United States* v. *Erie R. R. Co.*, 237 U. S. 402, 407–408.

The judgment of the Circuit Court of Appeals is reversed and that of the District Court affirmed.

Reversed.

3. "Railroad" and "Transportation"

ILLINOIS CENTRAL RAILROAD COMPANY *v.* RAILROAD COMMISSION OF LOUISIANA

236 U. S. 157 (1915)

Mr. Justice McReynolds delivered the opinion of the court.

After a full hearing and investigation the Railroad Commission of Louisiana, on August 8, 1903, promulgated the following, known as Order No. 295:

"No railroad company operating in the State of Louisiana shall refuse or decline to switch cars for any other railroad with which it connects or any shipper, or consignee, at rates approved or established by the Commission, whether such cars are to be loaded with freight to be shipped out of the State, or are loaded with freight shipped into the State. All tariffs for the 'service' of switching cars in the State of Louisiana, shall be filed with the Commission, within thirty days from the date of this order, and all the Commission's rules and orders relative to rates and changes in rates, will also apply to switching charges."

By a proceeding against the members of the commission, commenced in the United States Circuit Court, Eastern District of Louisiana, February 10, 1904, the appellant, a common carrier of freight and passengers operating lines in Louisiana, attacked the validity of this order upon the ground that it is an unlawful attempt to regulate interstate commerce and for other reasons, and prayed that defendants be restrained from enforcing it. Shortly thereafter a temporary injunction was granted to remain effective pending the cause or until otherwise directed; and on October 6, 1904, defendants answered denying all the alleged equities. The record discloses no further action by either party until April, 1913, when a rather meagre and unsatisfactory agreed statement of facts was filed. The trial court dismissed the bill without prejudice — January, 1914, — saying that the questions involved had been indirectly decided by this court in *Grand Trunk Ry.* v. *Michigan Railroad Commission,* 231 U. S. 457. From this decree a direct appeal was taken and a supersedeas was allowed.

The extraordinary delay in bringing the cause to final hearing is not explained; and in the circumstances we deem it quite sufficient briefly to indicate and decide the controlling question.

With the consent of the proper local authorities appellant constructed and now operates at New Orleans extensive terminals including switch and side tracks, warehouses and yards. These are essential to the proper conduct of its large interstate and foreign business; and when it brings freight there the cars are placed on its various switch tracks to be unloaded by the consignees. At New Orleans physical connections exist between appellant's tracks and the lines of competitive railroads leading therefrom to many States; if Order No. 295 is enforced its switch tracks will be subjected to use by such railroads; more cars will pass over them; and its power to comply with obligations to patrons will be hindered. Together with the various railroads appellant has published and now has in effect terminal tariffs covering switching; these include no rates for transporting freight to or from the city "but simply cover the charges made for switching cars from the depot or yard of one railroad company to points on its terminals." Upon orders of the consignees certain switch movements are made entirely within the switching limits of the city between points one or both of which may be located upon the terminals of the Illinois Central, and for these charges are made varying according to distance with an addition of three dollars per car for rental. When a car loaded with interstate freight arrives at New Orleans the consignee is first notified that the contents are ready for delivery at the carrier's depot or warehouse. After calling and paying the charges he gives to the agent of the railroad transporting the shipment an order directing that the cars be switched and placed on some terminal or industrial track for delivery. This order is then submitted to the Illinois Central Railroad and in due course is executed by it.

From the foregoing summary of the facts stipulated it fairly appears that obedience to Order No. 295 would require appellant, upon demand of a carrier or shipper and on terms fixed by the State Commission, to switch empty cars from any connection with a competing interstate railroad to a designated side track within its own terminals for the purpose of being loaded there with goods intended for interstate commerce, and when so loaded to move the same back to the competitor's line for continued transportation to another State. Likewise appellant would be required to accept from competing interstate lines at points within the city loaded cars brought from other States and place them on its own side track, although such track was the real destination contemplated at the time of the original shipment. Switching movements of this kind (we do not now inquire as to others) constitute a part of interstate commerce the regulation of which Congress has undertaken, and consequently the order of the State Commission transcends the limits of its powers.

When freight actually starts in the course of transportation from one State to another it becomes a part of interstate commerce. The essential nature of the movement and not the form of the bill of lading determines the character of the commerce involved. And generally when this interstate character has been acquired it continues at least until the load reaches the point where the parties originally intended that the movement should finally end. *McNeill* v. *Southern Railway*, 202 U. S. 543, 559; *Southern Pacific Terminal* v. *Interstate Commerce Commission*, 219 U. S. 498, 527; *Ohio Railroad Commission* v. *Worthington*, 225 U. S. 101, 110; *Texas & New Orleans Railroad* v. *Sabine Tram Co.*, 227 U. S. 111, 126; *Louisiana Railroad Commission* v. *Tex. & Pac. Ry.*, 229 U. S. 336, 341.

The contention for appellees that switching cars at junctions and terminals "is only interstate commerce when performed as a part of the interstate movement on a through rate or bill of lading under tariff authority" is contrary to the doctrine established by opinions of this court in the cases cited above. We cannot undertake as suggested to dissect the contested order and point out whether any part of it constitutes "a workable scheme for the regulation of intrastate traffic." Problems relating alone to commerce wholly within the State must be left to the discretion of the State Commission to be exercised upon a view of all existing, relevant facts and circumstances.

The present controversy is not controlled by *Grand Trunk Ry.* v. *Michigan Railroad Commission*, *supra*. The issues in the two cases are essentially different. There the attack was upon an order of the State Commission "suspensory only of the tariff of the appellants, not a final determination against it or of the conditions which might or might not justify it," and the question was "whether, under the statutes of the State of Michigan, appellants can be compelled to use the tracks it owns and operates in the city of Detroit for the interchange of intrastate traffic." The movement actually regulated was held to be intrastate commerce. It took place within Detroit but between points sufficiently far apart to constitute genuine transportation; and, treating it as a local matter, the Railway Company had applied special tariffs thereto until withdrawn because of disagreement with shippers and commission.

The original bill should have been sustained and a permanent injunction awarded. The decree below is accordingly reversed and the cause remanded for further proceedings in accordance with this opinion.

Reversed.

WESTERN TRANSIT COMPANY *v.* LESLIE COMPANY

242 U. S. 448 (1917)

Mr. Justice Brandeis delivered the opinion of the court.

The Western Transit Company, operating steamers between Buffalo and other points on the Great Lakes, formed, with the New York Central Railroad, a "lake and rail" line between Michigan and New York City. Among the privileges and facilities offered by this line was the right "in transit of free storage and diversion at Buffalo." That is, the shipper instead of sending his goods from Michigan through to New York City, was entitled, without the payment of any extra charge, to have them stored at Buffalo for a period, to await further orders and be forwarded later to New York. The shipper was also given the privilege of "diversion"; — that is of changing the ultimate destination of the stored goods upon proper adjustment of the rate. On September 23, 1908, A. C. Leslie & Co., Limited, the plaintiff below, delivered to the Western Transit Co., the defendant below, at Houghton, Michigan, for shipment over this line to New York City, 25 tons of copper ingots, with direction to store the same upon arrival at Buffalo to await further shipping directions. The copper arrived there September 30, and was placed in the Transit Company's warehouse. Nearly four months later about one ton of it was stolen from the warehouse. An action was brought by the shipper in the City Court of Buffalo to recover its value. The Transit Company denied all liability; but the court found that the loss was due to its negligence and held the company liable for the full value of the copper lost. The judgment of the City Court was affirmed by the Supreme Court of New York at special term and also by the Appellate Division of that court. 165 App. Div. 947. Applications for an appeal to the Court of Appeals of New York having been denied, both by the Appellate Division and by the Chief Judge of the Court of Appeals, a writ of error from this court was granted on the ground that the decision below involved a federal question, namely: the construction and effect of the bill of lading and of tariffs filed under the Act to Regulate Commerce as amended. Act 1906, c. 3591, 34 Stat. 584.

The question before this court relates solely to the measure of damages. The shipper contends that it is entitled to the full value of the copper lost, which was $271.38. The carrier contends that the damages recoverable are limited to $94.10; that is, the value *not to exceed $100 a ton.* In support of this limitation it relies upon the fact that freight was paid at the rate of 18 cents per ton, under a bill of lading and a tariff which names the following rates from Houghton, Michigan, to New York City:

"Copper ingots . . . . value not to exceed $100 a ton, 18c. per ton
Copper ingots . . . . value not expressed.................. 30c. per ton."

The shipper insists that it is enforcing the liability of the Transit Company not as carrier, but as warehouseman; and that the terms of its obligation as warehouseman are fixed, not by the bill of lading and the tariff provision quoted above, but wholly by the letter of November 26, 1908, and the circular therein referred to, which are copied in the margin.[1]

[1] The Western Transit Company, N. Y. C. & H. R. R. Line of Steamers.
Buffalo, N. Y., Nov. 26, 1908.

Messrs. A. C. Leslie & Company, Montreal, Que.

GENTLEMEN: Replying to your letter of 24th, instant, would advise you that we have in store here, lot 1036 ingot bars of copper, marked M. M. 102, as well as lot of 979 ingot bars, marked M. M. 97.

This copper came forward in our steamer, Buffalo, which unloaded here September 30th, and will be held here subject to our storage circular I. C. C. No. 236, copy of which I enclose.

Yours truly,
(Signed) EDWIN T. DOUGLASS,
General Manager.

I. C. C. No. 236, Superseding I. C. C. No. 231.
The Western Transit Company, New York Central & Hudson River R. R. Line.
General Office.
Copper and Copper Matte, Pig Lead and Spelter for Storage and Diversion at Buffalo.

The Western Transit Company will accept shipments of Copper and Copper Matte, Pig Lead and Spelter for storage and diversion at Buffalo, under the following rules:

1. The Western Transit Company, at request of owners, will furnish free storage on shipments of Copper and Copper Matte, Pig Lead and Spelter in transit, at Buffalo, for a period not exceeding four months.

The Transit Company filed with the Interstate Commerce Commission, in addition to its general tariffs covering "lake and rail" rates, a separate tariff known as I. C. C. No. 236, covering specifically storage and diversion privileges at Buffalo, as set forth in the circular copied in the margin. The filing of this tariff was required by the act (see *Goldenberg* v. *Clyde S. S. Co.*, 20 I. C. C. 527) since the general tariff did not specify the details of the storage and diversion privileges. The Act to Regulate Commerce as amended provides expressly (§ 1) that the term transportation includes storage. And § 6 provides that a carrier must file with the Interstate Commerce Commission tariffs "showing all the rates, fares, and charges for transportation" and "shall also state separately all . . . . storage charges, ... all privileges or facilities granted or allowed and any rules or regulations which in any wise change, affect, or determine any part or the aggregate of such aforesaid rates."

The bill of lading, in a form similar to that approved and recommended by the Interstate Commerce Commission (14 I. C. C. 346), contains the following, among other provisions:

"It is mutually agreed in consideration of the rate of freight hereinafter named, as to each carrier of all or any of said property over all or any portion of said route to destination and as to each party at any time interested in all or any of said property, that every service to be performed hereunder shall be subject to all the conditions, whether printed or written, herein contained, and which are hereby agreed to by the shipper, and by him accepted for himself and his assigns as just and reasonable."

. . . .

"To be held at Bflo. for orders.

---

2. If held longer than four months, it will be subject to a charge of one-half (½) cent per 100 pounds for each thirty (30) or part thereof so held.

3. Shipments held under this arrangement will be at owner's risk, and will not be accepted for storage unless arrangements are made with the undersigned previous to forwarding from Western Lake Ports.

4. Shipments ordered out of store will be charged at the through rate in effect at time the shipment originated, to points to which through rates are published by The Western Transit Company.

5. Shipments ordered to points to which no through rates are in effect via The Western Transit Company, will be charged at the local rate to and from Buffalo.

Issued May 15th, 1908.
Effective June 16th, 1908.

EDWIN T. DOUGLASS,
General Manager, Buffalo, N. Y.

"Value not to exceed $100.00 per net ton. Limited by written agreement.

"The consignor of this property has the option of shipping same at a higher rate without limitation as to value in case of loss or damage from causes which would make the carrier liable, but agrees to the specified valuation named in case of loss or damage from causes which would make the carrier liable, because of the lower rate thereby accorded for transportation."

. . . .

Conditions.

.

"The amount of any loss or damage for which any carrier becomes liable shall be computed at the value of the property at the place and time of shipment under this bill of lading, unless a lower value has been agreed upon or is determined by the classification upon which the rate is based, in either of which events such lower value shall be the maximum price to govern such computation."

The release valuation clause in an interstate bill of lading when based upon a difference in freight rates is valid. *Adams Express Co.* v. *Croninger*, 226 U. S. 491, 509. The limitation of liability by means of such valuation contained in the bill of lading continues although the service of carrying has been completed and the goods are held by the carrier strictly as warehouseman. *Cleveland, Cincinnati, Chicago & St. Louis Ry.* v. *Dettlebach*, 239 U. S. 588. The provisions of the bill of lading govern even where the goods are allowed to remain in the carrier's warehouse after giving receipt therefor and payment of freight. The carrier and the shipper can make no alteration of the terms upon which goods are held under a tariff, until there has been an actual delivery of the goods to the consignee. *Southern Ry. Co.* v. *Prescott*, 240 U. S. 632. The reasons are even more persuasive for holding that the terms of a bill of lading govern storage in transit, like that at Buffalo. The contention of the shipper that the letter of November 26 enclosing the circular created a contract of warehousing wholly independent of the contract of carriage is contrary to fact. The Transit Company's circular states "that free storage is furnished on shipments in transit" and that shipments "will not be accepted for storage unless arrangements are made with the undersigned previous to forwarding from Western Lake Ports." Obviously free storage in transit was granted only to those who shipped over this "lake and rail" line. The shipper had enjoyed nearly two months' storage when the circular was received in answer to a letter of inquiry. It stated only what was contained in the tariff filed, which every shipper was bound to take notice of.

The contention was also made that the judgment below was correct, even if the bill of lading be held to govern the warehousing at Buffalo; because the agreed valuation clause properly construed fixes an amount far greater than the actual value for which judgment was rendered. The "released" or agreed valuation is "$100 per net ton." There were 25 tons in this shipment. It is insisted that, as the 25 tons constituted a single lot, $2,500 is recoverable for loss of or damage to the whole or to any part of the lot. This construction does violence to the language used and is unreasonable. The valuation clause fixes not an arbitrary limit of recovery but a ratio. In *Kansas City Southern Ry. Co.* v. *Carl*, 227 U. S. 639, 656, where the released valuation clause was applied to a shipment consisting of two boxes and a barrel, and one box was lost, this court said, the consignor and carrier must have understood the agreed valuation to mean that the package contained "household goods of the average value per hundredweight of five dollars." The ratio is more naturally applied where the whole shipment is homogeneous. Under this bill of lading the shipper is entitled to recover not more than $100 a ton for each or any ton damaged or lost.

Judgment reversed and cause remanded for further proceedings not inconsistent with this opinion.

ERIE RAILROAD COMPANY *v.* SHUART *ET AL.*

250 U. S. 465 (1919)

Mr. Justice McReynolds delivered the opinion of the court.

Respondents delivered to the Toledo, St. Louis & Western Railroad at East St. Louis, Illinois, a carload of horses for transportation, under a Limited Liability Livestock Contract or bill of lading via petitioner's road, to themselves at Suffern, New York, their home. Among other things the contract provided:

"That the said shipper is at his own sole risk and expense to load and take care of, and to feed and water said stock whilst being transported, whether delayed in transit or otherwise, and to unload the same; and neither said carrier nor any connecting carrier is to be under any liability or duty with reference thereto, except in the actual transportation of the same." . . . . "That no claim for damages which may accrue to the said shipper under this contract shall be allowed or paid by the said carrier, or sued for in any Court by the said shipper, unless a claim for such loss or damage shall be made in writing, verified by the affidavit of the said shipper or his agent, and delivered to the General Auditor of the said carrier at his office in the City of Chicago, Ill., within five days from the time said stock is removed from said car or cars, and that if any loss or damage occurs upon the line of a connecting carrier, then such carrier shall not be liable unless a claim shall be made in like manner, and delivered in like time, to some proper officer or agent of the carrier, on whose line the loss or injury occurs."

Immediately after the car arrived at Suffern, petitioner placed it on a switch track opposite a cattle chute and left it in charge of respondents for unloading. By letting down a bridge they at once connected the chute and car and were about to lead out four horses when an engine pushed other cars against it and injured the animals therein. No written claim was made for the loss or damage as provided by the bill of lading; and when sued the carrier defended upon that ground. Respondents maintain that transportation had ended when the accident occurred and consequently no written claim was necessary. The courts below accepted this view.

Under our former opinions, the clause requiring presentation of a written claim is clearly valid and controlling as to any liability arising from beginning to end of the transportation contracted for. *Chesapeake & Ohio Ry. Co.* v. *McLaughlin*, 242 U. S. 142; *St. Louis, Iron Mountain & Southern Ry. Co.* v. *Starbird*, 243 U. S. 592; *Baltimore & Ohio R. R. Co.* v. *Leach*, 249 U. S. 217; *Cleveland, Cincinnati, Chicago & St. Louis Ry. Co.* v. *Dettlebach*, 239 U. S. 588, 593, 594; and *Southern Ry. Co.* v. *Prescott*, 240 U. S. 632.

In *Cleveland, Cincinnati, Chicago & St. Louis Ry. Co.* v. *Dettlebach* we pointed out that the Hepburn Act enlarged the definition of "transportation" so as to include "cars and other vehicles and all instrumentalities and facilities of shipment or carriage, irrespective of ownership or of any contract, express or implied, for the use thereof and all services in connection with the receipt, delivery, elevation, and transfer in transit, ventilation, refrigeration, or icing, storage, and hauling of property transported"; and we said from this and other provisions of the act "it is evident that Congress recognized that the duty of carriers to the public included the performance of a variety of services that, according to the theory of the common law, were separable from the carrier's service as carrier, and, in order to prevent overcharges and discriminations from being made under the pretext of performing such additional services, it enacted that so far as interstate carriers by rail were concerned the entire body of such services should be included together under the single term 'transportation' and subjected to the provisions of the Act respecting reasonable rates and the like."

In the instant case, when injured, the animals were awaiting removal from the car through a cattle chute alleged to be owned, operated and controlled by the railroad. If its employees had then been doing the work of unloading there could be no doubt that transportation was still in progress; and we think that giving active charge of the removal to respondents, as agreed, was not enough to end the interstate movement. The animals were in the car; no adequate time for unloading had transpired. The carrier had not fully performed the services incident to final delivery imposed by law. These included the furnishing of fair opportunity and proper facilities for safe unloading although the shippers had contracted to do the work of actual removal. See Hutchinson on Carriers, §§ 711, 714, 715.

Petitioner's request for an instructed verdict in its behalf should have been granted. The judgment below must be reversed and the cause remanded for further proceedings not inconsistent with this opinion.

Reversed.

MR. JUSTICE CLARKE dissenting.

I greatly regret that I cannot concur in the opinion and judgment of the court in this case, but I cannot consent to share in what seems to me a very strained construction of a definition in the Hepburn Act (34 Stat. 584, c. 3591, § 1) which will result in keeping alive a bill of lading, with the effect of excusing the carrier from liability for negligently damaging the live stock of a consignee, after it had been delivered, on the ground that a claim in writing for the damage, duly verified, had not been presented within five days.

My reasons for dissenting, stated as briefly as may be, are as follows:

It is shown by the opinion of the court that the consignee, a partnership of three members, was bound by the bill of lading to unload the horses at destination.

The consignee, being notified by the carrier as to the probable time of the arrival of the car, on the day before it arrived, paid what was supposed to be the full amount of the freight charges, and two members of the partnership were at the station at three o'clock in the morning to receive and unload it.

When the train came, the senior member of the consignee stood in the cattle chute with the conductor, while the latter was placing the car for unloading and approved as satisfactory the position in which it was placed. Thereupon, a brakeman set the brake, the engine was cut off and the conductor went away and left the car in the sole custody of the consignee, after saying to its representative, "You had better get them out as soon as you can, they have been on the road a good while and must be tired and hungry." Two members of the partnership, consignee, went to work at once to unload the horses, but it was necessary to get some boards to make the bridge from the car to the chute safe, and in about half an hour, when the two were in the act of leading two horses from the car, other cars were negligently thrown against it and caused the damage sued for.

I dissent from the opinion of the court because I agree with the three New York courts that the undisputed facts thus stated show that the transportation was ended and the delivery of the stock was so completely made as to end all liability of the carrier under the bill of lading, before the negligence of the company occurred which caused the damage complained of.

What constitutes delivery of goods or of live stock by a carrier is usually a mixed question of law and fact, but where, as here, the facts are not disputed, it is a question of law.

What more was there for the carrier to do, — what more could it have done — to make more complete the delivery necessary to fulfill its obligation as a carrier? The journey was ended, the freight charges were paid, and the car was placed on a side track in an appropriate place and position for unloading, which was approved by the consignee. It had been accepted by two members of the partnership, consignee, and had passed into their exclusive custody a full half hour before the accident. No assistance was asked for or needed after the conductor delivered the car and went away and thereafter the carrier owed to the consignee only the duty which it owed to any property lawfully upon or near to its tracks, — not to negligently or wilfully injure it, and it was for violation of that duty, not for failure to discharge duties imposed by the bill of lading, that this suit was instituted. The case is one of side track delivery, the equivalent of the familiar delivery of a car to an "industrial track" or "team unloading track" of a railroad, with possession taken by the consignee before the damage was done.

To the weighty authority of the New York courts which decided in this case that the delivery was complete before the damage was done, may be added, a few from many, the decisions of the Supreme Courts: of Michigan, in a strikingly similar case but with not so complete a delivery, in *Brown* v. *Pontiac, Oxford & Northern R. R. Co.*, 133 Michigan, 371; of Illinois, in *Gratiot Street Warehouse Co.* v. *St. Louis, Alton & Terre Haute R. R. Co.*, 221 Illinois, 418; of North Carolina, in *Reid* v. *Southern Ry. Co.*, 149 N. Car. 423; of Georgia, in *Kenny Co.* v. *Atlanta & West Point R. R. Co.*, 122 Georgia, 365. And see *Hedges* v. *Hudson River R. R. Co.*, 49 N. Y. 223.

The definition of "transportation" in the Hepburn Act (34 Stat. 584), relied upon in the court's opinion, seems to me quite irrelevant. That provision was incorporated into the act to prevent unjust discrimination by carriers in terminal delivery charges, as the context and the history of the act abundantly show. It defined "transportation" but did not define what should constitute delivery to a consignee, — that was left untouched and is governed by the prior decisions of courts and by those which have been developed since.

Equally beside the question involved seems to me the decision in *Cleveland, Cincinnati, Chicago & St. Louis Ry. Co.* v. *Dettlebach*, 239 U. S. 588, 593, 594, cited in the opinion of the court. The question there under consideration was, whether when goods carried to destination were lost, after they had been held more than a month uncalled for, the liability of the carrier was to be determined by the terms of the bill of lading or by the more limited liability of a warehouseman. Obviously there was no question in the case as to what constituted delivery, for there was no pretense of delivery, actual or constructive, and therefore the decision cannot be of service in determining this case.

The opinion of the court in this case concludes:

"The animals were in the car; no adequate time for unloading had transpired. The carrier had not fully performed the services incident to final delivery imposed by law. These included the furnishing of fair opportunity and proper facilities for safe unloading although the shippers had contracted to do the work of actual removal. See Hutchinson on Carriers, §§ 711, 714, 715."

I cannot find justification, in the sections cited, for such a statement of the law as is here made.

Section 711 deals with the obligation to unload carload freight, and, after saying that it is "the uniform rule and custom in this country" for the consignee to unload, the only other relevant statement of the writer is:

"All, therefore, that can be required of the railroad company is that it shall place the cars where they may be safely and conveniently unloaded."

This the carrier in the case before us had done to the satisfaction and acceptance of the consignee before the accident complained of.

Section 714 deals with the liability of the carrier pending removal (delivery) of the goods, and says:

"During this reasonable time [for delivery] the liability of the carrier remains unchanged; but so soon as it has elapsed he no longer stands in the relation of carrier to the goods, but in that of an ordinary bailee for hire."

The "reasonable time" here referred to is palpably that necessary for the carrier to wait before its obligation becomes that of a warehouseman when the consignee does not appear to claim the shipment, — it is not applicable to the time for unloading after the property has been accepted by the consignee.

Section 715 declares that:

"If the consignee is bound to unload the goods himself from the car, it is the duty of the carrier to place the car where it can be unloaded with a reasonable degree of convenience, and to furnish the consignee with safe and proper facilities for the purpose."

All of this the carrier in this case did, and the consignee not only approved as satisfactory, safe and proper, the position in which the car was placed and the facilities furnished for unloading it, but the delivery of the car was accepted and was in the actual possession and custody of the consignee for a very considerable time before the accident complained of happened. It was not in any attempt or effort on the part of the carrier to improve the unloading facilities or to assist the consignee that the damage was done, but it was the result of a tort, pure and simple, — of a negligent switching operation, entirely independent of the delivery of the shipment, occurring a half hour after it had been accepted.

The delivery having been completed and accepted by the consignee, the five-day limitation, so unreasonable in itself that it has been prohibited by congressional enactment (38 Stat. 1196, c. 176, § 1) has, in my judgment, no applicability to this case, and to bottom the conclusion announced upon the definition of "transportation" in the Hepburn Act is to convert what was intended for the protection of shippers of property in interstate commerce into an instrument of injury and injustice.

For the reasons thus stated I dissent from the opinion and judgment of the court.

MR. JUSTICE MCKENNA and MR. JUSTICE BRANDEIS concur in this dissent. MR. JUSTICE DAY also dissents.

INTERSTATE COMMERCE COMMISSION *v.* DIFFENBAUGH

222 U. S. 42 (1911)

MR. JUSTICE HOLMES delivered the opinion of the court.

These are appeals from injunctions issued upon bills brought by the appellees against the enforcement of two orders made by the Interstate Commerce Commission. 176 Fed. Rep. 409. The stages by which the Commission came to its present conclusion, against its earlier view, will be found reported in 10 I. C. C. Rep. 309, 12 *id.* 85, 14 *id.* 315. See 14 *id.* 317, 510, 551. In the Circuit Court these cases were tried upon the same evidence and they raise the same question; but as the Peavey suit presents that question in its initial and simplest form we will state the facts of that case first.

The Union Pacific Railroad, after passing through a grain country, has its eastern termini at Omaha and Kansas City, on the Missouri River. Much the greater part, nine-tenths, more or less, of the grain gathered and carried by the road passes beyond the termini, especially to points farther east. During the season the Union Pacific needs all its cars to collect the grain, and therefore wants to get them back as quickly as possible from the end of its line. Furthermore, the shipments eastward are made more profitably in heavier loads than can be collected from the local stations. For these reasons the Union Pacific sought to prevent its own cars being carried beyond the termini, over connecting lines, and to have the grain shifted to other cars. To make the change it is commercially necessary to pass the grain through an elevator, where also it is weighed, another necessary step in the transportation. See 14 I. C. C. Rep. 317, 318. An additional consideration is that Omaha and Kansas City are great grain markets where there are sales largely in excess of local needs, and this also requires the grain to pass through elevators at these points. If the Union Pacific could not use these instruments of transfer it could not compete with other roads that have through lines from the grain fields across the Missouri River to the East. See 14 I. C. C. Rep. 317, 327.

Acting on these motives, the railroad company in 1899 made a contract in good faith with Peavey under which he built an elevator at Council Bluffs on the other side of the river from Omaha. He was to receive not exceeding $1\frac{1}{4}$ cents per hundred pounds for the first ten years, and one cent for the next ten, for grain transferred through his elevator. Later another elevator was brought into the arrangement, now with Peavey & Co., a corporation. Peavey & Co. is a large dealer in grain and receives the same allowance for its own grain that it receives for that of others. It is important to remark that in no case is any additional charge made to the shipper for the elevator service. In 1904 the Interstate Commerce Commission investigated the matter and upheld the contract, including the allowance for Peavey & Co.'s own grain. 10 I. C. C. Rep. 309.

The Commission also made a report to Congress, and after further investigation, notwithstanding the fact that the incidental advantages to grain owners from such allowances had been made apparent, Congress passed the act of June 29, 1906, c. 3591, 34 Stat. 584. By this it was provided in § 1, amending the earlier statute, that "the term 'transportation' shall include . . . . all instrumentalities and facilities of shipment or carriage, irrespective of ownership or of any contract, express or implied, for the use thereof and all services in connection with the receipt, delivery, elevation, and transfer in transit, ventilation, refrigeration or icing, storage, and handling of property transported; and it shall be the duty of every carrier subject to the provisions of this Act to provide and furnish such transportation upon reasonable request therefor, and to establish through routes," etc. By § 6 the carrier was required to state separately in its schedules all terminal charges and all privileges or facilities granted or allowed, and by § 15 "If the owner of property transported under this

Act directly or indirectly renders any service connected with such transportation, or furnishes any instrumentality used therein, the charge and allowance therefor shall be no more than is just and reasonable, and the Commission may, after hearing on a complaint, determine what is a reasonable charge as the maximum to be paid by the carrier or carriers for the service so rendered or for the use of the instrumentality so furnished." Thus Congress clearly recognized that services such as those rendered by Peavey & Co. were services in transportation and were to be paid for notwithstanding the possibility that some advantage might be gained as a result. Meantime other elevators had sprung up, and in 1906 the Union Pacific extended the allowance made to Peavey & Co. to all elevators in Omaha, Council Bluffs and Kansas City.

But the Interstate Commerce Commission had begun to change its view upon further reflection. In 1907, upon rehearing, it cut down the allowance to Peavey & Co. to three-quarters of a cent, estimating that to be the actual cost, and being of opinion that to allow any profit would be in effect to permit a rebate. 12 I. C. C. Rep. 85. The order made required the railroad company to desist from paying more than three-fourths of a cent per hundred pounds, for service rendered in the transfer or elevation of grain at Council Bluffs or Kansas City, to any one interested in the buying, selling or shipment of grain at those places, especially naming the appellees. This is one of the orders complained of. The chief object of complaint, however, is an order made in the following year, on June 29, 1908. In that the Commission took the last step and ordered the Union Pacific to desist from paying any allowance to Peavey & Co. on grain in which they have any interest that is not reshipped from their elevators within 10 days, or that has been mixed, treated, weighed or inspected in any of their elevators at the above named points. 14 I. C. C. Rep. 315.

The ground on which the payment to owners of grain finally was held to be a rebate had been considered from the beginning and, as we have said, had been brought to the mind of Congress.

It is that when the owners of the elevators own the grain put into them they have the opportunity to perform other services to the grain in the way of treatment, or cleaning, clipping, and mixing the grain, which although not included under the term elevation or paid for by the railroad, it is an advantage to them to be able to perform at the same time. This advantage is thought to create an undue preference and unjust discrimination. Of course the opportunities for fraud are adverted to, but the ground of the decision is that even an honest payment of the bare cost of elevating grain in transit gives an undue advantage if the elevator owner also owns the grain. As was pointed out by the court below the final order is confined to grain that has been treated, weighed, inspected, or mixed.

We agree with the court below that this decision is erroneous in its conception of the grounds on which under the statute an advantage may be pronounced undue, and in its assumption that Congress has left the matter open by merely permissive words. The principle as to advantages is recognized in *Penn Refining Co.* v. *Western New York & Pennsylvania R. R. Co.*, 208 U. S. 208, 221. The law does not attempt to equalize fortune, opportunities or abilities. On the contrary the act of Congress in terms contemplates that if the carrier receives services from an owner of property transported, or uses instrumentalities furnished by the latter, he shall pay for them. That is taken for granted in § 15; the only restriction being that he shall pay no more than is reasonable, and the only permissive element being that the Commission may determine the maximum in case there is complaint (or now, upon its own motion. Act of June 18, 1910, c. 309, § 12, 36 Stat. 539, 551). As the carrier is required to furnish this part of the transportation upon request he could not be required to do it at his own expense, and there is nothing to prevent his hiring the instrumentality instead of owning it. In this case there is no complaint that the rate out of which the allowance is made is unreasonable, and it is admitted that three-quarters of a cent barely would pay the cost of the service rendered without any reasonable profit to Peavey & Co. for the work. See *Interstate Commerce Commission* v. *Stickney*, 215 U. S. 98.

In the Diffenbaugh case the order of the Commission bore the same date, June 29, 1908, as that against Peavey & Co. and the Union Pacific. It was directed against the Chicago, Burlington & Quincy Railroad Company and other competitors of the Union Pacific, and forbade their paying any sum as compensation for service rendered in the elevation of grain at Kansas City, Missouri, and other Missouri River points upon their lines. Competition, which was an element in the motives of the Union Pacific, led these other roads to make a similar arrangement. Probably, being through lines, they would not object to the Commission's order if that to the Union Pacific could be sustained. The opinion of Mr. Commissioner Prouty in this case takes somewhat different ground from that on which the orders in the Peavey case are based. 14 I. C. C. Rep. 317. See 15 *id.* 90, 93. See also *H. Gund & Co.* v. *Chicago, Burlington & Quincy R. R. Co.*, 18 I. C. C. Rep. 364. Especially it throws doubt upon the allowance being properly a transfer allowance at this present day. As the contract with Peavey & Co. purports to be only for grain transferred, it is not necessary to consider whether elevation could be allowed for as practically necessary under modern conditions even if the grain did not go on. For the purposes of this case so much of the order as meets the above-mentioned doubt by confining payments to grain reshipped within ten days seems proper enough and not open to review on the matter of fact. But when the grain has been treated the prohibition of an allowance is universal, and therefore the question that we have answered is raised by the record; the question, that is, of the power of the Commission to prohibit such allowances to grain owners in general terms. In this order it was stated expressly that the purpose of the Commission was to prohibit and stop the payment of the elevator allowances everywhere. 14 I. C. C. Rep. 510. *Ibid.* 551.

The Union Pacific made the allowances in question to elevators at its termini; it had no motive to make them anywhere else. The competitors of the Union Pacific concerned in the Diffenbaugh case were compelled by competition to make the same allowance at Missouri River points, but they also make it nowhere else. The Traffic Bureau, Merchants' Exchange of St. Louis, complained to the Commission that the result was a discrimination against St. Louis of $\frac{3}{4}$ of a cent per 100 pounds. But the principle of the decision is that the allowance to elevators upon their own grain is to be stopped everywhere unless they are prevented from using the opportunity for treating their grain. Therefore this question of preference between cities does not need to be discussed. But, as remarked below, the Union Pacific could not be complained of on this ground, 176 Fed. Rep. 424, and it would be impossible to deny the same right to competing roads, merely because as the result of the conditions one city would gain and another lose. *Louisville & Nashville R. R. Co.* v. *Behlmer*, 175 U. S. 648.

Although the order cutting down the allowance to Peavey & Co. to the estimated cost may have been influenced by erroneous views touching the powers of the Commission and the elements proper for consideration (see *Southern Railway Co.* v. *St. Louis Hay & Grain Co.*, 214 U. S. 297), we are of opinion that no sufficient reason appears for disturbing that. The Commission has decided what compensation is reasonable, and we infer that

Peavey & Co. would be content under the circumstances to render the service for three-quarters of a cent per hundred pounds rather than give it up.

The jurisdiction in the Diffenbaugh case was doubted, although the Commission did not press the point as it wishes a final decision. We are content to leave that matter on the statement of the court below. 176 Fed. Rep. 416, 417. The plaintiffs are affected by the order and it is just that they should have a chance to be heard, although not parties before the Commission.

The result is that the decree of the Circuit Court must be affirmed in its main point, but that the Commission's order of 1907, diminishing the allowance to three-quarters of a cent, and so much of the Peavey order of 1908 as confines allowances to grain reshipped within ten days, should be allowed to stand.

Decree of Circuit Court modified and affirmed.

MR. JUSTICE MCKENNA, with whom concurred MR. JUSTICE HUGHES, dissenting.

I am unable to concur in the opinion of the court.

The Commission did not hold that elevation may not properly be furnished by a railroad or be allowed for to a shipper, but held that "such elevation must be charged for at what it is reasonably worth," and without discrimination. And I understand elevation to mean "the transfer of the grain from the car of the inbound carrier, through an elevator to the car of the outbound carrier" within a given period. "In such elevation," Mr. Commissioner Harlan said, and his language I adopt, "there is nothing either preferential or discriminatory, whether done in an elevator operated by the carrier or in an elevator operated for it by the owner," but "any allowance by the carrier to the owner of an elevator on grain belonging to him that has been weighed, inspected, cleaned, mixed or otherwise treated in the process of elevation, is unlawful. As a facility for the convenience of the carrier free elevation is unobjectionable, but when the owner is permitted to and does use the elevation as a transit privilege for himself, by means of which to secure commercial advantages on his own grain, the result is an unlawful preference and discrimination."

The conclusion is not a misconstruction of the statute. Transportation simply is the business of the railroad company. Weighing, inspecting, cleaning and mixing, that is, raising the quality of the grain to suit the demand of the market, is the business of the grain dealer or others, and the two businesses are not to be confounded, and it was not, I think, the purpose of the statute to confound them. The statute makes the term "transportation" include "all instrumentalities and facilities of shipment or carriage," and it is only when the owner of property renders services "connected with such transportation, or furnishes any instrumentality used therein," that he may be compensated by the railroad. What goes beyond that transcends the statute and becomes, as the Commission held, a discrimination.

I am authorized to say that MR. JUSTICE HUGHES concurs in this dissent.

LEHIGH VALLEY RAILROAD COMPANY *v.* UNITED STATES

243 U. S. 444 (1917)

MR. JUSTICE HOLMES delivered the opinion of the court.

This is a proceeding instituted by direction of the Attorney General at the request of the Interstate Commerce Commission to prevent the appellant railroad from carrying freight at less than its published rates on file. The case was heard upon bill and answer and a stipulation, and the question is whether the facts warrant an injunction, as matter of law.

George W. Sheldon and Company is an Illinois corporation engaged in forwarding, or bringing goods for importers from the place of purchase in Europe to their destination in the United States and charging the importers for the transportation and such other services as it may perform. Of course the expectation is that it will make a profit from the transaction, although from the uncertainty of ocean freight charges it may lose, as the contract is made in advance. By arrangement with the appellant, so far as it is able it sends the goods over the appellant's line, and for doing so receives from it a varying percentage upon the published rates and also a salary of $5,000 a year. These payments by the appellant are the ground of the bill. The District Court issued an injunction as prayed. 222 Fed. Rep. 685.

As toward the railroad, George W. Sheldon and Company is consignor and consignee, and although it may be in no case the owner, that does not concern the appellant. Upon the admitted facts there can be no doubt and it is not denied that it is to all legal intents the shipper of the goods. *Interstate Commerce Commission* v. *Delaware, Lackawanna & Western R. R. Co.*, 220 U. S. 235. *Great Northern Ry. Co.* v. *O'Connor*, 232 U. S. 508. If the shipper were the owner an allowance to him of a percentage upon the freight as an inducement to ship by that line, however honest and however justifiable on commercial principles, would be contrary to the Act to Regulate Commerce as it now stands. Act of June 29, 1906, c. 3591, § 2, 34 Stat. 586, 587, amending § 6 of the original act, &c. See also the original Act of February 4, 1887, c. 104, § 2, 24 Stat. 379. *Wight* v. *United States*, 167 U. S. 512. But the above cases show that the carrier cannot inquire whether the shipper is the owner and therefore the statute expresses a necessary policy when it forbids in universal terms refunding in any manner any portion of the rates specified in the published tariffs or extending to "any shipper" any privilege not so specified. Of course it does not matter whether the allowance takes the form of a deduction or a crosspayment. Any payment made by a carrier to a shipper in consideration of his shipping goods over the carrier's line comes within the prohibiting words.

It is true no doubt that George W. Sheldon and Company in the performance of the services for which it is paid maintains offices here and abroad, advertises the Railroad, solicits traffic for it, does various other useful things, and, in short, we assume, benefits the road and earns its money, if it were allowable to earn money in that way. It is true also that in *Interstate Commerce Commission* v. *F. H. Peavey & Co.*, 222 U. S. 42, an owner of property transported was held entitled under § 15 of the Act to Regulate Commerce to an allowance for furnishing a part of the transportation that the carrier was bound to furnish. (So *Union Pacific R. R. Co.* v. *Updike Grain Co.*, 222 U. S. 215, and *United States* v. *Baltimore & Ohio R. R. Co.*, 231 U. S. 274.) But that case goes to the verge of what is permitted by the act. The services rendered by George W. Sheldon and Company, although in a practical sense "connected with such transportation," were not connected with it as a necessary part of the carriage — were not "transportation service," in the language of *Union Pacific R. R. Co.* v. *Updike Grain Co.*, 222 U. S. 215, 220 — and in our opinion were not such services as were contemplated in the Act of June 29, 1906, c. 3591, § 4, 34 Stat. 589, amending § 15 of the original act. On the other hand the allowance of them falls within the plain meaning of § 2 of the Act of 1906, to which we referred above.

There is some criticism of the form of the decree, but it prohibits with sufficient plainness all payments to George W. Sheldon and Company, whether by way of salary, commission, or otherwise, in consideration of the shipment of goods by George W. Sheldon and Company over the appellant's line.

Decree affirmed.

ATCHISON, TOPEKA & SANTA FE RAILWAY COMPANY *v.* UNITED STATES

232 U. S. 199 (1914)

In 1909, Associations, representing California fruit-growers, filed with the Commerce Commission complaints against numerous railroad companies attacking the freight and refrigeration charges on citrus fruit shipped from California to Eastern points. Much testimony was taken, from which it appeared that the orange crop amounted to about 50,000 cars per annum, of which the 20,000, shipped in warm weather, required some form of refrigeration in order to keep the fruit in condition for use at the end of the journey. At the close of the first hearing June 11, 1910, the Commission held (19 I. C. C. 148) that $1.15 per cwt. was a reasonable freight-rate on oranges. Other questions in the case were postponed until January 14, 1911, when the Commission made a report (20 I. C. C. 106) as to the reasonableness of the carriers' charges of $62.50 per car for refrigeration and $30 for services in shipments pre-cooled by the consignor.

The Commission found that in refrigeration by the carriers they furnished all the ice and performed all of the services, including re-icing en route. It found that there was a total of about 11 tons of ice furnished, but owing to the melting the average weight of ice hauled was 8,000 lbs., the freight on which to Chicago, was .25 per 100. It cost something to repair the bunkers, and the Commission recognized the right to include an additional sum to cover risk and profit.

The total revenue of $345.30 from such shipments was made up of the following items:

Freight on 27,200 lbs. of oranges @ $1.15		$312.80
Cost of 11 tons of ice	$30.	
Freight on 8,000 lbs. average weight of ice hauled @ .25	20.	
Damage to bunkers	5.	
Sum to cover risk and profit	7.50	
		62.50
Gross Receipt		$375.30
Less cost of ice		30.00
Freight and refrigeration charges		$345.30

The Commission found that the charge of $62.50 for refrigeration services was reasonable.

It further appeared that the Government had conducted certain experiments with a view of determining whether an advantage would not be derived from pre-cooling the fruit before the bunkers were filled with ice. There was testimony that the carriers had reached the conclusion that if the fruit was pre-cooled before the movement of the car began, there would be a corresponding saving in the amount of ice needed in the bunkers. They accordingly had erected plants at which the fruit could be pre-cooled and included such pre-cooling service in the regular refrigeration charge of $62.50.

Certain shippers claimed that better results were obtained where the fruit was pre-cooled immediately after it was taken from the grove and before it was placed in the car. They therefore adopted a method in which the shipper chills the fruit, cools the car, furnishes the ice and fills the bunkers at a cost to himself of $32.50. The carrier for its services in connection with hauling such pre-cooled shipment charged $30, intending thereby to make the rates on pre-cooled fruits the same, whether the pre-cooling was by the shipper or the carrier. In determining whether this $30 was a reasonable charge for service rendered by the carrier in hauling fruit pre-cooled by the shipper, the Commission said (20 I. C. C. 120) that no re-icing was necessary en route and that "it would be a liberal estimate to put the average weight of the ice during the entire journey at 5,000 lbs. For the hauling of this ice the carriers are entitled to fair compensation, as they are in the case of Standard Refrigeration." There is also an "expense in providing and keeping in repair the ice bunkers. . . . . The carrier is, therefore, entitled to this additional cost, which is about $5 per car per trip one way." (20 I. C. C. 120.)

Where the fruit is pre-cooled by the shipper, the boxes are packed so much closer together that the load is one-sixth greater than in case of shipments pre-cooled and refrigerated by the carrier. The result is that the revenue from a car of fruit pre-cooled by the shipper would be —

Freight on 33,000 lbs. of oranges at $1.15	$379.50
Freight on 5,000 lbs. of ice at 25 cents per hundred	12.50
Damage to bunkers (and profit allowed?)	7.50
	$399.50

or, $54 more than the revenue of $345.30 from a car pre-cooled and refrigerated by the carrier.

The Commission further said: "As bearing upon the reasonableness of the rate, the carriers showed the cost of the movement of these oranges per gross ton — that is, per ton of combined weight of car and of contents as compared with other articles — claiming that this was the true basis upon which to fix rates. So treating these pre-cooled shipments, it will be found that the carrier receives more per gross ton for handling the pre-cooled car than for either the ventilated or the refrigerated shipment. By every canon of rate-making which has been applied by carriers in the past, or which is relied upon by them now, these pre-cooled shipments at the standard rate without additional compensation are better business than either the ventilated or the refrigerated movement. Clearly these growers who have devised and perfected this system of shipment, should not be compelled to pay for the privilege of using it more than the fair cost to the carrier of providing the additional facilities which are not included in the ventilated rate with a fair profit." 20 I. C. C. 121.

The report concluded as follows: "We are of the opinion that the present pre-cooling charges of the defendants of $30 per car are unjust and unreasonable, and that these charges should not exceed for the future $7.50 per car, but the defendants may, as a condition of making this charge, require that pre-cooled cars be loaded seven tiers wide and two tiers high, and may provide by their tariffs a proper minimum to accomplish this result, the amount of which would depend upon the length of the car." 20 I. C. C. 123.

The carriers, in obedience to this order, put in a tariff of $7.50 for pre-cooling services, but at once filed another tariff, effective July 1, 1911, reciting that "the privilege heretofore permitted to shippers of citrus fruit to pre-ice carload shipments is withdrawn, the carriers retaining and exercising the exclusive right and control of furnishing and doing all icing and refrigeration of citrus fruit in all cases where shipper does not specifically request or direct shipments to move solely under ventilation."

Immediately thereafter the orange-growers' associations filed proceedings to cancel this withdrawal tariff and to compel the carriers to continue to extend to shippers the old privilege of pre-cooling at the new rate of $7.50. At the hearing the evidence and reports of the Commission in the former case were stipulated into the record and, on April 8, 1912 (23 I. C. C. 267, 271), the Commission held that the shippers had the right to the pre-cooling privilege and again ruled that $7.50 was a reasonable charge for the services rendered by the carriers.

The Railroad Companies then filed a petition in the Commerce Court attacking the original order of January 14, 1911 (fixing $7.50 as a reasonable charge on pre-cooled shipments) and the last order of April 8, 1912 (requiring the roads to permit pre-cooled shipments at that sum), contending that shippers had no right to ice the bunkers. They also insisted that the $7.50 rate was confiscatory and did not equal the $17.50, which the Commission itself had found to be the actual cost of services rendered in connection with pre-cooled shipments. The carriers, thereupon prayed that both orders should be annulled and set aside.

The Commerce Court (204 Fed. Rep. 647, 651) adopted the finding of the Commission that in pre-cooled shipments the revenue was $54 greater than in the Railroads' method of refrigeration, and concluded by saying that, in view of that fact, "we do not think that the petitioners have any valid complaint to make of the charge of $7.50 per car established by the Commission." It further held that under the facts appearing in the record, the shipper had the right to furnish the ice in pre-cooled shipments and thereupon it dismissed the petition. The case was then brought here by appeal.

MR. JUSTICE LAMAR, after making the foregoing statement of facts, delivered the opinion of the court.

There are many cases between shipper and carrier in which each insists that the other is bound to furnish service or facilities connected with the transportation of freight. The present record, however, presents an instance where both parties are contending for the privilege of supplying an article needed in the proper shipment of fruit — the consignor claiming that icing is a necessary part of the loading, which he is authorized to supply; while the carriers insist that icing is a part of refrigeration, by statute made transportation, which they are bound to provide and for which they are entitled to collect reasonable compensation. The determination of these conflicting claims necessitates an examination of the two methods under which, in warm weather, oranges are shipped from California to the East.

In what is called Standard Refrigeration, the boxes, of the aggregate weight of 27,200 pounds, are so placed as to leave spaces between them wide enough to admit of a free circulation of air chilled by ice in the bunkers. Subsequently the carriers put in a system of pre-cooling, under which after the cars had been loaded they were taken from the point of shipment to Refrigerating Plants owned by the carriers, where whole train-loads are pre-cooled at one time by means of blasts of very cold air driven into the car through and around the boxes. At the end of three or four hours the fruit is sufficiently chilled, the bunkers are then filled with about 10 tons of ice, furnished by the carrier, and the train is started on its journey to the East — the bunkers being re-iced from time to time as needed at stations along the route. For this entire service the Commission held that the carrier's charge of $62.50 was reasonable.

A different method obtains where the icing of the car is done by the shipper at his own expense. In that class of cases the oranges are taken from the grove directly to a cold room having a temperature of about 33° F. There the boxes are allowed to remain for periods of from 24 to 48 hours, and until the fruit is chilled to the center. When thus pre-cooled, the boxes are ready for shipment. A refrigerator car is then placed on the track opposite the door of the cold room of the warehouse with which it is connected by a collapsible enclosed passageway, so arranged as to exclude the outside air, while at the same time allowing that from the cold room to enter and cool the interior of the car. Through this passageway the oranges are trucked from the warehouse to the car and, as they have been chilled to the center, the boxes are packed close together forming a solid mass weighing 33,000 lbs., with a temperature of about 35° F. The doors and vents of the car are promptly and tightly closed, the bunkers are immediately filled with unusually large cakes of ice, in order to reduce the rate of melting, and the fruit is then forwarded under a filed tariff which provides that re-icing is unnecessary, and that the shipper will make no claim for damage occasioned by failure to re-ice in transit. For their services in connection with such pre-cooled shipments the carriers were allowed to charge $7.50 but the Commission refused to permit them to charge for the ice needed to keep the fruit cool between warehouse and destination.

1. This ruling is attacked by the appellants, who contend that icing is a part of refrigeration, which the Hepburn Act[1] makes a

[1] . . . . The term "transportation" shall include . . . . all services in connection with the receipt, delivery . . . . ventilation, refrigeration or icing, ... of property transported; and it shall be the duty of every carrier . . . . to provide and furnish such transportation upon reasonable request therefor. (Act of June 29, 1906, c. 3591, § 1, 34 Stat. 584.)

part of the transportation they are bound to furnish upon reasonable request. They insist that in order to meet the duty, thus imposed by statute, they have been compelled at great expense to erect immense plants where trainloads of fruit can be cooled and where an enormous quantity of ice is manufactured for refrigeration purposes. They argue that, being bound to furnish all necessary icing and re-icing and having at great cost prepared to furnish the supply, it is not only just, but a right given by statute, that they should be allowed to provide all needed icing or refrigeration at a rate to be approved by the Commission.

Whatever transportation service or facility the law requires the carrier to supply they have the right to furnish. They can therefore use their own cars, and cannot be compelled to accept those tendered by the shipper on condition that a lower freight rate be charged. So, too, they can furnish all the ice needed in refrigeration, for this is not only a duty and a right, under the Hepburn Act, but an economic necessity due to the fact that the carriers cannot be expected to prepare to meet the demand, and then let the use of their plants depend upon haphazard calls, under which refrigeration can be demanded by all shippers at one time and by only a few at another.

This contention was sustained by the Commission, which recognized that "the shipper has no right to provide refrigeration himself today and call upon the railroad company for that service tomorrow. To permit such a course is to demoralize the service of the defendants and prevent them from discharging their duty with economy and efficiency. . . . . It is the duty of the carrier to furnish refrigeration upon reasonable demand, and in so far as the furnishing of that refrigeration is a part of the service rendered by the carrier, the carrier may insist upon its right to furnish that service exclusively." 20 I. C. C. 116.

2. But of course this does not mean, that because the carriers have ice on hand, they can compel the shipper to have his fruit refrigerated, when, on account of the state of the weather or for other cause, he prefers to have it forwarded under ventilation only. When, however, ice is actually needed and is actually used, the question arises as to whether icing is a part of preparation which can be done by the shipper; or a part of refrigeration (transportation) which, by statute the carrier has the exclusive right to furnish.

To this question no answer can be given that will apply in all cases. For in the shipment of fruit, as in that of other articles, it is impossible to lay down a rule which definitely fixes what loading includes and by whom it must be done. Nor is there any consistent practice on this subject, since from reported cases it appears that the claims of the parties are based rather on interest than on some definite principle. Sometimes the shipper, as here, insists on the right to load and provide necessary appliances. At other times he demands that such service and appliances be furnished by the railroad company. Conversely the carriers sometimes claim, as here, the right to furnish service and facilities, while in other cases insisting that one or both must be supplied by the consignor. *Cf. National Lumber Dealers Association* v. *Atlantic Coast Line,* 14 I. C. C. 154; *Schultz* v. *Southern Pacific,* 18 I. C. C. 234; *In re Allowance for Lining and Heating Cars,* 26 I. C. C. 681; 25 I. C. C. 497.

These inconsistent and conflicting demands serve to emphasize the fact that, before the haul actually begins, the right or duty of each party, where not absolutely fixed by statute, must be decided with reference to the special facts of each case.

As a general rule, the carrier loads all freight tendered in less than carload lots while the consignor loads in all cases where, for his convenience, the car is placed at his warehouse or on public team tracks. This practice has grown up not only because the work can be more satisfactorily performed by the owner, but also because it is impossible for railroad companies economically to load cars at private warehouses or on those tracks where vehicles of the consignor or consignee come and go at the direction of the owner. 25 I. C. C. 490.

3. But loading may involve more than the mere placing of the freight on the car, since the character of the shipment may be such as to require the furnishing and placing of stakes, racks, blocks and binders needed to make the transportation safe; or, the freight may be such as to require special covering, packing, icing or heating, in order to preserve the merchandise in condition fit for use at the end of the journey. Who is to furnish these needed facilities, may be quite as uncertain as who is to place the freight on the car, and can only be determined by considering the character of the shipment, the place where the loading begins, and who can most economically perform the service required.

Neither party has a right to insist upon a wasteful or expensive service for which the consumer must ultimately pay. The interest of the public is to be considered as well as that of shippers and carriers — their rights in turn having been adjusted by a reduction in the rate, if the loading is done in whole or in part by the shipper; and by an increase in the rate where the loading is done in whole or in part by the carrier. But, by whomsoever done, the loading must be such as to fit the freight for shipment, and when — by statutory requirement, by valid order of the Commission, or by the carriers' voluntary act, — the car is placed at the consignor's warehouse to be loaded by the shipper, he may not only put the freight on the car but may do all other acts required to fit the freight for its proper shipment — at least, until under a tariff regularly filed, the carrier offers to do what is necessary to secure or preserve what has thus been placed on its car for transportation. The refrigeration and pre-cooling offered by the carrier to shippers of pre-cooled fruit was found not to be the equivalent of the method adopted by the shipper.

4. In the present case the carriers concede that in pre-cooling shipments the consignor had the right to take all of the steps for preparation except the last. They concede that he had the right to pre-cool the fruit, to pre-cool the car, to place the boxes on board the car, to stop the vents and seal the doors. But they deny that he could ice the bunkers, even though that was necessary to the complete preparation, or loading, needed in that particular class of shipments and without which the fruit would be damaged by the rise in temperature, occurring during the time the car is being hauled from the warehouse of the shipper to the icing station of the carrier. Such delay in filling bunkers would nullify most of the advantage of the expensive chilling of fruit and car necessary in the pre-cooling shipments, — permitted, if not originally encouraged, by the carrier. The privilege was withdrawn — not because the railroad companies were in position to furnish the ice at the proper time and place, but solely because the Commission had reduced the carriers' charge on pre-cooled oranges from $30 to $7.50 per car.

The icing may have been so related to refrigeration as to authorize the carriers to render that service. But manifestly they could not be expected to build refrigerating plants near each warehouse; and, the carrier not being in a position to do such icing, the consignor had the same right to provide the necessary supply that he would have had to ice a shipment of fish, to furnish and place standards to secure lumber on an open car, or to fasten to the floor articles which otherwise might be damaged by the jerks and jolts of a moving train. In the absence, therefore, of the carriers' offer, under a filed tariff, to furnish ice at the time and place needed in pre-cooled shipments, or to substitute a service of equal value at practically the same cost, they had no right to prevent the consignor from filling the bunkers so as to fit the freight for proper transportation. . . . .

INTERSTATE COMMERCE COMMISSION *v.* ILLINOIS CENTRAL RAILROAD COMPANY

215 U. S. 452 (1910)

MR. JUSTICE WHITE delivered the opinion of the court.

Whether a duty rested upon the Illinois Central Railroad Company to obey an order made by the Interstate Commerce Commission is the question here to be decided.

On the ground that preferences were created and discriminations engendered by regulations established by the railroad company concerning the daily distribution of coal cars to mines along its line in periods when the supply of such cars was inadequate to meet the demand upon it for the movement of coal, the order in question commanded the railroad company to desist from enforcing the regulations found to be preferential, and for a future period of two years to deliver cars to mines along its line in conformity with the rule announced by the commission.

A clearer perception of the questions to be considered will be afforded by giving a brief statement of the cause of car shortage referred to, accompanied with a mere outline of the steps generally taken by carriers to deal with the subject and the particular method applied by the Illinois Central Railroad Company prior to the date when the complaint was made against it, concerning which the order previously referred to was entered.

It is conceded in argument that bituminous coal mines, which are the character of mines here involved, must dispose of their product as soon as the coal is delivered at the surface, as it is not practicable for an operator to store such coal, and the amount that a mine will produce is therefore directly dependent upon the quantity that can be taken away day by day. As a result of this situation it is also conceded that railroads upon whose lines coal mines are situated pursue a system by which daily deliveries of cars, based upon requisitions of the respective mines, are made to such mines to permit of the removal of their available output for that day.

Notwithstanding full performance by railway carriers of the duty to have a legally sufficient supply of coal cars, it is conceded that unforeseen periods arise when a shortage of such cars to meet the demand for the transportation of coal takes place, because among other things, *a*, of the wide fluctuation between the demands for the transportation of bituminous coal at different and uncertain periods; *b*, the large number of loaded coal cars delivered by a carrier beyond its own line for transportation over other roads consequent upon the fact that the coal produced at a particular point is normally distributed for consumption over an extensive area; and, *c*, because the cars thus parted with are subject to longer detentions than usually obtain in the case of shipments of other articles, owing to the fact that bituminous coal is often shipped by mining operators to distant points to be sold after arrival, and is hence held at the terminal points awaiting sale, or because, owing to the cost of handling coal, and the difficulty of storing such coal, the car in which it is shipped is often used by the shipper or purchaser at the terminal points as a convenient means of storage or as an instrument for delivery, without the expense of breaking bulk, to other and distant points.

It is disclosed that the railroads of the United States generally, at various times, put in force regulations for the distribution of coal cars. Generally speaking, these regulations provide for fixing the capacity of coal mines in order to determine the number of cars to which each might normally be entitled to daily move its output of coal. And these regulations also provide for a method of determining the *pro rata* share of the cars daily allotted for distribution in times of car shortage. Neither the method by which capacity was to be ascertained nor the regulation for daily distribution upon the basis of such capacity in case of shortage was identical among the various railroad systems of the United States. The divergence, and even conflict, between those systems is illustrated by the cases of *Logan Coal Co.* v. *Pennsylvania R. R. Co.*, 154 Fed. Rep. 497; *United States ex rel. Pitcairn Coal Co.* v. *B. & O. R. R. Co.*, 165 Fed. Rep. 113; cases cited at pages 503 and 504 of the report of the Logan Coal Co. case, and the case of *Majestic Coal & Coke Co.* v. *Illinois Central R. R. Co.*, 162 Fed. Rep. 810.

In a general sense, however, all the regulations of the various railroads, either for ascertaining the capacity of coal mines or in order to determine the *pro rata* share for daily distribution of cars to the respective mines in case of shortage dealt with four classes of cars: 1, system cars, that is, cars owned by the carrier and in use for the transportation of coal; 2, company fuel cars, that is, cars belonging to the company and used by it when necessary for the movement of coal from the mines on its own line, and which coal had been bought by the carrier and was used solely for its own fuel purposes; 3, private cars, that is, cars either owned by coal mining companies or shippers or consumers, and used for the benefit of their owners in conveying coal from the mines to designated points of delivery; 4, foreign railway fuel cars, that is, cars owned by other railroad companies and which were by them delivered to the carriers on whose lines mines were situated, for the purpose of enabling the cars to be loaded with coal and returned to the company by whom the cars had been furnished, the coal being intended for use as fuel by such foreign railroad companies.

The various regulations, irrespective of minor differences between them, fell upon one or the other side of this broad line of division. One system took into account class 2, the fuel cars of the carrier, class 3, the private cars, and class 4, the cars of foreign railroads, and deducted from the rated capacity of the mine the sum of coal delivered by that mine in such cars, and upon the basis thus resulting apportioned ratably in case of shortage the system cars, that is, those embraced in class 1. On the other hand the other class of regulation not only took no account of the cars in classes 2, 3 and 4, as a means of rating the capacity of the mine, but moreover did not charge against any mine, for the purpose of ascertaining the daily *pro rata* of the cars to which such mine was entitled, any car whatever furnished such mine on such day embraced within classes 2, 3 and 4, that is, any company fuel car, foreign railway fuel car or private car. By this system, therefore, where a mine was entitled daily to a given *pro rata* of the cars subject to general distribution it received its full share of such cars, and in addition on that day also received such of the company fuel cars, foreign railway fuel cars and private cars as might have been sent to it for loading on that day. This absolute disregard in the allotment of the company fuel cars, foreign railway fuel cars and private cars was not in all respects common to all the systems which took no account of such cars in fixing capacity, since in some of the regulations one or the other of the classes was taken into account in fixing the *pro rata* for distribution.

Previous to 1907 the Railroad Commission of the State of

Ohio filed with the Interstate Commerce Commission two complaints against the Hocking Valley and another railroad company. These complaints were based upon the ground that the failure of the railroads in times of car shortage to include in the *pro rata* of cars for distribution foreign railway fuel cars and private cars, and to charge the mines which had received such cars with the same as part of their distributive share, created an undue preference and worked unjust discrimination in violation of the act to regulate commerce. On July 11, 1907, the report and opinion of the commission was announced in the cases referred to. *R. R. Comm. of Ohio* v. *Hocking Val. Ry. Co.*, 12 I. C. C. Rep. 398. It was declared that the complaints were well founded, and the relief prayed was awarded. Nine days afterwards — presumptively in ignorance of the finding of the commission just referred to — the Illinois Central Railroad Company promulgated rules governing the distribution of cars to coal mines. Although by these rules foreign fuel cars, private cars and company fuel cars were not taken into account in ascertaining the capacity of a mine or mines, such cars were expressly directed not to be counted for the purpose of the daily distribution of cars among the respective mines. On August 15 following, however, presumably to cause the regulations to conform to the interpretation of the Interstate Commerce Act adopted by the commission in the Hocking Valley case, a circular was issued by the Illinois Central Railroad Company, to go into effect September 1, 1907, cancelling the circular of July 20, 1907, and directing that account should be taken in the distribution of cars to a particular mine or mines of both foreign railway fuel and private cars. Before the date fixed for the going into effect of this last-named circular the Majestic Coal and Coke Company, a West Virginia corporation, filed a suit against the Illinois Central Railroad Company in the United States Circuit Court for the Northern District of Illinois, complaining that to charge against its distributive share of coal cars, in the event of a car shortage, the fuel cars and private cars furnished it would violate its legal rights. After hearing, a temporary injunction, preventing the going into effect of the regulations in the particulars mentioned, was issued. The distribution of coal cars thereafter continued to be made as provided in the prior circular.

With this prelude we come more immediately to the origin of the controversy before us.

On October 31, 1907, the Illinois Collieries Company filed with the Interstate Commerce Commission a complaint against the Illinois Central Railroad Company. The regulations of the railroad company as to the distribution of coal cars were assailed as unjustly discriminatory in violation of the act to regulate commerce, particularly as respected the practice of not taking into consideration foreign railway fuel cars and private cars in determining the distribution of coal cars among the various coal operators along the lines of the railroad on interstate shipments of coal. It appears that the complaint just referred to was heard before the commission, with two other complaints against other railroads involving the same general subject. In its report, which was filed in all three of the cases on April 13, 1908, *Traer* v. *Chicago & Alton R. R. Co.*, 13 I. C. C. Rep. 451, the commission held that not to count in times of car shortage when the daily distributions were made against the mine receiving the same company fuel cars, foreign railway fuel cars and private cars was a violation of the act to regulate commerce. In announcing this conclusion reference was made to the previous opinion of the commission in the Hocking Valley case, *supra*, and it was declared that the Illinois Central Railroad Company on the hearing before the commission had conceded the controlling effect of the previous ruling of the commission. Considering the temporary injunction issued by the Circuit Court of the United States for the Northern District of Illinois, the commission declared that in view of the decision of this court in the case of the *Texas & Pacific Ry. Company* v. *Abilene Cotton Oil Co.*, 204 U. S. 426, it was the duty of the commission to order the carrier to desist from the unlawful discrimination.

Although the complaint in the case of the Illinois Central Railroad Company differed from the complaints in the two other cases which were considered and passed upon by the commission at the same time, in that it did not assail the failure to take into account the company fuel cars in making distribution in times of car shortage, nevertheless the commission declared that the Illinois Central Railroad Company, both in its brief and argument, had conceded the importance of the subject to that company and had invoked the action of the commission thereon.

The order of the commission, as heretofore stated, therefore not only directed the desisting from the practice of failing to take into account the foreign railway fuel cars, private cars and the company fuel cars, but also required the carriers to establish regulations for a period of two years from July 1, 1908, providing for the counting of all such cars. The general scope of the order was, however, qualified by expressly authorizing a railroad company to deliver to a particular mine all the foreign railway fuel cars, the private cars and the company fuel cars consigned or assigned to said mine, even although the number thereof might exceed the *pro rata* share of the cars attributable to said mine when ascertained by taking into account all the cars which the order required to be considered. Where, however, the number of such cars was less than the *pro rata* share of the mine the order only permitted the carrier to add a sufficient number of system cars to make up the rightful *pro rata* number.

Being unwilling to comply with the order of the commission, the Illinois Central Railroad Company commenced the suit which is now before us to enjoin in all respects the enforcement of the order of the commission. It was averred that although the company was adequately equipped with coal cars and with sufficient motive power and operative forces, yet at times an inadequate supply of coal cars to meet the demand arose from the circumstances which we have previously stated. It was alleged that the regulations adopted by the company for ascertaining the capacity of the mines and for the distribution of cars were in all respects just and reasonable, and it was charged that the order of the commission, directing the taking into account of private cars in the distribution of cars, was unjust, unreasonable, oppressive and unlawful, because it deprived the owners of such cars of the right to the use of their own property. It was further alleged that, as to the foreign railway fuel cars, the order was also unjust, unreasonable, oppressive and unlawful, because such cars constituted no part of the equipment of the road, and, failing to count them, could not constitute an unlawful discrimination or the giving of an unjust preference within the intendment of the act to regulate commerce. Besides charging that the order to count the company fuel cars was unjust, unreasonable, etc., it was averred that the attempt of the commission to deal with such cars was beyond its power, and was but an effort to deprive the company of its lawful right to freely contract for the purchase of the fuel necessary for the operation of its road. In addition, the proceedings in the suit brought by the Majestic Coal Company were set out, the granting of a temporary injunction therein as to counting foreign railway fuel cars and private cars was alleged, and it was charged that in any event, as to those two classes of cars, the order of the commission was not lawful, since it compelled the company to violate the injunction which was yet in force. The commission answered by asserting the validity in all respects of the order by it made, substantially upon the grounds which had been set out in its report and opinion announced when the order was made. All the averments in the complaint as to want of power were traversed and it was expressly charged that the subject of the distribution of coal cars as dealt with by the order was within the administrative power delegated to the commission by the terms of the act to regulate commerce. The nature and character of the preferences and discriminations which had led the commission to conclude that unlawful discrimination and unjust preference arose from the failure to count the classes of cars referred to was alleged in subdivision XIV of the answer, a portion whereof is reproduced in the margin.[1] A certificate as to the public importance of the cause was filed by the Attorney General in compliance with § 16 as amended by the act of June 29, 1906, 34 Stat. 584, c. 3591, and the cause was thereafter submitted at the same time with one brought by the Alton Railroad, involving a similar question, to a Circuit Court held by Judges Grosscup, Baker and Kohlsaat. A single opinion was announced in both cases. 173 Fed. Rep. 930. While deciding that the complainants were not entitled to relief in so far as the order of the commission concerned the counting of foreign railway fuel cars and private cars, it was yet held that the railway companies were entitled to an injunction restraining the enforcement of the orders of the commission in so far as they directed

[1] XIV. Defendant avers that the allotment by complainant of said foreign railway fuel cars, private cars, and complainant's fuel cars to the mines receiving them in addition to the full distributive shares of such mines in the general distribution of cars by complainant and the failure by complainant to count and charge said foreign railway fuel cars, private cars, and company cars against the mines receiving them, in said general distribution, results in undue and unreasonable preference or advantage to the mines and operators receiving such cars and subjects the owners and operators of mines which do not receive such cars to undue and unreasonable prejudice and disadvantage in the following respects, to wit:

(*a*) That the operator receiving the foreign railway fuel cars, private cars, or company fuel cars thereby receives a higher percentage of cars than mines of equal capacity which do not receive such cars.

(*b*) That the operator receiving the foreign railway fuel cars, private cars, or company fuel cars may operate his mine to a fuller capacity and thereby reduce the cost of coal per ton, resulting in an increased profit on his commercial coal.

(*c*) That the operator receiving foreign railway fuel cars, private cars, or company fuel cars is enabled to increase the number of working places in

the taking into account of the cars employed by the company in hauling its own fuel. The conclusion on this latter subject was based upon the theory that, as the railroad companies took the coal which they bought for their own use from the tipple of a coal mine, and thereafter moved it for their own account and not for commercial purposes, the cars used for that purpose could not be treated as being engaged in commerce, as "commerce under these circumstances ends at the tipple." The court, however, observed:

"But this does not mean that these cars do not affect the problem of an equitable distribution of commercial equipment. The mine operators are objects of interest under the interstate commerce law, not as diggers of coal, but as shippers who tender a commercial product for transportation by interstate common carriers. The basis, therefore, on which the mines in a district should be rated is not their average output as a physical question, but the average output which they respectively tender for transportation in commerce."

And in accord with this reasoning it was in conclusion remarked that the complainants as to the cars used for hauling their fuel were entitled to an injunction "against their being compelled to take fuel cars into consideration except as a means in determining the true capacities of the mines to tender coal to them for transportation in commerce."

From the final decree enjoining the commission from enforcing its order, in so far as it directed the taking into account the com-

the mine, is enabled to develop his mine more rapidly, is enabled to increase his capacity rating, and in future reratings of such mine by complainant for the purposes of car distribution the mine would receive a higher rating and consequently a larger number of cars in complainants' general distribution of cars.

(*d*) That the operator receiving the foreign railway fuel cars, private cars, or company fuel cars is enabled thereby to secure and hold a larger, more efficient, and regular working force of miners and laborers.

(*e*) That the development of the mines which do not receive the foreign railway fuel cars, private cars, or company fuel cars is retarded in inverse ratio as the development of the mines receiving said cars is accelerated.

(*f*) That by the arbitrary allotment of the foreign railway fuel cars, private cars, or company fuel cars the complainant and the so-called foreign railways are enabled to secure low prices on railway fuel because the operator receiving such cars is enabled to produce his commercial coal at much lower prices than do the mines which do not receive such arbitrary cars.

(*g*) That the operator of the mine receiving the foreign railway fuel cars, private cars, or company fuel cars is thereby enabled to make contracts for the delivery of coal distributed over a long period, to an extent that the operator of the mines which do not receive such cars cannot do.

pany fuel cars in the distribution of coal cars in times of car shortage and in so far as it directed the future taking such cars into account, the Interstate Commerce Commission appeals. . . . .

When coal is received from the tipple of a coal mine into coal cars by a railway company, and the coal is intended for its own use and is transported by it, it is said there is no consignor, no consignee and no freight to be paid, and therefore, although there may be transportation, there is no shipment, and hence no commerce. In changed form these propositions but embody the reasoning which led the court below to its conclusion that, under the circumstances, commerce ended at the tipple of the mine. The deduction from the proposition is, as the movement of coal under the conditions stated is not commerce, it is therefore not within the authority delegated to the commission by the act of Congress, as all such acts have relation to the regulation of commerce, and do not, therefore, embrace that which is not commerce. It is to be observed, in passing, that if the proposition be well founded, it not only challenges the authority of the commission, but extends much further, and in effect denies the power of Congress to confer authority upon the commission over the subject. In all its aspects the proposition calls in question the construction given to the law by the commission in every case where the subject has been before it, and also assails the correctness of numerous decisions in the lower Federal courts, to which we have previously referred, where the subject, in various forms, was considered. It goes further than this, since it, in effect, seeks to avoid the fair inferences arising from the regulations adopted by the railroad company. Those regulations, in providing for the obligation of the railroad company to supply cars, and recognizing the duty of equality of treatment, found it necessary, by express provision, to provide that private cars, foreign railway cars and company fuel cars should not be counted against the mine on the day when furnished, thus implying that, under the general rule of equality, if not restricted, it was considered the duty would exist to consider such cars. The contention, moreover, conflicts with the rule which, as we have seen, obtains in other and great systems of railroad, by which, for the purpose of avoiding inequality and preference, foreign railway fuel cars, private cars and company fuel cars are made one of the factors upon which a mine is rated in order to fix the basis upon which its distributive share of cars is to be allotted in case of car shortage. And, from this, it must follow, if the proposition contended for be maintained, that it would not only relieve the railroad company, whose rights are here involved, from the obligation of taking into account its fuel cars in the making of the distribution, but from the duty even to consider them for the purpose of capacity rating. As a result, it would lead to the overthrow of the system of rating, prevailing on other railroads, by which, as we have said, such cars are taken into account, a consequence which is well illustrated by the case of *Logan Coal Co.* v. *Pennsylvania R. R. Co.*, 154 Fed. Rep. 497.

Under these conditions, it is clear that doubt, if it exist, must be resolved against the soundness of the contentions relied on. But that rule of construction need not be invoked, as we think, when the erroneous assumption upon which the proposition must rest is considered, its unsoundness is readily demonstrable. That assumption is this, that commerce in the constitutional sense only embraces shipment in a technical sense, and does not, therefore, extend to carriers engaged in interstate commerce, certainly in so far as so engaged, and the instrumentalities by which such commerce is carried on, a doctrine the unsoundness of which has been apparent ever since the decision in *Gibbons* v. *Ogden*, 9 Wheat. 1, and which has not since been open to question. It may not be doubted that the equipment of a railroad company engaged in interstate commerce, included in which are its coal cars, are instruments of such commerce. From this it necessarily follows that such cars are embraced within the governmental power of regulation which extends, in time of car shortage, to compelling a just and equal distribution and the prevention of an unjust and discriminatory one.

SWIFT & COMPANY *v.* HOCKING VALLEY RAILWAY COMPANY

243 U. S. 281 (1917)

Mr. Justice Brandeis delivered the opinion of the court.

The National Convention of Railway Commissioners, an association comprising the commissioners of the several States, adopted in November, 1909, a Uniform Demurrage Code. Its action was based upon extensive investigations and thorough discussion, participated in by the railroad commissioners, commercial organizations, representatives of railroads and individual shippers from all parts of the country. On December 18, 1909, the Interstate

Commerce Commission endorsed the rules so adopted and recommended "that they be made effective on interstate transportation throughout the country." *In re Demurrage Investigation*, 19 I. C. C. 496.

These rules provide that after two days' free time "cars held for or by consignors or consignees for loading" or unloading shall, (with certain exceptions not here material) pay a demurrage charge of $1 per car per day. Private cars are specifically included by the following note:

NOTE. — Private cars while in railroad service, whether on carrier's or private tracks, are subject to these demurrage rules to the same extent as cars of railroad ownership.

(Empty private cars are in railroad service from the time they are placed by the carrier for loading or tendered for loading on the orders of a shipper. Private cars under lading are in railroad service until the lading is removed and cars are regularly released. Cars which belong to an industry performing its own switching service, are in railroad service from the time they are placed by the industry upon designated interchange tracks, and thereby tendered to the carrier for movement. If such cars are subsequently returned empty, they are out of service when withdrawn by the industry from the interchange; if returned under load, railroad service is not at an end until the lading is duly removed.)

In 1910 the Hocking Valley Railway Company, an interstate carrier, inserted in its freight tariff duly filed and published as required by the Act to Regulate Commerce, the demurrage rules and charges, including that relating to private cars quoted above. Thereafter, Swift & Company, Chicago meat packers, established on the line of that railroad at Athens, Ohio, a warehouse to which it made, from time to time, shipments in private cars. These cars, which were placed on the switch used in connection with the warehouse, were not unloaded within the forty-eight hours' free time allowed by the tariff; and demurrage charges were assessed by the Railway Company. Payment being refused, this action was brought in the Court of Common Pleas of Cuyahoga County, Ohio, to recover the amount. The amended petition alleged, among other things, that the demurrage rules and charges had been "approved by the Interstate Commerce Commission, by a decision rendered by said Commission on the 14th day of November, 1910, in the case of Procter and Gamble Company against Cincinnati, Hamilton & Dayton Railway Company et al., which decision is reported in the 19th volume of the Interstate Commerce

Commission Reports, pages 556 to 560, inclusive thereof, and which decision, approving said car demurrage rules and charges, is hereby referred to and made a part hereof, as though the same were fully written out at length herein."

Swift & Company demurred; and defended on the single ground that the cars in question were its private cars standing on its "private track"; contended that the demurrage rule which required payment of charges under such circumstances was an arbitrary imposition; that it was unlawful and void; and that it was subject to collateral attack, even though included in a tariff duly filed and published under the Act to Regulate Commerce. Two days after the case had been heard on demurrer in the Court of Common Pleas, counsel filed a stipulation as follows:

"For the purpose only of reviewing the judgment of the Common Pleas Court on defendant's demurrer to the amended petition, it is stipulated by the parties hereto that the track on which the cars in question were placed was the private track of Swift and Company."

The next day judgment was rendered for the Railway Company. It was affirmed both by the Court of Appeals of Cuyahoga County and by the Supreme Court of Ohio. 93 Ohio St. 143.

The Supreme Court of Ohio assumed the track in question to be a "private track" as stipulated by the parties, and declared that "demurrage rules relating to private cars employed in interstate commerce and the charges assessable thereunder are matters properly included in the tariff or schedule required to be filed and published. This tariff containing the demurrage rule having been filed and published according to law, was binding alike on carrier and shipper, and so long as it was in force was to be treated as though it were a statute. . . . . This rule having been approved by a federal tribunal, acting within the scope of its authority, its decision must be followed by the courts of this state and be given full force and effect."

The case was then brought to this court on writ of error. The errors assigned were, in substance, that the demurrage rule was repugnant to the Act to Regulate Commerce and that the decisions below deprived Swift & Company of its property without the due process of law guaranteed by the Fourteenth Amendment.

Prior to the bringing of this action the Interstate Commerce Commission had held in *Procter & Gamble Co.* v. *Cincinnati, Hamilton & Dayton Ry. Co.*, 19 I. C. C. 556, that carriers were "within their lawful rights in establishing and maintaining" the above rule for demurrage charges on private cars. The Commerce Court approved the finding. *Procter & Gamble Co.* v. *United States*, 188 Fed. Rep. 221, 227. An effort to secure a review of these decisions by this court failed. *Procter & Gamble Co.* v. *United States*, 225 U. S. 282.

We do not find it necessary to decide whether the ruling of the Supreme Court of Ohio was correct; or whether the rule concerning demurrage charges on private cars is in all respects valid; or whether a shipper who has delivered private cars to a carrier knowing such rule to be in force is in a position to question its validity in an action for charges accruing thereunder. For the record discloses, contrary to the statement in the stipulation, that the track in question was *not* a "private track."

The facts which determine the character of the switch and the relation to it of carrier and shipper were carefully set forth in the amended petition and the "License" annexed, copied in the margin.[1] Under it Swift & Company occupied a part of the Railway Company's premises for its warehouse and office and en-

[1] Exhibit "B." — *License.* — Memorandum of agreement, made this twenty-second day of March, A. D. 1911, by and between the Hocking Valley Railway Company, a corporation existing under the laws of the State of Ohio, hereinafter known as the "Railway Company," party of the first part, and Swift & Company, a corporation whose principal place of business is in Chicago, County of Cook, State of Illinois, hereinafter known as the "Licensee," party of the second part, Witnesseth:

Whereas, the Licensee, at its own request, desires to occupy a tract of ground belonging to the Railway Company at Athens, Ohio, for the purpose of maintaining thereon a warehouse and office in connection with its business at that point, together with all the improvements and appurtenances thereto, in such a manner as not in any way to interfere with the premises, buildings, structures, tracks or business of said Railway Company, upon the following described premises, to wit:

The Northeast part of outlot No. 112 and the Northwest part of outlot No. 113, in the Village of Athens, Ohio, fronting 175 feet on the South side of State Street, immediately West of the premises occupied by the Standard Oil Company, said tract extending Southward from said street to the North side of the Railway Company's siding, known as the "Bank Track" as will more clearly appear shaded in yellow on blue print hereto attached and made a part hereof, for a period of five (5) years, beginning on the 1st day of November, 1910, at a rental of Thirty ($30.00) Dollars per annum, payable annually in advance on the following terms and conditions, to-wit:

First. This agreement shall not be assigned by the Licensee without the written consent of the Railway Company being first obtained, and in case the said Licensee shall permit its interests to be seized or sold under legal process, this agreement shall thereupon become null and void.

Second. The switch of the Railway Company hereby let and connected

joyed the rights in the switch from its main lines. The "License" recites, among other things, the Licensee's desire "to occupy a tract of ground belonging to the Railway Company . . . . for the purpose of maintaining thereon a warehouse and office . . . .

---

with its main line, shall at all times be under control of the Railway Company.

Third. The Railway Company shall have the right at all times to enter upon the premises hereby let, for the purpose of repairing or maintaining the track thereon, or switching or removing cars thereover.

Fourth. Either party hereto may terminate this agreement at any time, after giving to the other party thirty (30) days' notice in writing, and at or before the termination of said thirty (30) days said Licensee shall at its own expense remove all said improvements from said premises, without causing damage of any kind to the property of the Railway Company. Upon its failure to do so within said time the Railway Company may make such removal at the sole cost of the Licensee.

Fifth. The Licensee shall pay all taxes assessed upon improvements upon said premises or said premises by reason thereof and will at all times hereafter indemnify and save harmless the Railway Company, its successors and assigns, from and against all loss, costs, charges and accidents whatsoever, which it may suffer, sustain or in any wise be subjected to, on account of injuries accruing to its property, or loss or damage to the property of any other person or corporation, arising out of, resulting from or in any manner caused by the construction, erection, maintenance, presence or use of said improvements installed or existing under this agreement, and said Railway Company shall not be liable in any way for any loss or damage to said improvements or to any property belonging to or in the possession or control of said Licensee on or about said premises, resulting from the operation of and use of its railway, engines, cars or machinery, or by reason of fire or sparks therefrom, or any other casualty arising from the use and operation of its railway, and shall be held forever free and harmless by said Licensee from any such liability.

Sixth. The Licensee shall consign all products shipped to it, intended to be placed on the siding hereby let, where the rates and services are equal, via the line or lines of the Railway Company, and shall give said Railway Company the long hauls thereof.

Seventh. The Licensee hereby accepts the License herein made with the above specified terms and conditions, and agrees that any failure or default on its part as to either of the same, may be held and considered a forfeiture and surrender of this License by it.

In Witness Whereof, the parties hereto have caused this instrument to be executed in duplicate, on the day and year first above written.

THE HOCKING VALLEY RAILROAD COMPANY,

(Signed) BY W. L. MATTOON, *Real Estate Agent.*

SWIFT & COMPANY,

(Signed) BY L. B. SWIFT.

Witness:

(Signed) E. OSLER HUGHES.

Witness:

(Signed) D. E. HARTWELL.

in such a manner as not in any way to interfere with the . . . . tracks . . . . of said Railway Company . . . . "; that the premises lie on "the North side of the Railway Company's siding, known as the 'Bank Track' . . . ."; that "the switch of the Railway Company hereby let and connected with its main line, shall at all times be under control of the Railway Company"; and that "the Railway Company shall have the right at all times to enter upon the premises hereby let, for the purpose of repairing or maintaining the track thereon, or switching or removing cars thereover." A rental of $30 per annum is provided for; but the license is terminable on 30 days' notice.

These facts were admitted by the demurrer. Upon them the case was heard by the Court of Common Pleas; and upon them the case must be decided in this court, unaffected by stipulation of counsel made "for the purpose only of reviewing the judgment of the Common Pleas Court." The construction and effect of a written instrument is a question of law. *Dillon* v. *Barnard*, 21 Wall. 430, 437. Clearly the track in question was not a private track of the shipper but a track of the carrier — like the spur passed upon in *National Refining Co.* v. *St. Louis, I. M. & S. Ry. Co.*, 237 Fed. Rep. 347, affirming 226 Fed. Rep. 357.

If the stipulation is to be treated as an agreement concerning the legal effect of admitted facts, it is obviously inoperative; since the court cannot be controlled by agreement of counsel on a subsidiary question of law.[1] If the stipulation is to be treated as an attempt to agree "for the purpose only of reviewing the judgment" below that what are the facts shall be assumed not to be facts, a moot or fictitious case is presented. "The duty of this court, as of every judicial tribunal, is limited to determining rights of persons or of property, which are actually controverted in the particular case before it. . . . . No stipulation of parties or counsel, whether in the case before the court or in any other case, can enlarge the power, or affect the duty, of the court in this regard." *California* v. *San Pablo & Tulare R. R. Co.*, 149 U. S. 308, 314. See *Mills* v. *Green*, 159 U. S. 651, 654. The fact that effect was given to the stipulation by the appellate courts of Ohio does not conclude this court. See *Tyler* v. *Judges of Court*

[1] *San Francisco Lumber Co.* v. *Bibb*, 139 Cal. 325; *Owen* v. *Herzihoff*, 2 Cal. App. 622; *Aubuchon* v. *Bender*, 44 Mo. 560; *Prescott* v. *Brooks*, 94 N. W. Rep. 88, 94 (N. D.); *Holms* v. *Johnson*, 59 Tenn. 155. See also *Breeze* v. *Haley*, 11 Colo. 351, 362; *Lyon* v. *The Robert Garrett Lumber Co.*, 77 Kans. 823, 827; *Wells* v. *Covenant Mutual Benefit Assn.*, 126 Mo., 630, 639.

of Registration, 179 U. S. 405, 410. We treat the stipulation, therefore, as a nullity.

Consignors or consignees of freight shipped in private cars pay the same rates for transportation as if the commodities had been shipped in the cars owned by the carriers; but the owners or lessees of private cars are paid or allowed by the carriers (east of the Mississippi River) a sum equal to three-fourths of a cent per mile for refrigerator or tank cars and three-fifths of a cent per mile for other cars. The cars are returned by the railroads to the owners without extra charge. The mileage allowance is paid for the return trip as well as on the journey to destination with load. And if the private car owner does not furnish a load for the return journey the carriers have the right to load the cars. *Re Demurrage Charges on Tank Cars*, 13 I. C. C. 378, 379.

Swift & Company's cars were, therefore, though privately owned, still in railroad service while under lading. The cars while on the switch were on track owned by the Railway Company. The "transportation" within the meaning of the Act to Regulate Commerce had not ended. It cannot be said that a charge for detention of a private car and use of a railroad track under such circumstance is unreasonable. Even before the adoption of the Uniform Demurrage Code such a charge had been upheld by the Interstate Commerce Commission. *Cudahy Packing Co.* v. *Chicago & Northwestern Ry. Co.*, 12 I. C. C. 446. Defendant's argument was based wholly upon the assumption that the switch was a "private track"; and the propriety of such a charge for cars detained on a public track seems not to have been questioned.

Affirmed.

MR. JUSTICE MCKENNA, MR. JUSTICE VAN DEVANTER and MR. JUSTICE MCREYNOLDS dissent.

NEW YORK CENTRAL & HUDSON RIVER RAILROAD COMPANY *v.* BOARD OF CHOSEN FREEHOLDERS OF THE COUNTY OF HUDSON

227 U. S. 248 (1913)

MR. CHIEF JUSTICE WHITE delivered the opinion of the court.

The rails of the main line of the West Shore Railroad Company extend from Buffalo to Albany, New York, and beyond through the State of New York into New Jersey to the terminus of the road at Weehawken on the west bank of the Hudson river. From Weehawken steam ferries known as the West Shore Railroad ferries are operated over the river to several terminal points in New York City for the purpose of carrying railroad passengers and traffic from Weehawken to New York and from New York to Weehawken. Although these ferries are known as West Shore Railroad ferries and are operated as railroad ferries, their business is not limited to incoming persons or traffic carried over the lines of the railroad or to persons or traffic conveyed from New York to Weehawken to be transported from there over the railroad. Indeed, from both directions a very large number of persons besides considerable traffic "constantly move to and fro between the two States, not having used or intending to use the lines of the West Shore Railroad."

In 1905 the Board of Chosen Freeholders of Hudson County, New Jersey, adopted two ordinances, one fixing the rate for foot passengers ferried from New Jersey to New York and the other for a round trip commencing on the New Jersey shore, which rates were applicable to the ferries in question. The New York Central & Hudson River Railroad, engaged as a lessee in operating the lines of the West Shore Railroad and its railroad ferries, commenced this proceeding to prevent the enforcement of the rates fixed by the ordinances. The contention was that the ordinances were an unwarranted interference with the interstate business of the company and that the enforcement of the ordinances would constitute a direct burden on interstate commerce, which could not be done consistently with the Constitution. The Supreme Court of New Jersey maintained the contentions of the railroad company. The Court of Errors and Appeals reversed the judgment of the Supreme Court. 76 N. J. Law, 664. The case is now here, the writ of error having been directed to the Supreme Court, to which the record was remitted from the Court of Errors and Appeals.

At the outset it is to be observed that the contentions pressed in argument by both parties take a wider range than the necessities of the case require. We make a very brief reference to certain decisions of this court referred to in argument by both parties in order that they may aid us to mark plainly the boundaries of the real issues required to be decided, thus enabling us to put out of view irrelevant considerations and confine our attention to things essential.

Fanning v. *Gregoire*, 16 How. 524, required a consideration of the right of the legislature of Iowa to authorize a ferry across the Mississippi river at Dubuque. Without going into details it suffices to say that the subject was elaborately considered and the power of the State to grant the ferry right was sustained. In *Conway* v. *Taylor's Executors*, 1 Black, 603, the right of the State of Kentucky to grant franchises for ferrying across the Ohio river, was considered and the power was upheld, the general reasoning stated in *Fanning* v. *Gregoire* being reiterated and approved. It is undoubtedly true that in the course of the reasoning of both the cases just referred to expressions were made use of which give some support to the view that the power to regulate ferriage, even as to a stream bounding two States, was purely local, not transferred by the States to Congress, and therefore not within the grant of power to Congress to regulate commerce.

Gloucester Ferry Co. v. *Pennsylvania*, 114 U. S. 196, concerned the validity of a tax imposed by the State of Pennsylvania on a ferry company operating between Gloucester, New Jersey, and the city of Philadelphia. The tax was resisted on the ground that it was a direct burden on interstate commerce and therefore void as an interference with the power of Congress to regulate commerce. The contention was sustained. The whole subject of ferriage was elaborately considered, and in the course of the opinion it was expressly declared, after considering the decisions in *Fanning* v. *Gregoire* and *Conway* v. *Taylor's Executors*, that ferriage over a stream constituting a boundary between two States was within the grant to Congress to regulate commerce, and therefore not subject to be directly burdened by a State. It was also, however, held that in view of the character of such ferries and the diversity of regulation which might be required, the right to regulate them came within that class of subjects which although within the power of Congress the States had the right to deal with until Congress had manifested its paramount and exclusive authority.

In *Covington Bridge Co.* v. *Kentucky*, 154 U. S. 204, the right of the State of Kentucky to impose tolls for use of a bridge across the Ohio river, was challenged on the ground that the State had no authority to fix the tolls, because to do so was the assertion of a power to regulate commerce and therefore was an interference with the exclusive power of Congress on that subject. The tolls were held to be invalid. The opinion beyond question reasserted the principle enforced in the *Gloucester Ferry Case* that the movement across a stream, the boundary between two States, was within the grant of power to Congress to regulate commerce and therefore, generically speaking, not subject to the exertion of state authority. Indeed, in view of the fact that there was no act of Congress dealing with the subject of the tolls which were under review in the *Covington Case*, it is true to say that there are expressions in the opinion in that case which have been considered, whether rightly or wrongly we do not feel called upon to say, as qualifying or overruling the conclusion expressed in the *Gloucester Case* as to the power of a State to regulate ferries upon a stream bordering two States until Congress had manifested its purpose to exert its authority over the subject.

In *St. Clair County* v. *Interstate Transfer Co.*, 192 U. S. 454, the question considered was the liability of the Transfer Company to penalties imposed by the County of St. Clair, a municipal corporation of the State of Illinois, for having failed to obtain a license "for carrying on a ferry for transferring railroad cars, loaded or unloaded, over the county of St. Clair in Illinois to the Missouri shore and from the Missouri shore to the county of St. Clair." It was decided that there was no liability for the penalty (a) because the business of transferring freight cars in the sense disclosed was not ferriage in the proper meaning of that word, and was the transaction of interstate commerce not in any view subject to state control; and (b) because the particular ordinance relied upon as the basis for imposing the penalty was void because of provisions discriminating against interstate commerce which it contained. The cases of *Fanning* v. *Gregoire*, *Conway* v. *Taylor's Executors*, *Gloucester Ferry Co.* v. *Pennsylvania* and *Covington Bridge Co.* v. *Kentucky* were referred to. It was expressly declared in view of the special grounds upon which the case was decided that it was unnecessary to consider whether the decision in the *Covington Bridge Case* had established the doctrine that the interstate business of ferrying over navigable rivers bordering two States was exclusively within the authority of Congress to regulate, and therefore was not, as declared in the *Gloucester Ferry Case*, subject to state regulation until Congress had exerted its authority over the matter.

In the light of this statement we come to state the contentions of the parties. The plaintiff in error insists, not following the exact order of its argument, *a*, that the assailed ordinances are repugnant to the commerce clause because Congress has legislated concerning railroad ferries and thereby manifested its purpose that there should be no longer room for the exertion of state power on the subject; and, *b*, that if this is not so it is now necessary to pass on the question reserved in the *St. Clair Case*, and to decide that the ruling in the *Covington Bridge Case* affirmatively established that interstate ferriage like that here in question is so absolutely within the power of Congress as to exclude even in case of the inaction of Congress the presumption of a license for the exercise of state power. On the other hand, the argument for the defendant in error is this: That the carrying on of the business of ferriage on navigable rivers constituting a boundary between States is not interstate commerce, that the power to regulate it was not surrendered by the States and consequently no authority was given over the subject to Congress. This is sought to be shown by a copious review of adjudged cases, and by an analysis of what it is urged was the clear intendment of the opinion in *Gibbons* v. *Ogden*, especially as elucidated by the opinions in *Fanning* v. *Gregoire* and *Conway* v. *Taylor's Executors*. It is not denied that these theories are directly contrary to the ruling in the *Gloucester Ferry Case*, but it is urged that that case for the first time announced the doctrine of a national power over interstate ferriage and therefore practically amounted to making a new constitutional provision on the subject. Obviously, however, the views just stated are advanced in a mere academic sense, since the argument admits that the ruling in the *Gloucester Ferry Case* is now conclusive and has settled the significance of the Constitution contrary to the views mentioned. Thus, at the very outset of the argument, after stating and elaborating the theory of exclusive state power over interstate ferriage, it is said: "The decision of the *Gloucester Ferry Case*, 114 U. S. 196, decided in 1885, established Federal jurisdiction to legislate concerning ferriage over boundary streams, but did not turn what had been an exclusive state jurisdiction into an exclusive Federal jurisdiction. State laws on this subject are still valid until superseded by a Federal statute." Again, after copiously reiterating the conceptions as to the novelty of the ruling in the *Gloucester Ferry Case* and its assumed conflict with what had gone before, it is said: "The result of the *Gloucester Ferry Case*, therefore, with the other cases which have followed, has probably been to so extend the Federal authority over interstate ferriage as to bring the subject within the concurrent jurisdiction of Congress and of the States. It is a concurrent jurisdiction only, however, which has been established. In the absence of Federal legislation the States have all the power that they have been accustomed to exercise." Thus conceding the controlling force of the *Gloucester Ferry Case* and therefore not questioning the power of Congress which that case upheld, it is urged that the *Covington Bridge Case* should not be now held to have overruled or qualified the *Gloucester Ferry Case* so as to exclude the States from any right to regulate interstate ferriage before and until Congress has manifested its intention to exert its authority by dealing with the subject. Upon the assumption thus stated it is insisted that the court below rightly upheld the assailed ordinances because there has been no action by Congress exerting its authority over the subject with which the ordinances deal and therefore no room for the contention that it was not within the power of the State to enact them.

It is therefore apparent that the contentions of the plaintiff in error primarily invoke only the controlling effect of the ruling in the *Gloucester Ferry Case,* and insist that there has been action by Congress which destroys the presumption of authority in the State to act. It follows that the proposition that the *Covington Bridge Case* overruled the *Gloucester Ferry Case* is merely subordinate, and need not be considered unless it becomes necessary in consequence of an adverse ruling on the primary contention concerning the application of the *Gloucester Ferry Case.*

It is equally clear that the contention of the defendant in error as to the absence of all power in Congress over interstate ferries is merely academic. From this it necessarily arises that the only ground relied upon to sustain the judgment below is the ruling in the *Gloucester Ferry Case,* and the further proposition that there has been no action of Congress over the subject of the ferriage here involved which authorizes the holding that state power no longer obtains. As, therefore, the claim on the one side of an all-embracing and exclusive Federal power may be, temporarily at least, put out of view and the assertion on the other of an absolutely exclusive state power may also be eliminated from consideration because not relied upon or because it is both demonstrated and admitted to be without foundation, it follows that to dispose of the case we are called upon only, following the ruling in the *Gloucester Ferry Case,* to determine the single and simple question whether there has been such action by Congress as to destroy the presumption as to the existence in the State of vicarious and revocable authority over the subject. We say simple question because its decision is, we think, free from difficulty, in view of the express provision of the first section of the Act to Regulate Commerce (act of February 4, 1887, c. 104, 24 Stat. 379), subjecting railroads as therein defined to the authority of Congress, and expressly declaring that "the term railroad as used in this act shall include all bridges and ferries used or operated in connection with any railroad, and also all the road in use by any corporation operating a railroad, whether owned or operated under a contract, agreement or lease. . . . ." The inclusion of railroad ferries within the text is so certain and so direct as to require nothing but a consideration of the text itself. Indeed, this inevitable conclusion is not disputed in the argument for the defendant in error, but it is insisted that as the text only embraces railroad ferries and the ordinances were expressly decided by the court below only to apply to persons other than railroad passengers, therefore the action by Congress does not extend to the subject embraced by the ordinances. But as all the business of the ferries between the two States was interstate commerce within the power of Congress to control and subject in any event to regulation by the State as long only as no action was taken by Congress, the result of the action by Congress leaves the subject, that is, the interstate commerce carried on by means of the ferries, free from control by the State. We think the argument by which it is sought to limit the operation of the act of Congress to certain elements only of the interstate commerce embraced in the business of ferriage from State to State is wanting in merit. In the absence of an express exclusion of some of the elements of interstate commerce entering into the ferriage, the assertion of power on the part of Congress must be treated as being coterminous with the authority over the subject as to which the purpose of Congress to take control was manifested. Indeed, this conclusion is inevitable since the assumption of a purpose on the part of Congress to divide its authority over the elements of interstate commerce intermingled in the movement of the regulated interstate ferriage would be to render the national authority inefficacious by the confusion and conflict which would result. The conception of the operation at one and the same time of both the power of Congress and the power of the States over a matter of interstate commerce is inconceivable, since the exertion of the greater power necessarily takes possession of the field, and leaves nothing upon which the lesser power may operate. To concede that the right of a State to regulate interstate ferriage exists "only in the absence of Federal legislation" and at the same time to assert that the state and Federal power over such subject is concurrent is a contradiction in terms. But this view has been so often applied as to cause the subject to be no longer open to controversy. *Chicago, Rock Island & Pacific Ry. Co.* v. *Hardwick Farmers' Elevator Company*, 226 U. S. 426. Because in the *St. Clair Case, supra*, it was decided that a particular character of transportation of interstate commerce was not ferriage and not within state power, even where there had been no action by Congress, affords no reason for in this case extending state authority to a subject to which, consistently with the action of Congress, it cannot be held to apply.

The judgment of the Supreme Court of the State of New Jersey will be reversed and the case remanded for further proceedings not inconsistent with this opinion.

Reversed.

CHAPTER II

DUTIES OF CARRIER UNDER THE ACT

1. Services to be Rendered

LOUISVILLE & NASHVILLE RAILROAD COMPANY *ET AL.* v. UNITED STATES *ET AL.*

242 U. S. 60 (1916)

Mr. Justice Holmes delivered the opinion of the court.

This is an appeal from a decree, made by three judges sitting in the District Court, which denied a preliminary injunction against the enforcement of an order of the Interstate Commerce Commission and dismissed the appellants' petition. 227 Fed. Rep. 258, *id.* 273. See 33 I. C. C. 76, for the report of the Interstate Commerce Commission. The order complained of required the appellants, the Louisville & Nashville Railroad Company, the Nashville, Chattanooga & St. Louis Railway and the Louisville & Nashville Terminal Company to desist and abstain "from maintaining a practice whereby they refuse to switch interstate competitive traffic to and from the tracks of the Tennessee Central Railroad Company at Nashville, Tenn., on the same terms as interstate non-competitive traffic, while interchanging both kinds of said traffic on the same terms with each other, as said practice is found by the Commission in its said report to be unjustly discriminatory." It was further ordered, that "The Louisville & Nashville Railroad Company, Nashville, Chattanooga & St. Louis Railway, and Louisville & Nashville Terminal Company be, and they are hereby notified and required to establish, on or before May 1, 1915, upon notice to the Interstate Commerce Commission and to the general public by not less than 30 days' filing and posting in the manner prescribed in section 6 of the act to regulate commerce, and thereafter to maintain and apply to the switching of interstate traffic to and from the tracks of the Tennessee Central Railroad Company at said Nashville, rates and charges which shall not be different than they contemporaneously maintain with respect to similar shipments to and from their respective tracks in said city, as said relation is found by the Commission in its said report to be nondiscriminatory."

The appellants contend as matter of law that the relations between them exclude any charge of discrimination that is based only upon a refusal to extend to the Tennessee Central road the advantages that they enjoy.

The order is based upon discrimination and is limited by the duration of the interchange between the appellants found to be discriminatory, and the question argued by the appellants is the only question in the case. Therefore it is necessary to consider relations between the appealing railroads that were left on one side in *Louisville & Nashville R. R. Co.* v. *United States,* 238 U. S. 1, 18.

The Louisville & Nashville traverses Nashville from north to south, the Nashville & Chattanooga from, west to southeast, the Tennessee Central from northwest to east. They all are competitors for Nashville traffic. In 1872, contemplating a possible Union Station, the Louisville & Nashville acquired trackage rights from the Nashville & Chattanooga that connected its northern and southern terminals in the city (previously separate), and the terminal of the Nashville & Chattanooga. It now owns seventy-one per cent. of the stock of the latter. In 1893 these two roads caused the appellant Terminal Company to be organized under the general laws of Tennessee, with the right to let its property. The Louisville & Nashville owns all the stock of this company. In 1896 the two roads respectively let to the Terminal Company their several properties in the neighborhood of the original depot grounds of the Nashville & Chattanooga for 999 years, and shortly afterwards the Terminal made what is termed a lease of the same and subsequently acquired property to the two roads jointly for a like term. It covenanted to construct all necessary passenger and freight buildings, tracks and terminal facilities, the roads to pay annually as rental four per cent. of the actual cost, and to keep the properties in repair. The terminal Company then made a contract with the city for the construction of a Union Station, the two roads guaranteeing the performance, and the construction was completed in 1900; the tracks connecting with those of the two roads but not with those of the Tennessee Central. The Terminal Company as part of the improvements purchased large additional properties, the two roads advancing the funds, and the company executing a mortgage for three million dollars guaranteed by the roads. $2,535,000 of the bonds were issued and the proceeds used to repay the roads. On August 15, 1900, the two roads, at that time being the only two roads entering Nashville, made the arrangement under which they since have operated. They made an unincorporated organization called the Nashville Terminals which was to maintain and operate the property let to the two roads jointly by the Nashville Terminal Company and also 8.10 miles of main track and 23.80 miles of side track contributed by the Louisville & Nashville and 12.15 miles of main and 26.37 miles of side track contributed by the Nashville & Chattanooga. The agreement between the roads provided a board of control consisting of a superintendent and the general managers of the two roads, the superintendent having the immediate control and appointing under officers, &c. The total expense of maintenance and operation is apportioned monthly between the two roads on the basis of the total number of cars and locomotives handled for each. There is no switching charge to or from locations on tracks of the Nashville terminals within the switching limits on freight from or to Nashville over either road. The Tennessee Central tracks now connect with those of the Nashville & Chattanooga at Shops Junction in the western section of the city, within the switching limits, and with those of the Louisville & Nashville at Vine Hill, outside the switching limits and just outside the city on the south.

It should be added that in December, 1902, a further agreement was made purporting to modify the lease to the railroads jointly by excluding from it the property that came from them respectively, and remitting the roads to their several titles as they stood before the lease, subject only to the mortgage, with some other changes that need not be mentioned. This partial change from joint tenancy back to several titles does not affect the substantial equality of the contribution of the two roads, and the joint tenure of the considerable property purchased by the Terminal Company was left unchanged.

Another matter that seems immaterial to the case before us is that since the connection between the Tennessee Central and the appellant roads the latter have interchanged noncompetitive traffic with the former, but the Louisville & Nashville has refused to switch competitive traffic and coal except at its local rates and the Nashville & Chattanooga has refused to switch it at all. The switching of coal was dealt with by this court in *Louisville & Nashville R. R. Co.* v. *United States*, 238 U. S. 1. But the case now before us is not concerned with the effect of the carriers having thrown the terminals open to many branches of traffic. 238

U. S. 18. It arises only upon the question of the discrimination supposed to arise from the appellants' relations to each other, as we have explained — a question grazed but not hit by the decision in 238 U. S. See p. 19.

If the intent of the parties or purpose of the arrangement was material in a case like this, obviously there was none to discriminate against the Tennessee Central road. That road did not enter Nashville when the plan was formed, and the two appellants had a common interest although competitors — an interest that also was public and in which the City of Nashville shared. By § 3 of the Act to Regulate Commerce as it now stands, the Act "shall not be construed as requiring any such common carrier to give the use of its tracks or terminal facilities to another carrier engaged in like business." Therefore if either carrier owned and used this terminal alone it could not be found to discriminate against the Tennessee Central by merely refusing to switch for it, that is to move a car to or from a final or starting point from or to a point of interchange. We conceive that what is true of one owner would be equally true of two joint owners, and if we are right the question is narrowed to whether that is not for all practical purposes the position in which the appellants stand. They do still hold jointly a considerable portion of the terminals, purchased with their funds. They manage the terminals as a whole and in short deal with them in the same way that they would if their title was joint in every part. Of course they do not own their respective original tracks jointly and it is matter for appreciation that perhaps defies more precise argument whether the change back to a several tenure of those tracks changed the rights of the parties. We cannot see in this modification of the paper title any change material to the point in hand. Neither road is paid for the use of its tracks, but the severally owned and the jointly held are brought into a single whole by substantially equal contributions and are used by each as occasion requires.

The fact principally relied upon to uphold the order of the Commission is that instead of each road doing its own switching over the terminals used in common they switch jointly, and it is said that therefore each is doing for the other a service that it cannot refuse to a third. We cannot believe that the rights to their own terminals reserved by the law are to be defeated by such a distinction. We take it that a several use by the roads for this purpose would open no door to a third road. If the title were strictly joint throughout in the two roads, we can see no ground for prejudice in the adoption of the more economical method of a single agency for both, each paying substantially as it would if it did its own work alone. But, as we have indicated, a large part of the terminals is joint property in substance and the whole is held and used as one concern. What is done seems to us not reciprocal switching but the use of a joint terminal in the natural and practical way. It is objected that upon this view a way is opened to get beyond the reach of the statute and the Commission. But the very meaning of a line in the law is that right and wrong touch each other and that anyone may get as close to the line as he can if he keeps on the right side. And further, the distinction seems pretty plain between a *bona fide* joint ownership or arrangement so nearly approaching joint ownership as this, and the grant of facilities for the interchange of traffic that should be extended to others on equal terms. The joint outlay of the two roads has produced much more than a switching arrangement, it has produced a common and peculiar interest in the station and tracks even when the latter are not jointly owned. In our opinion the order was not warranted by the law; but in overturning it upon the single point discussed we do so without prejudice to the Commission's making orders to prevent the appellants from discriminating between competitive and noncompetitive goods, so long as they open their doors to the latter, the appellants being entitled to reasonable compensation, taking into account the expense of the terminal that they have built and paid for.

Decree reversed. Injunction to issue, without prejudice to further orders by the Interstate Commerce Commission as stated in the opinion.

MR. JUSTICE PITNEY, with whom concurred MR. JUSTICE DAY, MR. JUSTICE BRANDEIS, and MR. JUSTICE CLARKE, dissenting.

I am unable to concur in the opinion of the court, and, in view of the far-reaching effect of the decision upon the commercial interests of the country, deem it a duty to set forth the grounds of my dissent.

The Interstate Commerce Commission found as matter of fact (33 I. C. C. 76, 84): "Defendants [the two railroad companies, now appellants] unquestionably interchange traffic with each other and without distinction between competitive and noncompetitive traffic. The cars of both roads are moved over the individually owned terminal tracks of the other to and from industries on the other, and both lines are rendered equally available to industries located exclusively on one. The movement, it is true, is not performed immediately by the road over whose terminal tracks it is performed, but neither is it performed immediately by the road whose cars are moved. It is performed by a joint agent for both roads, and that being so, we are of the opinion that the arrangement is essentially the same as a reciprocal switching arrangement and accordingly constitutes a facility for the interchange of traffic between, and for receiving, forwarding, and delivering property to and from defendants' respective lines within the meaning of the second paragraph of section 3 of the act. [Interstate Commerce Act.] . . . . We can not agree with defendants' contention that they have merely exchanged trackage rights. But even if they have, we think the term 'facility,' as used in section 3 of the act, also includes reciprocal trackage rights over terminal tracks, the consequences and advantages to shippers being identical with those accruing from reciprocal switching arrangements."

The District Court, three judges sitting (227 Fed. Rep. 258, 269), after careful consideration, reached the following conclusions: "The operation jointly carried on by the Louisville & Nashville and the Nashville & Chattanooga under the Terminals agreement is not a mere exchange of trackage rights to and from industries on their respective lines at Nashville, under which each does all of its own switching at Nashville and neither switches for the other. It is, on the contrary, in substance and effect, an arrangement under which the entire switching service for each railroad over the joint and separately owned tracks is performed jointly by both, operating as principals through the Terminals as their joint agent, each railroad, as one of such joint principals, hence performing through such agency switching service for both itself and the other railroad. . . . . And, viewed in its fundamental aspect, and considered with reference to its ultimate effect, we entirely concur in the conclusion of the Commission that such joint switching operation 'is essentially the same as a reciprocal switching arrangement,' constituting a facility for the interchange of traffic between the lines of the two railroads, within the meaning of the second paragraph of section 3 of the Interstate Commerce Act. That each railroad does not separately switch for the other, but that such switching operations are carried on jointly is not, in our opinion, material. If it were, all reciprocal switching operations carried on by two railroads at any connecting point of several carriers could be easily put beyond the reach of the act, and its remedial purpose defeated, by the simple device of employing a joint agency to do such reciprocal switching. The controlling test of the statute, however, lies in the nature of the work done, rather than in the particular device employed or the names applied to those engaged in it."

With these views I agree. Elaborate argument is made in behalf of appellants in the effort to show that the method of operating the Nashville Terminals is not "reciprocal switching" within a certain narrow definition of that term. This is an immaterial point; the real question being whether it constitutes a facility for the interchange of traffic between the respective lines of appellants, and for the receiving, forwarding and delivering of property between connecting lines, within the meaning of § 3 of the Interstate Commerce Act (c. 104; 24 Stat. 380), so that it must be rendered to the patrons of the Tennessee Central upon equal terms with those of the Louisville & Nashville and the Nashville & Chattanooga. I cannot doubt that it bears this character.

It is clear, I think, that in the second paragraph of this section [3] the word "facilities" is employed in two meanings. Where it first occurs, it means those acts or operations that facilitate or render easy the interchange of traffic; while, in the final clause, "to give the use of its tracks or terminal facilities," the words "terminal facilities" are employed in a figurative sense and as equivalent to "terminal properties." This is obvious from the association together of tracks and terminal facilities as things subject to use. And the same words are used in the same sense in the 1906 amendment to § 1 of the Act (c. 3591; 34 Stat. 584), by which the definition of the term "railroad" was expanded so as to include "all switches, spurs, tracks, and terminal facilities of every kind used or necessary in the transportation of the persons or property designated herein."

There is nothing in the order of the Commission now under review that requires appellants or either of them, or their agency, the Nashville Terminals, to give the use of tracks or terminal facilities to the Tennessee Central, either physically or in any other sense, within the meaning of the final clause of § 3. It requires them merely to interchange interstate competitive traffic to and from the tracks of the Tennessee Central on the same terms as interstate non competitive traffic so long as they interchange both kinds of traffic with each other on the same terms;

and also to establish and apply to the switching of interstate traffic to and from the Tennessee Central rates and charges not different from those that they contemporaneously maintain with respect to similar shipments as between themselves. Undoubtedly the expenditures made by appellants in the construction of the joint terminal property, so far as that property is used in interchange switching, is an element to be taken into consideration in fixing the amount of the switching charges. And the same is true with respect to the value of the separately owned tracks of appellants, so far as necessarily used in mutual interchanges.

The practice of the Louisville & Nashville and the Nashville & Chattanooga in refusing to interchange competitive on the same terms as noncompetitive traffic with the Tennessee Central, while interchanging both kinds of traffic as between themselves, was found by the Commission to be unduly discriminatory, there being no substantial difference in the conditions of the interchange, nor any increased cost of interchanging competitive as compared with noncompetitive traffic.

The tracks included in the joint terminal arrangement of appellants include 8.10 miles of main and 23.80 miles of side tracks separately owned by the Louisville & Nashville, 12.15 miles of main and 26.37 miles of side tracks separately owned by the Nashville & Chattanooga, and some yard tracks owned by the Louisville & Nashville Terminal Company, whose entire stock is owned by the Louisville & Nashville R. R. Co. It may be conceded that by virtue of the lease from the Terminal Company to the appellant railroads, even as modified in December, 1902, there remains in some sense a joint tenure of the property of the Terminal Company. But, in my view, the question of the ownership of the property is entirely aside from the real point. The discrimination charged and found by the Commission is not so much in the use of terminal property as in the performance of interchange services; and for such discrimination a community of interest in the property affords neither justification nor excuse.

So far as the nondiscriminatory performance of those services requires that cars from the Tennessee Central shall be admitted to the terminal tracks of the Louisville & Nashville and the Nashville & Chattanooga and to tracks in which these companies have a joint interest, this is so only because appellants have, as between themselves, and also as regards traffic from the Tennessee Central, thrown their terminals open to the public use. The argument for appellants rests upon the essential fallacy that the terminal facilities are, in an absolute sense, and for all purposes, private property. But they, like all other parts of the railroad line, are, with respect to their use, devoted to the benefit of the public. And the final clause of § 3, while it protects each carrier to a certain extent in the separate use of its terminal property, does so not otherwise than it protects its particular use of the main line of railroad. "Tracks" are mentioned together with "terminal facilities," and the same rule is applied to both. The fact that a carrier owns its own terminals is no more an excuse for discriminatory treatment of its patrons with respect to services performed therein than its ownership of the main line is an excuse for discrimination with respect to transportation thereon.

It is said that if either of the appellants were the sole owner of the terminal properties in question and used them alone, it could not be deemed to discriminate against the Tennessee Central because of a mere refusal to switch for it in the interchange of traffic. Of course if it refused all connecting carriers alike it could not be held for discrimination. But whether it would be at liberty to refuse to switch for the Tennessee Central would depend upon circumstances; for instance, upon whether the Interstate Commerce Commission, pursuant to its authority under § 15 of the Act as amended in 1910 (c. 309; 36 Stat. 552), should establish the two lines as a through route, or (without that) should determine upon adequate evidence that the refusal of switching privileges was a failure to afford reasonable and proper facilities for the interchange of traffic between the connecting lines under § 3. Car interchange between connecting lines was made by the 1910 amendment of § 1 of the Act a positive duty on the part of the carrier, even without action by the Commission. 36 Stat. 545.

I deem it a most material fact that the appellants already interchange noncompetitive traffic with the Tennessee Central, upon terms like those upon which they interchange both competitive and noncompetitive traffic between themselves. So far as their method of doing this amounts to an interchange of trackage rights they have by their voluntary action thrown open the use of their terminals to all branches of traffic, excepting so far as they discriminate against competitive traffic over the Tennessee Central. Not only so, but the Commission has expressly found (33 I. C. C. 82) that the Louisville & Nashville will switch competitive coal and other competitive traffic to and from the Tennessee Central, the interchange being usually effected at Shops Junction and over the rails of the Nashville & Chattanooga. But the Louisville

& Nashville insists upon charging local rates as if for transportation between Nashville and Overton, Tennessee, which amount to from $12 to $36 per car, and are therefore in effect prohibitory. For a time the Nashville & Chattanooga in like manner offered to perform the same switching service to and from the Tennessee Central at its local rates, and published a terminal tariff December 14, 1913, expressly providing that such local rates would apply to competitive traffic from and destined to the Tennessee Central. This, however, was revoked shortly after the complaint in the present case was filed. There is here a very plain discrimination, found by the Commission to be an undue discrimination, not merely against the Tennessee Central but against a "particular description of traffic," which is distinctly prohibited by § 3. The conduct of appellants is quite analagous to the making of a discrimation in the charge for carriage not because of any difference inhering in the goods or in the cost of the service rendered in transporting them, but upon the mere basis of the ownership of the goods; a discrimination condemned by this court in *Int. Com. Comm.* v. *Del., Lack. & Western R. R.*, 220 *U. S.* 235, 252.

The present system of interchanging traffic between appellants was established in August, 1900, a year or two before the line of the Tennessee Central was constructed into Nashville. Emphasis was laid upon this, in argument, as refuting the suggestion that the arrangement could be deemed a "device" to avoid the discrimination clause of § 3 of the Interstate Commerce Act. The findings of the Commission show, however (33 I. C. C. 81), that when the Tennessee Central entered Nashville it was only after strong opposition from the Louisville & Nashville; and (p. 79) that prior to the year 1898 the people of Nashville had become desirous of better terminal facilities, particularly of a union passenger depot, and an ordinance authorizing a contract to that end between the City and the Terminal Company was proposed, containing a proviso that the terminal facilities should also be available on an equitable basis to railroads which might be built in the future. The present appellants opposed this proviso and an ordinance omitting it was passed, but was vetoed by the mayor on account of the omission. It clearly enough appears, therefore, that the agreement of August, 1900, was made by appellants in view of the probability of some other road entering Nashville thereafter.

But were it otherwise, the result should be the same. The obligation to avoid discrimination and to afford "all reasonable, proper, and equal facilities for the interchange of traffic" is not qualified by any rights of priority. The new road is a servant of the public, equally with the others; subject to the same duty and entitled for its patrons, to demand reasonable and impartial performance of the reciprocal duty from carriers that preceded it in the field.

In my opinion the present case is controlled by our decisions in the former case between the same parties (*Louis. & Nash. R. R.* v. *United States*, 238 U. S. 1, 18, 19), and the earlier case of *Pennsylvania Co.* v. *United States*, 236 U. S. 351, 366 *et seq.* In these cases many of the same arguments that are here advanced were considered and overruled by the court. The latter case concerned the switching of interstate carload traffic between industrial tracks and junction points within the switching limits at New Castle, Pennsylvania. The Pennsylvania Company undertook to sustain a practice of doing such switching at $2 per car for three railroads while refusing to do it for the Buffalo, Rochester & Pittsburgh, upon the ground of its sole ownership of the terminals and the fact that the three other carriers were in a position, either at New Castle or elsewhere, to offer it reciprocal advantages fully compensatory for the switching done for them in New Castle, whereas the Buffalo, Rochester & Pittsburgh was not in a position to offer similar advantages. The Interstate Commerce Commission (29 I. C. C. 114) overruled this contention, and in this was sustained by the District Court (214 Fed. Rep. 445), and by this court. We there held (236 U. S. 361) that the question what was an undue or unreasonable preference or advantage under § 3 of the Interstate Commerce Act was a question not of law but of fact, and that if the order of the Commission did not exceed its constitutional and statutory authority and was not unsupported by testimony, it could not be set aside by the courts; held (p. 363), that the provisions of § 3, although that section remains unchanged, must be read in connection with the amendments of 1906 and 1910 to other parts of the act, and that by these amendments the facilities for delivering freight at terminals were brought within the definition of transportation to be regulated; and also (pp. 368, 369) that the order did not amount to a compulsory taking of the use of the Pennsylvania tracks by another road within the inhibition of the final clause of § 3; no right being given to the Buffalo road to run its cars over the terminals of the Pennsylvania Company or to use or occupy its stations or depots for purposes of its own.

In the former case between the present parties (*Louis. & Nash. R. R.* v. *United States,* 238 U. S. 1), we sustained the District Court (216 Fed. Rep. 672) in refusing an injunction to restrain the putting into effect of an order of the Commission (28 I. C. C. 533, 540) requiring appellants to interswitch interstate coal with the Tennessee Central as they did with each other. The findings of the Commission (p. 542) recognized that the terminals were in part jointly owned and in part the separate property of the two appellants. The District Court (216 Fed. Rep. 682, 684) alluded to this fact. And this court (238 U. S. 17, 18, 19, 20) did not ignore that fact but laid it aside as immaterial, declaring: "If the carrier, however, does not rest behind that statutory shield [the final clause of § 3] but chooses voluntarily to throw the Terminals open to many branches of traffic, it to that extent makes the Yard public. Having made the Yard a facility for many purposes and to many patrons, such railroad facility is with the provisions of § 3 of the statute which prohibits the facility from being used in such manner as to discriminate against patrons and commodities."

If the decision reached in the present case is adhered to, and remains uncorrected by remedial legislation, it will open a wide door to discriminatory practices repugnant alike to the letter and the spirit of the Act to Regulate Commerce.

Mr. Justice Day, Mr. Justice Brandeis, and Mr. Justice Clarke concur in this dissent.

NORFOLK & WESTERN RAILWAY COMPANY *v.* DIXIE TOBACCO COMPANY

228 U. S. 593 (1913)

Mr. Justice Holmes delivered the opinion of the court.

This is an action brought by the defendant in error to recover for damage to tobacco shipped by it on the railroad at Bedford City, Virginia, to Marshall, Texas. The plaintiff got a verdict and judgment, which was affirmed by the Supreme Court of Appeals (111 Virginia, 813), the case having been taken there on the ground that the act of June 29, 1906, c. 3591, § 7, 34 Stat. 584, 595, amending § 20 of the Act to Regulate Commerce, of February 4, 1887, c. 104, 24 Stat. 379, 386, is unconstitutional. This section requires any common carrier receiving property for transportation from a point in one State to a point in another to issue a receipt or bill of lading for the same; makes the receiving carrier liable for loss caused by any common carrier *in transitu;* and provides that no contract shall exempt it from the liability thus imposed.

The bill of lading stipulated that no carrier should be liable for damages not occurring on its portion of the through route. There was evidence that the tobacco was damaged after it left the railroad company's hands; and the defendant asked an instruction that if the jury believe that it delivered the tobacco in good order to the next carrier the verdict should be in its favor. This instruction was refused and the defendant excepted. There was evidence also that the plaintiff chose the route for the tobacco, being partly by sea and a different one from that which the railroad would have adopted, which would have been all rail. The railroad had no through route or rate established with the line of steamers by which the tobacco went. Instructions were asked and refused, subject to exception, that the bill of lading controlled, and that the above statute, so far as it attempts to invalidate limitations or liabilities like that quoted above, is void.

The Supreme Court of Appeals followed the ruling in *Atlantic Coast Line R. R. Co.* v. *Riverside Mills,* 219 U. S. 186 (to which may be added *Galveston, Harrisburg & San Antonio Ry. Co.* v. *Wallace,* 223 U. S. 481), as conclusive. The plaintiff in error contends that these cases may be distinguished on the ground that in both of them it was to be presumed that the carrier was a voluntary party to a through route and rate, whereas here the stipulation against liability beyond its line and the fact that it had no through route with the steamship company exclude that presumption. It argues that as it was bound to accept goods destined beyond its line for delivery to the next carrier and was required by the statute to give a through bill of lading, if on such compulsory acceptance it is made answerable for damages done by others its property is taken without due process of law. But in the former case there was the same stipulation in the bill of lading, and the supposed through routes were only presumed. In the second case the carrier is spoken of as voluntarily accepting goods for a point beyond its line, but there too there was the same attempt to limit liability, and in the present case the acceptance was voluntary in the same degree as in that. There is no substantial distinction between the earlier decisions and this.

Judgment affirmed.

GEORGIA, FLORIDA & ALABAMA RAILWAY COMPANY *v.* BLISH MILLING COMPANY

241 U. S. 190 (1916)

MR. JUSTICE HUGHES delivered the opinion of the court.

The Blish Milling Company brought this action in trover against the Georgia, Florida & Alabama Railway Company and recovered judgment which was affirmed by the Court of Appeals of Georgia. 15 Ga. App. 142. The facts are these:

On May 13, 1910, the Blish Milling Company shipped from Seymour, Indiana, to Bainbridge, Georgia, a carload of flour consigned to its own order with direction to notify Draper-Garrett Grocery Company at Bainbridge. The bill of lading was issued by the Baltimore & Ohio Southwestern Railroad Company. The shipper's sight draft upon the Draper-Garrett Grocery Company, for $1,109,89 covering the price of the flour with a carrying charge, was attached to the bill of lading and forwarded to a bank in Bainbridge for collection. The flour was transferred to another car by the Central of Georgia Railway Company, a connecting carrier, and reached Bainbridge on June 2, 1910, over the line of the Georgia, Florida & Alabama Railway Company, the plaintiff in error, in accordance with routing. The plaintiff in error, without requiring payment of the draft and surrender of the bill of lading (which were ultimately returned to the Blish Milling Company), delivered the car to the Draper-Garrett Grocery Company immediately on its arrival by placing it on the side track of that company. In the course of unloading the grocery company discovered that some of the flour was wet and thereupon reloaded the part removed and returned the flour to the plaintiff in error. The subsequent course of events is thus stated by the Court of Appeals (*Id.*, pp. 144, 145):

"The railway company" (that is, the plaintiff in error) "retook possession of the car and unloaded it, and in a few days sold, as perishable property, a part of the flour alleged to be damaged, and on December 23, 1910, sold the remainder. On June 3, 1910, after the grocery company had turned the flour back to the railway company, B. C. Prince, traffic manager of the Georgia, Florida & Alabama Railway Company, telegraphed to the Blish Milling Company as follows: 'Flour order notify Draper-Garrett Grocery Company refused account damage. Hold at your risk and expense. Advise disposition.' On the next day the milling company replied by telegraphing to Prince, 'Sending our representative there. What is nature of damage?' To this Prince replied: 'Flour transferred in route. Slight damage by water, apparently rough handling. When will your representative reach Bainbridge?' The Blish Milling Company replied that their man would be there that night or the next day. On June 7 (after the milling company's representative had reached Bainbridge and conferred with the agents of the railway company and with the grocery company) the milling company sent a final telegram, saying, 'We will make claim against railroad for entire contents of car at invoice price. Must refuse shipment as we can not handle.' It appears, from the evidence of Mr. Draper, that the price of flour declined after his order was given and before the flour reached Bainbridge. There is conflict in the evidence as to a tender of the flour by the railway company to the milling company's representative. According to some of the testimony, about 18 barrels of the flour had been sold by the railway company before the alleged tender was made, and therefore it was not within the power of the carrier to tender the shipment in its entirety." The verdict in favor of the Milling Company was for $1,084.50 from which the Court of Appeals required a deduction of the amount of the unpaid freight which was held to have been erroneously included.

With other defenses, the Railway Company pleaded that the shipper had failed to comply with the following provision of the bill of lading, issued by the initial carrier: "Claims for loss, damage, or delay must be made in writing to the carrier at the point of delivery or at the point of origin within four months after the delivery of the property, or, in case of failure to make delivery, then within four months after a reasonable time for delivery has elapsed. Unless claims are so made, the carrier shall not be liable." This defense was overruled. The Court of Appeals stated that "so far as appears from the record, no claim was filed by the shipper," but deemed the provision to be inapplicable. *Id.*, p. 149.

There are only two questions presented here, and these are thus set forth in the brief of the plaintiff in error:

"1st. That the plaintiff's exclusive remedy was against the initial carrier, the Baltimore & Ohio Southwestern Railroad Company under the Carmack Amendment of Section Twenty of the Hepburn Bill.

"2nd. That under the stipulation in the bill of lading providing for the filing of claims for loss or damage the action was barred."

The first contention is met by repeated decisions of this court.

The connecting carrier is not relieved from liability by the Carmack Amendment, but the bill of lading required to be issued by the initial carrier upon an interstate shipment governs the entire transportation and thus fixes the obligations of all participating carriers to the extent that the terms of the bill of lading are applicable and valid. "The liability of any carrier in the route over which the articles were routed, for loss or damage, is that imposed by the act as measured by the original contract of shipment so far as it is valid under the act." *Kansas Southern Ry.* v. *Carl,* 227 U. S. 639, 648. See *Adams Express Co.* v. *Croninger,* 226 U. S. 491, 507, 508; *C. C. & St. L. Ry.* v. Dettlebach, 239 U. S. 588, 591; *Southern Railway* v. *Prescott,* 240 U. S. 632, 637; *Northern Pacific Ry.* v. *Wall, ante,* p. 87.

These decisions also establish that the question as to the proper construction of the bill of lading is a Federal question. The clause with respect to the notice of claims — upon which the plaintiff in error relies in its second contention — specifically covers "failure to make delivery." It is said that this is not to be deemed to include a case where there was not only failure to deliver to the consignee but actual delivery to another or delivery in violation of instructions. But 'delivery' must mean delivery as required by the contract, and the terms of the stipulation are comprehensive, — fully adequate in their literal and natural meaning to cover all cases where the delivery has not been made as required. When the goods have been misdelivered there is clearly a 'failure to make delivery' as when the goods have been lost or destroyed; and it is quite as competent in the one case as in the other for the parties to agree upon reasonable notice of the claim as a condition of liability. It may be urged that the carrier is bound to know whether it has delivered to the right person or according to instructions. This argument, however, even with respect to the particular carrier which makes a misdelivery, loses sight of the practical object in view. In fact, the transactions of a railroad company are multitudinous and are carried on through numerous employees of various grades. Ordinarily the managing officers, and those responsible for the settlement and contest of claims, would be without actual knowledge of the facts of a particular transaction. The purpose of the stipulation is not to escape liability but to facilitate prompt investigation. And, to this end, it is a precaution of obvious wisdom, and in no respect repugnant to public policy, that the carrier by its contracts should require reasonable notice of all claims against it even with respect to its own operations.

There is, however, a further and controlling consideration. We are dealing with a clause in a bill of lading issued by the initial carrier. The statute casts upon the initial carrier responsibility with respect to the entire transportation. The aim was to establish unity of responsibility (*Atlantic Coast Line* v. *Riverside Mills*, 219 U. S. 186, 199–213; *N. Y., P. & N. R. R.* v. *Peninsula Produce Exchange*, 240 U. S. 34, 38), and the words of the statute are comprehensive enough to embrace responsibility for all losses resulting from any failure to discharge a carrier's duty as to any part of the agreed transportation which, as defined in the Federal Act, includes delivery. It is not to be doubted that if, in the case of an interstate shipment under a through bill of lading, the terminal carrier makes a misdelivery, the initial carrier is liable; and when it inserts in its bill of lading a provision requiring reasonable notice of claims "in case of failure to make delivery" the fair meaning of the stipulation is that it includes all cases of such failure, as well those due to misdelivery as those due to the loss of the goods. But the provision in question is not to be construed in one way with respect to the initial carrier and in another with respect to the connecting or terminal carrier. As we have said, the latter takes the goods under the bill of lading issued by the initial carrier, and its obligations are measured by its terms (*Kansas Southern Ry.* v. *Carl*, *supra; Southern Railway* v. *Prescott*, *supra*); and if the clause must be deemed to cover a case of misdelivery when the action is brought against the initial carrier, it must equally have that effect in the case of the terminal carrier which in the contemplation of the parties was to make the delivery. The clause gave abundant opportunity for presenting claims and we regard it as both applicable and valid.

In this view, it necessarily follows that the effect of the stipulation could not be escaped by the mere form of the action. The action is in trover, but as the state court said, "if we look beyond its technical denomination, the scope and effect of the action is nothing more than that of an action for damages against the delivering carrier." 15 Ga. App., p. 147. It is urged, however, that the carrier in making the misdelivery converted the flour and thus abandoned the contract. But the parties could not waive the terms of the contract under which the shipment was made pursuant to the Federal Act; nor could the carrier by its conduct give the shipper the right to ignore these terms which were applicable to that conduct and hold the carrier to a different responsibility from that fixed by the agreement made under the published tariffs and regulations. A different view would antagonize the plain policy of the Act and open the door to the very abuses at which the Act was aimed. *Chi. & Alt. R. R.* v. *Kirby*, 225 U. S. 153, 166; *Kansas Southern Ry.* v. *Carl, supra; A., T. & S. F. Ry.* v. *Robinson*, 233 U. S. 173, 181; *Southern Ry.* v. *Prescott, supra.* We are not concerned in the present case with any question save as to the applicability of the provision and its validity, and as we find it to be both applicable and valid, effect must be given to it.

But, while this is so, we think that the plaintiff in error is not entitled to succeed in its ultimate contention under the stipulation for the reason that it appears that notice of the claim was in fact given. It is true that in the statement made by the Court of Appeals it is said that so far as appears from the record "no claim was filed by the shipper." We must assume, however, that this was in effect a construction of the provision as requiring a more formal notice than that which was actually sent. For the court had already set forth the uncontroverted facts in detail showing that the shipper (having made an investigation in response to the communication of the traffic manager of the Railway Company) had telegraphed to the latter, on June 7, 1910, only five days after the arrival of the goods at destination, as follows: "We will make claim against railroad for entire contents of car at invoice price. Must refuse shipment as we can not handle." In the preceding telegrams, which passed between the parties and are detailed by the state court in stating the facts, the shipment had been adequately identified, so that this final telegram taken with the others established beyond question the particular shipment to which the claim referred and was in substance the making of a claim within the meaning of the stipulation, — the object of which was to secure reasonable notice. We think that it sufficiently apprised the carrier of the character of the claim, for while it stated that the claim was for the entire contents of the car 'at invoice price' this did not constitute such a variance from the claim for the value of the flour as to be misleading; and it is plain that no prejudice resulted. Granting that the stipulation is applicable and valid, it does not require documents in a particular form. It is addressed to a practical exigency and it is to be construed in a practical way. The stipulation required that the claim should be made in writing, but a telegram which in itself or taken with other telegrams contained an adequate statement must be deemed to satisfy this requirement. See *Ryan* v. *United States*, 136 U. S. 68, 83; *Kleinhans* v. *Jones*, 68 Fed. Rep. 742, 745; *Godwin* v. *Francis*, L. R. 5 C. P. 295; *Queen* v. *Riley* [1896], 1 Q. B. 309, 314, 321; *Howley* v. *Whipple*, 48 N. H. 487, 488; *State* v. *Holmes*, 56 Iowa, 588, 590.

Judgment affirmed.

WESTERN TRANSIT COMPANY *v.* A. C. LESLIE & COMPANY, LIMITED

242 U. S. 448 (1917)

MR. JUSTICE BRANDEIS delivered the opinion of the court.

The Western Transit Company, operating steamers between Buffalo and other points on the Great Lakes, formed, with the New York Central Railroad, a "lake and rail" line between Michigan and New York City. Among the privileges and facilities offered by this line was the right "in transit of free storage and diversion at Buffalo." That is, the shipper instead of sending his goods from Michigan through to New York City, was entitled, without the payment of any extra charge, to have them stored at Buffalo for a period, to await further orders and be forwarded later to New York. The shipper was also given the privilege of "diversion"; — that is of changing the ultimate destination of the stored goods upon proper adjustment of the rate. On September 23, 1908, A. C. Leslie & Co., Limited, the plaintiff below, delivered to the Western Transit Co., the defendant below, at Houghton, Michigan, for shipment over this line to New York City, 25 tons of copper ingots, with direction to store the same upon arrival at Buffalo to await further shipping directions. The copper arrived there September 30, and was placed in the Transit Company's warehouse. Nearly four months later about one ton of it was stolen from the warehouse. An action was brought by the shipper in the City Court of Buffalo to recover its value. The Transit Company denied all liability; but the court found that the loss was due to its negligence and held the company liable for the full value of the copper lost. The judgment of the City Court was affirmed by the Supreme Court of New York at special term and also by the Appellate Division of that court. 165 App. Div. 947. Applications for an appeal to the Court of Appeals of New York having been denied, both by the Appellate Division and by the Chief Judge of the Court of Appeals, a writ of error from this court was granted on the ground that the decision below involved a federal question, namely: the construction and effect of the bill of lading and of tariffs filed under the Act to Regulate Commerce as amended. Act 1906, c. 3591, 34 Stat. 584.

The question before this court relates solely to the measure of damages. The shipper contends that it is entitled to the full value of the copper lost, which was $271.38. The carrier contends that the damages recoverable are limited to $94.10; that is, the value *not to exceed $100 a ton.* In support of this limitation it relies upon the fact that freight was paid at the rate of 18 cents per ton under a bill of lading and a tariff which names the following rates from Houghton, Michigan, to New York City:

"Copper ingots. . . . . value not to exceed $100 a ton,
18 c. per ton
Copper ingots . . . . value not expressed. . . . .
30 c. per ton."

The shipper insists that it is enforcing the liability of the Transit Company not as carrier, but as warehouseman; and that the terms of its obligation as warehouseman are fixed, not by the bill of lading and the tariff provision quoted above, but wholly by the letter of November 26, 1908, and the circular therein referred to, which are copied in the margin.[1]

[1] The Western Transit Company, N. Y. C. & H. R. R. Line of Steamers.
Buffalo, N. Y., Nov. 26, 1908

Messrs. A. C. Leslie & Company, Montreal, Que.

GENTLEMEN: Replying to your letter of 24th, instant, would advise you that we have in store here, lot 1036 ingot bars of copper, marked M. M. 102, as well as lot of 979 ingot bars, marked M. M. 97.

This copper came forward in our steamer, Buffalo, which unloaded here September 30th, and will be held here subject to our storage circular I. C. C. No. 236, copy of which I enclose.

Yours truly,
(Signed) EDWIN T. DOUGLASS,
General Manager.

I. C. C. No. 236, Superseding I. C. C. No. 231.
The Western Transit Company, New York Central & Hudson River R. R. Line.
General Office.
Copper and Copper Matte, Pig Lead and Spelter for Storage and Diversion at Buffalo.

The Western Transit Company will accept shipments of Copper and Copper Matte, Pig Lead and Spelter for storage and diversion at Buffalo, under the following rules:

1. The Western Transit Company, at request of owners, will furnish free storage on shipments of Copper and Copper Matte, Pig Lead and Spelter in transit, at Buffalo, for a period not exceeding four months.

The Transit Company filed with the Interstate Commerce Commission, in addition to its general tariffs covering "lake and rail" rates, a separate tariff known as I. C. C. No. 236, covering specifically storage and diversion privileges at Buffalo, as set forth in the circular copied in the margin. The filing of this tariff was required by the act (see *Goldenberg* v. *Clyde S. S. Co.*, 20 I.C. C. 527) since the general tariff did not specify the details of the storage and diversion privileges. The Act to Regulate Commerce as amended provides expressly (§ 1) that the term transportation includes storage. And § 6 provides that a carrier must file with the Interstate Commerce Commission tariffs "showing all the rates, fares, and charges for transportation" and "shall also state separately all . . . . storage charges, ... all privileges or facilities granted or allowed and any rules or regulations which in any wise change, affect, or determine any part or the aggregate of such aforesaid rates."

The bill of lading, in a form similar to that approved and recommended by the Interstate Commerce Commission (14 I. C. C. 346), contains the following, among other provisions;

"It is mutually agreed in consideration of the rate of freight hereinafter named, as to each carrier of all or any of said property over all or any portion of said route to destination and as to each party at any time interested in all or any of said property, that every service to be performed hereunder shall be subject to all the conditions, whether printed or written, herein contained, and which are hereby agreed to by the shipper, and by him accepted for himself and his assigns as just and reasonable."

. . . .

---

2. If held longer than four months, it will be subject to a charge of one-half (½) cent per 100 pounds for each thirty (30) or part thereof so held.

3. Shipments held under this arrangement will be at owner's risk, and will not be accepted for storage unless arrangements are made with the undersigned previous to forwarding from Western Lake Ports.

4. Shipments ordered out of store will be charged at the through rate in effect at time the shipment originated, to points to which through rates are published by The Western Transit Company.

5. Shipments ordered to points to which no through rates are in effect via The Western Transit Company, will be charged at the local rate to and from Buffalo.

Issued May 15th, 1908.

Effective June 16th, 1908.

EDWIN T. DOUGLASS,
General Manager, Buffalo, N. Y.

"To be held at Bflo. for orders.

"Value not to exceed $100.00 per net ton. Limited by written agreement.

"The consignor of this property has the option of shipping same at a higher rate without limitation as to value in case of loss or damage from causes which would make the carrier liable, but agrees to the specified valuation named in case of loss or damage from causes which would make the carrier liable, because of the lower rate thereby accorded for transportation."

. . . .

Conditions.

. . . .

"The amount of any loss or damage for which any carrier becomes liable shall be computed at the value of the property at the place and time of shipment under this bill of lading, unless a lower value has been agreed upon or is determined by the classification upon which the rate is based, in either of which events such lower value shall be the maximum price to govern such computation."

The release valuation clause in an interstate bill of lading when based upon a difference in freight rates is valid. *Adams Express Co.* v. *Croninger*, 226 U. S. 491, 509. The limitation of liability by means of such valuation contained in the bill of lading continues although the service of carrying has been completed and the goods are held by the carrier strictly as warehouseman. *Cleveland, Cincinnati, Chicago & St. Louis Ry.* v. *Dettleback*, 239 U. S. 588. The provisions of the bill of lading govern even where the goods are allowed to remain in the carrier's warehouse after giving receipt therefor and payment of freight. The carrier and the shipper can make no alteration of the terms upon which goods are held under a tariff, until there has been an actual delivery of the goods to the consignee. *Southern Ry. Co.* v. *Prescott*, 240 U. S. 632. The reasons are even more persuasive for holding that the terms of a bill of lading govern storage in transit, like that at Buffalo. The contention of the shipper that the letter of November 26 enclosing the circular created a contract of warehousing wholly independent of the contract of carriage is contrary to fact. The Transit Company's circular states "that free storage is furnished on shipments in transit" and that shipments "will not be accepted for storage unless arrangements are made with the undersigned previous to forwarding from Western Lake Ports." Obviously free storage in transit was granted only to those who shipped over this "lake and rail" line. The shipper had enjoyed nearly two months' storage when the circular was received in answer to a letter of enquiry. It stated only what was contained in the tariff filed, which every shipper was bound to take notice of.

Judgment reversed and cause remanded for further proceedings not inconsistent with this opinion.

WESTERN UNION TELEGRAPH COMPANY, PETITIONER *v.* ESTEVE BROTHERS AND COMPANY

256 U. S. (1921)

MR. JUSTICE BRANDEIS delivered the opinion of the court.

In September, 1917, the Western Union Telegraph Company delivered to Esteve Brothers & Company at New Orleans, Louisiana, an unrepeated cable message from the latter's main office at Barcelona, Spain, directing a sale for future delivery of two thousand bales of cotton. The message actually sent had directed the sale of two hundred bales. The error in transmission resulted in a loss to Esteve Brothers & Company of $31,095. To recover compensation for this loss they sued the Western Union in a state court of Louisiana. The case was removed to the Federal District Court and there was tried by jury upon these additional stipulated facts:

The message was sent over lines of the Spanish Government Telegraph from Barcelona to Paris and thence over lines of the French Government to Havre. There it was delivered to the Western Union, transmitted by its cable to New York City and thence over its land lines to New Orleans. The error in transmission occurred on these land lines. The charge of $6.60, paid at Barcelona for transmitting the message, represented the sum of the local rates on the several connecting lines. The Western Union's share was $4.65; and of this $3.75 was apportioned to the cable system and 90 cents to the land lines. This Western Union rate was established by its tariff of telegraph and cable rates, in force since some time prior to June 18, 1910. Under the Act of that date, Chapter 309, 36 Stat. 544, making telegraph and cable companies subject to the Act to Regulate Commerce, this tariff had been filed with the Interstate Commerce Commission in May, 1916, by its permission and pursuant to an appropriate resolution of the company. The tariff so filed embodied the long used classification of messages, rules and regulations, including the provision that the company "shall not be liable for mistakes . . . . in transmission . . . . of any unrepeated message, beyond the amount of that portion of the tolls which shall accrue to it." The plaintiffs did not in fact assent to this limitation of liability. They did not, in sending the message at Barcelona, use a blank containing the provisions so limiting liability. They did not have actual knowledge of the resolution of the company or of the filing of the tariffs with the Interstate Commerce Commission.

The plaintiffs contended at the trial that in view of the above facts they were entitled to a verdict for the full amount of their loss. The company contended that, since the message had not been repeated, the verdict should be limited to $4.65, the amount received by it as tolls. A verdict was directed for $31,095 with interest; judgment thereon was affirmed by the United States Circuit Court of Appeals for the Fifth Circuit. 268 Fed. 22; and a petition for writ of certiorari was granted. 254 U. S. The sole question presented for our decision is the amount of damages recoverable.

For more than fifty years prior to the transaction here in suit the Western Union had maintained these two classes of rates for general cable and telegraph service. The usual or basic rate was for service practically at the sender's risk, liability being limited to the amount of the toll collected. Another special rate entitled the sender to have the message repeated back to the point of origin and rendered the company liable in case of mistake or nondelivery up to fifty times the amount of the extra charge. The extra charge for this additional service was for telegrams one-half and for cables one-quarter of the basic rate. In *Primrose* v. *Western Union Telegraph Co.*, 154 U. S. 1, decided in 1894, this classification of rates and the limitations upon the company's liability were declared by this court to be reasonable and valid, in the absence of willful misconduct or gross negligence. The limitation upon the company's common law liability was held to be in the nature of contract; and this liability unlike that of a common carrier, was not an insurer's. It was merely for the damage flowing from failure to use due care in transmission. *Primrose* v. *Western Union Telegraph Co.*, *supra*, 14. Since the limitations of liability was in the nature of contract the provision had to be brought home to the sender of a message in order to be legally binding upon him. Assent by the sender was ordinarily established if the message was written upon one of the company's blanks which set forth the limitation of liability. *Primrose* v. *Western Union Telegraph Co., supra,* 25; compare *Cau* v. *Texas & Pacific Ry. Co.,* 194 U. S. 427, 431. Whether, in view of long established practice, the mere sending of a message although not written on such a blank imported assent to the usual terms of the rate involved then an issue of fact. See *New Jersey Navigation Co.* v. *Merchant's Bank,* 6 How. 344, 383. The question presented for our decision is whether since the amendment of June 18, 1910, to the Act to Regulate Commerce, the sender is, without assent in fact, bound as matter of law by the provision limiting liability, because it is a part of the lawfully established rate.

The Act of June 18, 1910, c. 309, sec. 7, 36 Stat. 539, 544, broadened the scope of the Act to Regulate Commerce to include "telegraph, telephone and cable companies (whether wire or wireless) engaged in sending messages from [a] State . . . to any foreign country." And whatever may have been the legal incidents of transmitting the message from Barcelona to Havre under Spanish and French law, the Western Union in sending the message over its own lines from Havre to New Orleans was governed by the provisions of that Act. *Galveston, Houston & San Antonio Ry. Co.* v. *Woodbury,* 254 U. S. . . . . In the third paragraph of Section 1 of the amended Act Congress provided that messages might be "classified into day, night, repeated, unrepeated, letter, commercial, press, Government and such other classes as are just and reasonable, and different rate [might] be charged for the different classes of messages." Acting, in May 1916, under the authority of that provision, the Western Union by appropriate action approved the tariff involved in the present case and by permission of the Interstate Commerce Commission filed with it the tariff, including the provisions here in question. The company was not required so to do by the terms of the act or by any order of the Commission; compare 25th Annual Report I. C. C. (1911) pp. 5, 6. But the rate, long before established, then formally adopted and filed, was thereafter the only lawful rate for an unrepeated message, and the limitation of liability became the lawful condition upon which it was sent. *Postal Tel.-Cable Co.* v. *Warren-Godwin,* 251 U. S. 27, 30; *Clay County Produce Co.* v. *Western Union Telegraph Co.,* 44 I. C. C. 670, 674.

The lawful rate having been established, the company was by the provisions of Section 3 of the Act to Regulate Commerce prohibited from granting to anyone an undue preference or advantage over the public generally. For, as stated in *Postal Tel.-Cable Co.* v. *Warren-Godwin Co., supra,* 30, the "Act of 1910 was designed to and did subject such companies as to their interstate business to the rule of equality and uniformity of rates." If the general public upon paying the rate for an unrepeated message accepted substantially the risk of error involved in transmitting the message, the company could not, without granting an undue preference or advantage extend different treatment to the plaintiff here. The limitation of liability was an inherent part of the rate. The company could no more depart from it than it could depart from the amount charged for the service rendered.

The Act of 1910 introduced a new principle into the legal relations of the telegraph companies with their patrons which dominated and modified the principles previously governing them. Before the Act the companies had a common law liability from which they might or might not extricate themselves according to views of policy prevailing in the several States. Thereafter, for all messages sent in interstate or foreign commerce, the outstanding consideration became that of uniformity and equality of rates. Uniformity demanded that the rate represent the whole duty and the whole liability of the company. It could not be varied by agreement; still less could it be varied by lack of agreement. The rate became, not as before a matter of contract by which a legal liability could be modified, but a matter of law by which a uniform liability was imposed. Assent to the terms of the rate was rendered immaterial, because when the rate is used, dissent is without effect. This principle was established in cases involving the limitation upon a carrier's liability for baggage by *Boston & Maine Railroad* v. *Hooker,* 233 U. S. 97, and *Galveston & San Antonio Ry. Co.* v. *Woodbury,* decided by this court December 13, 1920. In the former case it was said, "If the charges filed were unreasonable, the only attack which could be made upon such regulation [limiting liability] would be by proceedings contesting their reasonableness before the Interstate Commerce Commission. While they were in force they were equally binding upon the railroad company and all passengers whose baggage was transported by carriers in interstate commerce." So here the limitation of liability attached to the unrepeated cable rate is binding upon all who send messages to or from foreign countries until it is set aside as unreasonable by the Commission.

It is strongly argued that the rule is not applicable to the situation before us, because of the difference in the provisions of law which govern the establishment of railroad and of telegraph rates. The railroad rate is established, and can only be established by filing the tariff with the Commission. Telegraph companies may initiate rates without filing tariffs with the Commission, (*Clay County Produce Co.* v. *Western Union Telegraph Co., supra*). Plaintiffs insist that it is the filing and subsequent publication of the railroad rate which gives it the force of law and requires the shipper to take notice of it. But the contention, by dwelling unduly upon the procedural features of the Act, would defeat the end which Congress had in view. Both railroad and telegraph-cable rates are inititated by the carrier. It is true that a railroad rate does not have the force of law unless it is filed with the Commission. But it is not true that out of the filing of the rate grows the rule of law by which the terms of this lawful rate conclude the passenger. The rule does not rest upon the fiction of constructive notice. It flows from the requirement of equality and uniformity of rates laid down in Section 3 of the Act to Regulate Commerce. Since any deviation from the lawful rate would involve either an undue preference or an unjust discrimination, a rate lawfully established must apply equally to all, whether there is knowledge of it or not. Congress apparently concluded, in the light of discrimination theretofore practiced by railroads among shippers and localities, that in transportation by rail equality could be secured only by provisions involving the utmost definiteness and constant official supervision. Accordingly by ection 6 it forbade a carrier of goods from engaging in transportation unless its rates had been filed with the Commission; and it prohibited, under heavy penalties, departure in any way from the terms of those rates when filed. In the case of telegraph and cable companies Congress appears to have considered that such stringent provisions were not required to secure the end in view. It did not make filing with the Commission a condition precedent to the existence of a lawful telegraph and cable rate. When, therefore, the Western Union initiated and established this reasonable rate, the principle of equality and uniformity laid down in Section 3 required that it should have exactly the same force and effect as the rate initiated by a rail carrier and filed according to the provisions of Section 6.

It was suggested that the attempted limitation of liability must fail under the rule recently applied in *Union Pacific Railroad Co.* v. *Burke*, decided February 28, 1921; because both the alternative rates offered in the Western Union tariff for cable messages were for limited liability, and because, therefore, no offer was made to the sender of a rate under which the company would assume full liability for all losses suffered through its negligence. It is by no means clear that the rule of the *Burke* case — established for common carriers of goods — should be applied to telegraph and cable companies. See the *Primrose* case, *supra*, p. 14. In any event, it is not applicable here. The Western Union did not, as in the case of telegrams, offer to send cable messages upon a special valuation to be made by the sender and paid for by an extra charge "based upon such value equal to one-tenth of one per cent, thereof." But it offered alternative rates for repeated and for unrepeated cable messages. This long established classification was expressly recognised as just and reasonable for cable as well as for telegraph messages in the amendment made by the Act of June 18, 1910, to Section 1 of the Act to Regulate Commerce. The provision in the terms offered by the company is:

"To guard against mistakes or delays the sender of a cable message should order it repeated, that is, telegraphed back to the originating office for comparison. For this one quarter of the unrepeated message rate is charged in addition. Unless indicated on its face this is an unrepeated message and paid for as such.

" . . . this Company shall not be liable for mistakes or delays in transmission or delivery . . . . of any unrepeated message, beyond the amount of that portion of the tolls which shall accrue to this company, ... [nor] of an repeated message, beyond fifty times the extra sum received by this Company from the sender for repeating such message over its own lines. . . ."

The repeated rate, offering greater accuracy and greater liability in case of error, was open to anyone who wished to pay the extra amount for extra security. Whether the limitation of liability prescribed for the repeated message would be valid as against a sender who had endeavored, by having the message repeated, to secure the greatest care on the part of the company, we have no occasion to decide, because it is not raised by the facts before us. It is enough to sustain the limitation of liability attached to the unrepeated rate that another special rate was offered for messages of value and importance, and not availed of. The fact that the alternative rate had tied to it a provision which, if tested, might be found to be void, is not material in a case where no effort was made to take advantage of it.

Reversed.

MR. JUSTICE PITNEY and MR. JUSTICE CLARKE dissent.

CHICAGO, MILWAUKEE & ST. PAUL RAILWAY COMPANY *v.* McCAULL-DINSMORE COMPANY

253 U. S. 97 (1920)

Mr. Justice Holmes delivered the opinion of the court.

This is an action for the loss of grain belonging to the plaintiff and delivered on November 17, 1915, to the defendant, the petitioner, in Montana, for transportation to Omaha, Nebraska. The grain was shipped under the uniform bill of lading, part of the tariffs filed with the Interstate Commerce Commission, by which it was provided that "the amount of any loss or damage for which any carrier is liable shall be computed on the basis of the value of the property at the place and time of shipment under this bill of lading, including freight charges, if paid." The petitioner has paid $1,200.48, being the amount of the loss so computed, but the value of the grain at the place of destination at the time when it should have been delivered, with interest, less freight charges, was $1,422.11. The plaintiff claimed the difference between the two sums on the ground that the Cummins Amendment to the Interstate Commerce Act made the above stipulation void. The District Court gave judgment for the plaintiff, 252 Fed. Rep. 664, and the judgment was affirmed by the Circuit Court of Appeals. 260 Fed. Rep. 835.

The Cummins Amendment, Act of March 4, 1915, c. 176, 38 Stat. 1196, provides that the carriers affected by the act shall issue a bill of lading and shall be liable to the lawful holder of it "for any loss, damage, or injury to such property . . . . and no contract, receipt, rule, regulation, or other limitation of any character whatsoever, shall exempt such common carrier . . . . from the liability hereby imposed" and further that the carrier "shall be liable . . . . for the full actual loss, damage, or injury . . . . notwithstanding any limitation of liability or limitation of the amount of recovery or representation or agreement as to value in any such receipt or bill of lading, or in any contract, rule, regulation, or in any tariff filed with the Interstate Commerce Commission; and any such limitation, without respect to the manner or form in which it is sought to be made is hereby declared to be unlawful and void." Before the passage of this amendment the Interstate Commerce Commission had upheld the clause in the bill of lading as in no way limiting the carriers' liability to less than the value of the goods but merely offering the most convenient way of finding the value. *Shaffer & Co.*

v. *Chicago, Rock Island & Pacific Ry. Co.*, 21 I. C. C. 8, 12. In a subsequent report upon the amendment it considered that the clause was still valid and not forbidden by the law. 33 I. C. C. 682, 693. The argument for the petitioner suggests that courts are bound by the Commission's determination that the rule is a reasonable one. But the question is of the meaning of a statute and upon that, of course, the courts must decide for themselves.

We appreciate the convenience of the stipulation in the bill of lading and the arguments urged in its favor. We understand that it does not necessarily prevent a recovery of the full actual loss, and that if the price of wheat had gone down the carrier might have had to pay more under this contract than by the common law rule. But the question is how the contract operates upon this case. In this case it does prevent a recovery of the full actual loss, if it is enforced. The rule of the common law is not an arbitrary fiat but an embodiment of the plain fact that the actual loss caused by breach of a contract is the loss of what the contractee would have had if the contract had been performed, less the proper deductions, which have been made and are not in question here. It seems to us, therefore, that the decision below was right, and as, in our opinion, the conclusion is required by the statute, neither the convenience of the clause, nor any argument based upon the history of the statute or upon the policy of the later Act of August 9, 1916, c. 301, 39 Stat. 441, can prevail against what we understand to be the meaning of the words. Those words seem not only to indicate a broad general purpose but to apply specifically to this very case.

Judgment affirmed.

THE CHIEF JUSTICE dissents for the reasons stated by the Interstate Commerce Commission.

SOUTHERN PACIFIC COMPANY *v.* INTERSTATE COMMERCE COMMISSION

SOUTHERN CALIFORNIA RAILWAY COMPANY *v.* SAME

ATCHISON, TOPEKA AND SANTA FE RAILWAY COMPANY *v.* SAME

SANTA FE PACIFIC RAILROAD COMPANY *v.* SAME

SOUTHERN PACIFIC COMPANY *v.* SAME

200 U. S. 536 (1906)[1]

Prior to January 1900 there were in force over the Southern Pacific and the Santa Fe systems (hereafter called the initial carriers) through rates on citrus fruit from California to the East. Rivalry among connecting carriers to obtain this California fruit freight business led to systematic rebates to shippers to induce routing over the rebating roads. To end this practice, the initial carriers and several connecting carriers agreed upon a new through tariff, reserving the right to the initial carriers to route the goods beyond their own terminals. This new tariff was published to take effect January 1, 1900. On February 26, 1900 proceedings were commenced before the Interstate Commerce Commission, under sections 13, 14, 15 of the Interstate Commerce Act, on the part of corporations engaged in the business of shipping oranges and other citrus fruit from southern California to the Eastern markets to restrain the enforcement of the rule reserving to initial carriers the right to route. After hearing, the Commission (the chairman, Mr. Commissioner Knapp, dissenting) ordered the defendant carriers to cease from exacting from shippers the right themselves to make the route which the freight should take.

The initial carriers, believing the Commission had erred in its decision, refused to obey the order which it made, and thereupon the Commission, pursuant to the sixteenth section of the act, filed its bill in the Circuit Court for the purpose of enforcing its order.

The bill thus filed by the Commission was demurred to by the defendants, and the demurrer was overruled. 123 Fed. Rep. 598.

[1] The facts have been briefly restated. — ED.

The railroad companies then answered, and the case, after the taking of further evidence, came up for final hearing, when the order of the Commission was affirmed and directed to be enforced (132 Fed. Rep. 829), although the Circuit Court put the affirmance on the ground that the agreement as to routing showed that there was a violation of § 5 of the Commerce Act, in that such agreement amounted to a contract or combination for the pooling of freights. The court passed upon no other question raised in the case. A very full statement of facts is contained in the report in 132 Fed. Rep. *supra.*

A motion was made for a supersedeas pending the hearing of this appeal, which, for the reasons stated in the opinion of the Circuit Court, was denied. 137 Fed. Rep. 606.

MR. JUSTICE PECKHAM delivered the opinion of the Court.

Although there are separate proceedings in these various cases, the question arising in all is identical and the cases will hereafter be spoken of as if there were but one proceeding before the court. The single question presented is, has the carrier that takes the fruit from the shipper in California the right, under the facts herein, to insist upon the rule permitting such carrier to route the freight at the time it is received from the shipper?

The Commission has decided that the carrier has not the right, and that the rule denies to shippers the use of their transportation facilities, which such shippers are entitled to, and that in its application, by the initial carriers to the fruit traffic, the shippers are subjected to undue, unjust and unreasonable prejudice and disadvantage, and the carriers are given an undue and unreasonable preference and advantage. If this be the necessary effect of the rule, it may be assumed to be a violation of section 3 of the Interstate Commerce Act, and the Commission, therefore, rightly ordered the carriers to desist from observing it.

By section 16 of the act, the Circuit Court is given authority to enforce "any lawful order or requirement of the Commission." If the order be not a lawful one, the court is without power to enforce it. Whether or not such order was lawful is the matter to be determined.

The Commission does not find that any contract existed between the initial carrier and its eastern connections to bill the fruit according to certain proportions among the connecting railroads. The Commission said:

"The situation warrants the inference, however, that these

two initial carriers or systems, connecting with other carriers at various points, and they in turn connecting with numerous other carriers, as shown by the tariff, are able by acting in concert, and routing as they see fit, to only send traffic over the roads of such carriers as fulfilled an agreement to refrain from making any rate concession to the shippers, and some influence of like character could doubtless be exerted by them upon the car lines which are also hereinafter referred to."

Such statement simply shows that if any eastern railroad, with which an agreement for joint through rates existed, should give rebates on the joint through rate tariff, thus carrying freight below the rates agreed upon as the through rate tariff, that road would not get the freight.

We see nothing in the initial carrier endeavoring to maintain the rates agreed upon as a through rate tariff, and thereby preventing the payment of rebates, which in itself is a violation of the act. The act especially prohibits, in the sixth section, any alteration of the rates agreed upon, in favor of any person or persons. There is no finding that there has in fact, as a result of the rule, been any discrimination or unjust action as between the initial carriers and the shippers themselves, and there is no evidence that any was ever practiced.

In the examination of the rule it is well to bear in mind the situation of the companies and the business at the time of its adoption. It is fully set forth in the foregoing statement of facts. The payment of the rebates was a shame and was in truth unsatisfactory to all the railroads, besides being plainly a violation of the Commerce Act.

We think there is nothing in the act which clearly prohibits the roads from adopting the rule in question. The decision turns upon the construction of a statute which at least does not in terms prohibit.

In cases such as this a court is bound to consider the bearing of the result of either construction upon the general purposes of the act. In enacting the Commerce Act this court has stated that the object of Congress was to facilitate and promote commerce by the adoption of regulations to make charges for transportation just and reasonable, and to forbid undue and unreasonable preferences or discriminations. *Texas & Pacific Ry. Co.* v. *Interstate Commerce Commission*, 162 U. S. 197.

The importance of the rule in this case, so far as the shipper is concerned. is not so great as is its importance to the railroads in preventing rebates. If the right of routing be looked at alone, without any connection with the claimed right of diverting the freight, the rule itself would be generally of little importance to the shipper. In all probability the freight gets to its destination when routed by the carrier as early as if routed by the shipper, and in that event the particular route taken is not very important to the latter. The evidence before the Circuit Court shows that the routing, when done by the carrier, was fairly apportioned among the eastern connections, having an eye to good service and expedition, and the roads that the routing was done over were the best roads in the country; the roads that have been eliminated were the roundabout roads; there were no roads that were insolvent, so far as known by the witnesses. Now, as the fact appears that the actual routing is generally conceded the shipper, and also his request for a diversion allowed, there is nothing in the mere right of routing by the companies, separate from other facts, of which the shipper can properly complain. The Commission says it does not distinctly appear in testimony that a delivery by a particular terminal road has been denied in any particular case, yet the manifest evil results of an arbitrary application of the rule must be considered in determining its legality. If there is no such arbitrary application, we do not agree that the rule itself is to be held illegal, because a violation of the act may be committed, while the evidence is that none in fact was committed. It does appear that the mere existence of the right to route on the part of the company has ended the practice of rebating. But the opportunity to obtain rebates on the part of the shipper is surely not a ground for action by the Commission or by the court. Of course, if in attempting to cut off rebates there is a violation of the act, the act must be followed, and that means of prohibiting them must be abandoned. Courts may well look with some degree of care before so construing a statute, which confessedly does not in terms so provide, as to prohibit such a rule on the ground that it would be a violation of the statute. We are of opinion that the rule is not a violation thereof.

It is conceded that the different railroads forming a continuous line of road are free to adopt or refuse to adopt joint through tariff rates. The Commerce Act recognizes such right and provides for the filing, with the Commission, of the through tariff rates, as agreed upon between the companies. The whole question of joint through tariff rates, under the provisions of the act, is one of agreement between the companies, and they may. or may not, enter into it, as they may think their interests demand. And it is equally plain that an initial carrier may agree upon joint through rates with one or several connecting carriers, who between each other might be regarded as competing roads.

It is also undoubted that the common carrier need not contract to carry beyond its own line, but may there deliver to the next succeeding carrier and thus end its responsibility, and charge its local rate for the transportation. If it agree to transport beyond its own line, it may do so by such lines as it chooses. *Atchison &c. R. R. Co.* v. *Denver &c. R. R. Co.*, 110 U. S. 667; *Louisville & Nashville R. R. Co.* v. *West Coast Naval Stores &c. Co.*, 198 U. S. 483. This right has not been held to depend upon whether the original carrier agreed to be liable for the default of the connecting carrier after the goods are delivered to such connecting carrier. As the carrier is not bound to make a through contract, it can do so upon such terms as it may agree upon, at least so long as they are reasonable and do not otherwise violate the law. In this case the initial carrier guarantees the through rate but only on condition that it has the routing. It was stated by the late Mr. Justice Jackson of this court, when Circuit Judge in the case of *Texas &c. R. R. Co.* v. *Interstate Commerce Commission*, 43 Fed. Rep. 37, as follows:

"Subject to the two leading prohibitions that their charges shall not be unjust or unreasonable, and that they shall not unjustly discriminate, so as to give undue preference or disadvantage to persons or traffic similarly circumstanced, the act to regulate commerce leaves common carriers as they were at the common law, free to make special contracts looking to the increase of their business, to classify their traffic, to adjust and apportion their rates so as to meet the necessities of commerce, and generally to manage their important interests upon the same principles which are regarded as sound, and adopted in other trades and pursuits."

This statement was approved by this court in *Cincinnati &c. R. R. Co.* v. *Interstate Commerce Commission*, 162 U. S. 184, 197.

Having this right to agree on a joint through tariff on terms mutually satisfactory, we cannot find anything in the Commerce Act which forbids the agreement with such a condition therein as to routing. It is said that the sixth section, properly construed, prohibits such condition. We confess our inability to find anything in that section which does so.

The fact that the rate, when agreed upon, must be filed with the Commission and made public by the common carriers when directed by the Commission, does not prevent the adoption of an agreement for a through rate tariff with the condition as stated. Nor does the provision granting power to the Commission to prescribe forms of schedules of rates, as provided for in the sixth section, have any such effect. Where there is an agreed through rate tariff, and as part of such agreement, which is joined in by several railroads, the right to route cars is reserved to the initial carrier, we do not think that the shipper, by virtue of the sixth section, has the right to ignore the condition which is part of the agreement under which the through rate is made and is guaranteed.

We cannot see that the rule violates the third section of the act. All the facts referred to by the Commission are nothing but statements as to how, under such a rule, there might occur a violation of that section, but we find nothing in the facts stated by the Commission, showing that such violation had occurred. In truth, the companies did not always even enforce the rule, still less did they discriminate against shippers or in favor of carriers. On the contrary, the Commission stated that "while the initial carriers do not always route as requested by the shippers, they generally comply with their request." The mere failure to do so does not, however, prove a violation of the section.

The right to route is also complained of because the rule confined it to the fruit business, and therefore it was, as contended, a discrimination against those engaged in it or against the traffic itself. The transportation of this fruit is a special business, large interests are involved in it, and particular pains are taken to transport it as speedily as possible. With regard to all other freight it has substantially nothing in common. The cases are wholly unlike, and there has been no proof or complaint as to rebates being given in connection with other freight, and the witnesses for the railroad state if there were any evidence or complaint of such rebates, the same rule as to routing would be immediately adopted. As has been said, there is no pretense of discrimination under this rule between the shippers of freight themselves. There seems to be unanimous agreement that all shippers are treated alike and are granted the same privileges, and the routing is generally accorded them. It is the power to route, which rests with the initial carrier, that really takes away the motive for a rebate in the manner indicated, and, therefore, the granting of the request of the shipper as to a particular route may be, and is, generally conceded without danger that the rebate business may be again practiced.

The important facts that control the situation are that the carrier need not agree to carry beyond its own road, and may agree upon joint through tariff rates or not, as seems best for its own interests. Having these rights of contract the carrier may make such terms as it pleases, at least so long as they are reasonable and do not otherwise violate the law. We think the routing rule is not unreasonable under the facts herein and that it does not violate the third section of the act.

Because opportunities for the violation of the act may occur, by reason of the rule, is no ground for holding as a matter of law that violations must occur, and that the rule itself is therefore illegal. We are, consequently, unable to concur in the view taken by the Commission that the rule violates the third section of the act.

NORTHERN PACIFIC RAILWAY COMPANY *v.* SOLUM

NORTHERN PACIFIC RAILWAY COMPANY *v.* MONARCH ELEVATOR COMPANY

NORTHERN PACIFIC RAILWAY COMPANY *v.* DULUTH ELEVATOR COMPANY

247 U. S. 477 (1918)

Mr. Justice Brandeis delivered the opinion of the court.

These three cases were heard together. In each of them the plaintiff below sought to recover from the Northern Pacific Railway Company, in a state district court of Minnesota, an amount equal to that by which the freight collected for coal carried on an interstate route from Duluth to some other city in the State, exceeded the rate prescribed by the Minnesota law for carriage between those points on another route, wholly within the State. In each case judgment was entered in the trial court for the plaintiff for such amount; and the judgments were affirmed by the Supreme Court of Minnesota. Each case comes here on writ of error.

Carlton is situated on the Northern Pacific Railway, west of Duluth. Between these Minnesota cities that company operates two lines of railroad, each mainly single track. The northerly line, about 20.9 miles in length, lies wholly within Minnesota; the southerly line, 27.5 miles in length, extends for 11.7 miles through Wisconsin. The southerly is the original Northern Pacific line which was built in 1885. It has relatively light grades. The northerly line was built by the St. Paul and Duluth Railroad Company and came under the management of the Northern Pacific in 1900. It has a heavy upgrade from Duluth to Carlton. Since 1900 both lines have been operated continuously by the Northern Pacific. Because of these grades, the northerly route has been used almost exclusively for such Duluth shipments as are inbound and the southerly route has been used for such as are outbound. Until June, 1907, the rates were the same over the two routes. They were duly filed with the Minnesota Railroad and Warehouse Commission and with the Interstate Commerce Commission.

In 1907 the legislature of Minnesota fixed for intrastate carriage of coal, maximum rates which were lower than the published rates theretofore charged. The rates so fixed were to take effect June 1, 1907; but before that date their enforcement was enjoined by the proceedings which were reviewed in *The Minnesota Rate Cases*, 230 U. S. 352. This injunction remained in effect until July, 1913, when it was dissolved pursuant to that decision. Until then the Northern Pacific continued to charge the published rates (and therefore the same rates) on all shipments of coal from Duluth to Minnesota points, whether moving via the interstate route or the intrastate route. After dissolution of the injunction, the company refunded on the few shipments which had moved over the intrastate route, the amount by which the charges actually collected exceeded the charges which would have been collected had the rates fixed by the legislature been observed. It refused, however, to make refunds on shipments made over the interstate route, on the ground that the state statute did not affect them.

Among such shipments were those involved in these cases, from Duluth by the interstate route to three Minnesota points, Hitterdal, Battle Lake, and Hawley, cities on the Northern Pacific lying west of Carlton. The shipment in each case was delivered to the Railway without any instruction as to how it should be routed; but the plaintiffs contended that, in the absence of instructions, it was the duty of the carrier to select that route which was for the interest of the shipper, namely the intrastate route; because it would prove to be the cheaper, if the rates prescribed by the State were upheld. The several shippers claimed that they were entitled to the same refunds which would have been made if the coal had been carried on the intrastate route; and the suits were brought to recover these amounts.

The Railway answered in the first two cases, that, at the time of the shipments, the rates published were (because of the injunction in effect) identical on the two routes; that "in the ordinary and proper and economical operation of its property, it was necessary to move, and this defendant in general did and does now, move all out-bound shipments from Duluth via the interstate line and all in-bound shipments into Duluth via the intrastate line, and that to have carried the shipments referred to in the complaint to their destination . . . . via said intrastate line instead of via the interstate line, over which they were actually carried, would have entailed great additional expense upon this defendant"; and that these rates were just and reasonable for the service performed and were collected pursuant to the tariffs published and filed with the Interstate Commerce Commission. In the third case the answer alleged in addition, that, on December 24, 1915, and prior to the commencement of that action, the Interstate Commerce Commission had, in *Holmes & Hallowell Co.* v. *Great Northern Ry. Co.*, 37 I. C. C. 627, decided that the practice of defendant in routing its westbound shipments from Duluth over its interstate line was a proper and reasonable practice and had denied the application for reparation on shipments of coal made over that route.

The judgments entered were upon demurrers to the answers. That in number 205 was entered May 28, 1916; that in number 206 on May 23, 1916; that in number 526 on May 2, 1917. (133 Minnesota, 93; *Id.* 461; 136 *Id.* 468.) In each case it is assigned as error that the state court held that the cause of action therein is not affected by the federal statute regulating interstate commerce; and also that the state court assumed jurisdiction in advance of a determination by the Interstate Commerce Commission as to whether the practice of the Northern Pacific Railway, in sending via its interstate route all shipments of the character involved in these cases, was reasonable. In the third case the additional error is assigned that the court held that the intrastate rate should be applied, although the Interstate Commerce Commission had found that the practice of routing out-bound shipments from Duluth via the interstate route was proper and reasonable. The objection that the court lacked jurisdiction to entertain the proceeding was not made in the answers in the trial court; but it was insisted upon before the Supreme Court of Minnesota; was considered and overruled by that court (133 Minnesota, 93, 97); and is available here. In numbers 205 and 206 judgment was entered before the Act of September 6, 1916. A federal question is involved; and the cases are properly here under § 237 of the Judicial Code. In number 526 the judgment was entered after the Act of September 6, 1916, c. 448, 39 Stat. 726, took effect. In that case there was not drawn in question the validity of a statute or treaty nor the validity of any authority exercised under the State. *Philadelphia & Reading Coal & Iron Co.* v. *Gilbert,* 245 U. S. 162; *Ireland* v. *Woods,* 246 *U.* S. 323; *Stadelman* v. *Miner,* 246 U. S. 544. The writ of error in number 526 must therefore be dismissed; although the defendant in error has not objected to the jurisdiction of this court.

We proceed to consider numbers 205 and 206. In those cases the Supreme Court of Minnesota declared that the carrier's duty was governed by the common law and it stated the applicable principle as follows (p. 96):

"Where a railroad company operates two lines of railroad between the same points, and the freight rate over one line is less than such rate over the other line, if other conditions are reasonably equal, it is the duty of the company to transport shipments between those points over the line which will give the shipper the benefit of the cheaper rate. To justify transporting such shipments over the other line and thereby compel the shipper to pay the higher rate, the company must show that such line was chosen by the shipper or that the circumstances or exigencies were such that a proper regard for the interests of the shipper precluded the use of the cheaper line."

In the absence of shipping instructions it is ordinarily the duty of the carrier to ship by the cheaper route. But the duty is not an absolute one. The obligation of the carrier is to deal justly with the shipper, not to consider only his interests and to disregard wholly its own and those of the general public. If, all things considered, it would be unreasonable to ship by the cheaper route, the carrier is not compelled to do so. The duty is upon the carrier to select the cheaper route only "if other conditions are reasonably equal." Resort to the more expensive route may be justified. And the justification may rest either upon the peculiar circumstances of a particular case or upon a general practice. In the cases before us the justification is rested upon a general practice.

The answers allege that, because of the grades of the two lines, all outbound shipments were and are in general moved over the southerly route on account of the very great expense which another arrangement would entail. It may well be, under such circumstances, that carriage over the interstate route would be justified, even if it appeared that it was feasible to haul freight out of Duluth over the intrastate line. Whether the practice of the carrier of shipping over the interstate route was reasonable, when a lower intrastate route was open to it, presents an administrative question, one of perhaps considerable complexity.

PERE MARQUETTE RAILWAY COMPANY *v.* J. F. FRENCH & COMPANY

254 U. S. 538 (1921)

MR. JUSTICE BRANDEIS delivered the opinion of the court.

The Federal Uniform Bills of Lading Act of August 29, 1916, c. 415, 39 Stat. 538, provides by § 9 that a carrier is, subject to the provisions of §§ 10, 11 and 12, "justified . . . . in delivering goods to one who is"

(c) "A person in possession of an order bill for the goods by the terms of which the goods are deliverable to his order; or which has been endorsed to him, or in blank by the consignee, or by the mediate or immediate indorsee of the consignee."

The main questions presented for our decision in this case are, whether, upon the facts hereinafter stated, there was a delivery to one in possession of the bill, and, if so, whether the delivery exonerated the carrier, it having been made without requiring surrender of the bill of lading.

In 1917 J. F. French & Company shipped a carload of potatoes from Bailey, Michigan, to Louisville, Kentucky, by the Pere Marquette Railroad as initial carrier and the Big Four Railroad as connecting and terminal carrier. The shipment was made on a "consignor's order" bill of lading in the standard form by which the car was consigned to the shipper's order at Louisville; and there was a notation: "Notify Marshall & Kelsey, c/o Capt. Bernard, Commissary, Camp Zachary Taylor." The shipper attached the bill of lading to a draft on Marshall & Kelsey for the purchase price of the potatoes and sold and delivered both, duly endorsed in blank, to a bank at Grand Rapids. This bank transmitted for collection the draft, with bill of lading attached, to an Indianapolis bank. The latter, without obtaining payment of the draft, detached the bill of lading from it and wrongfully delivered the bill of lading to Marshall & Kelsey. The car having reached Louisville, its destination named in the bill of lading, it was physically delivered by the Big Four, upon request of one Bindner, to the Southern Railroad to be forwarded to Dumesnil, under the circumstances hereinafter set forth, without requiring surrender of the bill of lading. Later upon the refusal of Marshall & Kelsey to accept the potatoes and honor the draft, possession of the car and bill of lading was returned to the shippers who accepted them under protest and, without waiving any rights which they might have, proceeded to dispose of the potatoes elsewhere in order to make the damage as light as possible for all concerned. The shippers then brought this suit in a state court of Michigan against the Pere Marquette to recover compensation, contending that the carrier had by delivering the car upon request without requiring surrender of the bill of lading become liable for conversion of the potatoes. The court directed a verdict for plaintiff; and the judgment entered thereon was affirmed by the Supreme Court of Michigan. 204 Michigan, 578. The case comes here on writ of certiorari. 250 U. S. 637.

The following additional facts are material: Camp Zachary Taylor was located about six miles from Louisville on the Southern Railroad, near Dumesnil station. Marshall & Kelsey had contracted with the Government to supply a large quantity of potatoes at this camp; and had made a contract of purchase with J. F. French & Company. The car in question was shipped to Louisville to be applied on these contracts. The endorsed bill of lading for this, as for other cars shipped under like circumstances, had been left by Marshall & Kelsey at Dumesnil with one Bindner, an employee of the Southern Railroad, for safe-keeping. He, having the bill of lading in his possession at Dumesnil, telephoned from there, at Marshall & Kelsey's request, to the Big Four Railroad to ascertain whether the car had arrived at Louisville. Finding that it had, Bindner, knowing the Government's need of potatoes, told the Big Four trackage clerk that "he had the bill of lading and to let the car go out to the camp." Bindner had no specific instructions from Marshall & Kelsey to do this; but his action was later ratified by them. Upon receiving Bindner's further assurance that a small demurrage charge which had accrued would be paid, the trackage clerk, without requiring surrender of the bill of lading, released the car, changed the waybill so as to provide for delivery of the car at Dumesnil, and turned it over to the Southern. A charge of 6 cents per hundred pounds thereby became payable to the Southern Railroad for the local carriage from Louisville to Dumesnil; and it was left by the waybill payable by the consignee with the other freight charges upon receipt of the car at Dumesnil. The Big Four had no information that the draft covering the car had not been paid or of the circumstances under which Bindner obtained possession of the bill of lading. The car arrived at Dumesnil, but the Government did not accept it. Thereupon Bindner returned the bill of lading to Marshall & Kelsey upon their request; they returned it to the Indianapolis bank; this bank returned it and the draft to the Grand Rapids bank; which in turn surrendered both to J. F. French & Company, upon being repaid the sum originally credited to their account. The shippers then took possession of the car; disposed of the potatoes elsewhere, but at a lower price; and brought this suit to recover the amount of their loss. The evidence is in conflict concerning the reason for the failure of the Government to accept the potatoes, their condition, and the cause of deterioration in them, if any; and no finding of fact was made by the Supreme Court of Michigan on this issue. But, in an action for conversion the matter could affect only the question of damages and not that of liability; and it is not material in the view which we take of the case.

There is no controversy over the amount of the loss. Nor is it denied that suit was properly brought against the Pere Marquette as initial carrier. The shipment was interstate. The shippers sue the initial carrier under § 20 of the Act to Regulate Commerce as amended contending that there was a conversion of the goods by a misdelivery of them at Dumesnil instead of a delivery at Louisville; or, if it be held that there was a delivery at Louisville, that it was an unjustifiable delivery in violation of the contract of carriage, since a clause in the bill of lading declared: "The surrender of this original bill of lading properly endorsed shall be required before delivery of the property." The carrier defends on the ground that there was a delivery at Louisville which exonerated it under § 9 of the Federal Uniform Bills of Lading Act. Is the carrier liable for misdelivery, because the car was sent from Louisville to Dumesnil upon Bindner's request without requiring surrender of the bill of lading?

First. The Supreme Court of Michigan held that the Big

Four in sending the car over the Southern to Dumesnil at the request of Bindner made not a delivery but an irregular reconsignment. Whatever name be used in referring to the act of forwarding the car, the Big Four, when it surrendered possession of the car to the Southern at Bindner's request, terminated its relation as carrier; just as it would have done if, at his request, it had shunted the car onto a private industrial track or had given the control of it to a truckman on the team tracks. Having brought the goods to the destination named in the bill of lading the carrier's only duty under its contract was to make a delivery at that place; and it could make that delivery by turning the goods over to another carrier for further carriage. Compare *Bracht* v. *San Antonio & Aransas Pass Ry. Co., ante*, 489; *Seaboard Air-Line Railway* v. *Dixon*, 140 Georgia, 804; *Melbourne & Troy* v. *Louisville & Nashville R. R. Co.*, 88 Alabama, 443. The fact that in forwarding the car the Big Four used the original waybill, striking out the word "Louisville" under the "destination" and substituting "Dumesnil, Ky. So. R. R." is of no significance. The shipment from Louisville to Dumesnil was a wholly new transaction. In turning over the car for this new shipment the railway made a disposal of it in assumed termination and discharge of its obligations, which was, in legal contemplation, a delivery. Whether it was a justifiable delivery and did indeed discharge its obligations we must next consider.

Second. Was the delivery at Bindner's order one which the carrier was justified in making under the provisions of § 9 of the Federal Uniform Bills of Lading Act? Prior to the enactment of the Federal Uniform Bills of Lading Act, or of other applicable legislation, a carrier was not ordinarily relieved from liability to the consignor or owner for delivery of goods to a person not legally entitled to receive them, although such person was in possession of an order bill of lading duly endorsed in blank, and surrendered it to the carrier at the time of delivery. Delivery was held not to be a justification because the bill of lading, despite insertion therein of words of negotiability, did not become a negotiable instrument. Independently of statute (and, indeed, also under earlier state statutes) the insertion of words of negotiability had merely the effect of enabling title to the goods to be transferred by transfer of the document. See *Berkely* v. *Watling*, 7 A. & E. 29. But one who did not have a valid title to the goods could not by transfer of the bill of lading give a good title to a *bona fide* holder. *Shaw* v. *Railroad Co.*, 101 U. S. 557. When in the interests of commerce the Federal Uniform Bills of Lading Act extended to bills of lading certain characteristics of negotiable paper in order to protect a *bona fide* purchaser of such bills, it was deemed proper to afford also certain protection to the carrier. This was done, in part, by providing in § 9 that the carrier would be justified in making delivery to any person in possession of an order bill of lading duly endorsed, with certain exceptions to be noted below.

The shippers contend that Bindner was not "a person in possession" of the bill, because he held it as agent for Marshall & Kelsey and not on his own account. So far as the carrier is concerned that fact is entirely immaterial. Under § 9 it is physical possession of the bill which is made a justification for delivery of the goods by the carrier. Under that section it is immaterial in what capacity the person holds possession of the bill, and also whether he holds it lawfully or unlawfully, so long as the carrier has no notice of any infirmity of title. But the shippers' contention would not be advanced if it were held that the legal, not the physical, possession is determinative. For Bindner's request of the trackage clerk to have the car forwarded to Dumesnil was later ratified by Marshall & Kelsey. If his physical possession of the bill were deemed legally their possession of it, the physical delivery to him of the car would likewise be deemed legally a delivery of it to them and, hence, satisfy in this respect the requirements of § 9.

The only exception to the rule justifying the carrier in making delivery to one in possession of an order bill of lading endorsed in blank, which is urged as applicable here, is where the carrier has information that the person in possession of the bill is not lawfully entitled to the goods. The shippers contend that the Big Four when it made delivery of the car had such information regarding Bindner. For this contention there is not the slightest basis in the evidence. The Big Four had no such information. Nor was there in the circumstances anything which should even have led it to doubt that Bindner was lawfully entitled to request that the car be shipped to Dumesnil.

Concluding, therefore, that there was a delivery, that it was made to a person in possession of the bill of lading properly endorsed and that it was made in good faith, the important question remains: Does such a delivery exonerate the carrier upon suit by the shipper when it failed to require surrender of the bill of lading as provided in that instrument? In our opinion there is no exoneration where loss to shipper or subsequent purchaser of the bill results from such a failure; but where the loss suffered is not the result of the failure to take up the bill, mere failure to take it up does not defeat the exoneration.

The plaintiffs seek to establish the carrier's liability for its failure to take up the bill on two theories, — first, that they are *bona fide* purchasers of the bill left outstanding; and second, that as shippers and owners their goods were converted by a delivery in violation fo the terms of the bill of lading. But the shippers cannot claim the protection of § 11 of the act as *bona fide* purchasers of the bill, as those words are understood in the law, even if in taking back the draft and the bill of lading from the bank they can be deemed purchasers within the meaning of the act. They took back the bill of lading after the events here in question, with full knowledge of them, and because of them. The purchaser whom the act protects is he who is entitled to assume that the carrier has not delivered the goods and will not thereafter deliver them except to a person who holds the bill of lading. The purpose of §§ 10, 11 and 12 is to give bills of lading attributes of commercial paper. Here the plaintiffs were not buying commercial paper but a law suit.

There is nothing in the act which imposes upon the carrier a specific duty to the shipper to take up the bill of lading. Under § 8 the carrier is not obliged to make delivery except upon production and surrender of the bill of lading; but it is not prohibited from doing so. If instead of insisting upon the production and surrender of the bill it chooses to deliver in reliance upon the assurance that the deliveree has it, so far as the duty to the shipper is concerned, the only risk it runs is that the person who says that he has the bill may not have it. If such proves to be the case the carrier is liable for conversion and must, of course, indemnify the shipper for any loss which results. Such liability arises not from the statute but from the obligation which the carrier assumes under the bill of lading.

Does a delivery without compliance with the surrender clause of the bill of lading render the carrier liable for conversion under the facts shown here? Although there is a conflict of language in the cases in which a shipper sues a carrier for delivery of goods without requiring a surrender of the bill of lading, there appears to be no conflict of principle or in decision. Where the failure to require the presentation and surrender of the bill is the cause of the shipper losing his goods, a delivery without requiring it constitutes a conversion. *Babbitt* v. *Grand Trunk Western Ry.*

Co., 285 Illinois, 267; *Turnbull* v. *Michigan Central R. R. Co.*, 183 Michigan, 213; *Judson* v. *Minneapolis & St. Louis R. R. Co.*, 131 Minnesota, 5; see *First National Bank* v. *Oregon-Washington Railroad & Navigation Co.*, 25 Idaho, 58; compare *Georgia, Florida & Alabama Ry. Co.* v. *Blish Milling Co.*, 241 U. S. 190. But where delivery is made to a person who has the bill or who has authority from the holder of it, and the cause of the shipper's loss is not the failure to require surrender of the bill but the improper acquisition of it by the deliveree or his improper subsequent conduct, the mere technical failure to require presentation and surrender of the bill will not make the delivery a conversion. *Chicago Packing & Provision Co.* v. *Savannah, Florida & Western Ry. Co.*, 103 Georgia, 140; *Famous Mfg. Co.* v. *Chicago & Northwestern Ry. Co.*, 166 Iowa, 361; *Nelson Grain Co.* v. *Ann Arbor R. R. Co.*, 174 Michigan, 80; *St. Louis Southwestern Ry. of Texas* v. *Gilbreath*, 144 S. W. Rep. (Tex. Civ. App.) 1051. In the *Chicago Packing Co. Case*, *supra*, the court said, "The loss in the present case was not occasioned by the failure of the railway company to require the production and surrender of the bills of lading, but by the faithlessness of Hobbs & Tucker to their principal." Similarly, in the case before us, the failure of the carrier to require production and surrender of the bill of lading did not cause the loss. The same loss would have resulted if the bill had been presented and surrendered. The real cause of the loss was the wrongful surrender of the bill of lading by the Indianapolis bank to Marshall & Kelsey by means of which the car was taken to Camp Zachary Taylor and the shipper deprived of the Louisville market. Nor did the failure to take up the bill enable the buyer to throw back the loss upon the shippers. The shippers deliberately assumed the loss by their voluntary act in taking back the draft and the bill of lading which they had sold to the Grand Rapids Bank. Doubtless J. W. French & Company's relations with Marshall & Kelsey and with the Grand Rapids Bank and the relations of the latter with the Indianapolis Bank made this course advisable. But it is clear that they were under no duty to do so, since the tortious act of the Bank's agent for collection had occasioned the damage. Having assumed the loss of their own volition they should not be permitted to pass it on to the carrier merely because of its technical failure to take up the bill of lading. The delivery was made to one in possession of the bill of lading who could, and doubtless would, have surrendered it, had he not been prevented by distance from doing so.

To hold a carrier liable under such circumstances would seriously interfere with the convenience and the practice of business.

Reversed.

MR. JUSTICE HOLMES did not take part in the consideration and decision of this case.

---

2. EQUALITY OF SERVICE

WIGHT *v.* UNITED STATES

167 U. S. 512 (1897)

SECTION 2 of the interstate commerce act reads:

"That if any common carrier subject to the provisions of this act shall, directly or indirectly, by any special rate, rebate, drawback or other device, charge, demand, collect or receive from any person or persons a greater or less compensation for any service rendered, or to be rendered, in the transportation of passengers or property, subject to the provisions of this act, than it charges, demands, collects or receives from any other person or persons for doing for him or them a like and contemporaneous service in the transportation of a like kind of traffic under substantially similar circumstances and conditions, such common carrier shall be deemed guilty of unjust discrimination, which is hereby prohibited and declared to be unlawful." Act of February 4, 1887, c. 104, 24 Stat. 379.

Section 10 of the act as amended by the act of March 2, 1889, c. 382, 25 Stat. 855, makes the violation of any of the provisions of the act a misdemeanor and subject to punishment. On October 8, 1894, an indictment was found in the District Court of the United States for the Western District of Pennsylvania, charging the defendant with a violation of said section 2. The trial resulted in a verdict and judgment against him, to reverse which this writ of error was sued out.

In their brief his counsel make this statement of facts:

"The undisputed facts proved in evidence are as follows: F. H. Bruening was engaged, during the year 1892, in the business of a wholesale dealer in beer in the city of Pittsburgh; he purchased his beer in Cincinnati in carload lots, from the Moerlein Brewing Company of that city; Bruening's place of business was situated on the track of the Pittsburgh, Cincinnati and St. Louis Railroad Company, known as the 'Pan-handle,' and had a siding connection with that road, so that Mr. Bruening could ship his beer from Cincinnati over the Pan-handle Railroad, and have it delivered and unloaded directly into his warehouse. The rate by the Pan-handle Railroad for this service from Cincinnati to the warehouse was fifteen cents per hundred pounds. The station of the Baltimore and Ohio Railroad Company in Pittsburgh was at some distance from Bruening's warehouse, and there was no track connection between the Baltimore and Ohio Railroad and the warehouse, so that if Bruening shipped his beer from Cincinnati by the Baltimore and Ohio route it was necessary to haul it in wagons from the Baltimore and Ohio station to the warehouse, The rate charged by the Baltimore and Ohio route between Cincinnati and Pittsburgh, on beer in carloads, was likewise fifteen cents per hundred pounds.

"In the month of June, 1892, agents of the Baltimore and Ohio Railroad Company, subordinate to the plaintiff in error, made an arrangement with Mr. Bruening, by which it was agreed that, if Bruening would ship his beer via the Baltimore and Ohio route from Cincinnati to Pittsburgh, the railroad company would make the same delivery at the door of his warehouse that was made by the Pan-handle Railroad; that is to say, the railroad company would haul the beer from its station to Bruening's warehouse without extra charge. When, afterward, it was found that the cost to the railroad company for this hauling would be three and one half cents per hundred pounds, Bruening offered to do the hauling himself for that price, and his offer was accepted. This arrangement was reported to the plaintiff in error by his subordinates, approved by him, and continued in effect during the months of June, July, August and September, 1892. During these months Bruening made large shipments of beer in carloads via the Baltimore and Ohio route, paid the charge of fifteen cents per hundred pounds on delivery, hauled the beer from the station to his warehouse, and at the end of each month presented and collected a bill for three and one half cents per hundred pounds for the hauling. At the trial there was no question made of the good faith of the arrangement with Bruening; it was not questioned that the three and one half cents was the fair cost of the hauling; that the sole object of the arrangement was to make the same delivery which was made by the Pan-handle Railroad, and at the same charge of fifteen cents per hundred pounds.

"During the continuance of this arrangement with Bruening, as shown in the evidence, the Kaufman Brewing Company of

Cincinnati made several shipments of beer in carloads by the Baltimore and Ohio route, on bills of lading in the form shown at pages 73, 74 and 75 of the record. Each of these shipments was consigned to the 'Kaufman Brewing Company, care of or notify Henry Wolf, Pittsburgh, Pa., to order of shipper,' and was taken at the fifth class rate of fifteen cents per hundred pounds, as shown on the face of the bill. Henry Wolf was a wholesale dealer in beer in Pittsburgh, whose warehouse was near the station of the Baltimore and Ohio Railroad Company, but was not connected by track with any railroad. The bills of lading for the Kaufman Brewing Company's shipments were transmitted through bank with draft attached, and Mr. Wolf testified that, after he received notice from the railroad company of the arrival of each shipment, he went to the bank and paid the draft, received the bill of lading, and, on presenting it and paying fifteen cents per hundred pounds, received the beer, which he hauled to his warehouse at his own expense."

MR. JUSTICE BREWER, after stating the case, delivered the opinion of the court.

Accepting the statement of facts made by the defendant as correct (and there is nothing in the statement which makes to his prejudice, or omitted from that statement which would be to his advantage), we are of opinion that the verdict and judgment were right, and must be sustained. It is unnecessary to consider all the instructions given and those refused, or determine whether in those given there may or may not be some language open to criticism. In its general charge the court narrowed the case to the facts which, as stated by counsel, are undisputed, and correctly stated the law applicable to those facts. Indeed, while the question of guilt or innocence was submitted to the jury and passed upon by them it is one rather of law than of fact, and if the court properly stated the law applicable to the facts, then the verdict was right and ought to be sustained. With reference to all other matters it is enough to say that our attention is called to no errors in the admission of testimony, and we see nothing in the instructions asked and given or asked and refused which could injuriously affect the rights of the defendant or limit the specific interpretation by the court of the rules of law applicable to those facts.

It will be observed that, in order to induce Mr. Bruening to transfer his transportation from a competing road to its own line, the Baltimore and Ohio Railroad Company, through the defendant, in the first place, made an arrangement by which for fifteen cents per hundredweight it would bring the beer from Cincinnati and deliver it at his warehouse; that 'afterwards this arrangementwas changed, and it delivered the beer to Mr. Bruening at its depot, and allowed him three and one half cents per hundred for carting it to his warehouse. As Mr. Bruening had the benefit of a siding connection with the competing road, and could get the beer delivered over that road at his warehouse for fifteen cents, it apparently could not induce him to transfer his business from the other road to its own without extending to him this rebate. During all this time it was carrying beer for Mr. Wolf from the same place of shipment (Cincinnati) to the same depot in Pittsburgh, and charging him fifteen cents therefor. Mr. Wolf had no siding connection with the rival road, and, therefore, had to pay for his cartage by whichever road it was carried. His warehouse was in a direct line 140 yards from the depot, while Mr. Bruening's was 172 yards, though the latter generally carted the beer by a longer route, on account of the steepness of the ascent. Now, it is contended by the defendant that it was necessary for the Baltimore and Ohio Company to offer this inducement to Mr. Bruening in order to get his business, and not necessary to make the like offer to Mr. Wolf, because he would have to go to the expense of carting by whichever road he transported; that, therefore, the traffic was not "under substantially similar circumstances and conditions" within the terms of section 2. We are unable to concur in this view. Whatever the Baltimore and Ohio Company might lawfully do to draw business from a competing line, whatever inducements it might offer to the customers of that competing line to induce them to change their carrier, is not a question involved in this case. The wrong prohibited by the section is a discrimination between shippers. It was designed to compel every carrier to give equal rights to all shippers over its own road and to forbid it by any device to enforce higher charges against one than another. Counsel insist that the purpose of the section was not to prohibit a carrier from rendering more service to one shipper than to another for the same charge, but only that for the same service the charge should be equal, and that the effect of this arrangement was simply the rendering to Mr. Bruening of a little greater service for the fifteen cents than it did to Mr. Wolf. They say that the section contains no prohibition of extra service or extra privileges to one shipper over that rendered to another. They ask whether if one shipper has a siding connection with the road of a carrier it cannot run the cars containing such shipper's freight on to that siding and thus to his warehouse at the same rate that it runs cars to its own depot, and there delivers goods to other shippers who are not so fortunate in the matter of sidings. But the service performed in transporting from Cincinnati to the depot at Pittsburgh was precisely alike for each. The one shipper paid fifteen cents a hundred; the other, in fact, but eleven and a half cents. It is true he formallly paid fifteen cents, but he received a rebate of three and a half cents, and regard must always be had to the substance and not to the form. Indeed, the section itself forbids the carrier "directly or indirectly by any special rate, rebate, drawback or other device" to charge, demand, collect or receive from any person or persons a greater or less compensation, etc. And section 6 of the act, as amended in 1889, throws light upon the intent of the statute, for it requires the common carrier in publishing schedules to "state separately the terminal charges, and any rules or regulations which in any wise change, affect or determine any part or the aggregate of such aforesaid rates and fares and charges." It was the purpose of the section to enforce equality between shippers, and it prohibits any rebate or other device by which two shippers, shipping over the same line, the same distance, under the same circumstances of carriage, are compelled to pay different prices therefor.

It may be that the phrase "under substantially similar circumstances and conditions," found in section 4 of the act, and where the matter of the long and short haul is considered, may have a broader meaning or a wider reach than the same phrase found in section 2. It will be time enough to determine that question when it is presented. For this case it is enough to hold that that phrase, as found in section 2, refers to the matter of carriage, and does not include competition.

We see no error in the record, and the judgment of the District Court is

Affirmed.

MR. JUSTICE WHITE concurs in the judgment.

INTERSTATE COMMERCE COMMISSION *v.* ALABAMA MIDLAND RAILWAY COMPANY

168 U. S. 144 (1897)

On the 27th day of June, 1892, the Board of Trade of Troy, Alabama, filed a complaint before the Interstate Commerce Commission at Washington, D. C., against the Alabama Midland Railway Company and the Georgia Central Railroad Company and their connections, claiming that in the rates charged for transportation of property by the railroad companies mentioned and their connecting lines there was a discrimination against the town of Troy, in violation of the terms and provisions of the Interstate Commerce Act of Congress of 1887.

The general ground of complaint was, that Troy being in active competition for business with Montgomery, the defendant lines of railway unjustly discriminated in their rates against the former, and gave the latter an undue preference or advantage in respect to certain commodities and classes of traffic. The specific charges insisted on at the hearing, and to which the testimony related, were:

1. That the Alabama Midland Railway and the defendant roads forming lines with it from Baltimore, New York and the East to Troy and Montgomery charged and collected a higher rate of shipments of class goods from those cities to Troy than on such shipments *through Troy* to Montgomery: the latter being the longer distance point by fifty-two miles.

2. That the Alabama Midland Railway and Georgia Central Railroad and their connections unjustly discriminated against Troy and in favor of Montgomery in charging and collecting $3.22 per ton to Troy on phosphate rock shipped from the South Carolina and Florida fields and only $3.00 per ton on such shipments to Montgomery, the longer distance point by both of said roads; and that all phosphate rock carried from said fields to Montgomery over the road of the Alabama Midland had to be hauled through Troy.

3. That the rates on cotton, as established by said two roads and their connections, on shipments to the Atlantic seaports, Brunswick, Savannah and Charleston, unjustly discriminated against Troy and in favor of Montgomery, in that the rate per hundred pounds from Troy is forty-seven cents, and that from Montgomery, the longer distance point, is only forty cents, and

that such shipments from Montgomery over the road of the Alabama Midland had to pass through Troy.

4. That on shipments for export from Montgomery and other points, within the so called "jurisdiction" of the Southern Railway and Steamship Association to the Atlantic seaports, Brunswick, Savannah, Charleston, West Point and Norfolk, a lower rate was charged than the regular published tariff rate to such seaports, and that Montgomery and such other points were allowed by the rules of said association to ship through to Liverpool via any of these seaports at the lowest through rates on the day of shipment, which might be less than the sum of the regular published rail rate and the ocean rate via the port of shipment; that this reduction was taken from the published tariff rail rate to the port of shipment; that, this privilege being denied to Troy, was an unjust discrimination against that town in favor of Montgomery and such other favored cities, and that it was also a discrimination against shipments which terminate at such seaports in favor of shipments for export.

5. That Troy was unjustly discriminated against in being charged on shipments of cotton via Montgomery to New Orleans the full local rate to Montgomery by both the Alabama Midland and Georgia Central.

6. That the rates on "class" goods from Western and Northwestern points, established by the defendants forming lines from those points to Troy, were relatively unjust and discriminatory as against Troy when compared with the rates over such lines to Montgomery and Columbus.

The Commission, having heard this complaint on the evidence theretofore taken, ordered, on the 15th day of August, 1893, the roads participating in the traffic involved in this case "to cease and desist" from charging, demanding, collecting or receiving any greater compensation in the aggregate for services rendered in such transportation than is specified, as follows, to wit:

1. On class goods shipped from Louisville, Kentucky; Saint Louis, Missouri, or Cincinnati, Ohio, to Troy aforesaid, no higher rate of charge than is now charged and collected on such shipments to Columbus, Georgia, and Eufaula, Alabama.

2. On shipments of cotton from Troy aforesaid through Montgomery, Alabama, to New Orleans, Louisiana, no higher rate of charge than fifty cents per hundred pounds.

3. On shipments of cotton from Troy aforesaid for export through the Atlantic seaports, to wit, Brunswick, Savannah,

Charleston, West Point or Norfolk, no higher rate of charge to these ports than is charged and collected on such shipments from Montgomery aforesaid.

4. On shipments of cotton from Troy aforesaid to the ports of Brunswick, Savannah or Charleston, no higher rate of charge than is charged and collected on such shipments from Montgomery aforesaid through Troy to said ports.

5. On shipments of class goods from New York, Baltimore or other Northeastern points to Troy aforesaid, no higher rate of charge than is charged and collected on such shipments through Troy to Montgomery aforesaid.

6. On shipments of phosphate rock from South Carolina and Florida fields to Troy aforesaid, no higher rate of charge than is charged and collected on such shipments through Troy to Montgomery aforesaid.

The defendants having failed to heed these orders, the Commission thereupon filed this bill of complaint in the Circuit Court of the United States for the Middle District of Alabama, in equity, to compel obedience to the same. On the hearing in said court the bill of complaint was dismissed, and complainant, the Interstate Commerce Commission, appealed the cause to the United States Circuit Court of Appeals for the Fifth Judicial Circuit, at New Orleans, Louisiana. And, thereupon, in said last-named court, on the 2d day of June, 1896, the decree of the said Circuit Court of the United States for the Middle District of Alabama was in all things duly affirmed; and from this judgment and decree the appellant appealed to this court.

MR. JUSTICE SHIRAS, after stating the case, delivered the opinion of the court.

. . . .

Whether competition between lines of transportation to Montgomery, Eufaula and Columbus justifies the giving to those cities a preference or advantage in rates over Troy, and, if so, whether such a state of facts justifies a departure from equality of rates without authority from the Interstate Commerce Commission under the proviso to the fourth section of the act, are questions of construction of the statute, and are to be determined before we reach the question of fact in this case.

It is contended, in the briefs filed on behalf of the Interstate Commission, that the existence of rival lines of transportation and, consequently, of competition for the traffic, are not facts to be considered by the Commission, or by the courts, when de termining whether property transported over the same line is carried under "substantially similar circumstances and conditions," as that phrase is found in the fourth section of the act.

Such, evidently, was not the construction put upon this provision of the statute by the Commission itself in the present case; for the record discloses that the Commission made some allowances for the alleged dissimilarity of circumstances and conditions, arising out of competition and situation, as affecting transportation to Montgomery and Troy respectively, and that, among the errors assigned, is one complaining that the court erred in not holding that the rates prescribed by the Commission in its order made due allowance for such dissimilarity.

So, too, in *In re Louisville & Nashville Railroad*, 1 Int. C. C. Rep. 31, 78, in discussing the long and short haul clause, it was said by the Commission, per Judge Cooley, that "it is impossible to resist the conclusion that in finally rejecting the 'long and short haul clause' of the House bill, which prescribed an inflexible rule, not to be departed from in any case, and retaining in substance the fourth section as it had passed the Senate, both houses understood that they were not adopting a measure of strict prohibition in respect to charging more for the shorter than for the longer distance, but that they were, instead, leaving the door open for exceptions in certain cases, and, among others, in cases where the circumstances and conditions of the traffic were affected by the element of competition, and where exceptions might be a necessity if the competition was to continue. And water competition was beyond doubt especially in view."

It is, no doubt, true that in a later case, *Railroad Commission of Georgia* v. *Clyde Steamship Co.*, 5 Int. C. C. Rep. 326, the Commission somewhat modified their holding in the *Louisville and Nashville Railroad Company case*, just cited, by attempting to restrict the competition, that it is allowable to consider, to the cases of competition with water carriers, competition with foreign railroads, competition with railroad lines wholly in a single State; but the principle that competition in such cases is to be considered is affirmed.

That competition is one of the most obvious and effective circumstances that make the conditions, under which a long and short haul is performed, substantially dissimilar, and as such must have been in the contemplation of Congress in the passage of the act to regulate commerce, has been held by many of the Circuit Courts. It is sufficient to cite a few of the number: *Ex parte Koehler*, 31 Fed. Rep. 315; *Missouri Pacific Railway* v. *Texas & Pacific Railway*, 31 Fed. Rep. 862; *Interstate Com. Com.* v. *Atchison, Topeka &c. Railroad*, 50 Fed. Rep. 295; *Same* v. *New Orleans & Texas Pacific Railroad*, 56 Fed. Rep. 925, 943; *Behlmer* v. *Louisville & Nashville Railroad*, 71 Fed. Rep. 835; *Int. Com. Com.* v. *Louisville & Nashville Railroad*, 73 Fed. Rep. 409.

In construing statutory provisions, forbidding railway companies from giving any undue or unreasonable preference or advantage to or in favor of any particular person or company, or any particular description of traffic, in any respect whatever, the English courts have held, after full consideration, that competition between rival lines is a fact to be considered, and that a preference or advantage thence arising is not necessarily undue or unreasonable. *Denaby Main Colliery Co.* v. *Manchester, Sheffield & Lincolnshire Railway*, 11 App. Cas. 97; *Phipps* v. *London & North Western Railway*, 2 Q. B. D. 1892, 229.

But the question whether competition as affecting rates is an element for the Commission and the courts to consider in applying the provisions of the act to regulate commerce, is not an open question in this court.

In *Interstate Com. Commission* v. *Baltimore & Ohio Railroad*, 145 U. S. 263, it was said, approving observations made by Jackson, Circuit Judge, (43 Fed. Rep. 37,) that the act to regulate commerce was "not designed to prevent competition between different roads, or to interfere with the customary arrangements made by railway companies for reduced fares in consideration of increased mileage, where such reduction did not operate as an unjust discrimination against other persons travelling over the road. In other words it was not intended to ignore the principle that one can sell at wholesale cheaper than at retail; that it is not all discriminations or preferences that fall within the inhibition of the statute, only such as are unjust or unreasonable;" and, accordingly, it was held that the issue by a railway company, engaged in interstate commerce, of a "party-rate ticket" for the transportation of ten or more persons from a place situated in one State or Territory to a place situated in another State or Territory, at a rate less than that charged to a single individual for a like transportation on the same trip, does not thereby make "an unjust or unreasonable charge" against such individual within the meaning of the first section of the act to regulate commerce; nor make "an unjust discrimination" against him within the meaning of the second section; nor give "an undue or unreasonable preference or advantage" to the purchasers of the party-rate ticket within the meaning of the third section.

In *Texas & Pacific Railway* v. *Interstate Com. Com.*, 162 U. S. 197, it was held that "in passing upon questions arising under the act, the tribunal appointed to enforce its provisions, whether the Commission or the courts, is empowered to fully consider all the circumstances and conditions that reasonably apply to the situation, and that, in the exercise of its jurisdiction, the tribunal may and should consider the legitimate interests as well of the carrying companies as of the traders and shippers, and in considering whether any particular locality is subjected to an undue preference or disadvantage, the welfare of the communities occupying the localities where the goods are delivered is to be considered as well as that of the communities which are in the locality of the place of shipment; that among the circumstances and conditions to be considered, as well in the case of traffic originating in foreign ports as in the case of traffic originating within the limits of the United States, competition that affects rates should be considered, and in deciding whether rates and charges, made at a low rate to secure foreign freights which would otherwise go by other competitive routes, are or are not undue and unjust, the fair interests of the carrier companies and the welfare of the community which is to receive and consume the commodities are to be considered."

To prevent misapprehension, it should be stated that the conclusion to which we are led by these cases, that, in applying the provisions of the third and fourth sections of the act, which make it unlawful for common carriers to make or give any undue or unreasonable preference or advantage to any particualar person or locality, or to charge or receive any greater compensation in the aggregate for the transportation of passengers or of like kind of property, under substantially similar circumstances and conditions, for a shorter than for a longer distance over the same line, in the same direction, competition which affects rates is one of the matters to be considered, is not applicable to the second section of the act.

As we have shown in the recent case of *Wight* v. *United States*, 167 U. S. 512, the purpose of the second section is to enforce equality between shippers over the same line, and to prohibit any rebate or other device by which two shippers, shipping over the same line, the same distance, under the same circumstances of carriage, are compelled to pay different prices therefor; and we there held that the phrase "under substantially similar circumstances and conditions," as used in the second section, refers to the matter of carriage, and does not include competition between rival routes.

This view is not open to the criticism that different meanings are attributed to the same words when found in different sections of the act; for what we hold is that, as the purposes of the several sections are different, the phrase under consideration must be read, in the second section, as restricted to the case of shippers over the same road, thus leaving no room for the operation of competition, but that in the other sections, which cover the entire tract of interstate and foreign commerce, a meaning must be given to the phrase wide enough to include all the facts that have a legitimate bearing on the situation — among which we find the fact of competition when it affects rates.

In order further to guard against any misapprehension of the scope of our decision it may be well to observe that we do not hold that the mere fact of competition, no matter what its character or extent, necessarily relieves the carrier from the restraints of the third and fourth sections, but only that these sections are not so stringent and imperative as to exclude in all cases the matter of competition from consideration in determining the questions of "undue or unreasonable preference or advantage," or what are "substantially similar circumstances and conditions." The competition may in some cases be such as, having due regard to the interests of the public and of the carrier, ought justly to have effect upon the rates, and in such cases there is no absolute rule which prevents the commission or the courts from taking that matter into consideration. . . .

MR. JUSTICE HARLAN dissenting.

. . . .

The acts of Congress are now so construed as to place communities on the lines of interstate commerce at the mercy of competing railroad companies engaged in such commerce. The judgment in this case, if I do not misapprehend its scope and effect proceeds upon the ground that railroad companies, when competitors for interstate business at certain points, may, in order to secure traffic for and at those points, establish rates that will enable them to accomplish that result, although such rates may discriminate against intermediate points. Under such an interpretation of the statutes in question, they may well be regarded as recognizing the authority of competing railroad companies engaged in interstate commerce — when their interests will be subserved thereby — to build up favored centres of population at the expense of the business of the country at large. I cannot, believe that Congress intended any such result, nor do I think that its enactments, properly interpreted, would lead to such a result.

SEABOARD AIR LINE RAILWAY COMPANY ET AL. *v.* UNITED STATES ET AL.

254 U. S. 57 (1920)

MR. JUSTICE DAY delivered the opinion of the court.

In this case a petition was filed in the District Court of the United States for the Eastern District of Virginia to enjoin an order of the Interstate Commerce Commission concerning the absorption of switching charges on the lines of the Seaboard Air Line Railway Company, the Seaboard Air Line Railway, Southern Railway Company, and Atlantic Coast Line Railway Company within the switching limits of these roads as established at Richmond, Virginia.

The Commission's order was made upon a petition of the Richmond Chamber of Commerce averring that the practice of the railroads was discriminatory and unlawful and violative of § 2 of the Act to Regulate Commerce. From the facts found by the Commission it appears that the appellant railroad companies bring freight from the south to Richmond, Virginia, where the same is delivered to industries in the switching limits of that city. If the freight is received at a point served by any two or more of the carriers, the switching charge is absorbed if the freight be delivered on the line of either. But if the delivery is to an industry served only by a non-competitive carrier the switching charge is not absorbed. The Commission illustrated the point by an example: "Oxford, N. C., is a point reached both by the Southern and the Seaboard, but not by the Chesapeake & Ohio. Norlina, N. C., is a local point on the Seaboard. Assume that industries A, B, and C [referring to a diagram] on the Seaboard, the Southern, and the Chesapeake & Ohio, respectively, are similarly located with regard to the interchange tracks of the three carriers at Richmond. On traffic from Oxford to industry B on the Southern, the Seaboard will absorb the Southern's switching charges. But on traffic from Oxford to industry C, on the Chesapeake & Ohio, the Seaboard refuses to absorb the Chesapeake & Ohio's switching charges. On traffic from and to Norlina, a local point, however, the Seaboard refuses to absorb all switching charges whatsoever to any off-line industry."

The order complained of directed the three carriers to cease and desist on or before August 1, 1917, and thereafter to abstain from absorbing switching charges on certain interstate carload freight at Richmond, Virginia, while refusing to absorb such charges on like carload shipments for a like and contemporaneous service under substantially similar circumstances and conditions, such practices having been found in a supplemental report to be unjustly discriminatory and unlawful within § 2 of the Act to Regulate Commerce; and "to establish, on or before August 1, 1917, ... and thereafter to maintain and apply uniform regulations and practices for the absorption of charges for the switching of interstate carload freight at Richmond, Va., and to collect no higher rates or charges from shippers and receivers of such carload freight at Richmond, Va., than they contemporaneously collect from any other shipper or receiver of such carload freight at Richmond, Va., for a like and contemporaneous service under substantially similar circumstances and conditions." 44 I. C. C. 455.

The District Court denied the application for an injunction, and ordered that the petition be dismissed. 249 Fed. Rep. 368.

The contention of the appellants is that the carriage is not a like and contemporaneous service in the transportation of a like kind of traffic under substantially similar circumstances and conditions.

Section 2 of the Act to Regulate Commerce provides:

"That if any common carrier subject to the provisions of this act shall, directly or indirectly, by any special rate, rebate, drawback, or other device, charge, demand, collect, or receive from any person or persons a greater or less compensation for any service rendered, or to be rendered, in the transportation of passengers or property, subject to the provisions of this act, than it charges, demands, collects, or receives from any other person or persons for doing for him or them a like and contemporaneous service in the transportation of a like kind of traffic under substantially similar circumstances and conditions, such common carrier shall be deemed guilty of unjust discrimination, which is hereby prohibited and declared to be unlawful." (24 Stat. 379.)

Upon this controversy the Commission in its report said: "Complainant insists that when the line-haul carrier reaches the common point and competes for the traffic to or from Richmond proper, the absorption of the switching charges should not be confined to that traffic for which the switching line competes for the entire haul. That is, if the Seaboard absorbs the switching charges for the shipper on the terminal tracks of the Southern, it should also absorb the switching charges for the shipper on the terminal tracks of the Chesapeake & Ohio. Unless this is done, complainant contends that the two shippers are not upon an equality, since the Seaboard pays for a delivery service to shippers on the terminal tracks of the Southern and declines to pay for a similar delivery service to shippers on the terminal tracks of the Chesapeake & Ohio. . . . .

"Section 2 is primarily directed against discrimination between shippers located in the same community. It is aimed to put all shippers within a switching district upon a substantial equality. It provides that where a carrier receives from any person a greater compensation for any service rendered in the transportation of passengers or property than it receives from any other person for doing for him a 'like and contemporaneous service in the transportation of a like kind of traffic under substantially similar circumstances and conditions, such common carrier shall be deemed guilty of unjust discrimination,' a discrimination which is prohibited and declared to be unlawful. Under this section it is settled that the competition of rival carriers as such does not constitute substantially dissimilar circumstances to justify a difference in treatment."

We are of opinion that the Commission was correct in regarding the service in question as a like and contemporary service rendered under substantially similar circumstances and conditions, and amply sustained as matter of law in *Wight* v. *United States*, 167 U. S. 512, and *Interstate Commerce Commission* v. *Alabama Midland Ry. Co.*, 168 U. S. 144. The principle established in these cases is that the statute aims to establish equality of rights among shippers for carriage under substantially similar circumstances and conditions, and that the exigencies of competition do not justify discrimination against shippers for substantially like services.

Moreover the determination of questions of fact is by law imposed upon the Commission, a body created by statute for the consideration of this and like matters. The findings of fact by the Commission upon such questions can be disturbed by judicial decree only in cases where their action is arbitrary or transcends the legitimate bounds of their authority. *Interstate Commerce Commission* v. *Louisville & Nashville R. R. Co.*, 227 U. S. 88; *Pre-Cooling Case,* 232 U. S. 199; *Los Angeles Switching Case,* 234 U. S. 294, 311, 312, and cases cited; *Pennsylvania Company* v. *United States,* 236 U. S. 351, 361.

The Commission did not hold that switching charges must be always the same. But it did hold that they must be alike where the service was rendered under substantially similar circumstances and conditions. The Commission's report says:

"We do not consider that the carriers must absorb the switching charges indiscriminately to all industries within the switching limits of Richmond if they choose to absorb the switching charges to any one industry off their rails. The illegality herein found to exist is the receiving of a greater compensation for one service than for a like service under substantially similar circumstances and conditions. To take a concrete example and referring again to the diagram. Suppose industry C were 5 miles distant from the interchange tracks of the Seaboard, while industry B were only 2 miles distant. Suppose the Chesapeake & Ohio's switching charge amounted to $5, while that of the Southern was $2. If the Seaboard absorbed the Southern's $2 switching charge on traffic to industry B, we do not consider that it must absorb the entire $5 switching charge of the Chesapeake & Ohio on traffic to industry C, but only to the extent to which the service is similar. In other words, it would probably be necessary for the Seaboard to absorb $2 of the $5 charge of the Chesapeake & Ohio."

The practice condemned by the Commission, as its report and order show, was that of absorbing switching charges only when the line-haul carrier competes with the switching line; and refusing to absorb such charges when the switching line does not compete with the line-haul carrier; this the Commission held was discrimination within the meaning of § 2 of the Act to Regulate Commerce. We find no occasion to disturb this ruling as arbitrary in character or beyond the authority of the Commission.

We find no merit in the contention that the order of the Commission was too vague and uncertain to be enforced.

Affirmed.

THE CENTRAL RAILROAD COMPANY OF NEW JERSEY ET AL. *v.* THE UNITED STATES EL AL.

257 U. S. (1921)

Mr. Justice Brandeis delivered the opinion of the court.

This suit was brought in the Federal District Court for New Jersey to enjoin the enforcement of an order of the Interstate Commerce Commission on the ground that it exceeds the powers of the Commission, was arbitrary and is void. The plaintiffs were the Central Railroad of New Jersey, the Pennsylvania, and twenty-one other railroads located in Trunk Line territory and New England. The defendants were the United States and the Interstate Commerce Commission. The former filed a motion to dismiss; the latter an answer which admitted the material allegations of the bill of complaint. On these pleadings the case was heard before three judges on an application for a preliminary injunction. This was denied without written opinion; and the case is here on appeal under the Act of October 22, 1913, c. 32, 38 Stat. 208, 220.

The order of the Commission was entered upon a petition of the American Creosoting Company to which these twenty-three carriers — and no others [1] — were made respondents. *American Creosoting Co.* v. *Director General*, 61 I. C. C. 145. It alleged that the petitioner had a creosoting plant at Newark, New Jersey, which was connected by switch tracks with the Central and the Pennsylvania; that these carriers had failed to establish there the privilege known as creosoting-in-transit; that this failure was unjust and unreasonable in violation of Section 1 of the Act to Regulate Commerce of February 4, 1887 as amended; and that it was also unjustly discriminatory in violation of Section 3. The Commission found that failure to establish this transit privilege was not unjust or unreasonable and denied relief under Section 1. But it found on the facts hereinafter stated that this failure subjected the company to unjust discrimination; and, granting relief under Section 3, the Commission directed that the discrimination be removed by the respondents, who are the appellants here.

By the privilege called creosoting-in-transit forest products received for shipment may be stopped and unloaded at an intermediate point, there subjected to the process of creosoting, and later forwarded on the original bill of lading to the destination

[1] Except the New York, Ontario and Western Railway Company, another carrier in the Trunk Line territory, whose interests were presumably not affected by the order. The number of carriers is, therefore, referred to herein as being twenty-three.

therein named. Where the privilege is granted and availed of delivery is made of the commodity to the creosoting plant, as if that were the final destination. It is there unloaded and treated; and at some time thereafter it is redelivered to the carrier, as if there were an initial shipment of the creosoted product. Then it is forwarded to the final destination. Although some charge is made for the transit service, the shipper secures thereby a lower freight rate. For through rates are generally much less than the rate on the untreated forest product from point of origin to the transit point plus that on the treated product from there to destination.

The plant of the American Creosoting Company is not reached by lines of any of the twenty-three appellants except the Central and the Pennsylvania. Neither of these two carriers accords the creosoting-in-transit privilege at any point on its lines; and no competitor of the company has a plant on those of either. Nor is the privilege granted in Trunk Line territory by any carrier, with a single exception not here material. Some competitors of the American Creosoting Company have plants in Mississippi, Indiana, Illinois, Ohio and Pennsylvania; and the several railroads on which these plants are located have, each acting independently, established the privilege at the places where those plants are situated. Under the rules of the Commission governing the making, filing and publishing of tariffs, privileges like creosoting-in-transit are treated as a matter local to the railroad on which the transit point is situated. Whether the privilege shall be granted or withheld is determined by the local carrier. If granted, the local carrier determines the conditions; and these are set forth in the local tariff. Although a joint through route with joint rates is established by concurrent action of several carriers, the transit privilege may thus be granted by a carrier without the consent of, and without consulting, connecting carriers. And the whole revenue received for use of the privilege is retained by the local carrier. The appellants did not participate in any way in establishing the transit privileges enjoyed by competitors of the Newark concern on lines of the southern and midwestern carriers; and none of those carriers is controlled by any of the appellants. But appellants did join with those southern and midwest railroads in establishing joint rates on forest products over routes which pass through the points at which this privilege prevails and also through Newark. [1]

[1] The transit privilege so granted includes cutting of paving blocks into shape at creosoting plant. On some of the railroads the joint rates do not

The order entered by the Commission declares that the twenty-three carriers "in so far as they participate in tariffs carrying joint rates" on these forest products "through Newark from points in southern classification territory to points in northern New Jersey, eastern New York and New England" subject the American Creosoting Company to undue prejudice and disadvantage; and it directs these twenty-three carriers to avoid this undue prejudice. How the discrimination shall be removed is not prescribed. In effect the order directs that unless the Central and the Pennsylvania establish the privilege at Newark, the twenty-three carriers must withdraw from all tariffs establishing the joint rates. As to administrative orders operating *in futuro*, the Commission's findings of fact are conclusive, subject to qualifications here not pertinent; and a finding that the discrimination is unjust is ordinarily a finding of fact. *Manufacturers Ry. Co.* v. *United States*, 246 U. S. 457, 481, 482. But the question presented here is whether the discrimination found can be held in law to be attributable to the appellants, and whether they can be required to cancel existing joint rates, unless it is removed. No finding made by the Commission can prevent the review of such questions. *Interstate Commerce Commission* v. *Diffenbaugh*, 222 U. S. 42; *Philadelphia & Reading Ry.* v. *United States*, 240 U. S. 334.

Creosoting-in-transit, like other transit privileges, rests upon the fiction that the incoming and the outgoing transportation services, which are in fact distinct, constitute a continuous shipment of the identical article from point of origin to final destination. The practice has its origin partly in local needs, partly in the competition of carriers for business. The practice is sometimes beneficial in its results; but it is open to grave abuses. [1] To police it adequately is difficult and expensive. Unless adequately policed, it is an avenue to illegal rebates and seriously depletes the carriers' revenues. Railroad managers differ widely as to the policy of granting such privileges. The Commission clearly has power under Section 1 of the Act to Regulate Commerce as amended to determine whether in a particular case a transit privilege should be granted or should be withdrawn. For that section requires, among

---

apply through the transit point. On them the privilege includes an out-of-line movement and on some lines also a back haul to reach final destination. This broadened privilege was sought for Newark.

[1] See In Matter of Alleged Unlawful Rates and Practices, 7 I. C. C. 240; In Matter of Substitution of Tonnage at Transit Points, 18 I. C. C. 280; The Transit Case, 24 I. C. C. 340.

other things, that carriers establish, in connection with through routes and joint rates, reasonable rules and regulations. The Commission might, therefore, acting under Section 1, have directed the Central and the Pennsylvania to establish the creosoting-in-transit practice at Newark, if it deemed failure to do so unreasonable or unjust; or it might, in an appropriate proceeding, have directed the southern and midwestern carriers to discontinue the practice on their lines, if it deemed the granting of the privilege to be unreasonable or unjust. But it did neither. Instead it sought to accomplish by indirection either one result or the other and ordered under Section 3 that the discrimination found to exist be removed. Twenty-one of the appellants are powerless either to cause the Central and the Pennsylvania to instal the privilege at Newark or to cause the southern and midwestern carriers to discontinue the practice on their lines. The Central and the Pennsylvania are likewise powerless to cause these connecting carriers to withdraw the privilege. They can, it is true, equalize conditions by establishing the privilege at Newark. But to do so would involve departure from a policy to which they have steadfastly adhered and adhesion to which was held by the Commission not to be unreasonable. If they should establish the privilege at Newark, they would act contrary to their judgment and would adopt a practice which some connecting carriers had introduced without their concurrence or consent, and which may hereafter, upon appropriate enquiry, be held by the Commission to be unjust and unreasonable. Congress could not have intended that under such circumstances relief should be afforded under Section 3, when a direct remedy is available under Section 1.

It is insisted that the order leaves appellants the alternative of withdrawing from the tariffs which establish joint rates with the southern and midwestern carriers through Newark. The order does not so provide in terms; and in fact the alleged alternative is illusory. The undue prejudice found arises not from the existence of joint rates, but from conditions local to other railroads. Cancellation of the joint rates would not change those conditions. Although the joint rates were withdrawn, the established through routes would remain. The duty to provide such routes is specifically enjoined by paragraph 4 of Section 1; and, under the provisions of paragraph 1 of Section 6, the separately established rates of the several connecting carriers would, in the absence of joint rates, apply to through transportation. So far as appears the Newark concern would be under the same disadvantage as compared with its competitors, whether the traffic moved on the combination of the rates local to the several lines or on joint rates. Even the abolition of the through routes (which is not suggested) would leave the relative positions of the several creosoting concerns unchanged. Cancellation of the joint rates would, at most, relieve appellants from the charge that they are violating the provisions of Section 3.

It is urged, that while the undue prejudice found results directly from the individual acts of southern and midwestern carriers in granting the privilege locally, the appellants, as their partners, make the prejudice possible by becoming the instruments through which it is applied. Discrimination may, of course, be practiced by a combination of connecting carriers as well as by an individual railroad; and the Commission has ample power under Section 3 to remove discrimination so practiced. See *St. Louis & Southwestern Ry. Co.* v. *United States*, 245 U. S. 136, 144. But participation merely in joint rates does not make connecting carriers partners. They can be held jointly and severally responsible for unjust discrimination only if each carrier has participated in some way in that which causes the unjust discrimination; as where a lower joint rate is given to one locality than to another similarly situated. *Penn Refining Co.* v. *Western N. Y. & P. R. R. Co.*, 208 U. S. 208, 221, 222, 225. Compare *East Tennessee, Virginia & Georgia Ry. Co.* v. *Interstate Commerce Commission*, 181 U. S. 1, 18. If this were not so, the legality or illegality of a carrier's practice would depend, not on its own act, but on the acts of its connecting carriers. If that rule should prevail, only uniformity in local privileges and practices or the cancellation of all joint rates could afford to carriers the assurance that they were not in some way violating the provisions of Section 3. What Congress sought to prevent by that section as originally enacted, was not differences between localities in transportation rates, facilities and privileges, but unjust discrimination between them by the same carrier or carriers. Neither the Transportation Act 1920, February 28, 1920, c. 91, 41 Stat. 456, nor any earlier amendatory legislation has changed, in this respect, the purpose or scope of Section 3.

Reversed.

NEW YORK, NEW HAVEN AND HARTFORD RAILROAD COMPANY *v.* INTERSTATE COMMERCE COMMISSION

INTERSTATE COMMERCE COMMISSION *v.* CHESAPEAKE AND OHIO RAILWAY COMPANY

200 U. S. 361 (1906)

MR. JUSTICE WHITE delivered the opinion of the court.

Following an inquiry begun in consequence of a complaint to it made, the Interstate Commerce Commission, through the Attorney General of the United States, filed under the act to further regulate commerce (32 Stat. 847), in the Circuit Court of the United States for the Western District of Virginia, this proceeding against the Chesapeake and Ohio Railway Company, a Virginia corporation, and the New York, New Haven and Hartford Railroad Company, a corporation of the State of Connecticut. In this opinion we shall hereafter respectively speak of the parties as the Commission, the Chesapeake and Ohio, and the New Haven. The petition averred that the Chesapeake and Ohio was engaged in the carriage of coal as interstate traffic between the Kanawha district of West Virginia and Newport News, Virginia, for delivery thence to the New Haven in Connecticut, and charged that the traffic was being moved at less than the published rates, and in such a way as to produce a discrimination in favor of the New Haven road and against others, all in violation of the act to regulate commerce and the amendments thereto. Specifying the grounds of the complaint, it was alleged that in the spring of 1903 the Chesapeake and Ohio made a verbal agreement with the New Haven to sell to that road sixty thousand tons of coal, to be carried from the Kanawha district to Newport News, and thence by water to Connecticut, for delivery to the buyer at $2.75 per ton, and that a considerable portion had already been delivered and the remainder was in process of delivery. It was averred that the price of the coal at the mines where the Chesapeake and Ohio bought it and the cost of transportation from Newport News to Connecticut would aggregate $2.47 per ton, thus leaving to the Chesapeake and Ohio only about twenty-eight cents a ton for carrying the coal from the Kanawha district to Newport News, whilst the published tariff for like carriage from the same district was $1.45 per ton.

Referring to the developments before the Commission, and

annexing as part thereof the testimony taken on such hearing and the documents connected therewith, the petition further alleged that the Chesapeake and Ohio asserted that, although the total price which it received for the coal covered by the verbal agreement was less than the total outlay in delivering the coal, including its published rates, such fact did not amount to a departure from the published rates, and was not a discrimination for two reasons: First. Because if such difference existed, it was a loss suffered by the Chesapeake and Ohio, not from taking less than its published rates, but because it had received less as purchaser than the coal had cost. Second. That even if it had not the lawful right thus to impute the payment of the price of the coal, the Chesapeake and Ohio had, in fact, received much more for the coal than the price in money agreed on, because, at the time the verbal agreement to sell was made the New Haven had a claim exceeding one hundred thousand dollars against the Chesapeake and Ohio, arising from a previous written contract to deliver coal, which was to be extinguished by the completion of the delivery of the coal, and this caused that price largely to exceed the cost of the coal to the Chesapeake and Ohio, including its published rates. Averring that the prior contract was in itself void because it also embodied an agreement to take less than the published rates and was discriminating, it was charged that the New Haven had entered into both agreements with the Chesapeake and Ohio, knowing that they were in violation of the Interstate Commerce Law. The prayer was that the Chesapeake and Ohio and the New Haven be made parties; that both roads be enjoined, the one from further executing the verbal agreement to deliver coal and the other from seeking to enforce it; that the Chesapeake and Ohio be enjoined from "accepting or receiving any rebate, concession or discrimination in respect of the transportation of any property in interstate or foreign commerce carried by it," and be, moreover, enjoined from "doing anything whatever, whereby coal or any other property shall, by any device whatever, be transported .... at a less rate than named in the tariffs published and filed by such carrier, as is required by the act to regulate commerce and acts amendatory thereof or supplementary thereto, or whereby any other advantage may be given or discrimination practiced." And that the New Haven road "be enjoined and restrained from accepting or receiving any rebate, concession or discrimination in respect of the transportation of any property in interstate or foreign commerce carried by it."

A preliminary restraining order was issued conforming to the prayer of the petition. The Chesapeake and Ohio by its answer admitted that it had made, in the spring of 1903, a verbal agreement with the New Haven road for about sixty thousand tons of Kanawha coal for the price alleged in the petition, to be transported by it to Newport News, and thence delivered by ocean transportation to the New Haven in Connecticut. It was admitted that the purchase price agreed to be paid was less than the market price of the coal plus the published rates, and the cost of transportation and delivery from Newport News to Connecticut, but it was averred that this was only apparently the case, because the contract to sell included the discharge of a debt of about one hundred thousand dollars, arising from the previous written contract to which the petition referred. The validity of both the previous written contract and the later verbal agreement was averred. The right of the Chesapeake and Ohio to buy and sell coal, and to impute any loss on the sale of the coal to itself as dealer instead of to itself as a carrier, was averred. Both the original contract and the one of 1903 were averred to have been made in good faith, not with any intention to avoid the published rates, and it was charged that at about the time the original contract was made arrangements had been made by the railroad for a rate of transportation from Newport News to Connecticut which would have caused the contract price to be adequate to pay the market price of the coal and all other charges, including the published rates, but that, subsequently thereto, the persons with whom this contract for transportation was made had violated their agreement, and that by strikes the price of coal had advanced, and thereby the loss of one hundred thousand dollars to the Chesapeake and Ohio was occasioned.

The New Haven road in its answer asserted its good faith in making both the original contract and the verbal agreement. It alleged that by the original contract it was a mere purchaser of coal from the Chesapeake and Ohio, and not a shipper over that road; that the coal bought was intended for its own use in the operation of its railroad; that it had no knowledge of the price which the Chesapeake and Ohio would be obliged to pay for the coal or the sum which it would cost that road to deliver it, and therefore had no knowledge that the total cost would not equal the market price of the coal, the cost of delivery and the published rate of the Chesapeake and Ohio. It averred the validity of the agreement, the legality of the debt of one hundred thousand dollars which resulted from it, and charged that, taking that debt into consideration, the sum which is paid the Chesapeake and Ohio for the coal under the 1903 verbal agreement largely exceeded the market price and the cost of delivery, including the published rates of the Chesapeake and Ohio. It denied that there was any departure from the public rates or any discrimination, asserted that at the time the original contract was made the price was sufficient to have enabled the Chesapeake and Ohio to perform the contract without losing anything either as a seller or as a carrier, and that if in execution of the contract a condition arose where a loss was suffered by the Chesapeake and Ohio in either capacity, it was caused by subsequent events which could not affect the validity of the contract when made, and especially denied that in any way, directly or indirectly, had it knowingly lent itself to any discrimination, or any taking by the Chesapeake and Ohio of less than its published rates.

The case was heard on the testimony taken in the proceeding before the Commission and the documents forming a part of the same, and upon further documents and testimony stipulated by counsel.

For reasons to which we shall hereafter have occasion to advert, the court held that, considering both the original contract and the verbal agreement of 1903, there was no violation of the provisions of the second and sixth sections of the act to regulate commerce, forbidding the taking of less than the published rates. It, however, held that the contracts amounted to an undue discrimination and a violation of the third section of the act. The court, hence, permanently enjoined the Chesapeake and Ohio from discharging any obligation arising from the original contract of 1896, and from further executing or attempting to execute, in any manner whatever, directly or indirectly, the verbal agreement of 1903, and it permanently enjoined the New Haven from asserting or attempting to enforce any claim arising from the contract of 1896, or in any manner, directly or indirectly, attempting to enforce the verbal agreement of 1903. Thereafter the court denied a request made by the Commission, that the injunction be expanded so as in general terms to command the Chesapeake and Ohio perpetually to observe in the future its published rates.

The New Haven appealed. The Commission also prosecuted a cross appeal because of the refusal of the court to grant its prayer to make the injunction against the Chesapeake and Ohio general in its nature, and that company, in an elaborate and separate printed argument in its own behalf, assails the judgment below on the merits and, in effect, asks its reversal on the merits.

It is apparent from the case as thus stated that, in order to decide the issues which arise, we may not confine our attention to the verbal agreement of 1903, the execution of which it was the immediate object of the proceeding to enjoin, but must consider the prior contract of 1896, since primarily the rights, if any, which arose under the verbal agreement, are inextricably involved in and dependent upon the contract of 1896. In other words, the controversy as considered by the Commission on the inquiry by it conducted and as decided below, and as here presented, involves an analysis of all the dealings under both contracts and the legal rights, if any, which arose from them. We must, therefore, consider the subject in this aspect, and to do so we state at once the facts which are admitted or which are indisputably established, reserving such questions of fact as are in dispute for separate consideration when we approach the legal propositions which arise from the undisputed facts.

The Chesapeake and Ohio, chartered by the State of Virginia, operates a road which reaches both the New River and the Kanawha coal fields of West Virginia, and extends to Newport News. The New Haven, chartered by the State of Connecticut, operates a road principally situated in New England. On December 3, 1896, these two roads entered into a written contract, the one to sell and the other to buy between July 1, 1897, and July 1, 1902, not to exceed two million gross tons of bituminous coal to be taken from the line of the Chesapeake and Ohio road; deliveries to be made not exceeding four hundred thousand tons per annum. The price agreed upon was $2.75 per gross ton, New Haven basis, settlement to be made monthly. The coal was to be delivered by the seller on the line of the New Haven. The contract is reproduced in the margin. [1]

[1] Contract made between the Chesapeake and Ohio Railway Company and the New York, New Haven and Hartford Railroad Company.

Said Chesapeake and Ohio Railway Company, for the consideration hereinafter mentioned, hereby agrees to furnish to said railroad company not to exceed two million gross tons of bituminous coal from its line in such quantities monthly as wanted from July 1, 1897, to July 1, 1902, without charge for demurrage. Deliveries to be made not exceeding four hundred thousand tons per annum.

And said Chesapeake and Ohio Railway Company further agrees that all said bituminous coal shall be of the best quality, first-class in every respect, and

The Chesapeake and Ohio, not in its own name but through others who really although not ostensibly acted for it, made a contract with operators in the New River district of West Virginia, for the delivery to it of the coal to fulfill the contract which had been made with the New Haven. In consequence of failure of some of the operators to perform their part of the contract, changes were made at various times, which it is unnecessary to note. Deliveries of the coal were made to the New Haven as required up to the winter of 1900–1901, when, because of strikes and other difficulties, delivery ceased and the New Haven bought coal in the open market and presented to the Chesapeake and Ohio a bill for the increased price which it had paid, and the Chesapeake and Ohio paid one hundred and sixty thousand dollars to cover such loss. Subsequently in 1902 further strikes supervened and deliveries again ceased, at a time when about sixty thousand tons remained yet to be delivered. The New Haven again presented a bill for damages amounting to one hundred and three thousand dollars. Thereupon the verbal agreement of 1903 was made, by which it was provided that the shortage of sixty thousand tons upon the original contract might be discharged by delivery on the part of the Chesapeake and Ohio of that amount of coal from the Kanawha district at the contract

satisfactory to said railroad company, and said railway company has the right to terminate this contract at any time if said bituminous coal be of poor quality or if its delivery be unnecessarily delayed.

And said Chesapeake and Ohio Railway Company further agrees to deliver all said bituminous coal to said railroad company in its bins at such ports upon its lines as required by the monthly requisitions of its purchasing agent.

In consideration of the faithful performance by the said Chesapeake and Ohio Railway Company of all its agreements herein contained, said railroad company agrees to pay for said bituminous coal at the rate or two and seventy-five one-hundredths dollars per gross ton, New Haven basis, settlement to be made *monthly.*

Said railway company has the right to cancel any and all portions of said quantity of bituminous coal remaining undelivered on July 1, 1902.

Witness the names of the parties hereto this the 3d day of December, 1896

CHESAPEAKE AND OHIO RAILWAY COMPANY
By M. E. INGALLS, President.
The NEW YORK, NEW HAVEN AND HARTFORD RAILROAD COMPANY,
By C. E. MELLEN, Second Vice President.

For value received, I hereby guarantee that the Chesapeake and Ohio Railway Company shall not fail to deliver coal on account of strikes.

J. PIERPONT MORGAN

price of $2.75, and when this delivery was consummated it was agreed that the Chesapeake and Ohio would be absolutely relieved from the payment of the damage claim just referred to.

At the time this verbal agreement was made the contract price was, leaving out of view the claim for damages, inadequate to pay the market price, as admitted by the pleadings, of the coal plus the published rates of the Chesapeake and Ohio to Newport News, and the charges thence to the point of delivery. To put itself in a position to carry out the agreement an individual who represented the Chesapeake and Ohio made contracts in his own name with operators in the Kanawha district to furnish the desired coal. Without stopping to state the particular methods of accounting by which the result was accomplished, it is indisputable that the Chesapeake and Ohio bore the loss arising from the difference between the contract price, the price of the coal at the mines, the published rate to Newport News, and the cost of transporting thence to the point of delivery.

Undoubtedly long prior to the making of the first contract the Chesapeake and Ohio, besides its business as a carrier, bought and sold coal. This business was carried on by the company from about 1874 up to the time of the making of the contract of 1896, as testified by the president who made that contract, as follows:

"The coal was handled by a separate and distinct department of the railway company, the mine operators delivering for an agreed price at the mines to the coal agent of the railway company all coal mined by them, the net result realized from the selling price of the coal representing the freight earned by the railway company."

And the same official testified that he made the contract of 1896 as a continuation of this system.

In 1895, however, the State of West Virginia passed "An act to prevent railroad companies from buying or selling coal or coke and to prevent discrimination." The first section of this act made it unlawful for any railroad corporation to engage directly or indirectly in the business of buying and selling coal or coke. In consequence of this act, prior to the making of the contract of 1896, the coal department of the railroad was abolished. And it was the existence of the West Virginia statute which caused the Chesapeake and Ohio, when it contracted with operators in West Virginia to procure as to both contracts the coal for delivery to the New Haven, to do so not in its own name but through another.

Before applying to these undisputed facts the legal question arising for decision, we must determine a question of fact as to which there is some dispute; that is, was the price at which the Chesapeake and Ohio contracted in 1896 to sell the coal to the New Haven sufficient to pay the cost of the coal at the mines, as well as the expense of delivery, including the published freight rate? Without stopping to go into the evidence we content ourselves with saying that we think the court below correctly held that the price was not adequate to accomplish these purposes, and that from the inception of delivery under the contract and during the whole period thereof, except for a brief time, caused by a lowering of the freight rates, the contract price was inadequate to net the railroad its proper legal tariff.

We are brought then to determine whether the contract made in 1896 for the two million tons of coal was void because in conflict with the act to regulate commerce and its amendments. In approaching the consideration of the act to regulate commerce, we for the moment put out of view the provisions of the West Virginia statute and its influence upon the validity of the contract made in West Virginia for the purpose of acquiring the coal which the Chesapeake and Ohio had obligated itself to deliver. We shall also assume for the purpose of the inquiry that the Chesapeake and Ohio, although not expressly authorized, was not prohibited by its Virginia charter from buying and selling and transporting the coal in which it dealt. The case, therefore, will be considered solely in the light of the operation and effect of the provisions of the act to regulate commerce, and we shall not direct our attention to expressly determining whether the assertion by a carrier of a right to deal in the products which it transports would not be so repugnant to the general duty resting on the carrier as to cause the exertion of the power to deal in the products which it transports to be unlawful, irrespective of statutory restrictions.

The question, therefore, to be decided is this: Has a carrier engaged in interstate commerce the power to contract to sell and transport in completion of the contract the commodity sold, when the price stipulated in the contract does not pay the cost of purchase, the cost of delivery and the published freight rates?

The previous decisions of this court concerning the Interstate Commerce Act do not afford much aid in determining this question. This is the case, because, although that act was adopted in 1887, and questions concerning the import of the act have been often here, such questions have not generally involved the operation and effect of the act concerning the command that published rates be adhered to, and the prohibitions against discrimination, favoritism or rebates, but have mainly concerned the meaning of the act in other respects, that is, involved deciding whether powers asserted as to other subjects were vested by the act in the Interstate Commerce Commission.

There are several leading cases decided by the Commission, which are relied upon by the two railroads, directly relating to the question we have stated, but, as we shall have occasion hereafter to weigh their import, we shall not now pause to analyze and apply them.

It cannot be challenged that the great purpose of the act to regulate commerce, whilst seeking to prevent unjust and unreasonable rates, was to secure equality of rates as to all and to destroy favoritism, these last being accomplished by requiring the publication of tariffs and by prohibiting secret departures from such tariffs, and forbidding rebates, preferences and all other forms of undue discrimination. To this extent and for these purposes the statute was remedial and is, therefore, entitled to receive that interpretation which reasonably accomplishes the great public purpose which it was enacted to subserve. That a carrier engaged in interstate commerce becomes subject as to such commerce to the commands of the statute, and may not set its provisions at naught whatever otherwise may be its power when carrying on commerce not interstate in character, cannot in reason be denied. Now, in view of the positive command of the second section of the act, that no departure from the published rate shall be made, "directly or indirectly," how can it in reason be held that a carrier may take itself from out the statute in every case by simply electing to be a dealer and transport a commodity in that character? For, of course, if a carrier has a right to disregard the published rates by resorting to a particular form of dealing, it must follow that there is no obligation on the part of a carrier to adhere to the rates, because doing so is merely voluntary. The all-embracing prohibition against either directly or indirectly charging less than the published rates shows that the purpose of the statute was to make the prohibition applicable to every method of dealing by a carrier by which the forbidden result could be brought about. If the public purpose which the statute was intended to accomplish be borne in mind, its meaning becomes, if possible, clearer. What was that purpose? It was to compel the carrier as a public agent to give equal treatment to all. Now if by the mere fact of purchasing and selling merchandise to be transported a carrier is endowed with the power of disregarding the published rate, it becomes apparent that the carrier possesses the right to treat the owners of like commodities by entirely different rules. That is to say, the existence of such a power in its essence would enable a carrier, if it chose to do so, to select the favored persons from whom he would buy and the favored persons to whom he would sell, thus giving such persons an advantage over every other, and leading to a monopolization in the hands of such persons of all the products as to which the carrier chose to deal. Indeed the inevitable result of the possession of such a right by a carrier would be to enable it, if it chose to exercise the power, to concentrate in its own hands the products which were held for shipment along its line, and to make it, therefore, the sole purchaser thereof and the sole seller at the place where the products were to be marketed; in other words, to create an absolute monopoly. To illustrate: If a carrier may by becoming a dealer buy property for transportation to a market and eliminate the cost of transportation to such market, a faculty possessed by no other owner of the commodity, it must result that the carrier would be in a position where no other person could ship the commodity on equal terms with the carrier in its capacity of dealer. No other person owning the commodity being thus able to ship on equal terms, it would result that the owners of such commodity would not be able to ship, but would be compelled to sell to the carrier. And as by the departure from the tariff rates the person to whom the carrier might elect to sell would be able to buy at a price less than any other person could sell for, it would follow that such person so selected by the carrier would have a monopoly in the market to which the goods were transported. And that the result arising from an admission of the asserted power of the carrier as a dealer to disregard the published rates conduces immediately and not merely remotely to the production of the injurious results stated, is not only demonstrated by the very nature of things, but is established to be the case by the facts indisputably shown on this record. For here it is unquestioned that the Chesapeake and Ohio, as a result of its being a dealer, had become, long prior to the adoption of the Interstate Commerce Law and continued to be thereafter, up to the passage of the West Virginia statute prohibiting a carrier from dealing in coal, virtually the sole purchaser and seller of all the coal produced along the line of its road. That this result was not merely accidental, but was in effect engendered by the power of the carrier to deal and transport a commodity, is illustrated by the case of *The Attorney General* v. *The Great Northern Railway Company*, 29 Law Journal (N. S. Equity), 794. In that case Vice Chancellor Kindersley was called upon to determine whether dealing in coal by the railway company was illegal, because incompatible with its duties as a public carrier and calculated to inflict an injury upon the public. In deciding that the act of Parliament granting the charter to operate the railway implied a prohibition against the company's engaging in any other business, the reason for the rule was thus expressed (p.798):

". . . . These large companies, joint stock companies generally, for whatever purpose established, and more particularly railway companies, are armed with powers of raising and possessing large sums of money — large amounts of property — and if they were to apply that money, or that property, to purposes other than those for which they were constituted, they might very much injure the interests of the public in various ways."

Illustrating the danger to the public, as established by the case before him, the vice-chancellor said (p. 799):

"Here we find this company, having the traffic from the north of England, where the great coal fields are (at least some of the principal coal fields), supplying the country with coal, or capable of supplying it; this company buys the coal, which gives to the company an interest in checking, as much as possible, those who will not deal with them; and it is quite clear that it is possible, by the mode in which this company may (I will not say has), — but by the mode in which this company may exercise such powers as either it has or assumes to have — this company may get into their hands the traffic, that is, the dealing in all the coal in the large districts supplying coal to the country. They have to a considerable extent done so, and there is no reason why it should not go on progressing. I observe that in the eight(?) years from 1852 to 1857, inclusive, the amount of their coal business has increased from 73,000 tons to 794,000 tons; and there is no reason, as the affidavits show, why they should not — there is great danger that they may — get into their hands the entire business in the coal of all that district of country. If they can do that with regard to coal, what is to prevent their doing it with every species of agricultural produce all along the line? Why should they not become purchasers of corn, of all kinds of beasts, and of sheep, and every species of agricultural produce, and become great dealers in the supply of edibles to the markets of London; and why not every other species of commodity that is produced in every part of the country from which or to which their railway runs? I do not know where it is to stop, if the argument on the part of the company is to prevail. There is, therefore, great detriment to the interest of the public, for this reason, taking merely the article of coal."

It is apparent that the construction of the statute which is now claimed by the carriers would, if adopted, not only destroy its entire remedial efficacy, but would cause the provisions of the statute to accentuate and multiply the very wrongs which it was enacted to prevent.

Without a statutory requirement as to publication of rates and the imposition of a duty to adhere to the rates as published, individual action of the shippers as between themselves and in their dealings with the carrier would have full play, and thereby every shipper would have the opportunity to procure such concessions as might result from favoritism or other causes. Interpreting the prohibitions of the statute as it is contended they should be, it would follow that every individual would be bound by the published tariff, and the carrier alone would be free to disregard it. Thus the statute, whilst subjecting the public to the prohibitions, would exempt the carrier and would thereby enormously increase the opportunities of the latter to do the wrongs which the statute was enacted to prevent.

And the considerations previously stated serve also to demonstrate that the prohibitions of the act to regulate commerce concerning "undue or unreasonable preference or advantage," "undue or unreasonable prejudice or disadvantage" and "unjust discrimination" are in conflict with the asserted right of a carrier to become a dealer in commodities which it transports, and as such dealer to sell at a price less than the cost and the published rates. Certain also is it, when the reasons previously stated are applied to those prohibitions of the statute the possession of the power by a carrier to deal in merchandise and to sell and transport at less than published rates, would not only destroy the remedy intended to be afforded by the provisions in question, but would cause the statute to fructify the growth of the wrongs which it was intended to extirpate. In a general sense the considerations which we have previously stated, moreover, dispose of all the contentions urged at bar to establish the right of the carrier to become a dealer under the circumstances stated. Even although it may give rise to some repetition, we more particularly notice the various contentions.

(*a*) It is said that when a carrier sells an article which it has purchased and transports that article for delivery, it is both a dealer and a carrier. When, therefore, the price received for the commodity is adequate to pay the published freight rate and something over, the command of the statute as to adherence to the published rates is complied with, because the price will be imputed to the freight rate, and the loss, if any, attributed to the company in its capacity as dealer and not as a carrier. This simply asserted the proposition which we have disposed of, that a carrier possesses the power, by the form in which he deals, to render the prohibitions of the act ineffective, since it implies the right of a carrier to shut off inquiry as to the real result of a particular transaction on the published rates, and thereby to obtain the power of disregarding the prohibitions of the statute.

(*b*) It is said that, as in the case in hand, it is shown that there was no intention on the part of the carrier in making the sale of the coal to violate the prohibitions of the statute, and, on the contrary, as the proof shows an arrangement made by the carrier for transporting the coal from Newport News to Connecticut, which, if it had been carried out, would have provided for the full published rate, therefore an honest contract made by the carrier should not be stricken down because of things over which the carrier had no control. The proposition involves both an unfounded assumption of fact and an unwarranted implication of law. It is true the court below found that the proof did not justify the inference that the Chesapeake and Ohio had, in 1896, made the contract to sell the coal to the New Haven with the purpose of avoiding a compliance with the published rates. But in this conclusion of fact we cannot agree. Whilst it may be that the proof establishes that the contract for the sale of coal was not made as a mere device for avoiding the operation of the statute, we think the proof leaves no doubt that, in making the contract in question, the Chesapeake and Ohio was wholly indifferent to and did not concern itself with the prohibitions of the statute, of which, of course, it must be assumed to have had full knowledge. As we have seen, the president of the Chesapeake and Ohio, by whom the corporation was represented in making the contract, expressly testified that from the beginning that corporation had pursued the policy of acquiring all the coal mined on its line and sold it, relying upon the net result of such sales for its freight compensation, and that the particular contract was made in continuation of that policy. We find it impossible to conclude, from the proof, that the Chesapeake and Ohio could have made a contract for so large an amount of coal, to be delivered over so long a period, without taking into view the existing prices and the cost necessarily to be occasioned by the delivery of the coal, if the full published freight rates were to be realized. Indeed, the proof leaves no doubt upon our minds that, in making the contract, the Chesapeake and Ohio sought to accomplish results which it deemed beneficial by means which it considered effectual, even although resort to such means was prohibited by the Interstate Commerce Act. In other words, we think it is established beyond doubt that, desiring to stimulate the production of coal along its line and thereby, as it conceived, to increase the carriage of that commodity and to benefit the railroad and those living along its line by the reflex prosperity which it was deemed would arise from giving a stimulus to an industry tributary to the railroad, the Chesapeake and Ohio bought and sold the coal without reference to whether the net result to it would realize its published rates. And it would seem that this means of stimulating the industry in question was resorted to instead of attempting to bring about the same result by a lowering of the published rates, because to have so done would have engendered disparity between coal rates and the tariff on all the other articles contained in the same classification, and would besides have caused other and competing roads to make a similar reduction on the published rates, and thereby would have frustrated the very advantage to itself and those along its lines which the Chesapeake and Ohio deemed it was bringing about by the method pursued. That is to say, we think it is shown that the mode of dealing adopted was simply the result of a disregard by the Chesapeake and Ohio of the economic conceptions upon which the Interstate Commerce Law rests, and a substitution in their stead of the conceptions of the Chesapeake and Ohio, as to what was best for itself and for the public. Further, as the prohibition of the Interstate Commerce Act is ever operative, even if the facts established that at the particular time the contract was made, considering the then cost of coal and other proper times, the net published tariff of rates would have been realized by the Chesapeake and Ohio from the contract, which is not the case, it is apparent that the deliveries under the contract came under the prohibition of the statute whenever for any cause, such as the enhanced cost of the coal at the mines, an increase in the cost of the ocean carriage, etc., the gross sum realized was not sufficient to net the Chesapeake and

Ohio its published tariff of rates. This must be the case in order to give vitality to the prohibitions of the Interstate Commerce Act against the acceptance at any time by a carrier of less than its published rates. We say this because we think it obvious that such prohibitions would be rendered wholly ineffective by deciding that a carrier may avoid those prohibitions by making a contract for the sale of a commodity stipulating for the payment of a fixed price in the future, and thereby acquiring the power during the life of the contract to continue to execute it, although a violation of the act to regulate commerce might arise from doing so. Besides, all the contentions just noticed proceed upon the mistaken legal conception that the application of the statutory prohibitions depend not upon whether the effect of the acts done is to violate those prohibitions, but upon whether the carrier intended to violate the statute.

(*c*) It is urged that if the requirement of the act to regulate commerce as to the maintenance of published rates and the prohibitions of that act against undue preferences and discriminations be applied to a carrier when engaged in buying and selling a commodity which it transports, the substantial effect will be to prohibit the carrier from becoming a dealer when no such prohibition is expressed in the act to regulate commerce, and hence a prohibition will be implied which should only result from express action by Congress. Granting the premise, the deduction is unfounded. Because no express prohibition against a carrier who engages in interstate commerce becoming a dealer in commodities moving in such commerce is found in the act, it does not follow that the provisions which are expressed in that act should not be applied and be given their lawful effect. Even, therefore, if the result of applying the prohibitions as we have interpreted them will be practically to render it difficult, if not impossible, for a carrier to deal in commodities, this affords no ground for relieving us of the plain duty of enforcing the provisions of the statute as they exist. This conclusion follows, since the power of Congress to subject every carrier engaging in interstate commerce to the regulations which it has adopted is undoubted.

. . . .

We, therefore, conclude that the injunction below should be modified and enlarged by perpetually enjoining the Chesapeake and Ohio from taking less than the rates fixed in its published tariff of freight rates, by means of dealing in the purchase and sale of coal. And, as thus modified, the decree below is *Affirmed.*

UNITED STATES OF AMERICA, UPON THE APPLICATION OF THE ATTORNEY GENERAL, AT THE REQUEST OF THE INTERSTATE COMMERCE COMMISSION, *v.* UNION STOCK YARD & TRANSIT COMPANY OF CHICAGO

CHICAGO JUNCTION RAILWAY COMPANY *v.* UNITED STATES

226 U. S. 286 (1912)

MR. JUSTICE DAY delivered the opinion of the court.[1]

. . . .

As to the Pfælzer contract, both parties concede the authority of the Commerce Court to pass upon this subject and no objection was made as to the manner and form in which the jurisdiction of that court was invoked. There being no objection taken to the method of proceeding, we think, if this contract is within the prohibitions of the act, that the Commerce Court had the right to entertain the bill and to enjoin the performance of the contract. Sections 2 and 3 of the Elkins Act. It is contended that this contract is violative of certain features of the Act to Regulate Commerce and of the Elkins Act. Section 2 of the former and § 1 of the latter provide:

"SEC. 2. That if any common carrier subject to the provisions of this act shall, directly or indirectly, by any special rate, rebate, drawback, or other device, charge, demand, collect, or receive from any person or persons a greater or less compensation for any service rendered, or to be rendered, in the transportation of passengers or property, subject to the provisions of this act, than it charges, demands, collects, or receives from any other person or persons for doing for him or them a like and contemporaneous service in the transportation of a like kind of traffic under substantially similar circumstances and conditions, such common carrier shall be deemed guilty of unjust discrimination, which is hereby prohibited and declared to be unlawful."

"SEC. 1. . . . . It shall be unlawful for any person, persons, or corporation to offer, grant, or give or to solicit, accept, or receive any rebate, concession, or discrimination in respect of the transportation of any property in interstate or foreign commerce by

[1] The facts and first part of the opinion will be found on page 113, *supra.* — ED.

any common carrier subject to said Act to regulate commerce and the Acts amendatory thereto whereby any such property shall by any device whatever by transported at a less rate than that named in the tariffs published and filed by such carrier, as is required by said Act to regulate commerce and the Acts amendatory thereto, or whereby any other advantage is given or discrimination is practiced. . . . ."

This court has had frequent occasion to comment upon the purpose of Congress in the passage of these laws to require equal treatment of all shippers and to prohibit unjust discrimination in favor of any of them. *New York, New Haven & Hartford R. R. Co.* v. *Interstate Commerce Commission*, 200 U. S. 361; *Armour Packing Co.* v. *United States*, 209 U. S. 56; *Louisville & Nashville R. R.* v. *Mottley*, 219 U. S. 467; *Chicago & Alton R. R. Co.* v. *Kirby*, 225 U. S. 155.

By § 2 of the Act to Regulate Commerce the carrier is guilty of unjust discrimination, which is prohibited and declared unlawful, if by any rebate or other device it charges one person less for any service rendered in the transportation of property than it does another for a like service. The Elkins Act makes it an offense for any person or corporation to give or receive any rebate, concession or discrimination in respect to the transportation of property in interstate commerce whereby any such property shall be transported at a rate less than that named in the published tariff or whereby any other advantage is given or discrimination is practiced. By the very terms of the contract it is evident that the interest of the Stock Yard Company and also of the Junction Company is in the profit to be made in receiving and delivering, handling and caring for and transporting live stock, shipments of which, to the extent stated, are made in interstate commerce. The contract provides that if the Pfælzers construct a packing plant adjacent to the stock yards of the Stock Yard Company they shall receive $50,000, and it obligates them to maintain and operate the plant for a period of fifteen years and buy and use in their slaughtering business such live stock only as moves through such stock yards, and if not so bought to pay the regular charges thereon as if the same had moved into the stock yards and had been there purchased by them. In other words, this plant in effect may pay for the services of the Stock Yard Company, up to the sum of $50,000, with the bonus given to the Pfælzers for the location of their plant in juxtaposition to the stock yards.

The only interest which the Stock Yard Company has in Pfælzer

& Sons' interstate business is compensation for its services in handling their freight and its share of the profits realized by the Junction Company in rendering its service. Any other company with which it has made no contract would be compelled to pay the full charge for the services rendered without any rebate or concession. Another company might have a contract for a larger or smaller bonus, and thereby receive different treatment. Certainly as to the company which receives no such bonus there has been an undue advantage given to and an unlawful discrimination practiced in favor of Pfælzer & Sons. If these companies had filed their tariffs, as we now hold they should have filed them, they would have been subject to the restrictions of the Elkins Act as to departures from published rates — and we must consider the case in that light — and this preferential treatment, as we have said, would have been in violation of that act. It is the object of the Interstate Commerce Law and the Elkins Act to prevent favoritism by any means or device whatsoever and to prohibit practices which run counter to the purpose of the act to place all shippers upon equal terms. We think the Commerce Court should have enjoined the carrying out of this contract.

It follows that in case No. 621 the judgment of the Commerce Court should be reversed and the case remanded for the entry of a decree in conformity to this opinion. In No. 622 the judgment of the Commerce Court should be affirmed.

INTERSTATE COMMERCE COMMISSION *v.* BALTIMORE AND OHIO RAILROAD COMPANY

145 U. S. 263 (1892) [1]

The Interstate Commerce Commission found that "party-tickets" issued by the Baltimore & Ohio Railroad, *i. e.*, tickets to parties of ten or more at a reduced rate for each than that charged to single passengers between the same points, constituted an unjust discrimination and ordered the railroad to cease their issuances. Upon the railroad's refusal to obey the order the Commission brought a bill in the Circuit Court for the Southern District of Ohio for enforcement of its rule. Upon hearing before the Circuit Court upon pleadings and proofs the bills was dis-

[1] The facts have been briefly restated.—Ed.

missed. 43 Fed. Rep. 37. From this decree the Interstate Commerce Commission appealed to this Court.

MR. JUSTICE BROWN delivered the opinion of the court.

Prior to the enactment of the act of February 4, 1887, to regulate commerce, commonly known as the Interstate Commerce Act, 24 Stat. 379, c. 104, railway traffic in this country was regulated by the principles of the common law applicable to common carriers, which demanded little more than that they should carry for all persons who applied, in the order in which the goods were delivered at the particular station, and that their charges for transportation should be reasonable. It was even doubted whether they were bound to make the same charge to all persons for the same service; *Fitchburg Railroad Co.* v. *Gage*, 12 Gray, 393; *Baxendale* v. *Eastern Counties Railway Co.*, 4 C. B. (N. S.) 63; *Great Western Railway Co.* v. *Sutton*, L. R. 4 H. L. 226, 237; *Ex parte Benson*, 18 South Car. 38; *Johnson* v. *Pensacola Railway Co.*, 16 Florida, 623; though the weight of authority in this country was in favor of an equality of charge to all persons for similar services. In several of the States acts had been passed with the design of securing the public against unreasonable and unjust discriminations; but the inefficacy of these laws beyond the lines of the State, the impossibility of securing concerted action between the legislatures toward the regulation of traffic between the several States, and the evils which grew up under a policy of unrestricted competition, suggested the necessity of legislation by Congress under its constitutional power to regulate commerce among the several States. These evils ordinarily took the shape of inequality of charges made, or of facilities furnished, and were usually dictated by or tolerated for the promotion of the interests of the officers of the corporation or of the corporation itself, or for the benefit of some favored persons at the expense of others, or of some particular locality or community, or of some local trade or commercial connection, or for the destruction or crippling of some rival or hostile line.

The principal objects of the Interstate Commerce Act were to secure just and reasonable charges for transportation; to prohibit unjust discriminations in the rendition of like services under similar circumstances and conditions; to prevent undue or unreasonable preferences to persons, corporations or localities; to inhibit greater compensation for a shorter than for a longer distance over the same line; and to abolish combinations for the pooling of freights. It was not designed, however, to prevent competition between different roads, or to interfere with the customary arrangements made by railway companies for reduced fares in consideration of increased mileage, where such reduction did not operate as an unjust discrimination against other persons travelling over the road. In other words, it was not intended to ignore the principle that one can sell at wholesale cheaper than at retail. It is not all discriminations or preferences that fall within the inhibition of the statute; only such as are unjust or unreasonable. For instance, it would be obviously unjust to charge A a greater sum than B for a single trip from Washington to Pittsburg; but if A agrees not only to go but to return by the same route, it is no injustice to B to permit him to do so for a reduced fare, since the services are not alike, nor the circumstances and conditions substantially similar, as required by section 2 to make an unjust discrimination. Indeed, the possibility of just discriminations and reasonable preferences is recognized by these sections, in declaring what shall be deemed unjust. We agree, however, with the plaintiff in its contention that a charge may be perfectly reasonable under section 1, and yet may create an unjust discrimination or an unreasonable preference under sections 2 and 3. As was said by Mr. Justice Blackburn in *Great Western Railway Co.* v. *Sutton*, L. R. 4 H. L. 226, 239: "When it is sought to show that the charge is extortionate as being contrary to the statutable obligation to charge equally, it is immaterial whether the charge is reasonable or not; it is enough to show that the company carried for some other person or class of persons at a lower charge during the period throughout which the party complaining was charged more under the like circumstances."

The question involved in this case is, whether the principle above stated as applicable to two individuals applies to the purchase of a single ticket covering the transportation of ten or more persons from one place to another. These are technically known as party-rate tickets, and are issued principally to theatrical and operatic companies for the transportation of their troupes. Such ticket is clearly neither a "mileage" nor an "excursion" ticket within the exception of section 22; and upon the testimony in this case it may be doubtful whether it falls within the definition of "commutation tickets," as those words are commonly understood among railway officials. The words "commutation ticket" seem to have no definite meaning. They are defined by Webster (edition of 1891) as "a ticket, as for transportation, which is the evidence of a contract for service at a reduced rate." If this definition be applicable here, then it is clear that it would include a party-rate ticket. In the language of the railway, however, they are principally, if not wholly, used to designate tickets for transportation during a limited time between neighboring towns or cities and suburban towns. The party-rate ticket upon the defendant's road is a single ticket issued to a party of ten or more, at a fixed rate of two cents per mile, or a discount of one-third from the regular passenger rate. The reduction is not made by way of a secret rebate or drawback, but the rates are scheduled, posted and open to the public at large.

But, assuming the weight of evidence in this case to be that the party-rate ticket is not a "commutation ticket," as that word was commonly understood at the time of the passage of the act, but is a distinct class by itself, it does not necessarily follow that such tickets are unlawful. The unlawfulness defined by sections 2 and 3 consists either in an "unjust discrimination" or an "undue or unreasonable preference or advantage," and the object of section 22 was to settle beyond all doubt that the discrimination in favor of certain persons therein named should not be deemed unjust. It does not follow, however, that there may not be other classes of persons in whose favor a discrimination may be made without such discrimination being unjust. In other words, this section is rather illustrative than exclusive. Indeed, many, if not all, the excepted classes named in section 22 are those which, in the absence of this section, would not necessarily be held the subjects of an unjust discrimination, if more favorable terms were extended to them than to ordinary passengers. Such, for instance, are property of the United States, state or municipal governments; destitute and homeless persons transported free of charge by charitable societies; indigent persons transported at the expense of municipal governments; inmates of soldiers' homes, etc., and ministers of religion, in favor of whom a reduction of rates had been made for many years before the passage of the act. It may even admit of serious doubt whether, if the mileage, excursion or commutation tickets had not been mentioned at all in this section, they would have fallen within the prohibition of sections 2 and 3. In other words, whether the allowance of a reduced rate to persons agreeing to travel one thousand miles, or to go and return by the same road, is a "like and contemporaneous service under substantially similar conditions and circumstances" as is rendered to a person who travels upon an ordinary single-trip ticket. If it be so, then, under state laws forbidding unjust discriminations, every such ticket issued between points within the same State must be illegal. In view of the fact, however, that every railway company issues such tickets; that there is no reported case, state or federal, wherein their illegality has been questioned; that there is no such case in England; and that the practice is universally acquiesced in by the public, it would seem that the issuing of such tickets should not be held an unjust discrimination or an unreasonable preference to the persons travelling upon them.

But whether these party-rate tickets are commutation tickets proper, as known to railway officials or not, they are obviously within the commuting principle. As stated in the opinion of Judge Sage in the court below: "The difference between commutation and party-rate tickets is, that commutation tickets are issued to induce people to travel more frequently, and party-rate tickets are issued to induce more people to travel. There is, however, no difference in principle between them, the object in both cases being to increase travel without unjust discrimination, and to secure patronage that would not otherwise be secured."

The testimony indicates that for many years before the passage of the act it was customary for railroads to issue tickets at reduced rates to passengers making frequent trips, trips for long distances, and trips in parties of ten or more, lower than the regular single fare charged between the same points; and such lower rates were universally made at the date of the passage of the act. As stated in the answer, to meet the needs of the commercial traveller the thousand-mile ticket was issued; to meet the needs of the suburban resident or frequent traveller, several forms of tickets were issued. For example, monthly or quarterly, tickets, good for any number of trips within the specified time; and ten, twenty-five or fifty-trip tickets, good for a specified number of trips by one person, or for one trip by a specified number of persons; to accomodate parties of ten or more, a single ticket, one way or round trip, for the whole party, was made up by the agent on a skeleton form furnished for that purpose; to accomodate excursionists travelling in parties too large to use a single ticket, special individual tickets were issued to each person. Tickets good for a specified number of trips were also issued between cities where travel was frequent. In short, it was an established principle of the business, that whenever the amount of travel more than made up to the carrier for the reduction of the charge per capita, then such reduction was reasonable and just in the interests both of the carrier and of the public. Although 'the fact that railroads had long been in the habit of issuing these tickets would be by no means conclusive evidence that they were legal, since the main purpose of the act was to put an end to certain abuses which had crept into the management of railroads, yet Congress may be presumed to have had those practices in view, and not to have designed to interfere with them, except so far as they were unreasonable in themselves or unjust to others. These tickets then being within the commutation principle of allowing reduced rates in consideration of increased mileage, the real question is, whether this operates as an undue or unreasonable preference or advantage to this particular description of traffic, or an unjust discrimination against others. If, for example, a railway makes to the public generally a certain rate of freight, and to a particular individual residing in the same town a reduced rate for the same class of goods, this may operate as an undue preference, since it enables the favored party to sell his goods at a lower price than his competitors, and may even enable him to obtain a complete monopoly of that business. Even if the same reduced rate be allowed to every one doing the same amount of business, such discrimination may, if carried too far, operate unjustly upon the smaller dealers engaged in the same business, and enable the larger ones to drive them out of the market.

The same result, however, does not follow from the sale of a ticket for a number of passengers at a less rate than for a single passenger; it does not operate to the prejudice of the single passenger, who cannot be said to be injured by the fact that another is able in a particular instance to travel at a less rate than he. If it operates injuriously toward any one it is the rival road, which has not adopted corresponding rates; but, as before observed, it was not the design of the act to stifle competition, nor is there any legal injustice in one person procuring a particular service cheaper than another. If it be lawful to issue these tickets, then the Pittsburg, Chicago and St. Louis Railway Company have the same right to issue them that the defendant has, and may compete with it for the same traffic; but it is unsound to argue that it is unlawful to issue them because it has not seen fit to do so. Certainly its construction of the law is not binding upon this court. The evidence shows that the amount of business done by means of these party-rate tickets is very large; that theatrical and operatic companies base their calculation of profits to a certain extent upon the reduced rates allowed by railroads; and that the attendance at conventions, political and religious, social and scientific, is, in a great measure, determined by the ability of the delegates to go and come at a reduced charge. If these tickets were withdrawn, the defendant road would lose a large amount of travel, and the single-trip passenger would gain absolutely nothing. If a case were presented where a railroad refused an application for a party-rate ticket upon the ground that it was not intended for the use of the general public, but solely for theatrical troupes, there would be much greater reason for holding that the latter were favored with an undue preference or advantage.

In order to constitute an unjust discrimination under section 2, the carrier must charge or receive directly from one person a greater or less compensation than from another, or must accomplish the same thing indirectly by means of a special rate, rebate or other device; but in either case it must be for a "like and contemporaneous service in the transportation of a like kind of traffic, under substantially similar circumstances and conditions." To bring the present case within the words of this section, we must assume that the transportation of ten persons on a single ticket is substantially identical with the transportation of one, and, in view of the universally accepted fact that a man may buy, contract, or manufacture on a large scale cheaper proportionately than upon a small scale, this is impossible.

In this connection we quote with approval from the opinion of Judge Jackson in the court below: "To come within the inhibition of said sections, the differences must be made under like conditions; that is, there must be contemporaneous service in the transportation of like kinds of traffic under substantially the same circumstances and conditions. In respect to passenger traffic, the positions of the respective persons, or classes, between whom differences in charges are made, must be compared with each other, and there must be found to exist substantial identity of situation and of service, accompanied by irregularity and partiality resulting in undue advantage to one, or undue disadvantage to the other, in order to constitute unjust discrimination."

The English Traffic Act of 1854 contains a clause similar to section 3 of the Interstate Commerce Act, that "no such company shall make or give any undue or unreasonable preference or advantage to or in favor of any particular person or company, or any particular description of traffic, in any respect whatsoever, nor shall any such company subject any particular person or company, or any particular description of traffic, to any undue or unreasonable prejudice or disadvantage in any respect whatsoever."

In *Hozier* v. *Caledonian Railway*, 17 Sess. Cas. (2d Series) 302, (*S. C.* 1 Nev. & Macn. Railway Cases, 27,) complaint was made by one who had frequent occasion to travel, that passengers from an intermediate station between Glasgow and Edinburgh were charged much greater rates to those places than were charged to other through passengers between these termini; but the Scotch Court of Session held that the petitioner had not shown any title or interest to maintain the proceeding; his only complaint being that he did not choose that parties travelling from Edinburgh to Glasgow should enjoy the benefit of a cheaper rate of travel than he himself could enjoy. "It provides," said the court, "for giving undue preference to parties *pari passu* in the matter, but you must bring them into competition in order to give them an interest to complain." This is in substance holding that the allowance of a reduced through rate worked no injustice to passengers living on the line of the road, who were obliged to pay at a greater rate. So in *Jones* v. *Eastern Counties Railway*, 3 C. B. (N. S.) 718, the court refused an injunction to compel a railway company to issue season tickets between Colchester and London upon the same terms as they issued them between Harwich and London, upon the mere suggestion that the granting the latter, the distance being considerably greater, at a much lower rate than the former, was an undue and unreasonable preference of the inhabitants of Harwich over those of Colchester. Upon the other hand, in *Ransome* v. *Eastern Counties Railway*, 1 C. B. (N.S.) 437, where it was manifest that a railway company charged Ipswich merchants, who sent from thence coal which had come thither by sea, a higher rate for the carriage of their coal than they charged Peterboro' merchants, who had made arrangements with them to carry large quantities over their lines, and that the sums charged the Peterboro' merchants were fixed so as to enable them to compete with the Ipswich merchants, the court granted an injunction, upon the ground of an undue preference to the Peterboro' merchants, the object of the discrimination being to benefit the one dealer at the expense of the other, by depriving the latter of the natural advantages of his position. In *Oxlade* v. *North-eastern Railway*, 1 C. B. (N. S.) 454, a railway company was held justified in carrying goods for one person for a less rate than that at which they carried the same description of goods for another, if there be circumstances which render the cost of carrying the goods for the former less than the cost of carrying them for the latter, but that a desire to introduce northern coke into a certain district was not a legitimate ground for making special agreements with different merchants for the carriage of coal and coke at a rate lower than the ordinary charge, there being nothing to show that the pecuniary interests of the company were affected; and that this was an undue preference.

In short, the substance of all these decisions is that railway companies are only bound to give the same terms to all persons alike under the same conditions and circumstances, and that any fact which produces an inequality of condition and a change of circumstances justifies an inequality of charge. These traffic acts do not appear to be as comprehensive as our own, and may justify contracts which with us would be obnoxious to the long and short haul clause of the act, or would be open to the charge of unjust discrimination. But so far as relates to the question of "undue preference," it may be presumed that Congress, in adopting the language of the English act, had in mind the constructions given to these words by the English courts, and intended to incorporate them into the statute. *McDonald* v. *Hovey*, 110 U. S. 619.

There is nothing in the objection that party-rate tickets afford facilities for speculation and that they would be used by ticket brokers or "scalpers" for the purpose of evading the law. The party-rate ticket, as it appears in this case, is a single ticket covering the transportation of ten or more persons, and would be much less available in the hands of a ticket broker than an ordinary single ticket, since it could only be disposed of to a person who would be willing to pay two-thirds of the regular fare for that number of people. It is possible to conceive that party-rate tickets may, by a reduction of the number for whom they may be issued, be made the pretext for evading the law, and for the purpose of cutting rates, but should such be the case, the courts would have no difficulty in discovering the purpose for which they were issued, and applying the proper remedy.

Upon the whole, we are of the opinion that party-rate tickets, as used by the defendant, are not open to the objections found by the Interstate Commerce Commission, and are not in violation of the act to regulate commerce, and the decree of the court below is, therefore,

Affirmed.

PITTSBURGH, CINCINNATI, CHICAGO & ST. LOUIS RAILWAY COMPANY *v.* FINK

250 U. S. 577 (1919)

MR. JUSTICE DAY delivered the opinion of the court.

An action was brought by the Railway Company before a Justice of the Peace in Montgomery County, Ohio, to recover fifteen dollars, the freight charges upon a shipment in interstate commerce from Los Angeles, California, to Dayton, Ohio. The defendant, Fink, prevailed in the Magistrate's court, the judgment was reversed in the Court of Common Pleas, the case was taken to the Court of Appeals of Montgomery County where the judgment of the Court of Common Pleas was reversed and that of the Magistrate affirmed. 19 Ohio Circuit Court, New Series, 103. The Supreme Court of Ohio denied a motion to require the record to be certified to it by the Court of Appeals, and the case is here upon writ of error to the Court of Appeals of Montgomery County, Ohio.

The facts are that the railroad company on September 13, 1910, delivered to Fink, the consignee, two boxes of Indian relics shipped to him at Dayton, Ohio, from Los Angeles, California, the waybill specifying charges in the sum of fifteen dollars, which sum Fink paid upon receipt of the goods. The tariff rates filed with the Interstate Commerce Commission so classified this merchandise that the transportation charges should have been thirty dollars instead of fifteen. It is for the difference that this action is prosecuted.

It appears that Fink had dealt with the consignor at Los Angeles in suchwise that some old coins, belonging to Fink, were to be traded for a collection of Indian relics. Fink shipped the coins to the postmaster at Los Angeles to be held for his protection. At the time the action was brought, about one year after the shipment, the postmaster had released the coins, and Fink had sold some of the relics. Fink testified that he had no knowledge of the freight classification and rates, and simply paid the freight bill as it was presented to him. No agreement appears to have been made with the consignor that Fink should pay the freight charges.

Examination shows some conflict of authority as to the liability at common law of the consignee to pay freight charges under the circumstances here shown. The weight of authority seems to be that the consignee is *prima facie* liable for the payment of the freight charges when he accepts the goods from the carrier. (See the cases collected and discussed in 4 Elliott on Railroads, § 1559.) However this may be, in our view the question must be decided upon consideration of the applicable provisions of the statutes of the United States regulating interstate commerce. The purpose of the Act to Regulate Interstate Commerce, frequently declared in the decisions of this court, was to provide one rate for all shipments of like character, and to make the only legal charge for the transportation of goods in interstate commerce the rate duly filed with the Commission. In this way discrimination is avoided, and all receive like treatment, which it is the main purpose of the act to secure.

Section 6 of the Act to Regulate Commerce, which was in force at the time of this shipment, provides: "Nor shall any carrier charge or demand or collect or receive a greater or less or different compensation for such transportation of passengers or property, or for any service in connection therewith, between the points named in such tariffs than the rates, fares, and charges which are specified in the tariff filed and in effect at the time; nor shall any carrier refund or remit in any manner or by any device any portion of the rates, fares, and charges so specified, nor extend to any shipper or person any privileges or facilities in the transportation of passengers or property, except as are specified in such tariffs." It was, therefore, unlawful for the carrier upon delivering the merchandise consigned to Fink to depart from the tariff rates filed. The statute made it unlawful for the carrier to receive compensation less than the sum fixed by the tariff rates duly filed. Fink, as well as the carrier, must be presumed to know the law, and to have understood that the rate charged could lawfully be only the one fixed by the tariff. When the carrier turned over the goods to Fink upon a mistaken understanding of the rate legally chargeable, both it and the consignee undoubtedly acted upon the belief that the charges collected were those authorized by law. Under such circumstances consistently with the provisions of the Interstate Commerce Act the consignee was only entitled to the merchandise when he paid for the transportation thereof the amount specified as required by the statute. For the legal charges the carrier had a lien upon the goods, and this lien could be discharged and the consignee become entitled to the goods only upon tender or payment of this rate. *Texas & Pacific Ry. Co.* v. *Mugg,* 202 U. S. 242. The transaction, in the light of the act, amounted to an assumption on the part of Fink to pay the only legal rate the carrier had the right to charge or the consignee the right to pay. This may be in the present as well as some other cases a hardship upon the consignee due to the fact that he paid all that was demanded when the freight was delivered; but instances of individual hardship cannot change the policy which Congress has embodied in the statute in order to secure uniformity in charges for transportation. *Louisville & Nashville R. R. Co.* v. *Maxwell*, 237 U. S. 94. In that case the rule herein stated was enforced as against a passenger who had purchased a ticket from an agent of the company at less than the published rate. The opinion in that case reviewed the previous decisions of this court, from which we find no occasion to depart.

It is alleged that a different rule should be applied in this case because Fink by virtue of his agreement with the consignor did not become the owner of the goods until after the same had been delivered to him. There is no proof that such agreement was known to the carrier, nor could that fact lessen the obligation of the consignee to pay the legal tariff rate when he accepted the goods. *Pennsylvania R. R. Co.* v. *Titus*, 216 N. Y. 17. Nor can the defendant in error successfully invoke the principle of estoppel against the right to collect the legal rate. Estoppel could not become the means of successfully avoiding the requirement of the act as to equal rates, in violation of the provisions of the statute. *New York, New Haven & Hartford R. R. Co.* v. *York & Whitney Co.*, 215 Massachusetts, 36, 40.

In our view the Court of Common Pleas correctly held Fink liable for the payment of the remaining part of the legal rate upon the merchandise received by him. The judgment of the Court of Appeals of Montgomery County, Ohio, is reversed, and the cause remanded to that court for further procedings not inconsistent with this opinion.

Reversed.

VANDALIA RAILROAD COMPANY *v.* UNITED STATES

UNITED STATES CIRCUIT COURT OF APPEALS, SEVENTH CIRCUIT

226 Fed. 713 (1915)

In 1905, the Lumaghi Coal Company, whose property was located on the lines of the Vandalia Railroad Company, was desirous of purchasing additional property on some of which, at least, it held options. It had not the necessary money, and, as its president testified, it was not in a position to borrow it at 2 per cent. interest as a regular banking proposition or from any ordinary sources, and would not have undertaken the purchase of the 9,000-acre tract, at a cost of $260,000, if compelled to pay the ordinary rates for money at that time. And so it applied to the Vandalia Railroad Company for a loan. This company, being unable under its charter either to loan money or to buy and sell coal lands and because of other practical difficulties, caused the Vandalia Mineral Company to be organized, which had the necessary powers. Being, however, without charter power to own stock of this latter company, it caused the stock to be held for it by the Granite Improvement Company. The controlling interest in both the Granite Improvement Company and the Vandalia Railroad Company was owned by the Pennsylvania Company. It is conceded by appellant that, for the purposes of this case, all of the acts and doings of the Mineral Company and of the Granite Improvement Company are to be considered the acts of the Vandalia Railroad Company.

Thereupon, in 1905, supplemented in 1906, a contract was made between the Vandalia Railroad Company, Vandalia Mineral Company, Lumaghi Coal Company, and Louis F. and Joseph D. Lumaghi. Treating the Mineral Company as if it were the Vandalia Railroad Company, the contract, in substance, provided for a loan by the Vandalia Company to the Coal Company of $260,000, evidenced by notes of $20,000 each, bearing interest at 2 per cent. and falling due at the rate of one a year The coal lands in question were to be conveyed to the Vandalia practically as security for the loan and were to be proportionately conveyed to the Coal Company on payment of each note. The Railroad was to construct, without cost to the Coal Company, tracks to such coal openings as might be developed; but it retained the right to use such tracks for the general business of the road and to remove them on failure of the Coal Company to operate the mines for three years. The Coal Company agreed to furnish the necessary right of way without cost to the railroad. The Railroad Company agreed to haul the tonnage mined from this property and other property of the Coal Company to East St. Louis at as low a rate as the general rate for like tonnage of any railroad entering East St. Louis. The Coal Company agreed that the Railroad Company should be the exclusive carrier of all its coal and minerals from all of its property, and that a violation thereof should cause a forfeiture of its right to the property. A minimum tonnage was fixed for each year. The Coal Company agreed to sell to the Railroad Company such coal as it might desire to buy for company use at $1.20 per ton, based upon the then wage scale and mining scale, and subject to increase or decrease as such scales should increase or decrease, and to release the Railroad Company from liability for damage to any building located near the tracks, whether occasioned by fire from locomotive sparks or otherwise. It was further agreed that, if the Coal Company should default on any interest note for six months, the Railroad had the option of surrendering the notes and being released from any further obligation to convey the land. Every conveyance by the Railroad Company to the Coal Company was to contain a condition of forfeiture if the coal were not delivered exclusively to the Railroad Company for carriage.

At the time the contract was made, the Railroad was paying, not $1.20, but $1.10, per ton for its coal. It had never had any trouble in getting coal at market rates. Since the contract it had bought its coal from all the mines on its lines in proportion to the production by each during the prior year. While the price paid to the Coal Company was sometimes above and sometimes below the market, it was the same that was paid to the other companies. While, at one time, certain operators along its line had fixed a minimum price to be charged the Railroad, it had had no difficulty in buying in other markets. The chief clerk in the general manager's office of the Railroad, who testified to these facts, said on cross-examination that, if the contract in question had not been made, it would have been possible for all the coal owners in the vicinity to have combined into one association for the purpose of raising the price of coal to much in excess of $1.20 per ton.

The contract did not specify how the lender was to raise the money. In fact, it procured $240,000 from a bank, giving its notes, payable just as the Coal Company notes were payable, except that the interest was 4 per cent instead of 2 per cent. In each of the years, 1910, 1911, and 1912, shipments were made by the Coal Company pursuant to the contract. The notes falling due in each of these years were paid by the Coal Company to the Railroad Company and by the Railroad Company to the bank, with the result that the Railroad Company paid in each of these years, on account of the money borrowed by it, a considerable sum in excess of the interest that it received on the money loaned by it. The Coal Company paid the tariff rate at the time of and for each transportation transaction referred to in the indictment.

The Vandalia Railroad Company, which offered no evidence, was found guilty under an indictment charging it with having given the Coal Company a rebate by means of the device as hereinabove set forth in respect to the transportation of certain specified car loads of coal whereby they were transported at a less rate than that named in the published tariffs, in violation of section 1 of the Elkins Law (Act Feb. 19, 1903, c. 708, as preserved by the amendment in Act June 29, 1906, c. 3591, § 2, 34 Stat. 587). The several counts were based on shipments made in the years 1910, 1911, and 1912, respectively.

Before BAKER, KOHLSAAT, and MACK, Circuit Judges.

MACK, Circuit Judge (after stating the facts as above). While a number of errors are assigned, but two have been argued: (1) The refusal of the court to direct a verdict for defendant; (2) the refusal to charge as requested.

1. No question of discrimination, whether just or unjust, by the Railroad as between competing coal companies is involved. The indictment charges a concession or rebate — a departure from the tariff rate in respect to the transportation of certain car loads. Giving a rebate "whereby any such property shall by any device whatever be transported at a less rate than that named in the tariffs" is one of the offenses enumerated in section 1 of the Elkins Law. The contract, the execution of the 4 per cent notes and the 2 per cent notes, their payment, and the resulting payment of the excess interest for and during the year in which the acts of transportation mentioned in the indictment occurred, are alleged in the indictment to constitute the device by means of which the Railroad knowingly and willfully gave the Coal Company a

rebate in respect to the transportation in interstate commerce of the specified property "whereby said property was transported at a less rate and charge than that named in the tariffs."

The statute evidently aims to prohibit, not only discrimination as between shippers, but departure from the tariff rates, irrespective of its actual discriminatory effect. The history of this legislation demonstrates that both discriminations and rebates have ever been sought to be hidden under the most subtle disguises. Every device that seeks to cover up either a rebate or a discrimination in interstate transportation is denounced by the statute, provided only, as to a rebate, that thereby the property is actually transported at less than the tariff rate. That the full tariff rate is collected at the time of transportation does not negative the possibility of a rebate in respect thereto. The rebate may be in a lump cash sum in advance (*United States* v. *Union Stockyards*, 226 U. S. 286, 33 Sup. Ct. 83, 57 L. Ed. 226), or by later or earlier indirect payments (*G. R. & I. Ry. Co.* v. *United States*, 212 Fed. 577, 129 C. C. A. 113).

While it is conceded that, if the effect of a contract to purchase tonnage would be to give an undue preference or advantage, such a contract would come within the inhibition of the Elkins Law, it is contended that a similar result would not follow if the effect were to cause only a departure from the tariff rate. In the Union Stockyards Case, however, a cash bonus, paid to a shipper for locating next to the stockyards, and giving the stockyards the exclusive transportation of its property, was denounced, not merely as an unjust discrimination, but specifically as a departure from rates which were not, but ought to have been, and, for the purposes of the case, were treated as if, published; and the Grand Rapids & Indiana Railway Company was convicted under an indictment which charged the giving of a rebate alone, not a discrimination.

If, then, a direct cash payment for exclusive tonnage is a rebate in respect to property transported under such a contract, any device whereby a similar payment is made comes within the prohibition of the statute. A loan at less than the market rate of interest, like a lease at less than market rental (*C., C., C. & St. L. Ry. Co.* v. *Hirsch*, 204 Fed. 849, 853, 123 C. C. A. 145), is, in effect, a gift of the difference between the contract and the market rate, and is, in every respect, equivalent to a direct payment of that amount of money. The evidence detailed above shows clearly that, under all the circumstances, 2 per cent was far below the market rate, and that the payment of at least the difference between 2 per cent and 4 per cent, if given for the exclusive tonnage privilege, would be an unlawful rebate.

It is contended, however, that there were other considerations given by the Coal Company in addition to the exclusive tonnage; that the burden of proof is on the government to establish that these other considerations were not worth the entire difference between the 2 per cent and the market rate of interest; and that the government has failed to make any such proof. Specifically, the defendant claims that the agreement to furnish coal at $1.20 a ton, subject only to the change in the wage scale and mining scale, was a consideration of great value. The implication is that the jury was bound, in the absence of direct proof, to consider that this value exceeded what would otherwise have been a rebate. The jury, however, were not without evidence tending to show the very slight value of this alleged insurance against a combination of dealers to raise the price of coal to the railroad. The fact that the company was actually paying $1.10, and not the stipulated price of $1.20, at the time the contract was made; the further fact that the company had never had any actual difficulty in getting coal at the market price, in themselves would have justified the jury in regarding this clause as a mere subterfuge, and of no value whatsoever.

The other alleged advantages to the railroad might well have been deemed either offset by the advantages to the other parties, as shown by the contract, or of no substantial value whatsoever. We conclude, therefore, that the evidence fully sustains the charge that the defendant knowingly gave a rebate in respect to the interstate transportation whereby such property was transported at a less rate than that named in the tariff.

2. At the conclusion of the charge, defendant's attorney requested certain additional charges successively. To each of these in turn the trial judge either gave or refused his assent, or expressed his own modifying views. The last request and the action of the court thereon are thus presented in the bill of exceptions:

"Mr. Whitnel: If the court please, one further charge. I ask the jury be charged that devices or rebates are not contrary to law, and prohibited, unless by such devices or rebates property of the shipper, the Lumaghi Coal Company in this case, was transported at a less rate than that named in the tariffs published and filed by the Vandalia Railroad Company.

"The Court: Well, I refuse that instruction. It is not necessary, and add this to what I have said: It is not necessary for the government to show that the money that was paid, that specific money was rebating or reducing; that's all. It is sufficient, if from the whole evidence, as I have said before, you believe from the whole evidence that the defendant did pay one or more sums of money, for the purpose of reducing the costs of the transportation of this property, and that must be determined from the whole evidence.

"To which ruling of the court the defendant by its counsel asked for and was granted an exception."

Whether defendant excepted to the refusal so to instruct, or to the statement of the court, or to both, is not clear. Indeed, it is so vague that, in preparing the assignments of error, counsel deemed it to extend to the rulings on every request.

Waiving this, however, we consider the only error in regard thereto presented in the brief:

That "the jury were given to understand that thereby the Vandalia should be convicted of concocting a device, and not of transporting the property at less than the published rate."

While the request stated concisely a correct and applicable legal proposition, and might well have been given, the trial judge did not err in regarding it as not absolutely necessary, inasmuch as the court had theretofore pointed out the necessary elements of the offense.

After giving the language of the act and discussing the allegations as to a device and the purpose and intention of the parties, the court said:

"The indictment concludes with this sort of a charge. That is what you are to determine and try by the evidence in the case: 'And so the grand jurors aforesaid, upon their oaths aforesaid, do say that the said Vandalia Railroad Company, at the time and place and in the manner and form and through the device aforesaid, did conduct and transport property into and through said Eastern district of Illinois, and unlawfully did knowingly and willfully offer, grant, and give to said Lumaghi Coal Company a rebate in respect to the transportation of said property in interstate commerce from said Lumaghi Coal Company's mine in Illinois to the state of Missouri.'"

This is a direct statement that it was the duty of the jury to determine, among other things, whether or not the defendant did transport the property and did knowingly give a rebate in respect to such transportation. The jury could not have understood therefrom that the mere concoction of the device without the transportation at a reduced rate resulting therefrom would justify a verdict of guilty.

The additional statement made by the judge after refusing the request indicates that he believed defendant was endeavoring to have him hold that payment of a lump sum applicable to any and all subsequent shipments could not be deemed a rebate as to any specific transportation. The assertion that it was not necessary for the government to show that "the money paid, the specific money," was rebating, was intended as a denial of the supposed contention. In adding that "it is sufficient if the jury believe from the whole evidence that the defendant did pay one or more sums of money for the purpose of reducing the cost of the transportation of this property" the court neither held nor intended to hold that this was the only element necessary to be established, but only that, to establish the rebate element, it would be sufficient for the jury to find from the entire evidence, including as well the excess interest payment as the payment of the tariff rate at the time of shipments, that a reduction from the lawful rate had in fact been made.

Judgment affirmed.

CUDAHY PACKING CO. *v.* GRAND TRUNK WESTERN RY. CO.

United States Circuit Court of Appeals,

Seventh Circuit

215 Fed. Rep. 93 (1914)

Baker, Circuit Judge. Defendant in error, plaintiff below, recovered judgment against defendant for $3,637.75 on account of icing charges in transporting dressed meats for defendant.

A jury trial was duly waived, and the cause was submitted on an agreed statement of facts that showed: That plaintiff was a railroad corporation engaged in interstate commerce. That defendant was an interstate shipper of dressed meats. That plaintiff had duly published and filed its schedule of carriage charges for dressed meats, exclusive of icing charges. That defendant paid plaintiff the carriage charges. That plaintiff had duly published and filed a tariff sheet in which the following provision was made for icing charges over and above carriage charges: "Shippers desiring refrigerator service for freight in car loads must furnish at their own cost the necessary quantity of ice and salt, or this company, when requested, will obtain and furnish the same, charging therefor the actual cost including labor, but not less than $2.50 per ton of 2000 lbs., fractions of tons to be charged for pro rata." That defendant requested plaintiff to ice defendant's car load shipments. That plaintiff did so and charged therefor at the rate of $2.50 per ton of 2,000 pounds. That plaintiff procured some of the ice from Swift & Co., a competitor of defendant in the dressed meats trade, at a cost of $2.50 per ton of 2,000 pounds, and that defendant failed and refused to pay plaintiff for any of these icing charges.

In view of the Commerce Act's definition that transportation shall include all services in connection with refrigeration or icing of property transported, and of plaintiff's action under that definition in furnishing ice as a service in transportation, it is needless to consider plaintiff's contention that Congress lacked constitutional power to compel carriers to furnish ice, and that plaintiff could therefore recover the value of its icing services for defendant on an express or an implied contract, without making, publishing, and filing fixed and definite rates therefor. By holding itself out voluntarily as ready to ice car load shipments, plaintiff brought itself within the supervisory and regulatory provisions of the act with respect to reasonableness, certainty, and publicity of rates.

Under the Commerce Act (Act Feb. 4, 1887, c. 104, 24 Stat. 379 [U. S. Comp. St. 1901, p. 3154]) compensation for service in transportation cannot be a matter of bargaining between carrier and shipper, and no payment can lawfully be demanded or received except in accordance with a fixed and definite schedule of charges duly published and filed.

Is plaintiff's tariff provision, that the charge for icing shall be "the actual cost, but not less than $2.50 per short ton," void for uncertainty? If "cost" were published as the charge for a service in transportation, the tariff would in that respect undoubtedly be void, for cost is necessarily variant and is undeterminable with exactness until after the event, while the act contemplates that the shipper shall be informed of a fixed and definite rate in advance of his shipment. If the icing charge were stated to be "$2.50 per short ton," we conceive that no complaint would be made on the ground of uncertainty. If plaintiff had published that "the minimum rate for icing is $2.50 per short ton," without stating any higher rate or giving any fixed and definite basis on which a higher rate could be calculated in advance with certainty, it seems to us that the word "minimum" might well be disregarded as superfluous and $2.50 taken as the fixed rate under all circumstances. *Knudsen-Ferguson Co.* v. *Mich. Cent. R. Co.*, 148 Fed. 968, 79 C. C. A. 46. Quite evidently plaintiff has woven the idea of cost into its icing tariff. But does that element inhere throughout the structure? If the cost is less than $2.50 per short ton, the tariff explicitly provides that nevertheless $2.50 per short ton shall be the rate. In that part of the structure, therefore, the idea of cost as a condition to be taken into account has clearly been excluded. It is only in the part of the tariff which contemplates a charge above $2.50 per short ton that cost is made an element in the accounting. There is, consequently, we believe, a clean line of demarcation at $2.50 per short ton. Cost, if below or at that line, plays no part; if above, it is the sole basis given. And inasmuch as cost, for reasons heretofore stated, cannot be accepted as a published rate under the act, part of plaintiff's icing tariff is void for uncertainty. But, while the Commerce Act and all tariffs and doings of carriers should be strictly construed and enforced to accomplish the large purposes of fairness and uniformity, we are of opinion that the general principle in relation to statutes, wills, contracts, etc., that the illegal parts will be excised and the legal preserved unless the bad is so interwoven with the good that extrication is impossible, should be applied to the facts of this case. Plaintiff had duly declared that icing service was not included in the carriage rate, and had published an icing tariff, part of which was good and part bad. Where to cut seems clear, and what is left is without taint. And what is left is the only part that has been acted on by plaintiff.

Whether the carriage and icing charges separately or combined were reasonable, whether plaintiff could lawfully arrange to procure ice from defendant's competitor, and whether that arrangement brought about an undue preference, are matters beyond this case.

The judgment is affirmed.

UNITED STATES *v.* ERIE RAILROAD COMPANY

236 U. S. 259 (1915)

MR. JUSTICE MCKENNA delivered the opinion of the court.

These are direct appeals from decrees dismissing two bills filed by the United States to enjoin the railroad company from issuing passes to employés of common carriers not subject to the Act to Regulate Commerce.

The action of the railroad company is alleged to be in violation of §§ 2 and 3 of that act, Feb. 4, 1887, c. 104, 24 Stat. 379, and of §§1 and 6 as amended June 29, 1906, c. 3591, 34 Stat. 584, 586, prohibiting rebates and preferences.

The bills were filed in pursuance of § 3 of the Act to Further Regulate Commerce, Feb. 19, 1903, c. 708, 32 Stat. 847, 848, which authorizes proceedings in equity to prevent common carriers from departing from their published rates or from committing any discrimination forbidden by law, and the basic contention of the United States is that the giving of passes for free transportation constituted a departure from the carrier's published rates and a discrimination against other passengers. To this the railroad replies that the passes issued by it and which constitute the ground of suit were authorized by the so-called anti-pass provision of § 1 of the Act to Regulate Commerce. The question, therefore, is very direct and is, What does the act authorize or prohibit?

The charge in No. 493 is that the railroad company which is a common carrier subject to the act, in pursuance of a standing practice, issues passes to certain of the officers, agents and employés of various trans-Atlantic steamship lines, such lines not being carriers subject to the act, while other passengers who are transported between the same points are required to pay the published fares, and that the railroad company will continue the practice.

The railroad company admits the charges and avers that it solicits transportation over its lines of freight brought to this country by the steamship lines; that the latter in turn solicit from shippers on the line of the railroad company the transportation of their freight abroad; that large amounts of traffic moving by the steamship lines are transported by the railroad company after arrival in or before departing from the United States, as the case may be, some of it under through bills of lading; that the interchange of passes between the officers and employés of the railroad and such steamship lines to the limited extent alleged is one which as a matter of common knowledge has existed and been openly followed by the railroad company and other carriers generally for years; that its existence was commonly known long before the passage of the Interstate Commerce Act, by the terms of which its continuance is permitted; that it rests upon the same consideration, including considerations of business policy which have always been recognized as justifying the interchange of passes and is recognized and permitted by the proviso in § 1 of the act as amended and approved June 29, 1906. The provision is as follows:

"No common carrier subject to the provisions of this act, shall, after January 1, 1907, directly or indirectly, issue or give any interstate free ticket, free pass, or free transportation for passengers, ... provided, that this provision shall not be construed to prohibit the interchange or passes for the officers, agents, and employés of common carriers, and their families; nor to prohibit any common carrier from carrying passengers free with the object of providing relief in cases of general epidemic, pestilence, or other calamitous visitation."

The material facts in No. 494 are the same as in No. 493, with the exception that the passes there in controversy were issued by the railroad company to an employé of the Great Eastern Railway of England, and a defense of the passes is made not only under the proviso of § 1, above quoted, but under § 22 of the act as originally enacted, which reads as follows:

"Nothing in this Act shall be construed to prevent railroads from giving free carriage to their own officers and employés, or to prevent the principal officers of any railroad company or companies from exchanging passes or tickets with other railroad companies for their officers and employés."

In support of its contention the United States adduces certain rulings of the Interstate Commerce Commission and argues that Congress, having reënacted the statute, adopted the Commission's construction as the proper one. Counsel invoke a line of cases which decide, it is contended, that a contemporaneous construction of a statute by the officers upon whom is imposed the duty of administering it is entitled to weight, and, unless clearly wrong, to determining weight. The cases are familiar, the doctrine they announce a useful one, and we are brought to the inquiry, Does it apply in the case at bar?

The first of the rulings referred to was made upon petition of Frank Parmelee & Company. That company, which is a transfer company transferring passengers and packages from the railroads to the hotels in Chicago, and the reverse, asked for a ruling as to whether under the exception contained in the proviso of § 1 it had a right to interchange passes with the railroads. The Commission decided that the Parmelee Company was not a carrier subject to the act and that, therefore, an interchange of passes between it and the railroads was not permissible. In subsequent Conference Rulings the Commission decided that the right to issue passes coexisted with the obligation to file tariffs, and when the latter did not exist the former could not be exercised. These rulings received emphasis from the fact that "ocean carriers to non-adjacent foreign countries" were said to be among the carriers not subject to the act and, under the principle announced, not entitled to receive passes.

But these rulings were never enforced and the custom of carriers was uniformly the other way. Against a mere verbal construction, therefore, permitted to languish in inactivity, we have the unopposed practice of the companies. The Commission's action, therefore, cannot have the absolute effect that the Attorney General ascribes to it; but keeping it in mind, let us proceed to a consideration of the statute.

It is not denied that the words "carriers," "common carriers," "railroads" and "railroad companies" are used in the act with and without qualification "subject to the provisions of the act," and the number of times they are so used is compared. It will do no good to set forth the instances. The act was passed to regulate the conduct and affairs of the carriers of the country, and necessarily they are brought under its provisions and subject to them. It controls their relations, but the carriers subject to the act may have relation with other carriers, and special provisions would naturally be made to govern that relation. And certainly the reasoning is not impressive which justifies an interchange of passes between carriers subject to the act and denies it to those not so subject, the same business reasons existing in both cases.

Counsel for the United States sounds an alarm at such extension and lets imagination loose in portrayal of its consequences and sees included "tap lines and other industrial railroads, street car lines, local traction companies, omnibus transfer companies and herdic lines, hackmen, boatmen, ferrymen, truckmen, lumber flumes, bucket lines for ore, parcel deliveries, district messenger services, carriers of all descriptions, both in this country and abroad" — a formidable enumeration, it must be admitted. And there must be included, too, all their officers, all their employés and their families. There is, however, an opposing picture. It is conceded that carriers subject to the act may interchange passes, the officers and employés of each carrier receiving free transportation, and giving it to every other carrier subject to the act, making an army of the privileged with the same discrimination and the same burden on the passenger service of the railroads as in the illustration of the Government. There is no argument, therefore, in a comparison of the possibilities under one construction rather than the other. At best it is but a comparison of the excesses which may be but are not likely to be practiced. Counsel seem to think that the railroads have an eager desire to distribute passes and burden their transportation service with a crowd of free passengers. Congress certainly had no such view and gave power to exchange passes, considering that the best safeguard against its abuse was the interest of the carriers. The cases at bar are a typical instance of its exercise. It has its justification in a strictly business policy, and instead of being a burden upon the resources of the companies it is an aid to them. With these examples before us, and in view of the other reasons which we have adduced, we see no reason to disregard the literal terms of the statute. And this view is strengthened, not weakened, by the proviso inserted on June 18, 1910, which is as follows:

"And provided further, That this provision shall not be construed to prohibit the privilege of passes or franks, or the exchange thereof with each other, for . . . . employés . . . . of such telegraph, telephone and cable lines, and the . . . . employés . . . . of other common carriers subject to the provisions of this act." (36 Stat. 539, 546, c. 309.)

In such case the statute makes a special limitation, as will be observed; in other words, restricts the privilege of exchanging telegraph and telephone franks for employés, etc., of such lines and of other common carriers subject to the act — that is, there are words of explicit limitation.

Decree affirmed.

MR. JUSTICE MCREYNOLDS took no part in the consideration and decision of the case.

3. Maintenance of Competition

SOUTHERN PACIFIC COMPANY *v.* INTERSTATE COMMERCE COMMISSION

SOUTHERN CALIFORNIA RAILWAY COMPANY *v.* SAME

ATCHISON, TOPEKA AND SANTA FE RAILWAY COMPANY *v.* SAME

SANTA FE PACIFIC RAILROAD COMPANY *v.* SAME

SOUTHERN PACIFIC COMPANY *v.* SAME

200 U. S. 536 (1906)

Mr. Justice Peckham delivered the opinion of the court.[1]

. . . .

Upon the proceeding before the Circuit Court, that court did not pass upon the question decided by the Commission, but held that the routing rule agreed to between the initial carrier and the various eastern companies, and forming a part of the subsequent joint through tariffs which were filed with the Commission, was in itself a contract or combination for the pooling of freights.

The defendants object that the Circuit Court had no authority to decree the enforcement of the order upon any other ground than that taken by the Commission itself. We think that the court was not confined to those grounds, and if it found the rule was, in itself, for any reason illegal as a violation of the act, the order might be valid and be a lawful order, although the Commission gave a wrong reason for making it. If it held that the rule to be a violation of one section, the order to desist might be valid, if, instead of the section named by the Commission, the court should find that the rule was a violation of another section of the act. All the facts being brought out before the Commission or the court, the court could decide whether the order was a lawful one, without being confined to the reasons stated by the Commission. We therefore look to see the ground taken by the Circuit Court.

That court found that the rule was adopted to uphold their

[1] The facts and remainder of opinion will be found on page 000 *supra.* — Ed.

published rates, or in other words to maintain the rates on the joint through tariff. Although, under the previous through rate tariff, these rates had been secretly cut by the eastern connections of the initial carriers, yet when the routing rule was agreed to as part of the through rate tariff these rebates ceased. Hence, as the court said, the purpose of the rule was undoubtedly to maintain the through rate tariff, and that it was effectual. But the court held, as a result, that this routing provision, being part of the through rate tariff, agreed to by the various eastern roads, made a contract among those roads for the pooling of freights on competing railroads within the meaning of section 5 of the Commerce Act. It held that it was not necessary in order to form a pool, in violation of that section, that the contract or agreement should fix the percentages of freight the several railroads were to receive, or that the railroads should know in advance what the percentages should be; that it was sufficient to constitute a pool if the contract or agreement provided for special means of agencies for apportioning freights, which would destroy the rivalry which would otherwise exist between the competing railroads; and an agreement by which the apportionment was left to the will of the initial carrier accomplished that purpose as effectually as though definite percentages were fixed in the contract; that defendants' plan to maintain through rates through the operation of the routing rule necessarily destroyed competition, and the adoption of the routing rule put the shippers in a position where their patronage could not possibly be competed for by the defendants' eastern connections.

Thus the mere fact that the initial carrier was granted by this through tariff agreement the right to route the freight was held to result in the formation of a pool, in violation of the fifth section of the act. There was no other agreement proved in the case. It is stated by the Commission that the shipments are forwarded by the initial carrier so as to give certain percentages of the traffic to connecting lines. At the same time the Commission finds that initial carriers generally comply with the requests of the shippers to route the freight as desired. The substance of the report of the Commission is, therefore, that there is a certain percentage of the traffic given the connecting carriers when there is no request for routing given by the shippers. It amounts to the giving of fair treatment to the connecting carriers. It is true the Commission calls this a tonnage pool between the connecting carriers, to which the initial carriers give effect by their routing arrangement and that its object was not so much to prevent rebates, which was but an incident, as to effect the tonnage division. We are of opinion, however, that the evidence is substantially one way, and that is that the arrangement for routing was to break up rebating, and that it has been accomplished. The evidence before the Circuit Court was to the effect that there was no agreement whatever with the eastern connections that any of them should have any particular proportion of the freight, but the eastern roads entered into the routing agreement because they were satisfied that it would be better than the then present practice of rebating, and they thought that they would get a fair share of the business, or, in other words, would be fairly treated by the initial carriers, who gave them to understand that they would be so treated. The tonnage pool was, as the witnesses said, a myth, and it was testified to that there was not one of the eastern companies that knew what percentage of the whole business that company secured. They simply knew that the through rates were maintained under the operation of the routing agreement and that rebating ceased, and they were satisfied with the manner of their treatment by the initial carrier.

The Circuit Court, in order to arrive at its result, necessarily treated the connecting carriers as rival and competing transportation lines for this freight, and assumed that between these lines there would exist, but for the routing agreement, a competition for the fruit transportation which could not be extinguished by any agreement as to routing, as a condition for making through tariff rates; that as competition was destroyed by this rule, it was idle to say that such result was not intended by the defendant, and so it was held that the carrying out of the routing agreement violated the act.

We think these various roads were really not competing roads within the meaning of the fifth section of the Commerce Act, when the facts are carefully examined. That act recognizes the right of the carriers to agree upon and provides for the publication of joint through tariff rates between continuous roads, on such terms as the roads may choose to make, provided, of course, the rates are reasonable and no discrimination, or other violation of the act is practiced. The initial carrier did not, on its line, reach the eastern markets, but it reached various connecting railroads which did reach those markets. The initial carrier had the right to enter into an agreement for joint through rates, with all or any one of these connecting companies, though such companies were competing ones among themselves. And the agreements could be made upon such terms as the various companies might think expedient, provided they were not in violation of any other provision of the act.

Prior to the adoption of the routing rule these connecting railroads were already acting under a through rate tariff which continued up to the time when the agreement for the routing was adopted. When so acting it was no longer possible to compete with each other as to rates (and it is upon the rebates as to rates that this whole controversy is founded), provided the companies fulfilled their joint rate tariff agreements. The only way the rate competition could exist under the through rate tariff was by violating the law. This, unfortunately, was habitually done, and during that time the competition consisted in a rivalry between these roads, as to which would be the greatest violator of the law by giving the greatest rebates.

In truth, the only way in which these connecting lines could legally become competing railroads for this California fruit trade would be in the absence of all joint tariff rate agreements. The moment they made such agreements, and carried them out, rate competition would cease.

All that would be needed for the total suppression of rate competition among the connecting railroads would be the honest fulfillment of their agreement as to joint through rates. And just here is where they failed and where they violated their agreement and the law by granting rebates, or, in other words, by competing. as to rates, for the freight in violation of the joint rates. In such case we do not see any violation of the pooling section of the act, by putting in the agreement for joint through rates the provision for routing by the initial carrier. It achieved its purpose and stopped rebating, although it thereby also stopped rate competition which, in the presence of the through rate tariff, was already illegal. The railroads are no longer rate competing roads after the adoption of a through rate tariff by them, and they have no right to privately reduce their rates.

Now, while the most important, if not the only, effect of the routing agreement is to take away this rebating practice, and to hold all parties to that agreement as part of the joint through rate tariff, we think no case is made out of a violation of the pooling provision in the fifth section of the act, even where the initial carrier promises fair treatment to the connecting roads, and carries out such promises.

We must remember the general purpose of the act which is, as has been said, to obtain fair treatment for the public from the roads, and reasonable charges for the transportation of freight and the honest performance of duty, with no improper or unjust preference or discrimination. Under such circumstances, the court ought not to adopt such a strict and unnecessary construction of the act as thereby to prevent an honest and otherwise perfectly legal attempt to maintain joint through rates, by destroying one of the worst abuses known in the transportation business. The effort to maintain the published through joint tariff rates is entirely commendable.

We think that the agreement in question, upon its face, does not violate any provision of the Commerce Act, and there is no evidence in the case which shows that in fact there has been any such violation.

The decree of the Circuit Court is reversed and the case remanded with instructions to dismiss the bill.

Reversed, etc.

UNITED STATES *v.* DELAWARE, LACKAWANNA AND WESTERN RAILROAD COMPANY

238 U. S. 516 (1915)

The appellee was chartered not only as a Railroad Company, but was authorized to mine and sell coal. The Commodity Clause of the Hepburn Act of 1906 made it unlawful for the carrier to haul its own coal beyond the limits of the State of Pennsylvania, and desiring to continue the business of mining and transporting coal, the Railroad adopted a plan under which it was to make a sale and divest itself of title to the coal, at the mouth of the mines, before transportation began. Accordingly it caused to be incorporated, under the laws of New Jersey, the Delaware, Lackawanna and Western *Coal* Company with a capital stock of $6,800,000, — divided into shares of $50 each. The Railroad Company then invited its own stockholders to subscribe to the capital stock of the Coal Company at the rate of one share of the latter for each four shares of the former. Ninety-nine per cent. of these stockholders did, as was expected, subscribe for the stock of the Coal Company — their subscriptions being paid for in full out of a cash dividend of $13,600,000 previously declared by the Railroad Company. The new corporation was then organized by electing the Vice-President of the Railroad Company as President of the Coal Company and other officers and directors of the Coal Company were also officers and directors of the Railroad Company.

As soon as the organization was completed, the Railroad Company prepared and submitted to the Coal Company a contract by which the Railroad Company reserving what it needed for its railway locomotives 'agreed to sell and the Coal Company agreed to buy, f. o. b. the mines, all coal which, during the term of the contract, the Railroad Company should produce from its own mines or purchase from any one else.' The price for prepared sizes — the more important commercial coal — was fixed at 65 per cent. of the price in New York on the day of delivery at the mines. The Railroad Company also leased to the Coal Company all its trestles, docks and shipping facilities.

The contract — thus prepared by the Railroad Company — was then signed by both corporations and, on August 2, 1909, the Coal Company took possession of the leased property; those who had been Agents of the Railroad in its Sales Department became Agents of the Coal Company in its Sales Department and the two corporations, with managing officers in common, also had offices in common in the City of New York.

Thereafter the Railroad Company continued its mining business annually producing about 7,000,000 tons and purchasing about 1,500,000 tons from operators whose mines were located on its railway. After retaining what was needed for use on its railway engines, it sold the balance, aggregating about 7,000,000 tons, to the Coal Company at the contract prices f. o. b. the mines. The coal thus sold by the Railroad Company was then transported by the Railroad Company to destination where it was delivered to the Coal Company which paid the regular tariff freight rate and the contract prices on the 20th of each month. This course of dealing continued until February, 1913, when the Government filed a Petition, against both corporations, alleging that the two were practically one and attacking the validity of the contract.

The Petition alleged that the coal business was extremely profitable and in order to continue it, in all its branches, the Railroad Company (which was controlled by a group of 25 persons, owning a majority of its stock), had determined "to cause the organization of a new corporation to be under their own control — whose stockholders would be substantially the same as those of the Railroad Company — and through it to conduct the business theretofore carried on by the Railroad Sales Department, thus securing, in effect, the continued unity of mining, transporting and selling, in substance, as theretofore and depriving the public of the benefits which the Commodity Clause was intended to produce."

The Petition alleged that when the contract was made, in August, 1909, the stockholders of the two corporations were practically identical; that a large majority of the stock in both is still owned by the same persons and that by virtue of the terms and provisions of the contract the Railroad had such an *interest* in the coal as to make it unlawful for it to transport such commodity in interstate commerce.

It was further charged that the transportation of the coal sold to the Coal Company was not only a violation of the Commodity Clause, but that the contract tended to create a monopoly and unlawfully to hinder and restrain trade in coal in violation of the provisions of the Anti-Trust Act. In this connection it was also charged that the Railroad Company not only mined coal, but purchased the product of other mines located along its railway, and had acquired the output of other collieries on its line, giving to it the disposition of more than 90 per cent of the market, with power to arbitrarily fix prices. The Petition averred:

"By reason of the arrangements described, the support of the Railroad Company, and the peculiar advantages and facilities acquired, the Coal Company at once secured and has ever since maintained an unlawful monopoly of the sale of coal produced along defendant's railroad, and has completely dominated the markets at all points thereon not reached by any other railroad. Its position, power, and support render effective competition with it practically impossible, and the monopoly which it now holds will continue indefinitely unless restrained."

Both defendants answered. There was practically no dispute as to the facts, though both corporations contended that the facts alleged and proved did not support the legal conclusions sought to be drawn therefrom by the Government. Each insisted that the two corporations were separate in law and in fact; contended that the Railroad Company had no interest in the coal and insisted that the Coal Company acted independently of the Railroad Company and was not subject to its control.

At the hearing there was evidence that at the date of the making of the contract all except 2,249 shares in the Coal Company were held by those who held stock in the Railroad Company. By reason of sales of both stocks, it appeared that in October, 1913, 88,116 shares of the Railroad stock were held by those who were not then interested in the Coal Company and 6,907 shares of stock in the Coal Company were held by those who were not owners of the Railroad stock.

There was also evidence that many of the officers of the Coal Company were not officers of the Railroad Company; that the management of the two corporations was separate and distinct; that the Coal Company kept its own books, deposited its funds in its name in banks of its own choosing, and that the profits went solely to its own stockholders. The Coal Company paid the same rates of freight and demurrage as other shippers and received no discriminating favors from the Railroad Company. In 1910 the amount paid to the Railroad for the purchase price of coal under the contract was about $20,000,000, and for the freight thereon about $14,000,000. Since the contract was made the Coal Company has bought coal from other persons, the quantity being 3,847 tons in 1909; 2,267 tons in 1910; 6,600 tons in 1911; 92,004 tons in 1912; 310,645 tons in the first ten months in 1913.

There are about 70,000,000 tons of anthracite coal produced annually of which 20,000,000 tons are sold at tidewater. Of the 7,000,000 tons sold by the Delaware, Lackawanna and Western Railroad Company about 2,000,000 tons are transported to tidewater points and of this 500,000 tons are prepared sizes. The Coal Company at large expense bought land, built trestles and storage facility at various points in addition to those leased to it by the Railroad Company.

The District Court held that the business of the two corporations had not been so commingled as to make their affairs indistinguishable; that they are two distinct and separate legal beings actually engaged in separate and distinct operations and that the Railroad does not own the coal, either in whole or in part, during its carriage but has in good faith dissociated itself therefrom before the beginning of the act of transportation.

In answer to the claim that 'the Railroad will be the gainer from a high price at tide, since this will necessarily increase the price at the mines and therefore that this interest in the price is such an interest in the coal itself as is condemned by the statute,' the court said: "Undoubtedly it is correct to say that the Railroad has an interest in the price, but that 'interest' merely means that the Railroad will gain by a higher price at tide and does not mean that the Railroad has power to control the coal or the price for which it sells." The alleged power to increase the price by increasing the freight was held to be ineffective because freight rates were controlled by the Commerce Commission. "The Railroad Company does not fix prices. It does not decide how much coal is to go to New York Harbor, and it does not determine the sum for which the coal is to be sold at that point." 'The 65 per cent. basis had its origin many years ago and affords a convenient basis for calculating the price to be paid for future deliveries.' .... The Railroad retains nothing more after the title passes to the Coal Company at the mines than an interest in the price and this is not the same thing as an interest in the coal. The Commodity Clause deals with an "interest direct or indirect" in the commodities themselves and thus must mean some kind or degree of ownership in the thing transported or some power to deal with it or to control it. The Railroad Company neither owns nor controls the coal after it has been loaded on the cars at the breakers. Thereafter the Coal Company is the owner and the master, and fixes prices, routes and destination at its own will.

The court further said that 'the bill of complaint makes a formal charge against both defendants under the Anti-Trust Act, but the oral argument left us under the impression that this charge was not much insisted on. For that reason the Anti-Trust Branch of the complaint was regarded as comparatively unimportant, and for that reason we shall not undertake what we think would be the needless task of discussing the evidence bearing upon the charge of restraining or monopolizing commerce. If we are mistaken in this supposition the error can easily be corrected.'

The Petition was thereupon dismissed without prejudice to the Government's right to begin a second proceeding whenever it may be so advised. 213 Fed. Rep. 240. The Government then brought the case here by appeal.

In the Government's brief it is stated that while it did not now ask for a ruling as to the right of the Railroad Company to purchase and sell coal produced in mines along its Railroad, it did ask that if the decree was affirmed it should be without prejudice to the right of the United States to institute such proceedings.

MR. JUSTICE LAMAR, after making the foregoing statement of facts, delivered the opinion of the court.

The Commodity Clause of the Hepburn Act was intended to prevent railroads from occupying the dual and inconsistent positions of public carrier and private shipper; and, in order to separate the business of transportation from the business of selling, that statute made it unlawful for railroads to transport in interstate commerce any coal in which the company had "*any interest, direct or indirect.*" *United States* v. *Delaware & Hudson,* 213 U. S. 415; *Delaware &c. R. R.* v. *United States,* 231 U. S. U. S. 363, 371.

1. But mere stock ownership by a Railroad, or by its stockholders, in a producing Company cannot be used as a test by which to determine the legality of the transportation of such Company's coal by the interstate carrier. For, when the Commodity Clause was under discussion, attention was called to the fact that there were a number of the anthracite roads which at that time owned stock in coal companies. An amendment was then offered which, if adopted, would have made it unlawful for any such Road to transport coal belonging to such Company. The amendment, however, was voted down; and, in the light of that indication of Congressional intent, the Commodity Clause was construed to mean that it was not necessarily unlawful for a railroad company to transport coal belonging to a Corporation in which the Road held stock. *United States* v. *Delaware & Hudson Co.,* 213 U. S. 414. For a stronger reason, it would not necessarily be illegal for the Road to transport coal belonging to a Corporation whose stock was held by those who owned the stock of the Railroad Company.

Nevertheless, the Commodity Clause, of the Hepburn Act of 1906, rendered unlawful many transactions which prior to that time had been expressly authorized by the statutes of the States which had chartered the Coal Roads. And, while the Hepburn Act provided that, in the future, interstate railroads should not occupy the dual position of carrier and shipper, there was, of course no intent on the part of Congress to confiscate property or to destroy the interest of the stockholders. But, still, upon adoption of the Commodity Clause, this appellee Railroad was confronted with a difficult situation. To shut down the mines, because the coal could not be transported, would have meant not only a vast monetary loss to the Company and its stockholders, but would have been even more harmful to the interests of the public which required a constant supply of fuel. The character of coal property was such as to make it impossible to divide the same in kind among the railroad stockholders, while the value of the coal land was so great as to make it impracticable to find a purchaser in ordinary course of trade. It was, therefore, natural, if not necessary, to organize a corporation with which a contract could be made, and out of cash received or stock issued to pay for or preserve the equity which the railroad shareholders had in the coal.

In this situation there may have been no impropriety in the Railroad Company taking the preliminary steps of organizing such a corporation. Neither was it illegal for the stockholders of the Railroad Company to take stock in the Coal Company, for there are many instances in which the law recognizes that there may be diversity of corporate interest even when there is an identity of corporate members. A city and the county, in which it is located, may both have the same population but different corporate interests. Many private corporations have both stockholders and officers in common, yet they may nevertheless make contracts which will bind both of the separate entities. But whenever two such companies, thus owned or managed, make contracts which affect the interest of minority stockholders, or of third persons, or of the public, the fact of their unity of management must be considered in testing the validity and *bona fides* of the contracts under review.

2. That principle is to be specially borne in mind in the present case. For this is not an instance of a Coal Road and a Coal Company, both of which existed and had made contracts prior to the Commodity Clause; — but a case where a Coal Company was created with the express purpose that, with stockholders in common, it should be a party to a contract intended to enable the Railroad Company to meet the requirements of the Commodity Clause and at the same time continue the business of buying, mining, selling and transporting coal.

It is also to be noted that the Delaware, Lackawanna and Western Railroad Company did not part with title to its coal lands, mines and mining machinery as seems to have been done, on terms not fully stated [*United States* v. *Delaware & Hudson*, 213 U. S. 366, 398 (5), 392], in some of the instances discussed in the Commodity Cases. In them the ownership of the mines had passed completely from the railroads to the producing companies and the coal property was no longer subject to the debts of the railroad companies. After such sale of the coal lands there was both a technical and a practical separation of the legal interest of the two corporations in the coal under the ground, on the surface, when it was transported, and when it was sold. The fact that the Railroad held stock in the producing company, and received dividends thereon, did not give to the Railroad Company, any more than to any other stockholder in any other corporation, a legal interest in the property of the Coal Company. Nor would the fact that the Railroad Company had once owned it, have made any difference, if, — by a normal and *bona fide* sale at the point of production, — the carrier had lost all power of control and all right, title and interest in the coal before the transportation began. *United States* v. *Delaware & Hudson*, 213 U. S. 413, top.

3. But the decisions construing the statute, recognize that one corporation can be an agent for another corporation and that by means of stock ownership one of such companies may be converted into a mere agent or instrumentality of the other. *United States* v. *Lehigh Valley R. R.*, 220 U. S. 257, 273. And, this use of one by the other — or this power of one over the other — does not depend upon control by virtue of the fact that stock therein is held by the Railroad Company or by its shareholders. For dominance of the Coal Company may be secured by a carrier (*New Haven R. R.* v. *Int. Com. Comm.*, 200 U. S. 363) not only by an express contract of agency, but by any contract which in its practical operation gives to the Railroad Company a control or an "interest, direct or indirect" in the coal sold, at the mouth of the mines.

Assuming then that the incorporation and organization of the Coal Company under the auspices of the Railroad Company was legal; assuming that the election of railroad officers as the first managers of the Coal Company was not illegal; assuming that as officers of the Railroad they could contract with themselves as officers of the Coal Company; assuming that at the time of organization it was not unlawful for the Railroad Company and the Coal Company, not only to have officers but offices in common, and finally assuming that all these facts together did not, in and of themselves, establish an identity of corporate interest, still these facts taken together are most significant. They at least prove that the relation between the parties was so friendly that they were not trading at arm's length. And the further fact that one of the parties was under a statutory disability as to hauling coal makes it necessary to carefully scrutinize their arrangement in order to determine whether it was a *bona fide* and lawful contract of sale, or a means by which the Railroad though parting with the legal title retained an interest and control in what had been sold.

4. That contract is published in full in 213 Fed. Rep. 255–259. The provisions material in the present inquiry may be thus summarized:

(a) The Railroad Company agreed to sell and the Coal Company agreed to buy all of the coal mined or acquired by the Railroad Company during the continuance of the contract; (b) the price for the more important commercial grades was to be 65 per cent. of the New York price on the day of delivery; (c) the amount of coal to be sold and delivered was at the absolute option of the Railroad Company as its interests might determine; (d) the Coal Company was not to buy coal from any other person or corporation without the written consent of the Railroad Company; (e) the Coal Company was to conduct the selling of the coal so as best to conserve the interests, good-will and markets of the coal mined by the Railroad Company; (f) the Coal Company was to continue to fill the orders of present responsible customers of the Railroad Company, even if some of such sales might be unprofitable; (g) the Railroad leased to the Coal Company all of its trestles, docks and shipping facilities at a rental of 5 per cent. of their value; (h) the contract could be terminated by either party on giving six months' notice.

The most cursory examination of the contract shows that — while it provides for the sale of coal before transportation begins — it is coupled with onerous and unusual provisions which make it difficult to determine the exact legal character of the agreement. If it amounted to a Sales Agency the transportation was illegal because the Railroad Company could not haul coal which it was to sell in its own name or through an agent. If the contract was in restraint of trade it was void because in violation of the Sherman Anti-Trust Law. The validity of the contract cannot be determined by consideration of the single fact that it did provide for a sale. It must be considered as a whole and in the light of the fact that the sale at the mine, was but one link in the business of a Railroad engaged in buying, mining, selling and transporting coal.

5. By virtue of the fact that the Railroad Company bought, mined and sold, it — like any other dealer — was interested in maintaining prices, since the contract did not fix a definite sum to be paid for all of the coal sold, but provided that the Railroad Company was to receive 65 per cent. of the New York price on the

day the coal was loaded into the cars. The higher the rate in New York the better for the seller. And, by the contract, the Railroad reserved a power which, when exercised, could not only curtail production but shipments. Thus by decreasing the amount transported the supply in New York could be lessened. This would tend to raise New York prices and thus increase the sum the Railroad was to receive.

The Railroad Company was in the business of selling, and it is not to be presumed that its power to limit deliveries or to prevent the Coal Company from obtaining coal elsewhere would be often exercised. Yet the power did exist and it was reserved for some purpose — not, as argued, to prevent controversy as to failure to deliver in cases of strikes or accidents, for such is not the language or intent of the contract. Nor is room left for the implication [necessary to the validity of such an exclusive contract, *Chicago &c. R. R.* v. *Pullman*, 139 U. S. 80 (3), 89, 90], that the seller would deliver reasonable amounts at reasonable times. All such defensive arguments are excluded by the express and emphatic terms of the contract that "the amount of coal to be so delivered and sold to the buyer by the seller shall be at the absolute option of the seller as its interests may determine, and the seller shall be subject to no liability whatsoever for failure to supply the buyer with such amount of coal as it may desire."

It might be said that if such a power was exercised the Coal Company could then go into the market and purchase from other coal dealers. But this contract deprives the buyer even of that ordinary business privilege, declaring that the Coal Company "will purchase all coal to be sold by it from the seller, and will purchase no coal from any other person or corporation, except with the written consent of the seller."

6. Reading these two clauses together, it is evident that the Coal Company was neither an independent buyer nor a free agent. It was to handle nothing except the Railroad's coal and was the instrument through which the Railroad sold all its product. The Coal Company, though incorporated to do a general coal business, was dependent solely upon the Railroad for the amount it could procure and sell and was absolutely excluded from the right to purchase elsewhere without the consent of the Railroad Company, which, however, was under no corresponding obligation to supply any definite amount at any definite date.

Restrictive contracts should at least be reciprocal and mutual — for if A is bound to purchase only from B the latter should certainly be bound to furnish what A wishes to buy [*Chicago &c R. R.* v. *Pullman*, 139 U. S. 80 (3), 89, 90] — especially is this true when the subject of the contract is an article in which the public is interested. Even at common law, in passing upon the validity of contracts in restraint of trade, the "public welfare is first considered, and if it be not involved, and the restraint upon one party is not greater than protection to the other party requires the contract may be sustained." *Gibbs* v. *Baltimore Consolidated Gas Co.*, 130 U. S. 396, 409; *Fowle* v. *Park*, 131 U. S. 97.

In this case the subject of the contract was anthracite coal — an article of public necessity and of limited supply, one-tenth being controlled by the appellee. The Railroad Company might have justly insisted on contract provisions intended to secure payment for all that it produced. But going beyond what was required for its own protection, it restrained the Coal Company from buying from anyone else, and, — what is probably more significant in this case — thereby prohibited the Coal Company from competing with the Railroad Company for the purchase of coal mined on the Railroad lines. And, this was not a mere perfunctory provision, because the Railroad Company was a buyer of coal and purchased 1,500,000 tons per annum from mines on its system. By this contract it excluded from that market the Coal Company, which, with its capital of $6,000,000, could have been a strong competitor. Such a provision may not have actually effected a monopoly. But considering the financial strength of the carrier; its control of the means of transportation; its powers to fix the time when transportation of the very coal sold was to begin; its power in furnishing cars to favor those from whom it bought or to whom it sold — such a contract would undoubtedly have that tendency. In that respect it was opposed to that policy of the law, which was the underlying reason for the adoption of the Commodity Clause. *New Haven R. R.* v. *Int. Com. Comm.*, 200 U. S. 373.

7. There is another provision of the contract which shows that the Railroad had such an interest in the coal as enabled it to dictate to whom it should be sold, even at unprofitable prices. The agreement provides:

"Sixth. The buyer agrees that it will conduct the business of selling the coal of the seller in such manner as best to conserve the interests of and preserve the good will and markets of the coal mined by the seller, and to continue to fill the orders of all responsible present customers of the seller even though as to some of such customers the sales may be unprofitable, it being understood and agreed that at the prices above quoted the entire business of the buyer will be conducted at a profit."

This is not a mere stipulation that the Coal Company would not injure the reputation of the Railroad Company's coal; while the further provision that the Coal Company would 'continue to fill the orders of all responsible present customers, even though some of such sales might be unprofitable,' was a further indication of the fact that both parties recognized the Railroad had an interest in the coal and used the Coal Company to preserve and secure that interest even after transportation began.

The unusual, onerous and restrictive terms imposed by this contract may, as between the parties, have been negligible — certainly so as long as the stockholders remained the same, since a loss to the Coal Company would be presumably represented by a gain to the Railroad Company. But the Commodity Clause and the Anti-Trust Act are not conerned with the interest of the parties but with the interest of the public and it, therefore, makes no difference whether this contract dictated by the Railroad Company was for the permanent advantage of the Coal Company.

8. It is argued, however, that the contract has not operated to the injury of the parties or of the public. And, in answer to those urged by the Government, it is said that some of the objections now insisted on were not pressed in the lower court; that there is no complaint that the Railroad charged the Coal Company exorbitant prices; or, that it ever raised the New York prices; or, that it failed to make prompt deliveries; or, that it has prevented the Coal Company from buying coal from other operators; or, that the Railroad monopolized the coal mined on its railway, or that it deprived such mining companies of an open market. From this it is argued that the present objections to the contract are purely academic. But its validity depends upon its terms. And if, as a matter of law, the contract is in restraint of trade, or, if the Coal Company is practically the agent of the Railroad Company then the transportation of the coal by the latter is unlawful.

9. As already pointed out, the contract has in it elements of a sale and elements of a sales agency. It provides that the Railroad Company will sell and that the Coal Company will buy all coal that is mined during the continuance of the contract; but it prevents the Coal Company from buying from any one else.

It requires it to sell to present railroad customers at the old price, even though those prices may be unprofitable. The seller is not bound to make deliveries of fixed quantities at fixed dates and by decreasing what it will sell and determining when it will ship it has a power in connection with its power as a carrier, which, if exerted, would tend to increase prices in New York. Besides all this, the contract prevents the Coal Company from competing with the Railroad Company in the purchase of coal along the railway line. Taking it as a whole and bearing in mind the policy of the Commodity Clause to dissociate the Railroad Company from the transportation of property in which it is interested and that the Sherman Anti-Trust Act prohibits contracts in restraint of trade, there would seem to be no doubt that this agreement violated both statutes.

10. The Railroad Company, if it continues in the business of mining, must absolutely dissociate itself from the coal before the transportation begins. It cannot retain the title nor can it sell through an Agent. It cannot call that Agent a buyer while so hampering and restricting such alleged buyer as to make him a puppet subject to the control of the Railroad Company. If the Railroad sells coal at the mouth of the mines to one buyer or to many it must not only part with all interest direct or indirect in the property but also with all control over it or over those to whom the coal is sold at the mines. It must leave the buyer as free as any other buyer who pays for what he has bought. It should not sell to a corporation with officers and offices in common, — for the policy of the statute requires that instead of being managed by the same officers, they should studiously and in good faith avoid anything, either in contract or conduct, that remotely savors of joint action, joint interest or the dominance of one Company by the other. If the seller wishes — by a lawful and *bona fide* contract, whose provisions as to delivery and otherwise are not in restraint of trade — to sell all of its coal to one buying company, then that one buyer can be bound by reasonable terms and required to pay according to the contract. But such buyer should otherwise be absolutely free to extend its business to buy when, where and from whom it pleases, and otherwise to act as an independent dealer in active competition with the Railroad Company.

What has been said is sufficient to show that the contract was invalid. That makes it unnecessary to discuss other questions raised but not disposed of by the District Court, and the decision herein is without prejudice to the right of the United States to institute proceedings in reference thereto or to test the right of the Railroad Company to purchase coal for sale.

The decree is reversed with directions to enter a decree enjoining the Railroad from further transporting coal sold under the provisions of the contract of August 2, 1909, referred to in the Petition.

Reversed.

MR. JUSTICE MCREYNOLDS took no part in the decision of this case.

CHAPTER III

FUNCTIONS OF THE INTERSTATE COMMERCE COMMISSION IN THE ENFORCEMENT OF THE ACT

1. Constitutionality

INTERSTATE COMMERCE COMMISSION *v.* BRIMSON.

154 U. S. 447 (1894) [1]

Acting upon an informal complaint, the Interstate Commerce Commission of its own motion investigated into the alleged unreasonable rates and discriminations in favor of the Illinois Steel Company on the part of divers interstate carriers. Upon such hearing witnesses refused to obey the subpœna *duces tecum* of the Commission and to answer questions. The Commission thereupon petitioned the Circuit Court of the Northern District of Illinois for an order compelling to answer and produce the book called for by the subpœna. The Circuit Court held the twelfth section of the Interstate Commerce Act to be unconstitutional, upon which the petition was based, (53 Fed. Rep. 476), and from the judgment dismissing the petition this appeal was taken.

Mr. Justice Harlan delivered the opinion of the court. . . .

The answers of Brimson, Keefe, and Stirling in the present proceeding, besides insisting that the questions propounded to them, respectively, were immaterial and irrelevant, were based mainly upon the ground that so much of the Interstate Commerce Act as empowered the Commission to require the attendance and testimony of witnesses and the production of books,

[1] The facts have been briefly restated — Ed.

papers, and documents, and authorized the Circuit Court of the United States to order common carriers or persons to appear before the Commission and produce books and papers and give evidence, and to punish by process for contempt any failure to obey such order of the court, was repugnant to the Constitution of the United States.

Is the twelfth section of the act unconstitutional and void so far as it authorizes or requires the Circuit Court of the United States to use their process in aid of inquiries before the Commission? The court recognizes the importance of this question, and has bestowed upon it the most careful consideration.

As the Constitution extends the judicial power of the United States to all cases in law and equity arising under that instrument or under the laws of the United States, as well to all controversies to which the United States shall be a party, (Art. 3, sec. 2), and as the Circuit Courts of the United States are capable, under the statutes defining and regulating their jurisdiction, of exerting such power in cases or controversies of that character, within the limits prescribed by Congress, 25 Stat. 434, c. 866, the fundamental inquiry on this appeal is whether the present proceeding is a "case" or "controversy" within the meaning of the Constitution. The Circuit Court, as we have seen, regarded the petition of the Interstate Commerce Commission as nothing more than an application by an administrative body to a judicial tribunal for the exercise of its functions in aid of the execution of duties not of a judicial nature, and accordingly adjudged that this proceeding did not constitute a case or controversy to which the judicial power of the United States could be extended.

At the same time the learned court said: "Undoubtedly, Congress may confer upon a non-judicial body authority to obtain information necessary for legitimate governmental purposes, and make refusal to appear and testify before it touching matters pertinent to any authorized inquiry, an offence punishable by the courts, subject, however, to the privilege of witnesses to make no disclosures which might tend to criminate them or subject them to penalties or forfeitures. A prosecution or an action for violation of such a statute would clearly be an original suit or controversy between parties within the meaning of the Constitution, and not a mere application, like the present one, for the exercise of the judicial power in aid of a non-judicial body." *In re Interstate Commerce Commission*, 53 Fed. Rep. 476, 480.

In other words, if the Interstate Commerce Act made the refusal of a witness duly summoned to appear and testify before the Commission in respect to a matter rightly committed by Congress to that body for examination, an offence against the United States, punishable by fine or imprisonment, or both, a criminal prosecution or an information for the violation of such a statute would be a case or controversy to which the judicial power of the United States extended; while a direct civil proceeding, expressly authorized by an act of Congress, in the name of the Commission, and under the direction of the Attorney General of the United States, against the witness so refusing to testify, to compel him to give evidence before the Commission touching the same matter, would not be a case or controversy of which cognizance could be taken by any court established by Congress to receive the judicial power of the United States.

This interpretation of the Constitution would restrict the employment of means to carry into effect powers granted to Congress within much narrower limits than, in our judgment, is warranted by that instrument.

[The Court then considered the nature of the power to regulate commerce, and the conditions under which it may constitutionally be exerted.]

It was not disputed at the bar, nor indeed can it be successfully denied, that the prohibition of unjust charges, discriminations, or preferences, by carriers engaged in interstate commerce, in respect to property or persons transported from one State to another, is a proper regulation of interstate commerce, or that the object that Congress has in view by the act in question may be legitimately accomplished by it under the power to regulate commerce among the several States. In every substantial sense such prohibition is a rule by which interstate commerce must be governed, and is plainly adapted to the object intended to be accomplished. The same observation may be made in respect to those provisions empowering the Commission to inquire into the management of the business of carriers subject to the provisions of the act, and to investigate the whole subject of interstate commerce as conducted by such carriers, and, in that way to obtain full and accurate information of all matters involved in the enforcement of the act of Congress. It was clearly competent for Congress, to that end, to invest the Commission with authority to require the attendance and testimony of witnesses, and the production of books, papers, tariffs, contracts, agreements, and documents relating to any matter legally committed to that body for investigation. We do not understand that any of these propositions are disputed in this case.

Interpreting the Interstate Commerce Act as applicable, and as intended to apply, only to matters involved in the regulation of commerce, and which Congress may rightfully subject to investigation by a commission established for the purpose of enforcing that act, we are unable to say that its provisions are not appropriate and plainly adapted to the protection of interstate commerce from burdens that are or may be, directly and indirectly, imposed upon it by means of unjust and unreasonable discriminations, charges, and preferences, Congress is not limited in its employment of means to those that are absolutely essential to the accomplishment of objects within the scope of the powers granted to it. It is a settled principle of constitutional law that "the government which has a right to do an act, and has imposed on it the duty of performing that act, must, according to the dictates of reason, be allowed to select the means; and those who contend that it may not select any appropriate means, that one particular mode of effecting the object is excepted, take upon themselves the burden of establishing that exception." 4 Wheat. 316, 409. The test of the power of Congress is not the judgment of the courts that particular means are not the best that could have been employed to effect the end contemplated by the legislative department. The judiciary can only inquire whether the means devised in the execution of a power granted are forbidden by the Constitution. It cannot go beyond that inquiry without entrenching upon the domain of another department of the government. That it may not do with safety to our institutions. *Sinking Fund Cases,* 99 U. S. 700, 718.

An adjudication that Congress could not establish an administrative body with authority to investigate the subject of interstate commerce and with power to call witnesses before it, and to require the production of books, documents, and papers relating to that subject, would go far towards defeating the object for which the people of the United States placed commerce among the States under national control. All must recognize the fact that the full information necessary as a basis of intelligent legislation by Congress from time to time upon the subject of interstate commerce cannot be obtained, nor can the rules established for the regulation of such commerce be efficiently enforced, otherwise than through the instrumentality of an administrative body, representing the whole country, always watchful of the general interests, and charged with the duty not only of obtaining the required information, but of compelling by all lawful methods obedience to such rules. . . .

MR. JUSTICE BREWER dissented; the CHIEF JUSTICE [FULLER] and MR. JUSTICE JACKSON, concurring in the dissent.[1]

---

2. POWERS AND DUTIES

CONSOLIDATED CLASSIFICATION CASES

54 I. C. C. 1 (1919)

BY THE COMMISION:

In our annual reports to Congress we have from time to time mentioned our efforts to stimulate work in the direction of greater uniformity in freight classifications. Early in 1918 it was apparent, in view of the progress already made, that a complete unification of the rules and descriptions of articles in the official, southern, and western classifications was possible at a not distant date, and we accordingly inquired of the carriers why they could not by January 1, 1919, or sooner, effect a consolidation of the three general classifications into one volume containing one set of uniform commodity descriptions with three rating columns, one for each territory, subtended, and with one set of general rules.[2] Shortly thereafter the director of traffic of the Railroad Administration, after conference with us appointed a special committee of experienced classification men to carry out the work we had in mind. This committee prepared

[1] Reported in 155 U. S. 3.

[2] The term "descriptions" includes packing specifications and minimum and estimated weights. All provisions of the classification, other than ratisgm will hereinafter be referred to as rules and descriptions.

and submitted a volume entitled "Proposed Consolidated Freight Classification No. 1," which accomplishes the consolidation and uniformity sought, and, in addition thereto, proposes many increases and reductions in ratings, most of which, however, have no necessary connection with the work assigned to the committee. The volume was not filed with us as a tariff schedule.

The Director General requested that we make an investigation and give him our recommendations relative to the advisability of adopting it for application by carriers under federal control. We accordingly instituted this proceeding of inquiry and investigation into the reasonableness and propriety of its provisions. [1] We made respondents all of the carriers subject to the act and which were not under federal control, in order that the same classification might, if that course were found advisable, be prescribed for their use also. The special committee distributed about 14,000 copies of the volume among carriers, state commissions, interested shippers and shippers' organizations throughout the country, each copy accompanied by a notice of this proceeding. Hearings were held at Boston, Mass., New York, N. Y., Chicago, Ill., Omaha, Nebr., Portland, Oreg., San Francisco, Calif., Denver, Colo., Fort Worth, Tex., New Orleans, La., Atlanta, Ga., and Washington, D. C. Nearly 15,000 pages of testimony were taken and over 800 exhibits were filed. The evidence of objectors or protestants was generally confined to the proposed increases, changes in the nature of increases, and new items. In other words, objections to a particular item were not heard unless the item proposed to put some new or added burden upon shippers. Most of the evidence relates to the increased ratings. The consolidation of the classifications and the unification of the rules and descriptions, generally speaking, were received with favor.

As we understand it, the consolidated classification was proposed as a general standard classification to supersede not only the existing issues of the official, southern, and western classifications, but also all state classifications, and at the request of

[1] On the front cover page of the proposed consolidated classification was printed the following: "Prepared for filling with the Interstate Commerce Commission as an exhibit with an application under the 15th and 20th sections of the act to regulate commerce, as amended, for authority to publish and file a classification embodying these changes in lieu of the official, southern and western classifications specified." It was later decided, however, to handle the matter as above indicated instead of by application.

the director of traffic we have received evidence as to the general effect of canceling the various state classifications. That evidence will be referred to later in the report. We were advised by the director of traffic that he had under consideration also the advisability of canceling the exceptions to all classifications, but that commodity rates might be established in lieu thereof in proper cases. That matter, however, has not been referred to us for investigation and recommendation.

The consolidated classification is not a uniform classification in the full sense of the term, because all the ratings are not uniform. In a majority of the items, the ratings are the same as now. The consolidated classification would preserve the identity of the official, southern, and western classifications, and, as finally amended, is intended to be filed with the Commission, with a separate I. C. C. number for each territory. In other words, from a legal or technical standpoint, it is to be three classifications in one volume. It is not much larger and is no more complicated than any one of the three general classifications now in use.[1]

The consolidated classification is the result of effort toward uniformity extending over a long term of years, and since uniform rules and descriptions are necessary before uniformity in ratings is possible, it marks an important step toward a uniform classification. Definite action in the direction of uniformity was taken about 10 years ago, when the carriers created their committees on uniform classification, to which was assigned the duty of working out a common set of rules and descriptions for the three general classifications. This committee made disappointingly slow progress, largely because of technical considerations and the disposition of the carriers in each territory to force their views and measures of expediency upon the carriers in the other territories It was abolished shortly after the proposed consolidated classification was prepared.

The special committee which prepared the consolidated classification consisted of the chairman of the committee on uniform classification, the chairman of the Official and Western Classification Committees, a member of the Southern Classification Committee, now its chairman, and our classification agent.

[1] Included in the publication are the rules and regulations governing the transportation of explosives and other dangerous articles, which have been prescribed by this Commission. These are not involved in this case.

In consolidating the classifications and unifying the rules and descriptions the members of the special committee are understood to have been guided largely by their own ideas. They were not of one mind in respect to some of the charges they have proposed in the rules and descriptions. Numerous concessions were made and some long standing and deep rooted controversies growing out of territorial or local traffic policies were cast aside. There are instances in which the existing rules as to a given situation and the descriptions, even of like articles, differ widely in the three classifications, and in respect of certain items some radical changes were necessary in order to accomplish the desired uniformity.

As stated, the consolidated classification also proposes many changes in ratings. The special committee was not directed, however, to change ratings where that was not necessarily or reasonably incident to changes in descriptions. The task assigned to the special committee was merely the completion of the work begun years ago by the committee on uniform classification, which committee had nothing whatever to do with ratings. The changes in ratings were proposed, not by the special committee as a body, but by the representatives of the respective territorial committees, individually and on their own initiative. The representative of each classification committee undertook a realignment of the ratings in his own classification, in accordance with what he conceived to be proper principles and considerations. Our representative on the special committee had no voice in fixing any of the proposed ratings. There was no concerted effort to make the ratings uniform, but the desirability of uniformity seems to have been kept in mind, and as to a number of items where there were considerable differences in the existing ratings in the three classifications, changes were proposed which effected a greater degree of uniformity, particularly in the higher classes. Changes proposed for the purpose of attaining a greater degree of uniformity have more of an upward than a downward trend.

The classification committees generally have a large number of contemplated changes in ratings in the course of investigation, either before or after they are docketed by them for consideration at their meetings with the public. Some of the changes in ratings proposed in the consolidated classification grew out of such investigations and had been decided upon by the respective committees for publication. The great majority of the changes, however, were here laid before the public for the first time. So far as the western classification is concerned most of the increases proposed are of minor importance and comparatively few of them have been protested, but in the two other territories some of the increases would apply on important kinds of traffic and have been the subjects of vigorous protests. The chairmen of the three classification committees, as representatives both of the federal controlled and the nonfederal controlled lines, severally and jointly undertook the defense of their proposals. They have presented detailed written statements in explanation of each increased rating that was not covered by the oral testimony they offered in answer to the protests at the hearings.

Changes and new items are indicated in the consolidated classification by appropriate symbols. The special committee undertook to affix a proper symbol in every case where the classification provision might on any theory be construed as a change or new item. Based on these symbols the table below, showing the nature and number of changes and new items proposed, was prepared by the special committee and submitted with its report to the director of traffic.

Nature of changes	Number of changes in the classifications			
	Official	Southern	Western	Total
Increase in ratings	890	2,574	393	3,857
Reduction in ratings	478	898	464	1,840
Carload ratings eliminated [1]	136	1	4	141
Increases in minimum weights	342	599	194	1,135
Reductions in minimum weights	229	73	61	363
Carload minimum weights to which rule 34 is added, subjecting them to the graduate scale	39	49	132	220
Additions or new items	1,144	1,665	425	3,234
Total	3,258	5,859	1,673	10,790

[1] The number of carload ratings established does not appear, but they are included in the reductions.

As will be seen, the increases in ratings in the official classification greatly outnumber the reductions, there being 890 increases and 478 reductions. With respect to the western classification the situation is reversed, the reductions in ratings outnumbering the increases, there being 464 reductions and 393 increases. The greater number of increases in ratings in the official classification than in the western classification may be attributable in some measure to the fact that the official classification had not received as much upward revision in recent years as the western classification, probably because the official classification committee has only recommendatory powers, and was not free to make changes which it was convinced should be made. In the southern classification the increases in ratings far outnumber the reductions, there being 2,574 increases and 898 reductions. This is due to the fact that at present many articles that are in the higher classes in the official and western classification are rated lower in the southern classification, and it is proposed to bring a large number of ratings in the southern classification up to or nearer to the bases observed in the two other classifications. In the southern classification proposed increases of two classes are quite common, and there are some instances in which the increases are even greater.

An increase of one class in rating effects an increase in freight charges ranging generally from 15 to 25 per cent. Many of the protestants referred to the several recent general increases in freight rates and suggested that this was not a desirable time to require shippers to bear further increases, even though they might be reasonable when considered strictly from a technical classification standpoint. Many reductions are proposed, but it happens that upon the whole they do not apply to traffic of the same importance as do the increases, and so far as the individual shipper is concerned the reduction can not, as a rule, be said to neutralize or offset the increases, for the reason that the shipper who would suffer an increase probably would not, in most instances, be the one who would benefit by a reduction.

Owing to the fact that more increases than reductions are proposed and to the fact that the increases would apply on more important lines of traffic, or at least on a greater tonnage, than would the reductions, the consolidated classification would bring the carriers some additional revenue.

The changes enumerated in the above table, other than the increases and reductions in ratings, are generally of secondary importance and have been the subject of comparatively few protests. Additions and new items are numerous. In some cases they are for new articles of commerce, but in most cases they are merely specific provisions for articles that are at present rated by analogy or covered by indefinite or general provisions. It is impossible to say to what extent they represent increases or reductions.

The respective classification committees and territories will be hereinafter referred to as the official, western, or southern committee or territory.

In a number of instances the chairmen of the classification committees, and particularly the chairmen of the official and western committees, in the light of information developed upon the hearing, withdrew certain of their proposals or presented modified proposals which satisfied some of the protests in whole or in part. These concessions were incorporated in a supplement to the consolidated classification issued after the case was submitted, and given the same distribution as the original publication. In a few instances the revision made by the carriers in order to effect reductions that would satisfy the interested protestants of record resulted in new increases in related items or parts of items, which were not before the public when the hearings were in progress. These increases appear to be of minor importance and are generally of such a nature as to be unobjectionable, especially when considered in connection with the reductions to which they are related. . . .

We have stated that the consolidated classification marks an important step toward a uniform classification. Our hitherto most important case in which the matter of classification uniformity was considered was the *Western Classification Case,* 25 I. C. C., 442, decided December 9, 1912. In that proceeding the lines parties to the western classification sought to establish a large number of changes, including revised rules and descriptions which had been recommended by the committee on uniform classification. We there discussed classification matters rather fully and stated that in our opinion a uniform classification was practicable, but that there were great difficulties to be overcome, particularly in so far as uniform ratings are concerned. In the instant case several traffic organizations, one or two state commissions, and a number of the shippers who would be adversely affected by the changes proposed in the consolidated classification as a result of efforts toward uniformity went on record as being opposed to, or at least not advocating, a uniform classification, contending that there are such wide differences in conditions in the various parts of the country as to make a uniform classification impracticable and undesirable. We are now, as formerly, fully convinced that a uniform classification, with such exceptions or commodity rates as may be necessary in special cases, is practicable and desirable, and practical uniformity should not be unnecessarily delayed. Naturally there must be both increases and reductions, which may adversely or advantageously affect individual shippers and carriers, but a broad view of the situation justifies the statement that carriers and shippers alike will be amply repaid in the end by the benefits which will accrue from uniformity. The fact that a uniform classification would be of convenience is a consideration of relatively minor importance; we have advocated uniformity because it is an essential part of the general scheme which contemplates greater consistency in rate making and elimination of discriminations and inequalities.

Placing the ratings in juxtaposition in three parallel columns opposite the descriptions impresses us as never before with the great lack of consistency that exists among the three classification territories. Many of the inconsistencies are due to considerations of minor importance and could be removed without changes in rate scales and, in our view, without serious effect upon any one, particularly in so far as less-than-carload ratings are concerned. In large part different ratings in the three territories are not due to actual or substantial differences in circumstances and conditions, but are the result of mere differences of opinion and the natural inclination of traffic officials to give expression to their respective theories of classification. For instance, on furniture in less than carloads, the chairman of the official committee, following a practice of long standing in his territory, proposes the same rating for the articles wrapped as for the articles boxed or crated. The chairman of the southern and western committees in some instances do the same thing; in others they do not, but propose ratings one or two classes higher for articles wrapped than if boxed or crated. Moreover, the proposals of the three chairmen, even as to one and the same article of furniture, are in some cases directly opposed to each other. An interesting example of this is shown below. The ratings are for less than carloads.

Page	Item	Article	Ratings		
			Official	Southern	Western
		Furniture:			
180	8–9	Benches, dentists laboratory —			
		Wrapped in burlap	1½	1½	1½
		In boxes or crates	1½	1	1½
181	11–12	Kitchen cabinets, set up —			
		Wrapped in burlap	D1	1½	1¼
		Wrapped in fibreboard	D1	1½	1¼
		In boxes or crates	D1	1½	1
184	1–2	Chifforobes (chiffoniers and wardrobes combined), set up —			
		Wrapped in burlap	1½	1½	D1
		In boxes or crates	1½	[1] 1½	1½
185	13	Wooden desks, set up —			
		Wrapped in burlap or fibreboard	1½	1½	1¼
		In boxes or crates	1½	1	1
		Wooden desks, knocked down —			
		Wrapped in burlap or fibreboard	1¼	1¼	1
		In boxes or crates	1¼	1	2

[1] Conceded first class at hearing

Several other examples of lack of uniformity, most of which could probably be dealt with without great difficulty, are shown below. The ratings are for less than carloads

Page	Item	Article	Ratings		
			Official	Southern	Western
150	2	Electric exhaust fans	2	1	D1
322	10	Dressed poultry:			
		In barrels with cloth tops	[1] 1½	1	1
		In barrels or boxes	1¼	2	1
388	27	Canned vegetables, etc.:			
		In glass or earthenware, packed —			
		In crates	1	2	3
		In barrels or boxes	2	2	4
		In metal cans —			
		In crates	3	2	3
		In barrels or boxes	3	3	4

[1] Conceded 1¼ at hearing

We show below a few examples of lack of uniformity that probably had their origin in peculiar conditions of the distant past.

Page	Item	Article	Ratings		
			Official	Southern	Western
£115	[1] 9	Banana carriers, old, any quantity......	4 t 1	D1	4
£165	24	Rice flour:			
		Less than carloads..................	4	6	3
		Carloads..........................	6	C	5
£166	12	Fodder, in machine-pressed bales:			
		Less than carloads..................	1	5	3
		Carloads..........................	5	D	C

[1] In supplement

The instances cited in these tables are typical of thousands of others that probably would not exist but for the fact that the respective classification committees have for years followed precedents and have acted according to their different opinions or upon different information. Recently they have been working more in unison, and when additional provisions are established to cover new articles of commerce the ratings are generally made uniform, except when to do so would violate some unusually important and well-established policy in one or more of the territories.

The continued use of the intermediate or split classes of R–25 and R–26 in the official classification constitutes one of the principal difficulties in reaching uniform ratings on the higher classes of freight. R–25 is 15 per cent less than second class, subject to third class as a minimum. R–26 is 20 per cent less than third class, subject to fourth class as a minimum. These classes were formerly used to a rather limited extent, but additional articles have been assigned to them from time to time, until in the consolidated classification they are numbered by hundreds.[1]

[1] R–25 rating is proposed on 387 articles in less than carloads. The ratings proposed on these articles in southern territory are second class or higher in about 44 per cent of the cases and third class or lower in the balance of the cases.

The ratings proposed on the same articles in western territory are second class or higher in about 54 per cent of the cases and third class or lower in the balance of the cases — (*Continued on page 354.*)

While it is possible to remove many of the present inconsistencies without changes in rate scales, it should also be borne in mind that an absolutely uniform classification could be prepared and proposed only in connection with a universal system of rate scales having a uniform number of classes. In our view a desirable arrangement would be to have in each scale at least ten classes related somewhat as shown below; practically all less-than-carload traffic to be confined to the first four classes, and a redistribution made of the articles in the carload classes:

Classes	1	2	3	4	5	6	7	8	9	10
Percentages	100	85	70	60	45	35	30	25	22½	20

Many articles that now move under commodity rates and under exceptions to the classifications could be assigned ratings in such a scale that would result in the application of rates not substantially higher or lower than now apply. This would be particularly true of the official and southern territories. The percentages in the above scale do not differ greatly from those observed in a large portion of the country. . . .

As we have pointed out, most of the increases proposed have no necessary connection with the work of consolidating the rules and descriptions. None of them, except such as were necessarily or reasonably incident thereto, were contemplated by us when we suggested a unification of the rules and descriptions, and, as we understand it, were not in the mind of the director of traffic when he appointed the special committee. When the case was assigned for hearing we did not realize that there was such a vast number of changes that had no necessary connection with the work required of the special committee, and, as we understand it, the executive authorities of the Railroad Administration themselves were not fully cognizant of the magnitude of the proposal which had been put forward.

R-26 rating is proposed on 401 items in less than carloads. The ratings proposed on these items in southern territory are third class or higher in about 43 per cent of the cases and fourth class or lower in the balance of the cases.

The ratings proposed on the same items in western territory are third class or higher in about 66 per cent of the cases and fourth class in the balance of the cases.

We have no figures as to the articles that are rated R-25 and R-26 in carloads.

The Director General did not intend that the consolidated classification should be a revenue measure, and the chairmen of the classification committees disclaim any purpose on their part to make it such. While in fact it would yield the carriers some additional revenue, the record is convincing that, in the main, the proposed increases reflect conscientious efforts to bring about a proper relationship of ratings and to fairly distribute transportation expenses over the various articles of traffic.

A study of the changes in ratings proposed by the classification chairmen disclosed inconsistencies in each territory which apparently we could not endorse. We therefore made a comprehensive analysis of the existing and proposed ratings to ascertain whether or not we could properly recommend, with modifications, the somewhat general revision of ratings proposed, or an amplification of those proposals. We find that we can not properly recommend either, for the reason that many and important changes as to which interested shippers have had no notice or opportunity to be heard would be included.

Our analysis of existing and proposed ratings was made with a view of also ascertaining what changes in existing ratings other than those proposed would, in the judgment of our classification and general traffic experts, formed without fully hearing shippers or carriers that would be affected thereby, be proper to propose in any general revision of ratings having for its principal purpose attainment of a higher degree of uniformity. The results of this analysis apear in Appendix No. 6, and constitute practically a uniform classification so far as the first four classes are concerned. The results of this laborious work are thus preserved. They will be available and valuable in the future as efforts in the direction of uniformity progress. They must be understood to be the tentative views of our expert assistants who heard the case and in no sense as findings or conclusive suggestions by us. However, the suggestions in this appendix, so far as they affect descriptions, packing specifications, and minimum and estimated weights are adopted as recommendations by us without prejudice.

We cannot recommend the increased ratings as proposed, nor can we recommend, with modifications, those proposed unaccompanied by many others that have not been proposed and as to which no opportunity for hearing affected parties has been afforded. We shall not recommend any changed ratings except as the establishment of new items may indirectly effect changes, and such changes, as may be a necessary part of the establishment of uniform descriptions of articles, uniform minimum weights, or uniform packing requirements. Our recommendations as to such changes will not prejudice any complaint that may be filed as to individual changes that are believed by complainant to result in unreasonable rates or in undue prejudice. . . .

SOUTH BEND CHAMBER OF COMMERCE *v.* DIRECTOR GENERAL

57 I. C. C. 215 (1920)

MEYER, *Commissioner:*

This case was made the subject of a proposed report which was served upon the parties. Exceptions were filed by the complainants and the Michigan City intervener and oral argument had.

The initial complainant herein is a corporation organized to further the commercial, industrial, and municipal interests of South Bend, Ind. Its members and the other complainants herein are corporations, partnerships, and individuals having their principal places of business for the manufacture and sale of various commodities at South Bend, Mishawaka, Elkhart, Goshen, and Napanee, Ind. The complaint of these cities is that for the transportation of class and commodity traffic between those cities and points in trunk line territory and New England territory shippers are subjected to the payment of rates which are unjust and unreasonable, absolutely and relatively, in violation of the act to regulate commerce and the federal control act; and which are unjustly discriminatory and unduly prejudicial and in violation of the long-and-short-haul provision of the fourth section of the act to regulate commerce.

The class rates paid by the complainants between South Bend and the associated cities and New York, N. Y., are, in cents per 100 pounds, for the six classes, as follows:

Classes	1	2	3	4	5	6
Rates	108	95	72	50.5	43	36

Between trunk line territory and central territory, rates are adjusted in relation to the scale of rates applicable between Chicago and New York, which are regarded as base rates and Chicago as a 100 per cent point. Points in central territory are placed in groups which take percentages of the base rates, theoretically in the proportions that the short-line distances between such points and New York bear to the short-line distance between Chicago and New York. The percentages on eastbound traffic are not always the same as on westbound traffic. Rates between points in central territory and points in trunk line territory, other than New York, are made differentially higher or lower than rates to or from that point.

Under this adjustment the complaining cities are grouped with other points in northern Indiana taking 96 per cent of the base rates. Complainants contend that their manufacturers and jobbers compete with manufacturers and jobbers of similar character, particularly those located in the central and northern portions of the states of Ohio and Indiana and that portion of the southern peninsula of Michigan lying immediately north of the complaining cities; that the revenue per mile of haul under rates between the competitive territory specified and New York is lower than that under rates paid by the complaining cities; that their favorable location on the great channels of through transportation between Chicago and New York entitle them to rates made 92 per cent of the base rates, which would reduce their rates to and from New York in cents per 100 pounds on the respective classes in the following amounts:

Classes	1	2	3	4	5	6
Amounts	4.5	4	3	2	1.5	1.5

The Chamber of Commerce of Michigan City, Ind., composed of merchants and manufacturers of that city, filed a similar complaint, which was permitted to be filed as of the nature of an intervention. Michigan City is grouped with Chicago and other points in the 100 per cent group. It, too, is seeking a reduction of its percentage to 92 per cent, which would result in reductions in the rates in the following amounts:

Classes	1	2	3	4	5	6
Amounts	9	8	6	4	3.5	3.5

In the *Michigan Percentage Cases,* 47 I. C. C., 409, we held that rates to certain points in Michigan were unduly prejudiced to such cities, and that the prejudice could be removed only by reducing the percentages of the Michigan groups. Grand Rapids, Kalamazoo, Marshall, Battle Creek, and other points in Michigan in the 96 per cent group were reduced to 92 per cent. One effect of our order in that case was the division of the former 96 per cent group at the Indiana-Michigan state line. After the filing of the complaint in this case, in a petition to reopen the *Michigan Percentage Cases, supra,* the Director General averred, among other things, that the discrimination alleged by the complainants herein, if any existed, was due solely to the fact that the defendants in that case had obeyed our order and that the only proper method of removing such discrimination was to change the percentage bases in effect in Michigan, and especially in the 92 per cent group. The petition was denied. Some of the complainants in that case, interested in the preservation of the adjustments there obtained, intervened in the present case.

South Bend, Mishawaka, Elkhart, and Goshen are in the central portion of northern Indiana near the Indiana-Michigan state line. South Bend is less than 7 miles south, and Niles, Mich., in the 92 per cent group, is 5 miles north of that line. South Bend is 96 miles east of Chicago. By railroad Mishawaka is 4 miles east of South Bend, but its suburbs adjoin those of South Bend and the two cities are practically one industrial community. Elkhart is 11 miles and Goshen 31 miles east of Mishawaka. The complaining cities are located between Chicago and Toledo, Ohio, on the main line of the New York Central Railroad. South Bend and Mishawaka are also on the line of the Grand Trunk Western Railway between Chicago and Kalamazoo, Mich. Goshen and Elkhart are served by the Michigan division of the Cleveland, Cincinnati, Chicago & St. Louis Railroad operating from Benton Harbor, Mich., to Louisville, Ky. A branch of the Michigan Central connects South Bend with the main line of that company. In addition other north-and-south lines such as those of the Lake Erie & Western, New Jersey, Indiana & Illinois railways and the Pennsylvania Company reach South Bend, and in connection with eastern lines of the Baltimore & Ohio Railroad, Wabash Railroad, and the Pennsylvania Company form other routes. Napanee is on the main line of the Baltimore & Ohio Railroad between Chicago and Baltimore, Md. It is 9 miles west of Milford Junction, Ind., which is 11 miles south of Goshen.

Michigan City is located on the shore of Lake Michigan, 56 miles east of Chicago and about 10 miles southwest of New Buffalo, Mich., a point in the 92 per cent group. It is on the main lines of the Michigan Central and Pere Marquette railroads. It is also served by the north-and-south lines of the Lake Erie & Western and the Chicago, Indianapolis & Louisville railroads and by traction lines.

Under the formula used in making these percentage-group rates, the desired percentage is obtained by deducting a fixed terminal charge of 6 cents per 100 pounds from an assumed rate from Chicago to New York of 25 cents per 100 pounds; the remainder is divided by the short-line distance from Chicago to New York; the result is multiplied by the short-line distance of the point from which the percentage is sought from New York, the terminal allowance is again added and the percentage which the resulting rate bears to the 25-cent rate is the percentage to be used. Prior to *The Five Per Cent Case,* 32 I. C. C., 325, the sixth-class rate from Chicago to New York was 25 cents per 100 pounds. Due to the increases allowed in that case, in *The Fifteen Per Cent Case,* 45 I. C. C., 303, and General Order No. 28 of the Director General of Railroads, the present sixth-class rate from Chicago to New York is 37.5 cents per 100 pounds, or 50 per cent higher than the 25-cent rate. Consequently in their exhibits complainants have deducted 9 cents as a terminal allowance from the sixth-class rates, and, following the formula described, compared the resulting revenue per mile of haul at the complaining cities with that at points in Ohio and Michigan, and showed that the revenue under rates to the complaining cities is higher than that from rates to points in Ohio and many of the Michigan points. Defendants contend that this manner of obtaining rates does not correctly disclose the relative situation for the reason that the revenue per ton per mile decreases as the distance increases only because the terminal allowance, a constant factor, is necessarily proportionately diminished as the distance increases. They therefore compare the revenue per ton per mile under the fifth-class rates, and the revenue per 100 pounds per mile under the sixth-class rates, showing that with few exceptions the revenue per ton per mile and per 100 pounds per mile from rates to the complaining cities is lower than from rates to points in Ohio.

The fifth-class rates were used for the reason that over 50 per cent of the carload ratings in the official classification are of that class, whereas but 11 per cent are of sixth class.

In many instances the western edges of the rate groups are north-and-south lines of railroad, and many important points formerly recognized as basing points, such as Cleveland and Toledo, are in the western part of the groups. In a grouping system, it necessarily follows that rates at such points are lower, distance considered, and the revenue per ton per mile less than at other points in the group.

Michigan City is on the extreme eastern edge of the 100 per cent group. To grant it the relief prayed, a 92 per cent basis, would make the revenue per ton per mile under rates between New York and Michigan City lower than that under rates between New York and Chicago. Rates between New York and Michigan City are the same as the rates between New York and Chicago. Rates between Michigan City and the west are higher than those between Chicago and the west. Gary, East Gary, and Porter, Ind., are in the Chicago switching limits, Michigan City is not. Each case must be considered on its merits and whether the adjustment between Michigan City and the west is unreasonable or prejudicial is not in issue here.

West of the line of the New York Central running north from White Pigeon to Grand Rapids, lie 10 cities which have rates that yield lower revenue per ton per mile from the fifth-class rates from and to New York than do the rates to and from South Bend and associated cities and Michigan City. It is practically admitted by the defendants that these points have a basis of rates which is lower than that to which their location entitles them. That the rate disparity between Michigan City in the 100 per cent group, and New Buffalo in the 92 per cent group, is indefensible is admitted.

Because of deflation in the percentages and consequent lower rates to and from points in Michigan beyond South Bend, Elkhart, and Goshen, departures from the provisions of the fourth section exist. The Cleveland, Cincinnati, Chicago & St. Louis Railroad runs from Benton Harbor, through Niles, Elkhart, and Goshen, and south through Claypool, Bolivar, and New Paris, Ind., its junctions with the New York, Chicago & St. Louis, Erie, and Wabash railroads. These junctions, also Marion, Milford Junction, and Plymouth, Ind., in connection with eastern carriers, are used in making through rates via which Niles and Benton Harbor are accorded through rates on the basis of 92 per cent of the base rates.

The Grand Rapids branch of the New York Central Railroad from Elkhart to Grand Rapids runs through White Pigeon, Three Rivers, Kalamazoo, and Allegan. To and from the territory along this branch, in the 92 per cent group, through traffic is handled via Goshen and Elkhart, because it is more economical to do so than to move it via the shorter route of the same line via Grand Rapids, Lenawee Junction, and Toledo. After the *Michigan Percentage Cases, supra,* the interested carriers represented to us that departures from the long-and-short-haul provision of the fourth section of the act would be created and departures increased at intermediate points in Ohio and Indiana in complying with the decision. We accordingly authorized temporary relief from the application of the fourth section in this respect.

Defendants urge that if the basis sought by complainants is granted, other cities and towns in central territory, the percentages of which are not exactly upon the formula basis, would seek similar relief, and that a strict application of the percentage formula through the territory would involve serious reductions of revenue. They also call attention to the fact that many of the railroads serving the complaining cities are among those which failed in 1918 to earn their standard returns. While these are proper elements for consideration in determining the reasonableness of rates, they constitute no bar to the granting of relief if rates are shown to be relatively unreasonable or unduly prejudicial.

Defendants also urge that the preponderance of tonnage is eastbound rather than westbound; that overhead tonnage transported from the western edge of central territory, through Illinois, Indiana, and Ohio, increases very materially in the latter state; that the Mahoning and Shenango Valleys in Ohio and Pennsylvania, the great iron and steel producing section of the country, produce enormous volumes of tonnage both for eastbound and westbound movements far in excess of all tonnage produced in Indiana, and that basing points in Ohio may logically be accorded rates which are related more closely to those which an exact application of the percentage formula would afford them than could be claimed by the cities of Indiana with their comparatively lighter tonnage.

Upon consideration of the whole record, we are of the opinion and find that the rates between Michigan City, South Bend, Mishawaka, Elkhart, Goshen, and Napanee, on the one hand, and points in eastern trunk line and New England territories, on the other, are relatively unreasonable and unduly prejudicial to such cities and unduly preferential of cities in central and northern Ohio, and in Michigan, west of the line of the New York Central Railroad from Elkhart to Grand Rapids and south of the line of the Grand Trunk Western from Grand Rapids to Grand Haven.

The undue prejudice with respect to Ohio points should be removed by reducing the percentage of South Bend and associated cities to 94 per cent, and of Michigan City to 96 per cent, and with respect to the southwestern Michigan points can be removed by increasing the percentage of Niles, Buchanan, Hartford, Holland, and points east thereof to the line above described to 94 per cent, and points west thereof to 96 per cent.

The short-line routes to Kalamazoo and Grand Rapids and points on and east of the line above described do not pass through the complaining cities, and with rates to both groups properly adjusted, it is not apparent that the complaining cities would be injured by allowing traffic destined to points properly entitled to lower rates to move over routes through the higher-rated group, and as to these points we shall allow the temporary relief granted in Fourth Section Order No. 7149 to stand.

The routes and distances to points west and south of the lines above described from Elkhart to Grand Haven are not such as to justify lower rates than at the complaining cities, and that portion of the fourth section order permitting the maintenance of lower rates to such points than to intermediate points will be revoked.

Appropriate orders will be entered.

Hall, *Commissioner,* dissents.

NORTH IOWA TRAFFIC ASSOCIATION
v.
DIRECTOR GENERAL

58 I. C. C. 491 (1920)

DIVISION 2, COMMISSIONERS CLARK, MEYER, AND WOOLLEY

CLARK, *Chairman:*

A report in this case was proposed by the examiner. Exceptions thereto were filed by complainant.

This proceeding is in substance a continuation of *The Mississippi River Case,* 28 I. C. C., 47, 29 I. C. C., 530, as supplemented by *R. R. Comm'rs of Iowa* v. *A. A. R. R. Co.,* 46 I. C. C., 20, and of *Interior Iowa Cases,* 46 I. C. C., 39. In those cases, supplemented by a condition in supplemental order of December 29, 1914, in *The Five Per Cent Case,* 31 I. C. C., 351, 32 I. C. C., 325, we prescribed, with certain modifications, between points in official classification territory east of the Indiana-Illinois state line, hereinafter termed eastern points, and upper Mississippi River crossings, class rates not in excess of those contemporaneously maintained between eastern points and lower Mississippi River crossings; also proportional distance class rates between Mississippi River crossings and interior Iowa points applicable on traffic to and from eastern points. In the cases referred to Dubuque, Iowa, was considered the northernmost river crossing. The distance proportionals to points in northern Iowa therefore are generally based on the distance beyond Dubuque and through class rates between the east and northern Iowa are made by adding to the rates between the east and the Mississippi River the Iowa distance proportionals beyond.

Complainant is an association composed of the commercial organizations of 27 towns located in the two northern tiers of counties in the state of Iowa. Among these towns are North McGregor, on the west bank of the Mississippi River opposite Prairie du Chien, Wis., 54 miles north of Dubuque, and Mason City, Iowa, 117 miles west of North McGregor via the Chicago, Milwaukee & St. Paul Railway, hereinafter called the Milwaukee. It is alleged that the class rates between eastern points and points in northern Iowa are unreasonable and unduly preferential of cities in Iowa on the Mississippi River and in the central and southern portions of the state. Complainant asks primarily the establishment of North McGregor as a Mississippi River crossing and basing point for the contruction of through class rates. It asks that proportional class rates in northern Iowa be based on the distances from North McGregor where such distances are less than those from Dubuque. Originally the same rates were requested between eastern points and North McGregor as between eastern points and Mississippi River crossings, Dubuque and south, the rates between New York, N. Y., for instance, and the Mississippi River being 117 per cent of the New York-Chicago rates. However, complainant would be satisfied if rates were established between North McGregor and eastern points based on the relation of the Chicago and North McGregor distances. For the purpose of comparison New York may be taken as a representative point in the east and Mason City as a representative point in northern Iowa. As the propriety of the relationship between the various classes is not in issue, it will be sufficient to show the first-class rates. The rates apply in both directions, and for convenience in statement only those applying westbound will be referred to. Rates are stated in amounts per 100 pounds.

The evidence relates almost entirely to all-rail rates. We have previously recognized 912 miles as the short-line distance via all-rail routes from New York to Chicago. We have thought it proper in the discussion of this case to adopt the distance via the Milwaukee from Chicago to North McGregor used by complainant, which is 239 miles by way of Madison, Wis., aggregating 1,151 miles from New York, or 126 per cent of the distance to Chicago. The Milwaukee is the only road which crosses the Mississippi River at North McGregor, and it serves most of the northern Iowa points.

The following statement shows the rates and distances from New York to Chicago, North McGregor, Mason City, and a few of the interior Iowa cities located in the central and southern portions of the state:

STATEMENT OF RATES AND DISTANCES FROM NEW YORK TO CHICAGO AND VARIOUS POINTS IN IOWA.

Destination	Rate	Distance in miles	Ton-mile revenue, in cents
Chicago	$1.125	912	2.47
North McGregor	[1] 1.515	1,151	2.62
Do	[2] 1.42	1,151	2.47
Mason City	[1] 1.765	1,268	2.78
Do	[2] 1.72	1,268	2.71
Cedar Rapids	1.515	1,127	2.69
Marshalltown	1.715	1,197	2.87
Des Moines	1.715	1,253	2.74
Fort Dodge	1.815	1,274	2.85
Waterloo	1.565	1,173	2.67
Ottumwa	1.515	1,170	2.59

[1] Present rate. [2] Rate sought

The distances to cities in central and southern Iowa are based on the short-line routes to the Mississippi River shown at page 49 of the first report in *The Mississippi River Case, supra.* The present rates to North McGregor and Mason City are $1.315 to Dubuque, which takes Mississippi River rates, plus the Iowa proportionals of 20 and 45 cents for distances of 54 miles and 171 miles, respectively, beyond Dubuque. The rate sought to North McGregor is 126 per cent of the New York-Chicago rate, and the rate sought to Mason City is 30 cents higher, which is the Iowa proportional for 117 miles, the distance beyond North McGregor.

The Milwaukee crosses the Mississippi at Davenport, Sabula, and North McGregor, Iowa; La Crosse and Wabasha, Wis.; and St. Paul, Minn. There are steel bridges at all of these points except Wabasha and North McGregor, where pontoon bridges are used. Through traffic for southeastern Iowa is handled over the Davenport bridge. Substantially all through traffic for the remainder of Iowa, including the northern portion of the state, is handled over the bridge at Sabula, 44 miles south of Dubuque. Through traffic for St. Paul, Minn., and points beyond moves over the La Crosse bridge. Generally speaking, only traffic local to the Prairie du Chien and the Iowa and Dakota divisions of the Milwaukee is handled across the river at North McGregor. Those divisions extend to the east and west of North McGregor. There is no through train service from Chicago over the Prairie du Chien division and across the North McGregor bridge. The movement via that route would require set-outs at three transfer points. It is testified for defendants that the bridge at North McGregor and the lines in Wisconsin east thereof are no more a factor in the handling of through traffic from eastern points to northern Iowa than if they had never been constructed.

The pontoon bridge at North McGregor is single track and is in two sections — one over the east channel, 209 feet long, and one over the west channel, 276 feet long. The tracks connecting these pontoons with each other and with the banks of the river run over embankments and bridges, most of which are of wooden-piling construction, with a few steel spans. A locomotive of 90 tons is the largest that can be used over the bridge. Smaller locomotives are generally used, on account of lack of traffic. The Prairie du Chien division is a single-track line of relatively light construction. The line of the Milwaukee from Chicago to Sabula, however, is part of the main line to the Mississippi River and carries a very large volume of tonnage. It has double track, with 100-pound rails, the entire distance. The density of traffic is also heavy on the line of the Milwaukee from Sabula to North McGregor.

The pontoon bridge at Wabasha serves the Chippewa Falls branch of the Milwaukee in Wisconsin. The only other pontoon bridge operated by that road [is] across the Missouri at Chamberlain, S. Dak., and serves that portion of the line ending at Rapid City, S. Dak. Each of these pontoon bridges is located at a point where the cost of constructing a permanent steel bridge would be great and where the traffic is not handled in such volume or with such regularity as to justify the establishment of permanent structures.

A pontoon bridge has been maintained at North McGregor since 1874 and has been replaced at intervals of approximately 15 years. Occasionally this bridge is closed to traffic for short periods, due to ice in the river or adverse weather conditions.

The record shows that 406 loaded cars were moved westbound over the McGregor bridge in March, 1918; 555 in September, 1918; and 545 in May, 1919. Of these cars 52 originated east of the Indiana-Illinois state line; the remainder moved almost exclusively from Wisconsin points. For the calendar year 1918 the Milwaukee handled 1,194,961 long tons over the North McGregor bridge; 11,569,099 over the Sabula bridge, and 2,765,476 over the Davenport bridge; the Chicago Great Western handled 2,843,502 tons; and the Illinois Central 2,508,515 tons over the bridge at Dubuque.

The rates between eastern points on the one hand and Mississippi River and interior Iowa points on the other have been the subject of several complaints, and the present rates are the result of a gradual process of readjustment. The Mississippi River rates are the result of competition for traffic between the east and the Missouri River. In previous cases we have given in detail the history of these rates. Rates to the Missouri River from the east were originally on basis of the combination of single-line rates to St. Louis and local rates beyond. Several lines from the east terminated at Chicago and certain western lines operated between Chicago and the Missouri River by way of the upper crossings. The combination rates by way of these routes were higher than the combinations through St. Louis, Mo. To induce the movement of traffic via the upper crossings, proportional rates lower than the local rates were established to and from those crossings. In *The Mississippi River Case, supra,* we originally prescribed class rates between the upper crossings and the east slightly in excess of the rates to and from the lower crossings. In *The Five Per Cent Case, supra,* we permitted increases in rates to and from the Mississippi River crossings and restricted the increases to the upper crossings to amounts which would equalize them with the lower crossings. This parity of rates has since been maintained. The Illinois Central Railroad is the most northerly line which has its own rails between Chicago and the Missouri River, and it fixes the northern boundary of the so-called prorating territory. The Illinois Central crosses the Mississippi at Dubuque, and Dubuque has been recognized as the northern-most river crossing.

With respect to Mississippi River crossings, Dubuque and south, we said, in *Interior Iowa Cities Case,* 28 I. C. C., 64:

" The proportional rates to the Mississippi River are not made, and never have been made, with special reference to the traffic of interior Iowa points. On the contrary, they are made largely to meet the conditions of through traffic to the Missouri River and to the territory beyond."

In *The Wisconsin Rate Cases,* 44 I. C. C., 602, we said with respect to La Crosse, which is 66 miles north of North McGregor: "It is with relation to the rates to the twin cities and not to Dubuque that the La Crosse rates are constructed." In that case we prescribed class rates from the east to La Crosse based on 145 per cent of the New York-Chicago rate, the distance from New York to La Crosse being 1,175 miles, or 129 per cent of the New York-Chicago distance. The present first-class rate from New York to La Crosse is $1.625.

To the south of North McGregor, beginning with Dubuque, are the Mississippi River crossings to which rates from the east are based on the rates to St. Louis. To the north, beginning with La Crosse, is another group of Mississippi River points to which rates have been influenced by entirely different circumstances and conditions, although a certain relationship between the two is recognized by the finding in *The Wisconsin Rate Cases, supra.*

Complainant contends that the rates to North McGregor should be made with relation to the rates to Mississippi River crossings. It asserts that from approximately the northern one-third of central freight association territory and the northern two-thirds of eastern trunk line territory the distances to North McGregor are less than the average distances to St. Louis, Mo., and other lower Mississippi River crossings. Class rates from North McGregor and from the Mississippi River crossings are maintained upon a parity to Pacific coast points and points in the far west. To many points in New Mexico, Texas, Oklahoma, Kansas, and Nebraska the class rates from North McGregor are the same as from certain Mississippi River crossings, and higher than the rates from others in amounts ranging from 6 cents to 25 cents, first class. The situation is substantially the same with respect to class rates to North McGregor and Mississippi River crossings from the points referred to. In *Iowa State Board Railroad Commissioners* v. *A. E. R. R. Co.,* 28 I. C. C., 563, we approved a grouping under which rates from Utah and Colorado common points to North McGregor were made the same as to the Mississippi River crossings. The combination class rates from several eastern cities to North McGregor and the class rates from North McGregor to the principal cities in Kansas, Nebraska, and a number of other western states are higher in practically every instance than similar combinations of class rates to and beyond Chicago, St. Louis, and Dubuque.

While certain traffic is handled across the river at North McGregor, it is asserted for defendants that a consideration of the nature of the traffic, the character of the crossing, and the operating conditions upon the lines east and west of that point precludes from a physical standpoint the establishment of North McGregor as a river crossing for rate-making purposes. Competitive conditions which brought about the extension of the lower basis of rates to Dubuque do not exist at North McGregor. The rate assailed from New York to North McGregor is 135 per cent of the Chicago rate, whereas the distance to North McGregor is 126 per cent of the distance to Chicago, but in *The Wisconsin Rate Cases, supra,* and *Chamber of Commerce of Freeport, Ill.,* v. *Ry. Co.,* 33 I. C. C., 673, we prescribed the following class rates which were higher than rates based on the relative distances from Chicago:

From New York to —	Per cent of New York-Chicago rate	Distance miles	Per cent of New York-Chicago distance
La Crosse, Wis	145	1,175	129
Madison, Wis	125	1,042	114
Beloit, Wis	118	1,003	110
Freeport, Ill	114	1,026	112.5
Rockford, Ill	112	999	109.5

A reduction in the rates to North McGregor would disrupt the rate adjustment to southern Wisconsin and northern Illinois, especially to Madison, which is directly intermediate to North McGregor by way of the Milwaukee, and which is 100 miles nearer Chicago than is North McGregor.

Mason City is served by five railroads — the Milwaukee, Chicago & North Western, Chicago Great Western, Chicago, Rock Island & Pacific, and the Minneapolis & St. Louis. It is the largest and commercially the most important of the northern Iowa cities. It produces a large volume of traffic, which is explained by complainants to be due to the fact that its four large industries — namely, brick and tile, cement, meat packing, and beet sugar — use raw materials which are produced in the territory immediately surrounding Mason City, and that the carriers provide commodity rates for the outbound movement of the finished products.

Manufacturers and shippers at Mason City and various other northern Iowa towns, who are in active competition with similar enterprises located at Iowa cities in the central and southern parts of the state and on the Mississippi River, assert that the advantage in class rates from the east enjoyed by competing towns restricts the growth of industries in the northern part of the state. The Iowa proportional rates applying from the Mississippi River to northern Iowa points are compared with the proportionals from the river to cities in central and southern Iowa located substantially similar distances west of the Mississippi River. The differences thus shown, which are always in favor of the central and southern cities, grow out of the differences in distances of the respective points from an established Mississippi River crossing. For example, to Garner, Iowa, 137 miles west of North McGregor, the Iowa first-class proportional is 50 cents, based on the distance from Dubuque of 191 miles, while to Des Moines, Iowa, the proportional is 40 cents, based on the distance of 158 miles from the nearest crossing. Des Moines is almost due south of Garner. Notwithstanding the fact that these proportional rates are determined by applying the same distance scale from Mississippi River crossings, ton-mile earnings to northern Iowa points are uniformly higher than those to points in the central and southern part of the state, approximately the same distances from the Mississippi River. This is due to the comparison of the actual distances of the central and southern Iowa points from the nearest river crossings, which are also the rate-making distances, with the distances of the northern Iowa points from North McGregor, which are shorter than the rate-making distances. The combined first-class rates from various eastern cities to Mason City and Dubuque, plus the first-class rates from those points to Iowa destinations for approximately equal distances indicate an adjustment in favor of Dubuque.

It is asserted for defendants that the present basis of class rates prescribed by us from the east to interior Iowa, as applied by the carriers to the stations in northern Iowa, results in reasonably low rates. To Mason City the proportional rates from the Mississippi River are based on the distances from Dubuque of 171 miles by way of the Milwaukee. From the Milwaukee's crossing at Sabula, over which traffic from the east moves, to Mason City the distance is 215 miles, or 44 miles in excess of the rate-making distance. The distances from the crossings used by the other lines serving Mason City range from 40 miles to 71 miles in excess of the rate-making distance. A finding for the complainant in this case would not change the routing of through traffic, and if the Iowa proportionals to Mason City were based on 117 miles, the distance from North McGregor, the distances of the five roads serving that point from the points at which their traffic from the east crosses the Mississippi River would be from 94 miles to 125 miles in excess of the rate-making distance. The complaint, as modified, seeks rates to North McGregor based on 126 per cent of the New York-Chicago rates, to which are to be added the Iowa proportionals, based on the distances of the interior points from North McGregor. It is contended for defendants that the points in northern Iowa are located off the main routes of traffic; that the lines serving these points from the east could properly be termed branch lines; and that the northern Iowa stations should be on a somewhat higher basis than stations in the central and southern parts of the state. In *Corn Belt Meat Producers' Asso.* v. *C., B. & Q. R. R. Co.*, 17 I. C. C., 533, we approved rates on live stock from stations in northern Iowa to Chicago upon a relatively higher basis than from the central portion of the state. In that case we stated that the northern section of Iowa is not on what might be considered the main line of traffic. If the basis originally sought by complainant were established and the rates to stations on the Chicago & North Western, just across the line in Minnesota, remained the same, the following spread in rates would result: The first-class rate from New York to Scarville, Iowa, would be $1.525 and to Kiester, Minn., $1.95; to Sibley, Iowa, $1.74; and to Bigelow, Minn., $2.125. Under complainant's modified proposal the first-class rate from New York to North McGregor, and therefore to the Iowa points shown, would be 10.5 cents higher. The proportional rates from the Mississippi River to Mason City are generally lower than those in effect on March 30, 1914. At that time the average of the first-class proportionals from the Mississippi River to Mason City was 83 per cent of the first-class proportional from the Mississippi River to the Missouri River, but the present Mason City proportional is only 65 per cent of the Missouri

River proportional. The proportional of 45 cents from the river to Mason City is compared with proportional rates from St. Louis to points in Missouri ranging from 48½ cents to 66½ cents for distances of 115 to 188 miles. The through class rates from Pittsburgh, Pa., Cincinnati, Ohio, and New York to points in Minnesota and Missouri for distances substantially equal to those to Mason City are uniformly higher than the present rates to Mason City. Several exhibits were presented to show the extent of the territory which would be affected and the amount of the reductions in rates if the prayer of the complaint were granted, which it will not be necessary to discuss other than to say that they are based on the complaint as originally filed and not as modified with respect to the rates to North McGregor.

Upon consideration of all the facts of record, we find that the rates assailed are not shown to be unreasonable or unduly prejudicial. The complaint will be dismissed.

BURNHAM, HANNA, MUNGER DRY GOODS CO.

v.

CHICAGO, ROCK ISLAND & PACIFIC CO.

14 I. C. C. 299 (1908)

CLARK, *Commissioner:*

Complainants are individuals, partnerships, and corporations engaged in jobbing trade at Kansas City and St. Joseph, Mo., and Omaha, Nebr., to which points they ship via the lines of the defendants large quantities of goods from the Atlantic seaboard, largely under class rates, and from which points they distribute such goods throughout a large teritory to the southwest, west and northwest and also to a comparatively small and limited territory east of the Missouri River.

In sale and distribution of their goods, complainants come in competition with jobbers located at Minneapolis and St. Paul, hereinafter referred to as the Twin Cities, and the complaint alleges unjust and unreasonable discrimination in favor of the Twin Cities and undue prejudice against Kansas City, St. Joseph, and Omaha, hereinafter referred to as the Missouri River Cities, due to and measured by the difference in the class rates from the Atlantic seaboard to the Twin Cities, as compared with like rates from same points to the Missouri River Cities.

In testimony, briefs, and argument complainants make a strong attack upon the long-established system of rate making under which rates to points west of the Mississippi River are made upon the basis of the rates to the Mississppi River crossings.

As railroads were constructed into the undeveloped west and, for a time at least, had their western termini at the east bank of the Mississippi River, it seems natural that when the river was crossed, and rates were established to points beyond, they should be constructed by adding certain sums to the rates already established to the river, and as additional lines were built and additional railroad crossings over the Mississippi River were constructed, competition between carriers and localities naturally established common rates to the Mississippi River crossings, especially when applied to traffic going beyond.

As the west was further developed, this same condition and like results followed at the several crossings of the Missouri River, so that to-day the rates from the Mississippi River crossings to the Missouri River crossings, Kansas City to Omaha, inclusive, are the same, and from points east, to the Missouri River Cities, are the same via any of the Mississippi River crossings, East St. Louis to East Dubuque, inclusive.

Complaint alleges unreasonableness of the class rates from the Atlantic seaboard, and the defendants named in the complaint were the Chicago, Rock Island & Pacific Railway Company, the Chicago, Burlington & Quincy Railway Company, the Chicago, Milwaukee & St. Paul Railway Company, the Chicago & Northwestern Railway Company, and the Chicago Great Western Railway Company. All of these are carriers whose lines do not extend east of Chicago, and all of them have lines from Chicago through the several Mississippi River crossings, to the Missouri River Cities. The defendants whose lines are east of Chicago were made defendants upon application of the Chicago & Northwestern Railway Company. It will, however, be seen that the complaint, the testimony, and the argument are all against the rates charged west of Chicago and the Mississippi River crossings.

The Sioux City Commercial Club intervened and supported the complainants' request, introducing and emphasizing, however, the view that whatever might be done for Omaha should likewise be done for Sioux City, and arguing that as Sioux City was also a Missouri River crossing it should be placed upon a parity with Omaha. The St. Paul Jobbers and Manufacturers' Association of St. Paul, and the Commercial Club of Minneapolis intervened and in substance joined with and supported the defendants. The Chicago Association of Commerce and the Merchants' Traffic Bureau and the Business Men's League of St. Louis appeared at the hearings on behalf of the commercial interests of their respective cities, offered evidence and were heard on brief and in oral argument in defense of the system of rate construction based upon the Mississippi River, and in opposition to a rate adjustment that would give the Missouri River Cities an advantage at the expense of Chicago and St. Louis.

Complainants allege that the class rates from the Atlantic seaboard, of which New York will be taken as representative, to the Missouri River Cities, to wit, in cents per 100 pounds,

Class	1	2	3	4	5
Rate	147	120	93	68	57

are unjust and unreasonable; that they are unjustly discriminatory against the Missouri River Cities as compared with the class rates from New York to the Twin Cities, to wit, in cents per 100 pounds,

Class	1	2	3	4	5
Rate	115	99	76	53	46

and they ask that the Commission establish from New York to the Missouri River Cities the following through class rates in cents per 100 pounds,

Class	1	2	3	4	5
Rate	110	95.25	72.5	51.5	44

together with proportionate reductions from eastern producing points as shown in Western Trunk Line Tariff No. 786, I. C. C. No. 678, or such other rates as may be found just and reasonable.

Defendants, Chicago, Rock Island & Pacific Railway; Chicago, Burlington & Quincy Railway; Chicago, Milwaukee & St. Paul Railway; Chicago & Northwestern Railway, and Chicago Great Western Railway are parties to the tariff so referred to. It contains rates on classes and commodities from "Atlantic seaboard and points west thereof, east of the western termini of the trunk lines" to St. Paul, Minneapolis, etc., and the term "Atlantic seaboard" is used herein in that sense.

Defendants admit the correctness of the rates stated in the complaint, and the divisions thereof between the several carriers, and the distances via the various routes, but they deny that such rates are unjust and unreasonable, or unjustly discriminatory in comparison with the rates to the Twin Cities. Of the five original defendants, the Rock Island, the Northwestern, and the Great Western, allege justification for the lower rates to the Twin Cities on the ground of competition by water as well as of competition via the Canadian Pacific and the Minneapolis, St. Paul & Sault Ste. Marie Railway, hereinafter referred to as the Soo line.

Of the numerous complainants only representatives of the dry goods interests appeared to give evidence at the hearings, with the exception of one wholesale grocer, introduced by the intervenor, Sioux City Commercial Club. The jobbers of Sioux City sell goods in northwestern Iowa, southern Minnesota, South Dakota, northern Nebraska, and a part of Wyoming. They come into competition with jobbers at Chicago, Omaha, the Twin Cities, and other intermediate jobbing points, their strongest competition being with Omaha on the south and the Twin Cities on the north.

With the exception of North Dakota, western and northwestern Minnesota, and Canada it may be said in general that the drys goods concerns in the Missouri River Cities compete in all the territory from the Missouri River to the Pacific Ocean and from the Canadian boundary to the Gulf, and in much of this territory they meet competition more or less keen from jobbers at Chicago, St. Louis, the Twin Cities, Denver, San Francisco, and various smaller jobbing points. In Montana, Washington, and common-points territory the Missouri River Cities jobbers meet strong competition from jobbers in the Twin Cities, New York, Chicago, St. Louis, and San Francisco; New York and the Twin Cities having an advantage in that territory of the difference between the rates from New York to the Missouri River Cities and from New York to the Twin Cities. In the west and southwest the strongest competitors of the Missouri River Cities are New York, Chicago, and St. Louis. In Iowa, southeastern Dakota, and southwestern Minnesota the rates equalize at greater distances from the Twin Cities than from the Missouri River Cities.

While the Missouri River Cities jobbers are at a disadvantage as compared with the Twin Cities jobbers in Minnesota, North Dakota, northeastern South Dakota, and Canadian territory, the Twin Cities jobbers are at a like and apparently equal disadvantage in the territory immediately west and southwest of the Missouri River Cities and in the Black Hills district of South Dakota. There are points west of the Missouri River which can be reached by the jobber at St. Louis or at New York, under a combination rate based on St. Louis, cheaper than they can be reached by the Missouri River Cities jobbers under a combination rate based on the Missouri River, but the evidence seemed to show that in general this was where the application of a through rate at an intermediate point on the same line had that effect.

The record shows that 3 wholesale dry goods houses at Kansas City, 4 at St. Joseph, and 2 at Omaha do an aggregate annual business of about $40,000,000. They estimate that their inbound freight charges amount to about 3¼ per cent of the total sales; that their total expenses amount to 13 per cent of the total sales and that on an annual business of $5,000,000 the Twin Cities jobbers would have an advantage of approximately $40,000 over the jobbers at the Missouri River Cities by reason of the difference in freight rates. This estimate presumably assumes that the total of the year's sales is made in territory strictly competitive between the Missouri River Cities and the Twin Cities, and that it all moves under the first class rate.

Complainants insist that the system of basing rates to the Missouri River Cities and points beyond upon the Mississippi River crossings is improper. Their expert testified that the Mississippi River basis should be abolished, but he did not think the Missouri River basis should be abolished because, in his opinion, the country west of the Missouri River had not developed sufficiently as yet to warrant that change.

As has been noted, the Missouri River Cities have a certain territory naturally tributary to them in which the Twin Cities are apparently unable to compete with them, but in certain other territory naturally tributary to the Twin Cities, the Twin Cities jobbers have an advantage over the Missouri River Cities jobbers, and this must necessarily be so as to all distributing centers if the cost of the service and the distance which goods are transported are to be given any consideration in determining transportation rates. It is not possible to place all commercial centers on an equality in the cost of transportation except by basing transportation charges upon the same principle that underlies the Government's charges for the transmission of mail matter.

It is therefore proper for us to here look into the question of not only what the rates are but upon what principles they are constructed, by what conditions they are controlled, and what would be the effect of important changes therein. Chicago is 912 miles and St. Louis is 1,063 miles from New York, Kansas City is 280 miles northwest of St. Louis, St. Joseph is about 65 miles northwest of Kansas City, and Omaha is approximately 200 miles northwest of Kansas City. The short line mileages from New York to the Missouri River Cities are via St. Louis to Kansas City, 1,342 miles; to St. Joseph, 1,390 miles; to Omaha, 1,477 miles, and via Chicago to Kansas City, 1,370 miles; to St. Joseph, 1,382 miles, and to Omaha, 1,405 miles. The short line mileage from Chicago to Kansas City is 458 miles, to St. Joseph 470 miles, and to Omaha, 492 miles. The short line mileage from Chicago to Minneapolis is 420 miles and to St. Paul 409 miles. The average distances, however, between Chicago and the Missouri River Cities and between Chicago and the Twin Cities are approximately the same.

For a long time the rates from New York to points east of Chicago and to points between Chicago and the Mississippi River have been established on a percentage basis, the New York-Chicago rate being taken as 100 per cent. The rates from New York to points east of Chicago are fixed at certain percentages below the New York-Chicago rates and from New York to points beyond Chicago up to the Mississippi River crossings at certain percentages above the New York-Chicago rates.

Rates from New York to the Mississippi River crossings were fixed by the establishment of the New York-East St. Louis rate at 116 per cent of the New York-Chicago rate, and it will be seen that the mileage from New York to East St. Louis is substantially 116 per cent of the mileage from New York to Chicago. On January 1, 1908, the bridge tolls between East St. Louis and St. Louis were taken into the through rates and St. Louis, Mo., and East St. Louis, Ill., were placed upon the basis of 117 per cent of the New York-Chicago rates, which resulted in increasing the class rates 1 cent in each of the first three classes. The rates and divisions quoted herein, however, are those in effect at the time of the hearing of this case.

East St. Louis being a Mississippi River crossing, and the rates having been established at 116 per cent of the New York-Chicago rates, the rates from New York to all of the other Mississippi River crossings to and including East Dubuque, Ill., were fixed the same as to East St. Louis on traffic moving through them and to points beyond. This resulted in establishing class rates from New York to the several Mississippi River crossings, in cents per 100 pounds, as follows:

Class	1	2	3	4	5
Rate	87	75	58	4	35

The local class rates under Western Classification applying from the several Mississippi River crossings on traffic moving through them from New York and destined to the Missouri River Cities were, in cents per 100 pounds:

Class	1	2	3	4	5
Rate	60	45	35	27	22

It will, therefore, be seen that the through class rates from New York to the Missouri River Cities made by combination of the class rates to the Mississippi River crossings applicable on business beyond and the class rates from the Mississippi River Crossings to the Missouri River Cities resulted in class rates in cents per 100 pounds as follows:

Class	1	2	3	4	5
Rate	147	120	93	68	57

It should be understood that these rates apply on traffic moving via Chicago and that much of the traffic moving through the upper Mississippi River crossing moves via Chicago, and it should be remembered that the rates west of the Mississippi River crossings are not constructed upon percentages of the New York-Chicago rates, or upon any other percentage basis. They are the independently established class rates applying between the Mississippi River crossings and the Missouri River crossings and are made without reference to any methods employed in fixing the rates from the Atlantic seaboard to the Mississippi River crossings.

The local class rates from Chicago to the several Mississippi River crossings are on scales which range from 35.3 to 43.3 cents first class, and it will therefore be seen that the proportional rate from New York to the Mississippi River crossings applicable on business going west of the Mississippi is considerably less than the full combination of class rates on Chicago. The proportionals from New York to the Mississippi River crossings through Chicago are divided as follows:

Lines east of Chicago:

Class	1	2	3	4	5
Rate	72.3	62.4	48.4	34.3	29.4

Lines west of Chicago:

Class	1	2	3	4	5
Rate	14.7	12.6	9.6	6.7	5.6

In addition to the above divisions of the proportional rate up to the Mississippi River crossings the lines west of Chicago on business destined to the Missouri River Cities get their full class rate local giving them as earnings on this traffic for their service between Chicago and the Missouri River Cities the following, in cents per 100 pounds:

Class	1	2	3	4	5
Rate	74.7	57.6	44.6	33.7	27.6

The through class rates from New York to the Twin Cities in cents per 100 pounds are divided as follows:

To the lines east of Chicago:

Class	1	2	3	4	5
Rate	75	65	50	35	30

To the lines west of Chicago:

Class	1	2	3	4	5
Rate	40	34	26	18	16

And it is thus seen that in this division the lines east of Chicago get their full New York-Chicago rates. The division going to the lines west of Chicago constitute a line of proportional rates applicable only upon through business, the local class rates between Chicago and the Twin Cities being established on a scale of 60 cents first class.

Complainants allege that the operating and transportation conditions between Chicago and the Missouri River Cities and between Chicago and the Twin Cities are not substantially different and in no sense justify the existing differences in rates.

As has been seen, the defendants allege the controlling influence of competition by water and via the Soo Line in the fixing of the Chicago-Twin Cities proportionals. Complainant argues that this claim is not possessed of any merit, and in support of that argument cites the fact that these Chicago-Twin Cities rates have been increased during the season of lake navigation and reduced at a time when navigation was closed. There is much conflict in the testimony as to the effect of the competition of the Soo Line and as to when that became a factor in the situation. Complainants went to great trouble to locate the facts, but a careful inquiry into the records of the Commission shows that in some respects complainants' witnesses were mistaken on this point.

The reports of the Commission disclose that in 1886 there were class rates between Chicago and the Twin Cities, in cents per 100 pounds as follows:

Class	1	2	3	4	5
Rate	40	30	20	15	10

These rates were in effect at the time the Chicago, Burlington & Northern Railway (now Chicago, Burlington & Quincy Railway) began its operations in that year. From that time to June 4, 1888, these rates were sometimes higher and sometimes lower than above quoted. A short time prior to the date last mentioned, the Northwestern Association, made up of all the lines between Chicago and the Twin Cities, excepting the Chicago, Burlington & Northern, increased these rates to the basis of 60 cents first class. The Chicago, Burlington & Northern assented to the 60-cent scale, but claiming an alleged violation of the agreement it said:

Finding that many of our patrons would be discriminated against by the 60-cent scale, and owing to the extremely low rates from the seaboard prevailing by Lake Superior lines, we have decided upon the scale,

which was:

Class	1	2	3	4	5
Rate	40	33	26	18	12½

At the same time the same carrier established all-rail proportional class rates, applicable only upon traffic originating at or east of the western termini of the Trunk Lines, as follows:

Class	1	2	3	4	5
Rate	31	22	23	17	11

In re C. St. P. & K. C. Ry., 2 I. C. C. Rep., 231.

The Minneapolis, St. Paul and Sault Ste. Marie Railway Company completed its line from Sault Ste. Marie to Minneapolis in January, 1888.

In July, 1889, all of the roads between Chicago and the Twin Cities established the 60-cent scale between Chicago and the Twin Cities on traffic from the Atlantic seaboard; on September 25 it was again reduced to the 40-cent scale and remained there until November, when the 60-cent scale was again restored. This remained in effect until in February, 1890, when the 40-cent scale was again adopted. It was raised to a 50-cent scale in August and to the 60-cent scale in November of the same year. This continued in force until January, 1897, when the Soo Line, against the vigorous protests of the other lines, issued a tariff which became effective in February, 1897, and which established proportional class rates from Sault Ste. Marie to the Twin Cities on all traffic originating south of Ogdensburg and east of Newport, Vt., when routed via the Soo Line, and on traffic originating at or east of Pittsburg when routed via Mackinaw City destined to Minneapolis and St. Paul in cents per 100 pounds as follows:

Class	1	2	3	4	5
Rate	40	35	26	18	16

This line of differentials in connection with the Canadian Pacific rates to Sault Ste. Marie materially reduced the through class rates, and all of the lines between Chicago and the Twin Cities followed this reduction in May of 1897. In June, 1899, the Chicago-Twin Cities lines advanced these proportionals to a 50-cent scale and at a time when lake navigation was open. This scale remained in effect until January, 1901, when it was again reduced to the 40-cent scale at a time when navigation was closed. It is thus seen that these carriers have made numerous, persistent, and vigorous efforts to maintain proportional rates between Chicago and the Twin Cities higher than the 40-cent scale, and that they have been unable to do so.

The Canadian Pacific Despatch tariff referred to by defendants as showing maintenance of a 40-cent scale by the Soo Line, at the same time it was party to the tariffs fixing the 50-cent scale, taken in connection with Boston & Maine Railroad's joint west-bound tariff, show that class rates from Boston and points taking same rate to the Twin Cities were established via the Canadian Pacific Railway and the Soo Line in cents per 100 pounds as follows:

Class	1	2	3	4	5
Rate	105	91	70	49	42

The Chicago-Twin Cities lines were named as parties to these tariffs as well as the Soo Line, but it should be understood that these rates applied via a differential line upon which the same rates are now in effect.

With further reference to the influence of the water transportation upon the Chicago-Twin Cities proportionals, it is found that the class rates from New York to Buffalo in cents per 100 pounds are:

Class	1	2	3	4	5
Rate	39	33	28	19	16

And that the class rates from Duluth to the Twin Cities in cents per 100 pounds are:

Class	1	2	3	4	5
Rate	35	30	23	17	10

The through first class rate New York to the Twin Cities is $1.15. The sum of the rail rates New York to Buffalo and Duluth to the Twin Cities on first class is 74 cents, leaving 41 cents that could be applied to the cost of transportation by water between Buffalo and Duluth. It seems safe to say that if the all-rail through rates were materially increased with any assurance that the increases would be maintained for a long period, there would be every inducement for the interested jobbers to arrange for independent water transportation from Buffalo to Duluth and avail themselves of the combination that could be so constructed. The lake-and-rail rate on first class New York to Duluth is 68 cents per 100 pounds, which added to the first class rate Duluth to the Twin Cities of 35 cents makes a combination rate of $1.03 as compared with the all-rail rate via Chicago of $1.15. There are now in effect lake-and-rail rates from New York to the Twin Cities on a scale of 83 cents per 100 pounds on first class via Duluth.

The controlling influence of the water and Canadian competition over the rates from the Seaboard to the Twin Cities is apparent, and it is also apparent that the defendant carriers west of Chicago must meet the force of that competition or refrain from participation in that business. Their local class rates from Chicago to the Twin Cities are on the basis of 60 cents first class, as compared with a 55-cent scale via lake and rail from Chicago to the Twin Cities via Gladstone and the Soo Line, and a 50-cent scale from Chicago to the Twin Cities via Duluth.

The joint through class rates from New York to the Twin Cities apply up to the Missouri River crossings on traffic from the Atlantic seaboard destined through them to Montana common points and to Spokane, Wash., and common points, as well as upon traffic through the Twin Cities to the same destinations. The locals from the Missouri River crossings and from the Twin Cities are added thereto to make up the combination through rates. The local class rates from the Twin Cities to Montana common points, and to Spokane, Wash., and common points, are the same as from the Missouri River crossings to the same destinations. This adjustment is forced by competition. If the lines via the Missouri River crossings did not make the same rates to Montana and Washington points that are available via the Twin Cities they could get none of that business.

The class rates from Chicago to Oklahoma City moving via Kansas City are on a scale of $1.50 per 100 pounds first class, of which the carriers between Chicago and Kansas City receive as their division 48 cents.

The class rates from Chicago to Texas common points applying via Kansas City are on a scale of $1.57 per 100 pounds first class, of which the carriers between Chicago and Kansas City receive 47.1 cents. The class rates from Chicago through Kansas City to El Paso, Tex., are on the scale of $1.69 per 100 pounds, first class, of which the carriers between Chicago and Kansas City receive as their division 47.1 cents. The distance from New York to the Missouri River Cities is substantially the same as from Chicago to El Paso.

On transcontinental traffic from the Atlantic seaboard to the Pacific coast terminals, carriers west of Chicago receive as their division of the class rates for the haul between Chicago and the

Missouri River crossings on the first five classes in cents per 100 pounds the following:

Class	1	2	3	4	5
Rate	33	28.50	24.75	22.50	19.50

From these divisions of through rates accepted by the carriers between Chicago and the Missouri River crossings and from the admission of the Chicago, Burlington and Quincy Railway Company in its answer that they give said carriers some profit, complainants argue that the rates charged from the Mississippi River crossings to the Missouri River crossings are unreasonably and unjustly high.

Defendants answer this by asserting that a low division of the through rate for a long haul is not fairly comparable with the local rate between the same points; that the through rates are not made or controlled by them; that they are frequently made in competition with water transportation to the Pacific coast terminals or to the Gulf ports, and that while none of them can be said to represent less than the actual cost of the service they can not be considered in and of themselves as remunerative and can not be fairly taken as a measure of their rates. Manifestly, a carrier may not properly or lawfully engage in transportation at a rate less than the cost of the service. So to do would place an improper and unlawful burden upon other traffic, but if a carrier elects to accept a low division of a through rate for a long haul rather than to stay out of that business it can not be held to have thereby committed itself to that division as a measure of the reasonableness of its other rates for transportation between the same points on business from or to different destinations or of a different character.

Complainants argue that the cost of transportation on eastern and western roads is about the same; that the average rate per ton per mile received by the western roads is greater than that received by the eastern roads, and that the conditions of transportation are so substantially similar that it would be entirely fair to project to the Missouri River the same rate per ton per mile that represents the rates from the Atlantic seaboard to the Mississippi River. There are, however, differences in the physical conditions. The density of population and of traffic is materially less west of the Mississippi River, and the cost of operation is greater, due among other things to higher wages and higher cost of fuel and other necessary supplies. It seems clear that the lines west of the Mississippi River are entitled to a somewhat higher charge than would be received for the same service on the lines east of the Mississippi River and it seems that the only question to be determined here is whether or not the class rates of the defendant carriers between the Mississippi River and the Missouri River Cities on business from the seaboard and destined to the Missouri River Cities are too high. It seems patent that any change in the rates east of the Mississippi River, even if warranted, would fail to accomplish what the complainants desire, because whatever of advantage accrued therefrom to the Missouri River Cities would accrue to a like degree or extent to their principal competitive commercial centers to wit, New York, Chicago, St. Louis, and the Twin Cities.

The average short-line distance between the nearest Mississippi River crossings and the individual Missouri River Cities is about 275 miles. The average distance between the Mississippi River crossings, via which the rates apply, and the Missouri River Cities is 325 miles. As has been before stated, the local class rates between the Mississippi and the Missouri River crossings are in cents per 100 pounds:

Class	1	2	3	4	5
Rate	60	45	35	27	22

And these are the rates that are added to the rates up to the Mississippi River crossings to make up the through rates from the Atlantic seaboard to the Missouri River Cities. Are these rates as so used and the through rates resulting therefrom, unwarrantedly high or unduly discriminatory or unjustly prejudicial? Can they be changed with out doing injustice elsewhere?

As has been seen, the first class rate from the Atlantic seaboard to Chicago is 75 cents, and to the Mississippi River crossings is 87 cents. From Chicago to the Missouri River crossings the first class rate is 80 cents, and from the Mississippi River to the Missouri River is 60 cents. The through first class rate from the seaboard to the Missouri River is, therefore, $1.47; the combination on Chicago is $1.55 and on St. Louis is $1.47. The St. Louis jobbers can, so far as freight charges are concerned, purchase in the east and sell at all points east of the Missouri River Cities cheaper than can the jobbers in the Missouri River Cities, while at the same time the St. Louis dealers can sell in the Missouri River Cities themselves and at some points beyond them just as cheaply as can the dealers located in the Missouri River Cities. The Chicago dealer seems to have a handicap of 8 cents on the first class rate as compared with St. Louis. This no doubt is due to the fact that direct lines from the seaboard to St. Louis, belonging to one system, make the rate to St. Louis.

The class rates from the Atlantic seaboard to Sioux City when made upon the Mississippi River combination through any crossing East Burlington to East Dubuque, inclusive, are the same as to Omaha. The combination on Chicago is the same to Sioux City as to the Missouri River Cities. The combination on Mississippi River crossings south of East Burlington is higher to Sioux City.

If the local class rates of defendants between the Mississippi and Missouri rivers were reduced, it would give the same degree of advantage to all the producing and distributing centers on and east of the Missouri River, and their relative advantages or disadvantages would not be changed, while a very serious inroad upon the revenues of the carriers would inevitably result, and at a time of industrial depression when it could not well be borne. Such a change would necessitate corresponding changes in the rates to and from intermediate points and would probably be reflected in changes in commodity rates as well. The local class rates between the rivers are high, but this is not the time to precipitate such a violent change as would follow an important reduction of them. The first class rate from Buffalo to Chicago, about 540 miles, and from Pittsburg to Chicago, about 465 miles, is 45 cents. From Cincinnati to Chicago, 306 miles, it is 40 cents.

Complainants urge that defendant carriers west of Chicago and the Mississippi River crossings have, from their operations, accumulated enormous surpluses and that therefore they can not fairly present the plea of financial difficulty. Especial attention is called to the reports of the defendant, Chicago, Burlington & Quincy Railway Company, which show a surplus of nearly $42,000,000. The carrying of this item in reports is certainly misleading to those who are not otherwise acquainted with the true facts. This surplus is in no sense available cash or free surplus. The record in this case shows that it simply represents the amount of earnings that have been expended in past years for betterments and improvements in the road, and additions to its equipment.

An abundant share of the prosperity and development of the trans-Mississippi and trans-Missouri territories has come to the Missouri River Cities, from which this complaint comes, but the fact that they have prospered in the past as a result of rapid expansion and development of new territory may not be taken as conclusive evidence of the correctness or justice at this time of the rate adjustment that has prevailed in the past. We are not impressed with the view that the system of making rates on certain basing lines should be abolished. No system of rate making has been suggested as a substitute for it, except one based upon the postage-stamp theory, or one based strictly upon mileage. Either of these would create revolution in transportation affairs and chaos in commercial affairs that have been builded upon the system of rate making now in effect. It must not, however, be assumed that a basing line for rates may be established and be made an impassable barrier for through rates, or that cities or markets located at or upon such basing line have any inviolable possession of, or hold upon, the right to distribute traffic in or from the territory lying beyond. Development of natural resources, increase in population, growth of manufacturing or producing facilities, and increased traffic on railroads create changed conditions which may warrant changes in rates and in rate adjustments in order to afford just and reasonable opportunity for interchange of traffic between points of production and points of large consumption.

We can not agree with the argument that the rates from the Atlantic seaboard or from Chicago to the Missouri River Cities should be the same as or lower than rates from same points to the Twin Cities. As has been seen, the rates to the Twin Cities can not escape the influence of the water and Canadian competition.

As has been stated, the through rates from Atlantic seaboard territory to the Missouri River Cities are made by adding together the rates from points of origin to the Mississippi River crossings, using proportional rates when such are available, and the local class rates from the Mississippi River crossings to the Missouri River Cities. The through rates so established are, in our opinion, unreasonably high. This is so because those portions of the through rates which apply between the Mississippi River crossings and the Missouri River Cities are too high. These are defendants' "separately established rates" which are "applied to the through transportation," and, therefore, the through rates should be adjusted by reduction of those factors or parts thereof which are found to be unreasonable.

Out of consideration for long-established custom in rate construction and publication, involving different classifications, we refrain from establishing joint through rates, and, permitting the rates from Atlantic seaboard territory to the Mississippi River crossings to remain as at present, we conclude that the separately established rates of the defendants, Chicago, Rock Island & Pacific; Chicago, Burlington & Quincy; Chicago, Milwaukee & St. Paul; Chicago & Northwestern, and Chicago Great Western Railway companies, applied between the Mississippi River crossings and the Missouri River Cities to the through transportation of shipments moving under class rates and coming from the Atlantic seaboard, taking New York as representative, should be reduced to the following scale:

Class	1	2	3	4	5
Rate	51	.38	30	23	19

and that these rates should also be applied to the transportation of through shipments which move under class rates and which originate at points of origin specified on pages 3 and 4 of complainants' Exhibit A, same being the aforesaid Western Trunk Line Tariff No. 786, I. C. C. 678, or at points taking the same rates.

These rates should also be applied on traffic from same points of origin destined to Sioux City, Iowa, when it moves through any of the Mississippi River crossings, East Burlington to East Dubuque, inclusive.

As to the other defendants, the complaint should be dismissed.

An order will be entered in accordance with these views.

CLASS AND COMMODITY RATES TO SALT LAKE CITY

32 I. C. C. 551 (1915)

By the Commission:

The present class rates, in both directions, and some 210 commodity rates, westbound, as also a few eastbound, between Chicago, Mississippi River, Missouri River, and intermediate territory, on the one hand, and Utah common points on the other, were prescribed by this Commission in *Commercial Club, Salt Lake City,* v. *A., T. & S. F. Ry. Co.,* 19 I. C. C., 218; 21 I. C. C., 400; hereinafter referred to as the *Salt Lake case.* They became effective November 15, 1911.

The class rates are on the scale per 100 pounds, first class, of $2.45 from or to Chicago, $2.27 from or to Mississippi River points and $1.90 from or to Missouri River points.

The commodity rates so prescribed attach to commodity descriptions which follow in the main those in use to the Pacific coast.

The respondents have filed their joint freight tariff, Trans-Missouri No. 20–H, I. C. C. No. 287, effective April 1, 1914, revising the existing class and commodity structure with general trend upward. Against these proposed rates protests have been lodged with us by representatives of Salt Lake City, Missouri River, Iowa, Mississippi River, and Chicago interests, as well as on behalf of a large number of other eastern points which are affected. This tariff is under suspension in this proceeding until January 30, 1915.

Upon petition of respondents the proposed rates on iron and steel articles were, by order of June 26, 1914, eliminated from this proceeding and transferred to another.

The following table shows the relation of class rates in effect prior to November 15, 1911, present rates, and those proposed. In this report all rates are stated in cents per 100 pounds.

To Utah common points.

From —	1	2	3	4	5	A	B	C	D	E
Missouri River points:										
Prior	205	175	153	128	106	106	83	75	50.5	42
Present	190	162	142	119	98	98	77	70	50	42
Proposed	200	170	150	126	100	105	80	70	50	42
Mississippi River points:										
Prior	265	220	188	155	128	130.5	102.5	92	64	53
Present	227	189	163	134	111	111	88	80	57	48
Proposed	247	205	177	143	116	102.5	94	81	59	49
Chicago:										
Prior	285	240	198	160	133	138	110	97	69	58
Present	245	207	172	139	115	115	95	84	62	52
Proposed	265	223	185	149	121	128	101.5	86	64	54

Utah and Montana common points are said to be competitive territories, with rate adjustments which have always been interrelated. The first-class rate from Chicago to Montana common points is $2.65. Taking this as base, the respondents construct the proposed class scale as follows:

They deduct from the Chicago-Montana rate of $2.65 the differential of 65 cents between Chicago and Missouri River points, as fixed by the Commission on traffic moving to Colorado in *Colorado Mfrs. Asso.* v. *A., T. & S. F. Ry. Co.*, 28 I. C. C., 82; 29 I. C. C., 544, and thus arrive at $2 as the first-class rate, Missouri River-Utah. The lower class rates on this $2 scale are made by application of the following percentages:

Class	1	2	3	4	5	A	B	C	D	E
Percentage	100	85	75	65	50	55	40	35	25	21

Subject, however, to observance of the St. Paul-Montana common-point class rate as maximum. The class rate from and to the Mississippi River and Chicago, respectively, are then constructed by adding to these Missouri River-Utah rates the Mississippi River and Chicago differentials over the Missouri River, as fixed or approved by the Commission in the *Colorado Manufacturers case, supra.* These differentials are:

Class	1	2	3	4	5	A	B	C	D	E
Mississippi River	47	35	27	20½	16	18	14	13	9	7
Chicago	65	53	36	25	20	24½	21	17	14	11

The resulting sums constitute the class rates from or to these points, respectively, to or from Utah common points. But here, also, the Chicago-Montana rates are observed as maxima between Chicago and Utah.

The class rates from Peoria, Ill., are fixed midway between the Chicago and the Mississippi River rates. Those from St. Paul, Minn., are transferred from the Chicago to the Mississippi River basis, thus observing the suggestions made in *Minneapolis Traffic Asso.* v. *C., B. & Q. R. R. Co.*, 22 I. C. C., 259. Those from Duluth, Minn., and Memphis, Tenn., are retained on the Chicago basis as at present.

Class A rates are made higher than fifth class, as shown by the percentage table. This accords with our ruling in the *Colorado Manufacturers case, supra.*

The present commodity rates, where not prescribed in the

Sale Lake case, are those voluntarily established by respondents, subject to observance of two alternative clauses, one fixing the Spokane rate as maximum and the other fixing the Montana common-point rate as maximum.

The proposed tariff eliminates these clauses and states the specific rate in each instance. It revises the descriptions and restores differential adjustments from different territories of origin in effect for many years prior to the order in the *Salt Lake case, supra,* by taking as base the proposed commodity rates from Chicago and adjusting with relation thereto the proposed rates from Mississippi River territory, Peoria, St. Paul, Memphis, and Duluth. In this adjustment commodity rates from Chicago to Spokane and Montana common points still operate as maxima to Utah common points, and rates from Missouri River territory are generally held at 80 per cent of the Chicago rate, following the relation prescribed in the *Salt Lake case, supra.*

As thus proposed, many of the Chicago-Utah commodity rates are less than the Chicago-Montana, and the Missouri River-Utah commodity rates are in most instances less than the St. Paul-Montana commodity rates. The commodity list, both in the existing and in the proposed tariffs, is unusually large, due in part to the effect of water competition to the Pacific coast and the resulting need of commodity descriptions corresponding to those used by water competitors, and by transcontinental lines meeting that competition. The present commodity list is, as to rates, on a basis lower than that generally obtaining in western classification territory. Rates to Utah common points from the Mississippi River and Missouri River territories were made on the basis of 96 per cent and 80 per cent, respectively, of the commodity rates from Chicago. This gave to Utah rates relatively lower than to Kansas and Colorado, and actually lower than to Montana.

It will be observed from the foregoing comparative table of prior, present, and proposed class rates, that in some of the class rates no increase is sought.

So also in commodity rates, increase is not without exception. Respondents estimate that of the commodities in question, 187 show increase, 158 reduction, and 68 no change at all. But changes in descriptions and mixtures make the comparison somewhat uncertain. The correctness of this estimate is challenged by protestants.

The justification by respondents rests largely upon comparison of the proposed rates with those now in effect to Montana, Arizona, Nevada, Colorado, and Kansas, and the bearing of the Pacific coast adjustment upon intermediate territory which is affected by operating conditions more severe than those obtaining east of Colorado common points.

Protestants claim that the existing adjustment to Utah was fixed by the Commission after thorough investigation and should not be disturbed; that rates to Montana were not fixed by the Commission, and hence should not be taken as a basis for comparison; that the rate relation is not improved by the proposed adjustment; that the reductions do not compensate for the increases; that these increases are not warranted by change in conditions or any showing that present rates are not remunerative; and that for these and other reasons respondents have failed to sustain the burden of proof imposed by statute.

Much evidence was adduced in support of these and other contentions, but we shall content ourselves with reference to some of the more significant facts.

The short-line distance from Chicago to Butte is 1,512 miles, and to Salt Lake City, 1,528 miles. These destinations are fairly representative of the Montana and Utah common points, respectively. Between Chicago and Butte the highest elevation on any line is about 6,400 feet. Between Chicago and Salt Lake City the Union Pacific rises to over 8,000 feet and the Denver & Rio Grande to over 10,000 feet in crossing the continental divide. Distance, grade, and curvature are important elements in cost of service, especially on mountain lines.

Mention has been made of the relation between class rates to and from Montana and the proposed class rates to and from Utah.

As to commodity rates, comparison of those proposed to Utah which show increases, with rates on the same commodities to Montana for equivalent hauls, discloses a lower average commodity rate to Utah.

The Arizona comparison shows that Chicago-Phoenix class rates, fixed by the Commission in *Maricopa County Commercial Club* v. *S. F., P. & P. Ry. Co.*, 19 I. C. C., 257, average 116.45 per cent of the proposed Chicago-Utah class rates. The distance from Chicago to Phoenix is 115.3 per cent of the distance to Salt Lake City.

The Nevada comparison is as to rates from Omaha. Class rates from that city to Elko and Winnemucca, Nev., were fixed by the Commission in *Railroad Commission of Nevada* v. *S. P. Co.*, 19 I. C. C., 238. Their average is 122.6 per cent of the proposed class rates between Omaha and Utah. The average distance between Omaha and these Nevada points is 1,295 miles, or 124 per cent of the 1,037 miles between Omaha and Salt Lake City.

It will be observed that the resulting per ton-mile earnings on the proposed class rates to Utah are less than to Arizona, although the distance is shorter, and very little higher than those to the more distant points in Nevada.

Since our decision in the *Salt Lake case, supra,* class rates to and from Colorado points, and certain commodity rates westbound to those points from Chicago, Mississippi River, and Missouri River territory, as there defined, being the territories of origin here involved, were prescribed by this Commission in the *Colorado Manufacturers case, supra.* The haul to Colorado common points is a prairie haul; the farther haul to Utah common points in a mountain haul. On the line of the Union Pacific the rise and fall west of Cheyenne, Wyo., which is in the Colorado common-point group, is over twice that east of Cheyenne, despite an expenditure during recent years of over $10,000,000 in improvement of the line west. The other main line between Colorado and Utah common points, the Denver & Rio Grande, has also, and even more recently, expended millions in the improvement of its mountain road. On both lines the adverse mountain conditions compel higher operating expenses than on the prairie lines, because of decreased locomotive efficiency, necessity for helper service, constructive mileage and slower schedules resulting in higher wages to train crews, increased inspection and repair of both track and equipment, and other exceptional conditions.

The average class rate proposed between the territories of origin involved and Utah is 169 per cent of the average class rate to and from Colorado, as so fixed by this Commission. The average distance to Utah is 166 per cent of the average distance to Colorado. Similar comparisons made with respect to each main point of origin, except Omaha, show similar results. It thus appears that the Utah class rates are, on a distance basis, about 102 per cent of the Colorado class rates.

Comparison of the proposed commodity rates to Utah, which show increases, with rates on the same commodities to Colorado approved by us, disclosed that as to either Chicago, Mississippi River, or Missouri River traffic, Utah would have an average commodity rate which is lower on a per ton-mile basis than that to Colorado. The excess of such Utah commodity rates over the corresponding Colorado rates would be almost exactly 50 per cent. The present Commission made Utah class rates exceed the present Commission made Colorado class rates by almost 60 per cent.

The rule is well recognized that ordinarily the per ton-mile yield should decrease with distance. But this rule should find full application only where the conditions of haul are substantially similar, and where a prairie haul is compared with a mountain haul, as here, the general rule may well be qualified.

Further justification of these proposed rates is to be found in the *Colorado Manufacturers case, supra,* and *State of Kansas* v. *A., T. & S. F. Ry. Co.*, 27 I. C. C., 673, when read together. In the *Colorado case* this Commission regarded it as obvious that the spread between the Kansas rates and the Utah rates was not sufficient to afford Colorado the relief to which it was entitled without seriously impairing the revenues of the carriers. They were confronted with the alternative of lowering the rates from Colorado common points to jobbing territory lying farther west or of increasing the rates to Utah. Adoption of this latter alternative has resulted in the filing of the tariff under suspension in this proceeding.

Evidence adduced by merchants of Salt Lake City shows that while Denver can job westward on the line of the Denver & Rio Grande toward Salt Lake City more than 500 miles, Salt Lake City in jobbing back east against Denver is under the that distance. But in the west a normal jobbing territory usually lies largely to the west of the jobbing point, and Salt Lake City in jobbing back east against Denver is under the handicap of a back haul.

It is true, as urged by these merchants, that the proposed class rates to and from Utah show a higher percentage of lower to first than obtains in the class rates to and from Colorado. The illustrative table which follows gives these percentages to the points specified.

Comparative percentage relations of lower class rates to first-class rates applying from Missouri River points to the destinations shown.

TO—	1	2	3	4	5	A	B	C	D	E
Salt Lake City:										
Present.........	100	85.3	74.7	62.6	51.6	51.6	40.5	36.8	26.3	22.1
Proposed.......	100	85.0	75.0	65.0	50.0	55.0	40.0	35.0	25.0	21.0
Denver...........	100	80.0	64.3	52.5	40.9	48.7	36.5	32.2	28.7	25.2
Phoenix.......... } Reno .... }	100	86.8	73.2	63.2	53.2	53.2	41.6	33.2	31.6	28.4
Winnemucca......	100	86.5	73.1	63.0	52.9	52.9	41.6	33.2	31.5	28.2

From this table it appears that Utah is fairly treated in this respect; indeed, the percentages proposed by the respondents in the new rates are, on the whole, slightly lower than the percentages in the rates now prevailing. These latter, and the Colorado rates as well, were prescribed or approved by the Commission.

The objection is urged, and properly so, against the use of the Chicago-Montana rates as a measure of comparison, because they are not the rates of this Commission. The rates which it is now proposed to increase were fixed by this Commission after long and exhaustive investigation. They were made effective only after thorough test and a fair ascertainment that they were nonconfiscatory. It is elementary that Utah should not be compelled to pay increased rates merely to relieve Colorado. Nor should it pay rates which are merely the outcome of a compromise between the carriers and the Colorado interests. But it would appear that Utah common points, under the present adjustment, are really in a position of exceptional advantage, and we find it unnecessary to rely upon the Chicago-Montana comparison in reaching our conclusions. Those conclusions are dictated by the Colorado, Arizona, and Nevada comparisons, as also by the comparison of conditions affecting cost of service and competition east of Colorado common points with such conditions west, and the application of the result of this latter comparison to our finding in the *Colorado Manufacturers case, supra.* While the fact that a proposed revision of general upward tendency will remove present inequalities as between competing points may not of itself prove the reasonableness of the increased rates, it is certainly entitled to serious consideration as tending thereto.

The present rates to Utah were, as stated above, fixed in large part by this Commission; but it must also be remembered that we have since considered and fixed corresponding rates to Kansas and Colorado, and those rates have their bearing on the whole western adjustment. The statute itself, in giving to our rate orders a life of only two years, recognizes that conditions which determine reasonableness are subject to change. Even in the *Salt Lake case* we intimated that it was "perhaps probable that the effect of increased wages and increased cost of supplies will be more seriously felt in the future than it has been in the past." Since the *Salt Lake case* the Union Pacific has voluntarily observed the rates there prescribed as maxima to points east, in accordance with the long-and-short-haul clause, and the Denver & Rio Grande, upon order of this Commission, has observed the Utah maxima on traffic to points east of Westwater, Utah. *Grand Junction Chamber of Commerce* v. *D. & R. G. R. R. Co.*, 23 I. C. C., 115. In the *Salt Lake case* we made it clear that the latter line should receive consideration in fixing rates, even though the other main line, the Union Pacific, was the short line, and therefore on the plane of first importance. The return earned by the Denver & Rio Grande on its property investment in recent years has been small. This the protestants do not deny, but they question the efficiency of its management. We find it unnecessary to consider this here.

The record before us contains some evidence showing that under the proposed rates Rockford, Ill., together with other points in northern Illinois and some in southern Wisconsin, have been placed upon the Chicago basis, and it is urged that they should take the lower Peoria basis. We are not prepared to say that the showing by respondents in justification of group changes is overcome by the evidence of protestants on this point.

The evidence before us does not reach every individual rate, or set of rates, in the suspended tariff, and those on iron and steel articles have been expressly reserved for consideration in another proceeding.

The protestants who represent Iowa show that the proposed class and commodity rates do not preserve to interior Iowa points the zone basis prescribed by this Commission in *Iowa State Board of Railroad Commissioners* v. *A. E. R. R. Co.*, 28 I. C. C., 193, at 201. The respondents recognize the merit of this protest and say of record that whatever class rates this Commission finds to be justified between Missouri River points and Mississippi River points on the one hand, and Utah points on the other, will be made the basis for such zone rates.

It was also agreed of record that the respondents will make proper adjustments on the zone basis of the commodity rate structure in so far as the needs of interior Iowa demand. The Commission expects these Iowa rates to be adjusted immediately.

Upon all the facts of record we are of opinion, and so find, that the respondents have sustained the burden of justifying the proposed tariff, subject to any revision which may become necessary through application of our Fourth Section Order No. 124, in *City of Spokane* v. *N. P. Ry. Co.*, 21 I. C. C., 400, or any modification thereof, excepting, however, the proposed rates on iron and steel articles, which are reserved for consideration elsewhere, and the Iowa zone rates, which are to be adjusted as agreed of record.

An order will be entered accordingly vacating the suspension, except as to the rates comprised in the iron and steel schedule, and effective January 30, 1915.

TEXAS COMMON POINT CASE

26 I. C C. 528 (1913)

HARLAN, *Commissioner:*

In view of the vigorous protests made by commercial organizations representing the towns affected, the Commission by its order of June 1, 1912, suspended certain commodity tariffs filed by the southwestern lines, the respondents herein, for the avowed purpose of restricting the area of what is known as the common point territory of Texas. The necessary consequence of the tariffs, if allowed to become effective, will be to put outside that territory and into the so-called differential territory a number of towns that for years have enjoyed common point rates.

The rate adjustment to Texas points has often been referred to as unusual and peculiar; as a matter of fact, it is unusual only in the extraordinary extent of the territory affected by the adjustment. It is really nothing more or less than a very broad rate group, not duplicated elsewhere in the country except by the even larger rate group established under the tariffs of the transcontinental lines. The competitive conditions out of which the common point rates grew have been explained in *Dallas Freight Bureau* v. *M., K. & T. Ry. Co.*, 12 I. C. C., 427, and need not be repeated here. It will be sufficient to say that the common point territory, as now constituted under the tariffs of interstate carriers, comprises all that part of Texas lying east of a line commencing at Quanah on the north and running thence in a southerly direction through Big Springs and San Angelo to Corpus Christi on the Gulf of Mexico. This western boundary is indicated on the accompanying map by the dotted line. In general, all points in this very large territory, 500 miles in extent from north to south and 450 miles from east to west, take the same commodity rates from any point in the United States on or east of the Missouri and Mississippi rivers. In the northern part of the territory is an area commonly known as the burnt district, to which lower rates are in effect from Kansas City and intervening territory. The territory lying west and south of the common point territory is known as differential territory, and to all points within it rates are made by adding differentials to the common point rates. There is also a territory in the vicinity of Galveston and Houston to which rates lower than the common point rates are applied; but with these rates we are not concerned here. The average distance from St. Louis to Texas common points is 800 miles; this was our finding in the *R. R. Commission of Texas* v. *A. T. & S. F. Ry. Co.*, 20 I. C. C., 463, and it is submitted here to be approximately correct at this time.

The common point rate adjustment in Texas has been a matter of comparatively slow development. It originated out of the fact that interior Texas is accessible through so many gateways; traffic flows into all parts of the state not only by way of the ocean and gulf and on the Red River, but over the rail lines entering the state through its eastern and northern boundaries. The competition of the carriers reaching the state from these different directions resulted in putting a large part of the state on the same rate level, and was largely, if not altogether, responsible for the successive extensions of the common point territory toward the west. Possibly the orders of the state commission respecting state traffic may have contributed to the extension of the common point territory for interstate traffic; but an experienced railroad witness said on the hearing that this was not the case. It is altogether clear, however, that this is an accurate view of the situation. Nevertheless, it is true that the successive extensions of the territory, so far as interstate traffic is concerned, have voluntarily been made by the carriers in the

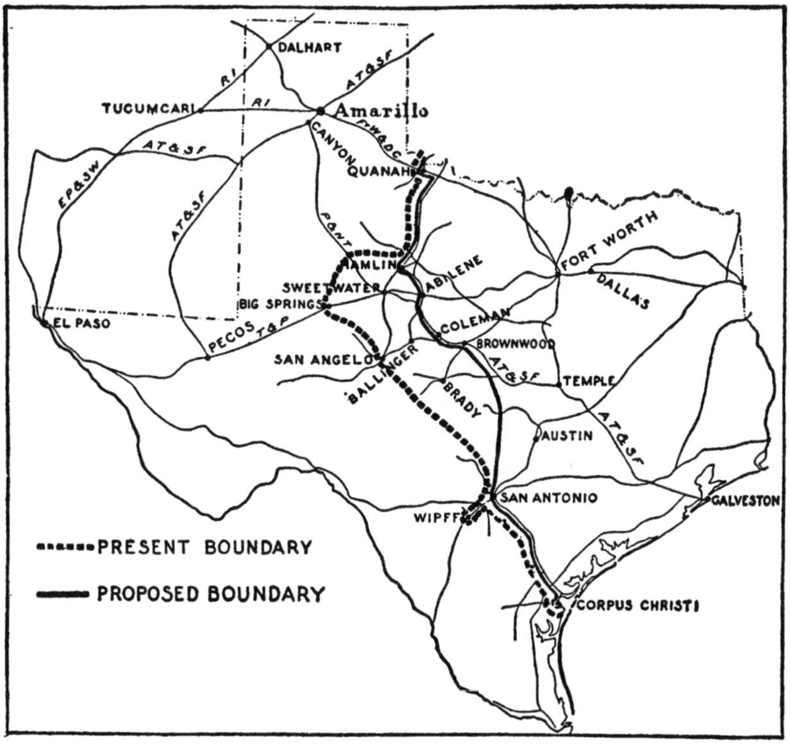

sense that they have not been required under any order of this Commission. In a number of cases before us communities in differential territory have demanded that they be included in common point territory, but in none of them did we find the record sufficient to justify such an order. So far as interstate traffic is concerned it appears, therefore, that the carriers have been forced by competition among themselves and by other conditions to enlarge the common point territory. The last extension was made on September 19, 1904, at which time the present western boundary line was established.

That extension took out of differential territory and put into common point territory certain towns, among which the most important were Sweetwater, Big Springs, San Angelo, Brady, and Ballinger. These communities have therefore enjoyed the common point rates for more than eight years. By the tariffs under suspension it is proposed now to raise their rates by restoring them to differential territory. As heretofore stated the present common point territory has been a matter of slow development. But the changes that have taken place in it have been in the direction of enlargement; there has been no restriction or drawing in of its boundaries. There is of record some vague impression that a restriction was attempted in 1906; but if it was made effective at all it was for a period of less than 40 days. The tariffs under suspension here are the first definite undertaking on the part of the carriers to narrow the area; it is proposed to do this by establishing the western boundary line farther toward the east, thus taking certain towns out of common point territory and to that extent broadening the so-called differential territory.

It is substantially admitted of record that the proposed increase in the rates of these towns, by taking them out of common point territory and putting them into differential territory, was not based on any real consideration of the merits of the new rates or upon any substantial consideration of the rate relation of those communities to other communities in common point territory. The fact is that recent railroad construction has left the respondents on the horns of a dilemma; they must either raise the rates of the towns in question by putting them out of common point territory and into differential territory, or they must lower the rates of Amarillo by taking it out of differential territory and putting it in common point territory. Being compelled by new conditions to accept one of these alternatives, the respondents frankly state of record that they took the course that would have the least effect upon their revenues. In other words, Amarillo has grown to such importance and has so large a traffic that the loss of revenues attending the lowering of its rates by putting it in common point territory would be substantially greater than the gain resulting from raising the rates of the points in question by putting them back into differential territory. The latter course was therefore adopted and is the purpose underlying the tariffs under suspension.

Should Amarillo be brought into common point territory the direct effect on its revenues, as estimated by the Santa Fe, will not exceed $25,000 a year. But the indirect effect, it is thought, will be of greater consequence for the reason that the Amarillo rates will have to be graded back into Oklahoma and Kansas. The Roswell rates, and rates into Roswell territory, will also be affected to some extent, a relation of rates between Roswell and Amarillo having been established in *Roswell Commercial Club* v. *A., T. & S. F. Ry. Co.*, 12 I. C. C., 339. It is clear that the effect on the revenues of the other southwestern lines will not be so great as upon the revenues of the Santa Fe. The estimates offered by the Santa Fe of the effect on its revenues from the inclusion of Amarillo in common point territory include both class and commodity traffic. It may be well to add that the class rates to common point territory are still under the control of our orders in the *R. R. Commission of Texas* v. *A. T. & S. F. Ry. Co.*, 20 I. C. C., 463; it is understood, however, that upon the expiration of the order in May next the respondent lines propose to take similar steps to narrow the common point area with respect to class traffic also.

Practically the only effort made by the respondent carriers to meet the burden cast upon them by the statute, of justifying this proposed increase in the rates of a number of more or less substantial communities, was by showing that unless the rates are increased another and a competing community will be entitled to lower rates than it now enjoys. It was suggested that the logical western boundary of the common point area would be the line established by the carriers in 1887, just west of Fort Worth; that, however, is not the line proposed by the tariffs under suspension. It was also said that the country surrounding the towns in question had been so affected by droughts during the past four or five years as to modify its outlook as an agricultural country and cause the farmers to some extent to revert to cattle grazing. But an earnest protest was made at the hearing against this view, and certainly the enthusiastic descriptions of the country by some of the witnesses gave no indication of any lack of hope in its steady and sound development. It was also asserted that new settlers are no longer coming into the country and that there has been an actual decline in the population of some of these towns. It must be remembered however, that the towns in question have long been in common point territory; that they were put there voluntarily by the carriers, and because, in the judgment of the carriers, their relation to competing points in the territory not only justified but required them to be put on the same rate basis. It is true that the absence of rain for some years has slowed up their growth, which prior to that time had been rapid and continuous. This burden these communities have been compelled to bear, and must continue to bear should it develop that there has been a permanent change in climatic conditions. The effect of the drought is also shown in the revenues of the carriers; but, apparently on the assumption that the droughts will continue for the indefinite future, the carriers, instead of sharing the consequences with the shippers, now seek to relieve themselves of the burden by increasing their rates. These climatic conditions have been emphasized by the respondent lines, but they have not undertaken to show any other change in the relations between the towns in question and other communities that are to remain in common point territory. All these trading centers are still in competition with one another, and the conditions which caused the carriers to put them on the same rate basis with one another still exist.

An attentive examination of the record has led us to the conclusion that the carriers have not justified the proposed increased rates for these towns, and have therefore failed to meet the burden of proof imposed upon them by the statute. When first put into common point territory the traffic of these communities was substantially less in volume than at this time. They contend, therefore, that if they were then entitled to common point rates they are much more entitled to them now. They also call attention to the fact that they were voluntarily put in common point territory by the carriers, and that their business had been adjusted to that rate basis. They regard it as an especial hardship now to have higher rates added to the burdens that the successive droughts have put upon them. Moreover, it appears that in some cases the short-line mileage is less now than when they were first put into common point territory. The short-line distance from Kansas City to San Angelo, for example, was then 857 miles. It is now 732 miles. From St. Louis the short-line distance was 1,059 miles. It is now only 940 miles. There is another fact upon which some stress is laid: Most of these towns have contributed to the new construction of the carriers, and in addition have subscribed for substantial amounts of bonds. Ballinger paid $80,000 to the Abilene & Southern; Brady gave $45,000 in cash to the Santa Fe, and in addition donated to it its entire right of way through the county and town and also its station grounds, at an additional expense of $45,000. San Angelo contributed to the Kansas City, Mexico & Orient $100,000 in money; it also donated its right of way through the county and bought $300,000 of its bonds. When the Santa Fe built its line from San Angelo to Sterling City in 1910, San Angelo donated the right of way and $40,000 in cash. The droughts have interfered with the payment of some of these amounts; in other cases the carriers have extended the notes, and in some instances have canceled the pledges. It is but proper to state these facts, although we have attached no importance to them in reaching the conclusion that the plan proposed by the respondents, of putting these towns back into differential territory, has not been justified of record. We find from the evidence adduced of record that the rates proposed by the respondents on the traffic of the communities in question are excessive and unreasonable, and that any rates upon such traffic for the future in excess of the rates on the traffic of adjacent points in the common point territory of Texas will also be unduly discriminatory.

The common point territory is perhaps unduly large and we have so intimated on various occasions. Its extension has not been favored by this Commission. Nevertheless when the southwestern lines prepare to narrow its boundaries they must do so in fair regard to the rights of the communities which they propose to exclude, in their relation to the communities which they propose to retain within the favored area. They have failed to do this in these tariffs. They have simply attempted to keep Amarillo out of common point territory by excluding its immediate competitors, overlooking the fact that these competitors of Amarillo have rights growing out of their relation with other communities that are still to remain in common point territory. The difficulty here is that the respondent lines have not gone far enough; they have made no effort to reform the boundaries of the common point territory on proper and consistent grounds but only an effort so to reform it as to keep Amarillo out.

The intervention of Amarillo herein asking that it be given common point rates is the real issue before us. The tariffs by which it is proposed to exclude certain competing towns from common point territory were filed by the southwestern lines simply in anticipation of a demand on the part of Amarillo for common point rates. The same relief was demanded by Amarillo in 1906 in *Nobles Bros. Grocer Co.* v. *F. W. & D. C. Ry. Co.*, 12 I. C. C., 242; and a proper understanding of the present situation requires a brief reference to the conditions then existing.

At that time the rails of the Santa Fe and of the Texas & Pacific in this part of Texas were substantially 250 miles apart; between Amarillo on the Santa Fe and Sweetwater on the Texas & Pacific was a vast stretch of country without a railroad and devoted almost exclusively to grazing. There were a few small settlements but no town of importance. On this record it is shown that there were no wholesale houses at Sweetwater until after our decision in that case, and only two jobbing houses at Big Springs. There was no town of commercial importance on the Texas & Pacific, and the wagon roads, leading from Amarillo into this country to the south, were substantially better than the country roads extending northward from points on the Texas & Pacific. The result of these conditions was that the merchants of Amarillo with their wagons were early in control of the jobbing business throughout this area. In consequence Amarillo's population rapidly increased, numerous jobbing houses were established there, and in 1906 we were asked in the case cited to extend the limits of common point territory by including Amarillo within it. We denied relief, but because of its proximity to Kansas City we held that Amarillo ought to have the so-called burnt district rates.

Even while that case was pending before us the relation of Amarillo to the general situation had begun to change. The Pecos & North Texas, now a branch of the Santa Fe, was building southward from Amarillo in the direction of Sweetwater; and shortly after our decision was announced that line was operating trains into Plainview, 74 miles south of Amarillo. It reached Lublock, 121 miles south of Amarillo, at the close of the year 1909, and entered Sweetwater in July, 1911. As construction progressed settlers came into the country in large numbers, ranches were broken up into farms, and agriculture took the place of cattle grazing as the principal occupation in the country districts. In the meanwhile Sweetwater has grown from a hamlet of 1,000 persons to a thriving town with a population of 5,000 inhabitants. Jobbing houses have been established there, and they reach out into the territory to the north as keen rivals of the merchants of Amarillo. At this time it in fact appears that Sweetwater is the most active competitor of Amarillo in the country that lies between them. Sweetwater has an advantage over Abilene and Big Springs in that it has a direct route, over one line only, into this territory to the north, while the route from the other two points is indirect and involves a two-line haul; under the state tariffs their distributing rates are therefore higher. The most important factor in the general situation, however, is that Sweetwater also has an advantage over Amarillo in that it is within the common point territory while Amarillo is in differential territory. Amarillo's rates are higher, although its haul is shorter. The indication of record is that a large part of the merchandise distributed in this extensive territory between Amarillo on the north and Sweetwater on the south moves over the Santa Fe rails through Amarillo. The Amarillo rates being higher than those of Sweetwater and therefore in conflict with the fourth section, although protected for the present by fourth-section applications.

These very material changes in conditions at Amarillo and in its relation to the surrounding territory prepared the carriers for the demand made upon them by the merchants of Amarillo, soon after our decision in the case last cited, for an entire readjustment of the rate situation. There can be no doubt at all from the record that the southwestern lines serving Amarillo felt that there was some justice in its demands. It is not necessary, however, to recount the history of the negotiations that followed. They were somewhat protracted, but finally reached a point where both sides were ready to make concessions. Growing out of the negotiation came a suggestion by the carriers that if the commercial interests of Amarillo would select a list of the commodities in which they were most interested the carriers would endeavor to establish rates upon them on a parity with the common point rates. It should be borne in mind that the jobbers of Amarillo were not contending that their rates were unreasonable, but only that they were discriminatory as compared with the rates enjoyed by Quanah, Sweetwater, and other points in common point territory. The merchants therefore presented such a list of commodities, and we think it fairly established by the record that there was practically an understanding that, on these commodities, rates would be fixed on a parity with common point rates. This plan, however, was never made effective.

Although there are some indications that the severe droughts of the last five years retarded the development of Amarillo as they have retarded the development of the surrounding country, nevertheless during the last 10 years its population has increased from 1,400 to 14,000. It is one of 11 first-class post-offices in the state of Texas; it has five banks, with aggregate deposits in November, 1912, of over $3,000,000; it is reached by four lines of railroad, the Rock Island, the Fort Worth & Denver City, the Southern Kansas of Texas, and the Pecos & North Texas, the last two being now in the Santa Fe system. It is a large jobbing center, distributing in less-than-carload shipments traffic that comes inbound in carload lots. There are five or six wholesale groceries there, one of them doing a business of over $1,000,000 a year. One hardware firm has a business approximating $425,000 a year. In addition there are wholesale dealers in dry goods, fruits, bicycles, agricultural implements, and other substantial articles of commerce. It is a common point with respect to state traffic and has been since 1905; it therefore enjoys common point rates from Galveston and other Texas ports. A hardware merchant testified that 40 per cent of his shipments came through the gulf ports. It takes burnt-district rates along with Sweetwater and Quanah. But on traffic from St. Louis and defined territories it takes a differential over common point rates, to its substantial disadvantage as a jobbing point.

The merchants and shippers of Amarillo have presented their case with great earnestness and in the confident belief that the relief prayed must necessarily be granted on the showing made. On the other hand, the defense offered by the respondents is directed largely to the consequences of such a step rather than to the merits of the demand. Moreover, although in their conferences and correspondence with the representatives of Amarillo the southwestern lines have shown a clear appreciation of the changed conditions above described and of the necessity of giving Amarillo some relief, nevertheless they have hesitated to make it a common point, not because of the direct effect of such a readjustment of rates upon their revenues but rather because of its indirect effect. They point out that the present area of the common point territory is larger than any state in the Union except Colorado, Montana, and New Mexico, and embraces a large part of the population and area of the state. The fear expressed by the carriers is that, if Amarillo is given common point rates, the result will be finally to extend such rates to the entire state. Dalhart, for example, on the Rock Island, 82 miles northwest of Amarillo, has always had the same rates as Amarillo; and in *Roswell Commercial Club* v. *A. T. & S. F. Ry. Co.*, 12 I. C. C., 339, as hereinafter stated, we fixed a relation of rates between Amarillo and Roswell; lower rates to Roswell would therefore follow a lowering of the rates to Amarillo. It is contended also that towns on the Rock Island between Amarillo and Texola, and on the Fort Worth & Denver City between Quanah and Amarillo, would have to be put in common point territory; and that points westward and southward, now taking differentials grading up from Amarillo, would require revised rates. The estimated loss for the past year, of the Southern Kansas of Texas and the Pecos & Northern, on the basis of all these rate revisions that the carriers assert would necessarily follow the granting of common point rates to Amarillo, was $25,517.76.

After a careful examination of the record we are not prepared fully to grant the prayer of the intervening petition of Amarillo. We have said that the common point territory of Texas has been enlarged from time to time, but has never been restricted. The statement is not altogether accurate. As a matter of fact an effort to force a reduction in its divisions caused the Fort Worth & Denver City to make certain arrangements with its connections that finally resulted in extending common point rates to Amarillo. This took place in November, 1891, and Amarillo continued to have the benefit of a rate parity on interstate traffic with towns in common point territory until June 10, 1895, a period of nearly four years. But this occurred many years ago and the conditions that brought it about were special in character. It is an incident in the rate history of Amarillo to which we can attach little importance now. The rights of Amarillo must be determined in the light of present conditions. Viewed from that standpoint there can be no doubt that we would not hesitate on this record to put Amarillo on a parity with Quanah, for example, on traffic moving from such a distance as St. Louis and the defined territories, if those two points could be considered by themselves and wholly apart from other points in Texas. But the rights of Amarillo can not be considered without giving some heed to the conditions that surround it. Quanah is in the common point territory, an already unusually extensive rate group which on strong grounds we have been and still are reluctant to enlarge. Such rate structures must have boundaries somewhere. Their limits must be prescribed and definitely located; and wherever the line may be drawn the point next beyond it is necessarily on a higher rate level. In some cases the increase is harshly abrupt. This is the plight of Amarillo. But now to put it in the favored territory, not improbably would soon result in making the common point area coterminous with the boundary lines of the state. This we think should be avoided and we are disinclined to take any step tending toward such a result. On the contrary there are substantial reasons, although not developed on this record, for thinking that the present common point territory, so far from being enlarged, could well be broken up into several different zones or groups, and this some day may be found to be necessary.

Nevertheless we think on this record that Amarillo is entitled to some relief. Although located well to the north in that part of the state commonly called the Panhandle, it is a gateway through which flows a growing volume of traffic into Sweetwater and other jobbing points in the common point area; and apparently it is the route over which a large part of the traffic now moves when destined to the territory intervening between Amarillo and Sweetwater. All these and other facts of record, as well as the principle involved in the fourth section, lend no small force to Amarillo's contentions. But in view of the far-reaching consequences of an order putting it in common point territory we are not prepared to take that course. As we have just stated it is entitled on the record to some relief; this is clearly demonstrated. But substantial justice will be done, we think, by requiring the southwestern lines to carry out the suggestion, at one time practically agreed upon, of giving to Amarillo rates upon certain commodities on a parity with common point rates; to that extent violations of the fourth section will be avoided. We shall expect the respondents to arrange to do this promptly without an order; but we shall reserve the record for such further consideration as the attitude of the carriers with respect to this suggestion may seem to make necessary.

RAILROAD COMMISSION OF NEVADA
v.
SOUTHERN PACIFIC COMPANY

19 I. C. C. 238 (1910)

Lane, *Commissioner:*

The highest main-line rates to be found in the United States are those from eastern points to stations in Nevada. For carrying a carload of first class traffic containing 20,000 pounds from Omaha to Reno the Union Pacific-Southern Pacific line charges $858. If a like carload is carried 154 miles further, to Sacramento, the charge is but $600. The first class rate to the more distant point, Sacramento, is $3 per 100 pounds, and to the nearer point, Reno, $4.29 per 100 pounds. If a like carload of freight originates at Denver, 500 miles west of Omaha, the same rates to Reno and Sacramento apply; and if the freight originates at Boston, 1,700 miles east of Omaha, the rates are the same. This interesting rate condition arises out of two simple facts: (1) The whole of the United States from Colorado common points to the Atlantic seaboard, barring a few of the southeastern states, is one wide group or zone from which practically uniform rates to the Pacific coast water points are made, and (2) the rates to Reno are based upon these blanket rates to coast cities, and amount to the sum of the rates to the coast plus the local rates back to point of destination.

This great zone, extending from the Rocky Mountains to the Atlantic, a distance of over 2,000 miles, from which practically uniform rates are made to Pacific coast terminal cities, is probably without parallel in the railroad world, excepting for a similar eastward blanket extended to Pacific coast producing points. The zone in which the same rates apply on California citrus fruits, for instance, extends from Salt Lake City on the west to Portland, Me. It is manifest that the transcontinental railroads have made a near approximation to the postage-stamp system of rate making. Their policy has been to give to all eastern producing markets an opportunity to sell to the terminal cities upon a parity as to transportation charges and to give to Pacific coast producing points access to all eastern markets upon a like basis. To the great basin lying between the Rocky Mountains and the Sierra Nevadas the carriers have in a limited degree extended this same policy by making rates into Nevada based on the coast cities, and thus, the carriers say, they give to this territory the advantage of its proximity to the Pacific seaboard; that the rates to the latter are made low because of water competition between the Atlantic and Pacific ports — lower than would be justified were Sacramento and San Francisco not upon the water — and that Nevada rates would be still higher but for its nearness to the Pacific coast.

The state of Nevada, through its railroad commission, now comes asking that Nevada points be given the same rates as are now given to Pacific coast terminals, urging that these coast rates are not unreasonably low in themselves, and are not the product of any real water competition.

The complaint originally filed in this case made the Southern Pacific the sole defendant; the reasonableness of the rates from the east to Nevada were not attacked, excepting in so far as they are based on the rates to further western points, and include a back-haul charge. As the complaint then stood the petition was that this Commission should hold it to be unreasonable for the Southern Pacific, delivering freight at Reno and other points in Nevada, to charge for a back-haul which is not in fact given, and that we should adjudge the rates to Sacramento to be unreasonable as applied to the intermediate points. Later the complaint was amended by adding carriers east of Ogden forming a single through route from the Atlantic coast. So that the petition of Nevada now is that from all points upon this through route reasonable rates shall be fixed which shall not exceed those now applicable on shipments from such points to the more distant coast terminals. It is suggested by the complainant that we bring in other carriers as defendants, so that the entire eastern territory may be covered by our order. This we think unnecessary, assuming, as we do, that the conclusions here reached as to a through route from the east to the west will be adopted and established by other lines similarly situated.

CONSTRUCTION OF NEVADA RATES.

To reach a clear understanding of the basis upon which Nevada rates in general are now fixed, it is necessary to bear primarily in mind the fact before referred to, that the carriers of the country have united in establishing a zone 2,000 miles in width from which rates are practically uniform to what are known as "coast terminals." There are 152 of these coast terminals, 97 of which are in California. They are points more or less arbitrarily established by the carriers, but which are either upon inlets from the ocean or rivers running to such inlets, or are but slightly removed from such water points. The most prominent coast terminals are Seattle, Tacoma, Portland, Sacramento, San Jose, Stockton, Oakland, San Francisco, Los Angeles, and San Diego. To these coast terminals are extended what are known as "terminal rates" on westbound transcontinental traffic. These rates apply either from all of eastern defined territory or from separate groups therein. The shaded portion of the accompanying map indicates eastern defined territory and the groups into which it is divided. These groups are lettered from A to J. A is limited to New York City piers, and has to do only with shipments by steamship via Gulf ports; B covers New England territory; C, New York territory and the middle states, with New York City as the principal point; D, Chicago and adjacent territory; E, the Mississippi River, with St. Louis as the principal city; F, the Missouri River; G, Kansas; H, Oklahoma; I, Texas; and J, Colorado, with Denver as its central point.

Class rates. — Coming, then, to the construction of the Nevada class rates, we find that the carriers have employed three methods of construction during the past two years. Prior to January 1, 1909, there existed a body of what were known as intermediate class rates to Reno from certain designated eastern points. These rates were, on first class —

From Chicago-Milwaukee common points	$3.90
From Mississippi River common points	3.70
From Missouri River common points	3.50
From Colorado common points	3.00

An alternative clause gave Reno the right to the combination rate based on Sacramento whenever that should be lower. This indefinite method of stating rates the Commission condemned in a general ruling. The tariffs were then changed so as to cancel the alternative clause and the intermediate class rates and thus to make all Nevada rates base on Sacramento. This was the

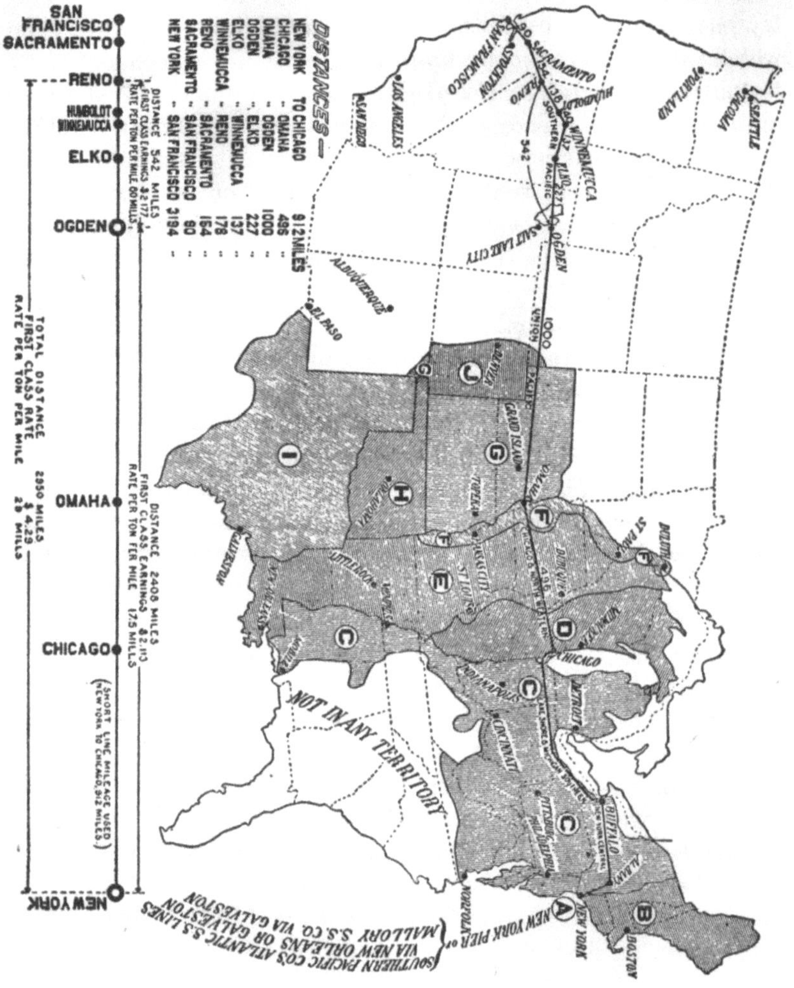

situation when the case was heard. Later, however, in June of last year, a third plan was adopted, and that now obtains, viz., to divide Nevada into two zones with Humboldt as the dividing point. Points west of Humboldt take the Sacramento combination. Points east of Humboldt take generally the Ogden combination. It is unnecessary herein to trace the history and the effect of these various changes in the method of rate basing. We shall deal with the rates to all Nevada points as joint rates. And inasmuch as rates on all ten classes were quoted by the carriers' tariffs from all eastern defined territory to coast terminals and therefore by combination to interior points, at the time when this proceeding was brought, we shall consider that our jurisdiction extends to the installation of such rates to all of such territory.

To ascertain the rate upon a shipment from New York to Reno one looks in vain for any one tariff in which such rate is to be found. By examination of the tariff of the Transcontinental Freight Bureau, to which the Southern Pacific Company is a party, this note is discovered:

Rates to intermediate points.

"When no specific rate is named to an intermediate point shown in Transcontinental Freight Bureau Circular No. 16–C (I. C. C. No. 864), supplements thereto, or reissues thereof, rate to such an intermediate point will be made by adding to the rate shown to the point designated herein as "Terminal," which is nearest destination of shipment, the local rate from nearest terminal point to destination."

Turning to Transcontinental Freight Bureau Circular No. 16–C (the issue at the date at which this complaint was brought), we find Reno named as an intermediate point, and that the nearest terminal to Reno is Sacramento, 154 miles west of Reno. We find, then, by returning to the Transcontinental Freight Bureau west bound tariff, the rate applicable upon the shipment to Sacramento. Then, having ascertained this from a tariff to which all of the carriers from New York to Sacramento are parties, we must next find the local rate from Sacramento to the destination of the freight, which is east of Sacramento. This local rate, Sacramento to Reno, we find in a tariff to which the Southern Pacific Company alone is a party. Thus we have, through a maze of tariffs, at length discovered the rate from New York to Reno, which is made up of a joint through rate to Sacramento and a local rate of the Southern Pacific Company alone from Sacramento back to Reno.

The all-rail class rates, in cents, per 100 pounds from eastern defined territory to coast terminals were, when this case was brought, as follows:

	Class									
	1	2	3	4	5	A	B	C	D	E
Groups B, C, D, E, F, G, H, and I...	$3.00	$2.60	$2.20	$1.90	$1.65	$1.60	$1.25	$1.00	$1.00	$0.95
Group J..........	3.00	2.60	2.00	1.75	1.60	1.40	1.20	.95	.85	.80

An examination of present tariffs will show that from New England and New York territories (Group B and C) no class rates below fourth class are now extended. Prior to January 1, 1909, however, and at the time this complaint was brought, rates were given for the full 10 classes from these groups, and such rates upon the $3 scale are now given to coast terminals from Group A, the freight being carried from the New York City piers to New Orleans and Galveston by ocean carriers and thence by rail. It will also be seen that from Group J slightly lower rates are made on all classes below second class than are made from other groups. With these exceptions, however, the rates are uniform throughout the whole eastern defined territory as to classified freight.

The local rates on classes from Sacramento to Reno are as follows:

Class........	1	2	3	4	5	A	B	C	D	E
Rate........	129	112	102	87	78	78	24	23.5	25.5	25.5

The result of the combination on Sacramento is therefore to produce the following rates to Reno:

From Groups B, C, D, E, F,, G, H, and I:

Class........	1	2	3	4	5	A	B	C	D	E
Rate........	429	373	322	277	243	238	159	133½	125½	120½

From Group J:

Class........	1	2	3	4	5	A	B	C	D	E
Rate........	429	373	302	262	238	218	154	128½	110½	105½

Rates to points east of Humboldt, such as Winnemucca and Elko, under the present method of making rates on the Ogden combination, vary as the rate from point of origin to Ogden.

The effect of this change in method of making rates may be illustrated briefly by the statement that the first class rate to Reno from Chicago prior to January 1, 1909, was $3.90, whereas it is now $4.29; from Missouri River $3.50, and now $4.29. To Elko, on the other hand, the first class rate from Chicago is now $4.27, as against a previous rate of $4.72½, when the rate based on Sacramento.

For many years the class rates to interior points, such as Reno, were no higher than to the terminals. On April 11, 1893, the practice of maintaining lower terminal rates was instituted. The first line of figures in the table below shows the Reno rates when this case was brought; the second line, the rates in 1892; and the third line, the difference, or the amount by which the rates have been increased.

To Reno from —	Class									
	1	2	3	4	5	A	B	C	D	E
Missouri River common points	429	373	322	277	243	238	159	133½	125½	120½
1892 rates	350	300	250	200	175	175	155	125	110	100
Difference	79	73	72	77	68	63	4	8½	15½	20½
Mississippi River common points	429	373	322	277	243	238	159	133½	125½	120½
1892 rates	370	320	260	205	180	182	163	130	115	105
Difference	59	53	62	72	63	56	...	3½	10½	15½
Chicago common points	429	373	322	277	243	238	159	133½	125½	120½
1892 rates	390	340	270	210	185	190	170	135	120	110
Difference	39	33	52	67	58	48	...	....	5½	10½

Commodity rates. — While there are many hundred commodity rates extended to coast terminals, there are but few given to intermediate points. On the following articles the commodity rates are the same to Utah and Nevada points as to Pacific coast terminals from Group D, E, F, G, H, I, and J of eastern defined territory, which include all points from Chicago west:

Apples; bananas; beer, in wood; bones; broom corn; butter, butterine, oleomargarine, eggs, cheese, and dressed poultry; cars, street; barley, corn, rye, oats, and speltz, c. l. and l. c. l.; bran and shorts, c. l. and l. c. l.; brewer's grits, brewer's meal, corn meal, corn chop or chop feed, chopped corn, cracked corn, and hominy; buckwheat, c. l. and l. c. l.; wheat, c. l. and l. c. l.; cooperage, cranberries; fertilizers, n. o. s.; household goods, c. l. and l. c. l.; live stock; machinery, mining; mineral-water bottles, returning; oil cake and oil-cake meal; onions; onion sets, l. c. l.; packing-house products; pineapples; plaster, building; poultry, alive; railway equipment; and staves and headings.

As to all but two or three of these commodities, the rates are the same to Reno as to Sacramento from Chicago. That is to say, the blanket rate made from all eastern defined territory to coast terminals on these commodities is applied from Chicago to Reno. There are a few other commodities upon which commodity rates are given to Reno which are somewhat higher than the rates from Chicago to Sacramento, viz., automobiles, buggies, carriages, wagons, vehicles, and coal, coke, and guano from certain far western points. From an examination of the tariffs it appears that the transcontinental commodity rates — rates from eastern defined territory to the coast terminals — are at the present time higher than they were ten years ago by a very considerable percentage and this regardless of the fact that the base of supplies has been constantly moving westward, thereby narrowing the distance between point of production and consumption.

VOLUME OF NEVADA TRAFFIC.

Nevada is colloquially known as the "Sage Brush State," and from the car window it presents the spectacle of an almost uninterrupted waste. Railroad men speak of it as a "bridge"— unproductive territory across which freight must be carried to reach points of consumption. The figures of the Southern Pacific demonstrate, however, that while Nevada traffic may at one time have been negligible such is no longer the case.

Some time before this proceeding was brought the Southern Pacific Company, which is the lessee of the Central Pacific running from Ogden west into California, brought suit in the United States circuit court for the district of Nevada attacking certain rate schedules upon state traffic established by the state commission. In support of its case the Southern Pacific Company filed an affidavit made by Mr. C. B. Seger, auditor of the Southern Pacific Company, showing the earnings of the Central Pacific on business wholly within the state, on business passing through the state, on business originating in and passing out of the state, and on business originating outside and having its destination in the state, for the fiscal year ending June 30, 1907. Mr. Seger said by way of explaining his figures:

"The freight earnings accruing to and made by said Southern Pacific Company in Nevada, being the revenue itself, without reference to its disposition under any lease, agreement, or otherwise, are derived for the said fiscal year 1907 from through and local business, understanding by local business such as is strictly intrastate in character, picked up and laid down within the limits of the state of Nevada, and understanding by through business such as is interstate in character. Further differentiating, said interstate business consists, first, of business originating outside and coming into the state; second, of business originating in and passing out of the state; and, third, of business originating outside the state, having destination beyond the state, and, in relation to the state itself, simply passing through the state. The freight earnings for said fiscal year, and pertaining to the said business as above classified, are set forth under the appropriate heads, and are, in fact, as follows:"

	Revenue	Percentage of total
Intrastate	$159,791.40	0.02
Originating outside and coming into the state	1,683,687.69	.20
Originating in and passing out of the state	831,802.96	.10
	2,675,282.05	.32
Passing through the state	5,578,282.28	.68
Sum total	8,253,564.33	1.00

Surprising as these figures are they apparently do not fully set forth the extent of Nevada business at this time, as is shown by an exhibit filed by the Southern Pacific Company in the present case, giving the business west of Ogden for the single month of February, 1909, which may be epitomized thus:

	Revenue	Percentage of total	Tonnage	Percentage of total
Intrastate	$29,001.00	0.03	4,715	0.04
Into and out of Nevada and Utah west of Utah	314,379.65	.38	64,367	.50
	343,380.65	.41	69,182	.54
Passing through the state	495,128.37	.59	60,271	.46
Total for month of February, 1909	838,509.02	1.00	130,453	1.00

Another most interesting showing is made by the Seger affidavit as to passenger business on the Southern Pacific in the state of Nevada for the year 1907, the figures given being these:

	Revenue	Percentage		
Intrastate	$286,235.65		10	
Originating outside and coming into the state	357,511.55	9		
Originating in and passing out of the state	267,582.85	13		
			22	
				32
Passing through the state	1,962,915.33			68
Sum total	2,874,245.38			100

The statement for the month of February, 1909, referred to above, sets forth very clearly not only the volume of business going into and out of Nevada and the earnings of the Southern Pacific thereon, but also gives a specific analysis of the sources of the traffic, showing the volume which comes into Nevada from the east and that which comes from California. Under "Question 2" below will be found a statement of the freight received at Nevada and Utah points from points west of Calvada, which is a station directly on the California-Nevada state line. This table, however, should not mislead; a considerable percentage of the traffic from California is traffic of eastern origin reshipped from California to Nevada. The table also includes coal and other commodities of very large tonnage (approximately one-half of the total in weight) coming from points west of eastern defined territory.

Territorial movement	Total	
	Tons	Southern Pacific earnings
Gross total tonnage and earnings of the Southern Pacific Co. for the month of February, 1909...	913,302	$3,422,529.00
Question No. 1		
Freight via Ogden to California................	37,886	320,220.55
Freight via Ogden from California..............	22,385	174,907.82
	60,271	495,128.37
Question No. 2		
Freight via Ogden to points in Nevada and Utah..	17,485	66,284.88
Freight received at Nevada and Utah points from points west of Calvada.....................	16,823	144,965.00
Freight via Ogden from points in Nevada and Utah	18,381	33,462.77
Freight forwarded from points in Nevada and Utah to points west of Calvada..................	11,678	69,667.00
	64,367	314,379.65
Question No. 3A		
Freight received in California, San Francisco and north, from all points in California, including interchange with connecting lines in California....	189,827	365,168.00
Question No. 3B		
Freight picked up and laid down in Nevada and Utah and freight moving between Nevada and Utah —		
Nevada to Nevada.......................	4,046	21,839.00
Utah to Utah...........................	144	948.00
Utah to Nevada.........................	499	5,122.00
Nevada to Utah.........................	26	1,092.00
	4,715	29,001.00

There was a time, doubtless, when Nevada traffic, save to the mines on its westernmost border, was but trifling. At present, however, it has a traffic, both freight and passenger, which is far too considerable to be overlooked under the rule *de minimis.* And it is to be remembered that the figures given apply to but one road, whereas a second is in operation across the state to the south, and a third is beginning operations on the north.

SOURCES OF EASTERN TRAFFIC.

It is interesting in this connection to regard the point of origin of this eastern freight. The railroad commission of Nevada had access to the billing of all shipments reaching Reno, and from these compiled a series of statements which appear to show that the great body of Nevada traffic which comes directly from the east via Ogden originates west of the Indiana-Illinois state line.

From one exhibit it appears that of the 1,063,687 pounds of less-than-carload shipments originating in eastern defined territory and delivered at Reno during the months of January, February, March, and April, 1908, only 10 per cent originated at the Atlantic coast cities of New York, Boston, and Philadelphia, and only 25 per cent in Connecticut, District of Columbia, Maine, Maryland, Massachusetts, New Jersey, New York, Pennsylvania, and Virginia. This exhibit further shows that on the traffic moved the charges were $32,719.30; that if terminal rates had been applied charges would have been $21,956.24; and that the difference is $10,748.07. In other words, the charges on these shipments to Reno were 48.3 per cent higher than would have been the charges on the same shipments had they been carried over the mountains to Sacramento.

Another exhibit shows that of 21,000,000 pounds of carload freight, earning $278,000, moved from eastern defined territory into Reno, 9,500,000 pounds, earning $120,000, moved in at rates no higher than terminals. It further shows that only 4,500,000 pounds of the 21,000,000 originated east of Chicago. This exhibit shows, aside from the products carried to Reno at terminal rates, that the charges were, for the year 1908, $157,824.94; that the terminal charge would have been $99,679.90; and the difference, $58,524.40. In other words, the charges on carload shipments to Reno were 59 per cent higher than the charges on the same shipments would have been had they been carried to Sacramento.

Commissioner Thurtell estimated from the figures at his hand that the total receipts under present rates upon business brought into Reno via Ogden for the year 1908 amounted to $454,343.69 and under terminal rates the revenue would have been $363,865.23, a reduction of $90,478.46. The statement also shows that the revenue to the Southern Pacific from this business was $268,516.40 and would have been under terminal rates $178,037.94, a reduction of $90,478.46, or about 33 per cent. Expressed in revenue the Southern Pacific on the haul from Ogden to Reno earned $11.51 per ton, while if terminal rates had been charged its earnings would have been $7.63 per ton.

On the whole, the figures given in this case, which are the most authoritative thus far presented to the Commission with reference to the sources of westbound transcontinental traffic, indicate that less than 25 per cent of the traffic into Reno from the east originates east of Chicago, while 75 per cent originates between Chicago and Denver. In other words, the needs of the people on the west coast may be and are in great part supplied from sources nearer home than the Atlantic seaboard.

The manufacturing center of the country has moved westward and rates from the Atlantic seaboard that were once necessary are now almost unused. It may be historically the fact, as the carriers assert, that the transcontinental blanket rates given to the Pacific coast cities were put in to meet water competition from the Atlantic coast points, and that these rates were extended westward from the Atlantic as matter of grace to western manufacturers and producers; to-day, however, it might well be said that this blanket is extended not westward, but eastward, so as to give the eastern manufacturer or jobber some opportunity to reach the far western markets.

WATER COMPETITION.

As we have seen, the rates are higher on almost all commodities from eastern producing points to Reno than on these same commodities to Sacramento, the more distant point. Without explanation this constitutes a violation of the long-and-short-haul clause of the act. The carriers justify the lower rates to the more distant point upon the ground of water competition. They say that the rates charged to Reno and other Nevada cities are reasonable in themselves measured by the cost of the service to the carrier or the value of the service to the shipper, and that rates to the coast cities measured by these standards are too low to be considered reasonable and would not be in effect but for the force of water competition. The Nevada commission, on the other hand, contends that while some commerce does move from the Atlantic seaboard by water, the volume is so small that it is not influential in determining the present rate to the coast terminals; that the coast rate itself is reasonable, and therefore that the application of a higher rate to an intermediate point can not be justified. The making of higher intermediate rates, they strongly urge, is a matter of railway policy and not of railway necessity, in that the railways wish to develop the coast cities as jobbing centers to the exclusion of interior points; that the revenues of the carriers would not be seriously impaired were this policy abrogated and as low rates given to the intermountain country as are now extended to the coast cities.

It is no reflection upon the traffic manager of a railroad to say that he bases his rates upon some line of policy. He deals directly, and in most cases exclusively, with the producer or the jobber. His concern is to keep these patrons satisfied and at the same time bring to his railroad the greatest possible revenue. This is what he means by saying that he charges what the traffic will bear. He regards as reasonable whatever rate will make for the best interest of his road, and in determining this he adopts a line of policy which affects either favorably or unfavorably the industrial growth of the communities which the carrier serves. The restrictions of the act to regulate commerce are governmental limitations placed upon the unlimited and arbitrary discretion of traffic officials. While the latter may adopt policies which they regard as most favorable to their roads, such policies must be restricted by the inhibitions of the law which this Commission must enforce. The policy of making Reno rates base upon those extended to the more distant point may not be justified upon the ground that Reno traffic will bear that imposition, but may be justified by conditions obtaining at the more distant point which the carrier may meet without offense to any provision of the act.

And this brings directly to our consideration the question of water competition at Sacramento and other coast terminals. It is, of course, a physical fact that commerce may be carried by water from the eastern seaboard to the Pacific coast. It is admitted by all, and substantiated by the evidence in this case, that some commerce does actually so move. An estimate has been made by complainant that approximately 3,000,000 tons of transcontinental traffic reaches the coast terminals during each year by rail, while the highest figure given as the volume of traffic reaching those points by water from the eastern seaboard is under 10 per cent of the rail movement. The fact, however, that it moves in large or small quantities does not of itself sustain the contention that the present rates from eastern defined territory to coast terminals are so low as not to make a reasonable return to the carrier for the service performed. A movement of traffic may be affected by water competition at a more distant point and yet a rate made up of the combination of the rate by water plus the rate back be unreasonable and unjust. Nevada, Utah, Arizona, and Idaho are nearer to the Pacific coast than to the Atlantic, but this does not of itself justify charging them overland rail rates which will give them none of the advantages arising out of their shorter distance to an eastern base of supplies. Nor does it follow that a rate to a point on the seaboard is lower than would be justified if that point were not so situated. In short, it is not sufficient to state that the terminal points are situated on the water to excuse the imposition of higher rates at intermediate points.

There has been little difficulty experienced from time to time by the rail carriers in raising rates to the Pacific coast; the only live water competitor on the Pacific to-day is a line which bases its rates on the rail tariffs, and the rates of both the rail and the water lines change simultaneously. Ways can be found, and have been found, by which the presence of the ocean as a controlling, or even greatly meddlesome, factor in the fixing of railroad rates can be nullified. There is no doubt but that rail rates have been influenced at times to all the Pacific ports by water carriers, and of course there is the possibility that at any time this water competition may become seriously aggressive and potent. The United States is not a maritime nation at present, and her coast line on the Pacific side is served in great part by such water carriers as the railroads permit to live.

While, therefore, physical conditions at the coast are dissimilar to those at interior points the rates to the coast are not necessarily less than in fairness the traffic should carry. The water carriers between the Atlantic and the Pacific coasts at present charge rates from 25 to 40 per cent less than their railroad rivals. To get this business the water carrier at the eastern port reaches inland and absorbs a rail rate of 20 cents upon commodities which carry more than a 50-cent water rate to the Pacific coast. The American-Hawaiian Steamship Company then transports the freight by water to the Tehuantepec road, where it is transshipped across the Isthmus, and being loaded again is carried to a Pacific coast port and there reshipped either by rail or water to certain designated points of destination inland from the port. In such a movement there is involved a rail haul of 400 or 500 miles, at least six, and possibly more, separate handlings of each parcel of freight, and a haul by water of fully 5,000 miles. Freight moving via Panama is subject to even heavier conditions. It is insisted by the Nevada commission that water competition of this character is not sufficiently aggressive or formidable to compel the railroads to make any other rates to the coast terminals than those which from reasons of policy they are at present making. The suggestion is not without pertinence that if four different transportation services, three by rail and two by water, involving at least six handlings of the freight and a total haul of 5,500 miles, can be furnished profitably at from 60 to 75 per cent of the rail rate, the compensation to the rail carrier for an all-rail haul of 2,500 miles, with no handling and but two terminal charges, should produce ample revenue to the rail carrier.

There are many interesting developments in this and other transcontinental cases touching this matter of competition by water. For instance, the lowest rate does not in all cases apply to and from the seacoast points. There are many commodities upon which the rates from Chicago and Kansas City to Sacramento and San Francisco are less than they are from New York. And yet it is said to be the competition from New York that produces the low rate. In no case is the rail rate from New York less than is the rate from other portions of eastern defined territory, while of course in all cases New York is nearer the source of the competing force, the ocean. This is accounted for by the carriers on the ground that by taking the same, or a lower, rate from the interior points to the coast terminals the rail carrier avoids the longer rail haul, the points of origin and destination being nearer together. This is an application of what the carriers term " market competition," but it is not a strong argument to sustain the theory of water competition.

As usually applied by carriers market competition results in the hauling of commodities produced at places distant from the point of consumption to compete with the same commodities from points nearer to the point of consumption. In this case, however, market competition is said to be the controlling factor which justifies a rate from an interior point less distant from destination. Thus we have a $3 rate from New York to Sacramento to meet water competition, and a $3 rate from Kansas City to meet market competition. We also have a $4.29 rate from Kansas City and from New York, to Reno, as a reasonable rate because of water competition from New York to Sacramento.

We do not regard the divisions of rates as in any wise conclusive as to the reasonableness of rates between certain points, but such divisions are sometimes of significance. In the present case we find that if 100 pounds of freight is shipped from Boston, or New York, or Chicago, or St. Louis, or Omaha to Sacramento on the $3 rate, and another 100 pounds of the same kind of freight is shipped from the same points to Reno on the same day, the carriers east of Ogden receive precisely the same earnings upon both shipments; but the Southern Pacific, west of Ogden, receives far more upon the Reno shipment than on the Sacramento shipment. This is illustrated in the following table:

From —	To —	Rate	Earnings east of Ogden	Earnings of Southern Pacific Company (west of Ogden)
		Cents	*Cents*	*Cents*
Group B, Boston	Sacramento	300	211.3	88.7
	Reno	429	211.3	217.7
Group C, New York	Sacramento	300	211.3	88.7
	Reno	429	211.3	217.7
Group D, including Chicago, etc.	Sacramento	300	181.9	118.1
	Reno	429	181.0	248.0
Group E, including Mississippi River	Sacramento	300	174.5	125.5
	Reno	429	174.5	254.5
Group F, including Missouri River	Sacramento	300	159.3	140.7
	Reno	429	159.3	269.7

Neither at the hearings nor in the argument did the carriers east of Ogden contend that their divisions of these rates were unreasonable. The Southern Pacific, however, the carrier which makes the last 700 miles of a 3,100-mile haul, strenuously insists that its rates to the more distant points are compelled by water competition for the purpose of defending higher rates to intermediate points; while the carriers performing 2,400 miles of that service appear to regard the rate as entirely reasonable. The line from New York to Sacramento and Reno constitutes a through route and in law the carriers engaging therein constitute one line. If the Sacramento rate is less than a reasonable rate and the result of competition then it would seem fair to assume that all of the carriers engaging in the transportation so consider it and would accordingly demand a lesser division than the division they would be justified in requiring out of the higher rate to the intermediate point. The fact remains, however, that for the 2,400-mile haul from New York to Ogden the New York Central, the Lake Shore, the North Western, and the Union Pacific secure the same revenue out of the $3 rate to Sacramento that they do out of the $4.29 rate to Reno. This is graphically illustrated by the following diagram showing the division of the rate:

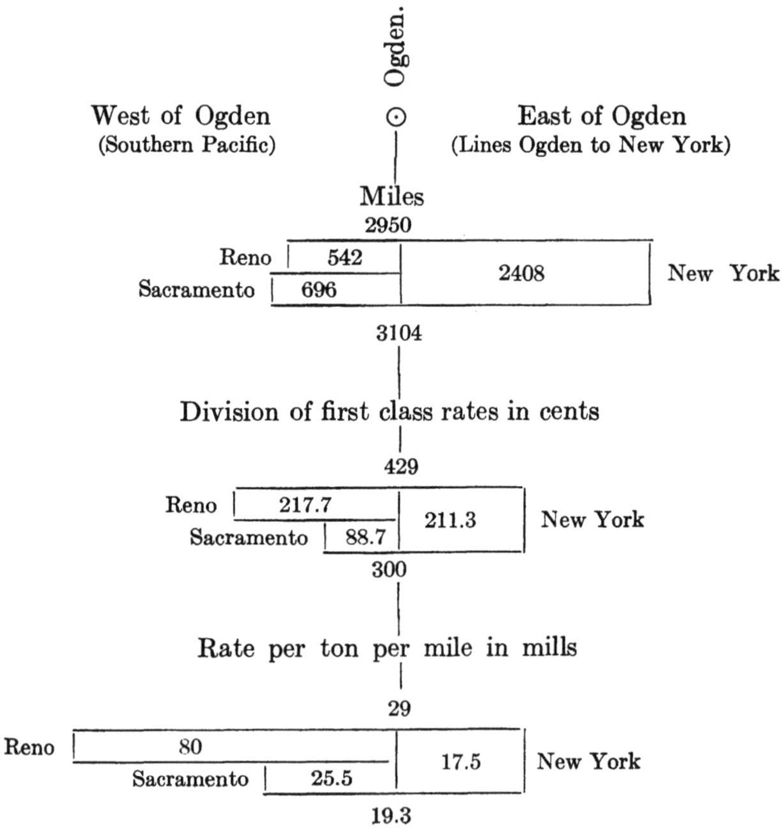

PRODUCTIVE FREIGHT TERRITORY.

We have gone extensively into an investigation of the conditions surrounding this traffic and in anywise governing the basis upon which the rates to Nevada from the east should be governed. What has been said herein gives little more than a suggestion of the extent of the inquiry which has been made. We have, for instance, had reports made upon the financial condition of the carriers involved, and their ability to meet any reduction which the Commission might direct without serious impairment of their revenues, an interesting fact in this connection being this: During the past two years the operating revenues of the Southern Pacific Company's Pacific system have increased $8,000,000 while its operating expenses have decreased $5,000,000, thus producing an increased operating income of over $12,000,000, or a net increase of about $2,000 per mile of road.

There appears in the record a compilation from the statistics of this Commisison for the years 1898–1907 in which it is shown that in these ten years the carriers in the Pacific coast territory doubled their freight tonnage, which rose from 18,000,000 to 35,000,000 tons; almost doubled their gross revenue; their receipts per mile increased over 70 per cent; their receipts per ton per mile increased from 1.07 to 1.25, or about 20 per cent; while the relation of expenses to earnings remained practically constant at 62.50 per cent. These figures are for all the roads in the Pacific territory. But if we take the Central Pacific alone we find it third in the list of Pacific coast roads in tons carried and the highest of all in freight earnings per mile ($13,453 per mile in 1907). While it is one of three railroads in the west carrying over a million tons of freight per mile of road — the average for the United States — the earnings of the Central Pacific per mile are 65 per cent greater than the average for the United States and 100 per cent greater than the average of the roads west of Chicago.

CONCLUSIONS.

The time has come, in our opinion, when the carriers west of the Rocky Mountains must treat the intermountain country upon a different basis from that which has hitherto obtained.

Nevada asks that she be given rates as low as those given to Sacramento. The full extent of this petition can not be granted. In making rates to Reno from a territory broader than the whole of continental Europe we have necessarily given consideration to existing rates to other intermediate points and to points upon the Pacific.

We are of opinion that the class rates to Reno, Winnemucca, and Elko, and other points in Nevada upon the main line of the Southern Pacific Company, from stations on the lines of the defendants between New York and Denver and other Colorado common points are unreasonable and unjust and that for the future no higher rates than those set forth below should be charged to Reno and points east thereof to, but not including, Winnemucca:

From —	Class									
	1	2	3	4	5	A	B	C	D	E
Denver and other points in Group J *a*	$2.10	$1.82	$1.54	$1.33	$1.12	$1.12	$0.87	$0.70	$0.66	$0.60
Grand Island and other points in Group G *a*	2.30	2.00	1.68	1.45	1.22	1.22	.96	.76	.73	.65
Omaha and other points in Group F *a*	2.50	2.17	1.83	1.58	1.33	1.33	1.04	.83	.79	.71
Clinton and other points in Group E *a*	2.80	2.42	2.03	1.71	1.43	1.46	1.14	.91	.86	.78
Chicago and other points in Group D *a*	2.90	2.51	2.09	1.75	1.47	1.50	1.18	.94	.89	.80
Toledo and other Cincinnati-Detroit common points *b*	3.05	2.63	2.19	1.81	1.52	1.56	1.23	.98	.92	.83
Buffalo and other Pittsburg-Buffalo common points *b*	3.20	2.76	2.29	1.87	1.57	1.62	1.28	1.03	.96	.86
New York and common points *b*	3.50	3.01	2.49	2.00	1.67	1.75	1.38	1.11	1.03	.93

a As designated in Transcontinental Freight Bureau Westbound Tariff 1-K, I. C. C. No. 920.
b As designated in Nor. Pac. No. 23500, I. C. C. No. 3295.

And that for the future no higher rates than those set forth below should be charged to Winnemucca and points east thereof to the Nevada-Utah state line:

From —	Class									
	1	2	3	4	5	A	B	C	D	E
Denver and other points in Group J *a*	$2.00	$1.72	$1.46	$1.26	$1.06	$1.06	$0.83	$0.67	$0.63	$0.57
Grand Island and other points in Group G *a*	2.19	1.90	1.60	1.38	1.16	1.16	.91	.72	.69	.62
Omaha and other points in Group F *a*	2.38	2.06	1.74	1.50	1.26	1.26	.99	.79	.75	.67
Clinton and other points in Group E *a*	2.66	2.30	1.93	1.62	1.36	1.39	1.08	.86	.82	.74
Chicago and other points in Group D *a*	2.75	2.38	1.99	1.66	1.40	1.43	1.07	.89	.85	.76
Toledo and other Cincinnati-Detroit common points *b*	2.90	2.50	2.08	1.72	1.44	1.48	1.17	.93	.87	.79
Buffalo and other Pittsburg-Buffalo common points *b*	3.04	2.62	2.18	1.78	1.49	1.44	1.22	.98	.91	.82
New York and common points *b*	3.33	2.86	2.37	1.90	1.59	1.66	1.31	1.05	.98	.88

a As designated in Transcontinental Freight Bureau Westbound Tariff 1–K, I. C. C. No. 920.
b As designated in Nor. Pac. No. 23500, I. C. C. No. 3295.

In directing the carriers to establish these class rates we have taken into consideration the fact that the general policy of the carriers is to make commodity rates somewhat lower than class rates on commodities, the movement of which is regarded as necessary to the development of mercantile interests and industries. There are at present, as we have seen, a considerable number of such commodity rates into Reno, but these are entirely insufficient to meet the needs of Nevada if she is to become in any way an independent business community. There is no foundation in the record in this case for the establishment of such commodity rates. The theory upon which the case was presented eliminated all other considerations excepting the claim that all rates extended to Sacramento were reasonable as to Reno and other Nevada points. The Nevada petition was tantamount to a request that under our legal authority to establish reasonable rates we should fix the same rate from Denver as from Boston. We do not so construe our authority as to permit this Commission to make rates upon such a basis. Without doubt the commodity rates made to the coast terminals are reasonable from a great portion of eastern defined territory, but a governmental authority may not exercise the latitude in fixing a rate blanket which the carriers themselves have here exercised.

In the *Spokane case,* 19 I. C. C. Rep. 162, some 600 commodity rates had been established voluntarily by the carriers, and the petition in that case was for the reduction of those rates to a reasonable figure. The carriers had made a special series of zones across the continent to meet the exigencies of the Spokane situation. In the case before us, however, no such favorable condition is presented. We have neither a schedule of commodity rates with which to deal as to which specific complaint is made, nor have the carriers so divided the continent into groups of originating territory, save in the sense that the transcontinental groups to the coast terminals, which are entirely different from those found in the *Spokane case, supra,* furnish a foundation for present combination rates to western Nevada.

In view of this situation we shall make no order as to commodity rates in this case at the present time, but shall direct the carriers to make a record of all shipments into Nevada from eastern defined territory during the months of July, August, and September, 1910, or during such other representative months as may be determined upon by the Commission after conference with the carriers, and furnish the Commission with a statement showing as to each shipment the following facts:

(1) The commodity; (2) the weight, carload or less than carload; (3) point of origin and the transcontinental territorial group in which the same is situated; (4) rate that would be applied under the tariffs in effect July 1, 1910; (5) the gross charges thereunder; (6) the rate applicable under the order made in this case; (7) the gross charges thereunder; (8) the rate that would be applied were the movement to Sacramento; (9) the gross charges thereunder.

The complainant will be ordered in this case, on or before October 1, 1910, to furnish to the Commission and to the defendant Southern Pacific Company a list of commodities upon which commodity rates are desired, together with an outline of the various territories or groups from which commodity rates should apply.

We are of the opinion that justice can not be done to Nevada unless Nevada points are put on a practical parity with points in eastern Washington and eastern Oregon, and a further hearing will in due course, be held after the data here requested have been furnished by carriers and complainant.

ARLINGTON HEIGHTS FRUIT EXCHANGE
v.
SOUTHERN PACIFIC COMPANY

22 I. C. C. 149 (1911)

PROUTY, *Commissioner:*

During a portion of the years 1902 and 1903 the defendants maintained a blanket rate on lemons from Southern California to most territory east of the Rocky Mountains of $1 per 100 pounds, and beginning with 1904 that rate was made applicable for the entire year. In November, 1909, this rate was advanced to $1.15.

In 1902 the corresponding rate on oranges was $1.25, but this was voluntarily reduced by the carriers in 1907 to $1.15, at which figure it was maintained during the year 1909.

In 1905 this Commission held, as the result of an elaborate investigation, that the rate on oranges ought not to exceed $1.10, but inasmuch as the Commission at that time had no authority to prescribe a reasonable rate for the future this rate was never established.

Upon the advance of the lemon rate, as above stated, California growers began proceedings attacking both rates as unreasonable, and asking that the same be materially reduced. After careful investigation the Commission reached the conclusion that while in its opinion the rate of $1.15 upon oranges was a liberal one, it ought not at the present time to be disturbed. It did hold that the lemon rate ought not to exceed $1, and so ordered. 19 I. C. C. Rep., 148.

From this order the carriers appealed to the Commerce Court and that court enjoined the order for reasons stated in its opinion of October 5, 1911. *A., T. & S. F. Ry. Co.,* v. *U. S.,* 190 Fed. Rep., 591.

Thereupon this Commission struck off its former order and set the case down for further hearing with a view to making such new order as might be required in the premises. All parties have been heard both in evidence and upon argument, and the case is now before us for a final disposition.

The ground upon which the Commerce Court enjoined the enforcement of our order, as stated in its opinion, was that the Commisssion in establishing a rate of $1 on lemons was not attempting to determine what would be a just and reasonable rate of transportation, but was rather endeavoring to protect California lemon growers against Sicilian competition. Its reason for reaching this conclusion was because:

"An examination of the report of the Commission, reproduced so far as it bears on the lemon rate, in its entirety, demonstrates that except for two brief paragraphs suggesting grounds for lowering the lemon while maintaining the orange rate, it deals entirely with matters tending to show the need in this industry of a high-protective tariff against Sicily and, not on traffic considerations, but to compensate for the tariff insufficiencies, a low transportation rate especially to eastern territory."

The complainants, in making out their case, relied in part upon the fact that for parts of two years and for the entire preceding six years these defendants had voluntarily maintained a rate of $1, and this, certainly, was a strong admission against the carriers, unless explained. The carriers attempted to explain it by stating that the rate of $1 had been established, not as a reasonable rate, but to enable California producers to meet the competition of Sicily. Thereupon the complainants replied that notwithstanding the additional duty, owing to increased cost of production in California, Sicilian competition under the advanced duty was as strong as it ever had been under the old duty, so that whatever rate had been reasonable for the past eight years was still reasonable.

The Commission in its opinion did not attempt to indicate the grounds upon which it based its judgment in any particular. It simply stated, in the briefest possible manner, the issues of fact made before it and the claims of the contending parties. We did not suppose that we had any authority to correct tariff insufficiencies by the freight rate, nor to protect, in that way, the American against the foreign grower, nor did we attempt to do so; the fact that this rate had for eight years been voluntarily maintained by the defendants was before us, together with whatever either party desired to say in relation to that circumstance.

Had we understood that the Commerce Court would attempt to look into the mind of the Commission for the purpose of ascertaining the reasons upon which its order was based; that the mere statement of the claims of the parties was to be taken as evidence of the assent of the Commission to those claims; and that the number of lines used in stating the issue was to indicate the weight attached by us to that particular consideration, we should have been more careful in the phrasing of our opinion. In this case the court reproduces in the margin of its opinion what the Commission said touching the lemon rate, but it refrains from reproducing what had gone before in the same opinion touching the orange rate. The Commission had already stated at considerable length the various elements entering into a determination of the reasonableness of the rate on oranges. In the main, the transportation conditions under which oranges and lemons move from Southern California to eastern markets are identical, and whatever had been said as to oranges applied as to lemons. It only remained to note those points in which the parties claimed that the two articles differed. As showing this difference, the complainants pointed to the fact that for the better part of eight years the defendants had of their own free will maintained a rate on lemons, at first 25 cents, and subsequently 15 cents lower than that contemporaneously in effect upon oranges. Upon this point voluminous testimony was given by both parties, and the Commission simply stated that issue in as brief terms as possible.

The Commission also mentioned two other reasons advanced by the complainants why a lower rate might properly be maintained upon lemons than upon oranges. No attempt was made in the original opinion to amplify any of these reasons, but it seems proper to refer to them somewhat more in detail here in the light of what has since transpired.

The first of these, and that one probably entitled to the greatest consideration, was the fact that the average haul upon the lemon was materially shorter than the average haul upon the orange. The rates in question were blanket rates, applying to all territory east of the Rocky Mountains, except the southeast. Manifestly, in passing upon the reasonableness of a rate to this wide territory we must consider it as a whole; that is to say, we must consider the average haul. Now, the testimony tended to show that, owing to the fact that the lemons consumed upon the Atlantic seaboard, and even as far west as Chicago, were to a considerable extent imported, while this was not true in case of oranges, the average haul upon the lemon was much shorter than upon the orange, and that, therefore, the cost of the service to these carriers was materially less in case of the average movement of lemons than of oranges.

It was said upon the former hearing that this difference in distance was 500 miles. The testimony of the complainants upon the last hearing tends to show that it is approximately 450 miles. The evidence of the Santa Fe Railway Company tends to show that comparing the average haul on all oranges and lemons handled by that company during the season of 1910–11, the average haul was only slightly over 300 miles greater in case of oranges than in case of lemons.

It appeared in the former case that the average haul on oranges was not far from 2,300 miles. A rate of $1.15 per 100 pounds would yield ton-mile earnings of 1 cent on the average; 15 cents per 100 pounds is 1 cent per ton-mile for 300 miles. If therefore, the average haul upon lemons was 300 miles less than the average haul upon oranges, and we had reduced the rate in proportion, the resulting rate for the lemon would have been $1.

It is perfectly true, as stated by the Commerce Court, that ordinarily, in case of long distances, the rate does not increase with the distance, but it would not be an extravagant difference, although perhaps more than we should make, if in establishing graded rates upon this commodity we were to allow 15 cents per 100 pounds for a haul of 500 miles.

The second transportation difference pointed out by the Commission in its previous report was that a much larger percentage of oranges moved under refrigeration than of lemons. It appears from the testimony introduced upon the last hearing that 14 per cent of all lemons, as compared with about 50 per cent of all oranges, were refrigerated during the season of 1910–11.

It is well understood that refrigeration is not ordinarily furnished by the transportation company, but by a separate refrigeration company, which retains the entire charge for the service. The carrier itself receives no more, if the rate is the same, when the commodity moves under refrigeration than when it moves without, although it does haul a certain additional weight of ice. In justifying charges made for the transportation of articles sometimes moved under refrigeration and sometimes not, carriers have uniformly insisted that the Commission should consider the fact that with respect to a portion of the transportation service an additional weight of ice was carried. These same transcontinental defendants have repeatedly urged upon this Commission, and did most earnestly insist in the present case, in justification of their rate of $1.15, that in the movement of approximately one-half of this citrus-fruit crop an additional weight of ice must be transported. In this view the complainants apparently concurred, and the Commission adopted it.

This was probably error. When we later came to examine in this very case the reasonableness of the refrigration charge we reached the conclusion that, whatever the parties might say, we must treat the additional cost of hauling the ice as an additional refrigeration expense, to be charged, not against the entire movement from California, but only against that part of the movement under refrigeration. We held that there was no ground upon which the shipper who shipped under ventilation could be required to help pay the transportation charge of the shipper who required refrigeration. *Arlington Heights Fruit Exchange* v. *So. Pac. Co.,* 20 I. C. C. Rep., 106.

Considering this matter in the light in which it was presented to us by both parties, and in which it was disposed of in the former case, the fact that a much larger per cent of oranges move under refrigeration than of lemons would justify a somewhat lower rate upon lemons than upon oranges If the matter is to be considered in the light of our subsequent holding, it must follow that in fixing the rate upon oranges we have taken account of an element in favor of the carriers which ought not to have entered into our conclusion, and that therefore the rate of $1.15 is somewhat too high. If this lemon rate is to be measured by the orange rate, then we think that the orange rate should be reduced in determining a fair relationship, not that the lemon rate should be advanced.

And we desire to call attention to the fact, upon that aspect of the case, that in our opinion the rate of $1.15 applied to the movement of oranges is an extremely liberal one. This Commission held in 1905 that this rate should not exceed $1.10. The production of these citrus fruits in California is almost twice to-day what it was at that time, which makes for a lower rather than for a higher rate.

Considering all the facts which are now before us, those developed in the second hearing as well as in the first, we are of the opinion and find that the $1.15 rate as applied to the transportation of lemons is unjust and unreasonable, and that it should not exceed $1. We do not base this decision upon any consideration that the American producer should be protected against foreign competition.

The Commission in its previous report called attention to the fact that the refrigerator cars in which these lemons are moved may be so constructed that the bunkers which contain the ice can be thrown into the upper part of the car, thereby leaving available for loading, when under ventilation, the space occupied by the bunker when the movement is under refrigeration. At the time of the former hearing it was said that about 1,000 of these collapsible bunker cars were in service, but that others were in process of construction. It appeared upon the last hearing that of the 18,000 cars used in the citrus-fruit traffic about 5,500 were then provided with this style of bunker. The Santa Fe, which handles fully 50 per cent of this traffic, uses 6,500 cars, of which 2,500 have the collapsible bunker.

It further appeared upon the last hearing that the lemon is less subject to decay in transportation than the orange. Experiments made with these collapsible bunker cars indicate that the ventilation obtained with that style of equipment is not as good as with the standard refrigerator car, and shippers, so far as we are at present advised, object to loading oranges in such cars when the bunkers are up, for the reason that the fruit does not carry equally well. But since the lemon is not as susceptible to decay as the orange, the complainants, representing 90 per cent of the lemon growers of California, state that they are willing to load these collapsible bunker cars to their full capacity with lemons, if presented for loading with the bunkers thrown up.

Such a car, of standard length, can be loaded with 34,000 pounds of lemons. The present minimum is 26,200 pounds; in case of oranges, 26,700 pounds. A car loaded to the minimum with lemons at a rate of $1.15 produces a car revenue of $301.30, while if loaded to a minimum of 34,000 pounds the earnings upon that same car, at a rate of $1, would be $340. There can be little doubt that from a purely transportation standpoint, having reference mainly to the cost of the service, a $1 rate with a minimum of 34,000 pounds is better business than a minimum of 26,200 pounds at a rate of $1.15.

It is in the public interest that these lemons should be transported at the lowest possible cost to the railway, and we feel that under the present circumstances carriers should be allowed to require of shippers the loading of these collapsible bunker cars to their capacity. The carriers will therefore be permitted to provide, by proper minima in their tariffs, that when these cars are presented with the bunkers thrown up they shall be loaded to the capacity of the car, not exceeding, however, two tiers in height. We do not base our opinion that $1 is a reasonable rate upon the fact that a minimum of 34,000 pounds can often and perhaps usually be carried, but we do think that, considering the whole situation, it is reasonable that the shipper should be required to load this minimum, when, without damage to himself, he can do so.

This Commission prescribed by its order, which the Commerce Court enjoined, a blanket rate extending from the Rocky Mountains east, and one ground of attack upon our order was that the Commission was without authority to establish a blanket of that extent.

The carriers themselves had voluntarily established, and for years maintained this blanket rate, which is applied to most of the products of California. They expressed the opinion upon the hearing that this was, upon the whole, the most satisfactory rate to them. The shippers concurred in this idea, so that we were virtually requested by both the railroad and the shipper to establish a rate of that kind. The question presented to us was not, What would be a reasonable rate if the Commission were for the first time establishing such rates, but, rather, is $1.15, or $1, or some other figure reasonable as a blanket rate?

It was in that aspect of the case that we prescribed the $1 blanket rate.

The courts might perhaps have held that the carriers, having tendered a rate of this kind, were estopped from contesting it upon the ground that the Commission had acted upon the rate presented and had prescribed the kind of rate which all parties asked for, but we did not believe that we were invested with authority to fix a blanket rate of this dimension, since that was really a question of public policy for Congress, and we did not care to go before the courts or the country in that light. For this reason the Commission struck off its order and took the matter under further advisement.

Upon the recent hearing carriers were asked whether it was their desire that the Commission should establish reasonable graded rates or should establish what in its opinion was a reasonable blanket rate. They requested the establishment of a blanket rate, and in that request the complainants joined. While the carriers did not in any way agree not to contest the order of the Commission upon other grounds, they did state that it would not be contested upon the ground that the establishment of so wide a blanket was beyond the jurisdiction of the Commission.

What is a reasonable freight rate can not, strictly speaking, be the subject of agreement between carriers and shippers, nor between carriers and this Commission. If in a given case, after hearing all that is to be said by the parties, we are clearly of the conviction that rates in effect are wrong, it is our duty to substitute for those rates others which we believe to be right. But we are not required to interfere unless clearly convinced that the present schedule is unlawful.

When the United States Government transports a package 10 miles for one citizen for 10 cents, while it charges his neighbor the same amount for transporting a like parcel 3,000 miles, a clear discrimination is made, but it is a discrimination of that character which by universal consent is in the public interest. So, here, it is by no means certain that these postage-stamp rates as applied to the distribution of the products of the Pacific coast states are not upon the whole for the general public good. Under this system the producers upon the Pacific coast are given the widest possible market for their products; the carriers obtain a certain amount of long-distance business at remunerative rates, which they would not otherwise have; the freight rate does not so far enter into the cost of these articles to the consumer that any noticeable burden is imposed upon any section of the country. If this Commission were required to establish a reasonable schedule of rates for the transportation of citrus fruits from southern California to eastern destinations, we should not feel at liberty to put in this blanket; but to establish graded rates at this time upon lemons would be to break up this rate system which is highly satisfactory to all parties concerned, and while the action of the court may in the end compel us to do this, we feel that we can, for the present, properly leave this situation as it is.

The complaint prays for reparation, which will be awarded upon the basis of the $1 rate established, all questions as to the parties who may recover such damages and the time within which they can be awarded being reserved for further consideration.

An order will be issued.

LANE, *Commissioner,* concurring:

The act to regulate commerce provides that if we find the rates made by the railroads to be unjust and unreasonable we shall have power to fix just and reasonable rates. It also declares that there shall be no advantage or preference given to any locality. We are called upon in this case to pass upon the reasonableness of a rate on lemons that is the same from Los Angeles to Denver as from Los Angeles to Boston. Manifestly if there is any direct relation between cost of service and the rate charged such method of making rates is in conflict with the law. These great blankets, however, are made as a matter of policy; they are instituted by the carriers for their own benefit, to develop the industry and to extend and simplify the marketing of the fruit. Such a blanket is a benefit to the railroads, because, as is fairly established in this case, the $1 rate is higher than is just and reasonable on a very considerable percentage — perhaps from 50 to 70 per cent — of the fruit which ends its journey to the west of the point to which a $1 rate would carry it. The shippers object to the breaking up of this blanket, because to do so would be an inconvenience to them, and as the rate is paid by the consignee and does not come out of the consignor's pocket, excepting in competitive territory in the east, they are indifferent as to the amount of the rate in and of itself excepting as it so increases the price of lemons that demand will decrease. The result of this mutuality of interest is a blanket rate which imposes on the consignees in some parts of the country a higher rate than would be charged under a scheme of graded rates, in order that a lower rate than otherwise would be reasonable may be made into a small section of the country which is intensely competitive. Now, this may be good policy. I am not prepared to say that it is not, and therefore concur in the opinion of the Commission.

This case, when broadly regarded, involves a question of the highest national importance. What is to be our policy with respect to the movement of traffic? Shall the country be treated as a whole for commercial purposes, or shall it be infinitely divided? In our postal service we deal with the country as a unit. As to our railroads there is no uniform policy, even upon the same lines or systems. In some parts of the country rates are on an almost strictly mileage basis, every 10 miles that is passed adding to the rate. In other territory we have a system of small zones or groups which are placed upon a common basis — a scheme of rate making that has worked most happily in the country to the east of the Mississippi River and which, it seems to me, should be extended westward. The whole continent for a zone of 2,000 miles is made to serve the Pacific coast terminal cities at uniform rates, while the states between the mountains are not given such advantage. So, too on California products generally, and not alone upon citrus fruits, the United States east of the Rockies is placed in a great zone to which a uniform rate is made. At the same time, the lumber of the far northwest is not so treated, nor the wool or hides of the interior.

Perhaps the United States will one day declare a policy of its own in this regard. Primarily it is a matter of national concern and not of railroad policy as to what system of rate making shall obtain so long as the carriers receive a reasonable return upon the value of their property. The people may say (1) that railroad rates shall be made so as to carry all products into all markets within the four lines of the country; or (2) that after a certain narrow limit is passed the whole of the land shall be one zone; or (3) a system of rates that will keep producers and consumers as near together as possible and eliminate waste in transportation. These are national questions. They go to the very future of our industrial life. Upon their determination depends the character of the farm products and the nature of the industries in the various sections of the country. The railroad by its rates may make each portion of the country largely independent of the remainder or it may make of the Nation one economic and industrial unit, each portion thereof doing best what nature has fitted it to do best. This is fundamentally the difference in the philosophy which underlies the two methods of making rates which have been given consideration in this case. Without any expression of policy from Congress we accept the policy which the railroads themselves have made, considering that upon the whole the results arising from such policy do not conflict with the provisions of the law. There is no doubt in my mind but that the Commission could not itself prescribe a blanket similar to that obtaining here and which we are approving because neither the carriers nor the shippers wish it destroyed.

I am authorized to say that Commissioner MEYER concurs in the view herein expressed.

CLARK, *Commissioner*, concurring in part:

I am able to agree in full with the conclusions of the majority in this case. It appears on further hearing that the average haul performed on the lemons is more nearly that performed on the oranges than appeared in the former hearing, and while I think that is a feature to be given consideration, it does not seem to me to be controlling, for the reason that the blanket rate on the lemons covers the same territory covered by the blanket rate on the oranges, and the shippers have the same privileges thereunder. It appears that the California lemons command a higher price in New York than do the imported lemons. If, therefore, the lemons are hauled shorter distances than the oranges, it is because the shippers so elect.

It seems to me clear that it would be greatly to the disadvantage of the citrus-fruit growers and shippers if the blanket rate were broken up. The blanket rate, together with the extremely liberal reconsignment privileges granted thereunder, has contributed greatly to the development of the citrus-fruit industry in California. It is admitted that under present transportation conditions the California growers have driven the foreign oranges from the markets of the United States.

It appears that the reconsignment privilege is exercised on

about 50 per cent of the shipment of citrus fruits, and that as to some carloads the privilege is availed of four or five times. Every reconsignment costs the carrier something in extra services and in readjustment of accounts, and the reconsignment privileges under these citrus-fruit blanket rates are probably more liberal than are or ever have been accorded in connection with any other traffic.

I am unable to discover any substantial transportation difference between the movement of oranges and of lemons except that the lemons stand transportation better than the oranges do and are therefore shipped to a larger extent under ventilation, and apparently can be loaded to a heavier carload minimum.

In several cases the Commission has, and I think properly, approved higher rates upon perishable commodities shipped under refrigeration than upon the same commodities shipped under ventilation. *Florida Fruit and Vegetable Asso.* v. *A. C. L. R. R. Co.*, 17 I. C. C. Rep., 552; *Ozark Fruit Growers Asso.* v. *St. L. & S. F. R. R. Co.*, 16 I. C. C. Rep., 106. It has uniformly appeared that it is not practicable or possible to load as heavily under refrigeration as under ventilation, and, necessarily, care of shipments under refrigeration, reicing, etc., involve additional expenses to the carriers.

Maximum loading is clearly in the interest of economy, and a substantially increased minimum weight justifies a lower rate. I therefore agree with the finding as to the rate on the minimum of 34,000 pounds under ventilation.

BLUEFIELD SHIPPERS' ASSOCIATION

v.

NORFOLK & WESTERN RAILWAY COMPANY

22 I. C. C. 519 (1912.)

PROUTY, *Chairman:*

This complaint puts in issue rates both from the east and from the west, to Bluefield, W. Va. With respect to rates from New York, Philadelphia, and Baltimore the allegation is that they are unreasonable *per se*, while those from Cincinnati, Columbus, Chicago, and Pittsburgh are assailed as unreasonable and also as in violation of the fourth section.

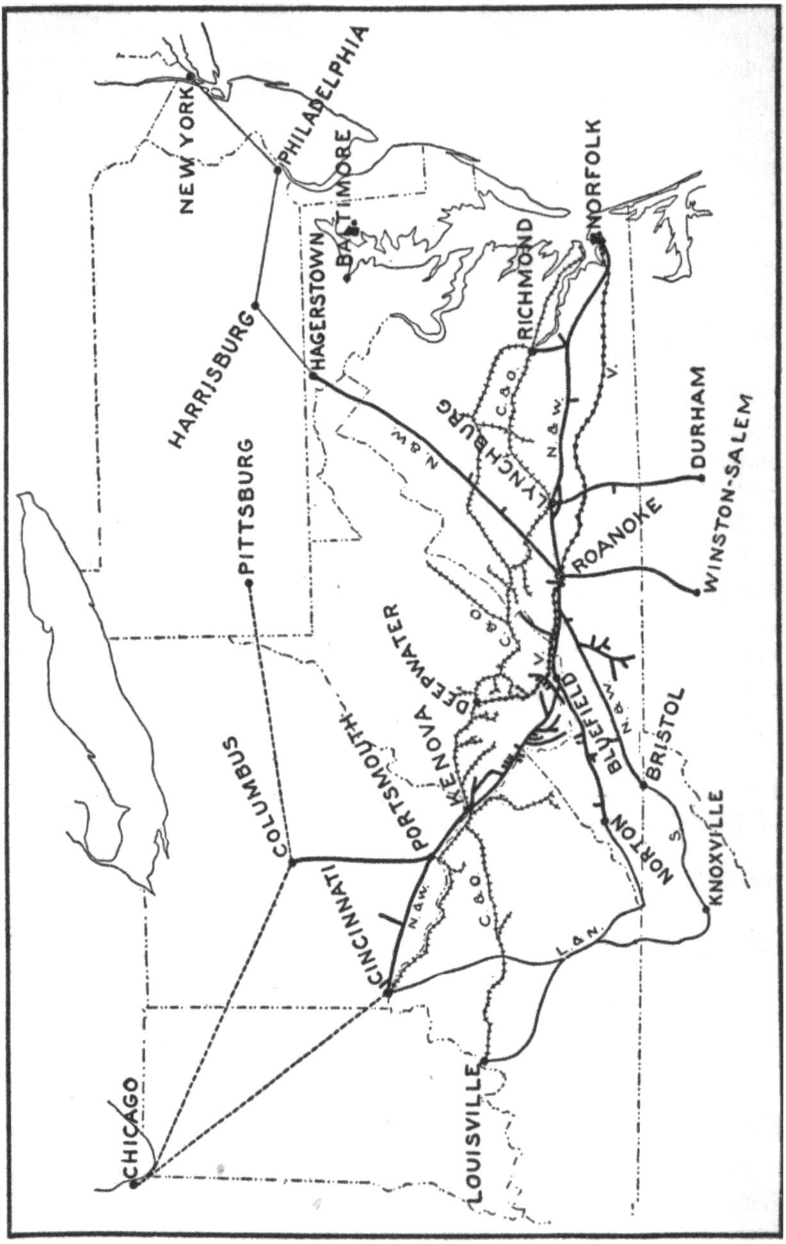
NEW YORK
PHILADELPHIA
BALTIMORE
NORFOLK
HARRISBURG
HAGERSTOWN
RICHMOND
PITTSBURG
LYNCHBURG
DURHAM
ROANOKE
WINSTON-SALEM
DEEPWATER
BLUEFIELD
BRISTOL
COLUMBUS
PORTSMOUTH
KENOVA
NORTON
KNOXVILLE
CINCINNATI
LOUISVILLE
CHICAGO
N.&W.
C.&O.
L.&N.

Bluefield is a local station upon the Norfolk & Western Railway, and the scheme of rates which is here under attack has been established by that carrier, which assumes, therefore, the burden of this defense.

The Norfolk & Western and its connections have filed an application under the fourth section for permission to continue to charge at intermediate points west of Roanoke, including Bluefield, higher rates than they apply at Roanoke. This fourth section application has been heard in connection with the complaint, and since the issue with respect to rates from the west is the same, the two will be considered together.

The accompanying map shows more clearly than any verbal description the exact issues presented in reference to these western rates. It will be seen that the Norfolk & Western Railway begins upon the west at Cincinnati and Columbus. From these points it extends to Portsmouth, Ohio, where it unites and proceeds easterly, crossing the Ohio River at Kenova and extending through Roanoke, Lynchburg, and Petersburg to Norfolk, its eastern terminus. The road from Columbus to Norfolk is known as the main line and is about 700 miles in length, but large amounts of traffic are handled from Cincinnati, which is also, to every intent, a main-line western terminus.

Bluefield is upon the main line, 205 miles east of Kenova and 105 miles west of Roanoke.

A branch of the Norfolk & Western extends from Radford southwest to Bristol, where a connection is made with the Southern Railway. Since the lines of this latter company reach Cincinnati, the Southern and the Norfolk & Western constitute together a second route from Cincinnati and points north through Bristol to Roanoke and other eastern destinations.

From Bluefield still another branch of the Norfolk & Western extends in the same general southerly direction to Norton, where it connects with the Louisville & Nashville. Since the lines of this company reach Louisville and Cincinnati, a third route is thus formed by which traffic between the west and the east passes over the Norfolk & Western to Roanoke and other points.

Joint rates apply and traffic is actually handled over all these routes by the Norfolk & Western Railway from Cincinnati, Chicago, and other points in central freight association territory to Roanoke and other eastern destinations, and all these routes are embraced in the fourth section application. Only the first or what may be termed the mainline route, is involved in the complaint, and that route will be first considered.

Rates from Cincinnati, Columbus, Chicago, and Pittsburgh to Roanoke and all points upon the main line of the Norfolk & Western east of Roanoke are the same. Many of these rates and perhaps all of them apply at Salem, a station 7 miles west of Roanoke, but Roanoke is the point of consequence, and will be used in this report as the most westerly point at which the blanket rate begins.

The relative rates from these points in controversy to Bluefield and Roanoke are as follows:

	Classes						Grain	Grain products
	1	2	3	4	5	6		
From Columbus to —	*Cents*	*Cents*	*Cents*	*Cents*	*Cents*	*Cents*	*Cents*	*Cents*
Bluefield	66½	55	42	31	26	21	17½	18
Roanoke	54½	47	35½	24	20	16	12½	13
From Cincinnati to —								
Bluefield	68	55	42	32	27	22	19	19½
Roanoke	62	53½	40½	27½	23	18½	14	14½
From Chicago to —								
Bluefield	84	72	55	39	33	27	18	18.7
Roanoke	72	62	47	32	27	22	13	13.7
From Pittsburgh to —								
Bluefield	86½	73	55½	39	34	26	....	....
On iron and steel articles	....	....	....	31	26	21	....	....
Roanoke	54½	47	35½	24	20	16	....	....

From an examination of these rates it will be seen that the rate to Bluefield is uniformly higher than that to Roanoke, although Bluefield is 105 miles nearer the point of origin, and although the traffic in all cases passes through that point. The Norfolk & Western justifies these rates by attempting to show, first, that its rate to Roanoke is compelled by competitive conditions which it does not control; second, that its rate to Roanoke is lower than would otherwise be reasonable; and, third, that the higher rate to Bluefield is reasonable.

A glance at the map will show that New York, Philadelphia, Baltimore, and Norfolk are all served from Chicago, Columbus, Cincinnati, and points in the central west by different lines of railway. Years ago all these lines competed for traffic to all these seaboard points. Freight would be carried, for instance, from Chicago to New York and from thence to Norfolk or Baltimore by water, and, conversely, it might go by rail from

Chicago to Norfolk and from Norfolk to New York by ship. This produced the most active competition between all points in the middle west and these different seaports.

The final outcome of this was an arrangement by which a certain relation of rates was established between the different ports. Taking New York as the base, Philadelphia was made 2 cents and Baltimore and Norfolk 3 cents lower. This adjustment was made many years ago, and while it has been somewhat modified as to export grain and grain products, is still in effect upon domestic business. This, it will be seen, fixes the rate from Chicago to Norfolk, for example, 3 cents below that to New York.

Of even greater importance in influencing the rates with which we are dealing has been commercial or market competition. Richmond, Lynchburg, Norfolk, and the other Virginia cities wholesale into surrounding territory in competition with Baltimore. If the business is done through Baltimore the freight may reach that point by the Baltimore & Ohio but not by the Chesapeake & Ohio. If, upon the other hand, the business is distributed from one of the Virginia cities, it may be brought there by the Chesapeake & Ohio but not by the Baltimore & Ohio. Since the ability of these different centers to job into intermediate territory depends upon the relative rate of freight at which the supplies of a given city can be obtained, the Chesapeake & Ohio, in the protection of the interests of the communities served by it, has insisted that rates from the west to the Virginia cities shall not be higher than to Baltimore. The most westerly of these Virginia cities served by the Chesapeake & Ohio is Lynchburg, and that city for many years has been accorded by the Chesapeake & Ohio the Baltimore rate, which is the same as that to Norfolk, and which is generally known as the Virginia cities rate.

The first business handled by the Norfolk & Western between the west and the east came through Bristol, and until 1890 that railway had no other western outlet. The Norfolk & Western did not create the Virginia city condition, but found it when it became a factor in business between the west and the east. It could not, if disposed, obtain a higher rate from these western points of origin than is applied by the Chesapeake & Ohio, which with its connections reaches the points in the west and offers equally good facilities of transportation.

The Chesapeake & Ohio has, ever since the passage of the

act to regulate commerce, observed the rule of the fourth section; that is, it makes no higher rate at any point upon its main line than that to a more distant point. Since it has in the past insisted upon maintaining the Baltimore rate at Lynchburg, notwithstanding that it was thereby compelled to reduce rates at all points west of Lynchburg, it must be assumed that this company will adhere to the same policy in the future and will maintain at Lynchburg the Baltimore or Norfolk rate. Clearly, the Norfolk & Western can not maintain a higher rate than its competitor between these points, and it must therefore be found that the Norfolk & Western does meet at Lynchburg competition which it can not control and which compels it to establish from these western points of origin the rates which it now observes.

The complainant insists that whatever may be the fact as to Lynchburg there is no such competition at Roanoke, and this is the serious question for determination in passing upon the fourth section application.

When the act to regulate commerce took effect, in 1887, the Norfolk & Western was to some extent handling business from the west through the Bristol gateway into and through Roanoke. At that time Roanoke was served by an additional railway known as the Shenandoah Valley and being the line from Hagerstown to Roanoke which is now operated by the Norfolk & Western. That line crosses the Chesapeake & Ohio some 40 miles north of Roanoke, and rates from the west into Roanoke were made jointly by the Chesapeake & Ohio and the Shenandoah Valley. The rates so established from the west were the Virginia cities rates, and no higher rate was made to any intermediate point by that route.

This case shows that the Norfolk & Western did not meet the rates so established by the Chesapeake & Ohio at the outset, but in 1890 the Norfolk & Western obtained control of the Shenandoah Valley, and it then determined to establish by its line the same rates which had been previously in effect by this competing line. The Norfolk & Western had, by acquiring the Shenandoah Valley, put an end to all possible competition by rail at Roanoke, and its management did not deem it good policy to signalize this event by advancing the rates previously in effect.

There was undoubtedly then and has ever since been the further thought of market competition. Roanoke lies 54 miles west of Lynchburg, and after 1890 was served for 20 years by the Norfolk & Western alone. Its position enabled it to intercept a great amount of trade which would naturally otherwise go to Lynchburg, and it was therefore in the interest of the Norfolk & Western to build up at that point a commercial center served by it exclusively which could compete with Lynchburg, where the Norfolk & Western must contest for the business with its rival, the Chesapeake & Ohio.

Whatever the motive, the Norfolk & Western did, after acquiring control of the Shenandoah Valley, establish by its own line from the west at Roanoke the Virginia cities rates, which it has ever since and is still maintaining.

In 1892 the route through Norton was opened for business and the same year saw the completion of the line through Kenova, which gave the Norfolk & Western access to the west over what thus became its main line. The rates already in effect to Roanoke were continued by all these routes.

From 1890 down to 1909 the Norfolk & Western was the only line serving Roanoke, but in this latter year the Virginian Railway, running from Deepwater to Norfolk, was opened for business. This line passes through Roanoke, as will be seen by reference to the map, runs westerly and parallel with the Norfolk & Western for some distance, and connects with the Chesapeake & Ohio at Deepwater. The Virginian Railway now forms, in connection with the Chesapeake & Ohio, another line from the west to Roanoke, and it now maintains via this line at Roanoke the Virginia cities rate. The Chesapeake & Ohio Railroad, as already said, observes the rule of the fourth section in the construction of its rates from these western points of origin to all points upon its main line east; that is, the rate to Deepwater, its junction with the Virginian Railway, is the same as to Norfolk and Lynchburg. The Virginian Railway does not observe the rule of the fourth section at points between Deepwater and Roanoke, but establishes to all these intermediate points rates which are higher than that to Roanoke. In this respect the practice of that railroad is exactly like that of the Norfolk & Western.

For many years that community has enjoyed the Virginia cities rate, and under the influence of that rate the commercial interests of Roanoke have developed. While the existence of a wrong can not, of itself, justify its continuance, and while the very purpose of the original fourth section and of this last amendment was to prevent discrimination like that before us, still, in determining what, under all the circumstances, is just and reasonable, in pursuance of the authority delegated to us by the amended section, we must certainly be to some extent guided by conditions as we find them.

This Commission has in two recent cases reached the conclusion that competitive conditions existed at Roanoke which did not obtain at points farther west and which compelled the observance of the rates now in effect. *Chicago Sash & Door Asso.* v. *N. & W. Ry. Co.,* 14 I. C. C. Rep., 594; *Corporation Commission of N. C.* v. *N. & W. Ry. Co.,* 19 I. C. C. Rep., 303.

In the latter case, which was carefully considered and but recently decided, we said:

"With respect of the contention of complainant that as Roanoke was served by but one railroad company, competitive conditions do not exist there which in any manner compel the making of lower rates than to the North Carolina cities in question, which are served by two or more railroads, it is to be said that the rates from the west to Roanoke were put in effect April 5, 1887, by the Kanawha Dispatch, which was a fast-freight line operating over the Chesapeake & Ohio and its connections. The rates were published from Chicago to Roanoke via Basic, Va., in connection with the Shenandoah Valley Railroad. In 1890 the Norfolk & Western acquired the Shenandoah Valley road, over which the Virginia cities rates were applied to Roanoke, and accepted the rates as it found them, and they have remained in effect substantially without change to the present time. The industries and business of Roanoke were built up and have been maintained under the existing rate adjustment, and we are of opinion that it should not be disturbed at this time."

Those cases both arose and were submitted previous to the amendment to the fourth section of June, 1910. But while that amendment may affect the use to be made of the facts found, it could not alter the facts themselves. Upon a further and perhaps fuller view of this entire situation we hold that there are to-day at Roanoke competitive conditions which do not obtain at Bluefield and which compel the maintenance at that point of the rates now in effect from the western points of origin here under consideration.

It should be noted that in deciding questions like that here considered, each case must stand upon it own facts, and no one situation can furnish an exact precedent for another.

The next question is, Have these competitive influences at Roanoke reduced the rates to that point from these points of origin in controversy below what would otherwise be reasonable? For if the rates to Roanoke are sufficiently high the same rates ought not to be exceeded at a point 105 miles west of that destination.

The Norfolk & Western crosses the Ohio River at Kenova. Generally speaking, rates from points in central freight association territory into territory south of the Ohio River are constructed by combination upon that river; that is, a rate to the river and a rate beyond are added together for the through charge. The defendant insists that this method might properly be followed in constructing rates from these points of origin to Roanoke, and that by this test the present rates to Roanoke are unreasonably low.

The distance from Kenova to Roanoke is 310 miles, and rates upon the classes and commodities involved are as follows:

Classes						Grain	Grain products
1	2	3	4	5	6		
Cents	*Cents*	*Cents*	*Cents*	*Cents*	*Cents*	*Cents*	*Cents*
54½	47	35½	24	20	16	12½	13

It will be seen that these rates, which are considerably lower than would result from the application of the Norfolk & Western mileage scale in force upon that part of its system, are the same as those from Columbus to Roanoke. If, therefore, it is proper to construct these rates by combination upon the Ohio River, and if the mileage scale of the Norfolk & Western, which is lower than that in effect upon most southern lines, is to be taken as reasonable, then, clearly, these Roanoke rates are below what would otherwise be proper.

We do not think, however, that rates from points of origin in central freight association territory to points upon the main line of this railway should be constructed upon that theory. The mere fact that the Norfolk & Western Railway crosses the Ohio River at Kenova does not, in this instance, fix a point at which any artificial building up of this kind can begin. We should treat the main line of this railroad as one continuous operation from Columbus and Cincinnati to Roanoke. The line from Kenova to Roanoke runs through a mountainous country. It was expensive to construct and is expensive to operate, but it is part of the main line of the Norfolk & Western, just as the mountainous sections of the Chesapeake & Ohio, the Baltimore & Ohio, and the Pennsylvania are parts of those systems. It originates an immense tonnage which is handled by that system, and it can not be said that the patrons of this railroad should pay rates of transportation which may be just and reasonable upon the general level of railroad rates in the south, where traffic is much less, than upon this part of the Norfolk & Western and where earnings are not at all comparable with those of this system. It is much more reasonable to compare the rates upon the main line with those upon the Chesapeake & Ohio and the Baltimore & Ohio, rôads operating largely in competition with the Norfolk & Western and under very similar conditions.

Below is a statement showing certain comparative statistics for the year 1910 upon these three systems, and also the averages of Group III and Group IV:

	N. & W.	C. & O.	B. & O.	Group III	Group VI
Average miles operated	1,945	1,937	4,434	26,054	13,896
Freight density ... tons..	3,456,296	3,161,307	2,711,666	2,020,779	1,098,029
Passenger density	93,095	117,051	172,165	157,573	82,260
Average distance freight hauled. miles..	265	267	191	116	192
Average rate per ton per mile..mills..	4.47	4.07	5.77	5.88	6.55
Average freight-train load ... tons..	635	701	442	457	423
Operating revenue per mile of road....	$18,028	$16,127	$20,048	$15,582	$9,132
Total operating expenses per mile of road	$10,821	$9,777	$13,831	$10,651	$5,655
Net operating revenues per mile of road	$7,207	$6,350	$6,217	$5,201	$3,477
Operating ratio ... per cent..	60.02	60.6	68.99	67.19	61.92

It will be seen from the above figures that the Norfolk & Western is fully as strong in every traffic and financial essential as either the Chesapeake & Ohio or the Baltimore & Ohio, that it is stronger than the average of Group III, which comprises the middle west, and very much above Group IV, embracing West Virginia, Virginia, and the Carolinas, in which the lines of the Norfolk & Western are mainly situated. It should also be observed that, territorially speaking, the Norfolk & Western is not properly a southern railroad, but that it either occupies, for the most part, a region peculiar to itself or competes with trunk roads like the Chesapeake & Ohio and the Baltimore & Ohio.

The favorable showing of the Norfolk & Western which appears from the above table does not result from the fact, as is sometimes the case, that this road consists of a single trunk line stem through which flows a great current of traffic which has been collected and is distributed by other lines of railway bearing to this line the relation of branches. The Norfolk & Western as a system has, as ordinarily stated, but a little over 700 miles of main-line track; treating Cincinnati as one of its western termini, 814 miles of main-line track, out of a total mileage of more than 1,900 miles. The heavy tonnage per mile and the very satisfactory earnings per mile are computed not upon this main-line mileage but upon the entire mileage of the whole system.

Nor is it true here, as is sometimes the case, that the earnings of the Norfolk & Western are artificially increased by the diversion to that line of traffic which might well follow, under a different state of control, other avenues. This system largely originates the enormous tonnage which it handles. From all of this the inference must be drawn that while the course of the Norfolk & Western is, during a greater part of its extent, through southern territory, the road itself as a system is much more comparable with those in trunk line and central freight association territories.

At the same time it must be remembered that a large part of its traffic is coal and coke and that it handles a considerable amount of other low-grade freight. That part of its business moving under class rates is rather small as compared with other roads which make a similar traffic and financial showing, and this class business may not be handled upon its system to the same relative advantage that it is upon roads generally which show the same earnings.

Nor is it meant that in fixing rates upon the branch lines of this system, like those extending to Durham and Winston-Salem upon the south or to Hagerstown upon the north where the traffic is much lighter and operating conditions entirely different, the same rule should be observed. The rates under consideration are from points in the middle west to points upon the main line of the Norfolk & Western.

Rates to Roanoke, which may be restated here for convenience, are as follows:

To Roanoke from —	Classes						Grain	Grain products
	1	2	3	4	5	6		
	Cents	*Cents*	*Cents*	*Cents*	*Cents*	*Cents*	*Cents*	*Cents*
Columbus..........	54½	47	35½	24	20	16	12½	13
Cincinnati..........	62	53½	40½	27½	23	18½	14	14½
Chicago............	72	62	47	32	27	22	13	$13\frac{7}{10}$
Pittsburgh.........	54½	47	35½	24	20	16	...	....

The distance from Columbus is 449 miles, from Cincinnati 456 miles, and for these distances the rates might well be the same. There is no standard by which these class rates can be exactly measured, and in determining what is reasonable or unreasonable a considerable latitude must of necessity be allowed to the carrier; but why rates over for the most part an identical route and for almost exactly the same distance should differ by one-eighth requires some explanation, and none is afforded by the present record.

From Chicago to Kenova the distance is 431 miles, the first class rate 45 cents, the grain rate 10 cents. These class rates are established, as we understand it, upon the regular mileage scale obtaining over railroads generally in central freight association territory. That may not be true of the grain rate.

From New York to Pittsburgh the distance is 440 miles, the first class rate 45 cents, the rate on grain and its products 15 cents.

These rates from Cincinnati and Columbus to Roanoke, if tested by the standards prevailing in territory where operating conditions, earnings, etc., are substantially the same upon the average as upon the Norfolk & Western, would be distinctly too high, but as already suggested we do not feel that they should be put upon quite that basis.

Exercising our best judgment upon the facts before us, we hold that the present rates from both Cincinnati and Columbus to Roanoke are lower than they might reasonably be were it not for the competition which has induced them, but we feel that in so holding as to Cincinnati the extreme limit has been reached. We have been to a degree influenced by the feeling that some relation probably exists, although not disclosed by this record, between these rates from Columbus and Cincinnati which might to some extent be disturbed by a contrary holding, although such holding, in view of the conclusion reached upon the reasonableness of the rates to Bluefield, could be of no importance to that community.

The distance from Chicago to Roanoke is about 741 miles. The first class rate from Chicago to Cincinnati is 40 cents, the grain rate 10 cents. In line with the conclusion just reached that 54½ cents, first class, and 12½ cents, on grain and its products, from Columbus to Roanoke is unreasonably low, we must hold that the present class rates, beginning with 72 cents, first class, and the present grain and grain-products rates, 13 cents and 13.7 cents, respectively, from Chicago to Roanoke are lower than they might properly be.

The class rates from Pittsburgh to Roanoke are the same as those from Columbus. Traffic moving under these rates goes west from Pittsburgh to Columbus, a distance of 191 miles, and thence via Kenova to destination. Having already held that the rates from Columbus are unreasonably low, the same conclusion must all the more follow as to those from Pittsburgh.

In passing upon this fourth-section application we must inquire, in the third place, whether the rates to the intermediate point are reasonable.

It has been earnestly urged in other cases, although not much insisted upon in this particular proceeding, that in determining whether relief shall be granted from the inhibition of the fourth section, this Commission should give no attention to the intermediate rate. If it be established that the long-distance rate is controlled by competition not existing at the intermediate point, which has forced the rate at the long-distance point below what it otherwise might properly be, then permission to make the higher charge at the intermediate point should be granted, without reference to the amount of that charge. It is said that this must be so, since the fourth section is aimed at the discrimination which results from the lower charge at the farther point and not at the inherently unreasonable intermediate charge.

To this view we do not assent. The statute forbids the making of the higher charge at an intermediate point, but provides that this Commission, upon investigation, may, in special cases, allow a deviation from that rule. We have held that the relieving power thus granted is not to be exercised arbitrarily, but that it is our duty to permit the higher intermediate charge whenever, under all the circumstances, the resulting rates will not contravene the act to regulate commerce in that they are unjust and unreasonable or unduly discriminatory. This embraces both the preference against the intermediate point and the rate which that point is required to pay. Congress has said to the carriers of interstate commerce by rail that they must not charge more for the short than for the long haul unless they can show to the satisfaction of this Commission that in so doing their rates do not violate the inhibition of the act as expressed in both the first and third sections.

It is said that we can deal directly, under the first section, with the intermediate charge if that be found unreasonable; but so can we deal directly with the discrimination under the third section, if that be found undue. It is no unreasonable burden to require a carrier to justify its rates at all points before it is permitted to practice this form of discrimination which has been particularly selected out and dealt with in the fourth section.

This does not mean that we should, in every case, undertake an exhaustive examination into the reasonableness of the intermediate charges, for this would be well nigh impossible. When no complaint exists as to the intermediate rates, and when an inspection of those rates by the Commission discloses nothing which seems to call for an investigation into their reasonableness, we may properly assume that they are just and reasonable, and proceed accordingly, but when, as here, complaint is made attacking the reasonableness of the intermediate charge, that must be investigated. If the present charge to Bluefield is found unreasonable a reasonable rate must be determined, and our order permitting a deviation from the fourth section must be conditioned that no higher intermediate charge shall be observed than that found to be just. If, in the absence of investigation, the intermediate charges are assumed to be reasonable, our relieving order should be conditioned that the present charges shall not be exceeded.

This form of order does not establish a relation between the long-distance and the intermediate rate. If for reasons over which the Norfolk & Western has no control the Roanoke rate should be further reduced, that company might meet this reduction without any corresponding reduction at Bluefield, and, conversely, if the Roanoke rate were advanced the Norfolk & Western could not at the same time advance the Bluefield rate.

It should be further noted that this form of order is only applicable in cases where the rate at the long-distance point is absolutely fixed by causes over which the applicant for relief under the fourth section has no control. We hold in this case that the Norfolk & Western could not, if it saw fit, apply at Roanoke other than the Virginia cities rate without an undue sacrifice of its revenues. If, upon the other hand, the applicant for relief does control the long-distance rate, if that carrier can determine what effect shall be given to the competitive conditions which are supposed to justify the reduction at the farther point, then this Commission may also determine whether the carrier is justified in giving to those competitive conditions the effect which it does — may determine the effect which such conditions might properly have, and may fix the extent to which those conditions shall be given effect.

It is possible that cases might arise where, even though the long-distance rate were beyond the control of the applicant for relief, nevertheless some relation ought to be established between the rate to the more distant and those to intermediate points. The intermediate rate should not, for example, exceed the long-distance rate plus a reasonable local charge from the more remote back to the intermediate point, and should perhaps, in some cases, be even less. These questions will be disposed of when they arise.

The present rates to Bluefield are as follows:

To Bluefield from —	Classes						Grain	Grain products
	1	2	3	4	5	6		
	Cents	*Cents*	*Cents*	*Cents*	*Cents*	*Cents*	*Cents*	*Cents*
Columbus	66½	55	42	31	26	21	17½	18
Cincinnati	68	55	42	32	27	22	19	19½
Chicago	84	72	55	39	33	277	18	$18\frac{7}{10}$
Pittsburgh	86½	73	55½	39	34	26	......	......
Iron and steel articles	......	......	31	26	21	......	......	......

Are these rates reasonable?

The distance from both Cincinnati and Columbus to Bluefield is substantially the same, being approximately 345 miles. We are of the opinion and find that the present rates from both Cincinnati and Columbus to Bluefield are unjust and unreasonable, and that the following rates are reasonable and ought not to be exceeded:

Classes						Grain	Grain products
1	2	3	4	5	6		
Cents 54½	*Cents* 47	*Cents* 35½	*Cents* 24	*Cents* 20	*Cents* 16	*Cents* 12½	*Cents* 13

As already noted, the first class rate from Chicago to Cincinnati is 40 cents, to Columbus 41 cents, and this would produce upon the basis of the rates which we have found to be reasonable a combination of 94½ cents upon Cincinnati and 95½ cents upon Columbus. This Commission has repeatedly said that through rates should not be constructed by using the full combination. In the *Burnham-Hanna-Munger case,* 14 I. C. C. Rep., 299, we established a first class rate of 51 cents when applied to through business as compared with a 60-cent local rate; but subsequently, and upon further reflection, this difference was reduced to 5 cents, 21 I. C. C. Rep., 546. To hold the present first class rate from Chicago to Bluefield, which is 84 cents, unreasonable, we must shrink by more than 10 cents the combination of an extremely low rate from Chicago to Cincinnati with a rate just found reasonable from Cincinnati to Bluefield. While these present class rates and grain rates from Chicago to Bluefield are ample, we do not hold at this time that they are excessive.

In declining to reduce the rates from Chicago to Bluefield we are somewhat influenced by the belief that the present adjustment into this territory as a whole is sufficiently favorable and ought not, unless that seem necessary, to be disturbed. To most points upon both the main line and the branch lines of the Norfolk & Western between Kenova and Roanoke rates are higher than the Virginia cities rate by certain arbitraries, beginning at 12 cents first class and ending with 5 cents sixth class. Rates so constructed are applied at all points upon the Bristol and the Norton lines and also upon other branch lines of the Norfolk & Western in that section. This was said to result in a blanket rate to between five and six hundred stations.

While it may be that these rates to certain points upon the main line of the Norfolk & Western are somewhat high, they are distinctly favorable to the points covered as a whole. If it clearly appeared that Bluefield was charged an unreasonable rate under this blanket adjustment, it would be our duty to reduce it, but since the greatest reduction which could properly be made, if Bluefield were considered by itself, would be so slight as to be almost inappreciable to the shippers of that locality, we feel that substantial justice is now being done, and that the present adjustment should not be disturbed.

Rates from Pittsburgh to Bluefield which are attacked by this complaint are made over the Pennsylvania lines from Pittsburgh to Columbus and from Columbus to Bluefield by the Norfolk & Western. Below are given the class rates which we have found reasonable from Columbus to Bluefield, the class rates from Pittsburgh to Columbus, the combination, and the present Pittsburgh rates:

	Classes					
	1	2	3	4	5	6
	Cents	*Cents*	*Cents*	*Cents*	*Cents*	*Cents*
Columbus to Bluefield	54½	47	35½	24	20	16
Pittsburgh to —						
Columbus..............	33	28½	22	15	12	9½
Combination............	87½	75½	57½	39	32	25½
Present rates............	86½	73	55½	39	34	26

We are of the opinion and find that the present class rates from Pittsburgh are excessive, and that the following rates are reasonable and should not be exceeded for the future:

Class............	1	2	3	4	5	6
Rate.............	79	68	53	35	29	22

There are at the present time in effect to Bluefield via this route, upon iron articles, classified as fourth, fifth, and sixth class, rates of 31, 26, and 21 cents, respectively, and these rates we hold to be just and reasonable. The above finding applies to the route via Columbus, no opinion being expressed as to what might be reasonable via Roanoke.

Under these holdings we shall permit the charging of higher rates at intermediate points than to Roanoke, and points east, from Pittsburgh, Columbus, Cincinnati, Chicago, and kindred points, so long as the present rates from these points to Roanoke and points beyond do not exceed those now in effect, and provided that no higher rates are charged at Bluefield and points to the west than have been found reasonable from Cincinnati, Columbus, and Pittsburgh.

The routes via Norton and Bristol, in which the Norfolk & Western is a link and with respect to which fourth section applications are now before us for disposition, are more circuitous than by the main line. Rates via these routes from Cincinnati, Chicago, and probably from Columbus are the same as via the direct line. Not only are the distances by these routes from points of origin upon the Ohio River and north greater than via the main line of the Norfolk & Western, but the roads handling the traffic from the Ohio River to Norton and Bristol show, for the most part, very much less favorable traffic and financial conditions than those exhibited by the Norfolk & Western. Taking all things into account, it is clear that rates via these routes to Roanoke from points of origin in the west, including Cincinnati, are lower than they might reasonably be.

No attack has been made upon the intermediate rates, and our examination of those rates in connection with those to Bluefield indicates that they are not probably excessive, certainly to points upon the Norfolk & Western. We shall assume that the intermediate rates are reasonable without prejudice to the right of the Commission to at any time further examine that subject, and shall permit carriers by these routes to deviate from the rule of the fourth section so long as neither the Virginia cities rate nor the intermediate rates are advanced. Should carriers desire to increase their present charges either at the more distant or the intermediate point, or should shippers conceive that these charges are unreasonable, that question can be presented to the Commission for further consideration.

The final question is upon the inherent reasonableness of the present rates from New York, Philadelphia, and Baltimore to Bluefield. Those rates, together with rates from the same points to Roanoke, are given below:

	Classes					
	1	2	3	4	5	6
To Bluefield from —	*Cents*	*Cents*	*Cents*	*Cents*	*Cents*	*Cents*
New York	99½	84	65½	46	40	30
Philadelphia	91½	78	60½	42	37	28
Baltimore	86½	73	55½	39	34	26
To Roanoke from —						
New York	68	59	51	32	28	23
Philadelphia	63	52	44	30	25	21
Baltimore	58	49	38½	27	23	19

An inspection of the above figures shows that rates from New York to Bluefield exceed those from New York to Roanoke by the following differentials:

Class	1	2	3	4	5	6
Differential	31½	25	14½	14	12	7

The differentials in case of Philadelphia and Baltimore are substantially, but not exactly, the same.

The present rates from Hagerstown to Bluefield and Roanoke are as follows:

From Hagerstown to —	Classes					
	1	2	3	4	5	6
	Cents	*Cents*	*Cents*	*Cents*	*Cents*	*Cents*
Bluefield	68	55	42	32	27	22
Roanoke	54½	46	35½	24	20	16

Here the differentials of Bluefield over Roanoke are:

Class	1	2	3	4	5	6
Differential	13½	9	6½	8	7	6

Apparently, rates from Hagerstown to Roanoke and Bluefield are not influenced by any competitive conditions. The distance from Hagerstown to Roanoke is 240 miles, and the rates in effect are normal for that distance. There is no reason why the Bluefield rate may not have been made as much higher than that to Roanoke as, under all the circumstances, would be reasonable, and the rates as we find them must be taken as an expression of the opinion of the Norfolk & Western to that effect.

The vice-president of the defendant was asked to explain how it happened that the first class rate from New York to Bluefield exceeded that to Roanoke by 31½ cents, whereas in case of Hagerstown that difference was but 13½ cents. He was unable to give any explanation, nor was any ventured upon the argument.

The distances from these eastern points of origin to Bluefield are as follows:

	Miles
New York	613
Philadelphia	523
Baltimore	408

We are of the opinion and find that the present rates from New York, Philadelphia, and Baltimore, via Hagerstown, to Bluefield are unjust and unreasonable, and that the rates given below are reasonable and ought not to be exceeded:

To Bluefield from —	Classes					
	1	2	3	4	5	6
	Cents	*Cents*	*Cents*	*Cents*	*Cents*	*Cents*
New York	81½	68	57½	40	35	29
Philadelphia	76½	61	50½	38	32	27
Baltimore	71½	58	45	35	30	25

If the disposition made of this case leaves in effect at Bluefield a discrimination, it may be observed:

First. The testimony before the Commission indicates that while, upon the face of the tariffs, there is a preference against Bluefield, still the effect of that preference is not especially noticeable. The rates paid by Bluefield are, or will be when our order in this case is complied with, just and reasonable in themselves, and jobbers at that locality do not seem to be seriously affected in competition with Roanoke and Lynchburg by the somewhat more favorable rates which those cities enjoy. In cases like this, where some one must suffer, it is pertinent to inquire how the least injury may be inflicted.

Second. If an undue discrimination is left in effect, it is because, under the law as it exists, no adequate method has been provided for its correction. Carriers are forbidden to agree upon competitive rates like those from the west to Roanoke and Lynchburg, and the Commission has no authority to fix a minimum charge. Under these circumstances it is impossible to establish and enforce rates which are relatively just to these different communities. The purpose of Congress seems to have been to keep alive competition of exactly the kind which is found at Roanoke, and which produces the lower rate at that point, upon the theory, probably, that while injustice may in some instances result the general effect is for the public good.

An order will be entered in No. 3753 establishing the rates found to be reasonable, and suitable orders will be made in the various fourth-section applications.

MURFREESBORO BOARD OF TRADE

v.

LOUISVILLE & NASHVILLE RAILROAD CO.

55 I. C. C., 648 (1919)

McCHORD, *Commissioner:*

The complaint in this proceeding alleges that the class and commodity rates to Murfreesboro, Columbia, Dickson, Gallatin, Lebanon, and Watertown, Tenn., from the points of origin hereinafter set forth are unreasonable and as compared to the rates to Nashville, Tenn., are unduly prejudicial to the points named. It is further alleged that certain rates involve departures from the long-and-short-haul clause of section 4 of the act to regulate commerce. Rates which shall not exceed those contemporaneously in effect to Nashville, and reparation, are asked. Intervening petitions were filed by the Traffic Bureau of Nashville and the Tennessee Manufacturers' Association. The former opposes the relief sought, and the latter does not support or oppose the prayer of complainants. Appropriate fourth section applications were set for hearing with the complaint.

On motion of the complainants we entered an order on September 19, 1918, permitting the filing of a supplemental complaint making the Director General of Railroads a party defendant. On October 4, 1918, answer thereto was filed on behalf of the Director General. Further hearing was not asked.

Murfreesboro is 32 miles southeast of Nashville, on the Nashville, Chattanooga & St. Louis Railway; Columbia is 46 miles southwest of Nashville, on the Louisville & Nashville Railroad and Nashville, Chattanooga & St. Louis Railway; Dickson is 42 miles west of Nashville, on the Nashville, Chattanooga & St. Louis Railway; Gallatin is 27 miles northeast of Nashville, on the Louisville & Nashville Railroad; Lebanon is 31 miles east of Nashville, on the Tennessee Central Railroad and Nashville, Chattanooga & St. Louis Railway; and Watertown is 45 miles east of Nashville, on the Tennessee Central Railroad. Nashville is on the Cumberland River, and is served by all of the railroads serving the various complaining points. The accompanying map illustrates the situation. In 1910 the population of these points was: Nashville, 114,899; Murfreesboro, 4,679; Columbia, 5,754;

Dickson, 1,850; Gallatin, 2,399; Lebanon, 3,659; and Watertown, 517.

The points of origin involved are the eastern ports; interior eastern cities; Buffalo-Pittsburgh territory; Virginia cities;

south Atlantic ports; interior southeastern points; Gulf ports St. Louis, Mo., Memphis, Tenn., and other lower Mississippi River crossings, and points beyond in western trunk line territory and points in the states of Texas, Oklahoma, and Arkansas and Ohio River crossings, Cairo, Ill., to Cincinnati, Ohio, inclusive, and points beyond in central freight association and western trunk line territories.

Unless otherwise noted, rates throughout this report will be stated in cents per 100 pounds. The table below shows the first-class rates in effect on June 24, 1918, which illustrate the rate situation, and distances from representative points of origin to Nashville and the complaining points. Under General Order No. 28 of the Director General these rates were increased 25 per cent, effective June 25, 1918.

From —	To Nashville		To Murfreesboro		To Columbia		To Dickson		To Gallatin		To Lebanon		To Watertown	
	Miles	Rate	Miles	Rate	Miles	Rate	Miles	Rate	Miles	Rate	Miles	Rate	Miles	Rate
New York, N. Y.	954	100	966	125	1,000	125	996	136	946	126	923	118	909	125
Norfolk, Va.	755	92	769	117	861	117	797	128	782	113	724	110	710	117
Savannah, Ga.	548	93	516	118	552	118	590	129	575	119	579	118	593	129
Atlanta, Ga.	288	72	256	72	292	83	330	93	315	93	319	90	333	97
Birmingham, Ala.	208	63	240	84	162	70	250	84	235	84	239	84	253	99
New Orleans, La.	608	90	640	115	577	108	566	119	635	113	639	115	653	126
Memphis, Tenn.	238	59	270	83	264	78	197	65	265	70	269	84	283	95
St. Louis, Mo.	323	70	355	95	369	95	365	85	350	96	354	95	368	106
Chicago, Ill.	447	98	479	107	493	107	441	102	452	108	478	100	492	134
Cairo, Ill.	209	47	241	72	255	72	167	57	236	63	240	72	254	83
Paducah, Ky.	181	47	213	72	227	72	139	53	208	63	212	72	226	83
Evansville, Ind.	157	47	189	72	203	72	193	79	163	63	188	72	202	83
Louisville, Ky.	186	47	218	72	232	72	221	80	159	55	217	72	231	83
Cincinnati, Ohio	300	62	332	87	346	87	335	88	273	78	331	87	345	98

The first-class rates in effect on June 24, 1918, from Nashville to the complaining points were as follows: Murfreesboro, 25 cents; Columbia, 25 cents; Dickson, 36 cents; Gallatin, 26 cents; Lebanon, 25 cents; and to Watertown, 36 cents. These rates also were increased under General Order No. 28. The through rates to the complaining points are generally based on the Nashville combination. The exceptions to this rule are usually due to the fact that the complaining points are intermediate to Nashville, in some instances, particularly as to Murfreesboro, Columbia, and Gallatin, and the application of the mileage scales results in lower rates than the combination on Nashville. In many instances the rates to Dickson are less than the combination on Nashville for the reason that the rates from points north of the Ohio and Missouri rivers are based upon Paducah.

Some of the rates under attack were increased on January 1, 1916, in connection with the revision of rates following our report in *Fourth Section Violations in the Southeast,* 30 I. C. C., 153, 313. In certain instances the rates to some of the intermediate points, particularly Gallatin, were not changed at the time the rates to Nashville were increased. The rates to points beyond Nashville were generally increased to the same extent as those to Nashville. In this readjustment the southern classification was made applicable in connection with the rates from eastern and interior eastern cities in lieu of the official classification, which also resulted in increased charges in some cases.

While it is alleged that the rates are unreasonable, the main contention of complainants is that the present rate adjustment is in violation of sections 3 and 4 of the act to regulate commerce, and on brief complainants practically abandoned the contention that the rates are unreasonable in and of themselves. Considerable evidence was introduced by the defendants for the purpose of showing that the rates to the complaining points are inherently reasonable. The rates attacked are compared with rates from the points of origin involved to other points in the southeast, also with rates in other sections of the country, some of which were prescribed by us. Defendants also refer to increased costs of operation.

The principal justification offered by the carriers for the maintenance of lower rates to Nashville than to intermediate points is that the rates are depressed by competition between the rail lines serving that point and by competition, actual or potential, with the boat lines operating on the Cumberland, Ohio, and Mississippi rivers.

It is asserted that the rail carriers serving Nashville are in active competition with each other for traffic to that point, which competition influences the rates; and that this situation does not exist at the complaining points. The record shows that the Tennessee Central is not a factor in making rates to Nashville, having met the rates in effect when it commenced operation in 1902, and since that time it has exercised little, if any, influence on the rates because of its light traffic, operating disadvantages, and financial condition. The Nashville, Chattanooga & St. Louis is controlled through stock ownership by the Louisville & Nashville. In *Financial Relations, etc., L. & N. R. R. Co.,* 33 I. C. C., 168, we found that the official record of these carriers clearly established that the purpose of control of the former by the latter was primarily to restrict competition and to maintain rates. We therefore find that the competition between the rail carriers serving Nashville is not of such a nature as to affect the measure of the rates to that point, and in determining whether the rates to Nashville are depressed we must consider the competition with the river lines only.

A very comprehensive record has been presented upon the

question of Cumberland River competition and its effect upon rates to Nashville. The Louisville & Nashville commenced operation from Louisville to Nashville in November, 1859. In 1857, 33 steamboats were engaged in transporting freight between Ohio and Mississippi river cities and Nashville, of which 6 were through boats operated from Pittsburgh, 7 from Cincinnati, 3 from Louisville, 2 from St. Louis, 4 from Memphis, 5 from New Orleans, and 6 from Paducah. In 1870, 15 steamboats transported freight to Nashville, 4 of which operated from Cairo, 3 from Cincinnati, 4 from Pittsburgh, and 1 from Evansville, and the points from which the remaining 3 boats operated were not shown. At the time of hearing, in March, 1917, 1 boat of 300-tons capacity operated weekly from Paducah to Nashville. At the same time there was a daily boat service from Cincinnati to Louisville, service twice a week from Louisville to Evansville, a somewhat irregular service from Evansville to Paducah, daily service from Cairo to Paducah, service twice a week from St. Louis and Memphis to Cairo, and regular boat and barge service between St. Louis and New Orleans, with stop at Cairo.

The following table shows the class rates published by the Louisville & Nashville from Louisville to Nashville from 1865 to and including January 1, 1916:

Date	1	2	3	4	5	6	A	B	C	D
Dec. 31, 1865	75	65	50	..	..	..	..	..	..	..
Aug. 1, 1869	70	60	45	35	..	..	..	..	..	..
July 1, 1872	55	45	42	30	..	..	..	..	..	.
Apr. 1, 1876	40	35	30	15	12	..	..	15	12	12
Aug. 12, 1878 [1]	..	..	..	..	..	..	..	..	..	...
Nov. 4, 1878	25	20	17	14	13	..	..	17	13	13
Dec. 3, 1879	35	28	24	19	15	15	15	19	15	15
Apr. 26, 1882	38	33	28	23	18	18	15	19	15	15
June 1, 1882	38	33	28	23	15	15	15	19	13	12
July 17, 1882	38	33	28	23	15	15	15	19	13	10
June 25, 1883	38	33	28	23	18	15	15	19	13	10
Mar. 15, 1886	38	33	28	23	18	15	15	19	11	10
Apr. 16, 1891	38	33	28	23	18	15	15	15	11	10
Aug. 1, 1908	38	33	28	23	18	15	15	18	11	10
Jan. 1, 1913	47	38	31	28	22	20	15	20	11	10

[1] A first-class rate of 20 cents was established on this date, but the rates for the lower classes were not given.

Specific instances are given by defendants of shipments of particular articles from competitive points to Nashville via the river lines. It is stated that the information in the possession of the defendants with respect to such shipments is not complete, and that recently the defendants have not attempted to check the movement of traffic via the river lines. The record shows conclusively that for many years after the Louisville & Nashville commenced operation to Nashville the competition with the river lines was very keen, and the witnesses testified at great length as to the various steps taken by the Louisville & Nashville to meet this competition. As hereinbefore shown, the first-class rate from Louisville to Nashville was reduced from 75 cents in 1865 to 20 cents in 1878 since which time the rate was gradually increased to 38 cents in 1882 and to 47 cents in 1916.

Complainants admit that the competition with the river lines influenced the rates to Nashville for some time, but contend that the question before us for determination is whether the present rates are affected by this competition. In support of this contention complainants cite *Commercial Club of Duluth* v. *B. & O. R. R. Co.*, 27 I. C. C., 639, wherein we stated at page 652 that —

"We not infrequently inquire into the origin and history of rates and of rate relations in order properly to interpret and to understand their significance; but when dealing with a rate or a relation of rates now in existence, and which is complained of as being either unreasonable or unduly discriminatory, we can neither justify nor condemn it on the basis of its origin or of the conditions surrounding the traffic in the past, but only on the basis of its present effect in the light of present conditions."

Complainants call attention to the fact that defendants refer specifically to but few shipments from competitive points to Nashville via the river lines since 1900. The defendants refer to 74 shipments of manufactured articles in 1901, 1905, and 1907 to 1913, inclusive, from competitive points to Nashville, and to shipments of grain in 1905 and 1915: Many of these shipments covered small quantities of freight. During 1911 and 1912 there was a considerable movement of merchandise and other manufactured articles which originated at various northern and eastern points. Complainants assert that this movement was artificially stimulated, as at that time the case of *Alanta Freight Bureau* v. *N., C. & St. L. Ry.*, 29 I. C. C., 476, in which the Nashville Traffic Bureau intervened, was before us. Complainants' assertion seems to be borne out by the fact that, as shown by the annual reports of the chief of engineers, United States army, hereinafter referred to, the movement of merchandise and manufactured articles via the river lines greatly decreased.

The following table is taken from the annual report of the chief of engineers, United States army, for the year 1916, and shows the tonnage transported via the Cumberland River below Nashville for the calendar years 1906 to 1915, inclusive:

Year	Total tonnage	Farm products	Forest products	Merchandise, including flour and meal	Fertilizer	Sand and Gravel	Miscellaneous, including coal, cement, iron, machinery, etc.	Rafted products
1906..........	223,899	29,185	159,346	2,000	....	31,680	....	1,688
1907..........	300,810	40,928	227,189	20,600	1,500	1,800	2,850	5,943
1908..........	259,734	24,176	217,272	6,300	....	8,520	1,778	1,688
1909.........	193,118	27,202	129,468	18,113	82	16,414	177	1,662
1910..........	327,757	56,365	168,909	42,513	....	45,000	9,770	5,200
1911..........	223,278	23,264	145,334	7,159	700	40,916	2,305	3,600
1912..........	176,659	21,431	59,373	10,800	....	26,780	1,542	56,733
1913..........	165,123	16,123	131,024	3,705	1,100	11,250	1,026	895
1914..........	153,458	6,151	99,266	4,140	851	38,976	1,337	2,737
1915..........	126,949	10,250	92,723	3,904	421	15,237	1,781	2,633

Of the traffic handled in the last year shown in the above table, 85,651 tons consisted of railroad ties, 9,707 tons of forest products other than railroad ties, 15,237 tons of sand and gravel. No figures are given showing separately the tonnage transported to or from local points and that transported to or from points also served by rail lines.

In an exhibit filed by the Louisville & Nashville it is stated that in the territory adjacent to the Cumberland River below Nashville large quantities of agricultural products, live stock, poultry, and eggs are produced, and that from Cumberland City, Tenn., to Eddyville, Ky., a distance of about 60 miles, the average distance across country to the nearest railroad is about 20 miles. It is also stated that in the territory adjacent to the river from Nashville to Burnside, Ky., a distance of 325 miles, large quantities of forest products are produced, and the movement of this traffic is absolutely dependent upon the river, as but two points are also reached by rail.

Improvements in the form of a series of locks and dams have been made in recent years in the Cumberland River channel, and prior to the hearing in 1917 the river below Nashville was navigable for boats drawing 6 feet or less from 8 to 10 months during the year. Further improvements of the same nature were then under way, and when completed the river will be navigable for boats drawing 6 feet or less during the entire year between its junction with the Ohio and Nashville.

The effect of the Cumberland River competition upon rates to Nashville has been under consideration by us in the following cases, and the conclusions reached in respect thereto in the various cases have not been altogether harmonious: *Phillips, Bailey & Co.* v. *Louisville & Nashville R. R. Co.,* 8 I. C. C., 93; *Payne-Gardner Co.* v. *Louisville & Nashville R. R. Co.,* 13 I. C. C., 186, and 35 I. C. C., 477; *Receivers & Shippers Asso.* v. *Commerce of Chattanooga* v. *S. Ry. Co.,* 10 I. C. C., 111; *Duncan & Co.* v. *N., C. & St. L. Ry. Co.,* 16 I. C. C., 590, 21 I. C. S, 186, and 35 I. C. C., 477; *Receivers & Shippers Asso.* v. *C., N. O. & T. P. Ry. Co.,* 18 I. C. C., 440; *Columbia Grocery Co.* v. *L. & N. R. R. Co.,* 18 I. C. C., 502; and *Atlanta Freight Bureau* v. *N., C. & St. L. Ry.,* 29 I. C. C., 476. Without discussing these cases in detail, it is sufficient to state that in some we held that the river competition influenced the rates and in others we held to the contrary. This question has been more fully covered in this proceeding than in those referred to, and the conclusions therein reached need not be considered here.

Before we can properly authorize the defendants to maintain lower rates to Nashville than to intermediate points it must be clearly shown that the circumstances and conditions surrounding transportation to Nashville are substantially dissimilar to those surrounding transportation to intermediate points. The testimony relied upon by defendants to support their allegation that the lower Nashville rates are necessary because of active and compelling competition with the river lines is not convincing. As stated above, defendants refer to some shipments of grain and manufactured articles from competitive points to Nashville via the river lines since 1900, but these shipments are comparatively few in number, and there is nothing in the record to indicate that this route is used regularly for the transportation of freight from competitive points in appreciable quantities. The competition with the river lines is almost entirely potential, and we are of the opinion that the competition disclosed by the record does not justify fourth section relief sought.

At the present time through rates to points beyond Nashville are generally made up of the rates to and from Nashville, so that Nashville merchants are usually enabled to compete for business at the complaining points on the same basis from a transportation standpoint as merchants located there, and when complainants undertake to compete with Nashville merchants at other competitive points they are at a serious disadvantage, as the combinations on the complaining points greatly exceed the combinations on Nashville. The defendants contend that the rates to Nashville are depressed by competition with the river lines, and that therefore the present basis of constructing through rates to points beyond Nashville is proper. We have already found that there is no compelling competition which justifies lower rates to Nashville than to intermediate points. Therefore in using the combination in constructing through rates to points beyond Nashville the defendants are applying the basing-point system, which has been repeatedly condemned by us. It appears from the record that it has been the purpose of defendants to maintain rates to Nashville which will enable that point to compete with other large commercial centers in the same general territory. The defendants can not lawfully extend such a basis of rates to Nashville, and at the same time ignore the rates to other points in the immediate vicinity.

Upon the facts of record we are of the opinion and find that the rates attacked have not been shown to be unreasonable, and that the defendants have justified the rates which have been increased since 1910; that the competition with the boat lines operating on the Cumberland, Ohio, and Mississippi rivers encountered by defendants in transporting freight to Nashville is not of such a character as to control or to affect materially the rail rates to Nashville, and the applications for authority to continue lower rates to Nashville than to intermediate points should be denied; that the present rates to the complaining points to which traffic moves through Nashville subjects such points to undue prejudice and unduly prefers Nashville to the extent that the through rates exceed the rates contemporaneously maintained to Nashville plus 75 per cent of the local rates contemporaneously maintained from Nashville to the complaining points.

The establishment of the percentage relation is not to be held as an approval by us of the existing local rates from Nashville to the complaining points as being reasonable to apply as factors of through rates even on the basis proposed. The complainants have established their right to relief from the undue prejudice. The relief granted is considered on the average, and in the absence of sufficient evidence to enable us to prescribe just and reasonable through rates in each instance.

There is no showing that complainants have been damaged because of the unlawful rate adjustment, and reparation is therefore denied.

Appropriate orders will be entered.

In Re INVESTIGATION OF ADVANCES IN RATES, etc.

20 I. C. C. 307 (1911.)

REPORT OF THE COMMISSION

Lane, *Commissioner:*

This proceeding, which is popularly known as the "Western Advanced Rate Case," involves the reasonableness of the rates upon some 200 commodities which the carriers west of Chicago have attempted to increase. No effort can be made to specify the individual rates, inasmuch as these number several hundred thousand, nor can the territory involved be precisely delimited, although a fair idea of its extent may be had by a survey of a map of the Burlington system which leads to most of the basing points upon which the rates concerned are fixed. More than 200 railroads operating in the states of Wisconsin, Minnesota, Iowa, Missouri, North Dakota, South Dakota, Nebraska, Kansas, and Montana are parties to these rates. It is needless to say that neither the carriers nor the shippers have throughout this investigation attempted to deal with all the specific rates between definite points of movement upon these lines of road. This investigation has been a general one, touching large and fundamental principles of law and governmental policy on the one hand, and of railroad needs, plans and policies on the other.

The rates concerned are under voluntary suspension by act of the carriers. It will be recalled that in June, 1910, the principal carriers in Western Trunk Line territory filed with the Commission tariffs increasing their rates upon a number of important articles of commerce. This action was taken through common agents. Before such rates, however, had gone into effect the Attorney General of the United States caused suit to be brought in the circuit court of the United States for the seventh circuit, alleging that such increased rates were the result of a combination and conspiracy in restraint of trade and in violation of the Sherman antitrust act. A temporary injunction having been secured, appeal was made by the carriers affected to the President of the United States, asking relief from such injunction and offering to voluntarily suspend the effectiveness of such rates pending a determination as to their reasonableness by the Interstate Commerce Commission. This appeal was made in view of a bill then pending before Congress amending the act to regulate commerce so as to vest in this Commission the power to suspend advanced rates. Such bill later became law. The carriers thereupon refiled their tariffs, suspending their effectiveness, however, until such time as the Commission could conduct the present investigation.

CONSTRUCTION OF NEW LAW

At the threshold of this inquiry we are required to give interpretation to a new provision of the act to regulate commerce, which reads:

"Whenever there shall be filed with the Commission any schedule stating a new individual or joint rate, fare, or charge, or any new individual or joint classification, or any new individual or joint regulation or practice affecting any rate, fare, or charge, the Commission shall have, and it is hereby given, authority, either upon complaint or upon its own initiative without complaint, at once, and if it so orders, without answer or other formal pleading by the interested carrier or carriers, but upon reasonable notice, to enter upon a hearing concerning the propriety of such rate, fare, charge, classification, regulation or practice; and pending such hearing and the decision thereon the Commission upon filing with such schedule and delivering to the carrier or carriers affected thereby a statement in writing of its reasons for such suspension may suspend the operation of such schedule and defer the use of such rate, fare, charge, classification, regulation, or practice, but not for a longer period than one hundred and twenty days beyond the time when such rate, fare, charge, classification, regulation, or practice would otherwise go into effect, and after full hearing, whether completed before or after the rate, fare, charge, classification, regulation, or practice goes into effect, the Commission may make such order in reference to such rate, fare, charge, classification, regulation, or practice as would be proper in a proceeding initiated after the rate, fare, charge, classification, regulation, or practice had become effective: *Provided,* That if any such hearing can not be concluded within the period of suspension, as above stated, the Interstate Commerce Commission may, in its discretion, extend the time of suspension for a further period not exceeding six months. At any hearing involving a rate increased after January first, nineteen hundred and ten, or of a rate sought to be increased after the passage of this act, the burden of proof to show that the increased rate or proposed increased rate is just and reasonable shall be upon the common carrier, and the Commission shall give to the hearing and decision of such questions preference over all other questions pending before it and decide the same as speedily as possible."

In the last sentence of this provision it is said that the burden of proof to show that "the increased rate" or proposed rate is just and reasonable shall be upon the common carrier. It is urged with much force and extensive citation of authority that the purpose of this provision was to limit the investigation of the Commission to the consideration of the necessity for "the increase in the rate." The purpose of Congress, it is said, was to regard all rates in effect on January 1, 1910, as the maxima, which could not be increased until it was shown that there was reason and necessity for the specific increase made. This would limit our investigations as to all rates increased since that time to the simple question, What additional expenses have attached to the movement of these articles which make proper an increase in the rate?

Such a construction of the statute is suggested by decisions of the English courts in interpreting the railway and canal act of 1894. We think, however, it is clear from the language of that statute, as well as its history, that the purpose of Congress differed from the purpose of Parliament. The English law was based on a legislative conclusion that existing rates were already sufficiently high and should not be increased excepting as transportation costs increased. Therefore, the English commission was to deal with the increase itself in the rate and not with the increased rate. This distinction is fundamental in the consideration of the laws of the two Governments.

The British Parliament in 1891 and 1892 passed a series of public acts establishing the maximum rates and charges assessable by the railway and canal companies of Great Britain and

Ireland. These acts became effective upon December 31, 1892. On the day immediately following, viz., January 1, 1893, the carriers took advantage of the liberal scale of class rates provided for in these parliamentary acts, and advanced a great number of such rates which were lower than the maxima allowed and which had obtained for many years. The Railway and Canal Commission was without authority to check such increases and restore previously existing schedules. At once, therefore, it was perceived that the effect of the new legislation by Parliament under which relief had been hoped for by the shippers was to place it within the power of the carriers to increase all rates up to the high class rates fixed by parliamentary act.

It was to remedy this situation that the railway and canal traffic act of 1894 was passed providing that " where a railway company has either alone or jointly with any other railway company or companies since the last day of December, 1892, directly or indirectly increased, or hereafter increase, directly or indirectly, any rate or charge, then, if any complaint is made that the rate or charge is unreasonable, it shall lie upon the company to prove that the increase of the rate or charge is reasonable, and for that purpose it shall not be sufficient to show that the rate or charge is within any limit fixed by an act of Parliament or by any provisional order confirmed by act of Parliament."

Lord Justice Smith gave the history of this act in the *Mansion House case*, 9 R. & C. T. Cases, p. 58, in these words:

" What the legislature did was obvious. We know how, when the new maxima came in, the companies put up their rates, and as regards many of them they put them up to their maxima, and it became a question for traders and the community at large, and the legislature said, when they found this had happened, we will go back two years and draw a line along there and say that is probably the proper rate two years ago, which they have been charging before they began putting up their rates to their maxima. We will just draw a line along there, and if they have increased them since that date, then we will put upon the railway company the onus of justifying that increase. That is the English of that act of Parliament, and that I have no doubt about."

The effect of this enactment was to cast upon the railway company the burden of proving " that the increase of the rate was reasonable." The act to regulate commerce, on the other hand, requires the carrier to show the reasonableness of the increased rate. Under the act of Parliament, the carrier is called upon to justify the difference between its previously existing rate and the rate established, while under the act of Congress the carrier is called upon to prove that the new rate as a whole is reasonable. This distinction is clearly recognized in the opinion of Smith, *L. J.* in the *Mansion House case,* 9 R. & C. T. Cases, at page 209, wherein it is said:

"There was an ingenious point taken by Mr. Russell, namely, that if the rate in the whole was reasonable, nothing more was to be inquired into. That really whittled the act of 1894 down to the procedure in vogue before 1894. The question then always was whether the rate or charge was reasonable, and this act, as I read it, makes the question whether the increase was fair and reasonable."

And, again, in the same case, Kay, *L. J.*, at page 201, says:

"That is where there has been an increase. If any complaint is made that the rate or charge is unreasonable it shall lie on the company to prove that the increase, not the rate or charge, but that the increase of the rate or charge, is reasonable."

And on page 200:

"What the company is bound to prove is that the increase has been reasonable, and they do not show that by merely showing that the present charge is reasonable."

There is, however, another and broader view by which we can determine the meaning of Congress. For more than 20 years Congress by express statutory declaration fixed the measure of a carrier's charge at "a just and reasonable rate." There was no check upon the initiative of the carrier. Any rate filed and published in accordance with the requirements of the law was presumed to be reasonable, and a direct proceeding of attack upon complaint was necessary to raise before this Commission the question whether or not it conformed to the standard set by the law. For a period of years the tendency of rates was downward, owing in great part to active competition between the carriers for traffic. Rates were made from day to day, and as between one shipper and another, by means of rebates from the standard published rate. This led to extreme dissatisfaction on the part of the public, and to the serious injury of the roads themselves. To meet this situation the carriers attempted to form traffic associations by which under severe penalties they were bound to each other by contract to exact the published rates. Under decisions of the Supreme Court of the United

States, however, these alliances were declared unlawful, and there then followed the development of the "community of interest" plan by which, through the medium of one group of financiers or another, the carriers of a certain territory became harmonized. They no longer competed by cutting rates, because they were subject to a common control, or at least were dominated by interests that were sympathetic. There resulted an era of unexampled prosperity among the railroads as a whole. Net revenues increased, the stronger roads of higher credit absorbed the smaller; new lines were projected by the greater roads; small lines were articulated into large and connected systems; and with the development on the part of the carriers of the advantages of concord came an evident determination not only to make rates stable but if possible to bring about their increase. Accordingly, for several years past the chief body of protest coming from shippers to this Commission has been against increases in rates, and the Commission being unable to stay these increases, the shippers sought from Congress the enactment of a law by which the power would be given to this Commission, when public reasons made advisable such a course, to lay a restraining hand upon the power and initiative which hitherto had rested with the carrier without limitation or constraint.

Moreover, the Federal courts found themselves embarrassed by the appeals made to their equity powers against such increases. The courts differed upon the fundamental question of jurisdiction. In the cases where the courts assumed jurisdiction there resulted the greatest discrimination as between individual shippers and carriers, for as to some the increased rate was in effect, while as to others it was not in effect. With such a history before it Congress deemed it advisable to lodge with this Commission, which alone under the *Abilene case*, 204 U. S., 426, has power to determine the reasonableness of a rate, the power to restrain for a time an increased rate until a determination can be had as to whether this rate conforms to the requirement of the statute or is but the evidence of the exercise of an arbitrary power.

The National Legislature has not fixed, as in England, a body of maximum rates. It has not declared that the rates of January 1, 1910, are to be regarded as either above or below the old and long established standard of reasonableness. The statute contains no intimation that we are to gauge an increased rate which is suspended by any other measure than that by which we would gauge any existing rate that might be complained of. The power to suspend is ancillary to the general power of investigation, it being the mind of Congress that it was a healthier and wiser policy that there should be a reasonable exercise of such power of suspension than that either the courts should continue to inadequately deal by injunctive process with a problem the ultimate solution of which did not rest within their purview, or that the shipping public should be subjected to continuing instability of rates and consequent commercial disturbance. Moreover, the duty having been laid upon the carriers to fix reasonable rates, it was neither harsh nor oppressive to require them to make justification when such rates were to be increased.

Regarded from this point of view, we cannot but conclude that Congress did not intend to say to this Commission: The rates obtaining on January 1, 1910, are maxima, and if a carrier attempts to increase them he must give the reason for the increase, showing what new burden of transportation expenses it has suffered which justifies such increase. The question before the Commission is that which would have arisen had these rates gone into effect and a formal complaint been made against them as unjust and unreasonable. We may establish the rates proposed as reasonable, one or all of them, or reduce the proposed rates. We may continue in effect the present lower rates, or we may reduce the existing rates. For " the Commission may make such order in reference to such rate . . . as would be proper in a proceeding initiated after the rate had become effective." The purpose of Congress was to give this Commission the same plenary power over increased rates that since the enactment of the Hepburn Act it has enjoyed over other rates.

BURDEN OF PROOF

Stress is further laid upon the use of the words " *the burden of proof* shall be upon the common carrier," and we are urged to a strict interpretation of this language along lines of judicial reasoning in civil and criminal cases. This language has a common-sense meaning which does not need elucidation by citation of authority.

It must be borne in mind that this Commission is not a court of law; its function is to apply the mandatory and restrictive provisions of the act to regulate commerce to stated conditions of fact. We must regard the problems presented to us from as many standpoints as there are public interests involved. The making of a rate is in ultimate analysis the exercise of a taxing power on commerce. 73 Fed., 409. The reasonableness of a rate is to be determined by no mere mathematical calculation, though figures of cost and revenue must play a not inconsiderable part in arriving at a final judgment. Wise men may differ as to what a "just and reasonable rate" is under given conditions. The courts recognize that there is abundant play for what the present Chief Justice so admirably described as "the flexible limit of judgment which belongs to the power to make rates." 206 U. S., 26. The unrestricted power to make rates, however, should not rest in the hands of those whose tendency must be, by reason of human nature, to exact to the limit the highest return that can be procured. Reasons of public policy demand that there shall be a check placed upon a power which may be perverted and thus brought to restrict and embarrass commerce rather than increase and develop it. Every rate question, therefore, is a public question — this is the underlying principle of the act to regulate commerce and of all similar legislation controlling public utilities. An examination into the specific provisions of the act, especially into those of section 13, will make clear to the candid mind that a complaint before this Commission was not intended to be regarded in the same strict and hard light as a complaint in an action of law, but was to be regarded as an appeal to the Government against oppressive, unjust, and illegal action. A shipper may not dismiss his complaint without consent. The fact that he has no interest in the traffic concerned in his complaint does not "put him out of court." These and similar provisions indicate that the purpose of Congress in enacting the act to regulate commerce was to establish a body whose function it should be to protect the public interest and not merely regard the technical rights of an individual shipper, and in this view of the law the act has been administered by the Commission. In accepting this theory, therefore, it is not within belief that Congress intended by the language now under consideration to convert this Commission into a tribunal which should merely determine as between two sides the preponderance of evidence and base its decisions upon technical and somewhat archaic rules of evidence.

By this, however, we are not to be understood as meaning that the language of the act is without significance, or has no binding authority upon us, or that it casts no burden upon the carriers. The assumption of the law is that the railroad which increases its rates takes such action knowing that the law casts upon it — if challenge is made either by this Commission or otherwise — the burden of justifying its action. Theirs, in the language of the learned Dean Wigmore, is "the risk of nonpersuasion." *Wigmore on Evidence,* sec. 2485. The railroad must assume to prove to this Commission that the new and the increased rates are within the words of description and limitation used in the act, that is, that they are just and reasonable. And to say that they must prove this is to say that they must satisfy our minds of this fact.

POSITION OF THE CARRIERS.

The carriers in the present proceeding have assumed this burden. They have laid before us their financial condition, their needs, their hopes, their fears. While the justification given by no one is precisely that given by all others, the common ground for these common advances may be epitomized in the language of the leading witness for the carriers, "We need the money."

Disregarding for the moment all other considerations, this statement that rates should be increased because the carriers need greater revenue than hitherto, sounds ominous, coming as it did in a year of unexampled railroad earnings. For it is a fact, demonstrable from the figures gathered by this Commission, that at no time in the history of American railroads have they yielded such profits or was their prospect more fair than in the fiscal year that closed June 30, 1910.

The primary impression of the Commission was that these increased rates were impelled by the "higher cost of living" to the railroads; that they were merely the outgrowth of the increased cost of supplies, fuel, and labor; but no sooner was the investigation under way than these matters were entirely subordinated. It became manifest that the purpose of the carriers was not so much to secure approval of these specific rates as to discover the mind of the Commission with respect to the policy which the carriers might in future pursue, and to secure if possible some commitment on our part as to a nation-wide policy which would give the carriers a loose rein.

No better expression of this thought can be made than is

found in the opening paragraph of the brief of the Atchison, Topeka & Santa Fe Railway Company:

"The case of The Atchison, Topeka & Santa Fe Railway Company is that American railway rates never have been high enough and that the public never has paid adequately for the service which it has received, that the railway company, with an extremely fortunate situation geographically, touching the Great Lakes, the Gulf of Mexico, and the Pacific Ocean, and penetrating states and territories yielding all varieties of traffic, has never, although most carefully managed, earned for its stockholders and its physical needs half the money to which it has been entitled from the public it has served; that this inadequate return has prevented it from properly keeping abreast of the development of the country or meeting the demands which the people had a right to make if they would pay for the things demanded; that the increased cost of operation and the increase of taxes have for years been encroaching upon its earnings at a pace which all the economies that could be practiced have been insufficient to withstand; that the demands of the region which it serves call for the annual expenditure of about $30,000,000, while under present conditions it can not procure the money; that for the reasons given it has never had the credit which it should have enjoyed as a great and constant borrower of money; and that to meet the needs of its territory henceforward by extending and improving its plant it must have more cash and higher credit, and both of these must come from higher rates.

It is doubtless true that in its control over the charges which our railroads may make this Commission exercises a power so extensive as to justify the broadest consideration of the economic and financial effects of its orders. By its decisions in the *Abilene Cotton Oil case, supra,* and in the *Illinois Central case,* 215 U. S. 452, the Supreme Court has erected this Commission into what has been termed "an economic court," or to give it a more commonplace definition, but one perhaps of stricter legal analogy, a select jury to pass upon the reasonableness and justness of railroad rates, rules, and practices. Within broad lines of discretion the courts regard the conclusions of the Commission on questions of fact as final. There is an appeal upon questions of law by the carriers to the courts, but unless a constitutional guaranty is violated the order of this Commission is final, provided, of course, the Commission does not overstep the jurisdictional limits placed upon it by the statute. And as to the shipper this tribunal is his one and only resort against injustice.

We must not regard too seriously, however, the effort of railroad counsel to establish this Commission *in loco parentis* toward the railroads. We must be conscious in our consideration of these rate questions of their effect upon the policy of the railroads and, ultimately, upon the welfare of the state. This country can not afford to have poor railroads, insufficiently equipped, unsubstantially built, carelessly operated. We need the best of service. Our railroad management should be the most progressive. It should have wide latitude for experiment. It should have such encouragement as would attract the imagination of both the engineer and the investor. Nevertheless, it is likewise to be remembered that the Government has not undertaken to become the directing mind in railroad management. We are not the managers of the railroad. And no matter what the revenue they may receive there can be no control placed by us upon its expenditure, no improvements directed, no economies enforced.

REGULATION *v.* LAISSEZ FAIRE.

The full significance of the opening sentence quoted, "that American railway rates never have been high enough and the public has never paid adequately for the service which it has received," can not be appreciated until one stops to think that for nearly seventy-five years after the first railroad was built the American Government did not choose to exercise the power of regulating the charges of interstate railroads. These carriers, charged with a public trust, were given a free hand in the institution of their own rates until within the last four years, and they now appear asking the protection of the law to increase their rates, which under the play of economic forces they say have never been high enough. Throughout this record it appears that a literary campaign has been conducted by the use of railroad money with the manifest purpose of establishing both at home and abroad the impression that the effect of railway regulation in the United States is injurious to the American Railroad. Widespread circulation has been given to the pessimistic utterances of railroad financiers who sought to fix the idea that injustice was being done our railroads by restrictive and oppressive legislation. Yet it is apparent that the carriers at present in this and similar cases are relying upon the restrictive provisions of the law which declare concessions from the published rate to be criminal and thus give stability to rates — at least as between carriers — to permit the elevation of rates to a standard which under the force of competition the carriers were unable to reach and maintain.

President Ripley, of the Santa Fe, in his testimony, which it may be said, was the broadest and most statesmanlike of any given herein, said that in the past the rates in the territory through which his road runs had not been sufficiently high, although they had been made without any substantial regulation. Being asked if in his opinion the result of operating railroads without regulation had resulted in not making a proper return to the carriers, he answered emphatically, " I do."

" And now, that we have regulation, rates should be put upon a paying basis, is that your opinion? " he was asked.

To which his answer was, " Yes."

Could there be any position less reasonable than to cry out against restrictive legislation and in the same breath ask benefits under this regulation which never were, and admittedly never could have been, won in the open field of unlimited competition?

The attitude of the American people toward their railroads is one of friendship, not enmity. Those who are familiar with the history of European and American railroads know that no other people have been more generous in their treatment of such great enterprises than have been the American people. Not only has the Federal Government granted extensive land concessions to many roads (an area estimated by a former Attorney General of the United States to be as large as nine states the size of Pennsylvania), but state and municipal governments have by grants of land for rights of way and terminal purposes, the voting of bonds in aid of construction, and by guarantees of bond issues promoted extensive lines of road, some of which were not justified at the time of their construction upon any reasonable basis of probable return. While there doubtless has been spasmodic and demagogic effort in various sections of our country, which made for the injury of the carriers, the trend of control and regulation as a whole has been conservative, wise, and sympathetic toward the investors in such enterprises.

If we contrast the action of the British Government toward its railroads with that of the Government of the United States toward our roads it will be manifest that we have allowed to American carriers far more play for the exercise of individual judgment and initiative than has our sister nation across the ocean. The act to regulate commerce grants to the Interstate Commerce Commission much less of power than is vested in the Canadian commission by our northern neighbor.

Whatever of doubt has arisen in the public mind respecting the value of our railroad securities has come, we are convinced, rather from the too reckless policy of stock manipulators parading under the title of financiers than from any course of governmental policy on the part of the American people.

The railroads make complaint that they no longer have a free hand. Yet the fact is that they have fared better under such control as that to which they are at present subjected than under a preceding régime of laissez faire. On July 1, 1901, there were in the United States reporting to this Commission 195,561 miles of railroad, yielding a gross operating revenue of $1,572,960,868, or $8,043 per mile. The net operating revenues of these roads amounted to $577,221,171, or $2,951 per mile. Coming forward ten years to July 1, 1910, we find that the mileage of our roads increased to 238,411 miles, which yielded for the preceding fiscal year a total gross income of $2,818,411,419, or $11,822 per mile. The net operating revenues reached the unparalleled figure of $932,848,978, or $3,913 per operated mile, an increase of 33 per cent in net per mile over the figures of but ten years ago. The advance year by year is shown in this table:

Year ended June 30—	Gross operating revenues.	Operating expenses.	Net operating expenses.	Number of miles of road operated on June 30[1]	Average per mile of road operated		
					Gross operating revenues.	Operating expenses.	Net operating revenues.
1901.....	$1,572,960,868	$995,739,697	$577,221,171	195,561.92	$8,043	$5,092	$2,951
1902.....	1,710,012,212	1,080,829,418	629,182,794	200,154.56	8,543	5,400	3,143
1903.....	1,882,695,212	1,217,909,213	664,785,999	205,313.54	9,170	5,932	3,238
1904.....	1,954,360,360	1,293,122,933	661,237,427	212,243.20	9,208	6,093	3,115
1905.....	2,062,763,957	1,344,778,305	717,985,652	216,973.61	9,507	6,198	3,309
1906.....	2,305,472,036	1,488,060,783	817,411,253	222,340.30	10,369	6,693	3,676
1907.....	2,564,701,422	1,690,080,341	874,621,081	227,454.83	11,275	7,430	3,845
1908.....	2,441,613,253	1,708,645,641	732,967,612	230,494.02	10,593	7,413	3,180
1909.....	2,473,827,401	1,650,494,318	823,333,083	235,402.09	10,509	7,011	3,498
1910.....	2,818,411,419	1,885,562,441	932,848,978	238,411.07	11,822	7,909	3,913

[1] Includes road operated under trackage rights.

The magnitude of this increase may be appreciated when one considers the column headed "Net operating revenues." A gain of over $109,000,000 in net revenue was made by the railroads of this country in the last year. A sum four times as great as the total paid by the United States for Alaska, the

Louisiana Purchase, and Florida, combined, was added to the net profits of our carriers in one year over and above the profits of the preceding year. And the mileage operated was but 3,000 miles greater in the one year than in the other. With an increase of 38,000 miles between 1902 and 1910 the net revenues received from the operation of our railroads increased over $300,000,000.

INCREASING DIVIDENDS.

Coming to a consideration of the return to the holders of American railroad stocks, we find a result equally gratifying. It is almost axiomatic that the investment in an American railroad is not represented by its capitalization. This generalization is subject to a few exceptions. This commission can not accept capitalization as representing either investment or value. As conservative an authority as Judge Noyes may be quoted to the effect that "Stocks are watered, anticipated profits are capitalized in advance, a large volume of securities is deemed desirable for speculative purposes. Therefore," he says, "fictitious capitalization is not an element of value. The amount of the outstanding stocks and bonds is seldom any true measure of worth. A railroad can not, by the manufacture of paper securities, impose upon the public the burden of making them pay real profits."

Bearing this thought in mind, let us glance at the following summary showing the amount and percentage of capital stock upon which dividends were declared between the years 1888 and 1910:

This table, it will be observed, begins with the first year after the act to regulate commerce took effect. At that time but 38 per cent of the stock of American railroads was paying dividends. The amount paid was, in round figures, $80,000,000 per year. Passing over the years of industrial panic and coming to the year 1900 we find 45 per cent of the stock paying dividends amounting to $139,600,000. These dividends were paid upon stock having a par value of $2,669,000,000 upon which the average rate paid was 5.23 per cent. In 1910, however, the amount of stock paying dividends had increased to nearly $5,500,000,000, or more than double what it was in 1900; the actual amount paid in dividends had increased to $405,000,000, or nearly three times the amount paid in 1900, and the average rate had increased over 42 per cent.

Years	Per cent of stock paying dividends	Amount of stock paying dividends	Amount paid in dividends	Average rate paid on dividend-paying stock
				Per cent
1910 [1]	67.20	$5,424,114,782	$405,131.650	7.47
1909 [1]	64.01	4,920,174,118	321,071,626	6.53
1908 [1]	65.69	4,843,370,740	390,695,351	8.07
1907	67.27	4,948,756,203	308,088,627	6.23
1906	66.54	4,526,958,760	272,795,974	6.03
1905	62.84	4,119,086,714	237,964,482	5.78
1904	57.47	3,643,427,319	221,941,049	6.09
1903	56.06	3,450,737,869	196,728,176	5.70
1902	55.40	3,337,644,681	185,391,655	5.55
1901	51.27	2,977,575,179	156,735,784	5.26
1900	45.66	2,668,969,895	139,597,972	5.23
1899	40.61	2,239,502,545	111,009,822	4.96
1898	33.74	1,818,113,082	96,152,889	5.29
1897	29.90	1,603,549,978	87,110,599	5.99
1896	29.83	1,559,024,075	87,603,371	5.62
1895	29.94	1,485,618,453	85,287,543	5.74
1894	36.57	1,767,925,565	95,515,226	5.40
1893	38.76	1,809,600,846	100,929,885	5.58
1892	39.40	1,825,705,437	97,614,745	5.35
1891	40.36	1,796,390,636	91,117,913	5.07
1890	36.24	1,598,131,933	87,071,613	5.45
1889	38.33	1,629,750,927	82,110,198	5.04
1888	38.56	1,490,267,149	80,238,065	5.38

[1] Does not include returns for switching and terminal companies.

Thus we see that at the very time that the carriers in the east and in the west were taking united action to increase their rates, they were compiling their annual statements, which show from the standpoint of net revenue and of dividends upon stocks the railroads of the United States as a whole have never before prospered — not even in the heyday of 1907 — as they did in 1910, which, be it remarked, was but two years removed from the financial panic of 1907–8. * * *

THE FIFTEEN PER CENT CASE

45 I. C. C. 303[1] (1917)

BY THE COMMISSION:

On March 22, 1917, carriers in official classification territory, hereinafter designated eastern carriers, represented to the Commission in a public conference that an emergency had arisen in their operation which required prompt remedial measures. Similar representations were similarly made on March 27 by the carriers in western classification territory, hereinafter referred to as western carriers, and on April 10 by carriers in southern classification territory, hereinafter referred to as southern carriers. In all of these conferences we were urged to act promptly, because, it was asserted, the situation had become critical and delay would detract from the beneficial effects of the remedial measures proposed.

Under authority delegated by the act the Commission has established rules governing the publications and filing of rate schedules, which rules have been modified from time to time. At the preliminary conferences we were asked to modify those rules so as to permit the filing in simplified form of schedules proposing a general and horizontal increase in all freight rates except upon certain designated commodities, and to permit such rates to become effective on less than statutory notice. The publication of all the necessary tariffs in the form required by the rules would have involved an expenditure of hundreds of thousands of dollars and consumed time. We were therefore urged to permit the filing of schedules providing for a percentage increase in rates. The request that increased rates be permitted to become effective on short notice was not granted.

On April 10 and 20, 1917, conferences between representatives of shippers and of carriers and the Commission were held to consider the form of the proposed publications. As a result of these conferences, at which practically no objections were raised to the proposed percentage form of publication, a permissive order was entered on April 23, 1917, granting to the carriers authority to publish and file supplemental tariffs proposing the increased rates in the simplified form requested. Such tariffs were filed on behalf of all, or practically all, the railways in the United States, to become effective July 1, 1917.

[1] The tables, set forth in the appendix to the report, have been omitted. — Ed.

Whether these tariffs shall be permitted to become effective as proposed or shall be suspended in whole or in part is the question immediately at issue.

In some quarters it has been alleged that the Commission has abrogated the law and the tariff rules in order to make the filing of these tariffs possible. It should be needless to state that nothing has been done by the Commission in violation of any provision of the statute. We were not asked to transgress or set aside the law and we would certainly not have done so if we had been asked.

We modified certain of our tariff rules as the act authorizes us to do. This we have done in other instances, and no doubt the future will develop instances in which further modifications of these rules will be warranted. The permissive order referred to authorized carriers to file the tariffs proposing horizontal increases in rates on not less than 50 days' notice, whereas the statutory period is not less than 30 days.

Many of the protestants requested us to suspend these tariffs in order that an investigation might be had, as in their view is contemplated by the statute, the implication being that an investigation would be impossible without suspension. This view is erroneous. We have sat as a body for practically a whole month listening to testimony and arguments favoring or opposing these proposed increased rates. More than 6,000 pages of testimony have been received and a mass of statistical and other exhibits has been made a part of this record.

The form of the investigation which we adopted fitted the subject to be investigated. Had these proceedings been conducted subsequent to a suspension of tariffs they could not properly have been materially different from what they have been. Everyone who appeared and expressed a desire to be heard was heard and no one was denied a fair hearing. We might have sat for months listening to detailed testimony relating to specific rates and localities, but such testimony could have been of little assistance to us in arriving at a proper conclusion with reference to the propriety and reasonableness of the increased rates here proposed covering the entire country. An investigation of such a detailed character is neither necessary nor useful in the exercise of the functions which we are called upon to perform in a case of this character.

During the preliminary conference above referred to authorized representatives of carriers in each of the three rate territorial districts expressed the willingness of all the carriers in the United

States to waive all technical requirements and guaranties in order that an expeditious and practicable procedure might be adopted. With this in view they agreed upon the record that if the Commission should authorize an increase on such a proceeding as we have conducted in the instant case they would, if at a later date the situation should change and the Commission should be of the opinion that the increased rates were, in whole or in part, no longer just and reasonable, reduce them on an expression from us to that effect, following a proceeding no more extensive than or different from that in which the increase was permitted. It was the desire of the carriers to bring the issue of the increased rates before us in the simplest, most direct, and economical manner. To this no substantial objection was expressed by any of the protestants.

As stated, the first representations were made on behalf of the eastern carriers on March 22. This is about the time in each month when the officials of the carriers generally get the statistical returns showing the results of operation during the preceding month. The operating results for the month of February, 1917, may well have startled the railway executives because, generally speaking, they were, for the eastern district especially, extremely unfavorable. The weather conditions had been severe. In many sections the difficulties of operation had been unprecedented. Furthermore, as a result of the congestion of traffic on the eastern roads and the various operating difficulties arising out of the shortage of cars, the movement of empty cars westward reached extraordinary proportions over some lines. Because of the severe weather conditions the expenses of the movement were greater than usual, and, of course, the movement of empties adds nothing to the revenues. Finally, increased wages directly and indirectly resulting from legislation first appeared in the operating accounts of a number of the carriers for the month of February. While some carriers made no charges in their accounts for increased wages, resulting directly or indirectly from the legislation referred to, other carriers charged estimated amounts for both January and February. These three causes, severe weather, relatively heavy movement of empty cars, and increased wages, together with increases in the cost of materials and supplies, and to some extent of fuel, made the operating results of the eastern carriers for February alarmingly unfavorable. Under stress of these conditions the railway executives made their first appeals for relief in the emergency in which they believed they found themselves. If these unfavorable tendencies had continued and the operating results for the succeeding months had perpetuated tendencies of the month of February, a problem very different from that which now confronts us would have been presented. That carriers have been obliged to pay increased prices for materials and supplies can not be questioned. It is difficult to characterize with moderation the increases in the prices of metals as well as the prices which have been demanded in various localities for fuel. Tables 1 to 7, inclusive, in the appendix, illustrate the prices of some of the more important commodities which the railways must purchase in large quantities and which consequently have an important effect upon their operating results.

The emergency which the carriers believed existed when these proceedings were initiated was attributed by some primarily to the war in Europe. Various statements relating to a casual connection between the war and the railway emergency led us to include in a circular of interrogatories submitted to the carriers a question relating to the burdens which it was believed the war would cast upon them. While a number of witnesses referred to the burdens to the carriers of the war, viewing the record as a whole no such burdens have been shown to exist nor has the probability of their development been demonstrated. It was not shown that military transportation had been in the past, or is likely to be in the future, a financial burden to the carriers. On the contrary, certain facts were referred to which indicated that the transportation of troops had been more remunerative during certain mobilizations in the past than ordinary passenger transportation. In so far as anything that is here asked of us might contribute to the success of the war we should respond unhesitatingly to the fullest extent of our lawful authority. We are not unmindful of the fundamental and immensely valuable service which the carriers perform in times of peace and even more in times of war. No one will deny that the successful operation of the railways is vital to our national welfare. We fully appreciate the services which the railways are performing, and the unusual efforts they are making to secure a maximum of efficiency. But this record does not convince us that the suspending or refusing to suspend the proposed rates, or the granting or refusing to grant increased rates, will facilitate or retard the successful prosecution of the war.

An examination of the results of operation during 1916 as

pictured in the reports of carriers to the Commission shows that that year was as a whole more profitable for the carriers than any preceding year, and it may be assumed that they might suffer some abatement of the prosperity of that year without being crippled or in any way incapacitated. In Tables 8 to 11, inclusive, in the appendix are shown monthly averages per mile of road for operating revenues and operating income for all class I roads in the United States and for those in the several districts before mentioned. The table for the country as a whole goes back to July, 1907. Owing to the fact that the reports for the earlier years were not classified with respect to districts, the figures by districts have been shown only from January, 1911. With respect, however, both to the country as a whole and to the several districts, the relation of the figures for operating revenues for each calendar year to those for the first four months, January to April, inclusive, is seen to be rather remarkably uniform, enabling one to expect with considerable confidence that the operating revenues for the calendar year 1917 will be in excess of those of any preceding calendar year covered by the series of reports. An estimate of operating income for the year is also shown, but, owing to the fact that a considerable number of increased costs that may reasonably be expected had not become effective prior to April 30, this estimate is not entitled to so much confidence as that of operating revenues.

A study of the figures contained in these tables suggests that, barring unforeseen contingencies and unusual disruptions of commercial affairs during the remainder of the year 1917, we shall find as results of the year's operations of class I roads figures about as follows:

	United States	Eastern district	Southern district	Western district
Average operating revenues per mile of road	$17,104	$29,432	$13,610	$12,597
Average operating income[1] per mile of road	4,334	5,802	3,872	3,813

[1] Based on costs represented in accounts to April 30, 1917. Anticipated increased costs, if realized, will operate to reduce somewhat the estimated figures for operating income per mile.

It is not practicable to determine from figures now compiled the book values of investment in road and equipment per mile of road prior to June 30, 1915, for roads in the several districts, but those for the United States cover a longer period. While these figures can not be accepted as reflecting accurately the actual cash investment they may be taken as significant for purposes of comparison. The figures for operating income per mile of road for calendar years when compared with those for book value of investment in road and equipment per mile of road at June 30, give for class I carriers for the United States as a whole the following ratios, using the estimated figures for 1917:

	1917	1916	1915	1914	1913	1912	1911	1910	1909	1908
Ratio of operating income to investment..........	*Per ct.* [1]5.817	*Per ct.* 6.400	*Per ct.* 5.240	*Per ct.* 4.091	*Per ct.* 4.683	*Per ct.* 5.300	*Per ct.* 5.070	*Per ct.* 5.519	*Per ct.* 5.866	*Per ct.* 4.941

[1] Based on an estimate of $4,334 operating income per mile of road and book investment of $74,500 per mile of road. Increasing costs subsequent to Apr. 30, 1917, will probably operate to diminish this figure somewhat.

The estimate of operating income for 1917 may be considerably diminished and still exceed the average for any three consecutive preceding years.

In Table 12 of the appendix the total number of tons of revenue freight originated by the carriers in the respective districts for the fiscal year 1916 is compared with the corresponding figures for the fiscal year ended June 30, 1913, the latter having been the largest prior year with respect to freight traffic. The totals for the respective districts show that the eastern roads originated 39,253,873 more tons during the fiscal year ended June 30, 1916, than in 1913; the southern roads 20,438,186 more tons, and the western roads 21,091,749 more tons. The increase in the tonnage of bituminous coal was 6,849,600 tons for the eastern district, 20,751,461 tons for the southern, while for the western there was a decrease of 1,949,606 tons. Similar increases are indicated in the tonnage of other commodities and groups of commodities originated in the respective districts, with the exception of forest products, with respect to which a decrease in the tonnage originated is observed for each of the districts. In this connection it should be recalled that the total number of revenue ton-miles of all carriers in the United States earning more than $100,000 per annum for the fiscal year ended June 30, 1916, was 343,099,937,805 compared with 301,398,752,108 revenue ton-miles for the fiscal year ended June 30, 1913, the largest preceding year with respect to freight traffic.

The consideration of a general increased rate case is necessarily a study of tendencies. The trend of the curves shown in the different diagrams for the respective period of time is unmistakably in a certain direction. It will be observed that there have been numerous ups and downs, but the general tendency has been favorable, including, for the country as a whole, the first four months of 1917. These figures and diagrams do not suggest a country-wide emergency. Emergencies of greater or less intensity may have existed with respect to individual carriers during various limited periods, but the direction of the curves shows recovery in each instance before the lapse of extended periods of time. The general trend has been distinctly favorable.

An examination of the operating results of individual carriers shows that certain of them have lacked prosperity while others have been affluent. The reasons for lack of prosperity on the part of some of them are well known. The great majority of them show a healthy condition from financial and operating standpoints. We must consider not only the successful and strong but also the unsuccessful and the weak. The needs of certain weak lines, however, can not justify a course of action that is unwarranted by the condition of the larger number of strong and successful lines. This record shows that many of the carriers are in a most prosperous condition. They have been managed by men of conspicuous ability and integrity, in whose achievement the whole nation may well take pride. It is certainly desirable that successes of this character which mean efficient service shall continue.

A number of witnesses laid stress on the land grants received by various carriers and upon large accretions to their property which many of them have been able to make out of earnings. Under the system of uniform accounts adopted by the Commission in 1907 all expenditures of this character out of earnings are shown in the annual reports. A compilation made from these reports shows that as of June 30, 1916, class I carriers had expended for "additions to property through income and surplus" a total of $503,651,510, of which the eastern carriers had expended $295,-476,596, the southern carriers $47,880,932, and the western carriers $160,293,982. These sums "include such amounts of income and surplus as have been definitely appropriated or set aside and expended since June 30, 1907, in the acquisition of property the cost of which is included in property investment accounts other than those for securities, etc."

The theory of this character of testimony seems to be that property donated and property paid for out of revenues of carriers does not in fact become their property in the sense that they may be permitted or are entitled to earn a reasonable return thereon, and that the public having donated certain property or having contributed to the revenues of the carriers through the payment of freight charges and passenger fares in reality owns such property and therefore can not lawfully be asked to pay rates and fares which will yield a return on such property. These are questions of large import which have been directly raised in valuation proceedings now pending before us and which will not be discussed here.

All the carriers expressed their willingness to begin immediately upon a revision of the horizontally increased rates with a view to reestablishing existing relationships between competitive localities, commodities, and territories, thus recognizing the commercial disturbances which would certainly follow the proposed increases. It was generally admitted that a percentage increase would destroy existing rate relations, and in all cases where the amount of the charge is appreciably large and where the differences in distance between competitive localities are relatively great a 15 per cent increase would seriously affect competitors in a common market. It is probably due to this fact that with respect to certain important commodities the protests came from persons located at the greater distances from the markets.

Only a most urgent and extraordinary situation would justify permitting tariffs carrying a large percentage increase to become effective. This record does not disclose the existence of a situation requiring so heroic a remedy.

The absence of protests against the proposed rates from many interests and localities affected received some attention upon the record. Certain witnesses were questioned respecting the extent of the clientele for which they were authorized to speak. The relative absence of protests from certain large traffic areas was likewise brought to our attention. The extent to which individuals, firms, and localities refrained from protesting against the increased rates on the theory that increased rates would result in an increase in the car supply and improvement in service can not be stated; nor can it be known to what extent public sentiment may have been influenced by those who could without serious difficulty pass along to others the burden of increased rates. The record also shows that some individuals and firms who could not so shift the burden favor the increases and are willing directly to bear the higher charges in the belief that such burden will be offset by advantages to them and to the country at large.

These facts are not without significance in so far as they indicate an existing state of the public mind. They are quite without significance as a basis for determining the propriety and reasonableness of the proposed rates. The statute does not authorize us to arrive at a decision with respect to the reasonableness of rates on the basis of preponderating views. It may be admitted that facts of this character reflected in the record indicate a somewhat different state of public opinion from that which has heretofore prevailed in connection with similar issues before us. Representatives of insurance companies and bankers appeared to favor permitting the rates to become effective as a means of stabilizing their investments in railroad securities and stocks.

While the instant case transcends all that have preceded it in the magnitude of the sums involved and the spontaneity and universality of its precipitation, it is in its essential characteristics and fundamental factors identical with other great rate-increase cases which have been considered.

From the proceedings of 1910 and 1911 to the present time all such cases have involved the consideration and weighing one against the other of certain fundamental factors. The essential character of these primary factors was the same in all the cases, but the attendant circumstances, the relation of the factors to one another, and certain significant secondary factors were not the same in all. This lack of identity in the relationship and surroundings of the individual factors accounts for the different conclusions arrived at in different proceedings.

In this connection we refer especially to Tables 13 to 21 in the appendix, which reflect operating results through the entire period embracing all of the important increased rate proceedings. They are the tables used in our reports of July and December, 1914, brought down to date. Tables 13, 14, 15, and 16 show those things which strikingly reflect the improvement in operating results following December, 1914.

From a technical standpoint the question at issue is that of suspension of the proposed increased rates. In substance the issue is the reasonableness of those rates. That is the issue which was tried on this record. The investigation which generally follows the suspension of tariffs in the instant case preceded their suspension. The reasons for this have been suggested in this report. As a matter of law we can not require cancellation of these rates at this time. From the beginning of this proceeding the carriers, the shippers, and the Commission alike have dealt with the essence of the economic problems presented rather than with legal questions.

We are not unmindful of the fact that plausible and persuasive arguments may be buttressed upon selected statistics taken from this record. The compilations upon which we rely in arriving at our conclusions were made in our division of statistics, based upon the sworn reports filed by the carriers. All the statistical exhibits introduced by carriers and protestants have been carefully checked, just as far as checking was possible, from the annual and other periodical and special reports filed with us by the carriers. There can be no question regarding the fundamental accuracy of the statistical summaries upon which we have primarily relied in this respect.

As we have said, if the unfavorable results of February had continued our conclusion must have been different. Those unfavorable tendencies, however, did not continue. The general operating results, looked at in the large through a series of years, show on the whole substantial improvement, general prosperity, and, by comparison with former years, ample financial resources with which to conduct transportation.

Increased prices of materials and supplies, the increased cost of fuel, and increased wages are all significant and extremely important factors in the situation which we are here considering. Some of the symptoms are unquestionably unfavorable. Much or all of what some of the railway officials believe will occur may occur in the future. No one can know in advance. Higher prices are being paid to-day, and still higher prices may have to be paid in the future, but that these higher prices will have that unfavorable effect on the general operating results which some believe they will have is by no means certain.

We have carefully considered the expenditures made by the carriers in 1916 for maintenance of way and structures and for maintenance of equipment. These indicate that no undue or disproportionate outlay was made in 1916 for these purposes. This question was carefully considered in the *1915 Western Rate Advance Case*, 35 I. C. C., 497, 514, 515. In the western districts the ratio of maintenance expenditures to total operating revenues in the fiscal year 1916 was less than for the average of the years 1914 and 1915; and in general we do not think that the outlay for maintenance has been excessive, either relatively or absolutely.

In a general way both the fiscal year ended June 30, 1916, and the calendar year 1916 were remarkable years in the history of American railroads. The volume of tonnage was never before equaled, and the gross receipts, as well as the net receipts, in each of the three districts were greater than ever before. Thus the average operating revenue per mile of road operated for the calendar year 1916 was $15,715 as against $13,455 for 1915, $12,885 for 1914, $13,819 for 1913, and $13,237 for 1912. Similarly, the average operating income per mile of road operated in 1916 was $4,723, as against $3,827, $2,964, $3,347, and $3,599 for the four preceding years, respectively. The ratio of operating income to average investment, or book cost, for the calendar year 1916 was 6.40 per cent, as against 5.24, 4.09, 4.68, and 5.30 per cent for the preceding calendar years, respectively.

A notable difference began to manifest itself in October, 1916, persisting, and on the whole growing accentuated, during the first four months of the current calendar year as between the eastern district and the southern and western districts. Table 22 in the appendix indicates per mile of road operated, the railway operating revenues, the railway operating expenses, the net revenue from railway operations, and the railway operating income for carriers in the United States as a whole, for carriers in the eastern, southern, and western districts, comparing each month beginning in July, 1916, through April, 1917, with the corresponding month of the previous year.

An inspection of the table will disclose that the carriers in the eastern district down through September, 1916, showed an increase in net revenue and in operating income over the corresponding month of the previous year. Beginning, however, with October, 1916, and continuing through April, 1917, this tendency is reversed for the eastern carriers, whereas with few exceptions southern and western carriers continued to show comparative increases in these items for each successive month. Thus, in October, 1916, the eastern carriers showed a decline in net revenue per mile of road from $840 to $821, and in operating income from $760 to $726.

For November, 1916, the eastern carriers showed a decline in these two items from $800 to $720 in net revenue, and from $721 to $623 in operating income.

For December, 1916, the same tendency persisted, showing a

decline in net revenue from $706 to $630 and a decline in operating income from $625 to $532.

The increasing tendency in these items for the months of July, August, and September, 1916, sufficed for the last six months of the calendar year 1916 to make a slightly better aggregate showing as contrasted with the last six months of the previous calendar year. But so far as the eastern carriers are concerned, the decline for the last quarter of 1916 was continued for the first four months of 1917 and in increasing ratio.

Thus, in January, 1917, net revenue per mile of road operated declined from $608 to $531, and operating income from $520 to $434.

For February, 1917, exceptional operating conditions exaggerated the decline and rendered it more pronounced. The February returns show a decline in net revenue from $576 to $271, and in operating income from $489 to $176.

March showed the same comparative decline, although upon a less intensified scale than in February. Net revenue declined from $666 to $557, and operating income from $578 to $460. The returns for April indicated the same tendency, net revenue declining from $686 to $611, and operating income from $599 to $512.

Summarizing the four months ended with April, 1917, the decline in net revenue per mile of road was from $2,536 to $1,970, and in operating income from $2,185 to $1,581. If we compare the relative decline in the last quarter of 1916 when this tendency became noticeable, we find that the falling off in operating income from the operating income of the last quarter of the previous year was approximately 17 per cent, whereas for the first four months of the current calendar year the decline in operating income as compared with the first four months of the previous calendar year amounts to about 27.5 per cent.

In interpreting these figures it must be borne in mind that the gross revenue in each of the three districts showed for each month from July, 1916, to April, 1917, a comparative increase, except only for the month of February in the eastern district. In the southern and western districts the results, so far as net revenue and operating income are concerned, show an almost unbroken contrast to the results for the eastern district.

If on the basis of the first four months of the current calendar year we estimate the total gross revenue in the eastern district for the entire year, we find indicated an average operating revenue per mile of road of $29,432, as against an average operating revenue for the preceding year of $27,688. Despite this increase in the gross operating revenue the average operating income per mile of road estimated for 1917, on the basis on the first four months of the calendar year, amounts to but $5,802, as against $7,782 for 1916. This indicates that the ratio of operating income to average investment in the eastern district will be but 4.893 per cent, as against 6.662 per cent for 1916.

In other words, using the actual figures for the first four months of the present calendar year, it would appear that although the gross revenue for the carriers in the eastern district would exceed that for the calendar year 1916 by approximately 7 per cent the operating income per mile of road will be but $5,802, as against $7,782 in 1916. This is only 75 per cent as much net income per mile of road in 1917 for performing about 107 per cent of the service performed in 1916.

The returns for the first four months of the calendar year 1917 for the roads in the southern district and in the western district disclose a different tendency and outlook. Common alike to the three districts is the probable increase in gross operating revenues. Thus, the first four months disclose average operating revenues per mile of $4,388 in the southern district as against $3,960 for the corresponding period in 1916, and $3,705 as against $3,288 in the western district. But in both the southern and western districts the first four months of the current calendar year presage not only an increase in the average operating income per mile of road, $1,222 as against $1,181 for the first four months of 1916 in the southern district and $930 as against $877 for the roads in the western district, but in both an increase in the ratio of operating income to average investment is indicated, rising in the case of the southern district from 6.390 per cent to 6.453 per cent and in the western district from 5.953 per cent to 6.217 per cent.

It may very pertinently be asked how it results that with the carriers in all three districts confronting increased expenditure for labor, fuel, and supplies, the prospective effect upon their respective net income is so markedly different. To this inquiry it is probably too early to make a completely satisfactory answer. Among the factors the following may be suggested as highly probable contributory causes. The ratio of increased wages may have been greater for the eastern carriers. The eastern carriers have encountered earlier and to a more complete degree the increase in prices of materials and supplies. The volume of traffic which has congested certain of the roads and terminals in the eastern district would seem to indicate that with their present facilities they can perhaps take on additional traffic only at an increasing cost per unit. In this respect they present a somewhat sharp contrast to roads in the southern and western districts. Congestion at eastern ports and terminals has led to the diversion of some traffic to Gulf and south Atlantic ports. Significant, too, is the testimony of Mr. Fairfax Harrison, president of the Southern Railway, who stated:

"I think I am quite safe in saying that we have no such troubles. We could get along with a much larger volume of business than we are doing to-day, and do it economically. Our trouble is that we are met by embargoes at boundary points, at Potomac Yard, at Cincinnati, and at other places where we have to get into the congested territory. For example, at the moment our normal preponderance of tonnage is northbound, but we are moving very little northbound to-day and our preponderance is southbound. It is an uneconomical displacement of our operating situation; it is more expensive. But we have not had in the south yet, fortunately for us, the causes of the congestions which have affected the whole country elsewhere."

In the western district the transcontinental roads, particularly the Southern Pacific and the Santa Fe, are now carrying a large volume of traffic which would normally move via the Panama Canal. This they are apparently able to handle without great difficulty. Whatever may be the other contributing causes to the divergent tendencies manifested in the three districts, the existence of agencies making for radically diverse results in the eastern district from those likely to appear in the southern and western districts would seem to be substantiated by the following table, which gives the ratio of net operating income to property investment in the three districts from 1900, with the probable results indicated for 1917. The estimates for 1917 are based on the monthly reports of carriers to the Commission, and thus relate to operating income rather than to net operating income, the distinction being that net operating income is derived from operating income by adjusting the last-named item for hire of equipment and other rents. For the purposes of this table the distinction is negligible, and the 1917 item is restricted to operating income only, because the monthly reports do not include data for rents.

Net operating income per cent of property investment

Fiscal years ending June 30 —	Eastern district	Southern district	Western district	Fiscal years ending June 30 —	Eastern district	Southern district	Western district
1900	5.27	......	.....	1910	6.16	5.19	5.06
1901	5.49	4.46	4.84	1911	5.13	6.22	4.68
1902	5.69	4.77	5.29	1912	5.10	4.40	4.24
1903	5.77	5.01	5.30	1913	5.28	4.55	4.91
1904	5.44	4.87	5.03	1914	3.95	4.25	4.24
1905	5.70	5.15	5.25	1915	4.42	3.41	4.14
1906	6.21	5.26	5.99		[1]6.64	[1]5.26	[1]5.43
1907	6.14	4.67	6.19	1916	[2]6.42	5.27	[2]5.29
1908	5.14	3.87	4.87		6.61	....	5.45
1909	5.43	4.72	5.34	1917 (estimated)	4.89	6.45	6.21

[1] Average based on gross property investment.
[2] Average based on property investment less reserves for depreciation.

The protestants do not dispute the fact of large increases in the prices of supplies, although there is, perhaps naturally, a divergence of opinion between the carriers and certain of the protestants as to the average percentage of such increases; but whether that percentage be taken at approximately 30 per cent, as certain of the protestants insist, or at 42 per cent or higher, as the carriers assert, the general increase is undeniable. The aggregate of the increased expenses thus imposed can not be predicted with any satisfactory degree of certainty. We can not know what the future fluctuations in the prices of such supplies may be. With respect to them, as with railway fuel, there is a remarkable difference in the figures and estimates of the various carriers. Some have contracted for fuel or supplies upon a lower price level, and others are without the protection of such contracts or have contracts to expire at an early date.

Without in any wise impugning the estimates of the carriers or criticisms thereof offered by the protestants, we prefer to confine our forecast to the basis of actual experience for the 10 months from July 1, 1916, including the first four months of the present calendar year.

For these reasons, necessarily stated in somewhat general terms, we are led to the conclusion that no condition of emergency exists as to the western and southern carriers which would justify permitting a general increase in their rates to become effective. In the eastern district increased rates have recently been permitted to become effective generally on bituminous coal, coke, and iron ore. We think that similar increases may properly be permitted in the southern district on coal, coke, and iron ore, and in the western district on coal and coke. This will preserve rate relationships between the several districts. In the southern district the proposed increased rates on coal are on the basis of 15 per cent, with a maximum of 15 cents per ton. These tariffs we shall permit to become effective. In the western district the increases are based upon 15 per cent, with a minimum of 15 cents per ton. These tariffs will be suspended, but the western carriers may, if they so elect, file new tariffs carrying increases in rates on coal and coke not exceeding in any case 15 cents per ton. All of the tariffs included in this proceeding of the western lines will be suspended. All of the tariffs included in this proceeding of the southern carriers will be suspended, excepting those applying on coal, coke, and iron ore.

In connection with our investigation as to rates on bituminous coal certain proposed increased rates on bituminous coal were suspended in Investigation and Suspension Docket No. 774. Subsequent to the institution of that proceeding conditions surrounding the production, transportation and sale of bituminous coal became so unusual that the principal protestants before us voluntarily conceded that the conditions were abnormal and that the rates might appropriately be increased, some of them, however, contending that the existing relationships of rates from certain coal-producing districts should be preserved. Pending further consideration of that proceeding and of the instant case, the carriers parties to the tariffs referred to voluntarily postponed the effective date thereof to August 1. Since that time increases have been filed, to become effective July 1, to destinations intermediate to those covered by the tariffs of which the carriers postponed the effective date to August 1. It is therefore consistent and appropriate that those carriers be permitted, on short notice, to advance the effective dates of such tariffs, and they are hereby authorized so to do.

For reasons indicated in this report, we shall suspend all of the tariffs before us in this proceeding of the eastern carriers, excepting those applying on iron ore. As has been indicated, however, the conditions confronting the eastern carriers are substantially different from those confronting the southern and western carriers, and we are persuaded that they are entitled to increased revenue beyond and above that which they are securing and will secure from the increased rates on bituminous coal, coke, and iron ore. By recent act of Congress we have been given jurisdiction over the movement, distribution, exchange, interchange, and return of freight cars. The obvious intent of this legislation is that cars shall be so used by the carriers as to secure the performance of the largest possible amount of transportation in needed and equitable ways. Shortly following the outbreak of the European war an unprecedentedly heavy movement of freight to the eastern district began, and that district in large part has been badly congested ever since. Hopeless congestion has been avoided only by a practically continuous condition of operating under embargoes. The result has been that while roads in other sections have generally been short of cars and in possession of less cars than they owned, the carriers in the eastern district have been in possession of substantially more than their ownership of cars. The hauling of empty cars is expensive and productive of no revenue. Railroad operating officials naturally and properly endeavor to avoid all unnecessary hauling of empties. There has been reason to believe that this disinclination to haul empties has caused the detention on the eastern roads of many cars that were badly needed in the west or south. It is probable, if not certain, that in administering the duties laid upon us by the legislation referred to we shall find occasion to require a very unusual haul of empty cars by the eastern carriers for the purpose of getting them promptly to western or southern localities where they are needed. In this way important additional expenses will probably fall upon the eastern carriers.

As we have indicated, percentage increases, especially where the percentage is substantial, can not fail to disrupt competitive commercial relationships. A general increase in class rates, which preserves existing relationships, distributes itself more generally and more equitably than would general increases on commodity rates. It also affords relatively equal benefits to all of the carriers parties thereto. Among the eastern carriers those located in New England appear to present the most serious condition. They are not carriers of large volumes of heavy loading commodities that move under commodity rates. It is not possible to estimate with confidence and accuracy the amount of additional revenue that will accrue from increased class rates, but from the best information at hand we conclude that the eastern carriers should be permitted to increase their class rates between New York and Chicago to the following scale, and to correspondingly increase their other class rates applying intraterritorially between points in official classification territory, observing the established relationships between ports and localities:

1	2	3	4	5	6
90	79	60	42	36	30

Such tariffs may be made effective upon not less than five days' notice, given in the usual way.

Special emphasis has been laid upon the unusually heavy increased expenses that have been laid upon the carriers by water, which, because of arrangements for through carriage with rail carriers, are subject, as to part or all of their rates, to our jurisdiction. Ordinarily rates via rail-and-water routes are maintained at a lower level than via all-rail routes. Largely increased costs of operation, the diversion of traffic to other channels because of war conditions, and the attendant increased marine insurance have laid upon such rail-and-water routes unusual burdens. We think that existing conditions justify the maintenance of rates via such routes on a level not higher than the all-rail rates between the same points. Carriers in the eastern, southern, and western districts parties thereto may, if they so elect, file and make effective, upon not less than five days' notice, tariffs increasing existing joint rates between rail-and-water carriers to a level not higher than the all-rail rates between the same points.

It is not improbable that some of the rates which we are authorizing to be increased are held by unexpired orders of the Commission. If that is true in any case, parties to such orders must, before filing such increased rates, apply for and secure specific modification of such orders.

The carriers were clearly within their rights in bringing these matters to our attention when they did. We do not question their good faith in anything they have done in this connection. Their action is an added evidence of the farsightedness and sense of responsibility in the performance of their duties toward the public with which so many of their officials are managing and administering the affairs of their respective properties. The things which they believed several months ago would happen have not happened. None of us know what the future may develop. We do not believe that it would be in the interests of anyone to now resume hearings in detail as to the suspended tariffs. As stated, we believe that the facts which have been developed constitute a full and sufficient basis for arriving at a just conclusion with respect to the proposed increased rates. We shall, through the medium of the monthly reports of the carriers, keep in close touch with the operating results for the future, and if it shall develop that the fears which have prompted the carriers are realized or that their realization is imminent, we shall be ready to meet that situation by such modification or amplification of the conclusions and orders herein reached and entered as are shown to be justified. If it shall develop that what has been accorded herein is more than is appropriate or that the increased rates are no longer warranted, we shall depend upon the pledges of the carriers to respond promptly to an announcement by us of a conclusion to that effect. Inasmuch as a general percentage increase is so undesirable because of its serious effect upon commercial conditions and established relationships, it would seem to be appropriate for the carriers to cancel the tariffs which we suspend herein, and permission is hereby accorded them so to do. The record will be available for consideration in any further proceedings that may be necessary or appropriate in this connection in the future, and any substantially changed conditions which may develop can be promptly, adequately, and fairly dealt with. The foundation for any such action can doubtless best be laid in conferences between the Commission and representatives of the carriers and of the shippers. The existing public sentiment to which we have referred and the manner in which the proposals of the carriers have been presented and handled by them indicate a feeling of mutual confidence, which at many times in the past has been regrettably absent.

An appropriate order of suspension of the proposed schedule will be entered.

HARLAN, *Commissioner*, concurring:

Under the law, this Commission may act only upon a concurring vote of at least four of its members, and, in view of the recent death of COMMISSIONER CLEMENTS and of the varying conclusions entertained among my colleagues on the important questions presented by the record, it became necessary, in order that some affirmative results might follow from this extended and laborious investigation, that I should concur in the course outlined in the Commission's report. I did this, however, because its findings are in the direction of what the record seems to me to justify and require and not because I regard the relief granted as adequate. Under the circumstances I venture briefly to explain my individual convictions in the case.

That a full hearing has been had, as the report finds, will be obvious to anyone who followed the proceeding or has examined the record. All shippers, either individually, by counsel, or through the traffic and commercial organizations to which they belong, were given an opportunity to be heard; and the shippers who testified were many in number and representative of their respective industries. In addition, a mass of statistical exhibits was introduced in evidence. In this way every aspect of the situation was carefully examined and illustrated. The result is a record that is entirely sufficient to enable us not only to decide whether or not the proposed rates should be suspended, but also to determine, as the Commission in fact has done, whether the present rates in any of the three great rate districts of the country might properly be increased and, if so, to what extent. The report of the Commission therefore brings the case to a conclusion at this point and, wisely in my judgment, does not undertake to continue the investigation as a suspension case under the suspension orders that are now to be entered.

From the mass of statistics offered in evidence on both sides it is not difficult, as the Commission's report indicates, to compile figures to illustrate almost any theory respecting the troubles of the carriers of the country. It is not my purpose, however, in this brief expression to deal much in statistics. It will suffice to say that laying some stress upon the figures for the last four months, the Commission's finding upon the whole record is that the fears of the railroad officials, when they laid their request for increased rates before us, have not been realized. The report, then, indicates the purpose of the Commission to follow the developments through the medium of the monthly reports of the carriers, and should their earnings make it appear that the dangers feared by the carriers are imminent, the Commission will then meet the situation by promptly amplifying the limited relief now permitted to them.

This month-to-month and purely statistical view of the matter seems to me to be wholly inadequate. Nor do I regard that course as altogether safe. We are facing a much larger problem, and it must be approached in a much broader way if we are to reach a sound solution. The report of the Commission states that some of the symptoms disclosed of record are unquestionably unfavorable. As I read the record, that is undoubtedly the case and, being so, the wisdom of deferring full relief is not apparent to me. What the country as a whole needs, as all participating in the hearings seemed to agree, is much larger terminals, more tracks, more cars, and more locomotives. This enlargement of our facilities is not required merely to meet the exigencies growing out of the war, but to keep our transportation facilities up to the measure of the country's growing volume of business. We are now a creditor nation, and it may reasonably be expected that the trade balance in our favor will continue at least for some years. With the aid of our new merchant marine, this may become a more or less permanent condition. With such a prospect before us, a foundation should be laid without delay for a definite plan for the development and building up of our transportation system. For seven or eight years, competent railroad officials have been warning us that the carriers are not keeping abreast of the requirements of the country. It is true that there are periods when a substantial part of the carriers' equipment is lying idle. On the other hand, the carriers can not prudently undertake to meet extreme and extraordinary demands. But a rough estimate of a billion dollars has been suggested as the yearly expenditure necessary to enable them to open up new territory and to enlarge and extend their present facilities in order to meet the rapidly growing volume of the general commerce of the country. No such investment, however, has been or is being made in our railroads. On the contrary an exhibit of record shows that beginning with 1895 the new construction increased year by year until 1910, while from the latter date it has steadily diminished. In other words, our population and commerce have largely expanded, but there has been no expansion, relatively speaking, in our transportation facilities.

For two years the commerce of the country has been moving under intermittent embargoes, an experience, as must be observed, that we have had in the past not only while we were at peace, but while the world at large was also at peace. Great losses have resulted to the whole country. The producer and manufacturer, with ample supplies which the public was demanding, have been unable to make deliveries. The coal operator, with no shortage of coal at the mine, has not been able to deliver it promptly to those needing it. Prices for the necessities of life have increased, partly at least because existing supplies could not be brought to the consumer; and the speculator has been enabled to demand unreasonable prices because inadequate facilities have prevented the competition in the consuming markets of those who were prepared to furnish the same commodities at lower prices. Large industries have been greatly embarrassed. It was stated of record, for example, that the producers of lumber in one territory alone, with the materials at hand, have fallen 30,000 carloads short in meeting their orders during the past 12 months. Many other instances of car shortage and of extraordinary delays in the delivery of traffic are related of record, but they need not be detailed here. It will suffice to say that, while the strains of the war have much to do with the present transportation conditions, the one outstanding fact during the hearing, as to which there was no disagreement, was that our transportation system is lacking in the capacity to meet the demands of the shippers and that the resulting loss to the general public has been very large. This condition is one of present danger, with a possibility that it may even become disastrous during the war period. But aside from this military influence, the record leaves no doubt that our transportation system, as a whole, must be promptly enlarged and expanded.

The shippers of the country recognize the danger and have given expression to this apprehension upon the record. They regard a prompt and sound cure of the trouble as being as vital to them as to the carriers. Representatives of some of the largest industrial centers, officers of some of the largest traffic organizations, and officials of some of the most important shippers of the country, availed themselves at the hearing of the opportunity to refer to the situation, and to point out that in their own interest as shippers, and in the interest of the general shipping public, the rates of the carriers might well be increased in order that they may be put in a position to increase their terminals and facilities. Many earnest objections were of course made to any increase. Other shipping interests were ready to acquiesce in an increase provided no discriminations against them were involved. But the whole discussion, unusually free from selfish contentions on the part of the shippers, and approached by the carriers, as I understand the record, in no selfish spirit, leaves me with the conviction that the shippers at large are ready for a substantial increase in their rates, provided it will result in an early betterment of their transportation service and in a rate structure free from discriminations. The record in my judgment demonstrates a proposition that has long been clear to me, namely, that a rate is a public question and that the existing rates, aside from any interest that the owners of our railroads may have in the matter, could well be advanced in the public interest, in order that assurance may thus be given for the early enlargement of our transportation facilities.

I express the thought in that way because it is clear that so long as we look to private interests to furnish a transportation service for the country we must see to it that the rewards are sufficient to attract capital for its further development. Under present conditions this appears not to be the case. Executives of great insurance companies and of great savings institutions testified during the hearings that the volume of their holdings in railroad securities has been steadily diminishing and that they and other large investors are looking with decreasing favor on railroad securities. Possibly this may result to some extent from an impression, which I think is very erroneous, that this Commission takes too narrow a view of such questions as are before us here. But, in any event, we must not overlook the fact that at this time, and apparently for the next few years, new capital must be sought by the carriers in competition with the demands of many governments for war loans and in competition with the very large returns of industrial companies. Nor must we overlook the fact that the returns on property investment in railroads, even under the unusually prosperous year 1916, were not such as to give any preference to the railway investor, and for the last 16 years this average return has been, using the principal and representative roads, for the eastern district 5.48, the southern 4.69, and the western 5.04 per cent.

Without extending this brief expression of my conception of the case, it will suffice to say that from the whole record it is clear to me that the 15 per cent increase proposed by the eastern carriers which in its actual results would probably not exceed 10 per cent should be permitted to become effective, subject, of course, to the understanding reached at the opening hearing that the carriers would later reduce them or restore the present rates if so requested by the Commission. The record shows that conditions with the western and southern lines are somewhat better than with the eastern carriers. Nevertheless, in my judgment, they also should be permitted some increase in their rates on the general grounds that I have attempted briefly to outline. In view, however, of the findings of the Commission's report, it will not be necessary to discuss the extent of the increase that they should have.

In the light of the refusal by the Commission of what, in my judgment, is sufficient additional revenues to the carriers, it seems appropriate again to call attention to the economies that may be and should be effected through the coordination of terminals, the elimination of unhealthy competition, the waste in service through the light loading of cars, and the performance of special services for particular shippers without charge. These matters

I have discussed at some length elsewhere, and since my views upon them are more or less understood I will not enlarge upon them here. Much of the service at the larger industrial centers and ports is special in character and the heavy terminal cost encountered by the carriers in performing them is spread over the rate structure instead of being compensated under a special charge. The smaller communities grouped with the larger centers thus bear burdens that should be borne by others. Sooner or later matters of this kind must have serious attention by the Commission, and they will open sources of substantial additional revenues to the carriers.

MEYER, *Commissioner*, dissenting in part:

I concur in the conclusions with respect to carriers in western and southern territories. I dissent from the conclusion of the majority that an emergency exists in regard to carriers in the eastern district of such a character as to make it imperative to authorize at this time the increased class rates sanctioned by the majority.

Five members of the Commission, including myself, have virtually addressed the carriers in the western and southern districts as follows: "The things that you believed several months ago would happen have not yet happened. You therefore have not justified these increased rates. If any or all of the untoward events upon which your application for increased rates was largely based should occur in the future you may then bring them to our attention. In the light of what we have learned in this proceeding and in the light of what we may learn from your monthly reports as they will reach us from time to time hereafter we will be in a position on short notice, and with only brief supplementary proceedings, to decide whether, as a matter of justice to all, our orders of suspension should be vacated with respect to some or all of the suspended tariffs carrying the increased rates. This will enable us to protect the interests which you represent, in so far as we may lawfully do so, and the entire people of this country against any possible situation which might cripple your respective properties in the performance of their public functions during this critical period of American history." This same language should be addressed to the eastern carriers.

I recognize freely that the results of operation for eastern carriers during recent months have been less favorable than for the western and the southern. Certain tendencies are unmistakably unfavorable. It is difficult to characterize with moderation many of the prices of materials and supplies and fuel which these carriers have paid and which apparently they will pay for some time to come. These together with higher wages tend with certainty toward more unfavorable operating results. We have authorized increases in the rates on bituminous coal, coke, and ore which will add to the operating incomes of these carriers many millions of dollars and which will bring the estimated return on the book cost of the carriers up to a level which in my judgment disproves the theory of an acute contemporary emergency demanding drastic action at this moment. In spite of increased and increasing expenses, there is nothing before us to prove conclusively that the net returns of carriers in the eastern district for the calendar year 1917 may not be more favorable than the net returns for all but a very small number of years during their entire history. But even if the contrary could be demonstrated, it does not necessarily follow that the increases authorized by the majority should be authorized at this time. Whenever the time may come, if it should come, that a real emergency can be shown to exist, we can then do promptly what justice and the law may demand. Before important action like this is taken the most conclusive proof of its necessity should be before the Commission. If I apply to the facts now before us the same test which I applied to the facts before the Commission in the great advanced rate cases that have preceded this one I am forced to a different conclusion regarding eastern carriers than that reached by the majority.

As stated in the majority report, while the instant case transcends all preceding ones in the magnitude of the sums involved, in its essential characteristics and fundamental factors it is identical with them.

From the proceedings of 1910 and 1911 to the present time all of these cases have involved the consideration and weighing one against the other of certain common fundamental factors. The relation of these factors to one another, and certain attendant features alone have varied, not the factors themselves. This lack of identity in the relationship and surroundings of the individual factors accounts for the differences in the conclusions arrived at by us in the successive proceedings.

In the advanced rate cases which terminated in February, 1911, we considered gross operating revenues, operating expenses, net operating income, operating ratios, rates of interest, rates of dividend, book costs and book values, the volume and character of securities, and allied factors during a succession of years, and interpreted these in the light of numberless other facts of record. As an attendant feature much consideration was given upon the record to questions of economy and efficiency. At that time we considered earnestly whether or not in the light of all the facts before us certain increases should be authorized. In a separate proceeding, involving the southwestern lines we then authorized increases, but finally concluded that conditions as a whole did not demand authorization of increases in the official and western classification territories. As is attested by the language used and unanimously approved by us in various proceedings affecting the rates on commodities which move in great volume, the facts established in the proceedings of 1910 and 1911 left their impress upon our minds, and to a certain extent shaped our action during the period intervening between February, 1911, and July, 1914, the date of the report in the second great advance movement.

In July, 1914, we again had before us a voluminous record upon which carriers based their claims for increased revenues. After considering the same group of factors which we had considered in 1911 but which had changed to a certain extent in their relative weight and relationship, and which were accompanied by the special features of allowances to industrial railways and the performance of accessorial services, we arrived at the conclusion that the increased rates prayed for had not been justified in their entirety.

Six months later, in December, 1914, in a further hearing, for the third time we had before us the same prayer of the carriers and the same group of factors which had been given consideration during the previous proceedings. The hearings which followed our decision of July, 1914, added to the record as made prior to July, 1916, certain significant facts. These, together with the intervening suspension of various tariffs in which it was proposed to assess charges on certain accessorial and so-called free services and the course of the proceedings with reference to industrial railways, compelled a modification of the conclusion reached in July, 1914, with respect to sources through which the carriers might augment their revenues and of our specific findings in that case. The relative weight of fundamental facts of record had changed, which in turn required a changed conclusion. In this connection I refer to Tables 13 to 21, inclusive, which reflect operating results through the entire period embracing all of the important increased rate proceedings. They are the tables used in our reports of July, 1914, and December, 1914 brought down to date. I direct especial attention to Tables 13, 14, 15, and 16, which clearly indicate the improvement in operating results following December, 1914 and likewise reflecting the decline since the fall of 1916.

During 1915 we dealt with two similar proceedings, one involving freight rates and the other passenger fares. Once more we considered the identical set of factors. We weighed and compared as we had weighed and compared in 1911 and 1914. Our conclusions differed from the conclusions in the earlier proceedings to the extent to which the weight and relationship of these factors differed from the weight and relationship of the factors in the antecedent proceedings.

In the instant case we have before us once more the now familiar aggregation of basic factors. Again we have considered them by themselves and in their relationship to one another, and we have assessed them in the light of the attendant facts and circumstances of record. Applying the same kind of reasoning and the same methods which have prevailed in the earlier proceedings to the facts upon the present record, I have reached the conclusion that the proposed increased rates have not been justified. The majority holds that the eastern carriers have justified certain increased rates. My convictions are to the contrary.

The year 1916 is admitted by all to have been an abnormally prosperous year for the class I railways of the eastern district, as well as for those of the entire country. The banner year prior to 1916 was 1913. In 1913 the operating revenues in the eastern district amounted, for the four months January to April, inclusive, to $7,241 per mile of road; the next best year prior to 1916 was 1915, in the corresponding four months of which this item was $6,653, although for these four months it was surpassed by 1914, in which the item amounted to $6,850. For the like period of 1916 the item had risen to $8,528, an increase of 17 per cent over 1913, and for the like period of 1917 it had further risen to $9,056, an increase more than 6 per cent over the figure for 1916.

It is argued, however, that expenses are rising much faster than revenues and that the outlook is so unfavorable that in the opinion of the majority it is necessary at once to authorize an increased class scale of rates.

The carriers are primarily interested not in operating revenues nor in operating expenses, but in the margin between them, in what remains of operating revenues after operating expenses and taxes have been deducted, or operating income. The operating income per mile of road in the eastern district for the first four months of 1916 was far in advance of that of any prior year for which the figures have been compiled from our monthly reports, being $2,188, as against $1,394 for the like period of 1911. The largest figure for this period for any of the intermediate years was $1,340 for 1913. The corresponding figure for the like period of 1917, within which the flood of increasing costs was expected to be upon us, was $1,582, an amount more than 13 per cent better than for that period of any of the preceding six years except the abnormal year of 1916.

It is too early for most of the May reports of the large carriers to have reached us, and at the time of writing only two of the principal carriers have filed their reports for May. While it probably would be incorrect to say that these two are typical, it is not without significance to point out that the operating income of the Southern Pacific Company for May, 1917, is more than 30 per cent greater than for May, 1916, and that while that of the Delaware, Lackawanna & Western, the only large eastern carrier whose last monthly report has been received, shows a falling off, it is yet substantially greater than for any May in the four years preceding 1916. The figures for the Delaware, Lackawanna & Western for the month of May for the last 10 years are shown hereunder:

May	Operating revenues	Operating income	Miles	May	Operating revenues	Operating income	Miles
1917....	$5,052,622	$1,546,259	955.12	1912....	$2,406,372	$ 353,995	958.60
1916....	4,463,151	1,618,061	955.06	1911....	3,110,664	1,075,911	930.09
1915....	3,713,265	1,243,873	958.63	1910....	3,079,225	1,200,412	930.79
1914....	3,706,838	1,046,880	959.81	1909....	2,819,060	1,142,954	893.18
1913....	3,569,323	1,166,203	958.20	1908....	2,955,361	1,162,602	893.18

In our reports relating to advanced rate cases which have preceded this one more or less has been said about operating ratios. I fully appreciate the limitations inherent in the use of operating ratios. However they have been among the more prominent factors which appear upon the respective records and in our reports. The table below states the operating ratios for all class I carriers in the eastern district for the first four months of each of the last 10 years:

Table of operating ratios for class I steam railways, eastern district

Month	1917	1916	1915	1914	1913	1912	1911	1910	1909	1908
January	76.35	70.66	80.91	83.68	76.44	79.16	77.34	72.44	74.71	79.75
February	86.15	71.78	79.77	88.97	78.01	77.10	77.97	73.12	75.01	80.82
March	77.04	69.98	74.04	78.31	78.87	71.94	71.47	68.47	68.88	73.99
April	74.79	68.73	70.97	76.47	78.06	77.61	69.23	70.30	68.52	71.85

An examination of this table shows conclusively that so far as operating ratios may be used as a barometer, the first four months of 1917 do not necessarily predict unfavorable results for the entire year. In fact it will be observed that for the banner year 1913, three out of the four operating ratios were more unfavorable than the corresponding ratios for 1917. I would be unwilling to state that this necessarily indicates that 1917 will result in larger net incomes than 1913, but I am equally unwilling to agree that the ratios for 1917 and the relatively unfavorable indications of certain other factors together support the conclusion that an emergency now exists which requires an immediate increase in the scale of class rates. Future events may justify this increase. Events up to the present have not done so.

McCord, *Commissioner*, dissenting:

Upon the facts before us, I concur in the dissent by Commissioner Meyer. The issue presented is in reality one largely of governmental policy, rather than a question whether the rates sought to be made effective July 1 are reasonable for the service of transportation. The nation is at war, costs of fuel and other commodities are abnormal, the conditions affecting the volume and movement of traffic are without precedent. The future of these conditions, immediate or remote, can not be predicted with even a fair degree of certainty. Thus the situation before us is not sufficiently normal or stable in character to make possible an intelligent inquiry into the reasonableness of rates. That the operating costs of certain carriers, particularly in eastern territory, have been substantially increased by the increased costs of fuel and supplies is apparent.

Should this Commission upon the showing here made approve an increase of rates predicated in a large measure upon prophecies for the future, to strengthen the credit of the carriers, or should the prices of fuel and supplies be supervised by governmental authority? It is argued with much force that this is a question for the Congress to determine and that until it is clear that such control will not be exercised and that the carriers' fears as to what may happen in the future have been realized, this Commission can not be justified in placing the burden upon the general public in the form of increased rates, especially in view of the showing made by the carriers as to their earnings. At the present moment it appears probable that the Congress will act in the matter. The Committee on Interstate and Foreign Commerce of the Senate is now holding hearings on the general subject of the control of prices. Coal operators have been in conference with the Federal Trade Commission and other government officers on the same subject. It appears that a special committee representing coal operators in all sections of the country has proposed that prices of coal during the war be fixed by a joint governmental commission. Congress has now before it the report and recommendations of the Federal Trade Commission on the bituminous coal situation. No report has yet been made to the Congress by the commission appointed by the President to observe the operation and effects of the so-called Adamson law. It may be fairly said that the matter of the governmental control of prices of various important commodities affecting these carriers is now before the Congress.

With reference to the assertion that prices of certain commodities are affected by car supply it should be remembered that by the car-service act, approved May 29, 1917, the Congress has given this Commission full authority over the movement, distribution, exchange, interchange, and return of cars, and I do not doubt that through a vigorous exercise of that authority substantially better transportation conditions and additional revenue can be secured.

It is my judgment, therefore, that this Commission should report to the Congress the essential facts disclosed by this record. If it should be determined by that body that the prices demanded of the carriers for fuel and supplies are reasonable under present conditions, or are not such as to warrant control by the government, and it should hereafter appear that the apprehensions expressed by the carriers have been realized, then I am prepared to sanction such rate increases as will permit the carriers to so equip themselves as to enable them to perform, in the most efficient manner, the transportation required of them. Those apprehensions were expressed by the chairman of the carriers' presidents committee on March 22, 1917, in the opening paragraph of his statement to the Commission in this case, as follows:

"Mr. Chairman and Gentlemen of the Commission: We are here on what we regard as a very serious question. We realize that the conditions of the railroads to-day present a menace to the country, not alone to the owners of the properties, but as affecting directly the international situation. It is absolutely essential that the railroads of this country shall be in splendid working order, not merely workable physically, but in a position to fulfill their full duties to meet what we all believe is coming — a crisis in our history; and to do it effectively and properly."

Operating revenues sufficient to enable the carriers to perform their full duties are unquestionably required. In the event that the apprehensions expressed by the carriers are realized and increased charges for transportation become necessary, I would not limit those increases to certain classes of traffic, nor, in the absence of very clear proof of differences in conditions, to particular sections of the country. Rate increases, made necessary by war conditions, should be borne by all sections of the country and all classes of traffic, in so far as influences of those conditions are national in scope.

It is admitted by the carriers that they do not seek the increase in freight rates for the purpose of purchasing additional equipment, motive power, or extension of terminals, but for the sole purpose of paying increased cost of wages, material, fuel, and supplies.

INCREASED RATES

58 I. C. C. 220 (1920)

By the Commission:

In this proceeding the carriers by railroad subject to our jurisdiction seek authority, pursuant to the provisions of section 15a of the interstate commerce act, to increase their freight revenues to a basis that will enable them to earn an aggregate annual net railway operating income equal, as nearly as may be, to 6 per cent upon the aggregate value of the railway property of such carriers held for and used in the service of transportation. The applications, which were filed in the latter part of April and the early part of May, 1920, were made at our suggestion to assist us in complying with the provisions of that section. Similar applications were filed on the part of certain carriers by water. Hearings were held in Washington in May, June, and July, 1920, and the case was submitted upon briefs and oral argument on July 6, 1920. In accordance with the provisions of paragraph 3 of section 13 of the interstate commerce act we invited the state commissions to cooperate with us in this proceeding, and there were appointed three representatives of those commissions, Hon. William D. B. Ainey, chairman of the Public Service Commission of Pennsylvania; Hon. Royal C. Dunn, of the Railroad Commission of Florida; Hon. Jno. A. Guiher, of the Railroad Commission of Iowa, who sat with us throughout the hearings and oral argument and joined with us in conferences antecedent to our determination of the matters in issue.

Section 15a of the interstate commerce act provides that in exercising our powers under that section we shall "initiate, modify, establish, or adjust" rates for the carriers as a whole, "or as a whole in each of such rate groups or territories as the Commission may from time to time designate." We accordingly assigned for oral argument on March 22, 1920, the question, among others, "whether for the purposes of said section 15a the rate adjustment shall be made for the carriers as a whole, or by rate groups or territories to be designated by the Commission, and if the latter, what rate groups or territories shall be so designated." The preponderance of opinion was that the boundaries of official, southern, and western classification territories should be observed, and that three groups should be designated accordingly. In making their proposals in this proceeding the carriers have observed generally those three groups, but the carriers in New England and in the southwest have brought to our attention the peculiar financial needs of the railroads in those territories. The New England carriers do not propose a change in the grouping suggested by the carriers generally, but certain of the southwestern lines ask that we carve out of the western territory a separate southwestern group. This separate application of the southwestern lines is opposed by many shippers served by these carriers and by other carriers in the western group.

The record shows that the principal railroads serving the territory west of the Colorado common points, especially the so-called transcontinental railroads as a whole, are in a substantially better financial condition than other carriers in the western territory. It also shows that the rates, generally speaking, are materially higher in the region west of the Colorado common points than in the part of the western territory lying east thereof. Considering the whole situation it is our view that the territory west of the Colorado common points and the traffic to and from that territory may properly be given separate treatment.

We find that for the purposes set forth in section 15a the groups should be as follows:

EASTERN GROUP

"Its limits for the purposes of this proceeding may be established as follows: The Atlantic seaboard from the Canadian border to Norfolk, Va., the main line of the Norfolk & Western Railway from Norfolk, Va., to Kenova, W. Va., the main line of the Chesapeake & Ohio Railway from Kenova, W. Va., to Cincinnati, Ohio, the Ohio River to Cairo, Ill., the Mississippi River to the mouth of the Illinois River, at or near Grafton, Ill., the Illinois River from Grafton, Ill., to Pekin, Ill., a line south and east of the Atchison, Topeka & Santa Fe Railway from Pekin, Ill., through Joliet and Streator, Ill., to Chicago, Ill., a line drawn from Chicago, Ill., to include the southern peninsula of Michigan, and thence following the international boundary to the Atlantic seaboard; including that portion of the Virginian Railway extending south of the southern boundary, and excluding those portions of the Southern Railway, Louisville & Nashville Railroad, Mobile & Ohio Railroad, Atlantic Coast Line Railroad, and Seaboard Air Line extending north of the southern boundary."

SOUTHERN GROUP

"The territory commonly known as the southern classification territory, embracing that section of the United States lying west of the Atlantic Ocean; south of the main line of the Norfolk & Western Railway from Norfolk, Va., to Kenova, W. Va., thence south of the Chesapeake & Ohio Railway to Cincinnati, and thence south of the Ohio River to Cairo, Ill., thence east of the Mississippi River to New Orleans, La., and the mouth of the Mississippi River; and north of the Gulf of Mexico from the Mississippi River to the Atlantic Ocean; including also those portions of the Southern Railway, Louisville & Nashville Railroad, Mobile & Ohio Railroad, Atlantic Coast Line Railroad, and Seaboard Air Line Railway extending north of the northern boundary and excluding that portion of the Virginian Railway extending south of the northern boundary."

WESTERN GROUP

"The territory lying west of the western boundaries of the eastern and southern groups as above described; south of Lake

Superior and of the international boundary line; north of the Gulf of Mexico and the Rio Grande, and on and east of a north and south line running as follows: Following the boundary line between the state of North Dakota and the state of Montana and the boundary line between the states of South Dakota and Wyoming and Nebraska and Wyoming to the line of the Union Pacific extending east from Cheyenne, and from Cheyenne running southward through Denver, Colorado Springs, Pueblo, and Trinidad, Colo.; then following the line of the Atchison, Topeka & Santa Fe Railway through Raton and Las Vegas, N. Mex., to Albuquerque, N. Mex., then south along the line of the Atchison, Topeka & Santa Fe Railway to El Paso, Tex."

MOUNTAIN-PACIFIC GROUP.

"All that territory lying between the line last described and the Pacific coast, not including Alaska."

The grouping herein approved differs somewhat from that proposed by the carriers, and, inasmuch as the record deals principally with the three major groups, it will be advisable to deal with the evidence as presented. In analyzing the results of operation for the various groups of carriers for the constructive year devised by them, and for the first four months of 1920, we shall group the carriers as they were grouped in the applications filed in this proceeding.

Paragraph (3) of section 15a is as follows:

"The Commission shall from time to time determine and make public what percentage of such aggregate property value constitutes a fair return thereon, and such percentage shall be uniform for all rate groups or territories which may be designated by the Commission. In making such determination it shall give due consideration, among other things, to the transportation needs of the country and the necessity (under honest, efficient, and economical management of existing transportation facilities) of enlarging such facilities in order to provide the people of the United States with adequate transportation: *Provided*, That during the two years beginning March 1, 1920, the Commission shall take as such fair return a sum equal to $5\frac{1}{2}$ per centum of such aggregate value, but may, in its discretion, add thereto a sum not exceeding one-half of one per centum of such aggregate value to make provision in whole or in part for improvements, betterments or equipment, which, according to the accounting system prescribed by the Commission, are chargeable to capital account."

In establishing rates for the two-year period we have no discretion as to the amount of the fair return except that we may add to the 5½ per centum provided by law "a sum not exceeding one-half of one per centum of such aggregate value to make provision in whole or in part for improvements, betterments, or equipment, which, according to the accounting system prescribed by the Commission, are chargeable to capital account." Having determined the per cent, we are called upon to perform the administrative task of establishing rates that will yield in the aggregate as nearly as may be that per cent until March 1, 1922.

Evidence has been submitted tending to show that we should accord to the carriers the maximum per cent authorized by the Congress. The high rates of interest now prevailing are cited by the petitioners, and our attention is called to prominent instances where large railroads with recognized financial standing have been obliged within recent months to pay interest rates well in excess of 6 per cent on new capital. The evidence shows that the New York Central Railroad Company recently sold $36,000,000 of 15-year equipment notes, carrying an interest rate of 7 per cent, and that notes carrying the same rate of interest were sold by other carriers, as follows: Pennsylvania Railroad Company, $50,000,000 of 10-year collateral notes; Northern Pacific Railroad, $4,500,000 of 10-year equipment notes; Atlantic Coast Line Railroad, $6,000,000 of 10-year collateral notes; Louisville & Nashville Railroad, $7,500,000 of 10-year collateral notes. Discounts and commissions raised the total cost of the capital to these carriers to 7½ per cent per annum.

EFFICIENCY IN OPERATION

Much has been said upon the present record concerning the necessity of additional equipment and the efficiency of the present management of the carriers. It is the view of the carriers that existing facilities are inadequate, and they state specifically that they need immediately at least 100,000 freight cars, 2,000 locomotives, and 3,000 passenger cars. Shippers are unanimously of the opinion that the transportation service has been and is unsatisfactory, and many of them urge upon us the necessity of granting such increased rates as may be necessary in order that the service may be improved. Others raise the question whether considerations other than inadequacy of facilities — notably labor difficulties — are not equally responsible for the admittedly poor service. Especially during recent months a shortage of labor at crucial points, due in part to strikes, has contributed more largely than any other single factor to the unsatisfactory condition that has existed and still exists. Witnesses for the carriers were unable to state explicitly what economies in operation, if any, may be presently effected. On the other hand, the opinion was expressed that certain increases in operating expenses are apparently unavoidable. During the war passenger traffic was unusually remunerative because of troop movements, elimination of unnecessary trains, and heavy loading of passenger cars. The movement of troops has practically ceased, and it is the view of the carriers that a larger number of passenger trains will have to be operated. During the war, in part because of war necessity, there was a marked increase in the loading of freight cars. It is apparent that there may be increases in expenses not related to the general increase in prices, which may offset any economies that may be effected in other directions.

PROPERTY INVESTMENT

The calculations of the carriers as to the increases in revenue needed by them are predicated upon the assumption that the Commission should permit a return of 6 per cent on the book figures for investment in road and equipment, improvements on leased railway property, materials, and supplies and government allocated equipment, hereinafter referred to as book cost. Their contention is that the aggregate value of the property of the carriers in each group, held for and used in the service of transportation, is substantially in excess of the aggregate of the amounts shown as their respective book costs.

The carriers recognize the infirmities inherent in the investment accounts as carried upon the books of the carriers, as a measure of the value of the respective properties taken separately; but they contend that it is appropriate for us to use the aggregate of such figures as the basis of our calculations, tested in the light of the work of our bureau of valuation as thus far progressed, the tendencies thereby shown, and the conclusions to be drawn therefrom by those familiar with the work so far done, and also by consideration of such matters of common knowledge or within the knowledge of the Commission as bear upon the subject.

The aggregate amount carried as book cost of road and equipment by all classes of carriers reporting to us, as of December 31,

1919, is set out below according to the territorial groups defined in the applications of the carriers:

Eastern group	$ 9,038,194,615
Southern group	2,183,923,124
Western group	8,818,454,872
Total, all groups	$20,040,572,611

In the administration of section 15a of the interstate commerce act it becomes necessary for us to determine, as nearly as may be, the aggregate value of the railway property of the carriers defined in that section, held for and used in the service of transportation. In making this determination, we are authorized to utilize the results of our investigation under section 19a of the act, in so far as we deem such results available; and we are required to give due consideration to all the elements of value recognized by the law of the land for rate-making purposes, and are required to give to the property investment account of the carriers only that consideration, which, under such law, it is entitled to in establishing values for rate-making purposes.

Considerable evidence of a general character as to the various elements of value has been produced herein, which we have carefully scrutinized.

While the valuation of the railroads under section 19a of the interstate commerce act is still incomplete, the work has progressed so far that the results are of value and informative in reaching the determination we are now required to make. So far as the work has produced results, either as to particular roads, or as showing general tendencies and principles, we have given consideration thereto. As will appear from examination of our various valuation reports, and from section 19a itself, our investigations under that section are designed to give information as to the original cost of the property, the cost of reproduction new, the accrued depreciation, the amount of the investment, the corporate histories of the properties, the values of the lands, and other values and elements of value, if any.

We have also before us the investment accounts of the carriers. Since 1907 there have been mandatory regulations by us as to the manner in which the investment accounts should be kept. In the administration of section 20 of the interstate commerce act we have had frequent occasion to investigate, and in many cases to correct, errors apparent in the investment accounts; other errors have been discovered and brought to our attention in the progress of the work of valuation under section 19a.

The probable earning capacity of the properties under particular rates prescribed by law and the sums required to meet operating expenses, separately and collectively, are indicated in the record.

There is also evidence which tends to show the amount and market value of the bonds and stocks of the carriers.

In properly appraising all these elements of value we are mindful of the fact that the carriers are operating units and going concerns. This fact has been given due consideration in the light of the financial history of the transportation system of the United States, as developed by the record and as known to us. The needs for working capital, and materials and supplies on hand have been considered and allowance therefor has been made.

From a consideration of all of the facts and matters of record, and those which, under section 15a of the interstate commerce act, we are both required and authorized to consider, we find that the value of the steam-railway property of the carriers subject to the act held for and used in the service of transportation is, for the purposes of this particular case, to be taken as approximating the following:

Eastern group, as defined by the carriers	$ 8,800,000,000
Southern group, as defined by the carriers	2,000,000,000
Western group, as defined by the carriers, including both the western and Mountain-Pacific groups herein designated	8,100,000,000
Total	$18,900,000,000

It is not deemed necessary, for present purposes, to apportion the aggregate value of the properties in the western group, as defined by the carriers, so as to show the value of the properties in the western and Mountain-Pacific groups as we have here defined them. Many of the important railroads are in and serve both groups into which we have divided the carriers' western group. It is not thought advisable to delay the decision of this matter to permit an accurate apportionment of the value of such properties, particularly as the result could not materially affect the determination we reach.

The record does not permit the estimation of the aggregate value of the properties of electric railways, other than those operated by steam roads, or of the boat lines, both of which have been made the subject of independent representations in this proceeding.

THE CONSTRUCTIVE YEAR

In estimating their financial needs for the immediate future the carriers have based their figures on the actual performance for the 12-month period ended October 31, 1919, with certain adjustments to be subsequently described. This period was considered by the carriers more representative of normal conditions than the calendar year 1919 for the reason, among others, that the bituminous coal strike began on November 1, 1919, ending early in December. Accounting committees were formed in the eastern, southern, and western groups, and in December, 1919, questionnaires were sent by those committees to the carriers in each group with a view to obtaining a "constructive" showing for the year ended October 31, 1919. Without discussing in too great detail the methods and bases employed in compiling the questionnaires it may be stated that an effort was made to devise a constructive year that would reflect increased prices of materials, wages, taxes and rates effective when the questionnaires were answered, to wit, January and February, 1920. This information was intended to show, as nearly as practicable, what increased revenues the carriers would require to enable them to earn 6 per cent on the book cost of their properties, on the basis of the tonnage actually moved during the year ended October 31, 1919, and on the basis of the prices, wages, taxes, and rates effective when the questionnaires were answered. Still further adjustments of the figures were subsequently made to make provision for increases in prices, additional railway-mail pay, and other items that became effective after the answers to the questionnaires were received.

The difficulty of making an accurate statistical analysis of the results of railway operation during the constructive year devised by the carriers is due in part to the incompleteness of their own figures. The questionnaire to which reference has already been made requested the individual railroads to follow the general instructions therein set forth. A number of small carriers failed to answer the questionnaire, and we are asked to assume that the directions — which were none too specific — were accurately and faithfully followed by the other carriers. The evidence indicates that such an assumption is unwarranted. An exhibit filed by the southern carriers shows that in adjusting freight revenue for the constructive year only six of them showed a credit to freight revenue; some of them made no adjustment whatever of freight revenue; and still others showed a debit.

There is no adequate explanation of record of such widely divergent results, but they strongly indicate that the method followed by the various carriers in responding to the questionnaire was not uniform. To the extent that different methods were employed the results are subject to criticism. A specific request by us that the carriers furnish "all underlying details and formulas upon which the constructive increases estimated for 1920 were based for the three groups" met with a response so general in character that it does not serve the purpose intended. Numerous other criticisms of the carriers' figures for the constructive year — some of which are justified by the facts — were made at the hearing. The inadequacy of the data furnished by the carriers increases substantially the difficulty of forecasting the results of operation for the two-year period.

Some of the important adjustments of revenues and expenses made subsequent to the filing of the questionnaire were based on data hastily obtained, in part by telegraph, from a few carriers regarded as typical. There is no assurance that this information was compiled on a uniform basis and no proof that it is accurate. The agents of the individual carriers by whom the information was originally compiled were not present at the hearing. Although an honest effort has apparently been made to provide the best information that could be obtained in the limited time available, it is necessary to call attention to the fact that the details of a number of the adjustments, both in the original questionnaire and subsequent thereto, can not be accepted as accurate.

The proposals of the carriers as originally presented and as considered throughout the hearings made no allowance for increased wages of railway employees not then effective. In the course of the hearings it was stated that a decision of the United States Railroad Labor Board would soon be forthcoming granting certain increases in the wages of railway employees, and it was generally agreed that we should give due consideration to the award of that board when made. On July 20, 1920, after the close of the hearings and oral argument, the Labor Board announced a decision awarding approximately $618,000,000 as increased wages. In discussing the results of operation in each group we shall deal first with the evidence as presented, without reference to the award of the Labor Board, and shall thereafter refer to the wage award and to its effect upon the operating expenses of the carriers in the several groups

REVENUE NEEDS OF CARRIERS IN EASTERN GROUP

The eastern carriers ask that they be permitted to earn an annual net railway operating income of $559,409,933, which represents 6 per cent on a book cost of $9,323,498,898.[1] That the rates of transportation now in effect fall far short of yielding the return sought by the eastern carriers is indicated by the following:

Net Railway Operating Income.[2]

As sought by the carriers	$559,409,933
Actual, year ended October 31, 1919	220,981,068
Year ended October 31, 1919, adjusted	112,465,003
Year ended October 31, 1919, finally adjusted	18,008,219

The figure in the next to last line is that compiled from the questionnaires, as previously explained. The figure in the last line reflects the further adjustments that were made subsequent to the receipt of the questionnaires, as has also been explained.[3] It will be noted that the eastern carriers estimate that on the basis of the costs effective when the adjusted figures were compiled they will fall short by over $500,000,000 annually of earning the net railway operating income to which they claim they are entitled.

[1] This represents the book cost of 51 class I systems, 39 class II, 30 class III, and 24 switching and terminal companies. The figures include additions and betterments to October 31, 1919, the estimated costs of equipment allocated by the government to the carriers, and the book value of material and supplies as of October 31, 1919. It has been explained elsewhere that the book cost can not be accepted, and is not accepted, as showing the fair value of the railroad property devoted to the service of transportation.

[2] Includes 51 class I, 39 class II, 30 class III, and 24 switching and terminal companies; aggregate mileage, 71,218.37.

[3] The adjustment based on the questionnaire reflected changes in certain items as follows: Decrease in railway operating revenue, $3,777,449; increase in railway operating expenses, $56,802,208; increase in railway tax accruals, $7,165,502; increase in uncollectible railway revenues, $27,678; increase in equipment rents, $13,996,332, net; increase in joint facility rents, $82,976, net. There were also included additions of $7,162,449 to corporate expenses and $17,693,800 to Federal income taxes. Miscellaneous items of increase aggregated $1,807,671. The adjustment made subsequent to the receipt of the questionnaires embraced the following: Estimated increased mail pay, $14,348,800; railway operating expenses, of which $34,094,687 represents increased wages and $54,811,580 increased fuel costs; railway tax accruals, $16,510,681; estimated increased allowance to private car owners, $3,888,636. In connection with the last item attention is called to the fact that there is no evidence showing that the carriers made allowances for increased earnings resulting from our decision in *Perishable Freight Investigation*, 56 I. C. 449.

As noted later herein, the carriers proposed to obtain all the additional revenue from freight traffic, and estimated that a general increase of 30 per cent in charges for freight transportation was needed. No detailed analysis of the carriers' adjusted figures will be attempted in this report.

The following table compares the "standard return" of class I carriers in the eastern group with the figures shown in the last preceding table:

Net railway operating income, eastern group.

Standard return	[4] $354,711,079
Actual, year ended October 31, 1919	[5] 220,981,068
Year ended October 31, 1919, adjusted	[5] 112,465,003
Year ended October 31, 1919, finally adjusted	[5] 18,008,219

Not only has there been a sharp decline in railway operating income during the last three or four years, but the operating ratio has increased at a rate that causes serious concern. For the period of five years, beginning with 1912 and ending with 1916, the eastern carriers were spending out of every dollar of operating revenue received approximately 71 cents for operating expenses. This increased to 75.03 cents in 1917, to 85.82 cents in 1918, to 88.51 cents in 1919, and to 97.68[6] in the first four months of 1920. When it is considered that operating expenses do not include railway tax accruals, uncollectible railway revenues, joint facility rents, hire of equipment, rents for lease of road, interest on funded and unfunded debt, and other fixed charges, dividends, and certain other items, the above figures are significant. The operating ratio for the first four months of 1920 means that during that period, after payment of operating expenses, there was left 2.32 cents out of each dollar for the payment of taxes and the other items just mentioned. During the period of six years, beginning with 1912 and ending with 1917, it took approximately 28.79 cents out of every dollar of operating revenue to pay the items mentioned which are not included in operating expenses and which are not considered in determining the operating ratio.

If the basis of the carriers' calculations be accepted as proper, an analysis of the results of operation for carriers in the eastern

[4] Represents the average net railway operating income of class I railroads, excluding switching and terminal companies, for the years 1915, 1916, and 1917.

[5] For 51 class I railroads, 39 class II, 30 class III, and 24 switching and terminal companies; aggregate mileage, 71,218.37.

[6] Not including Illinois Central north of Cairo.

group during the first four months of the calendar year 1920 indicates that the eastern carriers were conservative in estimating their revenue needs. It will be recalled that these carriers, after finally "adjusting" the figures for the constructive year, arrived at a net railway operating income of $18,008,219. The actual results of operation for the first four months of the current calendar year show a net railway operating deficit of $870,210.[7] Because of unusual conditions that obtained in the eastern group during the early part of the year it is unsafe to assume that the results for the first four months fairly indicate what the results will be for the year, and the figures are referred to merely to show that during this period the situation was even more unfavorable than the carriers predicted.

The number of ton-miles of revenue freight for class I carriers in the eastern group during the last eight years is shown below:

Year	Revenue, ton-miles
1912	[8] 149,609,767,908
1913	[8] 170,097,999,591
1914	[8] 161,263,328,467
1915	[8] 154,398,802,727
1916 (June 30)	[8] 193,530,008,573
1916 (December 31)	[9] 202,421,305,944
1917	[9] 212,660,648,483
1918	[9] 216,032,596,432
1918	[9] 190,744,545,350

It will be noted that the tonnage for the year 1919, the first 10 months of which were included in the carriers' constructive year, is the lowest since 1915.

It is estimated that the wage award made by the Labor Board under date of July 20, 1920, will add approximately $314,562,000 annually to the operating expenses of the carriers in the eastern group.[10] This is equivalent to 12.2 per cent of the total railway

[7] Includes estimate for Illinois Central north of Cairo, Ill., taken from carriers' figures, also data for Chesapeake & Ohio, Norfolk & Western, Virginian, Richmond, Fredericksburg & Potomac, and Washington Southern.

* See page 232 [528] *infra.*

[8] Compiled by the Commission's Bureau of Statistics.

[9] From carriers' exhibits.

[10] The carriers estimate that the wage award will add approximately $625,000,000 annually to the operating expenses of all carriers. A statement received from the Labor Board states the figure as approximately $618,000,000. For the purposes of this report we have used the latter figure.

operating revenue of the eastern carriers, as finally adjusted by them for the constructive year.

REVENUE NEEDS OF CARRIERS IN SOUTHERN GROUP

The financial condition of the carriers in the southern group as a whole is more favorable than that of the carriers in either of the other groups. The southern carriers ask that their rates be increased sufficiently so that they may earn a net railway operating income of $136,049,091, which represents a return of 6 per cent on a book cost of $2,267,484,847.[11] The extent to which present rates fall short of yielding the return sought by these carriers is shown by the following:

Net railway operating income as sought by the carriers	[12] $136,049,091 [1]
Standard return..	[13] 138,231,029 [2]
Net railway operating income actual, year ended October 31, 1919...	[12] 51,208,428 [1]
Adjusted net railway operating income, year ended October 31, 1919...	[12] 36,743,074 [1]
Finally adjusted net railway operating income, year ended October 31, 1919....................................	[12] 16,269,429 [1]

The amount $36,743,074 represents the actual income as adjusted in conformity with the questionnaire. The figure $16,-269,429 reflects further adjustments made subsequent to the questionnaire.[14]

[11] This represents the property investment account of 31 class I roads or systems, 34 class II, 49 class III, and 28 switching and terminal companies. The figures include additions and betterments to October 31, 1919, the estimated cost of equipment allocated by the Government to the carriers and the book value of material and supplies as of October 31, 1919. It has been explained elsewhere that the book cost is not accepted as indicating the fair value of the railroad property devoted to the service of transportation.

[12] Includes 31 class I roads or systems, 34 class II, 49 class III, and 28 switching and terminal companies; aggregate mileage, 38,901.15.

[13] Represents the average net railway operating income of class I railroads, excluding switching and terminal companies for the years 1915, 1916, and 1917.

[14] The adjustment based on the questionnaire reflected changes in certain items as following: Increase in railway operating revenues, $461,085; increase in railway operating expenses, $13,957,972; increase in railway tax accruals, $807,383; decrease in uncollectible railway revenue, $628; increase in joint facility rents, $161,712. The adjustment made subsequent to the preparation of the questionnaire changes embraced the following: Estimated increased mail pay, $3,671,941; railway operating expenses, $7,134,359, representing increased wages, and $7,820,000 representing increased fuel cost; railway

It will be noted that on basis of the predictions of the carriers the net railway operating income for this district will be approximately $120,000,000 lower annually than the sum which the carriers contend they should receive under the law. They estimated that a general increase of approximately 31 per cent in freight revenue would be necessary to return the amount claimed.

During the six years ended 1917 the railway operating income of these carriers averaged $126,000,000 annually; during the four years ended 1915 it averaged $108,000,000 annually; during 1916 and 1917 it averaged $163,000,000 annually; in 1918 it was $147,711,910, which was greater than in any previous year except 1916 and 1917. In 1919, however, it declined to $75,-546,591. During the six years ended 1917 the operating ratio of these carriers varied from 65.04 in 1916 to 74.1 in 1914. In 1916 it was 77.66, and in 1919 it rose to 86.08, and for the first four months of 1920 it was 86.22.[15] During the six years ended 1917, 27.05 cents out of every dollar of revenue earned by the carriers of this district was required to pay railway tax accruals, uncollectible railway revenues, rents for use of joint facilities, equipment, and leased roads, interest on funded and unfunded debt, dividends, and other miscellaneous income deductions.

The reports of class I carriers of this district to us for the first four months of 1920 show a net railway operating income of $23,399,151. Deducting the railway mail pay applicable to prior years stated by the carriers to have been taken into account in those months, in amount $8,287,241, leaves $15,111,910 as the actual result of operations. This figure should be compared with the estimate of $16,269,429 made by these carriers on the basis of a whole year's operations. The southern carriers substantially overestimated their needs, even assuming that the basis of their calculations is correct. As $15,111,910 covers only class I roads $80,519 may be added for the remaining carriers, which produces an aggregate of $15,192,429.

During the period 1914 to 1919, inclusive, the net railway operating income of the first four months in each year averaged 32.15

---

tax accruals, $4,000,000, based upon increased income taxes incident to greater income if rate increase is granted; estimated increased allowances to private-car owners, $943,920 (as corrected); and corporate expenses — net, $4,045,834. In connection with the last item attention is directed to the fact that there is no evidence showing that the carriers made allowances for increased earnings resulting from our decision in *Perishable Freight Investigation*, 56 I. C. C., 449.

[15] Illinois Central north of Cairo not included.

per cent of the aggregate for the year. Equating the actual results of the first four months of 1920 on this basis produces an estimated net railway operating income of $47,254,834. Subtracting from this figure the carriers' estimate of $943,920 for increased allowances to private car owners, and $7,820,000, their estimate of increased fuel costs, reduces it to $38,490,914. Comparing this result with $136,049,091, which the carriers urge they are entitled to receive under the law, indicates a deficiency of $97,558,177 in net railway operating income.

The amount of freight and other transportation revenue, excluding passenger, mail, and express, reported to us for the first four months of 1920 by class I carriers aggregated $152,443,828. To this amount $8,226,302 has been added to cover revenues of carriers other than class I carriers, resulting in a gross estimated revenue of $160,670,130. During the years 1915 to 1919 inclusive, freight and other transportation revenue, excluding passenger, mail, and express, for the first four months of each year averaged 31 per cent of the aggregate for the year. Equating the actual revenues of the first four months of 1920 upon this basis produces estimated revenues for an assumed period of twelve months of $518,290,742.

The number of ton-miles of revenue freight for class I carriers in the southern group during the past eight years is indicated in the subjoined statement:

Year	Revenue ton-miles
1912	[16] 27,483,661,188
1913	[16] 30,637,552,864
1914	[16] 31,376,537,497
1915	[16] 28,568,632,209
1915 (June 30)	[16] 34,183,991,890
1916 (December 31)	[17] 36,501,823,723
1917	[17] 42,825,200,670
1918	[17] 46,301,543,975
1919	[17] 41,527,854,002

It is estimated that the wage award made by the Labor Board under date of July 20, 1920, will add approximately $68,598,000 annually to the operating expenses of the carriers in the southern group. This is equivalent to 11.8 per cent of the total railway operating revenue of the southern carriers as finally adjusted by them for the constructive year.

[16] Compiled by the Commission's Bureau of Statistics.

[17] From carriers' exhibits.

REVENUE NEEDS OF CARRIERS IN WESTERN GROUP

The western carriers ask that their rates be fixed on a basis that will permit them to earn a net railway operating income of $537,833,024, which represents a return of 6 per cent on a book cost of $8,963,883,753.[18] The extent to which the rates of transportation now in effect fall short of yielding the return sought by these carriers is indicated by the following comparison:

Net railway operating income as sought by the carriers		[19] $537,883,024
Standard return		[20] 401,215,984
Actual net railway operating income year ended October 31, 1919	$293,212,870	
Less corporate income charges — net debit	28,027,616	
		[19] 265,185,254
Adjusted net railway operating income year ended October 31, 1919		[19] 226,831,658
Finally adjusted net railway operating income year ended October 31, 1919		[19] 184,939,759

The figure $226,831,658 represents the actual income, as adjusted in conformity with the questionnaire. The figure $184,939,759 reflects adjustments subsequent to the questionnaire.[21]

It will be observed that on the basis of the predictions of the carriers, the net railway operating income for this district will be approximately $350,000,000 lower than the annual sum to

[18] This represents the book cost of 59 class I systems, 53 class II, 41 class III, and 32 switching and terminal companies. The figures include additions and betterments to October 31, 1919, the estimated cost of equipment allocated by the government to the carriers and the book cost of material and supplies as of October 31, 1919.

[19] Includes 59 class I systems, 53 class II, 41 class III, and 32 switching and terminal companies; aggregate mileage, 138,243.74.

[20] Represents the average net railway operating income of class I railroads, excluding switching and terminal companies, for the years 1915, 1916, and 1917.

[21] The adjustment based on the questionnaire reflected changes in certain items, as follows: Increase in railway operating revenues, $678,907; increase in railway operating expenses, $35,689,425; increase in railway tax accruals, $7,733,128; decrease in equipment rents, $4,523,553, net; decrease in joint facility rents, $304,163, net; increase in corporate items, $437,666, net. The adjustment made subsequent to the preparation of the questionnaire changes embraced the following: Estimated increased mail pay, $13,513,600; railway operating expenses, $21,092,697 representing increased wages and $21,254,298 representing increased fuel costs; railway tax accruals, $11,242,557, based upon increased income taxes incident to greater income if rate increase is granted; estimated increased allowance to private-car owners, $1,815,947.

which they claim to be entitled. They estimated that a general increase of approximately 24 per cent in freight revenue was required to return the amount claimed.

During the six years ended 1917 the railway operating income of the carriers averaged $386,000,000 annually; during the four years ended 1915 it averaged $347,000,000 annually; during the years 1916 and 1917 it averaged $464,000,000 annually; in 1918 it dropped to $330,320,330; and in 1919 it declined further to $302,857,219. During the six years ended 1917 the operating ratio ranged from 62.69 to 67.68; in 1918 it rose to 78.14, in 1919, to 80.96, and for the first four months of 1920 to 86.06.

The reports of the class I carriers of this district to us for the first four months of 1920 show a net railway operating income of $56,104,721. Deducting the railway-mail pay applicable to prior years, stated by the carriers to have been taken into account in these months, in amount, $27,790,388, leaves $28,314-333 as the actual result of operations. Adding to this figure $1,209,969 to cover net railway operating income of carriers other than class I, produces $29,524,302.

During the period 1914 to 1919 the net railway operating income of the first four months in each year averaged 23.29 per cent of the aggregate for the year. Equating the actual results of the first four months of 1920 on this basis produces an estimated net railway operating income of $126,768,149, the net railway operating income of an assumed period of twelve months, on the basis of operating costs which prevailed during the first four months of 1920. Subtracting from this figure $3,789,728, which is the estimate of the carriers for increased allowances to private car owners, and $21,254,298, their estimate of increased fuel costs for the year, reduces it to $101,724,123.

The amount of freight and other transportation revenue, excluding passenger, mail, and express reported to us by class I carriers for the first four months of 1920, aggregated $498,001,006. To this amount $16,462,794 has been added to cover revenues of carriers other than class I carriers, resulting in a gross estimated revenue of $514,463,800. During the years 1915 to 1919, inclusive, freight and other transportation revenue, excluding passenger, mail, and express for the first four months of each year, averaged 28.52 per cent of the aggregate for the year. Equating the actual revenues of the first four months of 1920 upon this basis produces $1,803,870,266, as the estimated revenues of an assumed period of twelve months based on the operations of the first four months of 1920.

The number of ton-miles of revenue freight for class I carriers in the western group during the past eight years is indicated below:

Year	Revenue, ton-miles
1912	[22] 82,888,199,102
1913	[22] 96,986,976,238
1914	[22] 92,284,883,754
1915	[22] 90,945,571,633
1916 (June 30)	[22] 112,156,323,212
1916 (December 31)	[23] 123,250,722,123
1917	[23] 138,044,743,597
1918	[23] 142,335,128,414
1918	[23] 130,606,713,832

The carriers estimate that the wage award made by the Labor Board under date of July 20, 1920, will add approximately $234,-840,000 annually to the operating expenses of the carriers in the western group. This is equivalent to 11.2 per cent of the total railway operating revenue of the western carriers, as finally adjusted by them for the constructive year.

EXTENT AND METHOD OF OBTAINING ADDITIONAL REVENUE

As above noted, in the original applications the carriers proposed to obtain the desired additional revenue by general percentage increases in the respective groups, applicable to freight traffic only. No increases were suggested upon passenger, express, or mail traffic. In their amended proposals, following the wage award of the Labor Board, they propose to make increase upon all classes of traffic.

PASSENGER TRAFFIC

During the last nine years there has been substantial increase in the number of revenue passenger miles, as is indicated by the following figures, compiled by our bureau of statistics:

[22] Compiled by the Commission's Bureau of Statistics.
[23] From carriers' exhibits.

Number of revenue passenger miles for each year, 1911 to 1919, class I roads.

Year ended June 30	Eastern [24]	Southern [24]	Western [24]	United States
1911	15,161,685,623	4,072,229,173	13,137,530,997	32,371,444,793
1912	15,401,753,902	4,221,415,582	12,693,093,065	32,316,262,549
1913	16,087,159,298	4,384,239,446	13,403,687,214	33,875,085,958
1914	16,348,655,263	4,585,239,471	13,633,090,680	34,566,985,414
1915	14,960,949,033	3,988,171,076	12,840,808,078	31,789,928,187
1916	15,628,070,433	4,115,759,883	13,902,077,834	33,645,908,150
1916 [26]	16,627,329,935	4,573,888,153	13,384,733,938	34,585,952,026
1917 [26]	18,408,279,975	5,776,735,965	15,291,842,609	39,476,858,549
1918 [26]	19,516,672,752	7,404,952,632	15,754,953,815	42,676,579,199
1919 [26]	....	....	....	[25] 46,145,070,641

It will be noted that the increase for the country as a whole from 1911 to 1919 was over 40 per cent.

Passenger fares were increased to a minimum rate of 3 cents per mile on June 10, 1918, resulting in an increase of 50 per cent where 2 cents per mile was the basic fare, 20 per cent where 2½ cents applied, and no increase where the fare was 3 cents or higher. It appears that rates per passenger mile have increased since 1916, as follows: In the eastern group, 27 per cent; in the southern group, 27½ per cent; and in the western group, 22½ per cent. The relatively small increase in the western group is due to the fact that a 3-cent basis prevailed more generally in that territory than in other parts of the country.

In part because of conditions growing out of the war the passenger traffic has become relatively more profitable during the last three years. A reduction in the number of passenger trains occurred simultaneously with a substantial increase in the number of passengers carried, resulting in heavier loading of passenger cars and trains. In 1919 the number of passenger miles was 30 per cent greater than in 1916, but the number of passenger-train miles was 12 per cent less. Thus, in spite of the curtailment in service, the passenger revenue for the railroads as a whole was greater by $470,362,485 in 1919 than in 1916. This increase in revenue is regarded by the carriers as net, "almost more than net, because it was actually moved in fewer trains."

[24] The districts are those heretofore used for statistical purposes.

[25] As reported by the Director General of Railroads for carriers under federal control.

[26] Calendar year.

Following request of counsel for certain shippers, the carriers provided for the record an analysis of the freight and passenger earnings and expenses for certain designated railway companies for the calendar year 1919. In making this analysis, the expenses that could not be allocated solely to freight or passenger traffic were apportioned generally in accordance with instructions issued by us on January 1, 1920. A recapitulation of the figures showing the ratio of freight and passenger service expenses to freight and passenger revenues is as follows:

Railroad	Operating ratio, freight service	Operating ratio, passenger service
Atchison, Topeka & Santa Fe	74.53	67.84
Atlantic Coast Line	89.54	80.21
Baltimore & Ohio	97.88	75.96
Chicago & North Western	90.41	75.93
Chicago, Burlington & Quincy	85.8	67.98
Erie System	95.74	89.72
Great Northern System	80.70	84.08
Louisville & Nashville	95.3	76.9
New York Central	91.45	60.22
Cleveland, Cincinnati, Chicago & St. Louis	83.45	63.84
Pennsylvania Railroad, East	98.16	99.16
Michigan Central Railroad	81.20	58.50
Southern Railway	98.50	78.40

It will be noted that in the great majority of instances, the operating ratio was decidedly more favorable for the passenger traffic than for the freight traffic. However, there appears to be a wide discrepancy between the figures presented for the various lines, and too much reliance should not be placed upon this showing. Resumption of more frequent train service will tend to increase the operating ratio for passenger traffic. The carriers contend that it is uncertain whether an increase in the general level of passenger fares will yield increased revenue proportionate to the increase in the fare level, because of possible reduction in travel following a material increase in fare.

The foregoing would seem to indicate that such increase as is approved upon passenger traffic may properly be less than the percentage increase applied to freight traffic.

There has also been suggested the desirability of obtaining additional revenue for the rail carriers from an extra charge placed upon passengers in sleeping and parlor cars. Such a charge amounting to one-half cent per mile was in effect for a brief period during federal control. A charge of this character has much in its favor. Unquestionably the service is more valuable to the passengers, and more expensive to the rail carriers.

The Pullman Company opposes the reestablishment of a surcharge for Pullman occupancy on the ground that such a charge reduces the travel in cars of that type. It submitted a statement showing the revenues by weeks for the period March 1 to September 30, 1918, compared with corresponding weeks of the previous year. The surcharge imposed by the Director General was in effect from June 10 to November 30, 1918. The statement submitted by the Pullman Company shows that beginning with the third week of June there was a reduction in the revenue as compared with the same weeks of the previous year, whereas, during the period from March 1 to June 15, the earnings in 1918 were greater than in 1917. These figures appear in part at least to sustain the contention that the surcharge operated to reduce revenues.

An analysis of the situation, however, indicates that factors other than the surcharge were in part responsible for the decreased revenue from passengers in sleeping and parlor cars in 1918, as the very large reduction in service rendered during that year undoubtedly accounts for a portion of the reduction in revenue. It is well known that the policy of the Railroad Administration at that time was to discourage luxury travel and reduce the mileage of sleeping and parlor cars, particularly the latter.

Figures quoted above in this report indicate that the total number of passenger miles in 1918, notwithstanding that the surcharge was in effect for half the year, increased 8 per cent over the previous year and were greater than in any year prior thereto which indicates that travel on the whole was not materially affected by the surcharge.

In the amended application of the carriers following the wage award, it is proposed that a surcharge on passengers in sleeping and parlor cars be established amounting to 50 per cent of the charge for space occupied in either class of equipment. The carriers estimate that a charge of this amount will produce in their three groups respectively approximately the following amounts of revenue:

Eastern group	$17,556,108
Southern group	5,582,026
Western group	20,231,200
Total	$43,639,344

We conclude that increases as indicated next below may be made by all steam railroads subject to our jurisdiction serving the territory embraced in the groups hereinbefore designated.

1. All passenger fares and charges may be increased 20 per cent. The term "passenger fares" may be considered to include standard local or interline fares; excursion, convention, and other fares for special occasions; commutation and other multiple forms of tickets; extra fares on limited trains; club car charges.

2. Excess baggage rates may be increased 20 per cent, provided that where stated as a percentage of or dependent upon passenger fares the increase in the latter will automatically effect the increase in the excess-baggage charges.

3. A surcharge upon passengers in sleeping and parlor cars may be made amounting to 50 per cent of the charge for space in such cars, such charge to be collected in connection with the charge for space, and to accrue to the rail carriers.

4. Milk and cream are usually carried in passenger trains, and the revenue therefrom is not included in freight revenue. Rates on these commodities may be increased 20 per cent.

SWITCHING AND SPECIAL SERVICES

The carriers' original petitions asked for percentage increases in freight revenue only. In their reports to us, revenue from switching and certain other special services is stated separately from freight revenue, and therefore, accepted literally, the proposal would result in no increases on switching service. However, it is conceded that the submission of the proposal in this form was due to a misunderstanding, and it is now proposed to apply increases to switching and other special services as well as to freight rates proper.

No substantial reasons have been developed for exempting charges for switching from the general increases. It is our opinion that the charges for this service should be increased, together with the charges for transit, weighing, diversion, reconsignment, lighterage, floatage, storage (not including track storage), and transfer, where the carriers provide separate charges against shippers for such services. The charges for other special services are not to be subject to the general increases herein authorized. The percentage to apply should be determined by the percentage applicable in the group where the service is performed, except that at points on the boundary line between two groups taking different percentages the higher percentage should apply.

It should be understood that where tariffs now provide for the absorption by one carrier of the charges of another carrier in specific amounts such absorptions should be revised in harmony with the increases in charges herein authorized.

FREIGHT RATE INCREASES

In their original applications the carriers proposed general percentage increases in freight rates in the respective groups as follows: eastern, 30 per cent; southern, 31 per cent ; western, 24 per cent.

Following such general percentage increases, they indicate their willingness, where necessary, to revise rates to restore in so far as is deemed practicable existing recognized relationships and differentials, and as to coal and grain in certain important situations such readjustments are proposed in this proceeding. It is stated that the percentage method is not only on the whole the fairest to all interests by distributing the burden in proportion to the haul, but that it is the only way in which the desired increased revenue may be obtained without complications and delays due to tariff difficulties and to the lack of accurate statistics from which to determine the amount of revenue which may reasonably be expected from flat or maximum increases on particular commodities.

It would be desirable, if it were possible, to determine definitely the commodities, the sections of the country, and even the individual rates which can best bear the burden of increases, and the relationships of the rates and differentials which will be disturbed by a percentage increase. This is precluded by the necessity of prompt action upon the main issues presented.

PERCENTAGE INCREASES VERSUS FLAT INCREASES AND MAINTENANCE OF DIFFERENTIALS AND RELATIONSHIPS.

Many shippers have directed their testimony and argument principally to the method of increasing the rates rather than to the amount of the increases. Shippers are far from unanimous in their views and may be divided into three groups: (a) those who seek the preservation of existing relationships and differentials either by specific or flat increases or by applying the percentage increase to base rates and employing in connection therewith differentials from and to other points; (b) those who advocate a percentage advance in all instances, contending that differentials should increase in the same ratio as all other rates and charges; and (c) those who advocate a percentage increase with a maximum.

While established or "differential" relationships of rates are not general, there are many such adjustments; some fixed by the carriers and others by us, and it is contended by some shippers that in such cases it is desirable in readjusting the rates to maintain the differentials.

Many relationships in cents per unit were disturbed by the increases made by the Director General, except upon a few commodities of heavy movement which were subjected to specific increases in cents or dollars and cents per unit. A relatively small proportion of these relationships have subsequently been restored.

It is evident that there are many competitive situations where no recognized differentials have ever existed but where, nevertheless, the rates have been made to reflect competitive conditions. Such situations greatly outnumber those where "fixed relationships" have been established.

It is generally understood that on traffic to and from western trunk line territory and the southwest Chicago enjoyed for years a "differential" of 20 cents, first class, over St. Louis. This was thought to be a fixed, recognized, long-standing difference, and well entitled to bear the title "differential." Under General Order No. 28 it was increased to 25 cents. We are now asked on behalf of certain Chicago interests not to increase this differential. In this connection it is interesting to note that on traffic to and from the east the St. Louis rates are made uniformly 117 per cent of the Chicago rates, so that under any general increase in rates the spread between the St. Louis rates and the Chicago rates is automatically widened. In 1914 the first-class rate from New York to St. Louis was 13 cents higher than to Chicago. The difference is now 19 cents, although the percentage relationship is the same now as it was in 1914. There is apparently no more justification for maintaining Chicago's differential over St. Louis on traffic to the west than for maintaining the differential of St. Louis on traffic from the east. Practically all rates in official classification territory are constructed upon a percentage basis, and attention is directed to the important fact that not a single interest has here maintained, with the possible exception of Chicago, that we should depart generally from the percentage basis which has so long prevailed.

In favor of maintaining differentials, it is said that they have been fixed in most cases after careful investigation, and that they represent the proper measure of differences in the rates; that often they represent the maximum differences which will permit more distant shippers to compete with those in close proximity; that to increase rates by a percentage tends to decrease the radius in which goods are marketed, and thus by lessening competition prices are advanced; and that in all cases the margin of profit has not increased proportionately to prices.

Those who oppose maintaining differentials at this time contend that the value of the dollar expressed in terms of commodities shipped to-day is in reality but one-half its former value, and, therefore, a differential which was fixed at a given amount several years ago should, to have the same economic effect, be greater to-day; that there have been general increases in the prices of practically all commodities, and in wages and in the charges for all services, and that differentials should not be made an exception to the rule; and that as increased operating costs are the underlying reason for the proposed increased rates, the additional service represented by the differential, being more expensive than heretofore, should pay greater rates as well as other services.

The adoption of specific increases in cents per unit instead of percentage advances will, of course, maintain existing relationships. However, the carriers almost uniformly oppose this method and it is not generally advocated by shippers. Further, the difficulty of its adoption is apparent because of the lack of reliable statistics from which to determine the probable additional revenue from a given increase. It should also be noted that everyone who advocated this method insisted that flat increases be applied but once to combination rates. The complicated nature of tariff publication to make such an arrangement effective, when different percentages of increase are being made in different groups, is apparent.

Without attempting to pass finally upon the question whether in given cases differentials should or should not be maintained, it is evident that no general program of maintaining differentials can be made effective coincident with the increases here approved without materially delaying their effective date as definite testimony covering individual situations is before us in only a very few cases. To maintain differentials by applying the percentage increases to basing rates and adding thereto existing differentials can not be done without materially lessening the amount of additional revenue to be derived by the carriers, as generally differentials are added to rather than deducted from base rates.

After carefully considering the situation we find that with the exceptions hereinafter noted general percentage increases made to fit the needs of the groups of lines serving each of the four groups must be considered for present purposes the most practicable. This conclusion is without prejudice to any subsequent finding in individual situations.

PROVISIONS FOR IMPROVEMENTS, BETTERMENTS, OR EQUIPMENT

Section 15a of the interstate commerce act contains the following proviso:

"*Provided,* That during the two years beginning March 1, 1920, the Commission shall take as such fair return a sum equal to $5\frac{1}{2}$ per centum of such aggregate value, but may, in its discretion, add thereto a sum not exceeding one-half of one per centum of such aggregate value to make provision in whole or in part for improvements, betterments or equipment, which, according to the accounting system prescribed by the Commission, are chargeable to capital account."

The increases here authorized are intended to yield the additional one-half of 1 per cent. The record leaves no doubt as to the needs of the country for additional transportation facilities. All carriers participating in the increases will be expected to make appropriate provision for additional improvements, betterments, or equipment of a character chargeable to capital account and to make report to us semiannually, as of December 31 and June 30, showing what portion of the increased revenue resulting from the increases here authorized has been devoted to that purpose.

CONCLUSION AS TO GENERAL INCREASES.

We are of opinion and find that the following percentage increases in the charges for freight service, including switching and special services,[27] together with the other increases hereinbefore

[27] The increases should apply to special services in accordance with our findings under the caption "Switching and Special Services," *supra.*

approved, would under present conditions result in rates not unreasonable in the aggregate under section 1 of the act and would enable the carriers in the respective groups, under honest, efficient and economical management and reasonable expenditures for maintenance of way, structures, and equipment, to earn an aggregate annual railway operating income equal, as nearly as may be, to a return of 5½ per cent upon the aggregate value, for the purposes of this proceeding, of the railway property of such carriers held for and used in the service of transportation and one-half of 1 per cent in addition; eastern group, 40 per cent; southern group, 25 per cent; western group, 35 per cent; Mountain-Pacific group 25 per cent.

In view of the different percentages of increase herein approved, it becomes necessary to make provision for rates between the various groups.

(1) Where rates are constructed by the use of combinations upon gateways between any two groups, the through rates should be increased by applying to each factor its respective percentage.

(2) Rates between points within a group and points on the border line of such group should be increased according to the percentage applicable to the group. Where a river constitutes a boundary line between two groups, points on both banks thereof shall be considered as border-line points.

(3) Joint or single-line through rates between points in one group and points in other groups should be increased 33⅓ per cent.

(4) In cases where the rates over different routes between the same points would, by a strict application of the varying percentages of increase herein approved, be subject to different percentages, the lowest percentage applicable to any of the routes may be applied to the rates over all of such routes.

In the construction of rates in accordance with these findings it is not intended that the group boundaries hereinbefore designated should be strictly observed, but the territorial boundaries heretofore recognized should be observed. For example, Richmond, one of the so-called Virginia cities, should continue on the basis which it has heretofore enjoyed.

The above findings apply to all steam railroads subject to our jurisdiction, including so-called "short lines," but not to railroads in Alaska.

While the New England carriers are included in the eastern group and are subject to the percentage for that group, the evidence as to the disproportionate needs of the New England lines makes it desirable that the carriers give careful consideration to the divisions of joint rates accruing to these lines.

INDIVIDUAL COMMODITIES

Considerable evidence was presented with respect to the rates upon a number of individual commodities, including coal, lumber, cement, fruits and vegetables, petroleum, brick, sand, gravel and rock, asphalt, slag, grain, live stock, packing-house products, ore, bullion, potash, salt, fertilizers, and terra cotta.

Various issues have been raised or are presented as to these commodities, the principal of which are as follows: (a) Whether there should be departures from the general percentage increases by maintaining differentials or by the application of specific increases instead of percentages; (b) whether maximum increases should be provided in order to avoid the full percentage increase upon relatively high rates from distant points of production to important markets; (c) whether because of the high cost of production and marketing of some commodities, the percentage increases proposed by carriers will result in a cost delivered at points of market or consumption so great as to curtail production and distribution, an undesirable situation at this time of world shortage of commodities; (d) whether a more general necessary use warrants a lower transportation charge; (e) whether the rates effective June 24, 1918, before General Order No. 28 became effective, should be made the basis of readjustment now by applying thereto a 25 per cent increase and superimposing thereon the percentage increases now found reasonable. Our general conclusions as to the impracticability of specific increases or of attempting now to maintain differentials dispose of a number of these contentions. It should also be said that while we do not here sanction specific increases in lieu of percentages, we are not to be understood as expressing disapproval of increases of that character made by the Director General. Such increases were made under war conditions and under circumstances that do not now exist.

Our attention was called at the hearing to a number of formal complaints now pending, and we are asked to except from the general increase the rates in issue in those complaints. This would have the effect, during the pendency of those proceedings, of giving the rates in question a preferred standing and of exempting them from the general increase. In our opinion, a fairer disposition will be attained by applying the general increase to these rates, with the understanding that this action is without prejudice to any future findings.

Coal. — Carriers serving the Pennsylvania-Ohio-West Virginia coal fields propose to continue the existing differentials in coal rates, and have worked out a scheme of rates to effect that result. Carriers in the southern and western groups propose to ignore existing differentials in coal rates within those groups. The proposal of the eastern lines to preserve existing relationships is approved, and carriers in the other groups should work out a similar plan for restoring the relative adjustments of coal rates now obtaining in those groups. An effort should be made promptly to devise rates in each group that will yield, as nearly as practicable, the same revenue in the aggregate as would be afforded by a straight percentage increasd on the bases herein approved.

Lumber. — Lumber moves in large volume, and it is under ordinary conditions a commodity of comparatively low value and highly competitive in nature. It is produced in almost all parts of the country. The greatest consuming region is in the middle west and the states east of the Mississippi River and north of the Ohio, including New England. Lumber from both the west and the south is marketed in large volume in this region, and the competition between the two producing sections is keen.

There is no definite or fixed relationship in the rates from the south and the west to the consuming territory described, but carriers from each of these sections have endeavored to maintain rates relatively so adjusted as to permit free movement from each. The volume of production in the west has grown materially in the past decade, until to-day it is such that if excluded from eastern markets it is claimed a considerable curtailment of production will result.

The Director General applied a maximum increase of 5 cents upon lumber, which had the effect of maintaining in most cases the existing spread in cents per 100 pounds between southern and western lumber in the northern and eastern markets. The western lumber producers urge in this proceeding also the adoption of a maximum.

Most of the southern producers, including those in the Carolinas and others who ship on comparatively short hauls to the northern markets, urge the application of a straight percentage increase.

For the purposes of this report it is our opinion that the percentages hereinbefore approved should apply to this commodity.

Petroleum and its products. — The principal sources of the petroleum marketed in the United States are in the southwest, which will be termed the midcontinent field; in Wyoming, in California, and in Mexico.

In the past ten years many refineries representing a considerable investment have been established in the midcontinent field and the refined oil there produced is marketed to a considerable extent in the middle west and in the states east of the Mississippi and north of the Ohio.

In competition with the refineries of the midcontinent field in the northern and eastern markets are the refineries of Mexican petroleum located along the Atlantic coast and other refineries in the northern and eastern states, which obtain their crude oil in large part from the midcontinent and other fields through pipe lines, though some of these refineries use rail transportation for the movement of their crude oil.

The Director General imposed on petroleum a flat increase of $4\frac{1}{2}$ cents per 100 pounds in lieu of the standard 25 per cent. The midcontinent shippers claim that a percentage increase now applied without modification to petroleum will in probability tend to restrict the long-haul movement by rail. Other shippers contend that the percentage increase should be applied without exception.

It is concluded that no exception to the general percentage increases herein approved need at this time be made upon petroleum or its products. As has been observed in connection with other situations, the carriers should give careful consideration to the effect of the percentage increases approved on petroleum and, if necessity arises, should arrange for such modifications as the situation may seem to warrant.

Fruits and Vegetables. — Fruits and vegetables are produced in large volume in the far western states and in the south, particularly in Florida. These products are shipped in season to practically all sections of the country, but the most important consuming territory lies east of the Mississippi River and north of the Ohio. Comparatively long hauls to the latter territory are involved both from the south and from the Pacific coast states, and it has been contended that the effect of the proposed percentage increases applied to these rates will produce charges so high as to restrict consumption because of the resultant high delivered cost.

It has been shown that in some instances it has not been possible to market profitably some fruits and vegetables, but the facts before us in this proceeding do not warrant the conclusion that transportation charges are the controlling factor in producing this result, or that the percentage increases applied to the present rates will in fact have the effect feared by the fruit and vegetable shippers.

The western apple producers claim that in the past they have had difficulty in marketing in the east and that percentage increases will add materially to this difficulty. It appears, however, that the size, varying widely from year to year, of the eastern and western crops, respectively, is an important factor in determining the prices received by western growers and the ability to market in the east.

A number of the fruit and vegetable rates covering long hauls, upon which there is a heavy movement, are now before us in other proceedings, and our prior observations as to the effect of our present findings with respect to rates so pending upon complaint are applicable. It is concluded that no exceptions to the general percentage increases will now be made.

Sand, Gravel, Rock, and Slag. — The Director General increased rates on sand, gravel, and stone by specific amounts. Rates on slag in the east were increased 25 per cent and in the south generally by 1 cent per 100 pounds, the same as applied to sand and gravel.

Shippers of all of these commodities contend that the 1-cent increase made by the Director General averaged much more than 25 per cent and that to apply to the present rates the percentage increases proposed by the carriers will produce rates so high as to materially restrict movement. The eastern shippers of sand and gravel also contend that the different method under General Order 28 of increasing the rates on slag as compared with sand and gravel has resulted in preference of slag. The eastern carriers concede that rates on slag should not be less than upon sand and gravel.

We are not convinced that exceptions should be made at this time from the percentages approved for traffic generally. However, the record does suggest that rates in eastern territory are out of proportion to those in the other groups. The carriers have indicated a willingness promptly to readjust rates in cases where hardship results from the general percentage increases, and their special attention is called to these commodities to the end that such action may be taken as the facts may seem to warrant.

Live Stock and Packing-House Products.— Shippers contend that the condition of the live-stock industry is such as to make it probable that the full percentage increase proposed by the carriers will discourage production and distribution. Live stock is produced throughout the country, but the consuming markets in the north and east are to a considerable extent dependent upon the stock produced in the west and southwest. Drought conditions have prevailed here and there in recent years and the present condition of the producers does not appear favorable. However, it is not clear that this condition results from transportation charges.

The Director General in increasing rates on live stock applied a maximum of 7 cents per 100 pounds, while the full 25 per cent increase was applied to packing-house products. To apply again a maximum to live stock, as requested by shippers, without similar maximum upon packing-house products, will in all probability tend to lessen the movement of the southwestern and western stock to local packing plants and increase the movement to the larger and more distant plants in the middle west. One of the principal difficulties of which complaint has been made by the live-stock producers is the lack of prompt and efficient service. To encourage the long-haul movement as against the short-haul movement under present conditions of car supply would tend to increase rather than reduce the transportation difficulties.

From Montana to Chicago the rate on cattle is 55 cents and on hogs 62 cents per 100 pounds. These are among the highest rates now in effect applicable to heavy movements. Under the general basis of increase herein approved, these rates would be advanced 18 cents and 21 cents, respectively, approximately one-fifth cent per pound.

It is concluded that the facts before us at this time do not warrant any exception to the percentage method of increasing the rates on either live stock or packing-house products.

Iron Ore.— A considerable proportion of the iron ore consumed in the United States originates on ranges in Minnesota and Michigan near the head of Lake Superior. This ore moves to furnaces on Lake Michigan and Lake Superior; to furnaces on Lake Erie and in Pennsylvania, Ohio, and other states. The movement is by rail to the upper lake ports, and when destined beyond, by lake vessels to the lower lake ports.

Because of the keenly competitive situation between the respective furnaces, the Director General adopted a specific increase of 30 cents per ton upon iron ore in lieu of a percentage, which was applied to the movement from the Michigan and Minnesota ranges to the upper lake ports, but not from lower lake ports to eastern destinations, thus resulting in an equal increase in cents per ton for the rail transportation to each of the competing furnaces. Under this plan the rates of the western carriers up to the lake ports were increased approximately 57 cents, whereas the rates of the eastern carriers from the lower lake ports were not increased.

In this proceeding the eastern carriers propose first to apply an increase of 22 cents per ton and then impose thereon the general percentage increase. The testimony of ore shippers is conflicting, some proposing no further increase from the ranges to the lake ports, some favoring double increase in the rates from the lower lake ports, others proposing no exceptions to the general percentage increases proposed on traffic generally.

The returns made by the principal ore-carrying roads from the Minnesota ranges to Lake Superior ports indicate that such lines are in a much more prosperous condition than the western carriers generally.

It is concluded that at this time no increases should be made in the rates on iron ore from the Minnesota or Michigan ranges to Lake Superior or upper Lake Michigan ports. Other rates on iron ore may be increased according to the percentages herein approved.

Other Ores.— In some of the western states there is a considerable movement of low-grade ores, some of which are valued at $5 per ton or less. Shippers of these low-grade ores contend that further increases in the rates thereon will result in curtailing or destroying their movement. The evidence before us in this proceeding, however, does not warrant exceptions to the general percentage increases at this time.

Grain and Grain Products.— On grain and grain products we are asked to apply in connection with such percentages as may be approved a maximum increase. For the same reasons that have led to the conclusion that neither specific nor maximum increases are desirable, we find that upon this record no exception should be made of the general percentages upon these commodities, except as noted.

There are in the middle west a number of important grain markets through which it has been customary to maintain an equalization of the rates from important states to important consuming regions, under which the sum of the rates into and out of the various markets is in most cases equal. This adjustment differs from an ordinary differential basis in that it is in substance providing an equal through charge over various routes between the same points by the use of sums of proportional rates rather than the establishment of joint through rates or of transit. The application of different percentages in the various groups will result in dislocation of this equalization.

Carriers and shippers unite in recommending that this equalization be continued because of the keenly competitive situation of the various markets and of the lines of railway serving such markets. However, sufficient detailed information to cover fully the situation is not before us upon this record. We find that the grain rates into and out of these markets may be increased by the general percentages herein approved, with the understanding that the carriers will, within thirty days after the service of this report, file tariffs restoring the equalization through the grain markets now enjoying that basis. This should be done after conference with interested shippers, and, if desired, we will lend our cooperation in the premises.

PORT DIFFERENTIALS.

The eastern carriers express of record their willingness to preserve existing relationships between the rates to and from the eastern ports. No objection to this proposal was made. This result can be readily accomplished for the reason that all rates in official classification territory between the ports and points west of the Buffalo-Pittsburgh line are based on the New York-Chicago rates. The base rates may be increased and existing port differentials maintained. It is our view that in filing the increased rates here authorized a provision of this character should be made.

APPLICATION OF BOAT LINES.

There have been filed in this proceeding applications for increased rates by a number of boat lines. The record shows that the expenses of the boat lines have increased in general at least in the same proportion as expenses of the railroads. Authority is therefore granted to boat lines subject to our jurisdiction to increase their rates to the same extent as increases are herein granted to railroads operating between the same points or in the same territory. In the construction of rail-and-lake rates the present parity between Chicago and Duluth should be maintained.

FREIGHT RATES OF ELECTRIC LINES.

Petitions have been filed in this proceeding by a national organization of electric lines, seeking permission to increase their rates in the same proportion as the rates of trunk lines are advanced. The operating costs of these lines have, on the whole, increased in approximately the same ratio as those of steam railroads. In some instances there is competition between the electric lines and the steam railroads. We conclude that the freight rates of electric lines may be increased by the same percentages as are approved herein for trunk lines in the same territory. This is not to be construed as an expression of disapproval of increases, made or proposed in the regular manner, in the passenger fares of electric lines.

MINIMUM CARLOAD CHARGE, MINIMUM CLASS SCALE, AND MINIMUM CHARGE PER SHIPMENT.

There is now in effect, with certain important exceptions, a minimum charge of $15 per car on carload traffic, applicable to line-haul movements. There are also minimum class rates in the three classification territories. We find on the record no explanation of the underlying basis of the minimum carload charge or the minimum class scales and no justification for increasing them. It is our understanding that these minima were imposed as a revenue measure in connection with rates substantially lower than those authorized in this report. We also find that the minimum charge per shipment for less-than-carload traffic should not be increased.

SPECIFIC DIVISIONS.

In many cases divisions between carriers are in the form of specific amounts per unit. It is obvious that unless divisions of this character be increased, such lines will receive no benefit from the increases herein approved, while the other carriers will receive more than the respective percentage increases applicable to the traffic. It is concluded that where carriers earn specific amounts as their compensation out of through rates or fares, such amounts should be increased in the same percentages as the through rates or fares. Where the divisions of carriers participating in through rates or fares are in fixed amounts per unit and are absorbed by other carriers, such absorptions should be increased in the same percentage as the through rates or fares.

JOINT RATES TO AND FROM FOREIGN COUNTRIES.

Nothing herein should be construed as authorizing any increases in the proportions of joint through rates to or from points in foreign countries accruing in such foreign countries. The proportions of such rates accruing within the United States may, however, be increased to the extent herein approved for domestic rates in the same territory.

FOURTH SECTION DEPARTURES.

In instances where the approval herein of different percentages of increase results in departures from the provisions of the fourth section of the act the carriers will be expected either to correct such departures by tariffs filed not later than November 1, 1920, or to file on or before that date applications seeking permission to continue such departures. Temporary fourth section relief will be granted by appropriate order.

DISPOSITION OF FRACTIONS.

In computing and applying all increased rates authorized herein fractions will be treated as follows:

Where rates are stated in amounts per 100 pounds or any other unit, except as provided in the succeeding paragraph, fractions of less than $\frac{1}{4}$ of a cent will be omitted. Fractions of $\frac{1}{4}$ of a cent or greater but less than $\frac{3}{4}$ of a cent will be stated as $\frac{1}{2}$ cent. Fractions of $\frac{3}{4}$ of a cent or greater will be increased to the next whole cent. This rule will also be followed in computing passenger fares.

Where rates are stated in dollars per carload, including articles moving on their own wheels, when not stated in amounts per 100 pounds or per ton, amounts of less than 25 cents will be dropped; thus, $25.24 will be stated as $25. Amounts of 25 cents or more but less than 75 cents will be stated as 50 cents; thus, $25.65 will be stated as $25.50. Amounts of 75 cents or more but less than $1 will be raised to the next dollar.

OUTSTANDING ORDERS OF THE COMMISSION.

An order will be entered modifying outstanding orders of the Commission to the extent necessary to permit the carriers to make effective the increases herein authorized.

EFFECTIVE DATE OF NEW RATES AND SUBSEQUENT ADJUSTMENTS.

In view of the existing situation it is important that the increased rates be made effective at as early a date as practicable. The increases herein approved may be made effective upon not less than five days' notice to the Commission and to the general public by filing and posting in the manner prescribed in the interstate commerce act. The authority herein granted will not apply to any rates, fares, or charges filed with this Commission to become effective later than January 1, 1921.

Most of the factors with which we are dealing are constantly changing. It is impossible to forecast with any degree of certainty what the volume of traffic will be. The general price level is changing from month to month and from day to day. It is impracticable at this time to adjust all of the rates on individual commodities. The rates to be established on the basis hereinbefore approved must necessarily be subject to such readjustments as the facts may warrant. It is conceded by the carriers that readjustment will be necessary. It is expected that shippers will take these matters up in the first instance with the carriers, and the latter will be expected to deal promptly and effectively therewith, to the end that necessary readjustments may be made in as many instances as practicable without appeal to us.

An appropriate order will be entered.

EASTMAN, *Commissioner,* concurring:

I concur in the conclusions of the majority with respect to the increases in rates which should be permitted, but reach these conclusions by a somewhat different path.

In the transportation act, 1920, Congress has attempted to lay down a rule by which we may be guided in determining the general level of railroad charges. Briefly, we are to adjust rates so that the carriers, as a whole, or as a whole in such rate groups or territories as we may designate, may earn an annual aggregate railway operating income equal as nearly as may be to

$5\frac{1}{2}$ or 6 per cent upon the aggregate value of the railway property held for and used in the service of transportation. In my opinion this rule can not now be applied. Under present conditions any forecast of traffic and expenses for the next twelve months is largely a leap in the dark. But the controlling fact is that any valid determination of "aggregate value" is now impracticable.

For some time the Commission has been diligently engaged in the enormously difficult task of ascertaining and assembling the valuation data required by section 19a of the interstate commerce act; but it has not yet fixed final "value" for any road, and preliminary reports are available on but little more than 15 per cent of the mileage of the country. Nor have we as yet determined the principles by which "value" for rate-making purposes is to be estimated from the data accumulated. These principles are of vital consequence to the country. It is my conviction that the valuation doctrines which are prevalent in railroad and public utility circles and which have been urged upon us are fundamentally unsound in many respects and subversive of the public welfare. Discussion of this subject, however, must be reserved for another occasion. For the present it is enough to say that even if the controlling principles had been enunciated, upon the evidence now before us any present finding as to "aggregate value" is without adequate foundation. I know the good faith in which the majority have proceeded, but I feel sure that it is not in the public interest and I can not believe it necessary under the law, that such an estimate should now be made. It will almost certainly be misunderstood and misinterpreted and may have an unconscious influence upon our valuation work for the future from which it ought to be free. As a side light upon the situation, it will, I think, be conceded that something more than estimates of this kind will be necessary when it comes to enforcing the closely related portion of the act which provides for a division with the government of any income which a carrier may earn in excess of 6 per cent upon value.

I was one of those who opposed the early termination of federal control of railroads. The truth in regard to federal control was then obscured, in part by natural misunderstanding of circumstances arising out of war conditions and in part by propaganda which was often deliberately mendacious. The fact is that both the central and the regional organizations of the United States Railroad Administration were made up of men of wide railroad experience, chosen without regard to political considerations, and that they carried on pioneer work for their country in trying times, for the most part with an ability, fidelity, and patriotism for which they merit only honor and praise. It was my hope that federal control might be continued, because it was evident that the transition back to private operation would create additional disturbance in a time of unsettlement and unrest, that existing railroad facilities could be made to do more work and meet more nearly the transportation needs of the country under unified control than under the control of many separate companies, that the additional facilities which are so greatly needed could now be provided more easily and more economically by public than by private capital, and that disturbances resulting from both rate increases and labor difficulties could be reduced to a minimum if the government retained direct responsibility for the roads.

It was also my hope and belief, if federal control were continued for a reasonable period, that it could gradually be developed, in the light of experience and by genuinely constructive measures, into a system of administration which would preserve the manifest advantages of unified operation and direct governmental responsibility for the transportation system, avoid the dangers which are presumed to inhere in governmental operation by providing a management remote from political influences and free from undue centralization, and enlist the cooperation of labor by recognizing its just claim to some voice in the management.

The situation, however, received the careful consideration of Congress, and after long deliberation other conclusions were reached which were embodied in the transportation act, 1920. It is our plain duty to do everything possible to make the plan of operation adopted by Congress a success. Viewing the matter in this light, I am impelled to the conclusion that under existing conditions liberality in estimating the revenue needs of the carriers is desirable. Poor service is crippling our industries, curtailing production, and raising prices. As between high rates and poor service, the former is the lesser evil. While high rates will not at once bring good service, they may help to achieve this result. To provide good service the railroads greatly need additions and improvements and must secure large sums of capital for that purpose. They can only obtain such funds by the sale of their securities, and no private corporation is financially sound or can long continue to borrow unless it is able to market new stock. The war has depleted the resources of the world and produced profound disturbances in the money markets. Capital can only be obtained by the railroads in competition with demands from innumerable sources and at rates which would normally be regarded as exorbitant.

Summing the matter up, conditions are critical and they have not been made less so by the transition from federal to private control. The evil of poor service we have with us, and it is certain that the health of the nation will suffer seriously unless this evil is cured. It is my best judgment that the railroads can not function successfully without materially increased rates, and I am also persuaded that it is in the best interest of the country that the present plan of operation should receive without delay the best test that can be given it. Under all the circumstances, it follows that it would be a mistake if the railroads were now accorded rates designed to produce substantially less revenue than their responsible executives with unanimity assert that they need in order that good service may be provided. What revenue will actually be produced no one can tell. If the rates prove unduly high, they may later be reduced. The present proceeding has nothing of finality about it and in many respects is similar to a suspension case, where the question is whether or not certain proposed rates shall be permitted to take effect without suspension, a matter left by the act to the discretion of the Commission. I, therefore, concur in the increases of rates which the majority have approved.

I am authorized to say that COMMISSIONER WOOLLEY joins in this expression of opinion.

MCCHORD, *Commissioner:*

The concurring report of COMMISSIONERS WOOLLEY and EASTMAN injects into this case large political questions of governmental policy which are nowhere in issue here. The Congress has, for the time being, settled the question of government operation of the railroads by restoring them to private operation, hedged around by comprehensive laws vesting broad powers in this Commission to regulate them. It is the duty of this Commission to enforce the law as Congress has written it. The questions involved in this case are so great and so vital to the American people that no such suggestions as are here made should be injected to further complicate the extremely delicate and vital situations that now confront this Commission, the public, and the railroads.

For more than 30 years this Commission has stood four square to every wind that blows, confining its activities within the four corners of the law, and it is unwise in this critical period to complicate the real questions involved with extraneous issues. This is neither the time nor the place The Congress is the forum, and should Congress fail to meet the views of a dissatisfied public, if indeed it is dissatisfied, then the final remedy is to be found in that still greater forum, as was so well pointed out by the Supreme Court in 178 U. S., 548, 580:

" The august tribunal of the people, which is continually sitting, and over whose judgments on the conduct of public functionaries the courts exercise no control."

and further:

" This tribunal, therefore, should be the last to overstep the boundaries which limit its own jurisdiction. And while it should always be ready to meet any question confided to it by the Constitution, it is equally its duty not to pass beyond its appropriate sphere of action, and to take care not to involve itself in discussions which properly belong to other forums."

The Commission has attempted to deal with this case under the law in a broad, comprehensive, common-sense way, realizing that the primary responsibility for the future of our railroads rested upon its shoulders and that of the state railroad commissions who have throughout the case and are still cooperating in a most helpful way. They will, in my opinion, measure up to this responsibility to make fully effective what the Interstate Commerce Commission has, with their cooperation, done in this case. After this the gravest responsibility rests with the employees, for, after all, neither the Interstate Commerce Commission nor the state commissions can alone insure efficient railway service. The money derived from increased rates in and of itself will not solve the transportation problem. To enable the carriers to meet the present situation every man and group of men, whether employers or employees, must realize that they are in fact performing a public service. The spirit of duty and service must actuate all.

Had the decision in this case been left to my individual judgment, I would have arrived at the same general conclusion, but perhaps by a somewhat different route. However, I, in common with others, subordinate my individual views to the views of the majority as to the method to be adopted to raise the increased revenue regarding which there is no difference of opinion.

With respect to the criticism of aggregate value, I do not share the apprehension that what is said and done by the majority will result in misunderstanding, misinterpretation, or that it will have any influence upon the Commission's valuation work now being conducted. It will be recalled that in the discussion of this question the report, among other things, says:

"From a consideration of all the facts and matters of record, and those which, under section 15a of the interstate commerce act, we are both required and authorized to consider, we find that the value of the steam-railway property of the carriers subject to the act held for and used in the service of transportation is, for the purposes of this particular case, to be taken as approximating the following . . ."

WILLIAM WYLIE BEALL
v.
WHEELING TRACTION COMPANY

63 I. C. C. 220 (1921)

MEYER, *Commissioner:*

In our original report, 60 I. C. C., 600, we found, among other things, that the interstate passenger fares of the Wheeling Traction Company, hereinafter called the traction company, for the transportation of passengers between Steubenville, Ohio, and Wellsburg, W. Va., and between Steubenville and Weirton, W. Va., were just and reasonable fares, and that the intrastate fares of the traction company for the transportation of passengers in intrastate commerce between Steubenville and Brilliant, Ohio, were unduly preferential of intrastate passengers, unduly prejudicial to interstate passengers, and unjustly discriminatory against interstate commerce; and we prescribed intrastate fares which would remove such preference, prejudice, and discrimination. Upon petition of the intervening city of Steubenville and villages of Brilliant and Mingo Junction, Ohio, and motion of the National Association of Railway and Utility Commissioners, the case was reopened for reargument and said association was granted leave to intervene.

The essential facts are stated in our original report.

The contention of petitioners as stated upon reargument is that the traction company renders a strictly street-railway service, over the charges for which we have no jurisdiction. They point out that defendant has no station buildings along its line, does not do a freight business in the manner in which steam roads do, and has no through routes and joint freight rates.

In support of this contention counsel cite *Omaha Street Ry.* v. *Int. Com. Comm.*, 230 U. S., 324, in which the Supreme Court said:

"Ordinary railroads are constructed on the companies' own property. The tracks extend from town to town and are usually connected with other railroads, which themselves are further connected with others, so that freight may be shipped, without breaking bulk, across the continent. Such railroads are channels of interstate commerce. Street railroads, on the other hand, are local, are laid in streets as aids to street traffic, and for the use of a single community, even though that community be divided by state lines, or under different municipal control. When these street railroads carry passengers across a state line they are, of course, engaged in interstate commerce, but not the commerce which Congress had in mind when legislating in 1887. Street railroads transport passengers from street to street, from ward to ward, from city to suburbs, but the commerce to which Congress referred was that carried on by railroads engaged in hauling passengers or freight "between States," . . . The act referred to railroads which were required to post their schedules — not at street corners where passengers board street cars, but in "*every depot, station or office where passengers or freight are received for transportation.*" The railroads referred to in the act were not those having separate, distinct and local street lines, but those of whom it was required that they should make joint rates and reasonable facilities for interchange of traffic with connecting lines, so that freight might be easily and expeditiously moved in interstate commerce. . . .

"But it is said that since 1887, when the act was passed, a new type of interurban railroad has been developed which, with electricity as a motive power, uses larger cars and runs through the country from town to town, enabling the carrier to haul passengers, freight, express and the mail for long distances at high speed. We are not dealing with such a case . . . it affirmatively appears that the company was chartered as a street railroad, and hauls no freight and is doing only a business appropriate to a street railroad."

The traction company operates an electric railway system between several cities and villages in Ohio and West Virginia, serving several distinct communities, carrying passengers through the country from town to town long distances at a high speed, and rendering a service which can not properly be termed an "aid to street traffic." The record indicates that it uses cars of a type ordinarily employed in interurban service and transports some package freight. It has filed its interstate passenger and freight tariffs with us for many years. And in 1916, in *City of Steubenville, Ohio,* v. *Tri-State R. & E. Co.,* 38 I. C. C., 281, we exercised jurisdiction over the Steubenville, Wellsburg & Weirton Railway Company, the subsidiary line directly under consideration in this cause, on complaint by the city of Steubenville, one of the petitioners herein, and required that carrier to reduce its ticket fares between Steubenville and Follansbee, W. Va. Irrespective of the terms of incorporation we are convinced that the traction company is now rendering an interstate interurban service, the charges for which are within our jurisdiction.

Petitioners further contend that the record makes no showing of unjust discrimination or undue prejudice against interstate commerce or interstate shippers. They contend that section 15a of the interstate commerce act is not applicable to "street or suburban electric railways unless operated as a part of a general steam railroad system of transportation" or to "interurban electric railways" unless so operated "or engaged in the general transportation of freight." And they argue that "so far as section 13, paragraph 4 (of the interstate commerce act), applies to electric railroads that are interstate carriers, it is nothing more than a restatement of the effect of the Shreveport decision"; that that section when applied to steam railroads "is necessarily read in connection with section 15a; and that it has a broader meaning and means something quite different than it does when it applies to a class of carriers which are expressly excluded from section 15a." We can not accept the latter interpretation of the law.

Defendant's interstate passenger fares have been established in accordance with our findings in *Local and Joint Passenger Fares,* 59 I. C. C., 430. The record shows that defendant's intrastate fares are lower for the transportation of passengers for corresponding distances under substantially similar circumstances and conditions, in part in the same cars and over the same rails used by the interstate passengers. It shows that the imposition of these lower intrastate fares operates to prevent the collection of the higher interstate fares.

We have not attempted or asserted the right to regulate the fares of a street railway for travel within a municipality.

Upon consideration of the whole record we found in our original report that —

"the interstate passenger fares of the Wheeling Traction Company . . . between Steubenville and Wellsburg, and between Steubenville and Weirton are just and reasonable fares for interstate transportation over defendant's lines between those points; and that the maintenance of intrastate fares . . . between Steubenville and Brilliant lower than the just and reasonable interstate fares has resulted and will result in undue prejudice to persons traveling in interstate commerce over defendant's lines in the state of Ohio and between points in the state of Ohio and the above-mentioned points in the state of West Virginia; in undue preference of and advantage to persons traveling intrastate over defendant's lines between the points here involved in Ohio; and in unjust discrimination against interstate commerce.

"We further find that, whether the aforesaid passenger fares pertain to transportation in interstate commerce or to transportation in intrastate commerce, the transportation services are performed by the defendant under substantially similar circumstances and conditions."

We find no sufficient reason for modifying the findings stated in our original report, and they are accordingly affirmed.

EASTMAN, *Commissioner*, dissenting:

I approach this case with the conviction that the activities of this Commission should be confined, so far as the law permits, to matters of national consequence. The tendency to overcentralization, unless checked, can only lead to congestion here and to conditions which will sooner or later become intolerable to the people of the country. It is impracticable to handle from Washington with any degree of satisfaction matters which are chiefly of local importance. Nor is the fact that an evil exists which municipal or state authorities have not seen fit to abate necessarily a reason why we should be called or go to the rescue.

This was, I believe, the underlying thought when the Supreme

Court of the United States decided in the *Omaha Case* that street railroads, even when they cross state lines, are not engaged in the interstate commerce " which Congress had in mind when legislating in 1887," and hence are not subject to our jurisdiction. In the instant case the majority undertake to use the power of the federal government to raise two electric railway fares in Ohio which the local authorities will not permit to be raised. One of these fares applies between two small towns for a distance of about 9 miles; the second, between two other towns for a distance of about 7.5 miles. I am wholly persuaded that we ought not to undertake to use the power of the United States for such a purpose unless it is clear that Congress intended it to be so used, and that all doubts ought to be resolved against the assumption of such jurisdiction.

The Ohio electric lines in question are operated under franchises granted to the Bellaire, Bridgeport & Martin's Ferry Street Railway and to the Steubenville & Wheeling Traction Company. I am unable to discover any clearly marked distinction between these lines and the street railroad lines in the *Omaha Case* which the Supreme Court found were not within our jurisdiction. In our decision which the court reversed, *West End Improvement Club* v. *O. & C. B. Ry. & B. Co.*, 17 I. C. C., 239, we described the latter lines as follows, at page 243:

" In the instant case it should be remembered that the defendants have the characteristics of an interurban line as well as of a street railway. They operate 136 single-track miles of road; the rails are not all laid in public streets and highways, but for some distance run over private right of way; they operate over the bridge across the Missouri River, and through sparsely settled sections over expensive culverts not conforming to the level of the streets or roads; they carry the United States mail and do not serve the needs of a single city and its suburbs, but of two cities and several towns, villages, and resorts."

Certainly the electric lines in the present case do not possess the " characteristics of an interurban line " in any greater degree. Nor have I been able to discover any changes in the interstate commerce act since our order in the above-cited case which have with any degree of clarity or certainty extended our jurisdiction over street railroads.

However, my objections to the conclusions of the majority are not limited to this question of jurisdiction. I realize that there have been numerous decisions of the Commission which are inconsistent with a strict interpretation of the *Omaha Case.* But if we possess any power to override the will of Ohio municipalities and compel the raising of electric railway fares which these authorities, however mistakenly, will not permit to be raised, most assuredly it is only when unjust discrimination against interstate commerce or persons or localities engaged therein has been definitely established. In the instant case evidence of substance is wholly lacking that persons or localities engaged in interstate commerce are suffering injury because of the low intrastate fares or that the course of interstate commerce is in any way impeded. Such evidence as we have was presented chiefly by the ostensible defendant, the Wheeling Traction Company. No one else manifests serious concern for the protection of interstate commerce; its concern is clearly a matter of revenue; and its evidence is largely confined to a showing that the intrastate fares in question are unduly low.

I am unable to find in the interstate commerce act any intent of Congress that we should have power to raise the intrastate fares of electric railways which happen to be engaged to some extent in interstate commerce, as most of them are, merely because of a belief that such fares are lower than they ought reasonably to be and in the absence of evidence that the free course of interstate commerce is in any substantial way obstructed or hindered. The complaint should be dismissed.

I am authorized to state that COMMISSIONER CAMPBELL concurs in these views.

WHITAKER-GLESSNER COMPANY

v.

BALTIMORE & OHIO R. R. CO.

63 I. C. C. 47 (1921)

DIVISION 3, COMMISSIONERS CLARKE, HALL, AND EASTMAN.
HALL, *Commissioner:*

Exceptions were filed by complainant to the report proposed by the examiner and argument was had thereon.

Complainant, a corporation, manufactures pig iron and various steel articles at New Boston, near Portsmouth, Ohio. Its extensive plant adjoins the lines of defendants Baltimore & Ohio and Norfolk & Western, and includes an industrial railway which is not a common carrier or separately incorporated. Complainant operates this railway with its own power and crews in moving inbound and outbound carload traffic from and to interchange tracks connecting with the two trunk lines, and in intraplant movements of materials and supplies. The service performed on inbound or outbound traffic will be termed interchange switching; that in strictly intraplant movements, industrial switching.

The original complaint was filed March 24, 1919, and before and after amendment on May 19, 1919, was confined to interstate traffic. By supplemental complaint filed July 24, 1919, the scope of the proceeding was broadened to include intrastate traffic within Ohio. Our jurisdiction over the intrastate phase is limited to the period of federal control. Complainant alleges that the rates charged by defendants on shipments to and from its plant were and are unjust, unreasonable, unjustly discriminatory, and unduly prejudicial, in violation of sections 1, 2, 3, and 4 of the act to regulate commerce, and unjust and unreasonable in violation of section 10 of the federal control act. It prays that defendants be required to desist from these violations and to allow and pay to it the cost of performing the interchange switching service in the future, and, as reparation, the cost of that service in the past. At the hearing complainant's counsel indicated its willingness to accept, in lieu of an allowance, performance of the interchange switching by defendants without charge therefor in addition to the line-haul rate, if defendants would operate as one and render a service as satisfactory as that of complainant.

There is some evidence tending to show that ordinarily the cost to complainant of doing the interchange switching exceeds $100,000 per annum, but it was later agreed at the hearing that the amount of the allowance, past and future, if any is to be made, should be reserved for further hearing after complainant's right thereto shall have been determined by us.

Complainant's plant occupies some 120 acres separated from the Ohio River by the tracks of defendants. It is 1,625 miles long, 0.5 mile wide, and divided into two portions which are in most respects separate operating units, reached by separate tracks, but having track connection with each other. The steel-mills portion with its 10 open-hearth furnaces comprises 22 main buildings, not including engine rooms, outbuildings, sheds, and the like. There are five buildings in the blast-furnace portion.

The plant railway has over 20 miles of standard-gauge main line and sidings, in good condition, laid with 80 to 85 pound rails, all owned, constructed, and maintained by complainant at its own expense, except that certain of the interchange tracks just inside the plant entrance, where defendants receive and deliver complainant's traffic, were originally constructed by the carriers, but have since been renewed and increased by complainant. Ownership of these interchange tracks is said to be in doubt. The railway is equipped with 10 saddle-tank locomotives weighing from 35 to 55 tons apiece, 4 locomotive cranes, 51 freight cars, and 175 charging, ingot-mold, cinder, and hot-metal cars, all restricted to movement within the plant. Three overhead traveling cranes are operated over portions of the track used for interchange switching.

The greater part of the plant trackage is used for interchange switching. That used exclusively for industrial switching is in great part inside of or between buildings. The interchange switching far exceeds in amount the industrial switching. The two sets of track are closely interwoven and adjoin or connect at many points. Complainant's locomotives and crew in performing industrial switching must frequently go upon the tracks used for interchange switching, but in performing interchange switching need not ordinarily use the industrial tracks except for convenience. There are frequent movements of small train-loads of molten metal in ladle cars from the blast furnace to the ingot mills, in part over tracks which must be used for interchange switching. Whether or not this condition is a source of danger to crews engaged in interchange switching was the subject of some controversy at the hearing.

The spotting locations, or places where interchange traffic is loaded or unloaded, are about 75 in number, distributed throughout the plant. Much of the switching, especially of single carloads, consists of switchback movements because of the compactness and complexity of the plant and track layout. The tracks in the plant are numbered consecutively up to 172. There are 131 switches in those serving the steel mills and 54 in those serving the blast furnaces.

As given by complainant, the switching distances from the interchange tracks to the steel mills range from 1,100 to 3,900 feet, approximately, and to the blast-furnace spotting locations from 4,400 to 5,500 feet, with an average for the entire plant of 3,740 feet. The interchange tracks lie a few hundred feet from defendants' break-up yards, but cars are in fact switched by defendants a mile or more from the one to the other. Receipt and delivery of cars at the interchange tracks is comparatively simple and inexpensive for defendants.

Large quantities of limestone, coal, iron ore, scrap iron, and other raw materials are received by complainant, and semi-finished and finished products of steel in the form of billets, slabs, tie plates, sheets, roofing, drums, and range boilers are shipped out, as well as about one-half of the pig iron produced by its blast furnace, which is the excess over its steel-mill requirements. At the steel mills the inbound carloads of scrap iron, limestone, and coal are unloaded mainly at three spotting locations, and the outbound shipments of manufactured products move chiefly from four. Limestone and iron ore for the blast furnace are switched to two spotting locations and the pig-iron product moves from two. All the 75 spotting locations are used at one time or another. Complainant keeps on hand supplies and raw material for the steel mills in quantities sufficient for operation over extended periods, and thus obviates unnecessarily frequent service.

Much of the interchange traffic is assembled into cuts according to commodities and spotting locations within the plant. Where practicable each cut is switched and placed as a whole, to eliminate, where possible, individual movements of separate cars, although such movements are required for a considerable amount of traffic in single-car lots. The less important spotting locations will accommodate only a few cars, but the heaviest movement is to and from locations more amply provided. During February, 1919, the average number of interchange spotting locations served daily was about 2.5 for inbound and 5 for outbound shipments; during July about 6.3 and 5.2, respectively.

The interchange switching ordinarily requires the constant use of two locomotives day and night. The volume of carload traffic is considerable, and, as shown below, has developed rapidly. The heavy tonnage in 1917 and 1918 was due to the war. The figures for 1919 are an estimate based on actual figures for the first nine months:

1909	4,535 carloads.	1917	28,458 carloads.
1910	6,941 carloads.	1918	33,624 carloads.
1912	11,037 carloads.	1919	17,448 carloads.
1913	10,157 carloads.		

Complainant weighs nearly every every car that comes into its plant, loaded and empty. It has a scale on its main track leading from the interchange tracks to the spotting locations, and each loaded car is stopped there for weighing. The weights obtained on outbound traffic are accepted by defendants for waybilling purposes, but the scale is used principally to test the accuracy of the weights applied by the carriers in assessing freight charges, and otherwise for complainant's benefit. Empty cars are also weighed there. Cars unloaded in the plant are moved from the unloading locations to the scale, weighed, and then placed at another location for loading with outbound traffic.

The plant's history dates back to 1898. The property has changed hands several times since then, but for all practical purposes complainant may be regarded as the continuous owner. The plant was small at first and the track layout limited in extent and very simple. There were no intraplant tracks. The carriers did all of the switching with their own locomotives and crews and made no charge therefor in addition to the line-haul rate. This was done under contract. From time to time additions were made to the plant, and eventually the system of tracks became intricate and complex, especially because the intraplant tracks, additional sidings, and general track layout were made to conform to the location of many new buildings. The tracks were constructed mainly for plant convenience rather than for efficiency in railroad operation.

After the intraplant tracks had been constructed the industrial switching was done by complainant with its own locomotives and crews, but the interchange switching was still performed by the carriers. One carrier did the work one month and the other the next month. Complainant afterwards found it unsatisfactory to have the carriers' locomotives and crews within its plant and decided late in 1909 to do all of the switching itself. This was chiefly for reasons of efficiency and economy, combined with some expectation that it would be compensated by an allowance in money from the carriers. The carriers were accordingly notified that complainant would dispense with their services inside the plant inclosure, beginning January 29,

1910. Since then all of complainant's traffic has been received and delivered by the carriers on the interchange tracks just inside the plant entrance, and complainant's railway has been operated exclusively by it with its own locomotives and crews.

When complainant took over the interchange switching it apparently had some reason to believe that defendant, Baltimore & Ohio, might make an allowance in order to secure some of the heavy tonnage then moving over the Norfolk & Western. The matter was left in an unsettled state until, in May, 1912, complainant definitely requested the carriers to make it an allowance. They refused. Complainant then in October of that year suggested to the carriers that they do the interchange switching themselves. This they declined to do. In June, 1916, following our decision in the *Second Industrial Railways Case*, 34 I. C. C., 596, complainant again applied for an allowance, but in December, 1917, the carriers finally declined, with the suggestion that the matter be laid before us. Formal demand was made upon defendants in February, 1919, that they either grant an allowance or come into complainant's plant with their own locomotives and crews and perform the interchange switching. The demand was refused, and complainant promptly instituted this proceeding.

The foregoing summary of some salient facts disclosed by the record as to complainant's plant, and its relation hitherto with the carriers serving it, will suffice for an understanding of the issues raised by the complaint, as amended and supplemented. These will now be considered.

REASONABLENESS OF RATES AND FOURTH SECTION VIOLATIONS.

The line-haul rates to and from the plant are not attacked except as defendants' service of transportation ends or begins on the interchange tracks. Complainant contends that the rates should cover also the interchange switching or service between those tracks and the various spotting locations within the plant, and that this switching service should either be performed by defendants with their power and crews, or, if performed by complainant for defendants, should be paid for by an adequate allowance to be fixed by us. Reparation is sought in the amount which would represent such an allowance in the past.

Of the two alternatives, complainant prefers to do the interchange switching and receive an allowance, rather than to have it done by the carriers. It proposes in any event to continue to perform the industrial switching, in part over tracks needed for interchange switching, and for that purpose must maintain locomotives and crews. Complainant is not subject to full-crew laws and other statutes, state and federal, which place restrictions upon common carriers and often operate to increase the cost of performing service. But its principal reason seems to be that by doing the work itself it can assure unified operation over its tracks inside the plant and thus obviate controversies, congestion, delays, and other difficulties, such as seem to have prompted it to dispense with carrier service inside the plant in 1910. As a practical matter all the switching, industrial and interchange, must be under one direction or, at least, a scrupulously observed joint arrangement, difficult to formulate and still more difficult to enforce.

If each defendant should enter the plant with its own locomotives and crews, and at its own convenience, controversies and delays must result. Complainant would require much of the switching to be done at its own convenience and without interrupting the operation of the plant. Interference by each carrier with switching by the other, and with plant operations, would bring about a situation little short of intolerable. This is so manifest that defendants suggest it as valid ground for a finding by us that any demand for switching service by carriers within the plant is unreasonable. But it should be said that defendants indicated at the hearing their willingness to undertake, in fairness to complainant, to operate jointly or as a unit within the plant, and to effect with complainant reasonable operating arrangements, if we should find that their transportation duty extended to the spotting locations and they should elect to do the work themselves.

In doing this work defendants would encounter physical difficulties. Many of the curves and clearances, side and overhead, in the plant do not conform to the modern standards observed by them in constructing new tracks. There are some sharp curves where, as defendants assert, derailments would be likely if the usual type of switch engine were used, and some places where insufficient clearance would imperil defendants' crews and equipment. Some of the clearances, side and overhead, do not meet the requirements placed upon common carriers by the Ohio statute. Perhaps 50 per cent of the guard rails, switch points, and frogs lack the blocking prescribed by that statute, and the " ore dock," which is about 20 feet high, has no walk alongside the track for the use of switchmen, such as is required of common carriers by the Ohio law. As complainant owns the tracks it is not clear how defendants could either comply with the law or escape prosecution for noncompliance. As to the defects at the " ore dock," complainant says that defendants need feel no concern, because it intends to continue its own interchange switching of ore; but its complaint has not been amended so as to exclude ore.

Instances are shown where defendants perform switching service at other points under conditions by no means ideal in the matter of curves and clearances. To require them to increase the number of those instances would not be in the public interest or in theirs, but undue weight against complainant must not be given to operating conditions which are often disregarded where more important and practical considerations seem to justify that course. Such conditions can be remedied. Nevertheless it must be borne in mind that if the carrier duty extends beyond the interchange tracks throughout the ramifications of this plant to the various spotting locations, the common-carrier liability extends there also. Complainant owns the tracks as well as the ground they are on and the ground adjoining. It controls their location and maintenance, with their accessories. It uses them at pleasure for its industrial switching, whether of molten metal or of other matter, dangerous or not. On such a web of interlacing tracks, so dominated by complainant, the carriers would not have that control over the instrumentalities of carriage which corresponds with common-carrier liability for loss of or damage to the thing carried.

The switch engines used by defendants in complainant's plant prior to 1910 were the same in type as those ordinarily in use on their own lines at the time. Those of modern type are ill-adapted for such work because of its peculiar nature and the character of the tracks. In some instances the track could be straightened and danger from sharp curves lessened. Defendants might provide themselves with switch engines of special type, such as is used by complainant, which could be operated with greater safety. As to this, defendants contend that it is no part of their duty as common carriers to procure special facilities in order to accommodate themselves to the peculiarities of complainant's plant and business, and that if the service can not be performed efficiently with their ordinary facilities and without unusual risk, it is not a reasonable transportation service and therefore not one which they are obliged to perform.

Reference has been made to the location of complainant's track scale, and the use made of it for complainant's purposes. Defendants say that, if required to do the interchange switching, an inbound car should be deemed delivered when placed on the scale for weighing by complainant, and that they could not and should not be required to make a second delivery by placing it at some spotting location. They say, further, that if they should elect to make such second delivery they would be entitled to reasonable additional compensation for that extra service. If defendants, under compulsion, should do the switching between the interchange tracks and the spotting locations, without stopping the cars en route, loaded or empty, at the scale, the switching to and from the scale for weighing would then be left for complainant's engines and crews, and constant interference with defendants' operations on the same track would result. This might be obviated if the scale were used only for obtaining weights of outbound shipments for the carriers' billing purposes, or if it were shifted to a place where complainant's engines and crews could reach it without interfering with defendants' operations.

Whether defendants could do the work as satisfactorily as complainant is open to serious doubt. They contend that if complainant had difficulty in 1910 because of the dual operations on its railway, there is all the more reason now why defendants' engines and crews would be in the way. Complainant contends that operating conditions have improved, but whether that be so or not we must deal with the situation as it is.

A tariff feature is also presented as having some bearing on the reasonableness of the rate. In *Iron Ore Rate Cases,* 41 I. C. C., 181, we found that line-haul rates on iron ore should not include the service of placing carload shipments at the point of unloading on private industry tracks at destination, and that separate charges should be established for that service. Defendants have accordingly published a charge, in addition to the line-haul rate, to apply on iron ore switched by them from their yards to complainant's blast furnace, but this charge is not made, because complainant does the service itself. Complainant contends that the publication of this charge is a recognition by defendants that the service on iron ore is a common-carrier obligation and deduces therefrom that all of the interchange switching at complainant's plant is a transportation duty. It is true that so long as that charge is published defendants must, upon demand, perform the service. But it does not necessarily follow that they would be under any common-carrier obligation to do the switching if no charge were published. Carriers perform various services voluntarily or under stress of competition which are not within their duty as common carriers, and which they can not be required to perform in the absence of undue prejudice or unjust discrimination.

Complainant further contends that as a tariff matter the line-haul rates now in effect include interchange switching service, because the tariffs do not specifically exclude that service from the application of the rates except in the case of iron ore. It cites the provision of the interstate commerce act that "no carrier . . . shall extend to a shipper or person any privileges or facilities in . . . transportation . . . except such as are specified in such tariffs," and says that, since a charge is specifically published only for the switching of iron ore, it follows by natural inference and in legal effect that no charge will be made for that service on other commodities. It might be contended with equal force that, since receipt and delivery of carload shipments in general at spotting locations are not "specified in such tariffs," it is unlawful for defendants to receive and deliver them there.

Many instances can be found in official classification territory where carriers either pay allowances in money or perform switching without additional charge on extensive and complex industrial railroads. Many such were cited by complainant. In a number of them the Baltimore & Ohio is one of the carriers. The Norfolk & Western has quite consistently abstained from that practice. It makes no allowance to any industry, and performs no spotting service where industries have extensive or complex plant tracks, or where the industries have their own locomotives.

Defendants state that they will do the switching on plant-facility tracks wherever the service is found to be a common-carrier obligation incident to the line haul, provided the conditions are such that the service can be performed safely and conveniently with the power which they have available in that vicinity. Their policy appears to be that, except where they are already doing it, they will neither make allowances nor perform switching for shippers if any doubt exists as to their common-carrier obligation. Their purpose is to leave such cases to this Commission.

Notwithstanding complainant's present declared willingness to have defendants' engines and crews enter its plant, this case does not differ in principle from *General Electric Co.* v. *N. Y. C. & H. R. R. R. Co.*, 14 I. C. C., 237, and *Solvay Process Co.* v. *D., L. & W. R. R. Co.*, 14 I. C. C., 246, wherein we found that at these great industrial plants the obligation of the carriers in connection with the line-haul rates extended only to the receipt and delivery of cars at some reasonably convenient point of interchange. In *Marting Iron & Steel Co. Case,* 48 I. C. C., 620, and in *Virginia Portland Ry. Co.*, 49 I. C. C., 332, the tracks were much less complicated and extensive than those of complainant here. We found that the placing of cars on the tracks within the plant inclosure constituted delivery by the trunk lines under their line-haul rates, and that any allowance by the trunk lines for the service of spotting cars after such placement would be improper. In *United States Cast Iron P. & F. Co.* v. *Director General,* 57 I. C. C., 677, we said:

"Whenever a particular delivery service — spotting at some place of unloading within a plant — properly may be construed as the equivalent of either of these two services [typical team-track delivery or shunting of a car upon a siding of a shipper clear of the main track] and the rendition of such service practical, we may compel a carrier to perform such service with its own equipment as part of its legal obligation as to delivery of carload traffic. As the magnitude of the service becomes greater than the equivalent of team-track delivery or simple switching delivery, the demand on the carrier for its performance tends to exceed what may be regarded as a proper delivery service under transportation rates."

We can require the carriers to perform the interchange switching if we find it to be a reasonable transportation service incident to the line haul, but we can not compel them to act as a unit, or to do the work at the convenience and to the satisfaction of complainant. We can not order defendants to make an allowance. Whether a shipper shall receive an allowance in lieu of such switching service is optional with the carriers.

Complainant's plant is within the so-called southern Ohio rate district, which extends from Portsmouth to Huntington, W. Va. Points in this district take the same rates to and from most points in central territory. Following *Iron Ore Rate*

Cases, supra, delivery charges on ore were computed on the basis of the delivery service required at a given industry and separately published to cover the delivery service at that industry. This charge at complainant's plant was 4 cents per long ton, which was higher than that at most plants in the district. The total outlay of complainant on movements to or from the spotting locations in its plant, obtained by adding to the line-haul rates to Portsmouth the published delivery charge on ore, and on other traffic the cost of the interchange switching, was shown to be greater than that made by other industries on traffic to and from their plants in the same district when routed via Portsmouth. In like manner and under like circumstances the "rate per ton-mile" to Portsmouth could be computed as being higher than to more distant points in the district. Complainant relies upon such computations to support its allegation that the long-and-short-haul provision of the fourth section was violated. Its position is untenable.

Upon the record we are of opinion and find that complainant's railway was and is a plant facility; that the interchange switching service within the plant during the period covered by the complaint, as amended and supplemented, could not and can not be required of defendants; that the placing of cars upon the interchange tracks within the plant constituted and constitutes delivery at the industry by defendants under their line-haul rates; and that those rates were not and are not unjust, unreasonable, or in violation of the fourth section of the interstate commerce act.

UNJUST DISCRIMINATION AND UNDUE PREJUDICE.

Complainant competes with many other iron and steel manufacturers in the purchase of raw materials and sale of its products, and must meet prevailing prices. Any unjust discrimination or undue prejudice suffered at the hands of defendants would thus have a direct effect upon complainant's business. Unjust discrimination is alleged, but no evidence has been introduced tending to show violation of section 2 of the interstate commerce act. We therefore confine our discussion to the allegation under section 3.

In support of that allegation several plants were instanced in which the Baltimore & Ohio or the Norfolk & Western performs switching for industries in the southern Ohio rate district. These industries are engaged in much the same line of business as complainant, but the physical conditions at their plants are not in any substantial way similar to those at complainant's plant.

One illustration will suffice. The so-called Ironton plant of the Marting Iron & Steel Company is typical of the industries at which one or the other of defendants performs the interchange switching at the line-haul rates and respecting which complainant introduced detailed evidence and maps. It is a blast furnace at Ironton, Ohio, within the southern Ohio rate district, 27 miles from Portsmouth, and is served only by the Norfolk & Western. This plant is distinct from the Etna furnace at the same place, owned by the same company and operating the industrial railway considered in *Marting Iron & Steel Co. Case, supra.* The Ironton plant manufactures only foundry iron, which is one of complainant's products. To that extent, and because it uses the same kind of raw materials, it is said to compete with complainant. A witness for the latter estimated that some 12,000 cars, inbound and outbound, are handled there yearly.

The Ironton plant has 1 main lead with 7 branches, from which, in turn, other tracks diverge, making 16 in all upon which deliveries are made. The trackage within the plant aggregates about 2.25 miles. Some tracks are on ore trestles, but the carrier makes a separate delivery charge of 3 cents per long ton on iron ore. There are some 16 switches but no crossings. All spotting locations can be reached by simple and direct pulls. All structures are in one part of the plant area, and none of the tracks passes between buildings. The industry has no locomotives and there is no divided control over movements, no interference with the carrier's operations by industrial switching, and no hauling of molten metal in cars over the tracks. Six locomotives and crews perform all the switching within the Ironton switching limits for this and 22 other industries, the station siding, and the team tracks. It is obvious that the conditions at the Ironton plant are not comparable with those at complainant's plant and afford no basis for a finding of undue prejudice.

In a few instances the Baltimore & Ohio, but not the Norfolk & Western, performs switching for industries engaged to some extent in the same general line of business as complainant, but the evidence is general in character and fails to support the allegation.

Defendants' witness testified that all that portion of Ohio lying south of a line drawn through Union City, Ind., Columbus, Zanesville, and Bellaire is free from the spotting allowance practice, except in the Cincinnati switching district, and that where carriers spot for industries the conditions compare favorably with the ordinary team-track or private spur-track delivery.

Complainant's counsel, upon argument, confined himself to the issue of undue prejudice because of "the state of the evidence in the case, and the controlling motive of the industry in bringing this complaint." Counsel cited various decisions, and referred to instances in which defendants spot cars at the plants of complainant's competitors in the southern Ohio rate district. He urged that, although physical conditions at complainant's plant are more involved than at most of these competing plants, the cost of the service, because of the large amount of traffic handled, is probably not so great, and therefore, notwithstanding the complexity of complainant's facilities, there is no reason for according it less favorable treatment. The question whether prejudice is undue is not to be determined by relative costs alone. The situation as a whole at complainant's plant is plainly such as to put it in a different category from the others in the southern Ohio rate district.

Reference was made upon argument to the fact that several years ago, following *Car Spotting Charges,* 34 I. C. C., 609, and *Second Industrial Railways Case, supra,* the Baltimore & Ohio and the Pennsylvania concurrently established tariffs providing for allowance to the Wheeling Steel & Iron Company, which operates two locomotives in interchange switching at its plant in Wheeling, W. Va. From an exhibit showing the track layout, and from the testimony, it clearly appears that the Wheeling plant does not compare with complainant's plant in extent and character.

The Baltimore & Ohio performs interchange switching at Youngstown, Ohio, for the Republic Iron & Steel Company and the Youngstown Sheet & Tube Company. This was also pressed upon our attention but the evidence relating to their plants is too indefinite to afford a basis for comparison with complainant's plant.

Upon consideration of the record we are of opinion and find that the refusal of defendants to perform the interchange switching in complainant's plant beyond the interchange tracks or to grant in lieu thereof an allowance in money, was not and is not unjustly discriminatory or unduly prejudicial to complainant.

The complaint and supplemental complaint will be dismissed.

INTERMOUNTAIN RATE CASES

234 U. S. 476 (1914)

Mr. Chief Justice White delivered the opinion of the court.

We shall seek to confine our statement to matters which are essential to the decision of the case. The provisions of § 4 of the Act to Regulate Commerce dealing with what is known as the long and short-haul clause, the power of carriers because of dissimilarity of circumstances and conditions to deviate from the exactions of such clause and the authority of the Interstate Commerce Commission in relation to such subjects were materially amended by the act of June 18, 1910, c. 309, 36 Stat. 539, 547. Following the form prescribed by the Commission after the amendment in question, the seventeen carriers who are appellees on this record made to the Interstate Commerce Commission their "application for relief from provisions of fourth section of Amended Commerce Act in connection with the following tariffs." The tariffs annexed to the applications covered the whole territory from the Atlantic seaboard to the Pacific coast and the Gulf of Mexico, including all interior points and embracing practically the entire country, and the petition asked the Interstate Commerce Commission for authority to continue all rates shown on the tariffs from the Atlantic seaboard to the Pacific coast and from the Pacific coast to the Atlantic seaboard and to and from interior points lower than rates concurrently in effect from and to intermediate points. It was stated in the petition: "This application is based upon the desire of the interested carriers to continue the present method of making rates lower at the more distant points than at the intermediate points; such lower rates being necessary by reason of competition of various water carriers and of carriers partly by water and partly by rail operating from Pacific coast ports to Atlantic seaboard ports; competition of various water carriers operating to foreign countries from Pacific coast ports and competition of the products of foreign countries with the products of the Pacific coast; competition of the products of Pacific coast territory with the products of other sections of the country; competition of Canadian rail carriers not subject to the Interstate Commerce Act; competition of the products of Canada moving by Canadian carriers with the products of the United States; rates established via the shorter or more direct routes, but applied also via the longer or more circuitous routes." After full hearing the Commission refused to grant unqualifiedly the prayer of the petition but entered an order permitting in some respects a charge of a lower rate for the longer haul to the Pacific coast than was asked for intermediate points provided a proportionate relation was maintained between the lower rate for the longer haul to the Pacific coast and the higher rate to the intermediate points the proportion to be upon the basis of percentages which were fixed. For the purpose of the order in question the Commission in substance adopted a division of the entire territory into separate zones which division had been resorted to by the carriers for the purpose of the establishment of the rates in relation to which the petition was filed. Refusing to comply with this order the carriers commenced proceedings in the Commerce Court praying a decree enjoining the enforcement of the fourth section as amended on the ground of its repugnancy to the Constitution of the United States and of the order as being in any event violative of the amended section as properly construed. An interlocutory injunction was ordered. The defendants moved to dismiss and on the overruling of the motions appealed from the interlocutory order, the case being No. 136. Subsequently upon the election of the defendants to plead no further a final decree was entered and appealed from, that appeal being No. 162.

It suffices at this moment to say that all the contentions which the assignments of error involve and every argument advanced to refute such contentions, including every argument urged to uphold on the one hand or to overthrow on the other action of the Commission, as well as every reason relied upon to challenge the action of the court or to sustain its judgment, are all reducible to the following propositions:

(a) The absolute want of power of the court below to deal with the subject involved in the complaint because controversies concerning the fourth section of the Act to Regulate Commerce of the nature here presented were by an express statutory provision excluded from the cognizance of the court below. (b)

That even if this be not the case the action of the Commission which was complained of was purely negative and therefore not within the cognizance of the court because not inherently justiciable. (c) That correctly interpreting the fourth section the order made by the Commission was absolutely void because wholly beyond the scope of any power conferred by the fourth section as amended. (d) That even if in some respects the order of the Commission was within the reach of its statutory power there we intermingled in the order such an exertion of authority not delegated as to cause the whole order to be void. (e) That the order of the Commission was void even if the fourth section be interpreted as conferring the authority which the Commission exerted, since under that assumption the fourth section as amended was repugnant to the Constitution.

All the propositions, even including the jurisdictional ones, are concerned with and depend upon the construction of the fourth section as amended, and we proceed to consider and pass upon that subject and every other question in the case under four separate headings: 1, The meaning of the statute; 2, Its constitutionality; 3, The jurisdiction of the court; 4, The validity of the order in the light of the statute as interpreted.

1. *The meaning of the statute.*

We reproduce the section as originally adopted and as amended, passing a line through the words omitted by the amendment and printing in italics those which were added by the amendment, thus at a glance enabling the section to be read as it was before and as it now stands after amendment.

"Sec. 4. That it shall be unlawful for any common carrier subject to the provisions of this Act to charge or receive any greater compensation in the aggregate for the transportation of passengers, or of like kind of property, ~~under substantially similar circumstances and conditions,~~ for a shorter than for a longer distance over the same line *or route* in the same direction, the shorter being included within the longer distance, *or to charge any greater compensation as a through route than the aggregate of the intermediate rates subject to the provisions of this Act;* but this shall not be construed as authorizing any common carrier within the terms of this Act to charge and *or* receive as great compensation for a shorter as for a longer distance: Provided, however, That upon application to the *Interstate Commerce* Commission ~~appointed under the provisions of this Act,~~ such common carrier may in special cases, after investigation ~~by~~

~~the Commission,~~ be authorized *by the Commission* to charge less for longer than for shorter distances for the transportation of passengers or property; and the Commission may from time to time prescribe the extent to which such designated common carrier may be relieved from the operation of this section ~~of this Act:~~ *Provided, further, That no rates or charges lawfully existing at the time of the passage of this amendatory Act shall be required to be changed by reason of the provisions of this section prior to the expiration of six months after the passage of this Act, nor in any case where application shall have been filed before the Commission, in accordance with the provisions of this section, until a determination of such application by the Commission.*

"*Whenever a carrier by railroad shall in competition with a water route or routes reduce the rates on the carriage of any species of freight to or from competitive points, it shall not be permitted to increase such rates after hearing by the Interstate Commerce Commission it shall be found that such proposed increase rests upon changed conditions other than the elimination of water competition.*"

Before considering the amended text we state briefly some of the more important requirements of the section before amendment and the underlying conceptions of private right, of public duty and policy which it embodied, because to do so will go a long way to remove any doubt as to the amended text and will moreover serve to demonstrate the intent of the legislative mind in enacting the amendment.

Almost immediately after the adoption of the Act to Regulate Commerce in 1887 (February 4, 1887, c. 104, 24 Stat. 379), the Interstate Commerce Commission in considering the meaning of the law and the scope of the duties imposed on the Commission in enforcing it, reached the conclusion that the words "under substantially similar circumstances and conditions" of the fourth section dominated the long and short-haul clause and empowered carriers to primarily determine the existence of the required dissimilarity of circumstances and conditions and consequently to exact in the event of such difference a lesser charge for the longer than was exacted for the shorter haul and that competition which materially affected the rate of carriage to a particular point was a dissimilar circumstance and condition within the meaning of the act. We say primarily because of course it was further recognized that the authority existing in carriers to the end just stated was subject to the supervision and control of the

Interstate Commerce Commission in the exertion of the powers conferred upon it by the statute and especially in view of the authority stated in the fourth section. In considering the act comprehensively it was pointed out that the generic provisions against preference and discrimination expressed in the second and third sections of the act were all-embracing and were therefore operative upon the fourth section as well as upon all other provisions of the act. But it was pointed out that where within the purview of the fourth section it had lawfully resulted that the lesser rate was charged for a longer than was exacted for a shorter haul such exaction being authorized could not be a preference or discrimination and therefore illegal. *In re Louisville & Nashville R. R. Co.,* 1 I. C. C. 31. These comprehensive views announced at the inception as a matter of administrative construction were subsequently sustained by many decisions of this court, and to the leading of such cases we refer in the margin.[1] We observe, moreover, that in addition it came to be settled that where competitive conditions authorized carriers to lower their rates to a particular place the right to meet the competition by lowering rates to such place was not confined to shipments made from the point of origin of the competition, but empowered all carriers in the interest of freedom of commerce and to afford enlarged opportunity to shippers to accept, if they chose to do so, shipments to such competitive points at lower rates than their general tariff rates: a right which came aptly to be described as "market competition" because the practice served to enlarge markets and develop the freedom of traffic and intercourse. It is to be observed, however, that the right thus conceded was not absolute because its exercise was only permitted provided the rates were not so lowered as to be non-remunerative and thereby cast an unnecessary burden upon other shippers. *East Tenn. &c. R. Co.* v. *Interstate Com. Comm.,* 181 U. S. 1. As the statute as thus construed imposed no obligation to carry to the competitive point at a rate which was less than a reasonable one, it is obvious that the statute regarded the rights of private ownership and sought to impose no duty conflicting therewith. It is also equally clear that in permitting the carrier to judge primarily of the competitive conditions and

[1] *Int. Com. Comm. v. Balt. & Ohio Railroad,* 145 U. S. 263; *Cinn., N. O. & Tex. Pac. Ry. v. Int. Com. Comm.,* 162 U. S. 184; *Texas & Pac. Railway v. Int. Com. Comm.,* 162 U. S. 197; *Louisville & N. R. Co. v. Behlmer,* 175 U. S. 468; *East Tenn. &c. R. Co. v. Int. Com. Comm.,* 181 U. S. 1.

to meet them at election the statute lodged in the carrier the right to exercise a primary judgment concerning a matter of public concern broader than the mere question of the duty of a carrier to carry for a reasonable rate on the one hand and of the right of the shipper on the other to compel carriage at such rate, since the power of primary judgment which the statute conferred concerned in a broad sense the general public interest with reference to both persons and places, considerations all of which therefore in their ultimate aspects came within the competency of legislative regulation. It was apparent that the power thus conferred was primary, not absolute, since its exertion by the carrier was made by the statute the subject both of administrative control and ultimate judicial review. And the establishment of such control in and of itself serves to make manifest the public nature of the attributes conferred upon the carrier by the original fourth section. Indeed that in so far as the statute empowered the carrier to judge as to the dissimilarity of circumstances and conditions for the purpose of relief from the long and short-haul clause it but gave the carrier the power to exert a judgment as to things public was long since pointed out by this court. *Texas & Pac. Railway* v. *Interstate Com. Comm.*, 162 U. S. 197, 218.

With the light afforded by the statements just made we come to consider the amendment. It is certain that the fundamental change which it makes is the omission of the substantially similar circumstances and conditions clause, thereby leaving the long and short-haul clause in a sense unqualified except in so far as the section gives the right to the carrier to apply to the Commission for authority " to charge less for longer than for shorter distances for the transportation of persons or property " and gives the Commission authority from time to time " to prescribe the extent to which such designated common carrier may be relieved from the operation of this section." From the failure to insert any word in the amendment tending to exclude the operation of competition as adequate under proper circumstances to justify the awarding of relief from the long and short-haul clause and there being nothing which minimizes or changes the application of the preference and discrimination clauses of the second and third sections, it follows that in substance the amendment intrinsically states no new rule or principle but simply shifts the powers conferred by the section as it originally stood; that is, it takes from the carriers the deposit of public power previously lodged in them and vests it in the Commission as a primary instead of a reviewing function. In other words, the elements of judgment or so to speak the system of law by which judgment is to be controlled remains unchanged but a different tribunal is created for the enforcement of the existing law. This being true, as we think it plainly is, the situation under the amendment is this: Power in the carrier primarily to meet competitive conditions in any point of view by charging a lesser rate for a longer than for a shorter haul has ceased to exist because to do so, in the absence of some authority, would not only be inimical to the provision of the fourth section but would be in conflict with the preference and discrimination clauses of the second and third sections. But while the public power, so to speak, previously lodged in the carrier is thus withdrawn and reposed in the Commission the right of carriers to seek and obtain under authorized circumstances the sanction of the Commission to charge a lower rate for a longer than for a shorter haul because of competition or for other adequate reasons is expressly preserved and if not is in any event by necessary implication granted. And as a correlative the authority of the Commission to grant on request the right sought is made by the statute to depend upon the facts established and the judgment of that body in the exercise of a sound legal discretion as to whether the request should be granted compatibly with a due consideration of the private and public interests concerned and in view of the preference and discrimination clauses of the second and third sections.

2. *The alleged repugnancy of the section as amended to the Constitution.*

But if the amendment has this meaning it is insisted that it is repugnant to the Constitution for various reasons which superficially considered seem to be distinct but which really are all so interwoven that we consider and dispose of them as one. The argument is that the statute as correctly construed is but a delegation to the Commission of legislative power which Congress was incompetent to make. But the contention is without merit. *Field* v. *Clark,* 143 U. S. 649; *Buttfield* v. *Stranahan,* 192 U. S. 470; *Union Bridge Co.* v. *United States,* 204 U. S. 364; *United States* v. *Heinszen,* 206 U. S. 370; *St. Louis, I. M. & S. Ry. Co.* v. *Taylor,* 210 U. S. 281; *Monongahela Bridge Co.* v. *United States,* 216 U. S. 177. We do not stop to review these cases because the mere statement of the contention in the light of its environment suffices to destroy it. How can it otherwise be since the argument as applied to the case before us is this: that the authority in question was validly delegated so long as it was lodged in carriers but ceased to be susceptible of delegation the instant it was taken from the carriers for the purpose of being lodged in a public administrative body? Indeed, when it is considered that in last analysis the argument is advanced to sustain the right of carriers to exert the public power which it is insisted is not susceptible of delegation, it is apparent that the contention is self-contradictory since it reduces itself to an effort to sustain the right to delegate a power by contending that the power is not capable of being delegated. In addition, however, before passing from the proposition we observe that when rightly appreciated the contention but challenges every decided case since the passage of the Act to Regulate Commerce in 1887 involving the rightfulness of the exertion by a carrier of the power to meet competition as a means of being relieved from the long and short-haul clause of the fourth section before its amendment. While what we have already said answers it, because of its importance we notice another contention. As the power of carriers to meet competition and the relation of that right to non-competitive places may concern the fortunes of numberless individuals and the progress and development of many communities, it is said, to permit authority to be exerted concerning the subject without definite rules for its exercise will be to destroy the rights of persons and communities. This danger, the argument proceeds, is not obviated by declaring that the provisions of the second and third sections as to undue preference and discrimination apply to the fourth section since without a definition of what constitutes undue preference and discrimination, no definite rule of law is established but whim, caprice or favor will in the nature of things control the power exerted. And it is argued that this view is not here urged as the mere result of conjecture, since in the report of the Commission in this case it was declared in unequivocal terms as the basis of the order entered that the statute vested in the Commission a wide and undefined discretion by virtue of which it became its duty to see to it that communities and individuals obtained fair opportunities, that discord was allayed and commercial justice everywhere given full play. Let it be conceded that the language relied upon would have the far-reaching significance attributed to it if separated from its context, we think when it is read in connection with the report of which it but forms a part, and moreover when it is elucidated by the action taken by the Commission there is no substantial ground for holding that by the language referred to it was entitled to declare that the fourth section as amended conferred the uncontrolled exuberance of vague and destructive powers which it is now insisted was intended to be claimed. In any event, however, we must be governed by the statute and its plain meaning. After all has been said the provisions as to undue preference and discrimination, while involving of course a certain latitude of judgment and discretion, are no more undefined or uncertain in the section as amended than they have been from the beginning and therefore the argument comes once more to the complaint that because public powers have been transferred from the carriers to the Commission, the wrongs suggested will arise. Accurately testing this final result of the argument it is clear that it exclusively rests upon convictions concerning the impolicy of having taken from carriers, intimately and practically acquainted as they are with the complex factors entering into rate making and moreover impelled to equality of treatment as they must be by the law of self interest operating upon them as a necessary result of the economic forces to which they are subjected, and having lodged the power in an official administrative body which in the nature of things must act, however conscientiously, from conceptions based upon a more theoretical and less practical point of view. But this does not involve a grievance based upon the construction or application of the fourth section as amended but upon the wisdom of the legislative judgment which was brought into play in adopting the amendment, a subject with which we have nothing in the world to do. It is said in the argument on behalf of one of the carriers that as in substance and effect the duty is imposed upon the Commission in a proper case to refuse an application, therefore the law is void because in such a contingency the statute would amount to an imperative enforcement of the long and short-haul clause and would be repugnant to the Constitution. It is conceded in the argument that it has been directly decided by this court that a general enforcement of the long and short-haul clause would not be repugnant to the Constitution (*Louisville & N. R. Co.* v. *Kentucky,* 183 U. S. 503), but we are asked to reconsider and overrule the case and thus correct the error which was manifested in deciding it. But we are not in the remotest degree inclined to enter into this inquiry, not only because of the reasons which were stated in the case itself but also because of those already expounded in this opinion and for an additional reason which is that the contention by necessary implication assails the numerous cases which from the enactment of the Act to Regulate Commerce down to the present time have involved the adequacy of the conditions advanced by carriers for justifying their departure from the long and short-haul clause. We say this because the controversies which the many cases referred to considered and decided by a necessary postulate involved an assertion of the validity of the legislative power to apply and enforce the long and short-haul clause. How can it be otherwise since if this were not the case all the issues presented in the numerous cases would have been merely but moot, affording therefore no basis for judicial action since they would have had back of them no sanction of lawful power whatever.

3. *The jurisdiction of the court.*

The argument on this subject is twofold: (a) that as by the act creating the Commerce Court (June 18, 1910, c. 309, 36 Stat. 539) that court was endowed only with the jurisdiction "now possessed by circuit courts of the United States and the judges thereof" and provided that "nothing contained in this act shall be construed as enlarging the jurisdiction now possessed by the circuit courts of the United States or the judges thereof, that is hereby transferred to and vested in the commerce court" and as new powers were created by the subsequent amendment of the fourth section, therefore the Commerce Court had no jurisdiction. But we pass any extended discussion of the proposition because it is completely disposed of by the construction which we have given to the amended section since that construction makes it clear that the effect of the amended fourth section was not to create new powers theretofore non-existing, but simply to redistribute the powers already existing and which were then subject to review. The argument affords another manifestation of the tendency to which we have already directed attention in this case to seek to maintain and aggrandize a power by insisting upon propositions which, if they were accepted, would raise the gravest question as to the constitutional validity of the asserted power, a question which we need not at all consider in view of the want of foundation for the exercise of the power claimed in the light of the plain meaning of the act to the contrary which we have already pointed out.

(b) The second contention as to jurisdiction yet further

affords an illustration of the same mental attitude, since it rests upon the assumption that the order of the Commission refusing to grant the request of the carrier made under the fourth section was purely negative and hence was not subject to judicial inquiry. The contention therefore presupposes that the power which from the beginning has been the subject of judicial review by the mere fact of its transfer to the Commission was made arbitrary. Besides, the proposition disregards the fact that the right to petition the Commission conferred by the statute is positive and while the refusal to grant it may be in one sense negative, in another and broader view it is affirmative since it refuses that which the statute in affirmative terms declares shall be granted if only the conditions which the statute provides are found to exist. It is of course true as pointed out in *Interstate Commerce Commission* v. *Illinois Central Railroad,* 215 U. S. 452, 470, and since repeatedly applied that findings of fact made by the Commission within the scope of its administrative duties must be accepted in case of judicial review, but that doctrine, as was also pointed out, does not relieve the courts in a proper case from determining whether the Constitution has been violated or whether statutory powers conferred have been transcended or have been exercised in such an arbitrary way as to amount to the exertion of authority not given, doctrines which but express the elementary principle that an investiture of a public body with discretion does not imply the right to abuse but on the contrary carries with it as a necessary incident the command that the limits of a sound discretion be not transcended which by necessary implication carries with it the existence of judicial power to correct wrongs done by such excess. And without pausing to particularly notice it, we observe in passing that what has just been said is adequate to meet the contention that as violations of the fourth section were made criminal no power existed to enjoin an order of the Commission made under that section because the consequences would be to enjoin criminal prosecution. The right which as we have seen the act gives to test the validity of orders rendered under the fourth section is not to be destroyed by a reference to a provision of that section. The two must be harmoniously enforced.

4. *The validity of the order in the light of the statute as interpreted.*

The order is in the margin.[1] The main insistence is that there was no power after recognizing the existence of competition and the right to charge a lesser rate to the competitive point than to intermediate points to do more than fix a reasonable rate to the intermediate points, that is to say, that under the power transferred to it by the section as amended the Commission was limited to ascertaining the existence of competition and to authorizing the carrier to meet it without any authority to do more than exercise its general powers concerning the reasonableness of rates at all points. But this proposition is directly in conflict with the statute as we have construed it and with the plain purpose and intent manifested by its enactment. To uphold the

[1] FOURTH SECTION ORDER NO. 124

In the matter of the applications, Nos. 205, 342, 343, 344, 349, 350, and 352, on behalf of the Transcontinental Freight Bureau, by R. H. Countiss, agent, for relief from the provisions of the fourth section of the act to regulate commerce as amended June 18, 1910, with respect to rates made from eastern points of shipment which are higher to intermediate points than to Pacific coast terminals.

COMMODITY RATES.

These applications, as above numbered, on behalf of the Transcontinental Freight Bureau, ask for authority to continue rates from eastern points of shipment which are higher to intermediate points in Canada and in the States of Arizona, New Mexico, Idaho, California, Montana, Nevada, Oregon, Utah, and Washington, and other States east thereof, than to Pacific coast terminals.

Full investigation of the matters and things involved in these petitions, in so far as they concern westbound commodity rates, having been had,

It is ordered, That for purposes of the disposition of these applications, the United States shall be divided into five zones, as described in the following manner:

(The transcontinental groups hereinafter described are as specified in R. H. Countiss, agent's, transcontinental Tariff I. C. C. No. 929.)

Zone No. 1 comprises all that portion of the United States lying west of a line called Line No. 1, which extends in a general southerly direction from a point immediately east of Grand Portage, Minn.; thence southwesterly, along the northwestern shore of Lake Superior, to a point immediately east of Superior, Wis.; thence southerly, along the eastern boundary of Transcontinental Group F, to the intersection of the Arkansas and Oklahoma State line; thence along the west side of the Kansas City Southern Railway to the Gulf of Mexico.

Zone No. 2 embraces all territory in the United States lying east of Line No. 1 and west of a line called Line No. 2, which begins at the international boundary between the United States and Canada, immediately west of Cockburn Island, in Lake Huron; passes westerly through the Straits of Mackinaw; southerly, through Lake Michigan to its southern boundary; follows the west

proposition it would be necessary to say that the powers which were essential to the vivification and beneficial realization of the authority transferred had evaporated in the process of transfer and hence that the power perished as the result of the act by which it was conferred. As the prime object of the transfer was to vest the Commission within the scope of the discretion imposed and subject in the nature of things to the limitations arising from the character of the duty exacted and flowing from the other provisions of the act with authority to consider competitive conditions and their relation to persons and places, necessarily there went with the power the right to do that by which alone it could be exerted, and therefore a consideration of the one and the other and the establishment of the basis by

---

boundary of Transcontinental Group C to Paducah, Ky.; thence follows the east side of the Illinois Central Railroad to the southern boundary of Transcontinental Group C; thence follows the east boundary of Group C to the Gulf of Mexico.

Zone No. 3 embraces all territory in the United States lying east of Line No. 2 and north of the south boundary of Transcontinental Group C, and and on west of Line No. 3, which is the Buffalo-Pittsburg line from Buffalo, N. Y., to Wheeling, W. Va., marking the western boundary of Trunk Line Freight Association territory; thence follows the Ohio River to Huntington, W. Va.

Zone No. 4 embraces all territory in the United States east of Line No. 3 and north of the south boundary of Transcontinental Group C.

Zone No. 5 embraces all territory south and east of Transcontinental Group C.

It is further ordered, (1) That those portions of the above-numbered applications that request authority to maintain higher commodity rates from points in Zone No. 1 to intermediate points than to Pacific coast terminals be, and the same are hereby, denied, effective November 15, 1911; (2) that petitioners herein be, and they are hereby, authorized to establish and maintain, effective November 15, 1911, commodity rates from all points in zones numbered 2, 3, and 4, as above defined, to points intermediate to Pacific coast terminals that are higher to intermediate points than to Pacific coast terminals; provided, that the rates to intermediate points from points in zones numbered 2, 3, and 4 shall not exceed the rates on the same commodities from the same points of origin to the Pacific coast terminals by more than 7 per cent from points in Zone No. 2, 15 per cent from points in Zone No. 3, and 25 per cent from points in Zone No. 4.

The commission does not hereby approve any rates that may be established under this authority, all such rates being subject to complaint, investigation, and correction if they conflict with any other provisions of the act.

By the commission:

[SEAL] JUDSON C. CLEMENTS,
Chairman.

percentages was within the power granted. As will be seen by the order and as we have already said for the purpose of the percentages established zones of influence were adopted and the percentages fixed as to such zones varied or fluctuated upon the basis of the influence of the competition in the designated areas. As we have pointed out though somewhat modified the zones as thus selected by the Commission were in substance the same as those previously fixed by the carriers as the basis of the rate-making which was included in the tariffs which were under investigation and therefore we may put that subject out of view. Indeed, except as to questions of power there is no contention in the argument as to the inequality of the zones or percentages or as to any undue preference or discrimination resulting from the action taken. But be this as it may, in view of the findings of the Commission as to the system of rates prevailing in the tariffs which were before it, of the inequalities and burdens engendered by such system, of the possible aggrandizement unnaturally beyond the limits produced by competition in favor of the competitive points and against other points by the tariff in question, facts which we accept and which indeed are unchallenged, we see no ground for saying that the order was not sustained by the facts upon which it was based or that it exceeded the powers which the statute conferred or transcended the limits of the sound legal discretion which it lodged in the Commission when acting upon the subject before it.

It results that the Commerce Court in enjoining the order of the Commission was wrong and its decree to that end must therefore be reversed and the case be remanded to the proper District Court with directions to dismiss the bill for want of equity.

Reversed.

SKINNER & EDDY CORPORATION *v.* UNITED STATES ET AL.

249 U. S. 577 (1919)

Mr. Justice Brandeis delivered the opinion of the court.

The last paragraph of § 4 of the Act to Regulate Commerce, as amended by Act of June 18, 1910, c. 309, § 8, 36 Stat. 539, 547, declares that: "Whenever a carrier by railroad shall in competition with a water route or routes reduce the rates on the carriage of any species of freight to or from competitive points, it shall not be permitted to increase such rates unless after hearing by the Interstate Commerce Commission it shall be found that such proposed increase rests upon changed conditions other than the elimination of water competition."

On August 21, 1916, Skinner & Eddy Corporation brought this suit in the District Court of the United States for the District of Oregon to enjoin an increase in carload rates on iron and steel products from Pittsburgh to Seattle. The United States, the Commission and sixteen railroads were joined as defendants. The bill charged that the action of the carriers in increasing their rates and that of the Commission in authorizing such increase violated the above provision of the Commerce Act and, being beyond their respective powers, was void. The relief asked against the carriers was to prevent the collection of the proposed increased rates until the "Commission shall have held a hearing to determine whether the proposed increases rest upon changed conditions other than the elimination of water competition." The relief asked against the Commission was to prevent its taking any steps to enforce certain orders "so far as the same permit" such increases. An application for an interlocutory injunction heard before three judges on December 29, 1916, was denied; and later the bill and a supplemental bill, filed December 16, 1916, were dismissed on the ground that they do not state any cause of action. The case comes here by direct appeal. The essential facts are these:

After the decision by this court in *Intermountain Rate Cases*, 234 U. S. 476, and while the *Sacramento Case* (*United States* v. *Merchants & Manufacturers Traffic Association*, 242 U. S. 178) was pending in the District Court, carriers forming connecting lines between Pittsburgh and Seattle applied to the Commission in the same proceeding for further modification of Amended Fourth Section Order No. 124, so as to permit a reduction in carload rates on iron and steel products from Pittsburgh to Seattle without making such reduced rates applicable to intermediate points of destination. An order granting leave for a reduction from 80 cents [1] to 65 cents per 100 pounds was entered

[1] 80 cents was the specific published rate; but the combination of the Pittsburgh-Chicago rate of 18.9 cents and the Chicago-Seattle rate of 55 cents was 73.9 cents, and it was at this rate that the traffic from Pittsburgh actually moved.

March 1, 1916. *Rates on Iron and Steel Articles,* 38 I. C. C. 237. The carriers soon thereafter filed tariffs making that reduction effective April 10, 1916; and on that date, the 65-cent rate became operative.

During March, 1916, two applications had been made to the Commission in the same proceeding on behalf of shippers to reopen for further consideration other fourth section applications of carriers concerning westbound transcontinental rates and for modifications of orders issued thereon. The petitioners for such modification were the Spokane Merchants' Association and the Railroad Commission of Nevada, which had theretofore taken an active part in the proceedings (*Railroad Commission of Nevada* v. *Southern Pacific Co.,* 21 I. C. C. 329; *Commodity Rates to Pacific Coast Terminals,* 32 I. C. C. 611). Their prayer was for removal of the existing discrimination in transcontinental freight rates against the intermountain territory and in favor of the Pacific Coast ports. The ground alleged for seeking the modification was that by reason of slides in the Panama Canal and the increased demand for shipping due to the World War, water competition, which had theretofore been held to justify lower rates to the Pacific Coast ports, had in large part disappeared. Thereupon the Commission reopened on April 1, 1916, these applications, including that on which was entered the order of March 1, 1916, respecting iron and steel rates from Pittsburgh to Seattle; and a hearing was ordered "respecting the changed conditions which are alleged in justification of a modification of the Commission's orders."

None of the railroads had requested the reopening of the applications or the hearing; and when it was held, all opposed further modification of the transcontinental rates. No increased rates were proposed by them; and no specific increased rates were considered by the Commission. The petitioners introduced evidence respecting the changed conditions as a basis for modifying the several fourth section orders. On June 5, 1916, the Commission filed a report (*Reopening Fourth Section Applications,* 40 I. C. C. 35) in which it found that while the Panama Canal had been meanwhile reopened there was not then "any effective water competition between the two coasts" or likely to be any in the near future, and that "the war and an unparalleled rise in prices for ocean transportation have so changed the situation as to transform a relation of rates which was justified when established to one that is now unjustly discriminatory against intermediate points." It found also that these conditions were temporary. An order (amended July 13, 1916) was then entered, effective September 1, 1916, rescinding those previously entered on the several applications of carriers, including that of March 1, 1916, authorizing the 65-cent Pittsburgh-Seattle rate; and the carriers were directed to reduce the degree of discrimination then existing in favor of Pacific Coast ports as against intermediate territory.

Upon entry of this order the carriers filed tariffs effective September 1, 1916, raising, among others, the Pittsburgh-Seattle iron and steel rates from 65 cents to 94 cents. Promptly, on August 4, 1916, Skinner & Eddy Corporation protested, requested that the tariffs be suspended until a hearing could be had thereon, and alleged that the proposed increase violated, as later set forth in its bill of complaint, the last paragraph of the fourth section. Their request was not then granted. Thereafter, by action of the Commission and the carriers, not necessary to detail, the effective date of the tariff fixing the 94-cent rate was postponed to December 30, 1916; and meanwhile these tariffs were, with consent of the Commission, canceled upon the understanding that new tariffs fixing a 75-cent rate effective on that day would be filed. When the 75-cent rate was filed, Skinner & Eddy Corporation again protested on the same ground and made, as theretofore, the same request for a suspension of the tariffs and a hearing; and again the request was not granted.

First. The defendants contend that the District Court did not have jurisdiction of the subject-matter of this suit; because orders entered in a fourth section proceeding cannot be assailed in the courts; at least, not until after a remedy has been sought under §§ 13 and 15 of the Act to Regulate Commerce. This contention proceeds apparently upon a misapprehension of plaintiff's position. If plaintiff had sought relief against a rate or practice alleged to be unjust because unreasonably high or discriminatory, the remedy must have been sought primarily by proceedings before the Commission, *Loomis v. Lehigh Valley R. R. Co.*, 240 U. S. 43, 50; *Texas & Pacific Ry. Co.* v. *American Tie & Timber Co.*, 234 U. S. 138, 146; *The Minnesota Rate Cases*, 230 U. S. 352, 419; *Robinson* v. *Baltimore & Ohio R. R. Co.*, 222 U. S. 506; *Baltimore & Ohio R. R. Co.* v. *Pitcairn Coal Co.*, 215 U. S. 481; and the finding thereon would have been conclusive, unless there was lack of substantial evidence, some iregularity in the proceedings, or some error in the application of rules of law, *Manufacturers Ry. Co.* v. *United States,* 246 U. S. 457, 482; *Pennsylvania Co.* v. *United States,* 236 U. S. 351, 361; *Los Angeles Switching Case,* 234 U. S. 294, 311; *Kansas City Southern Ry. Co.* v. *United States,* 231 U. S. 423, 440; *Procter & Gamble Co.* v. *United States,* 225 U. S. 282, 297–298; *Interstate Commerce Commission* v. *Union Pacific R. R. Co.,* 222 U. S. 541. But plaintiff does not contend that 75 cents is an unreasonably high rate or that it is discriminatory or that there was mere error in the action of the Commission. The contention is that the Commission has exceeded its statutory powers; and that, hence, the order is void. In such a case the courts have jurisdiction of suits to enjoin the enforcement of an order, even if the plaintiff has not attempted to secure redress in a proceeding before the Commission. *Interstate Commerce Commission* v. *Diffenbaugh,* 222 U. S. 42, 49; *Louisiana & Pacific Ry. Co.* v. *United States,* 209 Fed. Rep. 244, 251; *Atlantic Coast Line R. R. Co.* v. *Interstate Commerce Commission,* 194 Fed. Rep. 449, 451. *The Sacramento Case, supra,* was a case of this character. Compare *Interstate Commerce Commission* v. *Louisville & Nashville R. R. Co.,* 227 U. S. 88, 92; *Southern Pacific Co.* v. *Interstate Commerce Commission,* 219 U. S. 433. The District Court properly assumed jurisdiction of this suit.

Second. The defendants contend, also, that if the subject-matter was within the jurisdiction of a District Court of the United States, it was not within that of Oregon. The objection is based upon the Act of October 22, 1913, c. 32, 38 Stat. 208, 219, which declares: "The venue of any suit hereafter brought to enforce, suspend, or set aside, in whole or in part, any order of the Interstate Commerce Commission shall be in the judicial district wherein is the residence of the party or any of the parties upon whose petition the order was made." And it is asserted that the parties upon whose petition the order was made, are the Merchants' Association of Spokane, a resident of the Eastern District of Washington, and the Railroad Commission of Nevada, a resident of the District of Nevada. The applications of these parties, filed in March, 1916, were doubtless instrumental in securing a reopening of the proceedings which resulted in the order complained of. But the proceedings in which the order was made were the original applications of carriers for relief under the fourth section. The report and the order are entitled, "In the Matter of Reopening Fourth Section Applications." One of the carriers which had made such application for relief from the provisions of the fourth section was a resident of Oregon, namely, the Oregon-Washington Railroad and Navigation Company; and as it was joined as defendant in the suit, the District Court for Oregon had jurisdiction over the parties.

Third. The main contention of plaintiff is that, as the carriers had in 1916 reduced the rate from 80 cents to 65 cents, neither the carriers nor the Commission had power to increase the rate without a prior finding by the Commission upon proper hearing "that such proposed increase rests upon changed conditions other than the elimination of water competition;" and that no such hearing had been had or finding made.

In construing this provision it is important to bear in mind the limits of the Commission's control over rates. Neither the Act to Regulate Commerce nor any amendment thereto has taken from the carriers the power which they originally possessed, to initiate rates; that is, the power, in the first instance, to fix rates or to increase or to reduce them.[1] Legislation of Congress confers now upon the Commission ample powers to prevent by direct action the exaction of excessively high rates. The original act, proceeding upon the common-law rule which prohibits public carriers from charging more than reasonable rates, gave the Commission power to declare illegal one unduly high; but even after such a determination the Commission lacked the power to fix the rate which should be charged. *Cincinnati, New Orleans & Texas Pacific Ry. Co.* v. *Interstate Commerce Commission*, 162 U. S. 184, 196–197; *Interstate Commerce Commission* v. *Cincinnati, New Orleans & Texas Pacific Ry. Co.*, 167 U. S. 479; *Interstate Commerce Commission* v. *Alabama Midland Ry. Co.*, 168 U. S. 144, 161. Effective control was not secured until the Act of 1906 had given to the Commission the power to fix, after such hearing, the rate which should be charged; *Interstate Commerce Commission* v. *Humboldt S. S. Co.*, 224 U. S. 474, 483; and the Act of 1910 had given it power to suspend, during investigation, tariffs for new rates, and placed upon the carrier the burden of proof to establish the reasonableness of the in-

[1] By Act of August 9, 1917, c. 50, § 4, 40 Stat. 270, 272, it was provided that until January 1, 1920, no increased rate or fare shall be filed except after approval thereof has been secured from the Commission. On the 28th day of December, 1917, the Government took control of the railroads, as a war measure, under Act of August 29, 1916, c. 418, 39 Stat. 619, 645. Proclamation of December 26, 1917, 40 Stat. 1733, 1734.

creased rates. *M. C. Kiser Co.* v. *Central of Georgia Ry. Co.,* 236 Fed. Rep. 573.

Congress, however, steadfastly withheld from the Commission power to prevent by direct action the charging of unreasonably low rates. The common law did not recognize that the rate of a common carrier might be so low as to constitute a wrong; and Congress has declined to declare such a rule. Despite the original Act to Regulate Commerce and all amendments, railroads still have power to fix rates as low as they choose and to reduce rates when they choose.[1] The Commission's power over them in this respect extends no further than to discourage the making of unduly low rates by applying deterrents. One such deterrent is found in the fact that low rates, because voluntarily established by the carrier, may be accepted by the Commission as evidence that other rates, actual or proposed, for comparable service are unreasonably high. *Board of Trade of Carrollton, Ga.,* v. *Central of Georgia Ry. Co.,* 28 I. C. C. 154, 164; *Sheridan Chamber of Commerce* v. *Chicago, Burlington & Quincy R. R. Co.,* 26 I. C. C. 638, 647. Compare *Louisville & Nashville R. R. Co.* v. *United States,* 238 U. S. 1, 11 *et seq.* The voluntary making of unremuneratively low rates in important traffic may also tend to induce the Commission to resist appeals of carriers for general rate increases on the ground of financial necessities. But the main source of the Commission's influence to prevent excessively low rates lies in its power to prevent unjust discrimination. Compare *Houston, East & West Texas Ry. Co.* v. *United States,* 234 U. S. 342. The order prohibiting the unjust discrimination, however, leaves the carrier free to continue the lower rate; the compulsion being that if the low rate is retained, the rate applicable to the locality or article discriminated against must be reduced. That is, the carrier may remove the discrimination either by raising the lower rate to the relative level of the higher, or by lowering the higher to the relative level of the lower, or by equalizing conditions through fixing rates at some intermediate point. *American Express Co.* v. *Caldwell,* 244 U. S. 617, 624.

A special group of cases in which the Commission may indirectly prevent unduly low rates through its power to prevent unjust discrimination is that provided for by the long and short haul clause. It was enacted to remedy one large class of dis-

[1] Subject only to the requirement of notice as provided in § 6 of the Act to Regulate Commerce, as amended.

criminations by creating a legislative presumption that the charge of more for a short haul under substantially similar circumstances and conditions than for a longer distance over the same line in the same direction was unjust. As originally enacted, the provision was construed to authorize the carrier to determine primarily whether the required dissimilarity of circumstances and conditions existed and also to authorize the acceptance of competitive conditions as a justification of a lower rate for the longer distance. So construed, the provisions proved inefficacious, and the act was amended in 1910 by striking out the "substantially similar circumstances and conditions" clause and making the prohibition absolute except to "the extent to which such designated common carrier may be relieved from the operation of this section" by the Commission. *Intermountain Rate Cases, supra.* But the lack of power to prevent by direct action excessively low rates remains; the carrier still having the option, if relief from the operation of the fourth section is denied, to keep in effect the low rate to the more distant point by lowering the rates to intermediate points.

The last paragraph of § 4, here in question, which was added by the Act of 1910, was designed to prevent the railroads from killing water competition by making exessively low rates. But again Congress refrained from prohibiting the carriers to reduce the rate and declined to confer upon the Commission power to prevent by direct action a reduction. The act still leaves the carrier absolutely free to make as low a rate as it chooses; and merely provides another deterrent, in declaring that, if the rate is once reduced in competition with a water route or routes, it cannot, thereafter, be increased, "unless after hearing by the Interstate Commerce Commission it shall be found that such proposed increase rests upon changed conditions other than the elimination of water competition." This provision may become operative in any case where there has been competition between a railroad and a water line, inland or coastwise. But we have now to determine merely whether the prohibition applies where the rates in question were reduced with the approval of the Commission given after hearing, by order entered upon application of the carrier for relief from the operation of the fourth section.

The language of the paragraph is general and read alone might compel that construction. But it may not be read alone. It must be construed in the light of the purpose of its enactment, of the earlier paragraphs of § 4, and of other sections in the

Act to Regulate Commerce designed to prevent unjust discrimination. The specific purpose of § 4 was to prevent discrimination by charging less for the longer haul, unless in the opinion of the Commission the circumstances make such action just. Discrimination, just when sanctioned, may become most unjust. Recognizing this fact, Congress provided that the judgment of the Commission should be exercised "from time to time" to determine "the extent to which [the] . . . carrier may be relieved from the operation of this section." In other words, the leave granted is not for all time. It is revocable at any time, either because it was improvidently granted or because new conditions have arisen which make its continuance inequitable. The specific purpose of the last paragraph of § 4 is to ensure and preserve water competition; to prevent competition that kills. A reduction made under the authority of a fourth section order after full hearing must have been found by the Commission to have been reasonably necessary in order to preserve competition between the rail and water carrier. A reduction so made is not within the reason of the prohibition declared by the last paragraph. Transportation conditions are not static; the oppressor of today may tomorrow be the oppressed. And in order to preserve competition between rail and water carriers it is necessary that the Commission's power to approve a modification of rates be as broad as it is to approve a modification in order to prevent unjust discrimination. Even a literal reading of § 4 would not require that the prohibition contained in the last paragraph be extended to reductions made with the approval of the Commission. The preceding paragraph declares that "the Commission may from time to time prescribe the extent to which such designated common carrier may be relieved from the operation of this section." The last paragraph is a part of the section. Why should not the Commission's power to relieve be extended to it?

The construction contended for by plaintiff would rather ensure monopoly than preserve competition. If a rail rate reduced in competition with a water route for the avowed purpose of preserving competition by rail should result, contrary to the Commission's expectations, in eliminating the water competition, because so low as to drive the water carrier out of business, then the prohibitively low rate would have to be continued permanently and other water competition be thereby prevented from arising; unless, perchance, some changed condition should develop which might make removal of the bar possible. Or, if the reduction in the rail rate, sanctioned by the Commission under the fourth section as not unjustly discriminating against intermediate points, because forced upon the rail carriers by oppressive water competition designed to destroy its business to the port, should become thereafter unjustly discriminatory, because the water carrier, destroyed by its own rate cutting, abandoned the route, still the low rail rate and resulting discrimination would have to continue. Only compelling language could cause us to impute to Congress the intention to produce results so absurd; and the language of the last paragraph of § 4 is clearly susceptible of the more reasonable construction contended for by defendants.

Fourth. The defendants further contend that, even if the prohibition of the last paragraph of § 4 be construed to apply also where the reduction was made with the authority of the Commission, the increase of the Pittsburgh-Seattle rate to 75 cents is valid, because the finding of the Commission complies with the prescribed condition that the increased rate must rest "upon changed conditions other than the elimination of water competition." It found in terms that: "the conditions formerly existing have materially changed"; that "the withdrawal of boats from this [coast to coast] service has not been on account of the rates made by the rail carriers with which the boats compete, but on account of slides in the Panama Canal and the extraordinary rise in ocean freights"; that the substantial disappearance of water competition was merely temporary; that competing water carriers "announced their intention ultimately to return to this service" and "that the time of such return depended in part upon the measure of the rates they would be able to secure for this service in competition with the rail lines." It is clear that the changed conditions so found are something other than the "elimination of water competition" which Congress intended should not justify raising the reduced rates. Compare *American Insulated Wire & Cable Co.* v. *Chicago & North Western Ry. Co.*, 26 I. C. C. 415, 416.

Fifth. The plaintiff attacks, however, the validity of the order of June 5, 1916 (amended July 13, 1916) also on the ground that it was not made upon application of the carrier — insisting that application by the carrier is not only a prerequisite to the original granting of relief under the fourth section, but also to the modification from time to time by the Commission of the relief afforded. This court expressed in the *Sacramento Case, supra,* at p. 187, its doubt whether such application was a prerequisite even to the original granting of relief. It is clear that application by the carrier is not a prerequisite to modification. As shown above, orders granting relief under the fourth section are not grants in perpetuity. Neither a carrier nor a favored community acquires thereby vested rights. Necessarily implied in each such order is the term, "until otherwise ordered by the Commission"; and the original application is always subject to be reopened, as it was here.

The District Court did not err in dismissing the bill (and supplemental bill) on the merits; and its decree is

Affirmed.

NATIONAL INDUSTRIAL TRAFFIC LEAGUE
v.
ABERDEEN & ROCKFISH R. R. CO.

61 I. C. C. 120 (1921)

MEYER, *Commissioner:*

Complainant is a voluntary organization composed of trade and traffic associations and individual shippers. By this complaint it alleges that defendants, which comprise practically all railroads subject to the interstate commerce act, have severally made numerous leases for the use of railroad property and consracts for the construction, maintenance, and use of industrial side tracks containing clauses limiting their liability for loss and damage caused by fire from locomotives while operating over such tracks. These liability clauses are attacked as unjust, unreasonable, unduly prejudicial, and otherwise unlawful in violation of sections 1, 3, and 20 of the interstate commerce act. We are asked, in the complaint, to require the defendants to insert in all their leases of railroad property and in their sidetrack agreements, uniform, reasonable, nondiscriminatory, nonpreferential, and otherwise lawful liability clauses.

Soon after the complaint was filed complainants and defendants entered into negotiations with a view to an amicable tolution of the matters in issue. As a result of these negotiations there was submitted to us jointly by counsel for complainant and for defendants the proposal that we approve the following liability clauses; that we recommend their general adoption and use in contracts for the construction, operation, and maintenance of industrial sidetracks; and that the complaint be dismissed:

"It is understood that the movement of railroad locomotives involves some risk of fire and the industry assumes all responsibility for and agrees to indemnify the railroad company against loss or damage to property of the industry or to property upon its premises, regardless of railroad negligence, arising from fire caused by locomotives operated by the railroad on said track, or in its vicinity for the purpose of serving said industry, except to the premises of the railroad and to rolling stock belonging to the railroad or to others, and to shipments in the course of transportation.

The industry also agrees to indemnify and hold harmless the railroad company for loss, damage, or injury from any act or omission of the industry, its employees or agents, to the person or property of the parties hereto and their employees, and to the person or property of any other person or corporation, while on or about said track; and if any claim or liability other than from fire shall arise from the joint or concurring negligence of both parties hereto it shall be borne by them equally."

The interveners filed a petition opposing the action urged by complainant and defendants.

After consideration of the matters presented we advised the parties that if the essence of the complaint is contained in the proposed liability clauses we inclined to the view that we were without jurisdiction to pass upon a contract of this character, and requested them to file briefs upon the question of our jurisdiction. Briefs have since been filed by the parties and by the National Association of Railway and Utilities Commissioners as *amicus curiæ.* No hearing has been had, and the case stands submitted on brief upon the jurisdictional question.

The allegation of unreasonableness is predicated on that part of section 1, paragraph (9), of the interstate commerce act, which provides:

"Any common carrier subject to the provisions of this Act, upon application of any . . . shipper tendering interstate traffic for transportation, shall construct, maintain, and operate upon reasonable terms a switch connection with any such . . . private side track which may be contructed to connect with its railroad, where such connection is reasonably practicable and can be put in with safety and will furnish sufficient business to justify the construction and maintenance of the same . . . . If any common carrier shall fail to install and operate any such switch or connection . . . , such shipper . . . may make complaint to the Commission, . . . and the Commission shall . . . determine as to the safety and practicability thereof and justification and reasonable compensation therefor, . . ."

This language clearly refers to the construction, maintenance, and operation of switch connections. We have held that under its provisions we have no authority to require a railroad to construct a private sidetrack, and that our authority is limited to requiring a carrier to make a switch connection with a private sidetrack. *Winters Metallic Paint* v. *C. M. & St. P. Ry. Co.*, 16 I. C. C., 587. Complainant refers to our report in *Imperial Wheel Co.* v. *St. L., I. M. & S. Ry. Co.*, 20 I. C. C., 56, and alleges that we there took jurisdiction of a similar question. We there said:

" We are therefore left to consider the single question whether a carrier, as a condition precedent to its undertaking to make a switch connection and to operate a spur track leading to an industry, may require the industry to indemnify it from liability and claim for loss and damage by fire caused by the sparks or burning coals from its locomotives on the spur track."

We found that the conditions respecting its liability for fire on the premises of the complainant, which defendant insisted upon, did not seem unreasonable, and dismissed the complaint. However, in that case the question of jurisdiction was not specifically raised. And subsequently in *Ralston Townsite Co.* v. *M. P. Ry. Co.*, 22 I. C. C., 354, we declined to take jurisdiction to enforce the performance of a sidetrack agreement. It was there pointed out that complainant failed to distinguish between the physical characteristics of a switch connection, which we can require in a proper case under authority conferred by section 1, and a private sidetrack, which we can not require a carrier to construct.

It is therefore apparent that we had no jurisdiction under section 1 of the act to regulate commerce to require the construction, maintenance, and operation of private sidetracks. Nor does it appear that the act as amended by the transportation act, 1920, enlarges our powers in that respect. While paragraphs

(18) to (21), inclusive, of section 1 of the interstate commerce act contain provisions for the extension or abandonment of the lines of common carriers by railroad upon authority from us and empower us under the conditions therein set forth to require any common carrier by railroad subject to the act, after hearing, in a proceeding upon complaint or upon our own initiative without complaint, "to provide itself with safe and adequate facilities for performing as a common carrier car service as that term is used in this act, and to extend its line or lines," paragraph (22) thereof specifically provides that:

"The authority of the Commission conferred by paragraphs (18) to (21), both inclusive, shall not extend to the construction or abandonment of spur, industrial, team, switching, or side tracks, located or to be located wholly within one state, or of street, suburban, or interurban electric railways, which are not operated as a part or parts of a general steam railroad system of transportation."

From this it is clear that industrial sidetracks, located or to be located wholly within one state, are excluded from the provisions of paragraphs (18) to (21), inclusive, of section 1 of the act.

The demands upon a carrier which lawfully may be made are limited by its duty. *Gt. Northern Ry.* v. *Minnesota,* 238 U. S., 340, 346. But it is not its duty as a common carrier to enter into a contract to lease a railroad siding to a shipper or to enter into an agreement to operate privately owned sidetracks. The liability clauses complained of do not involve the question of rates, nor the matter of facilities to be furnished by the railroad company for the transportation of property under its obligation as a common carrier, and section 1 does not confer upon us the power to pass upon liability clauses of leases or of agreements for the maintenance, use, and operation of such industrial sidetracks.

This brings us to a consideration of the allegation that the failure or refusal of defendants to establish and maintain uniform liability clauses in their leases and agreements for the construction, maintenance, and operation of industrial sidetracks results in undue and unreasonable prejudice and disadvantage. In *Guilford Lumber Mfg. Co.* v. *S. Ry. Co.,* 53 I. C. C., 669, 670, we said:

"The complaints allege violations of section 3, but fail to designate the individuals, organizations, communities, or traffic accorded undue or unreasonable preference or advantage, to the undue prejudice of complainants. Defendants were not put upon notice of the particular violations of law they were called upon to defend. Under these circumstances, and as we construe the record before us, no issue of undue prejudice under section 3 has been properly raised. . . ."

The allegation of undue prejudice is general in character and as no hearing has been had this issue can not be determined at this time. Whether undue or unreasonable preference or advantage exists in a particular case is a question of fact. It does not follow as a matter of law that the present practices of defendants are unduly prejudicial because they are not uniformly the same in all parts of the country and as to all shippers. Differences in conditions may justify variations in rules and practices. Uniformity is highly desirable with respect to many practices of common carriers. But where uniformity injuriously affects practices that are essentially local it is not desirable. In any event it can not be said that the failure of defendants to establish uniform liability clauses with respect to leases of industrial sidetracks is of itself unduly prejudicial. If notwithstanding the decision here made of the jurisdictional question complainant desires to press the issue of undue prejudice, the matter may again be brought to our attention for consideration.

It is also alleged by complainant that the liability clauses in existing leases for industrial sidetracks are in violation of section 20 of the act in that they unlawfully limit defendants' liability for loss, damage, or injury to property. Paragraph (11) of section 20 provides:

"That any common carrier, railroad or transportation company subject to the provisions of this act receiving property for transportation from a point in one State or Territory or the District of Columbia to a point in another State, Territory, District of Columbia, or from any point in the United States to a point in an adjacent foreign country shall issue a receipt or bill of lading therefor, and shall be liable to the lawful holder thereof for any loss, damage, or injury to such property caused by it or by any common carrier, railroad, or transportation company to which such property may be delivered or over whose line or lines such property may pass within the United States or within an adjacent foreign country when transported on a through bill of lading, and no contract, receipt, rule, regulation, or other limitation of any character whatsoever, shall exempt such common carrier, railroad, or transportation company from the liability hereby imposed. . . ."

The property referred to in this provision obviously refers to property offered for transportation, and does not relate to buildings or other property. The Supreme Court of the United States in *Chicago, R. I. & Pac. Ry.* v. *Maucher,* 248 U. S., 359, said: "But the Carmack Amendment deals only with the shipment of property." If the parties desire to make use of the liability clauses upon which they have agreed we think that in the second clause there should be inserted words similar to those in the first excepting shipments in the course of transportation. Complainant refers to our decision in *Bills of Lading,* 52 I. C. C., 671, and calls attention to what we said on the question of jurisdiction. It contends that "the terms of the statute and the interpretation thereof by the Commission are on all fours with the situation presented in this case." We there referred to the fact that the act specifically made it the duty of all carriers subject thereto to establish just and reasonable regulations and practices affecting the issuance, form, and substance of bills of lading, and said:

"Thus the Commission has power and authority under the act to determine the reasonableness of rules, regulations, and practices of the carriers, and to require them to cease and desist from the enforcement of rules and regulations, and the continuance of practices found to be unreasonable or unjustly discriminatory, or unduly prejudicial. And herein lies the Commission's power to lay hands upon the issuance, form, and substance' of bills of lading. The act specially requires carriers subject thereto to issue bills of lading. The Commission has undoubted authority to enforce this requirement in a proper proceeding."

The decision in that case has reference only to rules, regulations, and practices governing the transportation of property. It has nothing to do with liability clauses contained in leases or agreements involving property not offered for transportation. That report also points out that the act specifically requires carriers subject thereto to issue bills of lading. But it does not follow that we have like authority to prescribe the form and substance of liability clauses in leases and agreements affecting industrial sidetracks. We have repeatedly held that claims against common carriers for loss, damage, or delay to property are governed by general legal principles, and are determined by the courts.

An order will be entered dismissing the complaint.

RUTHERFORD-BREDE COMPANY
v.
DIRECTOR GENERAL, AS AGENT

61 I. C. C. 515 (1921)

DIVISION 3, COMMISSIONERS HALL, EASTMAN, AND FORD.

BY DIVISION 3:

At the argument complainants stated their exceptions to the report proposed by the examiner.

Complainants are A. C. W. Rutherford and Carl J. Brede, copartners trading as Rutherford-Brede Company, and wholesale dealers in potatoes at Minneapolis, Minn. By complaint filed January 19, 1920, they allege that the failure and refusal of defendants to equip cars with false floors to protect the lading from freezing in connection with the transportation of nine carloads of potatoes, shipped under " carriers' protective service," from Quamba, Minn., to various interstate destinations, between January 18 and March 8, 1918, inclusive, was in violation of section 1 of the act to regulate commerce and section 10 of the federal control act. They demanded a just and reasonable allowance under section 15 of the act to regulate commerce in order to reimburse them for the cost of supplying false floors.

The rules and regulations of the Director General of Railroads, hereinafter termed defendant, for protective service provide that during the period from October 15 to April 15 a shipper of specified perishable commodities, including potatoes, must declare at the time of ordering a car whether he desires the car moved under " option No. 1," termed " shippers' protective service," or under " option No. 2," termed " carriers' protective service." Under option No. 1, the carrier furnishes the equipment, and if the shipper desires to install false floors or stoves and send a caretaker in charge he is at liberty to do so. At the time the shipments moved the tariffs provided for outbound and return transportation of the fittings and caretaker under certain conditions without extra charge. Under option No. 2 the shipper pays an extra charge, varying from 5 to 7 cents per 100 pounds, for the protective service, the carrier assumes liability for damage to the commodity by freezing or overheating, and it is customary for the carriers to furnish in extremely cold weather cars with false floors and such other facilities and services as are necessary to prevent potatoes from freezing.

The tariff does not specify any particular type of equipment which the carrier must furnish under option No. 2, and does not authorize payment to a shipper of the expense of installing temporary false floors.

Complainants' buyer, at the beginning of the year 1918, ordered the nine cars from defendant's agent at Mora, Minn., to be placed at Quamba, a point on the line of the Great Northern, for the shipment of potatoes to move under option No. 2. Refrigerator cars were placed for loading, of which four were Great Northern cars equipped with permanent false floors; the others were not so equipped. Complainants' witness testified that he was advised by complainants' employee that defendant's local agent refused to accept the potatoes for shipment under option No. 2 unless the shippers installed temporary false floors in all cars; that as a consequence complaints supplied such floors at their own expense for the nine cars; and that defendant's agent told this employee that defendant would reimburse complainants for this expenditure. Defendant admits that the costs claimed by complainants, averaging $7.40 per car, are reasonable and represent the actual cost. Complainants paid a charge of 6 cents per 100 pounds for the special protection under option No. 2 in addition to the transportation charges.

Defendant's witness testified that a letter from this local agent stated: " shipper did not receive any permission from us to furnish linings," although he admitted that at certain stations in Minnesota in the vicinity of Quamba there had been "some specific arrangements " made between shippers and defendant's agent relative to furnishing temporary false floors.

Complainants' witness further testified, and defendant, conceded, that the permanent false floors in the Great Northern's refrigerator cars did not afford sufficient protection for potatoes during severely cold weather, which was true also of the refrigerator cars without permanent false floors, and that it was the custom of defendant to install temporary false floors in all such cars under option No. 2 during the time of year at which the nine cars moved. The initial line required its connecting lines to return these and similar false floors to it, or to pay to it $12 per car. During the winter of 1917–1918 other shippers of potatoes in Minnesota experienced difficulty in getting adequately equipped cars at points on the Great Northern and defendant was not able to furnish cars with proper false floors at such points.

Defendant contends that there is no competent evidence in the record of refusal to accept the shipments without the special floors; and that defendant, having taken the risk, had the right to furnish whatever equipment he considered necessary.

In view of the defendant's admissions that the cars were not and could not be properly equipped by him, and that damage was likely to result at that time unless temporary false floors were installed, complainants contend that they should not have been compelled to ship without such floors, knowing that the potatoes would be frozen in transit; and that such action on their part might have subjected them to criminal liability for deliberately destroying foodstuffs. They further contend that, having paid the charge of 6 cents per 100 pounds for the protective service, in addition to the usual transportation charges, a service which defendant failed fully to perform, they are entitled to a refund based upon the cost to them of furnishing the temporary false floors.

Section 15 of the act to regulate commerce contained the provision now found in paragraph (13) of section 15 of the interstate commerce act as follows:

"the Commision may, . . . determine what is a reasonable charge as the maximum to be paid by the carrier or carriers for the services so rendered or for the use of the instrumentality so furnished, and fix the same by appropriate order, . . ."

The United States Supreme Court, in *Interstate Com. Comm.* v. *Diffenbaugh,* 222 U. S., 42, 46, said that our power thereunder is to fix the maximum to be paid as an allowance. In exercise of this power we may not require a carrier to make an allowance or fix the precise amount, and it is doubtful whether we can award damages for failure to pay except in cases where the allowance is published in the carrier's tariffs and is not more than reasonable for the service. We think that the amount here claimed is reasonable, but any redress to which complainants may be entitled would seem to rest with the courts.

Upon this record we are of opinion and find that defendant's failure to equip these refrigerator cars with temporary false floors, or to reimburse complainants for supplying them, was not in violation of the act to regulate commerce or of the federal control act. The complaint will be dismissed.

CARNATION MILK PRODUCTS COMPANY *v.* ATCHISON, TOPEKA & SANTA FE COMPANY

63 I. C. C. 60, (1921)

DIVISION 2, COMMISSIONERS CLARK, DANIELS, AND ESCH.

ESCH, *Commissioner:*

The issues here presented were made the subject of a proposed report by the examiner; exceptions were filed by defendants, and oral argument has been had.

Complainant is a corporation engaged in the manufacture of condensed milk at various points in Washington, Oregon, Idaho, and other states. It alleges that the charges for heated-car service on shipments of condensed milk from the Pacific northwest to eastern points are unreasonable, unjustly discriminatory, and unduly prejudicial. It also alleges that the rules governing such service are unreasonable in not permitting a change in transit from shippers' to carriers' protection and from carriers' to shippers' protection. We are asked to prescribe reasonable rules and charges. The Puyallup & Sumner Fruit Growers Canning Company, of Puyallup and Sumner, Wash., intervened in support of the complaint.

The development of the heater service in the northwest was detailed at length in *Perishable Freight Investigation,* 56 I. C. C., 449, and need not be repeated. The service as it is now offered consists, briefly, in placing a portable heater in an insulated car, or in the bunker of a refrigerator car, and the maintenance of a sufficient degree of heat to prevent damage to the lading from cold. The shipper may perform the service himself, equipping the car at his own expense and assuming all responsibility for loss, or may elect to have it performed by the carriers, in which even certain charges, in addition to the transportation charges, are assessed, depending upon the points or territories of origin and destination. The protective service is offered on such commodities as fruits, vegetables, beverages, and certain groceries.

During the winter months condensed milk is shipped in refrigerator cars. In such cars it is not affected by ordinary cold weather unless delayed in transit. If delays occur and the cars remain stationary, freezing will result if the weather is extremely cold. Because of this immunity from damage by cold under ordinary conditions heater charges were not published on condensed milk at the time they were established on other perishable commodities. At the request of the shippers that commodity was later included in the list of articles which should be protected against cold, and is now specifically named in perishable tariff No. 1, agent Fairbank's I. C. C. No. 6, which became effective February 28, 1920.

Prior to the effective date of the tariff mentioned, heater charges between points in the northwest and points in the territory west of the Indiana-Illinois state line were stated in amounts per car and did not vary with the commodity or the weight carried. In other portions of the country, particularly in western trunk line territory and in New England, they were carried in amounts per 100 pounds with varying minima, depending upon the carload minima of the commodities, but not less than 30,000 pounds per car. Charges published in amounts per car were considered in *Perishable Freight Investigation, supra,* a proceeding instituted at the request of the Director General for advice concerning his proposed perishable protective freight tariff No. 1, which contained in one volume all the rules, regulations, and charges applicable to the protection of perishable freight from heat or cold on federally controlled lines. It was proposed in that tariff to publish all heater charges in amounts per car, without regard to weight, in order to harmonize all territories and encourage heavier loading, and because there is no substantial difference in the expense.

The charges proposed in perishable protective freight tariff No. 1 for heater service on traffic originating in the northwest were materially higher than those then in effect in transcontinental freight bureau tariff, agent Countiss' I. C. C. No. 1043. For example, the stated charge from points in Washington, Oregon, and northern Idaho to Chicago, in the latter tariff, was $27 per car, compared with proposed charges of $40 per car from Washington and Oregon and $37.50 from northern Idaho. Data relating to the cost of the service were submitted to show that the increased charges were reasonable, but proved to be of little or no value in determining their propriety. Accordingly, we were unable to find the proposed charges reasonable, and suggested that the charges then in effect be maintained until, through revised accounting methods and special studies made of the subject, the carriers were able to present more satisfactory evidence of cost.

Contrary to this recommendation, and contrary also to the views previously expressed by the carriers that the charges should be made without regard to weight, perishable protective tariff No. 1, made effective February 28, 1920, published heater charges in cents per 100 pounds, subject to minimum weights applicable to the different commodities but not less than 30,000 pounds. These charges range from 5 cents per 100 pounds to points in western Montana to 9 cents per 100 pounds to points in Wisconsin and Illinois. The charges per car on condensed milk would therefore range from $30 to $54, based on the minimum weight of 60,000 pounds. The average loading of condensed milk exceeds 60,000 pounds. The stated charges per car in effect at the time of the hearing in *Perishable Freight Investigation, supra,* ranged from $15 to $27 from Washington and Oregon, while those then proposed were $20 to western Montana and $40 to Wisconsin and Illinois. Under the present tariff the charges on shipments of fresh vegetables or fresh fruits would generally not exceed the minimum charges for heater service and would thus be the same as the former charges. This results from the fact that those commodities ordinarily load less than 30,000 pounds to the car. Vegetables and fruits are more susceptible to damage from cold than condensed milk, but are protected in transit for half the charge on the latter. In February, 1919, complainant forwarded 23 carloads of condensed milk from Chehalis, Wash., to Chicago, averaging 69,843 pounds in weight. These cars were forwarded under carriers' protection at a charge of $27 each, although at that time there was no heater charge applicable on condensed milk. Complainant requested the service and is satisfied with the charge assessed, but contends that the charge under the present tariff, which would average $62.85 per car, is unreasonable.

Little evidence was offered by defendants regarding the reasonableness of the present charges, particularly as applying on such heavy loading commodities as condensed milk. Attention was directed to the fact that the report in *Perishable Freight Investigation, supra,* decided February 4, 1920, was issued near the close of the heater season, which runs from October 15 to the following April 15, and therefore but little opportunity was afforded during the balance of the season to prepare reliable cost data. Beginning with the following season a record was kept of the details of the items entering into the cost of the service, but the results thereof were not available at the time of the hearing in November, 1920. In publishing the unified tariff, defendants chose to adopt the basis of charges applying between points in western trunk line territory rather than adhere to the per-car basis in effect from the Pacific northwest. The evidence relied upon by the carriers is the same as that introduced in the former proceeding. The present charges applied to shipments of condensed milk are higher than those then proposed.

At the argument defendants referred to the charges for heater service in New England found reasonable in *Transportation of Potatoes,* 25, I. C. C., 159, but those charges are not comparable because they were for the use of the Eastman heater car, a specially constructed car devoted to that service and always returned empty. They also referred to the charges in western trunk line territory which were found not unreasonable in *Northern Potato Traffic Asso.* v. *C. & A. R. R. Co.,* 44 I. C. C., 426, but those charges applied only on potatoes in connection with a minimum of 36,000 pounds. Defendants expressed a willingness to reduce the minimum on condensed milk to 50,000 pounds, but complainant loads its shipments above the present minimum and a reduction in the minimum would not affect the heater charges on such shipments. The carriers requested that if we are not willing to approve the present heater charges upon this record that they be given an opportunity to introduce the results of their cost study before the case is decided. Whatever the cost study might show, it could hardly justify heater charges on shipments of condensed milk which are 100 per cent greater than on shipments of fresh fruits and vegetables. In *Perishable Freight Investigation, supra,* we said, at page 540:

"We have the impression that the inherent qualities of the commodities should also be taken into consideration in determining the charges for protective service against cold. The element of hazard apparently varies materially with the commodity."

The record does not show the relative values of shipments of condensed milk and fresh fruits and vegetables, but assuming that the former have a higher value because of their greater weight, we are of the opinion that the difference in hazard is such that the heater charges on shipments of condensed milk should at least not exceed the charges per car on fruits and vegetables.

In support of its contention that the rules in perishable protective tariff No. 1 are unreasonable in not permitting change in transit from shippers' to carriers' protection and vice versa, complainant points out that the rules authorize change in transit from protection by refrigeration to protection by artificial heat, and from shippers' or carriers' protection against cold to refrigeration. The rule permitting such changes was established for the first time in the above tariff to cover shipments moving from a warm climate into a cold climate and vice versa. Complainant desires the privilege sought in order that it may avoid the charge for carriers' protection as much as possible and still be able to secure protection when required by a change in the weather during transit, especially where the shipment is unduly delayed. There are many difficulties that would surround the practical application of the rule sought, such as the shippers' inability to obtain information of a sudden drop in the temperature in time to instruct the carrier to afford protection before damage occurs, and the impossibility of determining whether damage occurred before or after the change, besides the additional expense of maintaining employees and equipment to make such changes whenever and wherever required.

A change from protection against heat to protection against cold and vice versa is sometimes essential, as in the case of shipments of fruits and vegetables from California to Canada. In the case of complainant's shipments, however, there is no such necessity for a change in transit and complainant has the option of calling for carrier's protection or affording its own protection for the entire movement covered by the heater service. The above rules in so far as they permit the change in one case and deny it in the other were approved in *Perishable Freight Investigation, supra.*

We find that the present charges for heated-car service on shipments of condensed milk from points in the Pacific northwest to points in the destination territories specified in perishable protective tariff No. 1 are unreasonable to the extent that they exceed those formerly in effect from and to the same points as carried in agent Countiss' tariff I. C. C. No. 1043 and supplements thereto. This finding is without prejudice to defendants' right to present in an appropriate manner new and reliable figures covering the cost of the service, and readjustment of their charges based thereon and in accordance with the views expressed herein will be given consideration. We further find that the rules governing such heated-car service are not unreasonable in failing to permit change in transit from shippers' protection to carriers' protection and from carriers' protection to shippers' protection.

An appropriate order will be entered.

CLASSIFICATION RATINGS AND CARLOAD MINIMUM WEIGHT ON GARDEN TRACTORS

64 I. C. C. 1 (1921)

DIVISION 3, COMMISSIONERS HALL, EASTMAN, AND CAMPBELL.

BY DIVISION 3:

At present the consolidated freight classification contains no specific ratings on garden tractors. They are generally shipped under the item " Machinery and Machines, Engines, Steam or Internal Combustion, Traction or Tractors, steam or internal combustion." By schedules filed to become effective May 25, 1921, respondents proposed to provide specific ratings for garden tractors. In so doing the less-than-carload ratings now applied on this article when shipped knocked down, in boxes or crates, would be changed from third to second class in southern, and from first to second class in western territory. No change is proposed in the less-than-carload rating of first class in official territory. The carload ratings, fifth in official, sixth in southern, and class A in western territory, would remain unchanged, but the minimum weight, when the article is shipped knocked down, in boxes or crates, would be increased from 20,000 pounds to 24,000 pounds for a standard 36-foot box car, subject to rule 34, which provides for graded minima for longer cars. Upon protest filed by the Associated Industries of Massachusetts in behalf of H. C. Dodge, Incorporated, of Boston, Mass., hereinafter referred to as protestant, the operation of the schedules was suspended until October 22, 1921.

It developed at the hearing that the proposed less than-carload ratings are satisfactory to protestant, and that the protest against the proposed increased minimum weights is based upon physical inability to load the garden tractor made by protestant to the required minima.

This tractor has one large front and two small rear balance wheels, and is driven by a gasoline engine. By the use of certain attachments, which are separate from the tractor itself, it can be converted into a cultivator, seeder, plow, sweeper, or lawn mower. The weight is approximately 135 pounds net, and from 185 to 190 pounds crated for shipment. In crating the small rear wheels are removed and the machine then rests on the frame, thus saving a loading space of about 40 per cent. When crated it measures about 70 inches in length, 24.5 inches in width, and 20 inches in height; and the weight per cubic foot is about 10 pounds. The record shows that 112 crates, weighing in the aggregate about 20,720 pounds, is the maximum loading for a box car 36 feet long by 8 feet 2 inches high. If the car is 8 feet 6 inches high, it will carry two crates more. Protestant insists that it is impracticable to ship its product in a smaller crate than at present, or any more disassembled, for the reason that if the handles, a part of the frame, are taken down, the direct connections between them and the engine, the gas tank and the gas feed pipe, the ignition control and the spark control also have to be taken down, and the average buyer would not know how to reassemble. Owing to the size of the package the weight which can be loaded does not increase as the size of the car increases. Protestant's tractor, first marketed in October, 1920, is sold chiefly to farmers in official and western territories, the price being $150. Carload shipments, which are now estimated at three per week, did not commence until March, 1921. At present more of these tractors are sold in carloads than in less-than-carloads.

The record affirmatively shows that all other garden tractors on the market load up to or in excess of 24,000 pounds. Respondents maintain that the propriety of a carload minimum weight must be considered in the light of loading possibilities of an entire line of the article to be covered rather than of either the lightest or heaviest type in the group and refer to *Thurber, et als.* v. *N. Y. C. & H. R. R. Co., and others,* 3 I. C. C., 473, 502. We there said —

"as classifications and rates must be general an injurious effect in some cases and to some interests is unavoidable, but so long as in the main they are satisfactory the rule applies that the good of the greater number is paramount."

The present classification item, which embraces garden tractors, also includes field, road, and, in fact, any kind of steam or internal-combustion tractor, irrespective of weight, and accords to them in each territory the same carload rating, minimum 20,000 pounds, whether shipped knocked down, or set up, loose, or in packages. The garden type ranges in weight from 135 to 1,100 pounds. Some field and road tractors weigh less than the heavy garden tractors, others exceed 8,000 pounds. Protestant contends that a line of demarcation based on rating can not be drawn at times between the heavy garden tractors and the light field or road tractors. But most, if not all, field and road tractors are shipped set up and can only be floor loaded.

We find that the schedules under suspension have been justified, and an order vacating the order of suspension will be entered.

LIMITATIONS OF LIABILITY IN CONNECTION WITH TRANSMISSION OF TELEGRAPH MESSAGES

61 I. C. C. 541 (1921)

Report of the Commission.

McChord, *Commissioner:*

The questions here presented for determination were made the subject of a proposed report by the examiner. Exceptions thereto have been filed by the respondent Western Union Telegraph and Postal Telegraph-Cable companies and by certain of the interveners, and the issues have been briefed and orally argued.

Pursuant to an order entered June 4, 1920, a general investigation has been made of the practices of telegraph companies subject to the interstate commerce act in adjusting claims for damages arising from errors or delays in the transmission or delivery, or from nondelivery, of interstate messages, and the reasonableness of their rules limiting liability on the several classes of messages, dependent upon the rates paid. All common carriers subject to the interstate commerce act engaged in the transmission of telegraph messages have been made respondents. Hearing was held on July 26, 1920, at which time appearances were filed on behalf of the Western Union Telegraph Company, the Postal Telegraph-Cable Company, the North American Telegraph Company, the Continental Telegraph Company, and the Commercial Pacific Cable Company. These companies, including those affiliated with the Postal Telegraph-Cable Company, but excluding the Commercial Pacific Cable Company, which is engaged in the transmission of cable messages only, perform substantially all the commercial telegraph business of the country. At this hearing various individuals and associations appeared for the purpose of expressing their views concerning the subject under investigation and to urge the establishment of more liberal rules and regulations. The record in No. 8917, referred to hereinafter as the *Unrepeated Message Case,* was made available for use in the proceeding, and one report will suffice for both cases.

The propriety of the rules established by the Western Union company to restrict its liability for damages arising from mistakes or delays in the transmission or delivery, or from non-delivery, of interstate messages was considered at length in the former report in the *Unrepeated Message Case,* 44 I. C. C., 670. That proceeding arose from the refusal of the Western Union to satisfy a claim for damages alleged to have resulted from the incorrect transmission of an unrepeated night-letter telegram. We were asked to determine, first, whether by the amended act to regulate commerce we had been invested with jurisdiction over matters of this kind, and, second, whether, if we had such jurisdiction, the rules governing liability were reasonable.

The rules in question, which are substantially the same as those published by the Postal Telegraph-Cable Company and its affiliated companies, except as hereinafter pointed out, are set out in full in the previous report, but for convenience are restated in the margin.[1] Briefly, they offer the sender his choice

[1] ALL MESSAGES TAKEN BY THIS COMPANY ARE SUBJECT TO THE FOLLOWING TERMS:

To guard against mistakes or delays, the sender of a message should order it REPEATED, that is, telegraphed back to the originating office for comparison. For this, one-half the unrepeated message rate is charged in addition. Unof three classes of messages, unrepeated, repeated, and valued, with different rates for each class, dependent upon the service to be performed and the liability to be assumed. As a condition attaching to the transmission of a message at the lowest, or unrepeated, rate it is stipulated that the company shall not be liable for mistakes, delays, or nondelivery beyond the amount received for sending it; and it appears that, unlike the Western Union, the Postal company steadfastly adheres to that limitation. But to protect the sender against possible loss in the event of errors in transmission, the respondents offer the second, or repeated, class of messages at a rate one and one-half times the rate for the same message if unrepeated. For this additional rate they agree to assume liability to the extent of 50 times the rate paid, with a maximum liability in the case of the Western Union of $50. The third class of messages, for the transmission of which the rate charged is the repeated rate plus a surcharge of one-tenth of one per cent of the valuation, is designed to insure the sender against any loss within the value placed upon the message. To afford protection against extravagant claims for damages on account of errors or delays which a repetition of the message would not have prevented, provision is made by the Western Union for a limitation of liability to $50, in practice applied both to unrepeated and repeated messages, and by the Postal company, in the case of repeated messages, to 50 times the repeated rate, which, unless a greater value is declared, is the agreed value of the message. This provision on the part of

---

less otherwise indicated on its face, THIS IS AN UNREPEATED MESSAGE AND PAID FOR AS SUCH, in consideration whereof it is agreed between the sender of the message and this company as follows:

1. The Company shall not be liable for mistakes or delays in the transmission or delivery, or for non-delivery, of any UNREPEATED message, beyond the amount received for sending the same; nor for mistakes or delays in the transmission or delivery, or for non-delivery, of any REPEATED message, beyond fifty times the sum received for sending the same, *unless specially valued;* nor in any case for delays arising from unavoidable interruption in the working of its lines; *nor for errors in cipher or obscure messages.*

2. In any event the Company shall not be liable for damages for any mistakes or delays in the transmission or delivery, or for the non-delivery, of this message, whether caused by the negligence of its servants or otherwise, beyond the sum of FIFTY DOLLARS, at which amount this message is hereby valued, unless a greater value is stated in writing hereon at the time the message is offered to the COMPANY for transmission, and an additional sum paid or agreed to be paid based on such value equal to one-tenth of one per cent thereof.

the Western Union is alleged to be necessary in jurisdictions where the unrepeated stipulation is held not to avail.

In *Primrose* v. *Western Union Telegraph*, 154 U. S., 1, decided May 26, 1894, the Supreme Court of the United States upheld the validity of a contract between the sender of a message and the telegraph company by which the latter assumed no liability for mistakes or delays, although arising from the negligence of its employees, beyond the toll charged for transmission unless repetition had been requested and the additional charge therefor paid. It was pointed out that a contract of this nature was not an effort on the part of the company to exempt itself wholly from liability for its negligence, but was a proper and lawful mode of securing a due proportion between the amount for which the company might be responsible and the toll received. Following the ruling announced in that case and applying the principles of the act to regulate commerce, to which act telegraph companies were subjected by the amendment of June 18, 1910, we held in the *Unrepeated Message Case* that the rules in question, being essentially part of the rates, were subject to our supervision and control, and that the classification of messages into unrepeated, repeated, and valued, " with the different rates and liabilities attaching to them, having affirmative recognition in the act itself, . . . when lawfully fixed and offered to the public, . . . are binding upon the defendant and upon all those who avail themselves of its services, until they have been lawfully changed."

The *Unrepeated Message Case* was decided May 17, 1917. By it common carriers engaged in the transmission of messages were apprised as to what, in our opinion, their practices should be in the settlement of damage claims arising through defaults in service. In order that we might be informed whether the general practice of the Western Union, defendant in the *Unrepeated Message Case,* was in conformity with its published rules and also to obtain further information relative to the reasonableness of the rules, that proceeding was set down for further hearing. Further hearing was had on February 20, 1918. On August 1, 1918, the President, under powers conferred upon him by Congress, assumed possession and control of the defendant company and appointed the Postmaster General his agent to continue its operation. Control of the property remained in the hands of the government until August 1, 1919, and consideration of the evidence taken at the hearing of February 20, 1918, was held in abeyance during that period. Thereafter, on March 1, 1920, a further hearing was had for the purpose of ascertaining whether changes had been made in the practices of the company since the date of the former hearing, and also to afford an opportunity to parties interested to present to us any new facts bearing on the propriety of the rules. At this later hearing petitions in intervention were filed on behalf of various stock, cotton, and grain exchanges and other associations. In the interest of uniformity the general investigation was subsequently instituted.

At the hearing on March 1, 1920, the contention was urged that a telegraph company, as a common carrier, may not lawfully undertake by contract, rule, regulation, or in any manner to exempt itself from full liability for errors or delays in the transmission of messages, and that all such rules restricting liability are void. This question is foreclosed by the decisions of the Supreme Court in the *Primrose Case* and in *Postal Telegraph-Cable Co.* v. *Warren-Godwin Co.*, 251 U. S., 27. In the latter case, decided December 8, 1919, which involved the extent of the liability of a telegraph company under an unrepeated interstate message, the court said:

"In the first place, as it is apparent on the face of the act of 1910 that it was intended to control telegraph companies by the act to regulate commerce, we think it clear that the act of 1910 was designed to and did subject such companies as to their interstate business to the rule of equality and uniformity of rates which it was manifestly the dominant purpose of the act to regulate commerce to establish, a purpose which would be wholly destroyed if, as held by the court below, the validity of contracts made by telegraph companies as to their interstate commerce business continued to be subjected to the control of divergent and it may be conflicting local laws.

"In the second place, as in terms the act empowered telegraph companies to establish reasonable rates, subject to the control which the act to regulate commerce exerted, it follows that the power thus given, limited of course by such control, carried with it the primary authority to provide a rate for unrepeated telegrams and the right to fix a reasonable limitation of responsibility where such rate was charged, since, as pointed out in the *Primrose case*, the right to contract on such subject was embraced within the grant of the primary rate-making power."

It is shown by the record that the practice of the Western Union in the settlement of damage claims, which is also followed by the Continental Telegraph Company, is not in accord with the rules it has established, but is founded upon a policy in which business considerations predominate. To secure and retain the good will of the public and to encourage a more liberal use of its facilities the Western Union makes it a point to adjust as promptly as possible at least a large percentage of meritorious claims presented to it, regardless of the class of message and of the admonition in the former report that its rules, as part of the rates, must be as strictly observed as the rates themselves. In other words, under its present practice the protection offered the sender under the repeated and valued message rates is voluntarily given for the unrepeated rate, the contractual limitations of liability being resorted to only when in the company's opinion the claim is without foundation, can not be settled for less than the cost of litigation, is unusually large, or is open to objection in some other respect.

In justification for departing from the strict and uniform enforcement of its rules it is urged that the courts of many states do not recognize the validity of the partial exemptions from liability, and, therefore, to avoid the expense of litigation claims arising in such jurisdictions are settled by agreement between the parties. This lack of uniformity among the courts in cases involving the restrictions upon the liability of the telegraph companies was referred to in our former report in the *Unrepeated Message Case.* It was there pointed out that one of the necessary consequences of the amended act was to put an end to all such diversity and attach to the respondent's error the same degree of responsibility in all the courts. The practice, however, is to adjust claims contrary to the rules, not only in the jurisdictions which heretofore have declined to sanction their validity but also in jurisdictions where they have been expressly upheld. It is frankly admitted that business considerations and equity dictate its policy.

On the other hand, the policy of the Postal Telegraph-Cable Company and its affiliated companies is the reverse of that of the Western Union. Since the amendment of June 18, 1910, and particularly since the former report in the *Unrepeated Message Case,* the Postal company has consistently declined to pay claims based on interstate messages if the amount involved is in excess of that contemplated in the contract of transmission. The effect upon its business can be readily appreciated. Unquestionably, the more liberal policy of the Western Union, when known, tends to induce patrons of the Postal company to withdraw or curtail their business with that company and transfer it to the Western Union.

It is clear that the policy of the Western Union is contrary to both the spirit and the terms of the interstate commerce act and must therefore be condemned. That the requirement of adherence to established rates and charges, as provided in the act, applies as strictly to telegraph companies as to other common carriers can not be questioned; yet that company makes it a practice, when a default occurs in connection with a message for which it charged the unrepeated rate, to assume a liability for which it holds itself out only at a higher rate. This is a plain departure from its published rules and stands on the same footing as an unlawful rebate. Those who rely upon the published rules are thus placed at a disadvantage, since others, either through ignorance of the rules or with knowledge that they are disregarded, are accorded unauthorized reimbursement for losses which they have sustained through the carrier's negligence.

The Western Union, while justifying its practice of adjusting claims in excess of its legal liability mainly on the grounds of business policy, equity, and fair dealing, nevertheless opposes a revision of its rules which legally impose upon it any greater degree of responsibility than it now holds itself out to assume. It urges that its financial condition will not permit the impairment of revenue that would follow if more liberal rules should be established. This view appears to be unfounded. Except for a short period following the amendment to the act in 1910, the practice of adjusting claims to the full extent of the actual loss suffered has been consistently followed, yet the surplus has been increased from $7,733,692.52 on June 30, 1910, to practice of adjusting claims to the full extent of the actual report to the stockholders. Dividends paid in 1910 were at the rate of 3 per cent, and in 1917 and 1918 at 7 per cent. During this period the funded debt was reduced from slightly over $40,000,000 to approximately $32,000,000.

In considering the reasonableness of the rule limiting liability in the case of an unrepeated message to the amount of the toll received for sending it, the evidential effect of the voluntary practices of the Western Union, which handles 75 per cent or more of the telegraph business of the country, can not well be overlooked. Prior to 1910 that rule was never observed, and all claims for damages were referred to and dealt with by the legal department without reference to its limited liability. Following the amendment of 1910 the conclusion was reached that thereafter there could be no latitude in the adjustment of claims, but that settlement would necessarily be made on a standard basis under fixed rules determined by the laws of the different states or the federal laws. Under date of May 8, 1911, authority was granted the general superindentents to settle all claims up to $500 when damage resulted from a fault in service and there was no valid contract limiting the company's liability. The superintendents were instructed to disregard the unrepeated-message condition, except in the case of claims arising or based on messages handled solely in New York, Massachusetts, California, or Rhode Island, where the validity of the stipulation was upheld except in the event of gross negligence. In 1913 the policy was altered, and claims were thereafter settled according to the discretion of the superintendents or managers. Since then adherence to the contractual limitations has not been required. It thus appears that the restricted-liability provisions are not resorted to in the case of meritorious claims which are reasonable in amount.

So far as the record shows there has been no substantial change in the Western Union's rule disclaiming responsibility for negligence in the transmission or delivery of unrepeated messages since it was first established, over 50 years ago, notwithstanding that the efficiency of the sending and receiving instruments has been greatly increased and that new appliances have been adopted which reduce the possibility of error to a minimum. Formerly all land-line messages were handled by Morse operation, which required manual transmission in the Morse code and receipt by sound. At the present time substantially one-half of all the messages transmitted by the Western Union, particularly between large cities, are automatically transmitted from the sending office and are received on machines which print the message directly upon the telegram blank. It is asserted by that company that the automatic printing system is the most accurate known for handling messages over long distances, and that the automatic sending instrument affords the most rapid and accurate method of transmission. Apparently, the experience of the Postal company with automatic devices has not been so satisfactory, as that company continues to employ manual transmission. From records prepared by the Postal company it is estimated that the ratio of errors in transmission to the number of messages handled is one to 25,000 or 30,000.

A repeated telegram differs from the ordinary telegram in that it is repeated back at each stage of transmission from point of origin to destination. This class of message is seldom used, an operator testifying that in 17 or 18 years' experience he had transmitted perhaps 200 such messages. Repetition of a message is a certain guard against errors in transmission, but is no protection against delayed delivery. To many patrons of the telegraph service a delay may have as serious consequences as a mistake in transmission, particularly in the case of commercial telegrams between members of boards of trade and exchanges. Rapid transmission and immediate delivery are frequently of such importance, dealers in perishable commodities argue, that they can not afford the delay incident to repetition of their messages. It is improbable, however, that the time required to repeat a message, estimated to be no more than three or four minutes over direct wires, could cause serious inconvenience or loss, except in very rare instances. The charge for an unrepeated message includes the cost incident to its receipt, transmission, and delivery, and a profit to the company. The repetition is but one additional element of the total service, and its cost, therefore, a relatively small proportion of the original cost, while the charge is 50 per cent higher. This additional amount is compensation for the greater care in handling and the extra liability assumed. So far as the record shows, a repeated message has never failed to accomplish its purpose, except in one instance where there was gross negligence. In that case the default was in delayed delivery. The fact that repetition is ordered should put the company on notice that the message is of unusual value, and thus insure the maximum degree of care in its transmission and delivery.

The valued message appears to be of no practical use in the great majority of instances, because of the impossibility of anticipating what default, if any, there may be in the service and thus determining in advance what loss may ensue. So far as a large proportion of the public is concerned this class of messages might be eliminated, as it never has been and probably never will be used to any considerable extent. If a valued message should be sent it would be handled in precisely the same manner as a repeated message; that is, repeated back at each stage of transmission, with extra care exercised in delivery. This class of message, however, is of importance to the carriers in that it places a limit upon unforeseen and unanticipated losses; and the contention pressed upon our notice, that senders can not well anticipate the results of defaults in the service, is at least no less true of the telegraph companies.

The present record amply demonstrates the need for a substantial revision of respondents' rules concerning their liability on interstate messages. All other common carriers subject to the act have been made fully liable for their errors or negligence, notwithstanding attempted limitations by contracts, rules, or otherwise, except in instances where they have been expressly authorized by this Commission to maintain varying rates dependent upon the declared or agreed value of the article transported: and the record herein offers no sound reason why telegraph companies should longer be permitted to avoid liability for their errors or negligence or to limit it to the nominal amounts now provided for in their rules. It has been shown that these rules are not observed by the Western Union, but that, on the contrary, meritorious claims arising in connection with unrepeated messages are adjusted either to the full extent of the loss suffered or on a basis satisfactory to the claimant. While that company declares that it is ready to abide by its rules as now published, it contends that its present practice is better from all viewpoints. That practice, as hereinbefore stated, contemplates full payment of claims by general superintendents or general managers up to $500 without submission to the legal departments and without reference to the contractual defenses.

The Postal company vigorously opposes any increase in its liability, principally on the ground that its revenues would be insufficient to meet the additional expense. No figures were presented, however, to indicate the probable effect upon the company of assuming liability for defaults in service due to its own negligence, subject to more reasonable limitations, and there is nothing of record to justify the assumption that its revenues would be seriously impaired. In any event we are not prepared to concede that a public-service corporation may rely upon its financial condition as a justification for refusal to establish reasonable rules and regulations. Certain information relative to revenues, expenses, surplus, dividends, etc., of the various companies affiliated with the Postal company was called for at the hearing, but has not been supplied.

Upon consideration of the record we find that the present rules of the respondents restricting their liability for negligence in the transmission or delivery, or for nondelivery, of unrepeated and repeated interstate messages are and for the future will be unreasonable; that the maximum liability in the case of a message for the transmission of which the unrepeated rate is charged should be not less than $500, and for a message received for transmission at the repeated rate, $5,000, which limitations we find to be reasonable as parts of the respective rates. Provision should be made for the transmission of valued messages under a liability limited to the value stated in writing by the sender of the message at the time it is offered for transmission upon payment of the repeated rate plus one-tenth of 1 per cent of the stated value in excess of $5,000.

An order in accordance with the foregoing findings will be entered.

POTTER, *Commissioner,* dissenting:

I can not concur in the view that the liability of the respondents should be increased. We have the right to make regulations designed reasonably to assure the performance by the respondents of their duties. Existing arrangements, I think, are sufficient to that end. As I see it, the Commission by its majority report has departed from the field of regulation and entered the field of corporate management and business policy. If the increased liability benefits the public and brings about an increase of burden to the respondents, that increased burden will be an expense which through increased rates will be passed along to all whom the respondents serve. The result of compliance with our report will be, therefore, to create a sort of insurance relation by which the individual sender of a message will be insured at the expense of senders in general. This might be a desirable arrangement, but whether it should be adopted as a part of the relation with the respondents and among those they serve is a business question rather than a matter of service regulation. To my mind, those who desire insurance should pay for it and should not be accorded it by us at the expense of others. Existing arrangements amply secure those who are willing to pay for their insurance.

HOBART MILL & ELEVATOR CO. *v.* DIRECTOR *v.* GENERAL AS AGENT

61 I. C. C. 192 (1921)

REPORT OF THE COMMISSION.

DIVISION 1, COMMISSIONERS MCCHORD, MEYER, AND AITCHISON.
AITCHISON, *Commissioner:*

The issues here presented were made the subject of a proposed report, to which complainants filed exceptions.

Complainants, Hobart Mill & Elevator Company and George B. Tarr, jointly own and operate a grain elevator at Cold Springs, Okla., and ship grain to interstate points. By amended complaint filed April 28, 1920, they allege that the St. Louis-San Francisco Railway, hereinafter called defendant, subjected them to undue prejudice in failing and refusing to furnish, from July 1, 1919, to December 1, 1919, the proportion of cars to which they were lawfully entitled, and unduly preferred other operators of grain elevators at near-by points by furnishing them a larger proportion of cars than was furnished to complainants. They ask for reparation, but for no other relief.

Cold Springs is on defendant's line between Enid, Okla., and Vernon, Tex. The alleged preferred elevators are located on the same line in Oklahoma at the following points; two at Roosevelt, about 5 miles north of Cold Springs; one at Mountain Park; and one at Snyder, about 8 and 10 miles, respectively, south of Cold Springs. During the wheat shipping season of 1919 there was an acute shortage of grain cars in this territory.

The capacity of complainants' elevator at Cold Springs is about 14 per cent of the total capacity shown. Had they received their proportionate share of the cars distributed, on the basis of grain on hand, they would have received not less than 25 cars out of the 183 furnished during the period in question.

The chief dispatcher was unable to explain the marked discrepancy between the number of cars furnished complainants and those furnished their competitors at the stations named. That defendant's officials were convinced that complainants had not been equitably dealt with in the matter of car distribution is indicated by the instructions given in December, 1919, after an investigation of the situation, that complainants be excepted from the operation of a general embargo which had been placed on shipments of grain from this territory in order that, as defendant's witness expressed it, they might have "a chance to catch up." This latter action of defendant was clearly unduly prejudicial to other shippers, who were held to the strict observance of the embargo, and could not justify any previous undue or unreasonable prejudice against the complainants.

Upon the record we find that the defendant's practice in the distribution of cars for grain loading during the period in question was unduly prejudicial to the complainants and unduly preferential of their competitors at Roosevelt, Mountain Park, and Snyder, Okla. The present record is not such that we can determine with any degree of certainty the amount of the damages, if any, sustained by complainants by reason of such undue prejudice. The defendant's subsequent distribution of cars is satisfactory to complainants and no relief for the future is sought. The complainants will be allowed 30 days from and after the service of this report within which to make a showing in support of an application for further hearing on the question of damages; in default thereof, the complaint will be dismissed.

NORTHERN WEST VIRGINIA COAL OPERATORS' ASSOCIATION *v.* PENNSYLVANIA RAILROAD COMPANY

60 I. C. C. 569 (1921)

REPORT OF THE COMMISSION.

DIVISION 5, COMMISSIONERS CLARK, DANIELS, AITCHISON, AND POTTER.

DANIELS, *Commissioner:*

The issues here presented were made the subject of a proposed report by the examiner. Exceptions were filed by complainant and the case was orally argued.

The complainant is an incorporated association whose members, hereinafter referred to as the operators, own and operate bituminous coal mines in northern West Virginia on the Monongahela Railway, hereinafter termed the Monongahela, and the Morgantown & Wheeling Railway, hereinafter termed the Wheeling. The operators sell and ship their coal to dealers and consumers at points served by or reached in connection with the Pennsylvania Railroad, hereinafter termed the Pennsylvania, and the Pittsburgh & Lake Erie Railroad, hereinafter termed the Lake Erie, and are in competition with coal operators on the lines of those railroads. The complaint, filed May 4, 1920, as amended, alleges in substance that the operators during a period of car shortage from July 1, 1919, to March 1, 1920, barring November, 1919, were not given their pro rata share of the cars available for loading as compared with operators of mines on the Pennsylvania and the Lake Erie; and that the acts and practices complained of were unreasonable, unjustly discriminatory, and unduly prejudicial in violation of the interstate commerce act and of the transportation act, 1920. It asks that we either (1) order the defendant carriers to " adjust and equalize " the alleged shortage or (2) award damages to the operators against the " agent acting for and in behalf of the President of the United States in winding up the affairs of federal control."

At the argument complainant withdrew the prayer that the Pennsylvania and the Lake Erie be ordered to equalize the shortage, leaving only the second prayer for consideration.

The Monongahela has its principal termini at Fairmont, W. Va., and Brownsville Junction, Pa. It has track connections with the Lake Erie, the Pennsylvania, and the Baltimore & Ohio railroads. Fifty per cent of its capital stock is owned by the Pennsylvania and 50 per cent by the Lake Erie, but it is separately operated under its own charter. The Wheeling, now in the hands of a receiver, is a short line, principally operated by electricity extending from a point near Randall, W. Va., where it connects with the Monongahela, northwestward toward the West Virginia-Pennsylvania state line. It has a separate organization from the Monongahela. Both of these railroads were taken under federal control. The Wheeling was released from federal control shortly after the taking over and was not operated by the government during the period with which the complaint is concerned. The Monongahela remained under federal control until March 1, 1920. Neither of these railroads owns coal cars used in interstate commerce, and the mines on their lines are consequently dependent upon the equipment of other carriers. There are joint rates on coal from points on the Monongahela and the Wheeling to points reached by and in connection with the Pennsylvania and the Lake Erie.

During the period in question the available supply of coal cars throughout the country generally was not sufficient for the demand. This shortage existed likewise in the region where the operators' mines are situated. A witness for complainant testified that during this period orders for coal cars desired by the mines on the Monongahela and the Wheeling were placed by the Monongahela with the Pennsylvania and the Lake Erie in the same manner as were orders for cars desired by mines on the latter two roads. Complainant's exhibits show that from July 1, 1919, to March 1, 1920, barring November, 1919, mines on the Monongahela and the Wheeling received 110,450 cars, or 72.2 per cent of the total number of cars ordered; that bituminous operators on the Pennsylvania Lines — East received 731,693 cars, or 84.3 per cent, and on the Lake Erie 81,713 cars, or 78.8 per cent, of the total number of cars ordered; and that mines on the Monongahela division, the Southwest branch, and the Pittsburgh west end division of the Pennsylvania received 263,933 cars or 94.1 per cent of the cars ordered. The defendants do not dispute the substantial accuracy of these figures. The record indicates that the mines on the Monongahela and the Wheeling were rated in accordance with the car-service regulations of the United States Railroad Administration, and that the cars ordered did not exceed the rated capacities of the mines.

Complainant's exhibits contain copies of letters and telegrams exchanged between it and officials of the Pennsylvania, the Lake Erie, and the eastern car pool, which show that complainant made frequent and repeated efforts during the period covered by the complaint to obtain a better supply of cars for the operators. Notwithstanding these efforts, and the promises of the officials in response thereto, the mines on the Monongahela and the Wheeling, month by month, received a substantially smaller percentage of cars ordered than was received by mines on the Pennsylvania and, except for July and September, 1919, than was received by mines on the Lake Erie. Complainant predicates its contention of discrimination largely on the showing of the combined total of cars furnished by the Pennsylvania and the Lake Erie for the entire period involved.

Car service circular C–S 31 of the United States Railroad Administration, which became effective October 10, 1918, after providing a method of determining the productive capacity of mines, in part read as follows:

"Whenever the available car supply is such that all orders for cars can not be filled, each mine shall be given its pro rata share of cars (grouping of mines or pooling of cars not being permitted) in accordance with the following rules:

"1. The daily rating, or the daily order for cars if less than the rating, shall be the basis for car distribution."

* * * * * * *

"9. If a mine receives more or less cars than it is entitled to during any period . . . it will be charged with a surplus or credited with a shortage accordingly and the discrepancy adjusted as promptly as practicable."

Car service circular C–S 31 (revised), which was promulgated January 10, 1920, and superseded C–S 31, also carried these rules in substantially the above form. These circulars were not filed with us as tariffs or in connection with a tariff. Complainant contends that the provision applied to the Wheeling as well as to the Monongahela, even though the former was not under federal control during the period in question. It appears that the Wheeling, along with the other three defendant carriers, was a party to and concurred in these rules.

The position of the Lake Erie is that there was no violation of any legal obligation toward the operators by the Director General in the matter of car supply either from the Pennsylvania or the Lake Erie, and that there is not even an allegation of a shortage of supply in connection with the operation of the Lake Erie; that, even admitting that the operators were not treated on an equality with mines on trunk lines, the determination of the question of car supply was a matter within the discretion of the operating officials of the Railroad Administration, who were at liberty to use their own judgment in regard thereto, provided only that they acted in good faith; and that complainant has not shown that prior to the transportation act, 1920, there was any obligation on the part of the railroads or of the Railroad Administration to give equal car supply to mines dependent on other lines. A witness for this defendant further testified that in his opinion the car distribution rules do not have any bearing on the duty of one railroad to supply empty equipment to another railroad, and that the provisions of these rules are confined to the railroad which issues them and obligate the issuing road to make equitable distribution of cars as between the coal mines on that railroad only; that during the time of the car shortage the Monongahela received from the rails of the Lake Erie as many cars as was consistent with equity; and that while the utmost was done to comply with orders of the car pool, the paramount thought in the minds of the officials operating the Lake Erie was equal distribution, not only to mines on its own line but to mines on so-called dependent lines, and equalization was attempted rather than strict compliance with orders of the pool.

As shown by complainant's exhibits, the cars supplied the Monongahela by the Lake Erie were 79.1 per cent of its orders as compared with 78.8 per cent furnished the mines on the Lake Erie. On the other hand, only 64.2 per cent of the cars ordered from the Pennsylvania were received from that road, while the deliveries of cars to mines on the Pennsylvania Lines–East, represented 84.3 per cent of those mines' orders, and mines on the Monongahela division, Southwest branch, and Pittsburgh west end division of that road received 94.1 per cent of their requirements.

The proper application of the car distribution rules as between the several defendant carriers does not appear to be controlling here. The question for us to determine is whether or not the law imposed a duty upon the defendant carriers, as agents of the Director General, to accord substantially equal treatment to the mines on the so-called dependent roads and on the trunk lines in the same region or district, and if so, whether or not that duty was discharged.

The failure to supply the Monongahela, and through it the operators, a pro rata share of available equipment apparently was due in part to the lack of full recognition on the part of the officials of the trunk lines that federally controlled roads were under unified operation, including the common use of equipment. The Pennsylvania, as the testimony shows, frequently objected to furnishing equipment to the Monongahela because it was short in its interchange of cars with the Lake Erie through the Monongahela. This question was a constant source of dispute between these two defendants. Although the acts and practices of the Pennsylvania and the Lake Erie in the matter of car distribution are referred to frequently of record, the liability of these carriers is not involved in the narrowed issues of the case. They were operated by the Director General and the acts complained of were the acts of his agents.

Defendants comment upon the fact that in arriving at the percentage of cars furnished complainant has considered the Monogahela and the Wheeling as one railroad. We perceive no objection to this. It is immaterial in this connection that the Wheeling was not under federal control during the period of the complaint. For the purposes of car distribution the Wheeling was treated by the Monongahela merely as a mine served by it and was given a rating in the same way that other mines were rated. Orders for cars needed on the Wheeling were placed with the Monongahela, and by it with the trunk lines. The Wheeling was as much dependent upon the connections of the Monongahela for equipment as was the Monongahela itself, and its mines were entitled to the same treatment as the mines on the Monongahela.

It is not possible always for carriers to furnish particular mines their exact quota of cars during periods of car shortage, and if shortages or overages are adjusted with reasonable promptness a carrier may be said to have fulfilled its duty. But where, as in this case, a substantial discrepancy as between groups of mines in the same locality continues over a period of several months a presumption arises, which is rebuttable, of course, that the carrier has not met its duty under the law to treat all of its patrons on a basis of equality. During the period in question the Monongahela and the Wheeling ordered 70,884 cars from the Pennsylvania and 69,899 cars from the Lake Erie, or a total of 140,783 cars. They were furnished 45,522 cars and 54,283 cars respectively, in response to these orders, or a total of 99,805 cars. The discrepancy between the latter figure and the figure previously given as representing the total number of cars received by the mines on the Monongahela and the Wheeling, 110,450 cars, is explained by complainant as probably due to the fact that the Monongahela was in possession of some empties, which it had received under load, and credited these against the orders from the mines, ordering the balance of the mines' requirements from the Pennsylvania and the Lake Erie.

Mines south of Pittsburgh, Pa., on the Lake Erie and mines served by the Monongahela division, Southwest branch, and

Pittsburgh west end division of the Pennsylvania are in the same general coal-producing region as are those served by the Monongahela and the Wheeling, and the transportation and other conditions in that region are similar. Nor does it appear that unfavorable weather conditions, not prevailing on the Pennsylvania divisions named and on the Lake Erie, were responsible for the different and less favorable treatment accorded the mines as a whole on the Monongahela and the Wheeling. The coals mined on these Pennsylvania divisions, and on the Lake Erie south of Pittsburgh, are of the same kinds as those mined on the Monongahela and the Wheeling and are used for the same purposes. The operators of these mines were in competition with each other and shipped to the same consuming markets, usually at the same freight rates to eastern markets.

The figures introduced by complainant show the total cars ordered by and delivered to the Monongahela, which also serves mines in Pennsylvania, and defendants raise the point in this connection that the mines of the operators in West Virginia on whose behalf the complaint is filed comprise only a small portion of the total number of mines on the Monongahela and the Wheeling. It was testified for complainant that its membership produces 75 to 80 per cent of the tonnage originating on the Monongahela in West Virginia and that the aggregate rating of the mines located on that road in Pennsylvania is slightly more than half of the aggregate rating of all its mines. It appears, therefore, that complainant's members produce a substantial part of the tonnage originating on the Monongahela. Out of 25 mines on the Wheeling complainant's members operate six.

Upon consideration of the record we find that the practices of the Director General during the period of this complaint in the distribution of coal cars as between the mines as a whole on the Monongahela and the Morgantown & Wheeling railways, on the one hand, and mines on the Pittsburgh & Lake Erie Railroad south of Pittsburgh and on the Monongahela division, Southwest branch, and Pittsburgh west end division of the Pennsylvania Railroad, on the other hand, subjected operators of coal mines on the first two named roads to undue prejudice and disadvantage to the extent that the percentage of cars furnished the mines as a whole on the latter roads was less than the average percentage of cars furnished the mines on the other lines named. There is no basis in the evidence for findings as to the extent of the damages, if any, suffered by the individual members of complainant as a result of the undue prejudice above found. The case will be held open and assigned for further hearing, as requested by complainant, upon that question.

NOTE

The pagination of Chapter IV, following, should run from pages 635–759 instead of as herewith, pages 589–713.

CHAPTER IV

FUNCTION OF COURTS IN THE ENFORCEMENT OF THE ACT

1. Primary Jurisdiction of the Commission

TEXAS AND PACIFIC RAILWAY COMPANY *v.* ABILENE COTTON OIL COMPANY

204 U. S. 426 (1907)

Mr. Justice White delivered the opinion of the court.

The oil company, the defendant in error, sued to recover $1,951.83. It was alleged that on shipments of carloads of cotton seed made in September and October, 1901, over the line of the defendant's road from various points in Louisiana east of Alexandria, in that State, to Abilene, Texas, the carrier had exacted, over the protest of the oil company, on the delivery of the cotton seed, the payment of an unjust and unreasonable rate, which exceeded in the aggregate, by the sum sued for, a just and reasonable charge. There were, moreover, averments that the rate exacted was discriminatory, constituted an undue preference, and amounted to charging more for a shorter than for a longer haul. Besides a general traverse, the railway company defended on the ground that the shipments were interstate, and were, therefore, covered by the act of Congress to regulate commerce. It was averred that as the rate complained of was the one fixed in the rate sheets which the company had established, filed, published and posted, as required by that act, the state court was without jurisdiction to entertain the cause, and even if such court had jurisdiction, it could not, without disregarding the act to regulate commerce, grant relief upon the basis that the established rate was unreasonable, when it had not been found to be so by the Interstate Commerce Commission.

The trial court made findings of fact. . . .

From the facts found the court stated the following as its conclusions:

"1st. The facts so found show that this was an interstate shipment.

"2d. The facts so found show that the defendant complied with the interstate commerce law, and said rates and classifications were thereby properly established and in force, except that the rate charged on cotton seed in carload lots was unreasonable and excessive.

"3d. I find that the rate charged by the defendant was that established under the interstate commerce law."

As nothing in these conclusions relates to the averments of discrimination, undue preference, or a greater charge for a shorter than for a longer haul, those subjects, it may be assumed, were considered to have been eliminated in the course of the trial.

There was judgment for the railway company. When the controversy came to be disposed of by the Court of Civil Appeals, to which the cause was taken, that court deemed there was only one question presented for decision; that is, whether, consistently with the act to regulate commerce, there was power in the court to grant relief upon the finding that the rate charged for an interstate shipment was unreasonable, although such rate was the one fixed by the duly published and filed rate sheet, and when the rate had not been found to be unreasonable by the Interstate Commerce Commission. In opening its opinion the court said (85 S. W. Rep. 1052):

"Adopting the construction of the pleadings evidently given them in the briefs, and treating it as presented, the case, briefly stated, is an action by appellant for damages for a violation of an alleged common law right, in that appellee demanded and coercively collected from appellant freight charges in excess of a reasonable compensation, for the transportation of a number of carloads of cotton seed from the town of Cotton Port and other designated towns in the State of Louisiana to the city of Abilene in the State of Texas."

After referring to the findings as to the unreasonableness of the charge exacted, and after pointing out that the railway company had not, by a cross assignment, challenged the correctness of the findings of the trial court as to the unreasonableness of the rate, it was said:

"So that we are relieved from a consideration of the difficulties discussed in some of the cases in ascertaining the fact, and therefore now have squarely before us the questions whether in a state court a shipper in cases of interstate carriage can, by the principles of the common law, be accorded relief from unjust and unreasonable freight rates exacted from him, or shall relief in such cases be denied merely because such unreasonable rate has been filed and promulgated by the carrier under the Interstate Commerce Act?"

Proceeding in an elaborate opinion to dispose of the question thus stated to be the only one for consideration, the conclusion was reached that jurisdiction to grant relief existed, and that to do so was not repugnant to the act to regulate commerce. Applying these conclusions to the findings of fact, the relief prayed was allowed. The court said:

"We therefore adopt the trial court's findings of fact, and, applying thereto the principles of law we have deduced, reverse the judgment, and here render judgment in appellant's favor for the said sum of $1,951.83, excessive freights charged, with interest. . . ."

The assigned errors are addressed exclusively to the operation of the act to regulate commerce upon the jurisdiction of the court below to entertain the controversy, and its power in any event to afford relief to the oil company, based upon the alleged unreasonableness of the rate under the circumstances disclosed. . . .

We are thus brought to the underlying proposition in the case, viz., the effect of the act to regulate commerce upon the claim asserted by the oil company. As presented below and pressed at bar, the question takes a seemingly two-fold aspect, the jurisdiction of the court below as affected by the act to regulate commerce and the right to the relief sought consistently with that act, even if jurisdiction existed. We say that these questions are only seemingly different, because they present but different phases of the fundamental question, which is the scope and effect of the act to regulate commerce upon the right of a shipper to maintain an action at law against a common carrier to recover damages because of the exaction of an alleged unreasonable rate, although the rate collected and complained of was the rate stated in the schedule filed with the Interstate Commerce Commission and published according to the requirements of the act to regulate commerce, and which it was the duty of the carrier under the law to enforce as against shippers. We come, therefore, first to the consideration of that subject.

Without going into detail, it may not be doubted that at common law, where a carrier refused to receive goods offered for carriage except upon the payment of an unreasonable sum, the shipper had a right of action in damages. It is also beyond controversy that when a carrier accepted goods without payment of the cost of carriage or an agreement as to the price to be paid, and made an unreasonable exaction as a condition of the delivery of the goods, an action could be maintained to recover the excess over a reasonable charge. And it may further be conceded that it is now settled that even where, on the receipt of goods by a carrier, an exorbitant charge is stated, and the same is coercively exacted either in advance or at the completion of the service, an action may be maintained to recover the overcharge. 2 Kent, Comm., 599, and note *a;* 2 Smith Lead. Cas., pt. 1, 8th ed., Hare & Wallace notes, p. 457.

As the right to recover, which the court below sustained, was clearly within the principles just stated, and as it is conceded that the act to regulate commerce did not in so many words abrogate such right, it follows that the contention that the right was taken away by the act to regulate commerce rests upon the proposition that such result was accomplished by implication. In testing the correctness of this proposition we concede that we must be guided by the principle that repeals by implication are not favored, and indeed that a statute will not be construed as taking away a common law right existing at the date of its enactment, unless that result is imperatively required; that is to say, unless it be found that the preëxisting right is so repugnant to the statute that the survival of such right would in effect deprive the subsequent statute of its efficacy; in other words, render its provisions nugatory.

Both parties concede that the question for decision has not been directly passed upon by this court, and that its determination is only persuasively influenced by adjudications of other courts. They both hence mainly rely upon the text of the act to regulate commerce as it existed at the time the shipments in question were made. The case, therefore, must rest upon an interpretation of the text of the act and is measurably one of first impression.

Let us, without going into detail, give an outline of the general scope of that act with the object of fixing the rights which it was intended to conserve or create, the wrongs which it proposed to redress and the remedies which the act established to accomplish the purposes which the lawmakers had in view.

The act made it the duty of carriers subject to its provisions to charge only just and reasonable rates. To that end the duty was imposed of establishing and publishing schedules of such rates. It forbade all unjust preferences and discriminations, made it unlawful to depart from the rates in the established schedules until the same were changed as authorized by the act, and such departure was made an offense punishable by fine or imprisonment, or both, and the prohibitions of the act and the punishments which it imposed were directed not only against carriers but against shippers, or any person who, directly or indirectly, by any machination or device in any manner whatsoever, accomplished the result of producing the wrongful discriminations or preferences which the act forbade. It was made the duty of carriers subject to the act to file with the Interstate Commerce Commission created by that act copies of established schedules, and power was conferred upon that body to provide as to the form of the schedules, and penalties were imposed for not establishing and filing the required schedules. The Commission was endowed with plenary administrative power to supervise the conduct of carriers, to investigate their affairs, their accounts and their methods of dealing, and generally to enforce the provisions of the act. To that end it was made the duty of the District Attorneys of the United States, under the direction of the Attorney General, to prosecute proceedings commenced by the Commission to enforce compliance with the act. The act specially provided that whenever any common carrier subject to its provisions "shall do, cause to be done, or permit to be done any act, matter or thing in this act prohibited or declared to be unlawful, or shall omit to do any act, matter, or thing in this act required to be done, such common carrier shall be liable to the person or persons injured thereby for the full amount of damages sustained in consequence of any such violation of the provisions of this act. . . ." Power was conferred upon the Commission to hear complaints concerning violations of the act, to investigate the same, and, if the complaints were well founded, to direct not only the making of reparation to the injured persons, but to order the carrier to desist from such violation in the future. In the event of the failure of a carrier to obey the order of the Commission that body, or the party in whose favor an award of reparation was made, was empowered to compel compliance by invoking the authority of the courts of the United States in the manner pointed out in the statute, *prima facie* effect in such courts being given to the findings of fact made by the Commission. By the ninth section of the act it was provided as follows:

"That any person or persons claiming to be damaged by any common carrier subject to the provisions of this act may either make complaint to the Commission, as hereinafter provided for, or may bring suit in his or their own behalf for the recovery of the damages for which such common carrier may be liable under the provisions of this act, in any District or Circuit Court of the United States of competent jurisdiction; but such person or persons shall not have the right to pursue both of said remedies, and must in each case elect which one of the two methods of procedure herein provided for he or they will adopt. . . ."

And by section 22, which we shall hereafter fully consider, existing appropriate common law and statutory remedies were saved.

When the act to regulate commerce was enacted there was contrariety of opinion whether, when a rate charged by a carrier was in and of itself reasonable, the person from whom such a charge was exacted had at common law an action against the carrier because of damage asserted to have been suffered by a discrimination against such a person or preference given by the carrier to another. *Parsons* v. *Chicago & Northwestern Ry.*, 167 U. S. 447, 455; *Interstate Commerce Commission* v. *Baltimore & Ohio R. R.*, 145 U. S. 263, 275. That the act to regulate commerce was intended to afford an effective means for redressing the wrongs resulting from unjust discrimination and undue preference is undoubted. Indeed, it is not open to controversy that to provide for these subjects was among the principal purposes of the act. *Interstate Commerce Commission* v. *Cincinnati, New Orleans & Texas Pacific Ry. Co.*, 167 U. S. 479, 494. And it is apparent that the means by which these great purposes were to be accomplished was the placing upon all carriers the positive duty to establish schedules of reasonable rates which should have a uniform application to all and which should not be departed from so long as the established schedule remained unaltered in the manner provided by law. *Cincinnati, New Orleans & Texas Pacific Ry. Co.* v. *Interstate Commerce Commission*, 162 U. S. 184; *Interstate Commerce Commission* v. *Cincinnati, New Orleans & Texas Pacific Ry. Co.*, 167 U. S. 479.

When the general scope of the act is enlightened by the considerations just stated it becomes manifest that there is not only a relation, but an indissoluble unity between the provision for the establishment and maintenance of rates until corrected in accordance with the statute and the prohibitions against preferences and discrimination. This follows, because unless the requirement of a uniform standard of rates be complied with it would result that violations of the statute as to preferences and discrimination would inevitably follow. This is clearly so, for if it be that the standard of rates fixed in the mode provided by the statute could be treated on the complaint of a shipper by a court and jury as unreasonable, without reference to prior action by the Commission, finding the established rate to be unreasonable and ordering the carrier to desist in the future from violating the act, it would come to pass that a shipper might obtain relief upon the basis that the established rate was unreasonable, in the opinion of a court and jury, and thus such shipper would receive a preference or discrimination not enjoyed by those against whom the schedule of rates was continued to be enforced. This can only be met by the suggestion that the judgment of a court, when based upon a complaint made by a shipper without previous action by the Commission, would give rise to a change of the schedule rate and thus cause the new rate resulting from the action of the court to be applicable in future as to all. This suggestion, however, is manifestly without merit, and only serves to illustrate the absolute destruction of the act and the remedial provisions which it created which would arise from a recognition of the right asserted. For if, without previous action by the Commission, power might be exerted by courts and juries generally to determine the reasonableness of an established rate, it would follow that unless all courts reached an identical conclusion a uniform standard of rates in the future would be impossible, as the standard would fluctuate and vary, dependent upon the divergent conclusions reached as to reasonableness by the various courts called upon to consider the subject as an original question. Indeed the recognition of such a right is wholly inconsistent with the administrative power conferred upon the Commission and with the duty, which the statute casts upon that body, of seeing to it that the statutory requirement as to uniformity and equality of rates is observed. Equally obvious is it that the existence of such a power in the courts, independent of prior action by the Commission, would lead to favoritism, to the enforcement of one rate in one jurisdiction and a different one in another, would destroy the prohibitions against preferences and discrimination, and afford, moreover, a ready means by which, through collusive proceedings, the wrongs which the statute was intended to remedy could be successfully inflicted. Indeed no reason can be perceived for the enactment of the provision endowing the administrative tribunal, which the act created, with power, on due proof, not only to award reparation to a particular shipper, but to command the carrier to desist from violation of the act in the future, thus compelling the alteration of the old or the filing of a new schedule, conformably to the action of the Commission, if the power was left in courts to grant relief on complaint of any shipper, upon the theory that the established rate could be disregarded and be treated as unreasonable, without reference to previous action by the Commission in the premises. This must be, because, if the power existed in both courts and the Commission to originally hear complaints on this subject, there might be a divergence between the action of the Commission and the decision of a court. In other words, the established schedule might be found reasonable by the Commission in the first instance and unreasonable by a court acting originally, and thus a conflict would arise which would render the enforcement of the act impossible.

Nor is there merit in the contention that section 9 of the act compels to the conclusion that it was the purpose of Congress to confer power upon courts primarily to relieve from the duty of enforcing the established rate by finding that the same as to a particular person or corporation was so unreasonable as to justify an award of damages. True it is that the general terms of the section when taken alone might sanction such a conclusion, but when the provision of that section is read in connection with the context of the act and in the light of the considerations which we have enumerated we think the broad construction contended for is not admissible. And this becomes particularly cogent when it is observed that the power of the courts to award damages to those claiming to have been injured, as provided in the section, contemplates only a decree in favor of the individual complainant, redressing the particular wrong asserted to have been done, and does not embrace the power to direct the carrier to abstain in the future from similar violations of the act; in other words, to command a correction of the established schedules, which power, as we have shown, is conferred by the act upon the Commission in express terms. In other words, we think that it inevitably follows from the context of the act that the independent right of an individual originally to maintain actions in courts to obtain pecuniary redress for violations of the act conferred by the ninth section must be confined to redress of such wrongs as can, consistently with the context of the act, be redressed by courts without previous action by the Commission, and, therefore, does not imply the power in a court to primarily hear complaints concerning wrongs of the character of the one here complained of. Although an established schedule of rates may have been altered by a carrier voluntarily or as the result of the enforcement of an order of the Commission to desist from violating the law, rendered in accordance with the provisions of the statute, it may not be doubted that the power of the Commission would nevertheless extend to hearing legal complaints of and awarding reparation to individuals for wrongs unlawfully suffered from the application of the unreasonable schedule during the period when such schedule was in force.

And the conclusion to which we are thus constrained by an original consideration of the text of the statute finds direct support, first, in adjudged cases in lower Federal courts and in the construction which the act has apparently received from the beginning in practical execution; and, second, is persuasively supported by decisions of this court, which, whilst not dealing directly with the question here presented, yet necessarily concern the same.

1. In *Swift* v. *Philadelphia &c. Ry. Co.*, 64 Fed. Rep. 59, it was held that in an action at law to recover damages for the exaction of an alleged unreasonable freight charge, the rate established in conformity with the act to regulate commerce must be treated by the courts as binding upon the shipper, until regularly corrected in the mode provided by the statute. And in *Kinnavey* v. *Terminal R. R. Association*, 81 Fed. Rep. 802, in an able opinion, the question was carefully considered and the same doctrine was announced and applied. When it is considered that the act to regulate commerce was enacted in 1887, and that neither the diligence of counsel nor our own researches have brought into view any case except the one now under consideration, holding that a court could, compatibly with the terms of that act, grant relief upon the basis that the established rate could be disregarded as unreasonable, it would seem to follow that the terms of the act had generally been treated in practical execution as incompatible with the existence of such power or right.

And this is greatly fortified when it is borne in mind that the reports of the decisions of the Interstate Commerce Commission show that many cases have been passed upon by that body concerning the unreasonableness of a rate fixed in an established schedule, which have resulted in awarding reparation to shippers and to the making of orders directing carriers to desist from future violation of the act; that is to say, in necessary legal effect correcting established schedules.

2. The cases of *Cincinnati, New Orleans & Texas Pacific Ry. Co.* v. *Interstate Commerce Commission*, 162 U. S. 184; *Louisville &*

Nashville R. R. Co. v. *Behlmer*, 175 U. S. 648, and *Interstate Commerce Commission* v. *Louisville & Nashville R. R. Co.*, 190 U. S. 273, involved the enforcement against carriers of orders of the Commission. After deciding that the orders of the Commission were not entitled to be enforced, because of errors of law committed by that body, this court declined to consider the question of the reasonableness *per se* of the rates as an original question; in other words, the correction of the established schedule without previous consideration of the subject by the Commission. It was pointed out that by the effect of the act to regulate commerce it was peculiarly within the province of the Commission to primarily consider and pass upon a controversy concerning the unreasonableness *per se* of the rates fixed in an established schedule. It was, therefore, declared to be the duty of the courts, where the Commission had not considered such a disputed question, to remand the case to the Commission to enable it to perform that duty, a conclusion wholly incompatible with the conception that courts, in independent proceedings, were empowered by the act to regulate commerce, equally with the Commission, primarily to determine the reasonableness of rates in force through an established schedule.

In *Gulf, Colorado &c. Ry.* v. *Hefley*, 158 U. S. 98, the facts were these: A rate had been fixed by a carrier in a bill of lading for an interstate shipment, which rate was less than that established under the provisions of the act to regulate commerce. On arrival of the goods at destination the carrier refused to deliver on tender of payment of the bill of lading rate, and demanded payment of and collected the higher established schedule rate. For so doing the carrier was proceeded against under a statute of the State of Texas, imposing a penalty upon a carrier for charging more than the rate fixed in a bill of lading. A judgment of the state court, enforcing the penalty, was reversed, upon the ground that the state statute, as applied, was repugnant to the act to regulate commerce, the court saying (p. 102):

"The carrier cannot obey one statute without sometimes exposing itself to the penalties prescribed by the other. Take the case before us. If, in disregard of the joint tariff established by the defendant and the St. Louis and San Francisco Railway Company and filed with the Interstate Commerce Commission, the latter company, as a matter of favoritism, had issued this bill of lading at a rate less than the tariff rate, both the defendant company and its agent would, by delivering the goods upon the receipt of only such reduced rate, subject themselves to the penalties of the national law, while, on the other hand, if the tariff rate was insisted upon, then the corporation would become liable for the damages named in the state act. In case of such a conflict the state law must yield."

In *Texas & Pacific Ry. Co.* v. *Mugg*, 202 U. S. 242, the facts were as follows: On an interstate shipment a given rate, less than the lawful schedule rate, was quoted to the shipper by the agent of the railroad at the point of shipment. On the arrival of the goods at their destination the road exacted the schedule rate, whilst the shipper insisted he was entitled to the lower and quoted rates. And a recovery of the excess collected over the quoted rate was allowed by a court of the State of Texas. Reversing the judgment, it was here held that the rate fixed in the schedule filed pursuant to the act to regulate commerce was controlling, that it was beyond the power of the carrier to depart from such rates in favor of any shipper, and that the erroneous quotation of rates made by the agent of the railroad did not justify recovery, since to do so would be in effect enabling the shipper, whose duty it was to ascertain the published rate, to secure a preference over other shippers, contrary to the act to regulate commerce.

In view of the binding effect of the established rates upon both the carrier and the shipper, as expounded in the two decisions of this court just referred to, the contention now made if adopted would necessitate the holding that a cause of action in favor of a shipper arose from the failure of the carrier to make an agreement, when, if the agreement had been made, both the carrier and the shipper would have been guilty of a criminal offense and the agreement would have been so absolutely void as to be impossible of enforcement. Nor is there force in the suggestion that a like dilemma arises from the recognition of power in the Commission to award reparation in favor of an individual because of a finding by that body that a rate in an established schedule was unreasonable. As we have shown, there is a wide distinction between the two cases. When the Commission is called upon on the complaint of an individual to consider the reasonableness of an established rate, its power is invoked not merely to authorize a departure from such rate in favor of the complaint alone, but to exert the authority conferred upon it by the act, if the complaint is found to be just, to compel the establishment of a new schedule of rates applicable to all. And like reasoning would be applicable to the granting of reparation to an individual after the establishment of a new schedule because of a wrong endured during the period when the unreasonable schedule was enforced by the carrier and before its change and the establishment of a new one. In other words, the difference between the two is that which on the one hand would arise from destroying the uniformity of rates which it was the object of the statute to secure and on the other from enforcing that equality which the statute commands.

But it is insisted that, however cogent may be the views previously stated, they should not control, because of the following provisions contained in section 22 of the act to regulate commerce, viz.: ". . . Nothing in this act contained shall in any way abridge or alter the remedies now existing at common law or by statute, but the provisions of this act are in addition to such remedies." This clause, however, cannot in reason be construed as continuing in shippers a common law right, the continued existence of which would be absolutely inconsistent with the provisions of the act. In other words, the act cannot be held to destroy itself. The clause is concerned alone with rights recognized in or duties imposed by the act, and the manifest purpose of the provision in question was to make plain the intention that any specific remedy given by the act should be regarded as cumulative, when other appropriate common law or statutory remedies existed for the redress of the particular grievance or wrong dealt with in the act.

The proposition that if the statute be construed as depriving courts generally, at the instance of shippers, of the power to grant redress upon the basis that an established rate was unreasonable without previous action by the Commission great harm will result, is only an argument of inconvenience which assails the wisdom of the legislation or its efficiency and affords no justification for so interpreting the statute as to destroy it. Even, however, if in any case we were at liberty to depart from the obvious and necessary intent of a statute upon considerations of expediency, we are admonished that the suggestions of expediency here advanced are not shown on this record to be justified. As we have seen, although the act to regulate commerce has been in force for many years, it appears that by judicial exposition and in practical execution it has been interpreted and applied in accordance with the construction which we give it. That the result of such long-continued, uniform construction has not been considered as harmful to the public interests is persuasively demonstrated by the fact that the amendments which have been made to the act have not only not tended to repudiate such construction, but, on the contrary, have had the direct effect of strengthening and making, if possible, more imperative, the provisions of the act requiring the establishment of rates and the adhesion by both carriers and shippers to the rates as established until set aside in pursuance to the provisions of the act. Thus, by section 1 of the act approved February 19, 1903, commonly known as the Elkins act, which, although enacted since the shipments in question, is yet illustrative, the willful failure upon the part of any carrier to file and publish "the tariffs or rates and charges," as required by the act to regulate commerce and the acts amendatory thereof, "or strictly to observe such tariffs until changed according to law," was made a misdemeanor, and it was also made a misdemeanor to offer, grant, give, solicit, accept or receive any rebate from published rates or other concession or discrimination. And in the closing sentence of section 1 it was provided as follows:

"Whenever any carrier files with the Interstate Commerce Commission or publishes a particular rate under the provisions of the act to regulate commerce or acts amendatory thereof, or participates in any rates so filed or published, that rate as against such carrier, its officers, or agents in any prosecution begun under this act, shall be conclusively deemed to be the legal rate, and any departure from such rate or any offer to depart therefrom shall be deemed to be an offense under this section of this act."

And, by section 3, power was conferred upon the Interstate Commerce Commission to invoke the equitable powers of a Circuit Court of the United States to enforce an observance of the published tariffs.

Concluding, as we do, that a shipper seeking reparation predicated upon the unreasonableness of the established rate must, under the act to regulate commerce, primarily invoke redress through the Interstate Commerce Commission, which body alone is vested with power originally to entertain proceedings for the alteration of an established schedule, because the rates fixed therein are unreasonable, it is unnecessary for us to consider whether the court below would have had jurisdiction to afford relief if the right asserted had not been repugnant to the provisions of the act to regulate commerce. It follows, from what we have said, that the court below erred in the construction which it gave to the act to regulate commerce.

The judgment below is, therefore, reversed, and the case remanded for further proceedings not inconsistent with this opinion.

PENNSYLVANIA RAILROAD COMPANY *v.* SONMAN SHAFT COAL COMPANY

242 U. S. 120 (1916)

Mr. Justice Van Devanter delivered the opinion of the court.

The coal company brought this action to recover damages from the railroad company upon two grounds, first, that for a period of four years, beginning April 1, 1903, the railroad company had failed to supply the coal company with a sufficient number of cars to meet the needs of the latter's coal mine; and, second, that during the same period the railroad company, in furnishing cars to the several mines in that district, had discriminated unjustly against the coal company and in favor of some of its competitors. The second ground was eliminated by the coal company at the trial and does not require further notice. The action was begun in a state court and resulted in a judgment for the coal company for $145,830.25, which the Supreme Court of the State affirmed. 241 Pa. St. 487.

The questions presented by the several assignments of error are: (1) What was the nature of the commerce involved? (2) If the commerce was interstate, was the action cognizable in a state court? (3) Was prejudicial error committed in excluding evidence presently to be mentioned?

The coal company sold its coal f. o. b. cars at the mine, and when the cars were loaded the coal was promptly forwarded to the purchasers at points within and without the State — largely to points in other States. This was well understood by both companies — by the coal company when it asked for cars and by the railroad company when it supplied them. Cars were not requested or furnished merely to be used in holding or storing coal, but always to be employed in its immediate transportation. While furnishing some cars for this service, the railroad company failed to furnish as many as the coal company needed and requested. It is plain that supplying the requisite cars was an essential step in the intended movement of the coal and a part of the commerce — whether interstate or intrastate — to which that movement belonged. It was expressly so held in *Pennsylvania R. R. Co.* v. *Clark Coal Co.*, 238 U. S. 456, 465–468. We there said of the sale and delivery of coal f. o. b. at the mine for transportation to purchasers in other States: "The movement thus initiated is an interstate movement and the facilities required are facilities of interstate commerce." Here the state court ruled that, as the coal was sold f. o. b. at the mine, the commerce involved was intrastate, even though the coal was going to purchasers outside the State. This was error, but it plainly was without prejudice unless it led the state court to exercise a jurisdiction which it did not possess.

In the courts below the railroad company contended that, in so far as the commerce involved was interstate, the action could not be entertained by a state court consistently with the Interstate Commerce Act, c. 104, 24 Stat. 379; and that contention is renewed here. It proceeds upon the theory, first, that the coal company was without any right to redress in respect of its interstate business unless the failure to supply it with the requisite cars was a violation of some provision of that act; second, that §§ 8 and 9 of the act prescribe the only modes of obtaining redress for violations of its provisions, and, third, that an action for damages in a state court is not among the modes prescribed.

It is true that §§ 8 and 9 deal with the redress of injuries resulting from violations of the act and give the person injured a right either to make complaint to the Interstate Commerce Commission or to bring an action for damages in a federal court, but not to do both. If the act said nothing more on the subject it well may be that no action for damages resulting from a violation of the act could be entertained by a state court. But the act shows that §§ 8 and 9 did not completely express the will of Congress as respects the injuries for which redress may be had or the modes in which it may be obtained, for § 22 contains this important provision: "Nothing in this act contained shall in any way abridge or alter the remedies now existing at common law or by statute, but the provisions of this act are in addition to such remedies." The three sections, if broadly construed, are not altogether harmonious, and yet it evidently is intended that all shall be operative. Only by reading them together and in connection with the act as a whole can the real purpose of each be seen. They often have been considered and what they mean has become pretty well settled. Thus we have held that a manifest purpose of the provision in § 22 is to make it plain that such "appropriate common law or statutory remedies" as can be enforced consistently with the scheme and purpose of the act are not abrogated or displaced, *Texas & Pacific Ry. Co.* v. *Abilene Cotton Oil Co.*, 204 U. S. 426, 446–447; that this provision is not intended to nullify other parts of the act, or to defeat rights or remedies given by earlier sections, but to preserve all existing rights not inconsistent with those which the act creates, *Pennsylvania R. R. Co.* v. *Puritan Coal Co.*, 237 U. S. 121, 129; that the act does not supersede the jurisdiction of state courts in any case, new or old, where the decision does not involve the determination of matters calling for the exercise of the administrative power and discretion of the Interstate Commerce Commission, or relate to a subject as to which the jurisdiction of the federal courts is otherwise made exclusive, *ibid.* 130; that claims for damages arising out of the application, in interstate commerce, of rules for distributing cars in times of shortage, call for the exercise of the administrative authority of the Commission where the rule is assailed as unjustly discriminatory, but where the assault is not against the rule but against its unequal and discriminatory application, no administrative question is presented and the claim may be prosecuted in either a federal or a state court without any precedent action by the Commission, *ibid.* 131–132; and that, if no administrative question be involved, as well may be the case, a claim for damages for failing upon reasonable request to furnish to a shipper in interstate commerce a sufficient number of cars to satisfy his needs, may be enforced in either a federal or a state court without any preliminary finding by the Commission, and this whether the carrier's default was a violation of its common law duty existing prior to law duty existing prior to the Hepburn duty prescribed by that act,[1] *ibid.* 132–135; *Eastern Ry. Co.* v. *Littlefield*, 237 U. S. 140, 143; *Illinois Central R. R. Co.* v. *Mulberry Hill Coal Co.*, 238 U. S. 275, 283; *Pennsylvania R. R. Co.* v. *Clark Coal Co.*, 238 U. S. 456, 472.

Applying these rulings to the case in hand, we are of opinion that a state court could entertain the action consistently with the Interstate Commerce Act. Not only does the provision in § 22 make strongly for this conclusion, but a survey of the scheme of the act and of what it is intended to accomplish discloses no real support for the opposing view. With the charge of unjust discrimination eliminated, the ground upon which a recovery was sought was that for a period of four years, during which the conditions were normal, the carrier had failed upon reasonable de-

[1] "SEC. 1. . . . and the term 'transportation' shall include cars and other vehicles and all instrumentalities and facilities of shipment or carriage, . . . and it shall be the duty of every carrier subject to the provisions of this Act to provide and furnish such transportation upon reasonable request therefor, . . . " c. 3591, 34 Stat. 584.

mand to supply to a shipper in interstate commerce a sufficient number of cars to transport the output of the latter's coal mine. Assuming that the conditions were normal and the demand reasonable, it was the duty of the carrier to have furnished the cars. That duty arose from the common law up to the date of the amendatory statute of 1906, known as the Hepburn Act, and thereafter from a provision in that act which, for present purposes, may be regarded as merely adopting the common law rule. There was evidence tending to show, and the jury found, that the conditions in the coal trade were normal and the demand for the cars reasonable. Indeed, without objection from the carrier, the court said when charging the jury: "There is no testimony disputing the claim of the plaintiff that these were normal times." The carrier insisted and the jury found that the carrier had a generally ample car supply for the needs of the coal traffic under normal conditions, and the jury further found that the failure to furnish the cars demanded was without justifiable excuse. Thus far it is apparent that no administrative question was involved — nothing which the act intends shall be passed upon by the Commission either to the exclusion of the courts or as a necessary condition to judicial action.

But there was testimony tending to show that the carrier was applying or following a rule for allotting cars which did not entitle the coal company to receive as many cars as it needed and requested, and because of this it is contended that the reasonableness of this rule was in issue and was an administrative question which the act intends that the Commission shall solve. We cannot accede to the contention. The conditions in the coal trade being normal, as just shown, the number of cars to which the coal company was entitled was to be measured by its reasonable requests based upon its actual needs. It is only in times of car shortage resulting from unusual demands or other abnormal conditions, not reasonably to have been foreseen, that car distribution rules originating with the carrier can be regarded as qualifying or affecting the right of a shipper to demand and receive cars commensurate in number with his needs. *Pennsylvania R. R. Co.* v. *Puritan Coal Co.*, 237 U. S. 121, 133. Such a rule being inapplicable in the conditions existing at the time, the rule mentioned in the testimony could not be a factor in the decision of the case, and whether in a time of unforeseen car shortage it would be reasonable or otherwise was not then material.

Upon the trial the carrier offered to prove by a witness then under examination . . . "that during all of the period of this action the defendant had in effect . . . through routes and joint rates to points outside the State of Pennsylvania on the lines of other common carriers; that it was obliged to permit cars loaded by its shippers with bituminous coal consigned to such points outside the State of Pennsylvania to go through to destination, even when on the lines of other railroad companies; that as a result of doing this it had continuously throughout the period of this action a large number of cars off its own lines and on the lines of other common carriers, which cars would otherwise have been available for shippers of coal on the railroad lines of the defendant and these cars if not on other railroad lines would have increased the equipment available for distribution to the plaintiff's mine and would consequently have diminished the damage which plaintiff claims to have sustained by reason of the fact that it did not receive more cars than it did receive."

But on the coal company's objection the evidence was excluded. We think the ruling was right. The offer did not point to any unusual or abnormal condition, not reasonably to have been foreseen, but, on the contrary, to a situation which was described as continuous throughout the four year period to which the action relates. It did not indicate that this condition was even peculiar to that period, or was caused by an extraordinary volume of coal traffic or an unusual detention of cars on other lines of railroad, or that it was other than a normal incident of the coal transportation in which the carrier was engaged. Without doubt the cars of this carrier when loaded with coal often went forward to destinations on the lines of other carriers. It is common knowledge that coal transportation has been conducted quite generally in this way for many years. Besides, a carrier extensively engaged in such transportation from mines along its lines, as this one was, naturally would expect to have a considerable number of cars on other lines in the ordinary course of business. Although possibly having a bearing upon the adequacy of the supply of cars provided by the carrier for the coal business as a whole, — a matter not within the contemplation of the offer, — it is certain that what was proposed to be proved had no tendency to show that the carrier had supplied to the coal company the number of cars to which it was entitled or to mitigate the carrier's default in that regard.

Judgment affirmed.

PENNSYLVANIA RAILROAD COMPANY *v.* STINEMAN COAL MINING COMPANY

242 U. S. 298 (1916)

Mr. Justice Van Devanter delivered the opinion of the court.

In a state court in Pennsylvania the coal company recovered a judgment against the railroad company for damages resulting, as was claimed, from unjust discrimination practiced in the distribution of coal cars in times of car shortage; and the Supreme Court of the State affirmed the judgment. 241 Pa. St. 509.

The suit related to both intrastate and interstate commerce, and whether, in respect of the latter, it could be brought in a state court consistently with the Interstate Commerce Act is the first question presented.

The coal company was engaged in coal mining on the carrier's line in Pennsylvania and was shipping the coal to points in that and other States. Other coal companies were engaged in like operations in the same district. A rule of the carrier provided for a *pro rata* distribution of the available supply of coal cars in times of car shortage, but did not require or contemplate that individual cars, owned or controlled by the shipper, should be charged against his distributive share. Without questioning the reasonableness of this rule, but, on the contrary, assuming that it was unobjectionable and became the true measure of the shipper's right and the carrier's duty, the coal company claimed that the carrier had unjustly discriminated against it to its damage by furnishing it a smaller number of cars, and some of its competitors a greater number, than the rule contemplated or permitted. In other words, the claim was, not that the rule was discriminatory, but that it was violated or unequally enforced by the carrier. Of such a suit we said in *Pennsylvania R. R. Co.* v. *Puritan Coal Co.*, 237 U. S. 121, 131–132, where the provisions of the Interstate Commerce Act were extensively considered: "There is no administrative question involved, the courts being called on to decide a mere question of fact as to whether the carrier has violated the rule to plaintiff's damage. Such suits, though against an interstate carrier for damages arising in interstate commerce, may be prosecuted either in the state or Federal courts." Adhering to this view, we think the suit was properly brought in a state court. See *Pennsylvania R. R. Co.* v. *Sonman Shaft Coal Co., ante,* [242 U. S.] 120.

But it is suggested that in the course of the trial an administrative question — one which the act intends the Interstate Commerce Commission shall solve — was brought into the suit and that this disabled the court from proceeding to a decision upon the merits. The suggestion is grounded upon the fact that one of the carrier's defenses at the trial was to the effect that the rule invoked by the coal company as fixing its quota of the cars was unjustly discriminatory and therefore not an appropriate test of the shipper's right or the carrier's duty. We think the suggestion is not well taken. The administrative question, which was whether the rule was reasonable or otherwise, was not then an open one. It had been theretofore determined in the mode contemplated by the act. Upon the complaint of other shippers, and after a full hearing, the Commission had found that the rule was unjustly discriminatory and had directed the carrier to give no further effect to it. See 19 I. C. C. 356, 392; 23 *ibid.* 186. This was shown by the reports and orders of the Commission, which were produced in evidence. Thus there was no jurisdictional obstacle at this point.

The Commission deemed it essential to a fair distribution in times of car shortage that individual cars, owned or controlled by the shipper, should be charged against his distributive share, and because the rule here took no account of such cars the Commission found that it was unjustly discriminatory. This occurred two years before the trial but after the period covered by the suit. As part of its defense the carrier claimed that the cars distributed to the coal company during that period included many individual cars controlled by the latter and that these were not charged against its distributive share. Evidently intending to recognize that this was so, and desiring to shorten the trial, the parties agreed that a verdict should be taken for the coal company in a designated sum, subject to the condition, among others, that, "if under the practice, the law and the rules," the court should conclude that "the plaintiff company should have been charged with individual cars," then judgment should be entered for the carrier *non obstante veredicto*. The verdict was taken and judgment entered thereon, the court concluding that the rule should be respected notwithstanding the Commission's finding. Complaint is made of this decision and we think it was wrong. That this shipper was not a party to the proceeding before the Commission hardly needs notice, no point being made of it in the briefs. And it is not a valid objection that the finding came after the period to which the suit relates. The act contemplated that the proceeding should be conducted in the interest of all the shippers who had been, or were likely to be, affected by the rule, and not merely in the interest of those who filed the complaint. The purpose was to determine the character of the rule for the equal benefit of all, to the end not only that discrimination thereunder in the future might be prevented, but also that such discrimination in the past might be redressed. So understanding the act, the Commission, upon finding the rule unjustly discriminatory, ordered the carrier to cease giving effect to it and also recognized that shippers who had been injured through its operation in the past were entitled to reparation. And the Commission proceeded to award reparation to such shippers as appeared and adequately proved their injury and the amount of damages sustained. Not only so, but the Commission's report makes it plain that the finding was not based upon any temporary or changeable condition existing at the time but upon what inhered in the rule and therefore was true from the time of its adoption. The legal propriety of the Commission's finding is not questioned, but only that it operates to discredit the carrier's rule as respects earlier transactions.

In the circumstances stated we are of opinion that effect must be given to the Commission's finding, even though it came after the transactions in question, and that a recovery by the coal company cannot be permitted without departing from the uniformity and equality of treatment which the act is intended to secure. Only through an enforcement of the discriminatory rule, and of the particular feature which made it discriminatory, can a recovery be had. A right to recover independently of that is neither shown nor claimed. In short, the coal company concedes that it received all the cars to which it would have been entitled under a reasonable rule and yet seeks to recover upon the ground that more cars were not delivered to it under a rule which was unreasonable, because unduly discriminatory in its favor. Consistently with the act this cannot be done.

Judgment reversed.

DIRECTOR GENERAL OF RAILROADS ET AL v. THE VISCOSE COMPANY

254 U. S. 498 (1921)

Mr. Justice CLARKE delivered the opinion of the court.

Silk, artificial and natural, had been accepted by the railway carriers of the country for transportation as freight for many years prior to the action which gave rise to the question which the Circuit Court of Appeals for the Third Circuit has certified herein to this Court and it had been classified in tariffs as first class. On January 21, 1920, Walker D. Hines, as Director General of Railroads, authorized an amendment or supplement to the appropriate freight tariff schedule so as to cancel the published classification and rates on such silk and to so amend rule 3 of "Consolidated Freight Classification No. 1" as to include it among the articles "that will not be accepted for shipment."

On the 28th of January, 1920, the supplement thus authorized was filed with the Interstate Commerce Commission, to become effective on the 29th day of February following, and if no other action had been taken the result would have been to have excluded such silks from shipment as freight after the effective date, for after that date there would not have been any published rate applicable to them.

The appellee, The Viscose Company, is an extensive manufacturer of artificial silk, eighty per cent of which "it maintains" must be shipped as freight, and, claiming that it would suffer great and irreparable damage if the supplement to the tariff proposed by the appellant were allowed to become effective, on February 26th, three days before it would have taken effect, the company applied for and obtained a temporary, and later on a permanent, injunction from the District Court of the United States for the Eastern District of Pennsylvania, restraining the Director General of Railroads and the other appellants:

(1) "From putting into effect and enforcing the provisions of the said supplement No. 2 to 'Consolidated Freight Classification No. 1, designed to cancel the existing classification of artificial silk as a commodity of freight,' and

(2) "From refusing to accept from The Viscose Company artificial or fibre silk for transportation under classifications which existed prior to the effective date of said supplement, or under such other classification as may be put into effect thereafter."

An appeal from the District Court carried the case to the Circuit Court of Appeals, which certifies to this court the question: "Did the District Court have jurisdiction to decide the matter raised by the complainant's bill and thereupon to annul the said action of the Director General of Railroads and enjoin the carriers from complying therewith."

Appellants contend that exclusive initial jurisdiction over the controversy here involved is in the Interstate Commerce Commission and that the appellees should have applied to that tribunal for relief. It is argued that the proposed supplement, striking silks from the first class in the tariffs filed was a change in classification and that the change in rule 3, adding them to the list of commodities which would not be accepted for shipment as freight, was a change of regulation and that over the reasonableness of both of these the Interstate Commerce Commission is given exclusive initial jurisdiction by sections 1, 3, 6, 13 and 15 of the Interstate Commerce Act (34 Stat. 584, as amended 36 Stat. 539).

On the other hand, it is argued by the appellees that for a common carrier to exclude a commodity from the tariffs and to refuse to accept it for shipment is neither classification nor regulation, and that an attempt to do such a thing presents a question of law for the courts, — that exclusion is not classification nor regulation.

Section 1 of the Interstate Commerce Act makes it the duty of all carriers subject to its provisions to provide and furnish "transportation upon reasonable request therefor" . . . "to establish, observe and enforce just and reasonable classifications of property for transportation" . . . "and just and reasonable regulations and practices affecting classification, rates or tariffs" . . . and all other matters relating to or connected with "the receiving, handling, transporting, storing and delivery of property." (36 Stat. 539, 545, 546.)

Section 3 of the act makes it unlawful for any carrier . . . to subject . . . "any particular description of traffic to any undue or unreasonable prejudice or disadvantage in any respect whatsoever." (24 Stat. 379, 380.)

Section 6 requires every carrier to print and file with the Commission schedules in form prescribed, showing . . . the classification of freight in force . . . and any rules or regulations which in any wise change, affect or determine . . . the value of the service rendered to the shipper. (34 Stat. 584, 586.)

Section 13 gives to any person or corporation the right to

apply to the Commission for relief on account of "anything done or omitted to be done" by any common carrier subject to the provisions of this act "in contravention of the provisions thereof." (36 Stat. 539, 550.)

And section 15 declares that whenever there is filed "a new individual or joint classification or any new individual or joint regulation or practice" the Commission shall have power to suspend the operation of such schedule, classification, regulation or practice until, upon complaint or upon its own initiative, an investigation shall be made, and if the proposed classification or regulation is found to be unreasonable or otherwise in violation of the act, the Commission may find what will be just and reasonable in the premises and may require the carrier thereafter to conform to its finding. (36 Stat. 539, 552.)

The power to suspend classifications or regulations when issued by the President was taken away from the Interstate Commerce Commission by the "Act to provide for the operation of transportation systems while under Federal control," etc. (40 Stat. 451, 456), but the power over them after hearing remained, and the power to suspend was restored when "The Transportation Act, 1920," approved February 28, 1920, became effective (41 Stat. 456, 487). The action of the Director General of Railroads, under consideration in this case, may, therefore, be treated as if it had been taken by a carrier subject to the act.

Without more, these references to the Interstate Commerce Act are sufficient to show that if the proposed change in the tariffs, and in the rule, which we are considering, constituted a change of classification or of regulation within the meaning of the Commerce Act, there was ample and specific provision made therein for dealing with the situation through the Commission, — for suspending the supplement or rule or annulling either or both if investigation proved the change to be unreasonable, and for providing for just treatment of shippers in the future. Strangely enough, it is a shipper not a carrier which here seeks to exclude the latter from this extensive jurisdiction of the Commission.

The certificate does not state what the purpose of the Director General of Railroads was in attempting to make the proposed change, but whether it was to permanently refuse to carry artificial silk as freight because of its value or of the risk involved, or for any other reason, or whether the action was taken to clear the way for putting into effect a commodity rate higher than the first-class rate (as might be done under appropriate conditions,

Chamber of Commerce, Houston, Texas v. *I. & G. N. Railway Co.*, 32 I. C. C. Rep. 247, 255; *Wheeling Corrugating Co.* v. *Baltimore & Ohio Railroad Co.*, 18 I. C. C. 125, 126), in either case it was necessary that the published classification of rates should be withdrawn by change of the tariffs on file and that notice should be given, through rule or regulation, that the silk would not be accepted for shipment in the future. Thus the supplement involved a change in the contents of previously filed classification lists and in a rule or regulation of the carriers.

That "exclusion is not classification" is an arresting but illusory expression. Classification in carrier rate-making practice is grouping, — the associating in a designated list, commodities, which, because of their inherent quality or value, or of the risks involved in shipment, or because of the manner or volume in which they are shipped or loaded, and the like, may justly and conveniently be given similar rates. To exclude a commodity from all classes is classification of it in as real a sense and with as definite an effect as to include it in any one of the usual classes. To strike artificial silk from the first class and to include it in the "prohibited list" which, for any cause, the carrier refuses to accept as freight, classifies it and sets it apart in a group subject to special treatment, as much as if it had been changed to the second class. We cannot doubt that the "exclusion in this case was an attempted "classification," and that the proposed change in rule 3 was an attempted change of regulation, applicable to artificial silks, and that when challenged by the shipper the reasonableness of both presented a question for decision within the exclusive initial jurisdiction of the Interstate Commerce Commission.

Confirmation of this conclusion may be found in *Lake-and-Rail Butter and Egg Rates*, 29 I. C. C. Rep. 45. There carriers on the Great Lakes issued a supplement to their tariffs (as was done here) adding to the list of commodities which would not be accepted for shipment, among other articles, butter, poultry and eggs. This was defended on the ground that such traffic required refrigeration at a cost greater than it would bear. Upon complaint by shippers to the Interstate Commerce Commission that the proposed action was unreasonable, the supplement was promptly suspended and upon full hearing it was held that the refusal to carry such commodities in the past and the attempt to fortify such refusal for the future by filing tariffs declining in terms to receive them, were unduly prejudicial to the traffic involved, and, the request of shippers for such transportation being held reasonable, an order that it be furnished was authorized.

The contention of the carriers, faintly made, that the common law and not the Interstate Commerce Act furnished the measure of their obligation to the public was promptly overruled by the Commission, informed, as it was, by wide experience in traffic affairs and in the administration of the Act.

The importance to the commerce of the country of the exclusive, initial jurisdiction which Congress has committed to the Interstate Commerce Commission need not be repeated and cannot be overstated (*Texas & Pacific R. R. Co.* v. *Abilene Cotton Oil Co.*, 204 U. S. 426; *Baltimore & Ohio R. R. Co.* v. *United States*, 215 U. S. 481; *Morrisdale Coal Company* v. *Pennsylvania R. R. Co.*, 230 U. S. 304; *Minnesota Rate Cases*, 230 U. S. 352; *Texas & Pacific Ry. Co.* v. *American Tie Co.*, 234 U. S. 138, 146; *Pennsylvania R. R. Co.* v. *Clark Coal Co.*, 238 U. S. 456, 469, and *Loomis* v. *Lehigh Valley R. R. Co.*, 240 U. S. 43, 49),and, concluding, as we do, that this case falls plainly within that jurisdiction, the question asked by the Circuit Court of Appeals must be answered in the negative.

Question answered, No.

Dissenting: MR. JUSTICE MCKENNA, MR. JUSTICE VAN DEVANTER, MR. JUSTICE PITNEY and MR. JUSTICE MCREYNOLDS.

---

2. JUDICIAL REVIEW

INTERSTATE COMMERCE COMMISSION *v.* ILLINOIS CENTRAL RAILROAD COMPANY

215 U. S. 452 (1910)

MR. JUSTICE WHITE delivered the opinion of the court.[1]

In consequence of one of the comprehensive amendments to the act to regulate commerce, adopted in 1906, § 15, Act June 29, 1906, c. 3591, 34 Stat. 584, 589, it is now provided that "all orders of the commission, except orders for the payment of money, shall take effect within such reasonable time, not less than thirty days, and shall continue in force for such period of time not exceeding two years, as shall be prescribed in the order of the com-

[1] The facts and remainder of opinion will be found on p. 189, *supra*. — ED.

mission, unless the same shall be suspended or set aside by a court of competent jurisdiction." The statute endowing the commission with large administrative functions, and generally giving effect to its orders concerning complaints before it without exacting that they be previously submitted to judicial authority for sanction, it becomes necessary to determine the extent of the powers which courts may exert on the subject.

Beyond controversy, in determining whether an order of the commission shall be suspended or set aside, we must consider, *a*, all relevant questions of constitutional power or right; *b*, all pertinent questions as to whether the administrative order is within the scope of the delegated authority under which it purports to have been made; and, *c*, a proposition which we state independently, although in its essence it may be contained in the previous one, viz., whether, even although the order be in form within the delegated power, nevertheless it must be treated as not embraced therein, because the exertion of authority which is questioned has been manifested in such an unreasonable manner as to cause it, in truth, to be within the elementary rule that the substance, and not the shadow, determines the validity of the exercise of the power. *Postal Telegraph Cable Company* v. *Adams*, 155 U. S. 688, 698. Plain as it is that the powers just stated are of the essence of judicial authority, and which, therefore, may not be curtailed, and whose discharge may not be by us in a proper case avoided, it is equally plain that such perennial powers lend no support whatever to the proposition that we may, under the guise of exerting judicial power, usurp merely administrative functions by setting aside a lawful administrative order upon our conception as to whether the administrative power has been wisely exercised.

Power to make the order and not the mere expediency or wisdom of having made it, is the question.

CHICAGO, MILWAUKEE & ST. PAUL RAILWAY COMPANY *v.* McCALL-DINSMORE COMPANY

253 U. S. 97 (1920)

Mr. Justice HOLMES delivered the opinion of the court.

This is an action for the loss of grain belonging to the plaintiff and delivered on November 17, 1915, to the defendant, the petitioner, in Montana, for transportation to Omaha, Nebraska. The grain was shipped under the uniform bill of lading, part of the tariffs filed with the Interstate Commerce Commission, by which it was provided that the "amount of any loss or damage for which any carrier is liable shall be computed on the basis of the value of the property at the place and time of shipment under this bill of lading, including freight charges, if paid." The petitioner has paid $1,200.48, being the amount of the loss so computed, but the value of the grain at the place of destination at the time when it should have been delivered, with interest, less freight charges, was $1,422.11. The plaintiff claimed the difference between the two sums on the ground that the Cummins Amendment to the Interstate Commerce Act made the above stipulation void. The District Court gave judgment for the plaintiff, 252 Fed. Rep. 664, and the judgment was affirmed by the Circuit Court of Appeals. 260 Fed. Rep. 835.

The Cummins Amendment, Act of March 4, 1915, c. 176, 38 Stat. 1196, provides that the carriers affected by the Act shall issue a bill of lading and shall be liable to the lawful holder of it "for any loss, damage, or injury to such property . . . and no contract, receipt, rule, regulation, or other limitation of any character whatsoever, shall exempt such common carrier . . . from the liability hereby imposed" and further that the carrier "shall be liable . . . for the full actual loss, damage, or injury . . . notwithstanding any limitation of liability or limitation of the amount of recovery or representation or agreement as to value in any such receipt or bill of lading, or in any contract, rule, regulation, or in any tariff filed with the Interstate Commerce Commission; and any such limitation, without respect to the manner or form in which it is sought to be made is hereby declared to be unlawful and void." Before the passage of this amendment the Interstate Commerce Commission had upheld the clause in the bill of lading as in no way limiting the carriers' liability to less than the value of the goods but merely offering the most convenient way of finding the value. *Shaffer* v. *Chicago, Rock Island & Pacific Ry. Co.*, 21 I. C. C. 8, 12. In a subsequent report upon the amendment it considered that the clause was still valid and not forbidden by the law. 33 I. C. C. 682, 693. The argument for the petitioner suggests that courts are bound by the Commission's determination that the rule is a reasonable one. But the question is of the meaning of a statute and upon that, of course, the courts must decide for themselves.

We appreciate the convenience of the stipulation in the bill of lading and the arguments urged in its favor. We understand that it does not necessarily prevent a recovery of the full actual loss, and that if the price of wheat had gone down the carrier might have had to pay more under this contract than by the common law rule. But the question is how the contract operates upon this case. In this case it does prevent a recovery of the full actual loss, if it is enforced. The rule of the common law is not an arbitrary fiat but an embodiment of the plain fact that the actual loss caused by breach of a contract is the loss of what the contractee would have had if the contract had been performed, less the proper deductions, which have been made and are not in question here. It seems to us, therefore, that the decision below was right, and as, in our opinion, the conclusion is required by the statute, neither the convenience of the clause, nor any argument based upon the history of the statute or upon the policy of the later Act of August 9, 1916, c. 301, 39 Stat. 441, can prevail against what we understand to be the meaning of the words. Those words seem not only to indicate a broad general purpose but to apply specifically to this very case.

Judgment affirmed.

The Chief Justice dissents for the reasons stated by the Interstate Commerce Commission.

INTERSTATE COMMERCE COMMISSION *v.* LOUISVILLE AND NASHVILLE RAILROAD COMPANY

227 U. S. 88 (1913)

Mr. Justice Lamar delivered the opinion of the court.

The New Orleans Board of Trade, in October and November, 1907, brought three separate proceedings against the Louisville & Nashville Railroad, asking the Commerce Commission to set aside as unfair, unreasonable and discriminatory certain class and commodity rates (local) from New Orleans to (1) Mobile, to (2) Pensacola, and (3) through rates, via those cities, to Montgomery, Selma, and Prattville. The Railroad answered. A hearing was had, the issue as to commodity rates was adjusted by agreement, and on December 31, 1909, the Commission made a single order in which it found the class rates complained of to be unreasonable, directed the old locals to be restored and a corresponding reduction made in the through rates. The Railroad thereupon, on January 26, 1910, filed a bill, in the United States Circuit Court for the Western District of Kentucky, praying that the Commission be enjoined from enforcing this order, which it alleged was arbitrary, oppressive and confiscatory, and deprived the company of its property and right to make rates, without due process of law.

After a hearing before three Circuit Court judges, the carrier's application for a temporary injunction was denied (184 Fed. Rep. 118). Testimony was then taken before an Examiner. Later the suit was transferred to the newly organized Commerce Court — the United States being made a party. There, in addition to the evidence in the Circuit Court, the Railroad exhibited all that had been introduced before the Commission, as a basis for the contention that this evidence utterly failed to show that the rates attacked were unreasonable. This view was sustained by the Commerce Court, which, in a lengthy opinion, held (one judge dissenting) that the order was void because there was no material evidence to support it.

On the appeal here, the Government insisted that while the act of 1887 to regulate commerce (24 Stat. 379, c. 104, §§ 14, 15, 16) made the orders of the Commission only *prima facie* correct, a different result followed from the provision in the Hepburn Act of 1906 (34 Stat. 584, c. 3591, § 15) that rates should be set aside if after a hearing the "Commission shall be of the opinion that the charge was unreasonable." In such case it insisted that the order based on such opinion is conclusive, and (though *Int. Com. Comm.* v. *Union Pacific R. R.*, 222 U. S. 541, 547, was to the contrary) could not be set aside, even if the finding was wholly without substantial evidence to support it.

1. But the statute gave the right to a full hearing, and that conferred the privilege of introducing testimony, and at the same time imposed the duty of deciding in accordance with the facts proved. A finding without evidence is arbitrary and baseless. And if the Government's contention is correct, it would mean that the Commission had a power possessed by no other officer, administrative body, or tribunal under our Government. It would mean that where rights depended upon facts, the Commission could disregard all rules of evidence, and capriciously make findings by administrative fiat. Such authority, however beneficently exercised in one case, could be injuriously exerted in

another; is inconsistent with rational justice, and comes under the Constitution's condemnation of all arbitrary exercise of power.

In the comparatively few cases in which such questions have arisen it has been distinctly recognized that administrative orders, quasi-judicial in character, are void if a hearing was denied; if that granted was inadequate or manifestly unfair; if the finding was contrary to the "indisputable character of the evidence." *Tang Tun* v. *Edsell*, 223 U. S. 673, 681; *Chin Yoh* v. *United States*, 208 U. S. 8, 13; *Low Wah Suey* v. *Backus*, 225 U. S. 460, 468; *Zakonaite* v. *Wolf*, 226 U. S. 272; or, if the facts found do not, as a matter of law, support the order made. *United States* v. *B. & O. S. W. R. R.*, 226 U. S. 14. Cf. *Atlantic C. L.* v. *North Carolina Corp. Com.*, 206 U. S. 1, 20; *Wisconsin, M. & P. R. Co.* v. *Jacobson*, 179 U. S. 287, 301; *Oregon Railroad* v. *Fairchild*, 224 U. S. 510; *I. C. C.* v. *Illinois Central*, 215 U. S. 452, 470; *Southern Pacific Co.* v. *Interstate Com. Comm.*, 219 U. S. 433; *Muser* v. *Magone*, 155 U. S. 240, 247.

2. The Government's claim is not only opposed to the ruling in *I. C. C.* v. *Union Pacific*, 222 U. S. 541, 547, and the cases there cited, but is contrary to the terms of the Act to Regulate Commerce, which, in its present form, provides (25 Stat. 861, § 17) for methods of procedure before the Commission that "conduce to justice." The statute, instead of making its orders conclusive against a direct attack, expressly declares that "they may be suspended or set aside by a court of competent jurisdiction." 36 Stat. 539 (15). Of course, that can only be done in cases presenting a justiciable question. But whether the order deprives the carrier of a constitutional or statutory right; whether the hearing was adequate and fair, or whether, for any reason, the order is contrary to law — are all matters within the scope of judicial power.

3. Under the statute the carrier retains the primary right to make rates, but if, after hearing, they are shown to be unreasonable, the Commission may set them aside and require the substitution of just for unjust charges. The Commission's right to act depends upon the existence of this fact, and if there was no evidence to show that the rates were unreasonable, there was no jurisdiction to make the order. *Int. Com. Comm.* v. *Northern Pacific Ry.*, 216 U. S. 538, 544. In a case like the present the courts will not review the Commission's conclusions of fact (*Int. Com. Comm.* v. *Delaware &c. Ry.*, 220 U. S. 235, 251), by passing upon the credibility of witnesses, or conflicts in the testimony.

But the legal effect of evidence is a question of law. A finding without evidence is beyond the power of the Commission. An order based thereon is contrary to law and must, in the language of the statute, "be set aside by a court of competent jurisdiction." 36 Stat. 551.

4. The Government further insists that the Commerce Act (36 Stat. 743) requires the Commission to obtain information necessary to enable it to perform the duties and carry out the objects for which it was created, and having been given legislative power to make rates it can act, as could Congress, on such information, and therefore its findings must be presumed to have been supported by such information, even though not formally proved at the hearing. But such a construction would nullify the right to a hearing, — for manifestly there is no hearing when the party does not know what evidence is offered or considered and is not given an opportunity to test, explain, or refute. The information gathered under the provisions of § 12 may be used as basis for instituting prosecutions for violations of the law, and for many other purposes, but is not available, as such, in cases where the party is entitled to a hearing. The Commission is an administrative body and, even where it acts in a quasi-judicial capacity, is not limited by the strict rules, as to the admissibility of evidence, which prevail in suits between private parties. *Int. Com. Comm.* v. *Baird*, 194 U. S. 25. But the more liberal the practice in admitting testimony, the more imperative the obligation to preserve the essential rules of evidence by which rights are asserted or defended. In such cases the Commissioners cannot act upon their own information as could jurors in primitive days. All parties must be fully apprised of the evidence submitted or to be considered, and must be given opportunity to cross-examine witnesses, to inspect documents and to offer evidence in explanation or rebuttal. In no other way can a party maintain its rights or make its defense. In no other way can it test the sufficiency of the facts to support the finding; for otherwise, even though it appeared that the order was without evidence, the manifest deficiency could always be explained on the theory that the Commission had before it extraneous, unknown but presumptively sufficient information to support the finding. *United States* v. *Baltimore & Ohio S. W. R. R.*, 226 U. S. 14.

As these contentions of the Government must be overruled, it is necessary to examine the record with a view of determining whether there was substantial evidence to support the order.

5. The Louisville & Nashville Railroad ran from New Orleans to Mobile and to Pensacola. From both of these cities it also had lines extending to Montgomery. When the road from Mobile to New Orleans was completed about 1871 there was in operation a boat line carrying freight from the latter city to Mobile and Pensacola. In order to meet this water competition a low rail rate was compelled and was put in force by the rail carrier.

In 1887 the through rate from New Orleans to Montgomery was adjusted so as to conform to an award by Judge Cooley, under which, rates from certain Ohio River points to Montgomery were to be the same, irrespective of any difference in distance. Rates to Montgomery from Kentucky points on the Mississippi were to be two cents lower, and rates to Montgomery from Memphis, Vicksburg and New Orleans were to be two cents lower still. With the exception of a change made necessary by the construction of a short line from Memphis to Birmingham, the class rates in that territory were, as a rule, maintained in conformity with the Cooley award, though, from time to time, commodity rates were made to meet special conditions.

Changes in rates from New Orleans to Mobile, to Pensacola, and from those cities to Montgomery were made in 1907. The carrier insists that the situation at Pensacola was not the same as at Mobile. But the controlling principle is applicable to the rates at all the points involved. And in order to prevent a treble discussion of the three cases the rates from New Orleans to Mobile to Montgomery may be regarded as typical. The increase in Class rates varied from 1 to 13 cents per 100 pounds. The increase in Class 3 was greatest, and it will therefore be taken as affording the best concrete example of the situation before and after the change of 1907.

Under the Cooley award the Tariff on Class 3 had been fixed as follows:

New Orleans to Mobile (local).....25
Mobile to Montgomery (local).....30
Combination of locals............55

But while these locals aggregated only 55 cents, there was, at the same time, a through rate:

New Orleans to Montgomery......68

The carrier's filed tariffs contained a provision that wherever the rates between two points, on its line, was greater than the sum of the locals between the same places the combination of the two locals should be collected. There was nothing to indicate that shipments from New Orleans to Montgomery were not entitled to this Combination rate; but it seems that the privilege was rarely, if ever, granted to New Orleans merchants who, in order to get the advantage of the low locals (25), were obliged to ship to Mobile, there unload, reload and rebill to Montgomery at the 30 cent rate. By this inconvenient method they could secure the 55-cent rate to Montgomery. Otherwise, they paid the rate of 68 cents on the same goods over the same line between the same points.

The carrier was notified that this practice was in violation of the Commission's ruling that, except in special cases, the through rate must not exceed the sum of the locals. An enforcement of this rule would have compelled the carrier to reduce the through rate (68) to the sum of the locals (55), and so, in less proportion, as to all other class rates involved in this case.

The company, however, met the situation by increasing the local, instead of reducing the through rate. For example, the rate on Class 3 from New Orleans to Mobile was raised from 25 to 38, so that, when added to the 30-cent rate from Mobile to Montgomery the Combination 68 equalled the existing through rate of 68 cents from New Orleans to Montgomery. Similar action was taken as to all other rates between New Orleans and Mobile and New Orleans and Pensacola and thence to Montgomery.

At the hearing the facts thus recited were established. The reports of the carrier, showing its earnings and expenses in detail, were in evidence. Its tariffs and those of other railroads were offered, as a basis for comparing the rates under attack with those charged by this and other companies for similar and longer distances. Numerous merchants from New Orleans testified that since the increase of August 13, 1907, they had been unable to sell in Mobile and Pensacola and that the through rate to Montgomery made it impossible to deal in that city. In its report the Commission found that the rates to Mobile, Pensacola and Montgomery from other and more distant points were actually or relatively higher than those for the shorter distance from New Orleans. That the ton-mile rate on the average of the first six classes was greater from New Orleans to Montgomery than from Memphis; that many departures had been made from the Cooley award; that the company's tariff contained a provision that the through rates should not exceed the sum of the locals; that while increasing the local on eastbound freight from New Orleans to Mobile and Pensacola no corresponding increase had been made on the westbound freight from those points to New Orleans; that the old low local out of New Orleans had been so long in force as to create a presumption that it was reasonable and compensatory. It concluded by entering an order adjudging that the rates in the tariff filed August 13, 1907, were unreasonable and directing the carrier to restore the old class rates (local) from New Orleans to Mobile and to Pensacola and to make a corresponding reduction in the through rates from New Orleans to Montgomery, Selma and Prattville.

This order was attacked generally and specially by a bill, which, at length and in minute detail, assailed each specific fact stated in the report on the ground, either that the fact found was without evidence to support it, or that it was irrelevant to the issue involved and furnished no basis whatever for the order which followed.

The Commerce Court rendered a lengthy and elaborate opinion in which it reviewed all of the matters referred to in the Commission's Report and held that the findings were irrelevant, or without evidence to support them, or contrary to the uncontradicted testimony; that the fact that rates from more distant points to Montgomery, Pensacola and Mobile were actually or relatively lower than from New Orleans to the same points, furnished no basis for the order, unless it was shown that the conditions were similar while it affirmatively appeared that these lower rates were compelled by water competition; that no conclusion could be drawn from the fact that such rates to Montgomery from other points were lower on the ton-mile basis, in view of the universal rule that the longer the haul the lower the rate. That the departures from the Cooley award related only to commodity rates, which were not involved in this hearing, and that the complaints of the merchants as to inability to sell in Mobile, Pensacola and Montgomery were referable only to Commodity rates and not to Class rates. It found that no legal inference could be drawn from the fact that the low locals had been maintained on westbound shipments after the carrier, on August 13, 1907, raised the locals on eastbound shipments from New Orleans to Mobile and Pensacola, inasmuch as there is no legal objection to having lower rates in one direction than in another. It found that the sole ground for making the order was the fact that the carrier had raised rates after they had been in force for more than twenty years; although the presumption of reasonableness disappeared in view of the uncontradicted testimony that the old rates had been compelled by water competition.

6. It is unnecessary in this case to review each of the matters discussed, ruled and found by the Commission in its Report and only the more salient facts will be mentioned. For the validity of the order does not necessarily depend upon the correctness of each of these findings, so that the breaking of one or many links by disproof would destroy the chain upon which the order depended. These findings are collateral and if correct might be confirmatory of the ruling, which, however, might still be sustained if some of these statements were eliminated. The question is whether there was substantial evidence to support the order.

7. The pleadings charged that the new rates were unjust in themselves and by comparison with others. This was denied by the carrier. The Commission considered evidence and made findings relating to rates which the carrier insists had been compelled by competition, and were not a proper standard by which to measure those here involved. The value of such evidence necessarily varies according to circumstances, but the weight to be given it is peculiarly for the body experienced in such matters and familiar with the complexities, intricacies and history of rate-making in each section of the country. So, too, the fact that a Commodity rate is low may cast some light on the reasonableness of the higher rate on the Class, from which that Commodity was taken or to which it might legally be restored.

It is true that the old low locals, Mobile (west) to New Orleans were maintained, while those from New Orleans (east) to Mobile were raised is not conclusive against the reasonableness of new tariff put in force in 1907. But it was a fact tending to support the conclusion unless the difference was shown to have been warranted by proper rate-making rules. Of the sufficiency of the explanation, including the extent of the difference in empty car movement, the Commission was authorized to judge. It also had before it the company's financial statement and general tariff sheets. Against which was the testimony for the carrier, tending to prove that the rate to New Orleans was low in fact, and by comparison with those in force over other parts of the carrier's system, and on other lines in the same territory, even though this particular part of the road ran through a sparsely settled country, with expensive trestles and bridges, frequently damaged by storms from the Gulf and expensive to maintain.

8. But these facts did not stand alone. It appeared that for

many years prior to 1907 the carrier had maintained low locals from New Orleans to Mobile and Pensacola. When first put in force they were abnormally low because compelled by water competition, and therefore furnish no just standard of reasonableness. And if when that competition disappeared the rates had been advanced, no inference adverse to the railroad could have been drawn from the increase. *Int. Com. Comm.* v. *Chicago G. W. Ry.*, 209 U. S. 108. The answer of the Railroad Company admits that this water competition had ceased to exist. The date is not definitely stated, but it is fairly inferable that the water competition was not potential for some years before the increase in rates in 1907. When made, the increase was not because of the absence of water competition, but to make the sum of the locals correspond with the through rates. Under the circumstances the maintenance of these low rates, after the water competition disappeared, tends to support the theory that by an increase of business or other cause they had become reasonable and compensatory.

9. From the appellee's standpoint, probably a principal objection to the order complained of, is that it will upset the Cooley award, under which rates have been adjusted throughout a large section. But that, too, was a matter for consideration by the Commission which by this order has not lost power to restore the old rates, or to make changes in the new if it shall be found that those put in force, unjustly discriminate in favor of New Orleans against other cities.

The order of the Commission, restoring a local rate that had been in force for many years, and making a corresponding reduction in the through rate, was not arbitrary but sustained by substantial, though conflicting evidence. The courts cannot settle the conflict nor put their judgment against that of the rate-making body, and the decree is

Reversed.

SPILLER *v.* ATCHINSON, TOPEKA AND SANTA FE RAILWAY COMPANY ET AL

253 U. S. 117 (1920)

Mr. Justice Pitney delivered the opinion of the court.

Plaintiff in error commenced an action against defendants in error jointly in the District Court of the United States for the

Western District of Missouri under section 16 of the Act to Regulate Commerce as amended (Act of February 4, 1887, Ch. 104, 24 Stat. 379, 384; June 29, 1906, Ch. 3591, 34 Stat. 584, 590; June 18, 1910, Ch. 309, 36 Stat. 539, 554), to recover certain amounts awarded to him against them respectively in a reparation order made by the Interstate Commerce Commission January 12, 1914. His petition contained also a count setting up a conspiracy between defendants for the restraint of interstate commerce, and claiming treble damages under section 7 of the Sherman Antitrust Act of July 2, 1890 (Ch. 647, 26 Stat. 209, 210); but this was abandoned at the trial. Defendants having filed separate answers, a jury was waived by stipulation, and a test case tried before the court — all defendants participating — with the result that a decision was rendered in favor of plaintiff, pursuant to which a combined judgment was entered, amounting in effect to as many judgments as there were defendants, each for the amount of the Commission's award against the particular defendant with interest and attorneys' fees. Defendants sued out separate writs of error from the Circuit Court of Appeals, where, by stipulation, the cases were heard together upon a single record. That court reversed the judgments, ordered the cause remanded to the District Court with directions to grant a new trial (246 Fed. Rep. 1), and refused an application for a rehearing (249 Fed. Rep. 677). Writs of error were prayed for and allowed for the review of the judgments of reversal in this court; and afterwards but in due season a petition for the allowance of a writ of certiorari was filed, the consideration of which was postponed to the hearing under the writs of error.

The jurisdiction of the District Court having been invoked not because of diversity of citizenship but because the suit was one arising under laws of the United States other than those particularly mentioned in sec. 128, Judicial Code, as amended (Act of January 28, 1915, Ch. 22, sec. 2; 38 Stat. 803), it follows that the judgments were not made "final" by the section referred to, and, if final in the sense of concluding the litigation, would be reviewable in this court by writ of error pursuant to sec. 241, Judicial Code, in each case where the matter in controversy exceeds one thousand dollars besides costs. In the cases of the Chicago & Alton and the Missouri Pacific Companies, the respective judgments with interest up to the issuance of the writs of error from this court were materially less than one thousand dollars; in each of the other cases substantially in excess of that amount; the aggregate of the judgments being more than $150,000. For want of a sufficient amount in controversy the two smaller judgments would not be reviewable here by writ of error even were they final in effect; but all the writs of error must be dismissed because the judgments call for further proceedings in the trial court; it being elementary that this writ will lie to review final judgments only. *McLish* v. *Roff*, 141 U. S. 661, 665; *Luxton* v. *North River Bridge Co.*, 147 U. S. 337, 341; *Heike* v. *United States*, 217 U. S. 423, 429.

However, upon consideration of the particular circumstances of the case, we have concluded that a writ of certiorari ought to be allowed, without further protracting the litigation to the extent that would be necessary in order to reach final judgments; the transcript of the record and proceedings returned in obedience to the writs of error to stand as the return to the writ of certiorari. This writ is allowable by virtue of section 240, Judicial Code, (derived from sec. 6 of the Act of March 3, 1891, Ch. 517, 26 Stat. 826, 828) in the case of the two smaller judgments, because the decision of the Circuit Court of Appeals is made final by the combined effect of sections 128 and 241; and in the case of the larger judgments it is allowable under section 262 of the Code (sec. 716, Revised Stat. U. S.), in aid of the ultimate jurisdiction of this court to review those cases by writs of error. *Lau Ow Bew* v. *United States*, 144 U. S. 47, 58; *In Re Chetwood, Petnr.*, 165 U. S. 443, 462; *Whitney* v. *Vick*, 202 U. S. 132, 135; *McClellan* v. *Carland*, 217 U. S. 268, 277, *et seq.*; *United States* v. *Beatty*, 232 U. S. 463, 467; *Meeker* v. *Lehigh Valley R. R. Co.*, 234 U. S. 749; 236 U. S. 412, 417.

Coming to the merits: The ground upon which the Circuit Court of Appeals reversed the judgments, and the ground principally relied upon to sustain its decision, was the refusal by the trial court of a motion made by defendants to hold: (*a*) That upon all the evidence plaintiff was not entitled to recover against any or all of the defendants; and (*b*) that there was not sufficient evidence before the Commission to sustain its order of reparation. The latter is the substantial question actually presented.

The course of proceedings at the trial, as appears from the bill of exceptions, was as follows: Plaintiff introduced the report of the Interstate Commerce Commission (unreported opinion No. A-583 in case No. 732, *Cattle Raisers' Association of Texas* v. *Missouri, Kansas & Texas Railway Co.*, dated January 12, 1914), and the order of reparation made pursuant to it and upon which the action was based. Defendants having admitted the service of the order, and that the money awarded had not been paid, plaintiff rested. The report makes an award in favor of Spiller, plaintiff in error, as assignee of a large number of claims for reparation by reason of excessive rates charged by the respective carriers on interstate shipments of cattle from points of origin in Texas, Oklahoma, New Mexico, Colorado, and Kansas, to destinations at Kansas City, St. Louis, Chicago, St. Joseph, and New Orleans, on various dates between August 29, 1906, and November 17, 1908; and a further award to named shippers in the case of certain unassigned claims pertaining to similar shipments; the several claims, assigned and unassigned, with distinguishing marks, being set forth in Appendix A, showing the delivering carriers against which the claims were allowed and, in each case, the consignor, points of origin and destination, number of cars shipped, weight, rate paid, the lower rate sanctioned by the Commission, amount of refund required, and the interest thereon. The report contains appropriate findings adequate to support the award, among them the following: That the persons named in Appendix A as consignors shipped from the points of origin to the points of destination specified, by the line of road named as the "delivering road," the number of cars and of the aggregate net weight stated; that the shippers paid to the delivering carriers freight upon the shipments at certain rates named; that in each instance this rate was unreasonable and excessive, and a reasonable rate to have been charged would have been the lower rate specified as having been subsequently established by the Commission, and that therefore the delivering carriers collected from the shippers unreasonable charges on account of the shipments in amounts named in the column headed "Amount of Refund"; that the shipments of live stock were in all cases consigned to some person at the delivering market, usually a commission firm; that the freight was paid in the first instance by the "consignor" (evidently a misprint for "consignee") to the delivering carrier, and subsequently the cattle were sold upon the market and the amount of the freight deducted from the purchase price, remittance being made for the balance, so that in all cases the owner and shipper of the cattle finally paid the transportation charges; and that by the unreasonable exactions of the carriers the shippers were damaged in the amounts stated in the appropriate column of Appendix A, since they received for the cattle less by those amounts than they would have received had the rate found reasonable been charged; that in the case of some of the claims the shippers made assignments to H. E. Crowley, then being secretary of the Cattle Raisers' Association, in a form set forth in the report; that subsequently Crowley ceased to be such secretary, and was succeeded by Spiller, the plaintiff, to whom Crowley assigned all claims previously assigned to him; and that other specified claims were assigned by the shippers to Spiller after he became secretary, the form of assignment being the same as that previously employed.

Defendants, endeavoring to show the insufficiency of the evidence upon which the findings and order of the Commission were based, introduced a transcript of the stenographer's notes of the testimony taken upon the hearing of the reparation claims; following this by introducing a sample page taken from one of the exhibits introduced before the Commission as illustrative of the form of exhibits there introduced. After other evidence not necessary to be mentioned, and a request for judgment in favor of defendants, and for certain rulings on points of law that would have produced that result, all of which were refused, the case was closed.

It appears that in February, 1904, the Cattle Raisers' Association of Texas, in behalf of its members and of others interested, petitioned the Interstate Commerce Commission under section 13 of the Commerce Act, alleging the rates in force in the territory in question to be unjust and unreasonable, they having been advanced some time before to the extent (in most cases) of 3 cents per hundred pounds. On August 16, 1905, the Commission held (*Cattle Raisers' Association of Texas* v. *Missouri, Kansas & Texas Ry. Co.*, 11 I. C. C. 296, 352) that the then existing rates were unjust and unreasonable by the amount of the advance. At this time the Commission was not empowered to fix rates for the future. This power having been conferred by the Hepburn Act of June 28, 1906 (Ch. 3591, 34 Stat. 584, 589), which, by Joint Resolution of June 30, (34 Stat. 838), took effect sixty days after its approval by the President, or on August 28, 1906, the Cattle Raisers' Association immediately thereafter applied for and obtained a reopening of the matter, to the end that reasonable rates might be established; and on April 14, 1908, the Commission decided that the former rates should be restored, but that reparation would not be allowed upon claims accruing prior to August 29, 1906 (date of the application). 13 I. C. C. 418, 435. The reduced rates finally were put into effect November 17, 1908.

The reparation claims in controversy appear to have been filed in due season by the Cattle Raisers' Association in behalf of its members and other shippers interested, and in the names of the alleged owners of the cattle shipped.

The transcript of the testimony taken by the Commission, as introduced in evidence in the District Court, forms the basis of the decision of the Circuit Court of Appeals that the reparation order was unsupported by evidence. But the transcript shows that important documentary evidence was introduced, and furnished the principal foundation for the findings made. This documentary evidence (except the single sheet offered for purposes of illustration) was not introduced in the District Court, in order, as stated by counsel, to "avoid introducing a number of papers that would almost fill a farm wagon." But obviously we hardly could sustain a decision rejecting the reparation order upon the ground that there was not sufficient evidence before the Commission to support it when the whole of the evidence that was before the Commission was not produced.

That this is a matter of substance will appear from a review of the course of the proceeding as disclosed by the stenographer's transcript. The evidence was taken by Mr. Commissioner Prouty at Chicago; there being three sessions, the first on September 19 and 20, 1912, the second on January 24 and the third on October 17 in the following year. They were held in the presence of counsel for the Cattle Raisers' Association, who appeared for the claimants, and counsel for the several carriers interested. If we were called upon to review the proceeding as upon a writ of error or appeal it might be difficult to say that no improper evidence was admitted, that production of the best available was insisted upon, or that a different conclusion might not have been reached upon that which was admitted. But the scope of the judicial review is not so extensive. Section 13 of the Act to Regulate Commerce (Act of February 4, 1887, Ch. 104; 24 Stat. 379, 383; amended June 18, 1910, Ch. 309; 36 Stat. 539, 550) requires the Commission on receipt of a claim for reparation to proceed on notice to the carrier to "investigate the matters complained of in such manner and by such means as it shall deem proper"; and by section 16 (34 Stat. 590; 36 Stat. 554), if, after such hearing, the Commission shall determine that any party complainant is entitled to an award of damages, the Commission is to make an order of reparation accordingly, and in a suit based thereon the "findings and order of the Commission shall be *prima facie* evidence of the facts therein stated." The same section contemplates that numerous parties may unite in a claim for reparation, and that numerous carriers may be joined as defendants; and similarly that in a suit brought upon such award there may be a joinder of parties plaintiff and defendant. And, by sec. 17 (24 Stat. 385; 25 Stat. 861), "the Commission may conduct its proceedings in such manner as will best conduce to the proper dispatch of business and to the ends of justice."

These provisions allow a large degree of latitude in the investigation of claims for reparation, and the resulting findings and order of the Commission may not be rejected as evidence because of any errors in its procedure not amounting to a denial of the right to a fair hearing, so long as the essential facts found are based upon substantial evidence.

In the present case, the hearing was informal, but not to the extent of sacrificing essential rights of parties; and it cannot be characterized as arbitrary or unfair. Many carriers were interested, and they were represented by counsel. Thousands of carload shipments were in question, but the points in real controversy were few, and there was a natural desire on all sides to expedite the hearing. In the main, counsel for the carriers coöperated in facilitating the investigation. It was not in dispute that all shipments under inquiry were made during a period when the tariff rates were under investigation, and that afterwards those rates were determined by the Commission to have been excessive. It appeared that itemized claims for reparation had been made out in duplicate (one copy of each being filed), in the names of the parties alleged to have made shipments of cattle as owners during the period in question, that these were based in most cases upon data furnished by the commission houses at the several points of destination, as taken from their books, in other cases by the shippers themselves, and that they were computed by applying the excess charges, as determined, to the actual weights of the shipments where known, in other cases to the minimum carload weights. There was evidence that few of the cattle shippers kept books, they relying upon the commission companies to do this, and that such companies were the consignees of the cattle, and made it a practice on receiving a shipment to pay the freight, sell the cattle, and remit the proceeds to the owner after deducting the freight paid and other charges. During the hearing, there was drawn off from the claims as made up and filed a summary for each carrier, purporting to show the consignor, consignee, originating road, point of origin, destination, date of delivery, number of cars moved, rate paid, rate established by the Commission, and the overcharge claimed. These were submitted to the several carriers for investigation by their accounting officers, and some months later were reported back to Commissioner Prouty by their counsel with the results of such investigation, which in a majority of instances verified the statements said to have been deduced from the records of the commission houses. In some cases, in addition to check-marks, "O. K." and other marks indicating that the items had been found correct, waybill references, car numbers, initials, etc., had been inserted, and where it had been found impossible to locate a shipment there were comments tending to add support to the verification of those that were located. No reparation was awarded by the Commission except with respect to such shipments as were acknowledged in the reports of the defendants to have moved as stated. These reports were introduced in evidence before Commissioner Prouty, but, as already shown, were not in evidence before the District Court. What we have said as to their contents is gathered from the stenographer's transcript; what else may have appeared upon their face, in the nature of admissions is left to be inferred. Counsel for some of the carriers undertook to qualify the effect of admissions contained in them, as by saying that the checking meant no more than that a particular car moved as stated, and that the carrier collected the amount of freight specified; that it was not intended to admit that remittance was made to the person named as claimant; that the statements were subject to confirmation by the books of the commission merchants, or the like. But the Commission was justified in according to the reports of the checking an evidential effect not limited by the qualifying statements, treating the latter as merely argumentative. It might regard the fact that the shipments could be and were identified from the records of the carriers, in the manner described, as evidence that the details respecting the shippers of the cattle and the particulars of the shipments were true, might take the movement and delivery of the freight thus acknowledged as evidence that the delivering carrier collected the freight charges according to the published tariffs, which of course included the overcharges; and might take this, in connection with the evidence as to the course of business, as showing that the shippers whose names were mentioned in the statements sustained damages to the extent of the excessive charge as determined by the Commission. The minutes show that until near the conclusion of the hearing it was the intention to appoint an examiner to investigate the books of the commission merchants at the various points of destination in order to verify the details of the several shipments, and that this purpose was abandoned in view of the admissions made by the carriers. Perhaps it ought to have been carried out; but the court was not justified in treating the report of the Commission as a nullity for this reason, if there was substantial evidence of the essential facts without such verification. We think that what we have detailed of the course of the hearing, taken in connection with what we know and what may be presumed as to the contents of the unproduced documentary evidence, shows there was substantial evidence that the owners specified in the claims had been subjected to the excessive charges with respect to the shipments acknowledged by the carriers; and, as already remarked, the award of reparation was confined to these shipments.

The opinion of the Circuit Court of Appeals severely criticizes the evidence on which these conclusions were based, characterizing it as hearsay. It is not to be disputed that much of the evidence, — including essential parts of it — is properly so characterized. The only witness sworn was Mr. Williams, assistant secretary of the Cattle Raisers' Association, who had gathered the data upon which the claims were based, obtaining it mostly from commission merchants, in some instances from the cattle shippers. He had prepared the claims, had spent much time and pains in investigating them, and in the course of his duties had visited several of the points of destination and examined the books and records of the commission merchants to ascertain the method in which their business was conducted and records kept. It was he who testified as to the customary course of business of cattle shippers and commission merchants. He had been connected with the Cattle Raisers' Association for about eight years, and might be presumed to have some general familiarity with the business in addition to that gained in the special study he had made of it while investigating the claims. His explanation of the method of business and the details of the claims was accepted, and accepted without objection, very much as the testimony of an expert witness might have been accepted. Whether he had shown such special knowledge as to qualify him to testify as an expert was for the Interstate Commerce Commission to determine; and its decision thereon is not to be set aside by the courts unless clearly shown to have been unfounded, which cannot be said in this case. *Stillwell Mfg. Co.* v. *Phelps*, 130 U. S. 520, 527; *Montana Ry. Co.* v. *Warren*, 137 U. S. 348, 353.

The evidence was not objected as hearsay when introduced, nor, indeed, at any time during the hearing before the Commission. Counsel did in some instances assert that there was a failure of proof and suggest that the proceeding ought to be dismissed. But the objections came too late, and were too general in character, to be equivalent to an objection to the reception of the evidence because hearsay. Even in a court of law, if evidence of this kind is admitted without objection, it is to be considered, and accorded its natural probative effect, as if it were in law admissible. *Diaz* v. *United States*, 223 U. S. 442, 450; *Rowland* v. *St. Louis & S. F. R. R. Co.*, 244 U. S. 106, 108; *Damon* v. *Carrol*, 163 Mass. 404, 408. And it is clear that the verification of the details of the claims by the carriers after full investigation by their auditing departments constituted primary evidence against them, and went far towards showing that the facts as disclosed by the hearsay evidence might be depended upon.

We are not here called upon to consider whether the Commission may receive and act upon hearsay evidence seasonably objected to as hearsay; but we do hold that in this case, where such evidence was introduced without objection and was substantially corroborated by original evidence clearly admissible against the parties to be affected, the Commission is not to be regarded as having acted arbitrarily, nor may its findings and order be rejected as wanting in support, simply because the hearsay evidence was considered with the rest.

In *Interstate Com. Comm.* v. *Baird*, 194 U. S. 25, 44, it was said: "The inquiry of a board of the character of the Interstate Commerce Commission should not be too narrowly constrained by technical rules as to the admissibility of proof. Its function is largely one of investigation and it should not be hampered in making inquiry pertaining to interstate commerce by those narrow rules which prevail in trials at common law where a strict correspondence is required between allegation and proof." In *Interstate Com. Comm.* v. *Louis. & Nash. R. R.* 227 U. S. 88, 93, the court recognized that "The commission is an administrative body and, even where it acts in a quasi-judicial capacity, is not limited by the strict rules, as to the admissibility of evidence, which prevail in suits between private parties." And the fact that a reparation order has at most only the effect of *prima facie* evidence (*Meeker & Co.* v. *Lehigh Valley R. R.*, 236 U. S. 412, 430; *Meeker* v. *Lehigh Valley R. R.*, 236 U. S. 434, 439; *Mills* v. *Lehigh Valley R. R.*, 238 U. S. 473, 482), being open to contradiction by the carrier when sued for recovery of the amount awarded, is an added reason for not binding down the Commission too closely in respect of the character of the evidence it may receive or the manner in which its hearings shall be conducted.

In this case the Commission did not act upon evidence of which the carriers were not cognizant and to which they had no opportunity to reply, as in the case supposed in *Interstate Com. Comm.* v. *Louis. & Nash. R. R.*, 227 U. S. 88, 91, 93. All the carriers participated in the hearing, and had full opportunity to object, to cross-examine, and to introduce evidence on their own part.

It results that the judgments of the Circuit Court of Appeals must be reversed, and those of the District Court affirmed.

Writs of error dismissed.

Writs of certiorari allowed.

Judgments of Circuit Court of Appeals reversed, and judgments of District Court affirmed.

FLORIDA EAST COAST RAILWAY COMPANY *v.* UNITED STATES

234 U. S. 167 (1914)

Mr. Chief Justice White delivered the opinion of the court.

The order of the Interstate Commerce Commission concerning which the appellant, hereafter called the East Coast Line, complained before the court below and which that court refused to enjoin was made on a second supplemental petition presented in controversies which had been long pending and twice before decided, such controversies involving many railroads and being concerned with the rates as to pineapples, citrus fruits and vegetables from places of production in Florida to exterior points of distribution or consumption. While the report here under consideration made on the second supplemental petition deals with only a few of the railroads concerned in the previous inquiries and with only a part of the controversies involved in the previous cases, yet the reports in the previous cases and the reasons stated by the Commission for its action in those cases are so connected with its action complained of in this case that it is impossible to understand this controversy without recurring to and stating the previous reports of the Commission in the controversies to which we have referred.

We observe before coming to make that statement that none of the testimony taken before the Commission in the cases prior to this one is in the record, it having been stipulated that the facts stated by the Commission in its reports in such previous cases should be taken as the facts of such controversies. For the purpose of the statement which we shall make the record therefore consists of the reports in such previous cases, of the report in this case and the testimony taken in this case before the Commission and in the court below. The future application of the facts which we shall state will be facilitated by giving a description of the East Coast Line as stated in the several reports of the Commission to which we shall immediately recur.

The East Coast Line is wholly within the State of Florida, the main line extending from Jacksonville south along the Atlantic coast to Miami, a distance of 366 miles, then to Homestead, 28 miles south, and thence across the Florida Keys to Key West. At the time of the final hearing before the Commission on March 2, 1911, the road was not fully constructed and was only completed and being operated to Knight's Key, about 83 miles below Homestead. The total mileage of the road was about 583 miles, including 477 miles of main line from Jacksonville to Knight's Key and about 106 miles of branch line above Miami. The cost of the construction from Homestead on was enormous, amounting to nearly $175,000 per mile, and the total cost of the extension from Homestead to Knight's Key, 83 miles, nearly equalled the entire cost of the balance of the road, 500 miles. On July 3, 1907, a petition was filed by the Florida Fruit & Vegetable Shippers' Protective Association against the Atlantic Coast Line, the Seaboard Air Line and Southern Railway Companies and the East Coast Line complaining of and asking a reduction in interstate rates on pineapples, citrus fruits and vegetables. The East Coast Line was the only one of the defendant railroads whose traffic was confined to the producing regions in Florida because while the other lines also undoubtedly penetrated to the area of production, their lines were not confined to Florida but were trunk lines carrying not only the product committed to them by producers in Florida, but also the products committed by producers to roads like the East Coast Line which did not extend beyond Florida and had therefore to be transshipped if destined to points beyond the State by other roads. In coming to make its report in the case thus referred to, the Commission thus stated the general situation of the railroad traffic of all the roads in Florida concerning the subjects under discussion (No 1168, 14 I. C. C. 483):

"The shape and location of the state of Florida is such that these railroads which handle this traffic from the point of production up to the base point necessarily do but a limited business. They extend south considerable distances through a sparsely settled country which neither originates nor consumes a considerable amount of traffic. Some of them reach the seacoast, but none of them connect or can connect with railroads leading beyond, and the amount of through business handled is extremely light. Their traffic is confined almost entirely to bringing out the products which originate upon their lines, and carrying in the supplies which are consumed in the territory served by them. Fruits and vegetables, lumber, naval stores, and in some cases cotton and phosphate rock are the principal commodities carried, and of these, fruits and vegetables produce the most revenue."

In the report by which the Commission disposed of this controversy (No. 1168, 14 I. C. C. 476) it divided the rates to be considered into two classes: (*a*) gathering charges from production points in Florida to base points of which Jacksonville was the only one on the East Coast Line, and (*b*) rates from base points to points of final destination in other States, the sum of the two rates being the joint through rate.

Considering the three products whose traffic charges were under consideration, the Commission said:

(*a*) Citrus fruits:

"From an examination of the elaborate figures which were introduced upon the trial showing the character of the traffic handled by these Florida roads, the conditions under which it is handled, their earnings, and the cost of operation running through a series of years, it is difficult to see how these railroads can be expected to transport in a suitable way this fruit and vegetable traffic from points of production to these basing points for a less sum than they now receive. It is difficult to see how, even upon the present traffic, those lines can in the immediate future expect to pay any considerable return upon their investment. We feel that these local rates, although they are high in comparison with other local rates, are as low as should be established under all the circumstances." (p. 484.)

(*b*) Vegetables:

"The same observations which have been made upon the orange rates to base points apply with equal pertinency to those upon vegetables. They are named by the railroad commission of Florida. They are made with the understanding that they are really parts of through rates from the point of production to the market of consumption. They are low in comparison with other rates because it is understood that this industry is an important one to the State of Florida, and that a low cost of transportation is essential to its development.

"While these local rates are essentially part of the through charge and should be dealt with by this Commission as such, it is difficult to see how these Florida railroads can render a proper service upon a lower scale of rates than is now applied. It must be remembered that without the railroad this industry could not exist at all, and that to its satisfactory carrying on the character of the service is fully as important as the rate: It is better that these fruits and vegetables should reach the market on time, and in good condition, than that a few cents per box should be subtracted from the carrying charge. There was very little complaint as to the service; nor did the shippers who testified manifest any desire that these carriers should be required to accept less than reasonable compensation for that service. Our conclusion upon this branch of the case is that the present rates up to the base points, while high in comparison with similar rates in other localities are as low as they ought to be under the conditions obtaining upon these Florida lines, so that here, as in case of oranges, the real question arises upon the rate from the base point to the northern market." (p. 496.)

(*c*) Pineapples:

"Pineapples are mainly produced in Florida, upon the line of the Florida East Coast Railway, which extends, as already said, down the east side of Florida. This industry has within recent years developed rapidly. Florida pineapples today sell in all the markets of the United States in competition with foreign pineapples, usually commanding much higher prices than the foreign article. While the period of production in the United States and in Cuba is not exactly the same, still it may fairly be said that the two products do compete.

"It was said that Jansen might be selected as a typical producing point upon the Florida East Coast Railway. This station is 257 miles south of Jacksonville and the rate on pineapples is 24 cents per box of 80 pounds. Rates from other points are relatively about the same as from Jansen; somewhat lower, it will be seen for the same distance, than from most producing points upon oranges." (p. 502.)

Presumably, deeming that the particular situation on the East Coast Line as to the character of its business, its location, its cost, etc., etc., required to be specially pointed out in addition to what was said in the passages quoted, the Commission said:

"The Florida East Coast Railway was built as part of a hotel scheme, and its principal business is the carrying of passengers who frequent these Florida winter resorts. Over 50 per cent of its total receipts are from passenger traffic. Its most important freight business is the transportation of fruits and vegetables, and of these pineapples afford the most considerable amount of revenue. The management of the railroad has paid great attention to the development of this business. In the pineapple region highways are few and transportation by wagon is therefore costly. To relieve this difficulty sidings have been put in the pineapple region at frequent intervals. The traffic representative of this railroad stated that it was possible to load pineapples every half mile upon his line in the pineapple-producing region. When once loaded great attention is paid to sending the fruit to Jacksonville upon a reliable and expeditious schedule.

"Very elaborate tables were introduced showing the cost of constructing this railroad and the financial results of its past operations. These statements and tables have been examined by the Commission, but it does not seem necessary to reproduce them here or to state in detail the grounds of our conclusions. But for this railroad the pineapple industry in Florida would not today exist. The quality of the service rendered that industry by this road is not criticised. The shippers of this fruit ought not to object, nor do they object to paying a fair compensation for the service, and in our opinion the present rates do not exceed such just compensation for the transportation of pineapples from various producing points to Jacksonville, and we so hold." (p. 503.)

And concerning the earnings of the East Coast Line, it was said:

"The total earnings of the Florida East Coast Railway for the same year (ending June 30, 1907) were $5,911 per mile, and its operating expenses $4,502. The greater part of the receipts of this railroad are from its passenger service. The evidence shows that a considerable portion of what little freight revenue it has comes from the transportation of fruits and vegetables. It has given in the past great attention to this service, and has apparently satisfied its patrons in this respect. It makes no through rates, but receives its full local in all cases up to Jacksonville." (p. 484.)

Giving effect to the foregoing, the Commission held that the complaint as to gathering charges was wholly unfounded, and they were maintained. A different conclusion, however, was reached as to charges from the base points to points of distribution or consumption, as to which some reduction was made. It consequently follows that all the other roads who were defendants were subjected to some reduction as to their rates, while the East Coast Line because of its being a purely gathering road was subjected to no reduction whatever.

Within a year after this action by the Commission the same complainant commenced a new proceeding (No. 2566) against two hundred railroads, including among others the East Coast Line, to establish carload rates from base points in Florida to interstate points. At the same time in No. 1168, which as we have seen had been previously passed upon by the Commission and decided in favor of the East Coast Line, a supplemental petition was filed against that road, the sole complaint against the East Coast Line in such petitions being as to its gathering rates on pineapples from points of production to Jacksonville. And it is to be presumed that the complaint as to pineapple-gathering rates was made only against the East Coast Line because as we have seen, as stated by the Commission, that road was almost the exclusive carrier of such product, and in fact had virtually built up that industry. The controversy while it involved a claim of reduction, in its broad aspect presented only a controversy as to whether there should be put in force carload and less-than-carload instead of any-quantity rates in the performance of its duty of gathering pineapples. On the filing of the new and original as well as of the supplemental petition the Commission directed the rescinding of its previous order concerning the reasonableness of gathering rates, as well as its finding on the subject of rates from base points and directed the matter to be reheard. Without referring to the conclusion of the Commission concerning the controversy as to the many railroads who were before it as to their interstate rates, we come to state the ruling of the Commission as to the East Coast Line (17 I. C. C. 552, 564):

"The evidence produced upon the present hearing suggests no change in what was said so far as that applies to the Florida East Coast Railway. That line operates at the present time 477 miles of main line and 106 miles of branches. It has a first mortgage of $10,000,000, a second mortgage of $20,000,000, and a capital stock of $3,000,000, making in all $33,000,000. This capitalization, with the exception of about $4,000,000, represents an actual cash investment.

"It is urged by the complainant that the portion of the line from Miami south, which has cost some $14,000,000, was not at the present time a paying investment and that the balance of the line from Jacksonville to Miami, which is used by the growers of pineapples, ought not to be taxed with the cost of this construction. Admitting this to be so, and laying out of view altogether the $14,000,000 which have been invested in that part of the property, it is still true that during the entire existence of the Florida East Coast Railway, so far as this record shows, that property has never earned in any single year 6 per cent upon the money invested, with the single exception of the year 1909. During much of the time its net earnings have been but little above its operating expenses. We certainly cannot hold that these rates should be reduced because for a single twelve months, under what may be termed abnormal conditions, this railway earned about 6 per cent on the money which has been actually invested in its construction. The years when no return has been received must certainly be given some consideration. Upon no other theory could private capital be induced to invest in the construction of railroads.

"While, however, we adhere to what was said in the previous case, we do think, upon more careful examination, that these rates of the Florida East Coast Railway on pineapples ought to be somewhat revised. They are not consistent with one another, and in our opinion those from the more distant points are too high as compared with rates from nearby points.

"The present rates are in any quantity. About 60 per cent of these pineapples move from the point of origin in carloads, 40 per cent in less than carloads. Carload shipments are stripped and loaded by the shipper and are not unloaded at Jacksonville, which probably saves the carrier not far from 2 cents per box. The less-than-carload shipment is loaded by the railway and usually unloaded at the station in South Jacksonville or Jacksonville. In our opinion carload rates should be established which are less than the present any-quantity rates by 3 cents per box.

"The establishment of such carload rates will not of a certainty work a decrease in the net earnings of the carriers. It is a false theory of transportation which seeks to force the shipper to avail himself of a less-than-carload service, which is more expensive to render, for the purpose of increasing the gross revenues of the carrier. The true object should be to perform the service in the most economical manner and to charge for that service reasonable compensation. In the end this makes to the advantage of both the carrier and its patron. The vice-president of the Florida East Coast Railway stated that he had always thought that carload rates should be established and that in his opinion to establish carload rates 3 cents per box less than the present any-quantity rates would not prejudice the net revenues of his company, since he would make up by saving in operating expenses what he lost in gross income."

The order of the Commission which gave effect to these views entered February 8, 1910, changed gathering charges on pineapples and citrus fruits on the East Coast Line from any-quantity to carload and less-than-carload rates and modified the mileage basis. On attention being directed to the fact that the complaint related only to pineapples, while the order applied to that product and to citrus fruits, the order was modified and restricted to the subject complained of, pineapples. The East Coast Line conformed to the order and indeed shortly after doing so also voluntarily put into effect carload and less-than-carload gathering rates on citrus fruits and vegetables, and although the rates thus fixed were somewhat higher than the rates on pineapples which the Commission had established, they were lower than the citrus fruit and vegetable rates which had been expressly sustained by the Commission. Some months after this was done the same complainant who had filed the previous petitions presented in No. 1168 a second supplemental complaint against the East Coast Line, and new petitions against the Seaboard Air Line and Atlantic Coast Line Railways (No. 3808). So far as the East Coast Line was concerned the complaint was against the citrus fruit and vegetable-gathering rates and asked that they be equalized with or made the same as the pineapple rate. The Florida Railroad Commission intervened and asked the same relief. The Commission in effect granted the prayer of this second supplemental complaint, found the rates of the East Coast Line on citrus fruits and vegetables to be unjust and unreasonable, and directed the putting into operation of a lower stated schedule of gathering rates which was made applicable not only to the East Coast Line but also to the other roads which were parties to the proceeding. And it is this order which the railroad refused to obey and to enjoin the enforcement of which this suit was brought.

Without going into detail it suffices to say that the report of the Commission concerning the action just stated did not purport to question the correctness of its previous findings sustaining the citrus fruit and vegetable rates of the East Coast Line, but was based upon what was deemed to be a change in conditions since the previous decisions. After pointing out that it had previously ordered a change from any-quantity to carload and less-than-carload rates on pineapples from gathering points to the base point on the East Coast Line and on all fruits and vegetables from base points outward, and that on both the Atlantic Coast Line and the Seaboard Air Line any-quantity rates yet remained from gathering points as to all fruits and vegetables, although such was not the case as to the East Coast Line because of the change which it had voluntarily made, it was said (22 I. C. C. 11, 14, 15):

"No material change has taken place since then (that is, since the previous decisions) so far as this record discloses which would lead to a different conclusion if the same subject were before us today. The volume of business transacted has increased, but the expenses of operation have also increased to an extent which offsets the greater amount of business. . . .

. . . .

"It appeared in the original case that citrus fruits to some extent, and vegetables to a much greater extent, were shipped in small lots to Jacksonville and there reloaded for movement beyond. It was our impression in establishing carload rates from the base point that this would permit the movement in small lots up to the base point and the consolidation at such point, and that the carload movement would in fact be mainly beyond the base point. Such has not been the result. In order to obtain the carload rate beyond the base point it seems to be necessary for the shipper, in actual practice, to present a full carload at the point of origin, and from this it follows that the movement up to the base point at the present time is entirely different from what it was when we approved these any-quantity rates. At that time the loading was by the carrier; now it is mainly by the shipper. The loading of the cars from the point of origin to the base points is much heavier now than formerly. In 1907 the average loading of citrus fruits and pineapples upon the Atlantic Coast Line up to the base point was 215 boxes. In 1910 this loading had increased to 279 boxes. In case of vegetables the increase is even more marked. The number of cars now required to transport the same amount of this traffic from points of origin to base points would be materially less than in 1908. Otherwise stated, it costs the shipper more to handle his business today and it costs the railroad less."

And upon that changed circumstance an order was awarded directing the change from any-quantity to car-load and less-than-carload and fixing a rate which was the same as that previously fixed for pineapples. Of course, as the East Coast Line had voluntarily put in carload and less-than-carload rates, it was only affected by this order to the extent that it lowered the traffic charge as contained in the schedule which had been previously voluntarily established.

It is insisted that the order of the Commission was wrongful and that the court below erred in not restraining its enforcement for the following reasons: (*a*) because the order complained of was rendered without any evidence whatever to sustain it; (*b*) because it confiscated the property of the railway in a two-fold aspect, first, by fixing a rate so unreasonably low as to afford no remuneration to the corporation for the use of its property, and second, because although the Commission in order to justify the rate which it fixed took into account the revenue derived from the extended road, it nevertheless declined to at all consider the value of the extended road and the right to earn a return thereon. We come as briefly as possible to consider these contentions separately.

(*a*) *That there was no evidence whatever tending to sustain the reduction of the rates on citrus fruits and vegetables as to the East Coast Line which the Commission ordered.*

While a finding of fact made by the Commission concerning a matter within the scope of the authority delegated to it is binding and may not be reëxamined in the courts, it is undoubted that where it is contended that an order whose enforcement is resisted was rendered without any evidence whatever to support it, the consideration of such a question involves not an issue of fact, but one of law which it is the duty of the courts to examine and decide. (*Int. Com. Comm.* v. *Louis. & Nash. R. R.*, 227 U. S. 88, 91, 92, and cases cited.)

In view of what we have said concerning the state of the record, the solution of the question must depend upon an examination and analysis of two subjects, the one the reports of the Commission in the previous cases, and the other, the testimony which was before it and the report made in this case. As to the first, in view of the statements made by the Commission in its report in the original case (No. 1168, 14 I. C. C. 476) as to the earning power of the road, the nature of its business and the reasonableness of its rates and the express finding that the citrus fruit and vegetable rates were just and reasonable and should not be changed and the further fact that they were not called in question in the second proceeding it follows that the inquiry narrows itself to the mere consideration of the testimony taken in this proceeding, and the report of the Commission in such proceeding, and the testimony taken before the court below in so far as it is proper to consider it in connection with the particular question under consideration. But coming to make a review of the testimony before the Commission on the issue raised by the second supplemental petition, we fail to find the slightest proof tending to sustain the reduction in rates as to the East Coast Line, which was made.

There are only three subjects referred to in the testimony which can in any view be considered as having any possible tendency to show such a change as would cause the rate which was found by the Commission in the past reasonable and not to justify a change to be unreasonable and therefore require reduction. The three subjects are these: (*a*) testimony by the chairman of the Florida Railroad Commission that there had been a considerable increase in the volume of traffic in citrus fruits and vegetables since the previous finding; (*b*) a further statement or admission made by an officer of the East Coast Line in a colloquy which took place at the hearing in this case to the effect that as shippers under carload rates loaded their own cars there was some difference in cost to the advantage of the road over the cost of loading when the any-quantity rates prevailed; (*c*) testimony with reference to the Atlantic Coast Line and the Seaboard Air Line (but none as to the East Coast Line) to the effect that on those roads it had come to pass that there was a saving in expense and an increase in earning capacity because even under the any-quantity rates carload shipments had greatly increased and cars so shipped were much more heavily loaded and moved from the point of production through the base point to their ultimate destination, when such was not the case at the time the previous order was made. Testimony which as we have seen was expressly declared by the Commission to be in effect the cause which gave rise to the reduction. But at once it is to be observed that so far as any inference alone from the difference between carload and less-than-carload rates and any-quantity rates is concerned it had no application to the East Coast Line since that road had put in the carload and less-than-carload rates while the other two roads had not. And so far as the consideration of the increased loading is concerned as stated by the Commission, whatever may have been the proof as to the Seaboard Air Line and the Atlantic Coast Line, it is beyond controversy that no such proof can be found in the record as to the East Coast Line except the vague intimation to which we have referred.

Thus by analysis the case comes to this: Did the facts as to the increased loading which the Commission found to exist in the case of the Seaboard Air Line and the Atlantic Coast Line support or tend to support the order as to the East Coast Line in the absence of all testimony in the record concerning the existence of such fact as to the traffic on that road? In other words, the question is, Because there was testimony as to the traffic of those roads, can such testimony be said to tend to establish the same condition on the East Coast Line? Conceding that from an abstract point of view an affirmative answer would have to be given to such question we think such is not the case here for the following reasons: (*a*) because of the difference in business carried on by the two roads named and the East Coast Line, they being not only gatherers of the local product but trunk line carriers; (*b*) because of the difference in the situation and traffic of the two trunk lines named and the East Coast Line, as deduced solely from the peculiar environment and movement of business on that road so aptly stated in the passages from the reports of the Commission which we have quoted. Differences which presumably gave rise to separate statements in the previous reports in considering that road. While we do not say that the conclusion is affirmatively sustained, nevertheless we think the state of the record at least tends to give some support to the suggestion in the argument that the greater magnitude and importance of the consideration of the business and rates of the two trunk line carriers concentrated attention in that direction and therefore caused the inquiry on that subject and the facts concerning the same to eclipse the distinctions between those lines and the East Coast Line — distinctions which if otherwise taken under consideration should have produced a different result.

As it follows from these views that the order in question as to the East Coast Line and its enforcement should have been enjoined by the court below, our duty is to reverse the action of that court and to remand the case to the proper District Court with directions to grant the prayer of the East Coast Line and restrain the enforcement of the order in question and it is so ordered.

Reversed.

THE LOS ANGELES SWITCHING CASE[1]

234 U. S. 294 (1914)

MR. JUSTICE HUGHES delivered the opinion of the court.

The Atchison, Topeka and Santa Fe Railway Company, the Southern Pacific Company and the San Pedro, Los Angeles and Salt Lake Railroad Company, brought this suit against the Interstate Commerce Commission in the Circuit Court of the United States for the District of Kansas, first division, to restrain the enforcement of an order of the Commission made in April, 1910. The order required these companies to desist 'from exacting their present charge of $2.50 per car for delivering and receiving carload freight to and from industries located upon spurs and sidetracks within their respective switching limits' in Los Angeles, California, when such carload freight 'is moving in interstate commerce incidentally to a system-line haul.' It also prohibited the exaction of any charge whatever, other than the charge for transportation from points of origin to destination, for delivering or receiving carload freight in such cases.[2]

[1] Docket title of this case is Interstate Commerce Commission, The United States of America, Associated Jobbers of Los Angeles, and Pacific Coast Jobbers and Manufacturers Association, appellants, *v.* Atchison, Topeka and Santa Fe Railway Company, Southern Pacific Company, and San Pedro, Los Angeles and Salt Lake Railroad Company.

[2] The order is as follows:

"This case being at issue on complaint and answer on file, and having been duly heard and submitted by the parties, and full investigation of the matters and things involved having been had, and the commission having,

After answer had been filed by the Commission, the suit was transferred to the Commerce Court, and the United States, the Associated Jobbers of Los Angeles and the Pacific Coast Jobbers' and Manufacturers' Association, intervened. The United States thereupon moved to dismiss the bill for want of equity and the petitioners asked for a preliminary injunction. The Commerce Court, denying the Government's motion, suspended the Commission's order until the further order of the court (188 Fed. Rep. 229, 929); and this appeal is prosecuted.

The complaint of the petitioners in substance is that they have established in the city of Los Angeles their public terminals, including what are known as team tracks and freight sheds, for the accommodation of the public in receiving and delivering carload freight; that these facilities are entirely adequate for the purpose, and are sufficient to handle all the carload freight shipped or delivered in the city, including that now received or delivered upon the industrial spur tracks in question; that the spur-track service has been established simply for the convenience of the shippers thus served; that it is a service essentially distinct from the line haul, and additional thereto, being of great benefit in the saving of cartage charges to the favored shippers for whose use the spur tracks were constructed; that the industries or

---

on the date hereof, made and filed a report containing its findings of fact and conclusions thereon, which said report is hereby referred to and made a part hereof, and having found that the present charge of $2.50 per car exacted by the several defendants for delivering and receiving carload freight to and from industries located upon spurs and sidetracks within their respective switching limits at Los Angeles, Cal., when such carload freight is moving in interstate commerce incidentally to a system-line haul, is in violation of the act to regulate commerce:

"It is ordered, That said defendants be, and they are hereby, notified and required to cease and desist, on or before the 1st day of July, 1910, and for a period of not less than two years thereafter abstain, from exacting their present charge of $2.50 per car for delivering and receiving carload freight to and from industries located upon spurs and sidetracks within their respective switching limits in the said city of Los Angeles, Cal., when such carload freight is moving in interstate commerce incidentally to a system-line haul.

"It is further ordered, That said defendants be, and they are hereby, notified and required to cease and desist, on or before the 1st day of July, 1910, and for a period of not less than two years thereafter abstain, from exacting any charge whatever, other than the charge for transportation from points of origin to destination, for delivering or receiving carload freight to or from industries located upon spurs or sidetracks within their respective switching limits in the said city of Los Angeles, Cal., when such carload freight is moving in interstate commerce incidentally to a system-line haul."

plants located upon the spurs are distant from the main tracks, in the case of the Atchison Company from 1–5 mile to 3½ miles, in that of the Southern Pacific Company from 200 feet to 7 miles, and in that of the San Pedro Company from 1–5 mile to 4 miles, and that the special switching service involves a much greater expense than if the carload freight were received or delivered on the team tracks or at the freight sheds of the carriers respectively; that the charge of $2.50 per car for this service is entirely reasonable and one which the carriers are entitled to make in addition to the line-haul rate; and that as such it has been duly specified in their published tariffs. It is also averred that, while in the contracts governing the construction and maintenance of the spur tracks no specific sum was prescribed for the service of receiving and delivering carload freight thereon, the charge above mentioned had been generally established; that at the time of the making of these contracts the shippers understood and willingly consented that, if the railway company performed this special service, there should be additional compensation and that such charge has generally been maintained and collected. The adequacy of the public terminal facilities for carload freight in Los Angeles (consisting of the team tracks and freight sheds of the carriers respectively), the facts set forth with respect to the construction of the spur tracks, their location, the acquiescence in the switching charge and its maintenance, were established before the Commission, it is alleged, by undisputed evidence. It is further stated that on account of water and other competition, the rates of transportation to and from Los Angeles have been forced to an exceedingly low basis so that the companies do not receive the amount to which they are justly entitled and that they ought not to be required to perform the service in question without reasonable reward. The Commission's order was assailed as beyond its authority, involving a discrimination in favor of the owners of plants located upon the spur tracks and a deprivation of the property of the carriers without due process of law.

The report of the Commission (18 I. C. C. 310) was made a part of the bill. It appears that the proceeding before the Commission was instituted by the Associated Jobbers of Los Angeles and was directed against two distinct practices, involving the spur-track switching charges incident to a system-line haul and to a foreign-line haul respectively. The propriety of such a charge when the line haul was by a foreign carrier was sustained, and the prohibitory order was confined to cases where the charge was made in connection with a system-line haul. The pertinent facts as found by the Commission are substantially as follows:

Each of the carriers has designated certain territory as within its switching or yard limits in the city of Los Angeles, extending for 6 or 7 miles in a general easterly and westerly direction, and including numerous tracks, main lines, branch lines, industry spurs, classification tracks, team tracks, freight-shed tracks, hold tracks, repair tracks, and others, and also their stations, freight sheds, derricks, roundhouses, and other structures. Freight moving in carloads is delivered at team tracks, at freight sheds, or at industry spurs. At team tracks and freight sheds no charge is imposed for the receipt or delivery of such carload freight over the freight rate named in the tariffs, while at industry spurs an additional charge of $2.50 is imposed on every loaded car moving either in or out. These industry spurs vary in length, some leading directly from the main track into or alongside of the industries served, while others are of greater length and branch at one or more points, short spurs running off from what is known as the 'lead' to serve other industries in the immediate neighborhood. These spurs have been constructed under substantially uniform contracts.[1] None of the industries at Los Angeles furnishes its own motive power, and interline switching is done from the interchange track to the industry by the locomotives of the delivering line, the carrier performing the switching service.

The Commission found that these spur tracks were portions of the terminal facilities of the carriers with whose lines they connected, being distinguished from mere plant facilities such

[1] The standard form of the Southern Pacific Company provides as follows:

"1. Undersigned (shipper) will pay cost of constructing above-described track (rails, splices, bolts, switches, frogs, switch stands, and connections to be furnished by and at the cost of Southern Pacific Company), whether such cost may be more or less than amount of foregoing approximate estimate.

"2. Said track shall be under full control of Southern Pacific Company, and may be used at discretion of said company for shipments or delivery of any freight, but the business of the undersigned shall always have preference.

"3. All material in said track furnished at expense of Southern Pacific Company, whether in original construction or by any way of replacements or repairs, shall be and remain exclusive property of Southern Pacific Company, and said Southern Pacific Company shall keep said track in repair.

"4. In case said track shall not be used by undersigned for period of one year, said Southern Pacific Company may, at its option, remove said track.

"5. All goods shipped from or to said track by rail, routing of which is controlled, or may be reasonably held to be controlled, by or through under-as were under consideration in *Chicago & Alton Ry. Co.* v. *United States*, 156 Fed. Rep. 558, and in the cases of the *General Electric Company* and *Solvay Process Company*, 14 I. C. C. 237, 246. Each of the spurs here considered, said the Commission, is in a real sense a railroad terminal at which the carrier receives and delivers freight. It further appears from the report that the charge for spur-track delivery has been made by all of the carriers at Los Angeles as long as the railroads have had access to that city; that it was first imposed by the Southern Pacific and as the other lines came in they adopted the policy of the line already there; that as to certain commodities the charge was not imposed until quite recently and at all times until the Hepburn Act went into effect there was great variation in charge as between individual shippers. It is added that there are 97 places in California to which what are known as coast terminal rates apply, rates lower than to intermediate points; only in Los Angeles, San Francisco and San Diego is there such a charge for spur-track delivery, though in many of these places such delivery is furnished. To the north, in Portland, Seattle, Tacoma, and a large number of other points which also enjoy coast terminal rates, the Southern Pacific, Northern Pacific and Great Northern lines, impose no such charge, and to the east where defendants' lines have their termini in cities competing with Los Angeles, this charge is also unknown.

The Commission thus described the character of the service in question: "Spur-track delivery is a substitute service, a service which it has solicited the right to give, as the evidence here shows, a service which costs the industry for the installation of

---

signed, shall, when forwarded, be over such railroads as may be selected by Southern Pacific Company, provided rate of charge shall be as low as that from or to point in question by any other rail route."

The Sante Fe contract contains this provision:

"The title to said track, and to all the rails, ties, bolts, switches, fastenings, and fixtures connected therewith, and to all other property which may be furnished by the railway company in the maintenance of said track, shall at all times be and remain in said railway company, and said railway company may use the same for other purposes than the delivery of freight to or the receipt of freight from the second party, provided that such use shall inconvenience the business of the second party as little as possible consistent therewith; and at any time after the termination of this contract or the obligation of the railway company, as herein provided, to maintain such track, the railway company shall have the right to remove said track and every part thereof."

the track and the use of its property as a railway terminal. It is a service over the carrier's own rails to a point where it yields possession of the property transported and which involves no greater expense than would team-track delivery. It relieves the carrier's team tracks and sheds, necessitating less outlay for expanse of yards in a crowded city, promotes the speedy release of equipment, and vastly aids in conducting a commerce which is greater than the carrier's own facilities could freely, adequately, and economically handle.

"Again it is not to be overlooked that the delivery given on an industry spur is not supplemental to any other delivery. Cars destined to industry spurs are not placed first at a spur, depot, or on the team tracks, or at the sheds, and later switched to oblige the consignee. A train of freight cars goes to the breaking-up yards which lie at the entrance to the city, and there it is divided up with respect to the character of the freight in the various cars and their destination. No one has access to the cars at this point. This yard is purely a railroad facility. After the cars are segregated they are taken to the tracks to which they are ordered — some to the various team tracks distributed along the main line, some to different industries, some perhaps to the railroad shops or to freight sheds or to the stock yards. Before the cars are placed the consignees are given notice of the tracks to which they are to be sent, so that there is no confusion, and the switch engines which place the cars on one track also served to haul the 'loads' in and 'empties' out at the other tracks. After a most exhaustive inquiry we cannot find, taking this service as a whole in the same way that it is treated by the carriers, that the service is more expensive to the carrier than if all cars were given team-track delivery.

"An additional charge may be made when an additional service is given. But the service here given is not additional to that for which the rate pays. If the shipper pays for team-track delivery and does not receive it, but asks instead and is given a sidetrack delivery which costs the carrier no more, he may not be compelled to pay an additional charge upon the assumption that he has received a terminal team-track service which has not been given. A carrier may not so construct its rates as to compel an extra charge for like service, and this, in our judgment, the defendants at Los Angeles have done." 18 I. C. C. pp. 317, 318.

1. It is urged that the Commission's order rests upon a construction of the statute which would forbid any carrier

from separating its terminal and haulage charges on the same shipment, and that this is a fundamental misconception of the law.

We do not think that the order is open to this objection. It is true that the Commission directed attention to the distinction between the American and English methods of stating rates, pointing out that the English practise of fixing separate schedules for 'conveyance' and 'station terminal' rates had not obtained in this country so far as the records of the Commission show. The opinion was expressed that the provisions of the Act to Regulate Commerce were enacted with reference to the American method of rate-making and that the rate which the statute requires to be published is 'a complete rate,' including 'not only the charge for hauling but the charge for the use of the terminals at both ends of the line.' 18 I. C. C. pp. 315, 316. We need not stop to consider whether this is a correct interpretation of the act, for the question of a segregation of haulage and terminal charges (meaning, by the latter, charges for the use of ordinary terminal stations in receiving and delivering goods) was not before the Commission and its propriety was not necessarily involved in the decision. No such segregation had been attempted by the carriers here. On the contrary, it was undisputed that the line haul carload rate comprehended receipt and delivery on team tracks or at freight sheds.

The Commission conceded the right of the carrier to charge for any terminal service that was accessorial. But it was held that an additional charge was not justified if additional service was not in fact rendered.

2. Nor do we understand that the Commission ruled that the receipt and delivery of goods at plants located upon spurs or side-tracks could not, in any circumstances, be regarded as a distinct service for which separate compensation might be demanded. Cases of an interior movement of plant traffic to and from various parts of the establishment, and of deliveries through a system of interior switching tracks constructed as plant facilities, were expressly distinguished by the Commission (18 I. C. C. pp. 313, 314); and it is apparent that the ruling of the Commission would not apply in any case where by reason of the location and extent of the spur tracks and the character of the movement the facts were essentially different from those upon which the decision was based. (*Interstate Commerce Commission* v. *Stickney*, 215 U. S. 98, 105.)

3. On the other hand, it cannot be maintained that the delivery and receipt of goods on industrial spur tracks within the switching limits in a city is necessarily an added service for which the carrier is entitled to make, or should make, a charge additional to the line-haul rate to or from that city, when the line-haul rate embraces a receiving and delivering service for which the spur-track service is a substitute. It is said that carriers are bound to carry only to or from their terminal stations. But when industrial spur tracks have been established within the carrier's switching limits, within which also various team tracks are located, these spurs may in fact constitute an essential part of the carrier's terminal system. It was stated by the Commission that carriers throughout the country treat industry spurs of the kind here in question 'as portions of their terminals, making no extra charge for service thereto when the carrier receives the benefit of the line haul out or in.' It was added that while this general statement covered perhaps ten thousand cities and towns in the United States, the carriers before the Commission could name only three exceptions, to wit, the cities of Los Angeles, San Francisco and San Diego. But, laying the generalization on one side, it is plain that the question whether or not there is at any point an additional service in connection with industrial spur tracks upon which to base an extra charge, or whether there is merely a substituted service which is substantially a like service to that included in the line-haul rate and not received, is a question of fact to be determined according to the actual conditions of operation.

Such a question is manifestly one upon which it is the province of the Commission to pass.

4. We must therefore take the findings of the Commission in the present case as to the character and manner of use of the industrial spurs in Los Angeles — that they constituted part of the carrier's terminals and that under the conditions there existing, the receipt and delivery of goods on these spurs was a like service as compared with the receipt and delivery of goods at team tracks and freight sheds — as conclusions of fact. Assuming that they were based upon evidence, they are not open to review. *Baltimore & Ohio R. R. Co.* v. *Pitcairn Coal Co.*, 215 U. S. 381, 495; *Interstate Commerce Commission* v. *D., L. & W. R. R. Co.*, 220 U. S. 235, 251; *Interstate Commerce Commission* v. *Union Pacific R. R. Co.*, 222 U. S. 541, 547, 548; *Interstate Commerce Commission* v. *Louisville & Nashville R. R. Co.*, 227 U. S.

88, 92; *Atchison, Topeka & Santa Fe Rwy. Co.* v. *United States* 232 U. S. 199, 221.

In this view, we find no ground for holding the order of the Commission to be invalid. It is not denied that the complaining shippers and these carriers were heard before the Commission and that evidence disclosing the terminal situation in Los Angeles, and the nature and use of the various tracks within the switching limits, was presented; and it cannot be doubted that the case demanded an appreciation of a variety of details, or minor facts, in order that the ultimate questions of fact could be determined. It is said that it was established by undisputed evidence that the team tracks and freight sheds provided by the carriers were fully adequate for all carload freight. Putting aside the denial by the Commission of this allegation, it is evident that the question was not simply as to such adequacy, but as to the actual use of the various tracks, the services thereon relatively considered, and whether there was really an extra service in the circumstances shown. Again, it is said that the Commission did not find the switching charge in itself, that is, taken separately, to be unreasonable, but the inquiry was whether in view of the conditions of the distribution of the carload freight through a large area there was in fact such a similarity of movement as to negative the basis for a separate charge. It is further urged that while the contracts for the construction of these spurs did not fix the charge, it was proved by undisputed evidence that at the time these contracts were made the shippers consented to a special charge, if freight were received and delivered thereon, and that the charge in question had been generally maintained. The service, however, was performed subject to the law of the land requiring that the carrier's charges should not be unreasonable or unjustly discriminatory. (See *Louisville & Nashville R. R. Co.*, v. *Mottley*, 219 U. S. 467, 482; *Phila., Balt. & Nash. R. R. Co.* v. *Schubert*, 224 U. S. 603, 613, 614.) If it became apparent that the shippers were subjected to an arbitrary and unwarranted exaction, they were in no way estopped from bringing the matter before the body created by law to deal with such questions and from securing its order directing the carriers to stop the objectionable practise.

But it is contended that the finding of the Commission is opposed to the admitted physical facts, and reference is made to the transportation to and from industrial plants located from 1–5 of a mile to 7 miles from the main track of the carrier. We find no such fundamental unsoundness in the Commission's conclusions. It appeared, as already stated, that the carrier had designated certain territory as within its switching or yard limits in Los Angeles extending for 6 or 7 miles and 'including numerous tracks, main lines, branch lines, industry tracks, team tracks, freight-shed tracks and various structures.' It does not appear how many industries were within a short distance or to how many the statement as to the greatest distance above-mentioned applied. The carrier did not fix a charge according to the comparative service in the case of these various industrial plants. It made the same switching charge whether the distance was 200 feet or 7 miles, that is, it dealt with the situation upon an average basis making the same charge for all this switching in a given area which constituted its terminal district. It was the service within these switching limits, that the Commission was considering. Manifestly it was permissible to establish such a district, and taking the team-track and freight-shed service in that area, and the average spur-track service, the Commission reached the conclusion set forth. It is said that the finding of the Commission as to the comparative cost of the service was not affirmative, but was merely a negative statement to the effect that the commission was unable to find that the cost of spur-track delivery was more expensive to the carrier. While this form of expression was used at one place in the Commission's report, at another the service in question was described as one which involved 'no greater expense than would team-track delivery' and we cannot but regard this as the Commission's finding upon the evidence. It is then insisted that the contrary of this finding is self-evident, but the facts with respect to the movement of freight in a great terminal district are by no means so simple that the deliberate judgment of the Commission can be regarded as contradicting the obvious.

The argument for the petitioners necessarily invites the court to substitute its judgment for that of the Commission upon matters of fact within the Commission's province. This is not the function of the court. We cannot regard the Act to Regulate Commerce as justifying an increased or extra charge for a substantially similar service and upon the case made it cannot be said that the Commission has overstepped its authority in forbidding the charge in question as one which was unjustly discriminatory.

In our opinion the Commerce Court erred in denying the Government's motion to dismiss and in granting the petitioner's motion for injunction. The order of the Commerce Court is therefore reversed and the cause is remanded to the District Court of the United States for the Southern District of California, southern division, with instructions to dismiss the bill. Act of October, 22, 1913, c. 32; Stat. 1913, p. 221.

It is so ordered.

SEABOARD AIR LINE RAILWAY COMPANY ET AL *v.* UNITED STATES ET AL

254 U. S. 57 (1920)

MR. JUSTICE DAY delivered the opinion of the court.

In this case a petition was filed in the District Court of the United States for the Eastern District of Virginia to enjoin an order of the Interstate Commerce Commission concerning the absorption of switching charges on the lines of the Seaboard Air Line Railway Company, the Seaboard Air Line Railway, Southern Railway Company, and Atlantic Coast Line Railway Company within the switching limits of these roads as established at Richmond, Virginia.

The Commission's order was made upon a petition of the Richmond Chamber of Commerce averring that the practice of the railroads was discriminatory and unlawful and violative of § 2 of the Act to Regulate Commerce. From the facts found by the Commission it appears that the appellant railroad companies bring freight from the south to Richmond, Virginia, where the same is delivered to industries in the switching limits of that city. If the freight is received at a point served by any two or more of the carriers, the switching charge is absorbed if the freight be delivered on the line of either. But if the delivery is to an industry served only by a non-competitive carrier the switching charge is not absorbed. The Commission illustrated the point by an example: "Oxford, N. C., is a point reached both by the Southern and the Seaboard, but not by the Chesapeake & Ohio. Norlina, N. C., is a local point on the Seaboard. Assume that industries A, B, and C [referring to a diagram] on the Seaboard, the Southern, and the Chesapeake & Ohio, respectively, are similarly located with regard to the interchange tracks of the three carriers at Richmond. On traffic from Oxford to industry B on the Southern, the Seaboard will absorb the Southern's switching charges. But on traffic from Oxford to industry C, on the Chesapeake & Ohio, the Seaboard refuses to absorb the Chesapeake & Ohio's switching charges. On traffic from and to Norlina, a local point, however, the Seaboard refuses to absorb all switching charges whatsoever to any off-line industry."

The order complained of directed the three carriers to cease and desist on or before August 1, 1917, and thereafter to abstain, from absorbing switching charges on certain interstate carload freight at Richmond, Virginia, while refusing to absorb such charges on like carload shipments for a like and contemporaneous service under substantially similar circumstances and conditions, such practices having been found in a supplemental report to be unjustly discriminatory and unlawful within § 2 of the Act to Regulate Commerce; and "to establish, on or before August 1, 1917, . . . and thereafter to maintain and apply uniform regulations and practices for the absorption of charges for the switching of interstate carload freight at Richmond, Va., and to collect no higher rates or charges from shippers and receivers of such carload freight at Richmond, Va., than they contemporaneously collect from any other shipper or receiver of such carload freight at Richmond, Va., for a like and contemporaneous service under substantially similar circumstances and conditions." 44 I. C. C. 455.

The District Court denied the application for an injunction, and ordered that the petition be dismissed. 249 Federal 368.

The contention of the appellants is that the transportation is not a like and contemporaneous service of a like kind of traffic under substantially similar circumstances and conditions.

Section 2 of the Act to Regulate Commerce provides:

"That if any common carrier subject to the provisions of this act shall, directly or indirectly, by any special rate, rebate, drawback, or other device, charge, demand, collect, or receive from any person or persons a greater or less compensation for any service rendered, or to be rendered, in the transportation of passengers or property, subject to the provisions of this act, than it charges, demands, collects, or receives from any other person or persons for doing for him or them a like and contemporaneous service in the transportation of a like kind of traffic under substantially similar circumstances and conditions, such common carrier shall be deemed guilty of unjust discrimination, which is hereby prohibited and declared to be unlawful." (24 Stat. 379).

Upon this controversy the Commission in its report said:

"Complainant insists that when the line-haul carrier reaches the common point and competes for the traffic to or from Richmond proper, the absorption of the switching charges should not be confined to that traffic for which the switching line competes for the entire haul. That is, if the Seaboard absorbs the switching charges for the shipper on the terminal tracks of the Southern, it should also absorb the switching charges for the shipper on the terminal tracks of the Chesapeake & Ohio. Unless this is done, complainant contends that the two shippers are not upon an equality, since the Seaboard pays for a delivery service to shippers on the terminal tracks of the Southern and declines to pay for a similar delivery service to shippers on the terminal tracks of the Chesapeake & Ohio. . . .

"Section 2 is primarily directed against discrimination between shippers located in the same community. It is aimed to put all shippers within a switching district upon a substantial equality. It provides that where a carrier receives from any person a greater compensation for any service rendered in the transportation of passengers or property than it receives from any other person for doing from him a 'like and contemporaneous service in the transportation of a like kind of traffic under substantially similar circumstances and conditions, such common carrier shall be deemed guilty of unjust discrimination,' a discrimination which is prohibited and declared to be unlawful. Under this section it is settled that the competition of rival carriers as such does not constitute substantially dissimilar circumstances to justify a difference in treatment."

We are of opinion that the Commission was correct in regarding the service in question as a like and contemporary service rendered under substantially similar circumstances and conditions, and amply sustained as matter of law in *Wight* v. *United States*, 167 U. S. 512 and *Interstate Commerce Commission* v. *Alabama Midland Railway Company*, 168 U. S. 144. The principle established in these cases is that the statute aims to establish equality of rights among shippers for carriage under substantially similar circumstances and conditions, and that the exigencies of competition do not justify discrimination against shippers for substantially like services.

Moreover the determination of questions of fact is by law imposed upon the Commission, a body created by statute for the consideration of this and like matters. The findings of fact by the Commission upon such questions can be disturbed by judicial decree only in cases where their action is arbitrary or transcends the legitimate bounds of their authority. *I. C. C.* v. *L. & N. R. R. Co.*, 227 U. S. 88; *Pre-cooling Case*, 232 U. S. 199; *Los Angeles Switching Case*, 234 U. S. 294, 311, 312 and cases cited; *Penn. R. R. Co.* v. *United States*, 236 U. S. 351, 361.

The Commission did not hold that switching charges must be always the same. But did hold that they must be alike where the service was rendered under substantially similar circumstances and conditions. The Commission's report says:

"We do not consider that the carriers must absorb the switching charges indiscriminately to all industries within the switching limits of Richmond if they choose to absorb the switching charges to any one industry off their rails. The illegality herein found to exist is the receiving of a greater compensation for one service than for a like service under substantially similar circumstances and conditions. To take a concrete example and referring again to the diagram. Suppose industry C were 5 miles distant from the interchange tracks of the Seaboard, while industry B were only 2 miles distant. Suppose the Chesapeake & Ohio's switching charge amounted to $5, while that of the Southern was $2. If the Seaboard absorbed the Southern's $2 switching charge on traffic to industry B, we do not consider that it must absorb the entire $5 switching charge of the Chesapeake & Ohio on traffic to industry C, but only to the extent to which the service is similar. In other words, it would probably be necessary for the Seaboard to absorb $2 of the $5 charge of the Chesapeake & Ohio."

The practice condemned by the Commission, as its report and order show, was that of absorbing switching charges only when the line-haul carrier competes with the switching line; and refusing to absorb such charges when the switching line does not compete with the line-haul carrier; this, the Commission held was discrimination within the meaning of section 2 of the Act to Regulate Commerce. We find no occasion to disturb this ruling as arbitrary in character or beyond the authority of the Commission.

We find no merit in the contention that the order of the Commission was too vague and uncertain to be enforced.

Affirmed.

LOUISIANA AND PINE BLUFF RAILWAY COMPANY *v.* UNITED STATES

257 U. S. (1921)

Mr. Justice BRANDEIS delivered the opinion of the court.

The Louisiana & Pine Bluff Railway Company, a common carrier owned by the Union Sawmill Company, serves it by means of a tap line which connects its mill at Huttig, Arkansas, with the Missouri Pacific Railway at Dollar Junction. The trunk line and the tap line joined in establishing through routes and joint rates from the mill to points on the trunk line and beyond. The division or allowance given to the tap line out of the joint rates was large. It was held by the Interstate Commerce Commission to amount to a rebate to the Union Sawmill Company and to discriminate unjustly against the Wisconsin Lumber Company, an independent concern also served by the tap line.[1] After proceedings before the Commission, which extended over many years, its supplemental order, entered June 10, 1919, limited the division receivable by the tap line for hauling lumber from the Union Sawmills to Dollar Junction to $3 per car.[2] The Louisiana & Pine Bluff Railway Company then brought this suit in the Federal District Court for Western Arkansas against the United States to enjoin enforcement of the order and to annul the same. The bill charged that the order deprived plaintiff of property without due process of law; that it discriminated against plaintiff by denying to it the same compensation which other carriers were allowed to charge for like service; and that the Commission was without authority in law or fact to make the order complained of. The Interstate Commerce Commission intervened. Answers setting forth the proceedings taken were filed; and by consent of parties, the case was submitted for final hearing upon the pleadings. The District Court entered a decree dismissing the bill,

[1] See The Tap Line Case, 23 I. C. C. 277; 23 I. C. C. 549; 31 I. C. C. 490; 34 I. C. C. 116; Louisiana & Pine Bluff Divisions, 40 I. C. C. 470; 53 I. C. C. 475.

[2] By the fifth supplemental order the maximum division for shipments after May 31, 1919 was raised to $3.50 per car; and a further increase to $4.50 per car was made by the sixth supplemental order. Increased Rates 58 I. C. C. 220. Corresponding increases were made for hauls greater than three miles. These increases do not affect the legal questions involved.

and the case comes here on appeal under the Act of October 22, 1913, c. 32, 38 Stat. 208, 220.

No claim is made here that the division allowed is so low as to be confiscatory. No claim is made that there was lack of notice or of opportunity to be heard before the Commission or that the proceedings before it were otherwise irregular. Nor could a claim that the order was unsupported by evidence be insisted upon. For only a part of the evidence taken before the Commission was introduced. *Manufacturers Railway Co.*, v. *United States*, 246 U. S. 457, 481; *Spiller* v. *Atchison, Topeka & Santa Fe Ry. Co.*, 253 U. S. 117, 125. The claim now urged is that the order was arbitrary and so unreasonable that it should be set aside.

After the decision in *The Tap Line Cases*, 234 U. S. 1, the Commission made, in respect to each of the many tap line companies which were party to the proceeding, an order, 40 I. C. C. 470, like that sustained in *O'Keefe* v. *United States*, 240 U. S. 294. By these orders the maximum division to a tap line for hauling a car from the mill to the junction with the trunk line for a distance of not more than three miles was fixed at $3. For a distance over three and not more than six miles the division to the tap line was fixed at 1½ cents per 100 pounds or approximately $9 a car. The plaintiff contends that it should be allowed to receive the division of 1½ cents per 100 pounds on the ground that its haul from the Union Sawmill plants to Dollar Junction was longer than three miles. Cars loaded with lumber at the platforms of the Union Sawmills, if hauled direct to Dollar Junction, would travel only 2.41 miles. But they are not hauled direct to the junction; they are taken first in the opposite direction to a track scale located on and controlled by the trunk line. Because of this fact the distance actually travelled is 3.42 miles. The Commission, interpreting its own order, directed that for this service the plaintiff could not be allowed by the trunk line more than $3. The contention is that weighing the car is an integral part of the transportation service. *In re Weighing of Freight by Carriers*, 28 I. C. C. 7; *Detroit Coal Exchange* v. *Michigan Central R. R. Co.*, 38 I. C. C. 79; and that to refuse to make an allowance for the out-of-line haul is arbitrary and so unreasonable as to invalidate the order. For the haul from the Wisconsin Lumber Company's mill to Dollar Junction, which is 3.24 miles in the direct line, the Commission authorized the division to the plaintiff of 1½ cents per 100 pounds.

The contention that the order is invalid ignores both the nature of the proceeding before the Commission and the findings upon which the order was made. The proceeding was one to remove unjust discrimination. The Commission's decision is based upon a consideration both of general conditions and of the particular situation. It finds that allowance of more than $3 a car for hauling the car from the Union Sawmill plant to Dollar Junction would result in unjust discrimination. That the finding was supported by evidence we must assume in this proceeding. And not only does plaintiff fail to show that the conclusion reached was arbitrary; but additional findings in the report afford abundant reason why the out-of-line haul to the scales should not be allowed for in fixing the division. The Commission finds, 53 I. C. C. 475, 476, that: "The evidence does not show that it is necessary that the shipments be weighed by the tap line rather than by the trunk line;" and, 40 I. C. C. 470, 471, that allowing the larger division on these facts would place the plaintiff in a more advantageous position than any other tap line in that territory performing a similar service and would "open the way in the case of many tap lines for a relocation of their track scales so as to require a long back haul, and in that way to lay a basis for divisions or allowances very materially in excess of those fixed by the Commission for the distance covered by a direct movement from the mill to the junction." In other words, divisions that would operate as rebates.

Affirmed.

PROCTOR & GAMBLE COMPANY *v.* UNITED STATES OF AMERICA, INTERSTATE COMMERCE COMMISSION, CINCINNATI, HAMILTON & DAYTON RAILWAY COMPANY, ET AL

225 U. S. 282 (1912)

MR. CHIEF JUSTICE WHITE delivered the opinion of the court.

Having three manufacturing plants, one at Ivorydale, Ohio, a second at Port Ivory, New York, and a third at Kansas City, Kansas, in which they carried on the business of refining cottonseed and other oils and of manufacturing soap and other products from grease and oil, the Procter & Gamble Company, to facilitate the transportation to their factories of the substances required for their operation and of shipping out the finished products, became the owner of about five hundred railroad tank cars. The cars were exclusively devoted to the business of the company in the following manner: On the property of the company in the yards about their factories there were railroad tracks belonging to the company which served for holding empty or loaded cars, the cars thus situated being held for storage and for movement from place to place, as business required. At each of the factories there was also an interchange track connected with the tracks in the yards and with the tracks of the railroad company or companies through whom the business of shipping in interstate commerce to and from the factories was carried on. The movement of cars to the interchange tracks for outward shipment and from the interchange tracks when they were left there by railroad companies was at two of the factories carried on by the company through its own employés and motive power. At the other one this work was done by a railroad company, who made an independent and special charge for the service. The transportation of the private tank cars of the corporation by the railroad companies was governed by established rules and the price paid to the railroads for transporting the commodities of the company in its private cars was the regular price fixed for such commodities in the established tariffs. The railroads, however, paid to the company for the use of its private cars a fixed sum per mile, this payment being also stated in the regular established tariffs in compliance with law. A portion of the carrier's rule (Rule 29), relating to the subject of compensation for hauling such private tank cars is in the margin.[1]

In 1910 among others the railroads engaged in transporting tank cars from the plants of the Proctor & Gamble Company adopted a system of rules governing the payment of demurrage

[1] Rule 29. (Sec. 1.) In providing ratings in this classification for articles in tank cars, the carriers whose tariffs are governed by this classification do not assume any obligation to furnish tank cars in cases where they do not own or have not made arrangements for supplying such equipment. When tank cars are furnished by shippers or owners, mileage at the rate of three-quarters (¾) of one cent per mile will be allowed for the use of such tank cars, loaded or empty, provided the cars are properly equipped. No mileage will be allowed on cars switched at terminals nor for movement of cars under empty freight car tariffs.

by shippers. The provisions of these rules pertinent to this case are excerpted in the margin.[1]

The rules in question were prepared by a committee of the National Association of Railroad Commissioners composed of a representative from each State having a railroad commission and a member of the Interstate Commerce Commission, and were adopted in convention by the National Association and were subsequently approved by the Interstate Commerce Commission, although putting them in force was not imperatively prescribed by that body.

The Proctor & Gamble Company, dissatisfied with the regulations concerning demurrage, in so far as they imposed in certain respects charges upon its tank cars, filed a complaint with the Interstate Commerce Commission charging the rules to be repugnant to the act to regulate commerce because unjust and oppressive and because to enforce them would create preferences and discriminations forbidden by the act. After hearing, the Commission made a report declaring that the rules complained of were in no sense in conflict with the act to regulate commerce, and on the contrary conformed to that act and tended to prevent and repress unlawful preferences and discriminations. An award of

[1] Rule I.

Cars subject to Rules.

Cars held for or by consignors or consignees for loading, unloading, forwarding directions, or for any other purpose, are subject to these demurrage rules, except as follows:

(*a*) Cars loaded with live stock.

(*b*) Empty cars placed for loading coal at mines or mine sidings, or coke at coke ovens.

(*c*) Empty private cars stored on carrier's or private tracks, provided such cars have not been placed or tendered for loading on the order of a shipper.

NOTE. — Private cars while in railroad service, whether on carrier's or private tracks, are subject to these demurrage rules to the same extent as cars of railroad ownership.

(Empty private cars are in railroad service from the time they are placed by the carriers for loading or tendered for loading on the orders of a shipper. Private cars under lading are in railroad service until the lading is removed and cars are regularly released. Cars which belong to an industry performing its own switching service are in railroad service from the time they are placed by the industry upon designated interchange tracks and thereby tendered to the carrier for movement. If such cars are subsequently returned empty, they are out of service when withdrawn by the industry from the interchange; if returned under load, railroad service is not at an end until the lading is duly removed.)

relief was therefore denied. In February, 1911, the Proctor & Gamble Company filed a petition in the Commerce Court of the United States making defendants the United States, the Interstate Commerce Commission and the railroads who had been complained of in the proceeding before the Commission. The petition recited the facts stated above as to the character of the business of the petitioner, the ownership of tank cars, etc., the establishment of the rules for demurrage, their repugnancy to the act to regulate commerce, the injury which had resulted from being compelled to pay the charges for demurrage in accordance with the rules, the application made to the Commission and the refusal of that body to award relief. The conception upon which the petition was based is shown in the excerpt in the margin,[1] wherein it was also charged that the order of the Commission dismissing the complaint as above set forth "is null and void and beyond the power of said Interstate Commerce Commission, in that it sustains the validity of . . . said demurrage rules."

The prayer was as follows:

"Wherefore, complainant prays that the aforesaid order of said Interstate Commerce Commission made in said cause No. 3208 on November 14, 1910, be set aside and annulled, and that the defendant railway companies, and each of them, be enjoined from collecting or attempting to collect any demurrage charges

[1] Complainant avers that said order of said Interstate Commerce Commission, in dismissing its complaint as above set forth, is null and void and beyond the power of said Interstate Commerce Commission, in that it sustains the validity of Rule I of said demurrage; that said Rule I in so far as it provides that privately owned cars under lading on private tracks are in railroad service and subject to the demurrage charges imposed by said tariffs until the lading is removed, is unjust and unreasonable, in that it deprives complainant of the right to use its said private cars upon private tracks for its own purposes without paying the defendant railway companies demurrage charges therefor, after said private cars have been delivered to complainant and have actually ceased to be engaged in railroad service; that the charges exacted by the defendant railway companies of complainant under said provision of said rule permit said defendants to take complainant's property without compensation, and deprive it of its property without due process of law, in violation of the Constitution of the United States, and particularly of Article V in amendment thereof, and that said provision of said rule is in violation of the said Act to Regulate Commerce and particularly of §§ 1 and 15 thereof as amended June 29, 1906; that said defendants are now exacting such demurrage charges under the provisions of said rule, and will continue to do so, unless the said order of said Interstate Commerce Commission is set aside and annulled by this court, and defendant railway companies are enjoined from enforcing the provisions of said rule.

upon complainant's loaded tank cars after said cars have been delivered to complainant and placed upon tracks owned or controlled by it; and further, that said defendant railway companies and each of them be required to repay to complainant herein all sums found to have been wrongfully collected by them, or any of them, under the rule here complained of; and that complainant be granted such other and further relief as it may be entitled to in the premises."

The railroads answered the bill. The United States and the Interstate Commerce Commission appearing for the purpose, challenged the jurisdiction of the court to entertain the cause, and moved to dismiss, upon this general ground: "Because the order of the Interstate Commerce Commission complained of directed no affirmative relief and the negative order of the Commission dismissing the complaint affords no ground for an action in this court;" and upon the following more detailed specifications filed on behalf of the United States:

"(*a*) It prays that the order of the Interstate Commerce Commission be enjoined, when said order directed no action against any party and therefore the same is not subject either to enforcement or to injunction.

"(*b*) It prays that the defendant common carriers, who are not proper parties to this proceeding except on their own motion, be enjoined from collecting the demurrage mentioned, when no order inhibiting the same has been made by the Interstate Commerce Commission, and in the absence of such an order this court has no power to grant such relief.

"(*c*) It prays that the defendant common carriers be required to repay to complainant all sums heretofore wrongfully collected as demurrage, when this court has no power or jurisdiction to grant such relief, either with or without an order of the Interstate Commerce Commission directing such repayment."

The court, declining at the threshold to consider the demurrers and motion to dismiss, postponed their consideration until the hearing on the merits. There was a consent by all the defendants except the United States and the Interstate Commerce Commission that the case be heard upon the evidence and documents introduced before the Commission and the report of that body. The United States and the Interstate Commerce Commission, however, on the overruling of its demurrer and a refusal to grant its motion to dismiss, elected to stand thereon and declined to plead further.

In disposing of the case, the court considered it in a two-fold aspect — first, as to its jurisdiction; and, second, as to the merits of the case. On the first subject it held, *a*, that it had jurisdiction of the cause, and that the refusal of the Interstate Commerce Commission to afford relief to the Proctor & Gamble Company was, for the purposes of jurisdiction of the court, the exact equivalent of an order of the Commission granting affirmative relief, and, *b*, as a corollary of this power it was further decided that there was jurisdiction to award pecuniary relief for demurrage if any was illegally exacted. On the merits, however, it was decided that the Interstate Commerce Commission had rightfully refused to grant relief and that there was no foundation for the contention that the property of the company in its private tank cars was taken without due process of law by the demurrage regulations. On this subject it was declared that as the company had accepted the provisions of the published tariffs concerning the use of the tank cars, therefore those cars were submitted to the regulations which the carriers had lawfully established. In other words, the court concluded that because the company had availed of the proffer of the railroads to use the cars in transportation and pay for their use a stated sum, the company had acquired no right to disregard restrictions against preferences and discriminations embodied in the act to regulate commerce.

The case was then brought here by the appeal of the Proctor & Gamble Company. That company insists that the court below erred in not awarding the relief which was asked and in dismissing the petition. On the other hand the Interstate Commerce Commission and the railroads insist that the court was right in refusing relief and dismissing the bill. Before we can come, if at all, to consider the merits, however, it is necessary to dispose of the question concerning the jurisdiction of the court below to entertain the petition, because the United States insists at bar, as it did in the lower court, that the court erred in overruling the demurrer to the jurisdiction and refusing to dismiss the cause for want of jurisdiction.

The provisions of the act to establish the Commerce Court fixing the jurisdiction of that court are stated in the first section of the act of June 18, 1910, 36 Stat. 539, c. 309, now § 207 of the Judiciary Act of March 3, 1911, 36 Stat. 1087, 1184. And in view of the necessity of having the provisions of the section immediately in mind we reproduce them. They are as follows:

"Sec. 207. The Commerce Court shall have the jurisdiction

possessed by circuit courts of the United States and the judges thereof immediately prior to June eighteenth, nineteen hundred and ten, over all cases of the following kinds:

"First. All cases for the enforcement, otherwise than by adjudication and collection of a forfeiture or penalty or by infliction of criminal punishment, of any order of the Interstate Commerce Commission other than for the payment of money.

"Second. Cases brought to enjoin, set aside, annul, or suspend in whole or in part any order of the Interstate Commerce Commission.

"Third. Such cases as by section three of the Act entitled 'An Act to further regulate commerce with foreign nations and among the States,' approved February nineteenth, nineteen hundred and three, are authorized to be maintained in a circuit court of the United States.

"Fourth. All such mandamus proceedings as under the provisions of section twenty or section twenty-three of the Act entitled 'An Act to regulate commerce,' approved February fourth, eighteen hundred and eighty-seven, as amended, are authorized to be maintained in a circuit court of the United States.

"Nothing contained in this chapter shall be construed as enlarging the jurisdiction now possessed by the circuit courts of the United States or the judges thereof, that is hereby transferred to and vested in the Commerce Court.

"The jurisdiction of the Commerce Court over cases of the foregoing classes shall be exclusive, but this chapter shall not affect the jurisdiction possessed by any circuit or district court of the United States over cases or proceedings of a kind not within the above-enumerated classes."

The question to be decided is this: Does the authority with which the Commerce Court is clothed in virtue of these provisions invest that body with jurisdiction to redress complaints based exclusively upon the conception that the Interstate Commerce Commission, in a matter submitted to its judgment and within its competency to consider, has mistakenly refused, upon the ground that no right to the relief claimed was given by the act to regulate commerce, to award the relief which was claimed at its hands? In other words, the important question is, Is the authority of the Commerce Court confined to enforcing or restraining, as the case may require, affirmative orders of the Commission, or has it the power to exert its own judgment by originally interpreting the administrative features of the act to regulate commerce and upon that assumption treat a refusal of the Commission to grant relief as an affirmative order and accordingly pass on its correctness?

Turning for the elucidation of the question to the jurisdictional provisions, it is plain that although all of the four numbered subdivisions composing the section may serve to throw light upon the issue for decision the solution of the question must intrinsically be found in a correct interpretation of the second subdivision. We say this because clearly the first deals alone with cases for the enforcement of orders of the Commission as therein described; the third deals only with cases brought under the act of February 19, 1903, which is wholly foreign to the subject here reviewed, since the act referred to relates only to proceedings to enjoin either discriminations or departures by carriers from their published rates, and the fourth refers exclusively to the right to mandamus conformably to § 20 or 23 of the act to regulate commerce, which sections are concerned with the performance of certain duties imposed upon carriers by the act to regulate Commerce. The words of this second subdivision are: "Second. Cases brought to enjoin, set aside, annul, or suspend in whole or in part any order of the Interstate Commerce Commission."

Giving to these words their natural significance we think it follows that they confer jurisdiction only to entertain complaints as to affirmative orders of the Commission; that is, they give the court the right to take cognizance when properly made of complaints concerning the legality of orders, rendered by the Commission and confer power to relieve parties in whole or in part from the duty of obedience to orders which are found to be illegal. No resort to exposition can add to the cogency with which the conclusion stated is compelled by the plain meaning of the words themselves. But if it be conceded for the sake of argument that the language of the provision is ambiguous a consideration of the context of the act will at once clarify the subject. Thus, the first subdivision provides for the enforcement of orders, that is, the compelling of the doing or abstaining from doing of acts embraced by a previous affirmative command of the Commission, and the second (the one with which we are concerned) dealing with the same subject from a reverse point of view, provides for the contingency of a complaint made to the court by one seeking to prevent the enforcement of orders of the Commission such as are contemplated by the first paragraph.

In other words, by the coöperation of the two paragraphs, authority is given on the one hand, to enforce compliance with the orders of the Commission if lawful, and, on the other hand, power is conferred to stay the enforcement of an illegal order. The other provisions of the act are equally convincing. Thus, § 3 (208), provides that the mere pendency of a suit to enjoin, set aside, annul or suspend an order of the Commission "shall not stay or suspend the operation of such order" but confers upon the court the power, under circumstances stated, to restrain or suspend in whole or in part the operation of an order. The same section, moreover, causes the meaning of the provision, if possible, to become clearer by making a finding that irreparable injury will result from the operation of an order sought to be enforced, essential to the granting of an order or injunction restraining or suspending its enforcement.

We might well be content to rest our conclusion upon the considerations just stated. In view, however, of the importance of the subject we do not do so, but shall consider the matter in a broader aspect for the purpose of demonstrating that to give to the statute a meaning contrary to that which we have found results from its text, and therefore to recognize the existence in the court below of the power which it deemed it possessed would result in frustrating the legislative public policy which led to the adopting of the act to regulate commerce, would render impossible a resort to the remedies which the statute was enacted to afford, would multiply the evils which the act to regulate commerce was adopted to prevent, and thus bring about disaster by creating confusion and conflict where clearness and unity of action was contemplated. It cannot be disputed that the act creating the Commerce Court was intended to be but a part of the existing system for the regulation of interstate commerce, which was established by virtue of the original adoption in 1887 of the act to regulate commerce, and which was expanded by the repeated amendments of that act which followed, developed in practical execution by the rulings of the body (Interstate Commerce Commission), upon whom was cast the administrative enforcement of the act, the whole elucidated and sanctioned by a long line of decisions of this court. That in adopting the provisions concerning the Commerce Court and making it part of the system, it was not intended to destroy the existing machinery or method of regulation, but to cause it to be more efficient by affording a more harmonious means for securing the judicial enforcement of the act to regulate commerce is certain. The act creating the Commerce Court (June 18, 1910, 36 Stat. 539, c. 309) was entitled "An Act to create a Commerce Court, and to amend the Act entitled 'An Act to regulate commerce,' approved February fourth, eighteen hundred and eighty-seven, as heretofore amended, and for other purposes." The first six sections, which called into being the Commerce Court and defined its powers, all demonstrate the purpose as above stated, that is, to adjust the powers and duties of the newly created court in such manner as to cause them to accord with the system of regulation provided by the act to regulate commerce as it then existed.

What was then the existing system and the functions which the new court was created to perform will be conclusively shown by a brief outline of the scope and purpose of the system which arose from the enactment of the act to regulate commerce (Act February 4, 1887, c. 104, 24 Stat. 379) and its development. By that act as originally enacted many regulations and consequent duties were imposed upon carriers in the interest of the public and of shippers which did not theretofore exist, and various administrative safeguards were formulated, all of which, in their very essence, required, first, for their compulsory enforcement the exercise of official functions of an administrative nature, and, second, for their harmonious development an official unity of action which could only be brought about by a single administrative initiative and primary control. To that end the act (§ 11) created an administrative body endowed with what may be in some respects qualified as *quasi*-judicial attributes, to whom was confided the enforcement of those provisions of the act which essentially exacted unity in order that they might beneficially operate. And for the purposes stated, to the body thus created was committed the trust of enforcing the act in the respect stated, of determining, limited as to the subject-matters to which we have referred, whether the provisions of the act had been violated and if so of primarily enforcing the act by awarding appropriate relief. The statute, therefore, necessarily, while it created new rights in favor of shippers, in order to make those rights fruitful as to the subjects with which the statute dealt coming within the scope of the administrative unity which we have mentioned primarily made the judgment of the administrative body to whom the statute confided the enforcement of the act in the respects stated a prerequisite to a resort to the courts. In other words, as to the subjects stated the act did not give to the courts power to hear the complaint of a party concerning a violation of the act, but only conferred power to give effect to such complaints, when by previous submission to the Commission, they had been sanctioned by a command of that body.

In the long interval which intervened between 1887 when the act to regulate commerce was enacted and June 18, 1910, when the Commerce Court act was passed we have learned of no instance where it was held or even seriously asserted, that as to subjects which in their nature were administrative and within the competency of the Commission to decide, there was power in a court, by an exercise of original action, to enforce its conceptions as to the meaning of the act to regulate commerce by dealing directly with the subject irrespective of any prior affirmative command or action by the Interstate Commerce Commission. On the contrary, by a long line of decisions, whereby applications to enforce orders of the Commission were considered and disposed of or where requests to restrain the enforcement of such orders were passed upon, it appears by the reasoning indulged in that it was never considered that there was power in the courts as an original question without previous affirmative action by the Commission to deal with what might be termed in a broad sense the administrative features of the act to regulate commerce by determining as an original question that there had been a compliance or non-compliance with the provisions of the act. The subject is illustrated and made clear by the rulings in *State of Washington, ex rel. Oregon Railroad & Navigation Co.* v. *Fairchild,* 224 U. S. 510; *Robinson* v. *Balto. & Ohio R. R.,* 222 U. S. 506; *Southern Railway Co.* v. *Reid,* 222 U. S. 424, and *Texas & Pacific Ry.* v. *Abilene Cotton Oil Co.,* 204 U. S. 426. The latter case especially will serve to point out that where the power of original action by a court without previous action of the Commission was insisted upon, it was based upon the conception that the particular subject-matter as to which such power was asserted was by the express terms of the act to regulate commerce not embraced within the subjects primarily confided by the act exclusively to the administrative authority of the Commission.

Originally the duty of the courts to determine whether an order of the Commission should or should not be enforced carried with it the obligation to consider both the facts and the law. But it had come to pass prior to the passage of the act creating the Commerce Court that in considering the subject of orders of the Commission, for the purpose of enforcing or restraining their enforcement, the courts were confined by statutory operation to determining whether there had been violations of the Constitution, a want of conformity to statutory authority, or of ascertaining whether power had been so arbitrarily exercised as virtually to transcend the authority conferred although it may be not technically doing so. *Int. Com. Comm.* v. *Union Pacific R. R.*, 222 U. S. 541, 547; *Int. Com. Comm.* v. *Ill. Cent. R. R.* 215 U. S. 452. So also at the time the law creating the Commerce Court was passed, suits to compel obedience to orders of the Commission or to restrain an enforcement of such orders were required to be brought in the Circuit Court of the United States in the district where a carrier or one of two or more carriers to whom the order was directed had its principal operating office.

In view of the provisions of the act to regulate commerce just referred to as originally enacted, of the legislative evolution of that act, its uniform practical enforcement and the constant judicial interpretation which we have thus briefly indicated, it is impossible, we think, in reason, to give to the act creating the Commerce Court the meaning affixed to it by the court below, since to do so would be virtually to overthrow the entire system which had arisen from the adoption and enforcement of the act to regulate commerce. First, because as the previous ascertainment by the Commission on complaint made to it as to whether violations of the act had been committed, with reference to the subjects as to which previous action was required, was an essential prerequisite to a right to complain in a court, the interpretation given below would, by destroying the necessity for the prerequisite action of the Commission, operate to create a vast body of rights which had no existence at the time the Commerce Court act was passed. Second, because the recognition of a right in a court to assert the power now claimed would of necessity amount to a substitution of the court for the Commission or at all events would be to create a divided authority on a matter where from the beginning primary singleness of action and unity was deemed to be imperative. Third, because the result of the interpretation would be to bring about the contradiction and the confusion which it had been the inflexible purpose of the lawmaker from the beginning to guard against, an interpretation which would seemingly create rights hitherto non-existent and yet at once proceed to destroy such rights by bringing about a confusion which would render the rights which the act creates practically valueless. Indeed, these inevitable results of the interpretation given by the court below to the act would necessarily amount to declaring that Congress in seeking to unify and perfect the administrative machinery of the act to regulate commerce and to make more beneficial its operation had overthrown the whole fabric of the system as previously existing.

The demonstration of the error of the construction adopted below is so additionally made manifest by a consideration of the general structure and the text of the act creating the Commerce Court, that in connection with the legislative history which we have previously stated, that we advert to that point of view, *A*. The first section of the act wherein is recited the jurisdiction of the Commerce Court which we have previously commented upon makes clear that the purpose was not to create a court with new and strange powers destructive of the previous well-established administrative authority of the Interstate Commerce Commission and in conflict with the general jurisdiction vested in the courts of the United States, but only to give to the new court the special jurisdiction then possessed by the courts of the United States for the enforcement of orders made by the Commission, and thus to unify the exertion of judicial power with reference to the enforcement of the orders of the Commission. The opening words of the section which make this result clear are as follows: It (the Commerce Court) shall "have the jurisdiction now possessed by circuit courts of the United States and the judges thereof over all cases of the following kinds: . . ." *B*. Because the enumeration as to the subject-matters of jurisdiction conferred which follows the words just quoted, which enumeration we have previously reproduced and commented upon, conforms to the existing law and evidently assumes its continued operation. *C*. Because the sedulous effort of Congress while creating the new machinery not to destroy the existing system finds expression in a two-fold way: (1) by the declaration that nothing in the fact that the existing power of the Circuit Courts as to the subjects of jurisdiction transferred to the new court should be deemed as an enlarging of those powers, and (2) by the provision that nothing in the transfer of the enumerated powers to the Commerce Court should be considered as limiting or abridging the existing jurisdiction possessed by the Circuit Courts as to things and subject-matters not embraced in the powers transferred. Thus the two provisos again serving to make clear the legislative intent that the creation of a new body to exercise a portion of the existing judicial power should not in any way enlarge the power as existing or be implied as destroying or minimizing the general scope of the judicial power possessed by the Circuit Courts where such power was not embraced within the authority transferred to the new body. *D.* Because the act which created the court contained in its latter sections provisions amending sections of the act to regulate commerce which when rightly interpreted were manifestly adopted to make that act more consistent with the new situation resulting from the creation of the new court and utterly inconsistent with the conception that that court had power not previously possessed by any court and the existence of which would serve to set at naught the whole system of interstate commerce regulation.

Some suggestion is made in argument concerning the alleged claim of constitutional right asserted in the petition filed below and which the court disposed of in the manner we have stated. But what we have said suffices to point out the fallacy which the contention involves, for the following reasons: If the claim of constitutional rights concerned a subject which from its very nature and effect dominated the act to regulate commerce and therefore was wholly independent of all questions of right or remedy created by or depending upon that statute, then the issue presented a controversy not cognizable in the Commerce Court, as it could not so be without violating the express reservation and restriction as to the general power of the Circuit Courts which we have just quoted. If, on the other hand, the constitutional question was involved in or depended upon the provisions of the act to regulate commerce that question in the nature of things was subject to the precedent action of the Commission on the subjects committed to it by the act to regulate commerce and as to which the court had jurisdiction alone to act in virtue of a prior affirmative order of the Commission.

The general considerations which we have stated establish the error committed by the court below in holding that it had jurisdiction over the claim of the Proctor & Gamble Company to recover on a money demand based on the illegality of the demurrage charges alleged to have been wrongfully exacted by the railroad companies. Through abundance of precaution, we, however, say that wholly irrespective of the general considerations stated we think the conclusion of the court as to its possession of jurisdiction over the subject referred to was clearly repugnant in other respects to the express terms of the act.

As it follows from what we have said that the court below

erred in taking jurisdiction of the petition, it results that our duty is to remand the cause to the court below with directions to dismiss the petition for want of jurisdiction,

And it is so ordered.

---

3. Proceedings for Enforcement

INTERSTATE COMMERCE COMMISSION *v.* BAIRD

194 U. S. 25 (1904)

This is an appeal from an order made in the Circuit Court of the United States for the Southern District of New York in the matter of the petition of the Interstate Commerce Commission for orders requiring the testimony of witnesses and the production of certain books, papers and documents. The petition recites that the Attorney General of the United States, at the request of the Interstate Commerce Commission, instructed the United States District Attorney for the Southern District of New York to present the petition and institute proper proceedings for the enforcement of the provisions of the acts to regulate interstate commerce as amended, and to invoke the aid of the court in requiring the attendance and testimony of witnesses and the production of books, papers and documents, pursuant to the provisions of said acts. The case grows out of a complaint of William Randolph Hearst, filed on November 2, 1902, with the Interstate Commerce Commission, against the Philadelphia and Reading Railway Company, Lehigh Valley Railroad Company, Delaware, Lackawanna and Western Railroad, Central Railroad Company of New Jersey, New York, Susquehanna and Western Railroad Company, Erie Railroad Company, New York, Ontario and Western Railroad Company, Delaware and Hudson Company, Pennsylvania Railroad Company and Baltimore and Ohio Railroad Company.

In the complaint it was charged: That the defendants are common carriers, engaged in the transportation of passengers and freight between points in different States of the United States, and are particularly engaged in the transportation of anthracite and bituminous coal mined in Pennsylvania, Maryland and West Virginia, and shipped as interstate traffic over said lines, and are carriers subject to the provision of the act of February 4, 1887, to regulate commerce, and the acts amendatory thereto; that the rates charged and exacted by the defendants for the transportation of anthracite coal in carloads from points in the anthracite coal region of Pennsylvania to New York city and New York harbor points and internal points of destination in the State of New York, to Boston and other points in the New England States, to Baltimore and other points in the State of Maryland, and to Washington, in the District of Columbia, are unreasonable and unjust, and subject consumers and producers of such coal, who are not common carriers or corporations owned and controlled by common carriers, to undue and unreasonable prejudice and disadvantage in favor of and to the undue and unreasonable preference and advantage of said defendants and companies under their control, in violation of sections 1 and 3 of the act to regulate commerce; that the rates charged and exacted by the defendants for the transportation of anthracite coal are relatively unreasonble and unjust, and unjustly discriminating against the interests of dealers and consumers of that commodity as compared with the rates contemporaneously charged by said defendants for transportation of bituminous coal for much longer distances and to the points of destination above mentioned, and also as compared with the defendants' rates and charges on other carload freight generally, all of which is a violation of §§ 1, 2, and 3 of the act to regulate commerce; that the defendant companies — Lehigh Valley Railroad Company, Central Railroad Company of New Jersey, Delaware, Lackawanna and Western Railroad Company, New York, Susquehanna and Western Railroad Company and the Philadelphia and Reading Railway Company — are, in the absence of agreement, natural competitors in the business of transporting anthracite coal from the coal fields of Pennsylvania to tide-water at New York, two of said defendants — the Lehigh Valley Railroad Company and the Central Railroad Company of New Jersey — being substantially parallel lines; that in 1896, 1897, 1898, 1899, 1900 and 1901 the six defendants last named, by an agreement and combination with one another, pooled and have during the year 1902 pooled freights and freight traffic in anthracite coal, so as to divide the same between their different lines in agreed proportions, in violation of § 5 of the act to regulate commerce. The prayer of the petition was that the defendants be required to make answer to the charges, and, after hearing, for an order or orders commanding the said defendants, and each of them, wholly to cease and desist from each and every of the alleged violations of the act to regulate commerce, and for such further order or orders and action by the commission as its duty under the act and the cause of petitioner and others similarly situated may require. Answers were filed by the railroad companies, taking issue with the allegations of the petition and denying violation of the law. In the course of the hearing certain witnesses refused to produce contracts and answer questions when required so to do by order of the commission, which refusal gave rise to the petition to the Circuit Court. The character of the testimony required by the order of the commission is sufficiently set forth in the opinion hereinafter given. To the petition answers were filed too lengthy to abstract, and in substance setting forth the right of the defendants to refuse the production of the papers and documents and to decline to answer the questions because the same did not relate to any subject which the commission had the right to investigate and the contracts relate to the private business of persons not parties to the proceedings before the commission; that the witnesses are protected in their right to refuse to produce the contracts or answer the questions by the Fourth, Fifth and Tenth Amendments to the Constitution of the United States; that the contracts were not relevant to the subject matter of investigation before the commission. The Circuit Court placed its decision on the latter ground, and dismissed the petition of the Interstate Commerce Commission.

MR. JUSTICE DAY delivered the opinion of the court.

A motion is made to dismiss the appeal upon the ground that no direct appeal lies to this court from the order of the Circuit Court. The act of February 19, 1903, (Comp. Stat. 1901, Sup. for 1903, p. 365,) to further regulate commerce with foreign nations and among the States, § 3, closing paragraph, enacts, "*Provided,* That the provisions of an act entitled 'An act to expedite the hearing and determination of suits in equity pending or hereafter brought under the act of July second, eighteen hundred and ninety, entitled 'An act to protect trade and commerce against unlawful restraints and monopolies,' 'An Act to regulate commerce,' approved February fourth, eighteen hundred and eighty-seven, or any other acts having a like purpose that may be hereafter enacted, approved February eleventh, nineteen hundred and three,' shall apply to any case prosecuted under the direction of the Attorney General in the name of the Interstate Commerce Commission."

The second section of the act of February 11, 1903, (Comp. Stat. of 1901, Sup. for 1903, p. 376,) provides "That in every suit in equity pending or hereafter brought in any Circuit Court of the United States under any of said acts [having reference to the anti-trust act of 1890 and the act to regulate commerce mentioned in the preceding section] wherein the United States is complainant, including cases submitted but not yet decided, an appeal from the final decree of the Circuit Court will lie only to the Supreme Court and must be taken within sixty days from the entry thereof."

In support of the motion to dismiss it is argued that the language of the proviso of section 3, above quoted, "shall apply to any case prosecuted under the direction of the Attorney General in the name of the Interstate Commerce Commission," must be read in connection with preceding paragraphs of the section, which provide for bringing actions by direction of the Attorney General in the Circuit Courts of the United States, and do not include proceedings of the character of the present action to compel the production of books and papers and the giving of testimony by witnesses called before the commission.

It is true that the office of a proviso, strictly considered, is to make exception from the enacting clause, to restrain generality and to prevent misinterpretation. *Minis* v. *United States*, 15 Pet. 423; *Austin* v. *United States*, 155 U. S. 417, 431; *White* v. *United States*, 191 U. S. 545, 551. It is apparent that this proviso was not inserted in any restrictive sense or to make clear that which might be doubtful from the general language used. It was inserted for the purpose of enlarging the operation of the statute so as to include a class of cases not otherwise within the operation of the section. It may be admitted that this use of a proviso is not in accord with the technical meaning of the term or the office of such part of a statute when properly used. But it is nevertheless a frequent use of the proviso in Federal legislation to introduce, as in the present case, new matter extending rather than limiting or explaining that which has gone before.

In *Chesapeake & Potomac Tel. Co.* v. *Manning*, 186 U. S. 238, 242, the subject was under consideration, and Mr. Justice Brewer, delivering the opinion, while recognizing the restrictive office of a proviso as stated by Mr. Justice Story in *Minis* v. *United States*, 15 Pet. 423, 445, added: "While this is the general effect of a proviso, yet in practice it is not always so limited. As said in *Georgia Banking Company* v. *Smith*, 128 U. S. 174, 181: 'The general purpose of a proviso, as is well known, is to except the clause covered by it from the general provisions of the statute, or from some provisions of it, or to qualify the operation of the statute is some particular. But it is often used in other senses. It is a common practice in legislative proceedings, on the consideration of bills, for parties desirous of securing amendments to them to precede their proposed amendments with the term "provided," so as to declare that, notwithstanding existing provisions, the one thus expressed is to prevail, thus having no greater signification than would be attached to the conjunction "but" or "and" in the same place, and simply serving to separate or distinguish the different paragraphs or sentences.' "

The provision in the statute under consideration being intended to enlarge rather than limit the application of previous terms should not receive so narrow a construction as to defeat its purpose. It extends the terms of the act of February 11, 1903, to "any case" brought under the direction of the Attorney General in the name of the Interstate Commerce Commission. The second section of the act of February 11, has reference, it is true, to a suit in equity under certain acts wherein the United States is complainant, and the argument is that the extension of the terms of this act in the act of February 19 is only to suits in equity. But for some reason Congress, in the act under consideration, saw fit not to limit the terms of the extension to suits or proceedings provided for in section 3 of the act of February 19, or to suits in equity, but broadly extended the rights and privileges of the act of February 11, to "cases" of the character designated. We cannot assume that this use of the broader term was without purpose. Before the passage of this act this court had held that a petition filed under section twelve of the interstate commerce act against a witness duly summoned to testify before the commission, to compel him to testify or to produce books, documents and papers relating to the matter in controversy, makes a case or controversy to which the judicial power of the United States extends. *Interstate Commerce Commission* v. *Brimson,* 154 U. S. 447. The object of construction, as has been often said by the courts and writers of authority, is to ascertain the legislative intent, and, if possible, to effectuate the purposes of the lawmakers. We cannot read these statutes without perceiving the manifest purpose of Congress to facilitate the disposition of cases brought under the direction of the Attorney General to enforce the provision of the anti-trust and interstate commerce statutes. The present proceeding is not merely advisory to the commission, but, as was said in *Interstate Commerce Commission* v. *Brimson, supra,* a judgment rendered will be a final and indisputable basis of action as between the commission and the defendant, and furnish a precedent for similar cases. While it has for its object the obtaining of testimony in aid of proceedings before the commission, it is evident that important questions may be involved touching the power of the commission and the constitutional rights and privileges of citizens. Congress deemed it imperative that such cases, affecting the commerce of the country as well as personal rights, should be promptly determined in a court of last resort.

If the appeal in the first instance was to the Court of Appeals the judgment of that court would not be final under the act of March 3, 1891, and in such case this court would still be required to consider the cases on final appeal. We think it was the purpose of the act to eliminate an appeal to the Circuit Court of Appeals and to permit the litigation to be shortened by a direct appeal to this court.

We pass now to the merits of the controversy. The record in this case is voluminous, and much of the discussion before the commission is printed. We shall endeavor to classify and consider the questions made so as to indicate our holdings with a view to a proper judgment in the case.

It is urged that the complainant before the commission did not show any real interest in the case brought, and that the proceeding should for that reason have been dismissed. It is provided in the act to regulate commerce, sec. 13, that "any person, firm, corporation," etc., complaining of anything done or omitted to be done by any common carrier subject to the provisions of this act, in contravention of the provisions thereof may apply to said commission by petition, etc. And certain procedure is provided for — and (said commission) "may institute any inquiry on its own motion in the same manner and to the same effect as though complaint had been made," and the section concludes: "No complaint shall at any time be dismissed because of the absence of direct damage to the complainant." In face of this mandatory requirement that the complaint shall not be dismissed because of the want of direct damage to the complainant, no alternative is left the commission but to investigate the complaint, if it presents matter within the purview of the act and the powers granted to the commission.

Power is conferred upon the commission, under section 12 of the act as amended March 2, 1889, and February 10, 1891, (3 U. S. Comp. Stat. of 1901, p. 3162,) to inquire into the management of the business of all common carriers subject to the provisions of the act, and to keep itself informed as to the manner and method in which the same is conducted, with the right to obtain from such common carriers full and complete information necessary to enable the commission to perform the duties and carry out the objects for which it was created.

In making the orders which were the basis of the application to the Circuit Court and in the petition filed therein it is set forth that the commission at the time when the witnesses refused to produce the contracts required, was engaged "in the discharge of its duty to execute and enforce the provisions of the act to regulate commerce and in the exercise of its authority to inquire into the business of common carriers subject to the provisions of the act, and to keep itself informed as to the manner and method in which said business is conducted, and to obtain from said common carriers full and complete information necessary to enable it to perform the duties and carry out the objects for which it was created; and your petitioner is of the opinion that said contracts are not only material and relevant to the issues on trial in said proceeding, but that the production thereof as required by it, as aforesaid, is necessary to enable your petitioner to discharge its duty and execute and enforce said provisions of said act to regulate commerce and to inform your petitioner as to the manner and method in which the business of said common carriers is conducted, and to enable your petitioner to obtain the full and complete information necessary to enable your petitioner to perform the duties and carry out the objects for which it was created."

But in the present case, whatever may be the right of the commission to carry on an investigation under the general powers conferred in section 12, this proceeding was under the complaint filed, and we will examine the testimony offered with a view to its competency under the allegations made by the complainant. . .

KNAPP *v.* LAKE SHORE AND MICHIGAN SOUTHERN RAILWAY COMPANY

197 U. S. 536 (1905)

MR. JUSTICE MCKENNA delivered the opinion of the court.

Petition for mandamus filed in the Circuit Court of the United States for the Northern District of Ohio by the Interstate Commerce Commissioners against the Lake Shore and Michigan Southern Railway Company. The railway company moved to dismiss the petition on the ground that the court had no original jurisdiction to issue a writ of mandamus. The motion was granted and the writ dismissed. A certificate was duly made showing that a question of jurisdiction was in issue, and recites that the court acted not only on the motion of the railroad but on its own motion in dismissing the petition for want of jurisdiction.

The petition alleges that the railroad company is a corporation created by the laws of the States of New York, Pennsylvania, Ohio, Michigan, Indiana and Illinois, and has its principal place of business in the State of Ohio, and is a common carrier engaged in interstate commerce, and as such is subject to the provisions of the act of Congress to regulate Commerce.

That under section 20 of said act the Interstate Commerce Commission is authorized to require any common carrier subject to the act to make reports of certain matters and things, and in pursuance thereof the Commission made an order on the third of June, 1903, prescribing the manner and form in which said reports should be made and the contents thereof, and directed each common carrier to file the same on or before the fifteenth. A copy of the order was served on the railroad company, but the company failed and neglected to make out and return a report in full, in that it failed to set forth in the report made and returned by it the data or information called for, namely, "the tonnage, ton-mileage, earnings and receipts per ton per mile on grain, hay, cotton, live stock, dressed meats, anthracite coal, bituminous coal, and lumber carried in carload lots; and that said data or information required by the Commission to be given in said report by respondent is necessary to enable the Commission to perform the duties and carry out the objects for which it was created, in the interest of the public, and that promptness by carriers in furnishing the same on or before the fifteenth day of September of each year, as required by the Commission, is essential for the purpose, among others, of enabling the Commission to make a full and complete annual report to Congress, which, by section 21 of said act to regulate commerce, is required to be transmitted to said body on or before December 1 of each year."

It is also alleged that there is no adequate remedy except that afforded by mandamus.

It is admitted that under the judiciary act of 1789, 1 Stat. 73, and the act of 1875, as construed by this court, a Circuit Court of the United States has no jurisdiction of an original proceeding seeking relief by mandamus. And counsel, not to minimize the admission, quotes the cases in which that has been laid down and the text books which have expressed the doctrine as settled. But, it is suggested, that under the act of 1887, 24 Stat. 552, a different ruling should be made. No change in language is pointed out which would justify such change in ruling, but we are urged to that radical course in view of the modern development of proceedings by mandamus, and the very great importance of the remedy thereby. We are not impressed by the invocation. We are unable to understand how language conferring jurisdiction on a court can take a new meaning from the circumstances suggested. Difference in remedies is conspicuous in our jurisprudence, and some remedies are of that nature that they can be enforced only under exceptional circumstances and under special grants of power. Of this kind is mandamus, and if Congress had intended by the act of 1887 to confer power on the Circuit Courts to issue mandamus in an original proceeding Congress would not have employed the language which had been construed from the foundation of the Government not to give such jurisdiction. We adhere, therefore, to the prior cases.

2. Congress has undoubtedly power to authorize a Circuit Court to issue a mandamus in an original proceeding. *Kendall* v. *United States*, 12 Pet. 524; *United States* v. *Schurz*, 102 U. S. 378. But has Congress done so, as contended, by sections 12 and 20 of the Interstate Commerce Act as amended? Under section 12 the Commission is given the authority to inquire into the management of the business of common carriers subject to the act, and have the right to obtain from the carriers full and complete information to enable it to perform its duties. It is also authorized to enforce the provisions of the act. By section 20 the Commission may require annual reports and fix the time and prescribe the manner in which such reports shall be made. And it is made the duty of any district attorney of the United States, to whom the Commission may apply, to institute in the proper court and to prosecute under the direction of the Attorney General all necessary proceedings for the enforcement of the provisions of this act. It is hence contended that the power of the Commission to require the report stated in the petition is undoubted, and having power to order the report to be made the Commission has the power to enforce obedience to the order.

But in what way? Manifestly only in such way as the courts

have jurisdiction to give. All powers are given in view of that jurisdiction, and the amendments of the Interstate Commerce Act are so framed. Jurisdiction to issue mandamus is conferred by section 6, to enforce the filing or publishing by a common carrier of its schedules or tariffs of rates, fares and charges. And such jurisdiction is also given to the Circuit Courts and District Courts upon the relation of any person or persons, firm or corporation, alleging a violation of any of the provisions of the act which prevents the relator from having interstate traffic moved on terms as favorable as any other shipper. The remedy is expressly made cumulative of the other remedies provided by the act. It is clear, therefore, when Congress intended to give the power to issue mandamus it expressed that intention explicitly. Such power cannot be inferred from the grant of authority to the Commission to enforce the act or from the direction to district attorneys or the Attorney General to institute "all necessary proceedings for the enforcement of the provisions" of the act (section 12). The proceedings meant are, as we have said, those within the jurisdiction of the court. And special remedies are given. For instance, by section 16 a summary proceeding in equity is authorized, and the form of the ultimate order of the court may be that of a "writ of injunction or other proper process, mandatory or otherwise."

Without attempting now to define the extent of that section, we may say, it seems adequate to enable the Commission to enforce any order it is authorized to make.

Judgment affirmed.

MR. JUSTICE HARLAN dissented.

UNITED STATES AT THE RELATION OF KANSAS CITY SOUTHERN RAILWAY COMPANY *v.* INTERSTATE COMMERCE COMMISSION

252 U. S. 178 (1920)

MR. CHIEF JUSTICE WHITE delivered the opinion of the court.

The Act of Congress of March 1, 1913 (37 Stat. 701), amending the "Act to regulate commerce," imposed the duty upon the Interstate Commerce Commission (section 19*a*) to "investigate, ascertain, and report the value of all property owned or used by every common carrier subject to the provisions of this Act."

Specifying the steps to be taken in the performance of the general duties thus imposed, the same section commanded as follows:

"First. In such investigation said commission shall ascertain and report in detail as to each piece of property owned or used by said carrier for its purposes as a common carrier . . . the cost of reproduction new, the cost of reproduction less depreciation, and an analysis of the methods by which these several costs are obtained and the reasons for their differences, if any . . .

"Second. Such investigation and report shall state in detail and separately from improvements the original cost of all lands, rights of way, and terminals owned or used for the purposes of a common carrier, and ascertained as of the day of dedication to public use, and the present value of the same, and separately the original and present cost of condemnation and damages or of purchase in excess of such original cost or present value.

. . . .

"Fifth. . . . (8th par.) Whenever the commission shall have completed the tentative valuation of the property of any common carrier, as herein directed, and before such valuation shall become final, the commission shall give notice by registered letter to said carrier, . . . stating the valuation placed upon the several classes of property of said carrier, and shall allow thirty days in which to file a protest of the same with the commission. . . .

"If notice of protest is filed the commission shall fix a time for hearing the same, and shall proceed as promptly as may be to hear and consider any matter relative and material thereto . . . All final valuations by the commission and the classification thereof shall be published and shall be prima facie evidence of the value of the property in all proceedings under the Act to regulate commerce as of the date of the fixing thereof, and in all judicial proceedings for the enforcement of the Act approved February 4th, 1887, commonly known as 'the Act to regulate commerce,' and the various Acts amendatory thereof, and in all judicial proceedings brought to enjoin, set aside, annul or suspend, in whole or in part, any order of the interstate commerce commission."

Pursuant to these requirements the Commission proceeded to investigate and report the value of the property of the Kansas City Southern Railway Company. Upon completing a tentative valuation, the Commission gave the notice required by the statute to the Railway Company, which thereupon filed a protest against such valuation on the ground that in making it the Commission had failed to consider and include the "present cost of condemnation and damages or of purchase in excess of such original cost or present value." Upon the subject of the protest, the Railway Company took a large amount of testimony and much was also taken by the Commission, both parties having incurred considerable expense in the matter.

Pending this situation, in order that the excessive expense of taking each individual parcel and showing what it would cost to acquire it or a right of way over it by purchase or condemnation might be avoided, an agreement was entered into between the Director of the Bureau of Valuation of the Commission, C. A. Prouty, and the Railway Company, that in the event the Commission should decide that evidence upon the cost of acquiring land by purchase or condemnation would be received by it, the Bureau of Valuation would recommend to the Commission the percentage or multiplier of the naked value of the land, to be used for the purpose of reaching the railway cost of acquiring the same.

At that time there was also pending a protest concerning a tentative valuation made by the Commission as to the property of the Texas Midland Railroad Company, raising the same question as to error committed in failing to carry out the provisions of the statute concerning the present cost of condemnation, etc., in which case the Commission overruled the protest, holding that the provision of the statute in question was not susceptible of being enforced or acted upon for reasons stated by the Commission in part as follows (I. C. C. Val. Rep. 1, p. 54 *et seq.*):

"However, the direction in paragraph 'Second' for the ascertainment of the present cost of condemnation and damages or of purchase in effect calls for a finding as to the cost of reproduction of these lands. Must this be done, and can this be done? It seems elementary that the cost of reproduction can be estimated only by assuming that the thing in question is to be produced again, and that if it is to be produced again, it is to be taken as not existent. It seems sophistry to contend that the lands of the railroad can be produced again at a cost to the railroad without first making the assumption that they are no longer lands of the railroad; and this necessary assumption carries with it the mental obliteration of the railroad itself.

"Considerable testimony was produced to the effect that in the acquisition of a railroad right of way it is necessary for the carrier to pay sums in excess of the value of the land if measured by the present or market value of similar contiguous lands, and this because of the elements which have been enumerated and embraced in the protest, such as cost of acquisition, damages to the severed property, cost of buildings and other improvements, accrued taxes and various incidental rights.

. . . .

"We are unable to distinguish between what is suggested by the carrier in this record and nominally required by the act and what was condemned by the court (in the *Minnesota Rate Cases*) as beyond the possibility of rational determination; nor is there any essential difference in the actual methods there employed and those now urged upon us. Before we can report figures as ascertained, we must have a reasonable foundation for our estimate, and when, as here, if the estimate can be made only upon inadmissible assumptions, and upon impossible hypotheses, such as those pointed out by the Supreme Court in the opinion quoted, our duty to abstain from reporting as an ascertained fact that which is incapable of rational ascertainment, is clear.

. . . .

"Because of the impossibility of making the self-contradictory assumptions which the theory requires when applied to the carrier's lands, we are unable to report the reproduction cost of such lands or its equivalent, the present cost of acquisition and damages or of purchase in excess of present value. The present value of lands as found by us appears in the final valuation, appended hereto."

Applying the ruling thus made to the protest which was pending in this case, the Commission gave notice to the Railway that the agreement made with the Director of the Bureau of Valuation concerning the method of proof would be treated as not further operative; and thereafter when an offer was made by the Railway before an examiner of the Commission of further testimony concerning the subject in hand, it was excluded because in conflict with the ruling announced in the *Midland* case. The Commission sustained this action of the examiner on the ground that that officer had rightly held that the ruling in the *Midland* case was controlling; and the Commission therefore decided that no further testimony on the particular subject would be heard in this case, and that it would make no report concerning that subject.

This suit was then brought to obtain a mandamus to compel the Commission to hear the proof and act upon it under the statute. The amended petition, after reciting the facts as we have outlined them and making the appropriate formal averments to justify resort to mandamus, alleged:

"That the refusal of respondent to investigate and find such present cost of condemnation and damages or of purchase in excess of original cost or present value of relator's lands will result in great wrong and injury to relator; by way of illustration, such refusal will result in a finding by respondent of a value of but $60,000 with respect to parcels of land acquired by relator by judicial award in condemnation proceedings during four years immediately preceding such valuation at an actual cost to relator of $180,000; and in the aggregate will result in a finding with respect to said lands at least $5,000,000 less than the value so directed by the Act of Congress above mentioned to be found."

It was further averred, with considerable elaboration, that the petitioner stood ready to produce proof to meet the requirements of the statute which was neither speculative nor impossible to be acted upon, since it would conform to the character of proof usually received in judicial proceedings involving the exercise of eminent domain.

The Commission in its answer, either stating or conceding the history of the case as we have recited it, and summarily reiterating the grounds for the refusal by the Commission to receive the proof or report concerning it, challenged the right to the relief sought. A demurrer to the answer as stating no defense was overruled by the trial court, which denied relief without opinion. In the Court of Appeals, two judges sitting, the judgment of the trial court was affirmed by a divided court, also without opinion, and the case is here on writ of error to review that judgment.

It is obvious from the statement we have made, as well as from the character of the remedy invoked, mandamus, that we are required to decide, not a controversy growing out of duty performed under the statute, but one solely involving an alleged refusal to discharge duties which the statute exacts. Admonishing, as this does, that the issue before us is confined to a consideration of the face of the statute and the non-action of the Commission in a matter purely ministerial, it serves also to furnish a ready solution of the question to be decided, since it brings out in bold contrast the direct and express command of the statute to the Commission, to act concerning the subject in hand, and the Commission's unequivocal refusal to obey such command.

It is true that the Commission held that its non-action was

caused by the fact that the command of the statute involved a consideration by it of matters "beyond the possibility of rational determination," and called for "inadmissible assumptions," and the indulging in "impossible hypotheses" as to subjects "incapable of rational ascertainment," and that such conclusions were the necessary consequence of the *Minnesota Rate Cases.* (230 U. S. 352).

We are of opinion, however, that, considering the face of the statute and the reasoning of the Commission, it results that the conclusion of the Commission was erroneous, an error which was exclusively caused by a mistaken conception by the Commission of its relation to the subject, resulting in an unconscious disregard on its part of the power of Congress and an unwitting assumption by the Commission of authority which it did not possess. And the significance which the Commission attributed to the ruling in the *Minnesota Rate Cases,* even upon the assumption that its view of the ruling in those cases was not a mistaken one, but illustrates in a different form the disregard of the power of Congress which we have just pointed out, since, as Congress indisputably had the authority to impose upon the Commission the duty in question, it is impossible to conceive how the *Minnesota Rate* ruling could furnish ground for refusing to carry out the commands of Congress, the cogency of which consideration is made particularly manifest when it is borne in mind that the *Minnesota Rate Cases* were decided prior to the passage of the Act in question.

Finally, even if it be further conceded that the subject-matter of the valuations in question which the Act of Congress expressly directed to be made necessarily opened a wide range of proof and called for the exercise of close scrutiny and of scrupulous analysis in its consideration and application, such assumption, we are of opinion, affords no basis for refusing to enforce the Act of Congress, or what is equivalent thereto, of exerting the general power which the Act of Congress gave, and at the same time disregarding the essential conditions imposed by Congress upon its exercise.

The judgment of the Court of Appeals is therefore reversed with directions to reverse that of the Supreme Court, and direct the Supreme Court to grant a writ of mandamus in conformity with this opinion.

ELLIS *v.* INTERSTATE COMMERCE COMMISSION

237 U. S. 434 (1915)

MR. JUSTICE HOLMES delivered the opinion of the court.

This is an appeal from an order of the District Court made upon a petition of the appellee, the Interstate Commerce Commission, filed under the act to regulate commerce, § 12, c. 104, 24 Stat. 379, 383. The order directs the appellant to answer certain questions propounded and to produce certain documents called for by the appellee. There is no doubt that this appeal lies. The order is not like one made to a witness before an examiner or on the stand in the course of a proceeding *inter alios* in court. *Alexander* v. *United States*, 201 U. S. 117. It is the end of a proceeding begun against the witness. *Interstate Commerce Commission* v. *Baird*, 194 U. S. 25. Therefore, we pass at once to the statement of the case.

The Interstate Commerce Commission, reciting that it appeared from complaint on file that the allowances paid for the use of private cars, the practices governing the handling and icing of such cars, and the minimum carload weights applicable to the commodities shipped therein, on the part of carriers subject to the act to regulate commerce, violated that act in various ways, ordered that a proceeding of investigation be instituted by the Commission of its own motion to determine whether such allowances, practices, or minimum carload weights were in violation of the act as alleged, with a view to issuing such orders as might be necessary to correct discriminations and make applicable reasonable weights. It ordered that carriers by railroad subject to the act be made parties respondent, and, later, that all persons and corporations owning or operating cars and other vehicles and instrumentalities and facilities of shipment or carriage of property in interstate commerce be made parties also. In the proceedings thus ordered the questions propounded were put to the appellant, the vice president and general manager of the Armour Car Lines.

The Armour Car Lines is a New Jersey corporation that owns, manufactures and maintains refrigerator, tank and box cars, and that lets these cars to the railroad or to shippers. It also owns and operates icing stations on various lines of railway, and from these ices and reices the cars, when set by the railroads at the icing plant, by filling the bunkers from the top, after which the railroads remove the cars. The railroads pay a certain rate per ton, and charge the shipper according to tariffs on file with the Commission. Finally it furnishes cars for the shipment of perishable fruits, &c., and keeps them iced, the railroads paying for the same. It has no control over motive power or over the movement of the cars that it furnishes as above, and in short, notwithstanding some argument to the contrary, is not a common carrier subject to the act. It is true that the definition of transportation in § 1 of the act includes such instrumentalities as the Armour Car Lines lets to the railroads. But the definition is a preliminary to a requirement that the carriers shall furnish them upon reasonable request, not that the owners and builders shall be regarded as carriers, contrary to the truth. The control of the Commission over private cars, &c., is to be effected by its control over the railroads that are subject to the act. The railroads may be made answerable for what they hire from the Armour Car Lines, if they would not be otherwise, but that does not affect the nature of the Armour Car Lines itself. The petition of the Interstate Commerce Commission to compel an answer to its questions hardly goes on any such ground.

The ground of the petition is that it became the duty of the Commission to ascertain whether Armour & Company, an Illinois corporation shipping packing-house products in commerce among the States, was controlling Armour Car Lines and using it as a device to obtain concessions from the published rates of transportation, and whether Armour Car Lines was receiving for its refrigerating services unreasonable compensation that enured to the benefit of Armour & Co., all in violation of §§ 1, 2, 3, and 15 of the act.

If the price paid to the Armour Car Lines was made the cover for a rebate to Armour & Co., or if better cars were given to Armour & Co. than to others, or if, in short, the act was violated, the railroads are responsible on proof of the fact. But the only relation that is subject to the Commission is that between the railroads and the shippers. It does not matter to the responsibility of the roads whether they own or simply control the facilities, or whether they pay a greater or less price to their lessor. It was argued that the Commission might look into the profits and losses of the Armour Car Lines (one of the matters inquired about), in order to avoid fixing allowances to it at a confiscatory rate. But the Commission fixes nothing as to the Armour Car Lines except under § 15 in the event of which we shall speak.

The appellant's refusal to answer the series of questions put was not based upon any objection to giving much of the information sought, but on the ground that the counsel who put them avowed that they were the beginning of an attempt to go into the whole business of the Armour Car Lines — a fishing expedition into the affairs of a stranger for the chance that something discreditable might turn up. This was beyond the powers of the Commission. *In re Pacific Railway Commission*, 32 Fed. Rep. 241; *Interstate Commerce Commission* v. *Brimson*, 154 U. S., 447, 478, 479; *Harriman* v. *Interstate Commerce Commission*, 211 U. S. 407. The Armour Car Lines not being subject to regulation by the Commission its position was simply that of a witness interested in but a stranger to the inquiry, and the Commission could not enlarge its powers by making the Company a party to the proceedings and serving it with notice. Therefore the matter to be considered here, subject to the qualification that we are about to state, is how far an ordinary witness could be required to answer the questions that are before the court.

We have stated the nature and object of the investigation, and it is to be observed that not every advantage that may enure to a shipper as the result of the position of his plant, his ownership or his wealth is a preference. *Interstate Commerce Commission* v. *Diffenbaugh*, 222 U. S. 42, 46. But the intervening corporation may be a means by which an owner of property transported indirectly renders the services in question, and in that event its charges are subject to the Commission by § 15. The supposed unreasonable charge may be used as a device to attain the forbidden end and therefore reasonable latitude should be allowed to see if any such device is used. *Interstate Commerce Commission* v. *Brimson*, 154 U. S. 447, 464. But still until Armour Car Lines is shown to be merely the tool of Armour & Company it has the general immunities that we have stated. With the foregoing general principles in view we proceed to dispose of the questions asked.

It is not necessary to repeat the many pages of questions at length. They are grouped by the Government into classes and numbered so that the result may be stated in comparatively few words. The first group concerning interlocking officers and relations between Armour Car Lines, Armour & Company and Fowler Packing Company, questions 1, 2, 3 and 7, should be answered. The only objection was on account of the general intent avowed as we have stated. So also questions 4, 5, 6, concerning the acquirement of cars previously owned by Armour and Company and Armour Packing Co., making the second group. Also questions 8, 9, 12 and 13, as to contracts of Armour Car Lines with Armour & Company and Colorado Packing Company for furnishing cars and icing service. The next group, so far as the questions concern the ownership, manufacture and repair of cars, Nos. 10, 11, 14, 16, 17 and 19, need not be answered, except 11 "where are the cars of Armour Car Lines repaired when not repaired in shops of railroads?" The last two groups concern matters into which the Commission was not authorized to inquire. The fifth, questions 15, 20, 21, 25, 26, 27, and 28, called for statements showing profit and loss, credits and debits to income &c., so far as the same related to transportation as defined in the act; and the sixth, Nos. 22, 23, and 24, for statements showing the amount invested in each icing plant and the detailed results of the operation of each, amount invested in each, cost per ton of ice at the source of supply &c., &c., all matters belonging to the private business of the Armour Car Lines and not open if our interpretation of the law is correct. Our decision, however, must be without prejudiced to the possibility that the case may be brought within §15 by evidence to the effect stated above.

Decree reversed without prejudice.

MR. JUSTICE DAY, while not differing from the general views taken by the court, is of opinion that the nature of the inquiry under § 15 made it proper that all the questions should be answered.

MR. JUSTICE MCREYNOLDS took no part in the consideration or decision of this case.

LOUISVILLE & NASHVILLE RAILROAD COMPANY *v.* OHIO VALLEY TIE COMPANY

242 U. S. 288 (1915)

MR. JUSTICE HOLMES delivered the opinion of the court.

This is a suit brought by the defendant in error in 1911 against the Railroad Company to recover for injury to business and other damages alleged to have been caused by the Railroad's acts. The most important feature at this state is that the Railroad maintained and collected a higher rate for cross-ties than it did for lumber when they were carried between States, although the state commission required the same rate upon both for carriage within the State, and although, as the Railroad knew, the Interstate Commerce Commission repeatedly had decided that the rates for cross-ties and lumber should be the same. It is alleged that these and the other acts complained of were done for the purpose of getting rid of the plaintiff as a competitive buyer, and, in that sense, maliciously. The plaintiff tried to meet the higher rate by directing delivery within the State of ties intended to go beyond, which attempt the defendant encountered by refusal to carry them except on its interstate tariff, and hampered the plaintiff by declining to let its cars leave its road, by deliveries at points requiring a haul by wagon and so forth, and, in short, it may be assumed that the Railroad did other acts to further the alleged end, not necessary to be stated here.

Shortly before bringing this suit the plaintiff complained to the Interstate Commerce Commission in respect of charges collected upon ninety-one carloads of ties, and in 1912 obtained an order that the Railroad pay to it $6198 as reparation for unreasonable rates, and establish a rate for ties not to exceed its contemporaneous one for lumber of the same kind of wood. This order was pleaded by an amendment to the petition and it appeared at the trial that the sum awarded had been paid. As the damage alleged was attributed mainly to the publication and exaction of excessive charges, the defendant insisted at the trial and before the Court of Appeals upon its rights under the Act to Regulate Commerce, and those rights were passed upon by the court, so that there is no doubt of the jurisdiction here, although some questions were raised that we think it unnecessary to discuss.

The defendant contended and asked for a ruling that in this action no damages could be allowed "on account of defendant having charged to and collected from plaintiff unreasonable rates of freight for the carriage of interstate shipments of cross-ties" and other rulings to similar effect. It also asked an instruction that under the Act to Regulate Commerce it was required to collect the rates fixed by its tariff on file and in effect. These requests were refused, and the jury were told that if they believed that the rates found by the Interstate Commerce Commission to be unreasonable were wilfully and maliciously maintained with intent to injure the plaintiff's business, and that the defendent knew them to be unreasonable, and that by its acts it tied up a part of the plaintiff's capital and so damaged the plaintiff's business, then upon this, as well as on several other possible findings stated, they would find for the plaintiff. The jury found a verdict for the plaintiff for certain itemized expenses and for $50,000 damage to plaintiff's business and credit as mentioned in the above instruction. Judgment on the verdict was affirmed by the Court of Appeals. 161 Kentucky, 212.

The Court of Appeals decided that the Act to Regulate Commerce committed to the Interstate Commerce Commission only the granting of special relief against the making of an overcharge and that the satisfaction of the Commission's award still left open an action in the state courts to recover what are termed general damages — such as are supposed to have been recovered in this case. In this we are of opinion that the court was wrong.

By § 8 a common carrier violating the commands of the act is made liable to the person injured thereby "for the full amount of damages sustained in consequence" of the violation. By § 9 any person so injured may make complaint to the Commission or may sue in a court of the United States to recover the damages for which the carrier is liable under the act, but must elect in each case which of the two methods of procedure he will adopt. The rule of damages in one hardly can be different from that proper for the other. An award directing the carrier to pay to the complainant the sum to which he is entitled is provided for by § 16. By the same section if the carrier does not comply in due time with the order the complainant may sue in a state court — which implies that if the order has been complied with and the money paid no suit can be maintained. It is to be noticed further that reparation before answer is contemplated as possible by § 13 and in that case the carrier shall be relieved of liability to the complainant though only of course for the particular violation of law. The decisions say that whatever the damages were they could be recovered; *Pennsylvania R. R. Co.* v. *International Coal Mining Co.*, 230 U. S. 184, 202, 203; *Meeker* v. *Lehigh Valley R. R. Co.*, 236 U. S. 412, 429; and that the statute determines the extent of damages. *Pennsylvania R. R. Co.* v. *Clark Brothers Coal Mining Co.*, 238 U. S. 456, 472. We are of opinion that all damage that properly can be attributed to an overcharge, whether it be the keeping of the plaintiff out of its money, dwelt upon by the trial court, or the damage to its business following as a remoter result of the same cause, must be taken to have been considered in the award of the Commission and compensated when that award was paid.

If at a new trial the plaintiff can prove that the defendant unjustifiably refused cars or caused it other damage not attributable to the overcharge of freight, our decision does not prevent a recovery; but it is evident that the present judgment embraces elements that cannot be allowed.

Judgment reversed.

SOUTHERN PACIFIC COMPANY ET AL. v. DARNELL-TAENZER LUMBER COMPANY ET AL.

245 U. S. 531 (1918)

MR. JUSTICE HOLMES delivered the opinion of the court.

This is a suit brought by the defendants in error to recover reparation from the railroads for charging a rate on hardwood lumber, alleged to be excessive. The Interstate Commerce Commission had found the rate to be excessive and had made an order for reduction from 85 to 75 cents, which was obeyed, and also one for reparation to the extent of the excess, which was not obeyed. 13 I. C. C. 668. A demurrer to the declaration was sustained by the Circuit Court on the ground that it was not alleged that the plaintiffs had paid the excessive rates or that they were damaged thereby. 190 Fed. Rep. 659. The declaration was amended, but at the trial the judge directed a verdict for the defendants, presumably on the ground argued here, that it did not appear that the plaintiffs were damaged. The judgment was reversed by the Circuit Court of Appeals. 221 Fed. Rep. 890. 137 C. C. A. 460. At a new trial the jury were instructed that if they found the rate charged unreasonable and that prescribed by the Interstate Commerce Commission reasonable, they should find for the plaintiffs in accordance with the Commission's award. The jury found for the plaintiffs and this judgment was affirmed by the Circuit Court of Appeals. 229 Fed. Rep. 1022. 143 C. C. A. 663.

The only question before us is that at which we have hinted: whether the fact that the plaintiffs were able to pass on the damage that they sustained in the first instance by paying the unreasonable charge, and to collect that amount from the purchasers, prevents their recovering the overpayment from the carriers. The answer is not difficult. The general tendency of the law, in regard to damages at least, is not to go beyond the first step. As it does not attribute remote consequences to a defendant so it holds him liable if proximately the plaintiff has suffered a loss. The plaintiffs suffered losses to the amount of the verdict when they paid. Their claim accrued at once in the theory of the law and it does not inquire into later events. *Olds* v. *Mapes-Reeve Construction Co.*, 177 Massachusetts, 41, 44. Perhaps strictly the securing of such an indemnity as the present might be regarded as not differing in principle from the recovery of insurance, as *res inter alios*, with which the defendants were not concerned. If it be said that the whole transaction is one from a business point of view, it is enough to reply that the unity in this case is not sufficient to entitle the purchaser to recover, any more than the ultimate consumer who in turn paid an increased price. He has no privity with the carrier. *State* v. *Central Vermont Ry. Co.*, 81 Vermont, 459. See *Nicola, Stone & Myers Co.* v. *Louisville & Nashville R. R. Co.*, 14 I. C. C. 199, 207–209. *Baker Manufacturing Co.* v. *Chicago & North Western Ry. Co.*, 21 I. C. C. 605. The carrier ought not be allowed to retain his illegal profit, and the only one who can take it from him is the one that alone was in relation with him, and from whom the carrier took the sum. *New York, New Haven & Hartford R. R. Co.* v. *Ballou & Wright*, 242 Fed. Rep. 862. Behind the technical mode of statement is the consideration well emphasized by the Interstate Commerce Commission, of the endlessness and futility of the effort to follow every transaction to its ultimate result. 13 I. C. C. 680. Probably in the end the public pays the damages in most cases of compensated torts.

The cases like *Pennsylvania R. R. Co.* v. *International Coal Mining Co.*, 230 U. S. 184, where a party that has paid only the reasonable rate sues upon a discrimination because some other has paid less, are not like the present. There the damage depends upon remoter considerations. But here the plaintiffs have paid cash out of pocket that should not have been required of them, and there is no question as to the amount of the proximate loss. See *Meeker* v. *Lehigh Valley R. R. Co.*, 236 U. S. 412, 429. *Mills* v. *Lehigh Valley R. R. Co.*, 238 U. S. 473.

An objection is taken to the jurisdiction of this court upon writ of error. An application is made for a certiorari in case the objection is held good, and as we should grant the latter writ in that event the question has no importance here except as a precedent. We are inclined to take the course followed *sub silentio* in *Mills* v. *Lehigh Valley R. R. Co.*, and to treat cases brought under § 16 of the Act to Regulate Commerce which authorizes the joinder of all plaintiffs and all defendants as standing on a peculiar ground.

Judgment affirmed.

THE VICKSBURG, SHREVEPORT & PACIFIC RAILWAY COMPANY ET AL. v. ANDERSON-TULLY COMPANY

256 U. S. 408 (1921)

Mr. Justice Clarke delivered the opinion of the court.

This is an action instituted by a shipper under the provisions of Section 16 of the Interstate Commerce Act, as amended June 18, 1910 (36 Stat. 539, 554), against various carriers based upon an order of the Interstate Commerce Commission for the payment of money found due as reparation for the exacting of an unreasonable rate for the transportation of "box shooks" in carload lots from Vicksburg, Mississippi, to Port Arthur, Texas, which the carriers refused to pay.

It will be necessary to consider only the liability of the defendant, the Vicksburg, Shreveport & Pacific Railway Company, hereinafter referred to as the Vicksburg Company.

The petition in the case was filed in the United States District Court for the Western Division of the Southern District of Mississippi, and the plaintiff therein, defendant in error, for the purpose of showing the venue, allowed in section 16, of the Interstate Commerce Act, *supra*, alleged that the defendant, the Vicksburg Company, was operating a part of its road within that district. The Vicksburg Company challenged the jurisdiction of the District Court by a plea in abatement, denying that it owned or operated a railroad in the district at the time or for many months before the petition was filed and averred that the person on whom summons was served was not at the time its agent.

The shipper prevailed in both lower courts.

The venue provision of the Interstate Commerce Act allows such an action as we have here to be commenced in any district "through which the road of the carrier runs," and it is contended, first, that the Vicksburg Company did not have a road running through the District of suit, and that, therefore, the court did not have jurisdiction over the case.

It is stipulated that the Vicksburg Company is a Louisiana corporation and that at the times involved it owned a railroad extending through Louisiana to Delta Point, a station on the west bank of the Mississippi River, opposite Vicksburg. Its cars were ferried to and fro across the river and were hauled by the Alabama & Vicksburg Railroad Company, hereinafter called the Alabama Company, over its rails to freight and passenger tations in Vicksburg. The Vicksburg and the Alabama companies shared the expense of freight and ticket offices in Vicksburg, at which tickets were sold and bills of lading issued by the Vicksburg Company from Vicksburg to various points on its line. The Vicksburg Company filed passenger and freight tariffs with the Interstate Commerce Commission without any division of rates with the Alabama Company, that company being paid on a mileage basis for the service which it rendered east of the river. It is also stipulated "that exactly the same arrangement is now in force between" the Vicksburg and Alabama companies "as was in effect before the United States Government took control of these two roads."

Thus the mileage, passenger, freight and tariff publication, arrangements which the Vicksburg Company had with the Alabama Company plainly were equivalent in practice to a lease of the road of that company to the Vicksburg Company for its transportation purposes, and the dealings of the Vicksburg Company with the public and with the Interstate Commerce Commission with respect to traffic to and from Vicksburg were precisely the same as if it had owned or had leased the Alabama Company's tracks. The applicable venue provision of the Interstate Commerce Act does not require that the carrier shall be the owner of a railroad in the District, but only that its road must run through it, and we agree with the Circuit Court of Appeals in concluding that the tracks of the Alabama Company east of the river, in the District of suit, under the circumstances of operation as the parties stipulated them to be, constituted them the road of the Vicksburg Company within the meaning of the Act.

It is next contended that the person on whom summons was served was not, at the time, an agent of the Vicksburg Company.

The return of the marshal is that he executed the writ "by handing a true copy of this summons and petition for judgment to Austin King, freight agent for the Vicksburg, Shreveport and Pacific Railway Company." The plea in abatement denied on "information knowledge and belief" of counsel that King was at the time of service an agent of either of the defendants. No evidence whatever was introduced to sustain this plea and in support of it sole reliance is placed upon the stipulation that the Government was in control of the lines of the Vicksburg Company at the time the petition was filed.

The unreasonable rate for which the reparation order was made was exacted on shipments moving long prior to the taking over of the railroads by the Government in December, 1917, and there being no evidence that King was not the agent of the Vicksburg Company, the return of the marshal was properly accepted by both lower courts as conclusive. He may not have been in the employ of the Director General of Railroads at all and it was entirely possible for him to have been serving as agent for both the Director and the Company.

Since the shipment for which reparation was allowed moved prior to the taking over of the railroads by the United States Government, as against the objection of government control, we think the provision of Section 10 of the Federal Railroad Control Act (40 Stat. 451, 456) is applicable and ample to support the jurisdiction, viz., that "actions at law or suits in equity may be brought by and against such carriers and judgments rendered as now provided by law; and in any action at law or suit in equity against the carrier, no defense shall be made thereto upon the ground that the carrier is an instrumentality or agency of the Federal Government."

It is further claimed that the Act of Congress abolishing the Commerce Court (38 Stat. 208, 219), repealed by implication the provisions of Section 16, *supra,* permitting such reparation suits as we have here to be filed in the District Court for any district "through which the road of the carrier runs" and that for this reason the District Court was without jurisdiction.

The plaintiff was a Michigan corporation and if the provisions of § 16 referred to had been repealed at the time the case was commenced the venue was improperly laid and the court was without jurisdiction.

The argument is that the act of Congress abolishing the Commerce Court, in restoring to the District Courts the jurisdiction which had been vested exclusively in that court provided that "The venue of any suit hereafter brought to enforce, suspend or set aside . . . any order of the Interstate Commerce Commission shall be in the judicial district wherein is the residence of the party or any of the parties upon whose petition the order was made;" (38 Stat. 219) and that this provision for venue is so inconsistent with that of Section 16, *supra*, allowing suit to be commenced, on an order for the payment of money, in any district through which the road of the carrier runs, that the latter must be regarded as repealed by implication.

This contention is much too artificial and unsubstantial for us to consider it in much detail. It is enough to say that the two principal amendments to the Interstate Commerce Act of 1887 show that it has been the plainly expressed policy of Congress to make the prosecution of suits upon reparation orders for the payment of money progressively easier and less expensive for the shipper by enlarging the venue provisions of them, doubtless because many such claims are so small that if suit could be maintained by the owners only in distant jurisdictions a large part of them would be abandoned. Act, 1887, 24 Stat. 379, 384, Sec. 16; Act, 1906, 34 Stat. 584, 590, Sec. 16; Act, 1910, 36 Stat. 539, 554, Sec. 16. The Commerce Court repealing act was a section of an appropriation act and dealt with venue only to the extent necessary to redistribute the jurisdiction of the court abolished and in terms it repealed only acts or parts of acts in so far "as they relate to the establishment of the Commerce Court" and again so far as "inconsistent with the foregoing provisions relating to the Commerce Court." 38 Stat. 219, 221. The venue provided for, and relied upon in this suit, was for suits in the Circuit (District) Court on an order for the payment of money, and of such suits the Commerce Court never had jurisdiction.

The contention that Congress intended by implication to repeal and cut down to such narrow limits the venue which has gradually been so liberally extended cannot be entertained. The terms of the repealing act do not justify it and we cannot doubt that if such purpose had been intended it would not have been left to inference and implication but would have been clearly expressed.

. . . .

It results that the judgment of the Circuit of Appeals is

Affirmed.

UNITED STATES *v.* NORTHERN PACIFIC RAILWAY CO

242 U. S. 190 (1916)

This is a civil proceeding brought by the United States in the United States District Court for the District of North Dakota, to recover $500 from the Northern Pacific Railway Company for the claimed failure to file, for five successive days, with the Interstate Commerce Commission, a report of violations of the Hours of Service Act, as required by an order of the Commission issued June 28, 1911. The order was made under authority of § 20 of the Act to Regulate Commerce, as amended June 18th, 1910, 36 Stat. 539, 556, and has the force of statute law. It requires the carrier to report "under oath" within thirty days after the end of each month, all instances where employees have been on duty for a longer period than that provided in said act, which in this case was sixteen hours.

The District Court rendered judgment for the Government, which was reversed by the Circuit Court of Appeals for the Eighth Circuit (213 Fed. Rep. 162). The case is here for decision on writ of certiorari.

The judgment of the District Court was rendered on the pleadings, the admitted facts of the case being as follows:

Five employees of the defendant were called to take charge of a wrecking train at 8.10 o'clock p. m. October 29, 1911, but, before they reported at the place of duty, it was ascertained that such train would not be needed and when they arrived they were notified that their services would not then be required, but that they should report for duty at 10.35 o'clock p. m. the same evening. From 8.10 to 10.35 o'clock they did not render any service "save that they kept alive the fire in the engine during said period." At 10.35 o'clock the five men entered upon a freight train run, which, because of hot boxes, was delayed so that it did not arrive at destination until 1.15 o'clock p. m. the next day.

If the service of the men were considered as beginning at 8.10 o'clock, the hour for which they were called, they were on duty for 17 hours and 5 minutes, but if the time were reckoned from 10.35 p. m., when the men actually took charge of the freight train, they were on duty less than sixteen hours. It is admitted that the officials of the railway company believed in good faith that the time of the men should be reckoned from 10.35 p. m., and not from 8.10 p. m., and that, for that reason, when next October 30th, 1911, they filed their report of employees subject to the act who had been kept on duty for a longer period than sixteen hours, the names of the members of this crew were omitted, although the names of many other employees who had been kept on duty longer than the statutory limit were stated in that report.

It was conceded at the hearing in the Circuit Court of Appeals that the United States had sued the company for the "forfeitures" prescribed for these excessive services under discussion in this case, and had secured a judgment which had been paid, and that thereby it was determined, for the purposes of this suit, that these employees were on duty from 8.10 o'clock p. m., and therefore for more than sixteen hours.

The Government's claim in the case is for the omission for five days to file the report and it prays judgment for "forfeitures" aggregating $500, although when the complaint was filed the report claimed to be defective had been on file from November 30th, 1911, to September 14th, 1912, and if the "forfeitures" of $100 per day prescribed by the law for each day of failure to file a proper report were allowed, the amount of recovery by the Government would be $28,900, and it is only by grace of the public officials that the claim in the suit was not for this amount instead of for $500.

MR. JUSTICE CLARKE, after making the foregoing statement, delivered the opinion of the court.

It will be seen from the foregoing statement of facts that the question presented by the record in this case for decision is: Assuming that the law required that in the report of the company filed on November 30th, 1911, the names of these five employees of the defendant should have been included as having been on duty for more than sixteen hours, and that their names were omitted from that report because it was in good faith believed that their hours of service should be computed from 10.35 o'clock p. m., and that, therefore, they had not been on duty in excess sixteen hours, is the company liable for the "forfeitures" prescribed by the statute, judgment for which was prayed for in the complaint?

Section 20 of the Act to Regulate Commerce of February 4, 1887, as amended June 18, 1910, 36 Stat. 556, requires the filing of elaborate annual reports by carriers and also the filing of such special reports as the Commission may, by general or special order, require. On the twenty-eighth day of June, 1911, the Commission ordered that all carriers subject to the provisions of the act should report "under oath" within thirty days after the end of each month all instances of employees who had been on duty for a longer time than that required by the act. It is for violation of this order, which has the effect of statute law, that this suit was instituted, it being admitted by the Government that the failure to mention these five men in the report by the defendant, filed at the proper time, and which contained a report of many men kept on duty for a period longer than the time allowed by law, was due to the fact that it in good faith believed that these men commenced their time of service at 10.35 instead of at 8.10 o'clock, and that therefore they were not on duty more than the sixteen hours prescribed by the statute. The defendant in the error contends that judgment is asked for an omission caused by an honest mistake with respect to a genuinely doubtful case in a report which was properly filed and this, it is claimed, is not a violation of the law. The statute is a penal one and should be applied only to cases coming plainly within its terms. *Steam Engine Co.* v. *Hubbard,* 101 U. S. 188. While the reports filed must be truthful reports (*Yates* v. *Jones National Bank,* 206 U. S. 158), yet, since they must be made under oath, the penalties for perjury would seem to be the direct and sufficient sanction relied upon by the law-making power to secure their correctness.

We are confirmed in this conclusion by the fact that the annual report required of carriers by this same § 20 of the act calls for so great an amount of detailed information that it would be difficult, if not impossible, for any one to prepare such a report without making some unintentional omission or mistake, and we cannot bring ourselves to think that Congress intended to punish such an innocent mistake or omission with a penalty of $100 a day.

There are, to be sure, many statutes which punish violations of their requirements regardless of the intent of the persons violating them, but innocent mistakes, made in reporting facts, where the circumstances are such that candid minded men may well differ in their conclusions with respect to them, should not be punished by exacting penalties, except where the express letter of the statute so requires, and we conclude that the section under discussion contains no such requirement. In reports in which a mistake is much more likely to prove harmful than in such a report as we have here, the national banking laws punish mistakes only where "knowingly" made.

It is argued that if good faith will excuse an omission or a mistaken statement in this report, it will be widely taken advantage of as a cover for making false and fraudulent statements in such reports in the future. Such a prospect seems quite groundless, since many, if not most, criminal laws imposing penalties are made applicable only in cases where corrupt intent or purpose is established to the satisfaction of a court or jury, yet such requirement has not been found in practice to be an encouragement to wrongdoing.

The fact that the Government sues for only one fifty-seventh part of the forfeitures which had accrued under the construction of the rule and statute contended for by it, should make us slow to attribute to Congress a purpose to exact what is thus admitted to be a punishment greatly disproportionate to the offense. Statutes should be construed, as far as possible, so that those subject to their control may, by reference to their terms, ascertain the measure of their duty and obligation, rather than that such measure should be dependent upon the discretion of executive officers, to the end that ours may continue to be a Government of written laws rather than one of official grace.

It being very clear that it is not the purpose of the law under discussion to punish honest mistakes, made in a genuinely doubtful case, the decision of the Circuit Court of Appeals is

Affirmed

LEHIGH COAL & NAVIGATION COMPANY *v.* UNITED STATES

250 U. S. 556 (1919)

MR. JUSTICE MCKENNA delivered the opinion of the court.

The case is here on certificate, an outline of which it is necessary to give.

The Lehigh Coal & Navigation Company, herein called the Company, is a miner and shipper of anthracite coal and was indicted, convicted and fined in the District Court of New Jersey for accepting rebates and concessions from the Central Railroad of New Jersey in violation of the Elkins Act, as amended in 1906, 34 Stat. 584.

It was charged in each count of the indictment that the Central Railroad Company was an interstate carrier of coal and as such filed tariffs and schedules with the Interstate Commerce Commission showing its rates and charges from the coal fields in Pennsylvania to points in New Jersey.

During 1912, 1913, 1914 and a part of 1915, the tariffs were in force and under them the Company shipped a carload (described in the indictment) from its colliery in Pennsylvania to a specified point in New Jersey and accepted from the railroad a portion of the rate due and payable so that the coal was carried at less than the rate and the Company thus received the advantage of an illegal rebate. Discrimination was not charged.

In accordance with circumstances which are detailed at length in the certificate, among which was the fact that the Company at one time operated a railroad of its own (the Lehigh & Susquehanna), the Company decided to lease its railroad properties to the Central Railroad, a connecting carrier. Accordingly, March 31, 1871, the Company made a lease to the Railroad, the 10th covenant of which provided as follows:

". . . on coal delivered for transportation by the Company on sidings at the northern end of the Nesquehoning tunnel, the rates of transportation shall not exceed the rates charged at the same time from Penn Haven to the same points on coal from the Lehigh region, either by the Central Railroad or by the Lehigh Valley Railroad Company."

In making the lease naturally the Company took into account the advantageous nearness of its mines to tide and sought to insure favorable rates for the coal from its collieries.

About 1878 the method of fixing rates was changed but the rate to be charged the Company was fixed at 86% of the rate charged to other mines in the Lehigh region, the reason being that there was that difference in distance. While this arrangement was in force the Company paid a net rate calculated on the basis of 86%. After 1887, the date of the first act to regulate commerce, this method of settlement was changed and the Company was charged the full tariff rate, but was rebated or credited with 14% thereof, this being done under the obligation or supposed obligation of the 10th covenant. And between 1887 and August, 1906, when the Hepburn Act went into effect, this arrangement for repayment did not appear in the tariffs filed by the Railroad with the Commission. But in August, 1906, and thereafter, the tariffs contained a footnote in the following form:

"(4) In compliance with the Tenth Covenant of the lease from the Lehigh Coal & Navigation Company under which the Central Railroad Company of New Jersey operates the Lehigh and Susquehanna Railroad, a lateral allowance is made out of herein-named rates to the Lehigh Coal and Navigation Company on all Anthracite coal originating on the latter's tracks in the Panther Creek, Nesquehoning, and Hacklebarnie Districts mined and shipped by it, when coming via the Hauto, Nesquehoning, and Mauch Chunk gateways."

All of the tariffs of the Railroad filed with the Commission after 1906 (262 in number) contained the footnote. The allowance was 19.18 cents per ton and this was credited in the monthly settlement of the Company's account with the Railroad, the credit being the point of the Government's attack.

"The verdict covers 27 shipments of coal in prepared sizes from Nesquehoning colliery for reshipment at Elizabethport. The foregoing facts were either proved or stipulated, and it appeared also without dispute that during the years in question the Companys' officers were familiar with the contents of the Central Railroad's tariffs, and knew that the allowance was being made and accepted. One of the Company's defenses was that it had not 'knowingly' accepted a rebate within the meaning of the Act — its contention being, that the allowance had been accepted in good faith, in the honest belief that the payment was justified by the 10th covenant, and also in the honest belief that the allowance was properly and legally noted and provided for in the filed and published tariffs."

The Company offered evidence that would support the following findings:

(1) At the time the note was made, the Company was informed of it, but was advised that the note had been made part of the tariff in full compliance with the Act of 1906, and that being so the payment and receipt of the allowance would comply with the tariff and the law and the officers of the Company relied on this judgment.

(2) Between 1906 and the date of the indictment 262 tariffs, all containing the note, had been filed and accepted by the Commission.

(3) In 1908 the Company had been informed by the Railroad that the Commission (acting through one of the Commission's important officers who was in charge of the tariffs) had specifically approved the form of the tariff containing the note, in spite of

the fact that the amount of the allowance had not been specified therein, the Commission at the time having the question under consideration. By reason of such information the Company honestly believed that the receipt of the allowance was not in violation of the tariff or the act, but was in compliance therewith.

(4) The Company's books, records and accounts were examined by the Commission's investigators in 1909, and the Commission was thereby informed that the Company had received and was receiving the allowance, but the Commission did not object either to the form or the substance of the practice.

"The Company's evidence concerning good faith was received under the Government's objection, and the Government offered evidence in contradiction thereof. At the close of the trial the court struck out all the evidence on this subject from the record, and refused to submit the question of good faith to the jury, holding that the Company's honest belief that the allowance was permitted by the tariffs and the footnote thereto could not affect the issue, for the reason that the Company knew the contents of the tariffs, and knew also that the allowance was actually made and received."

The certificate asks the following questions:

"1. In the criminal prosecution of a shipper for knowingly accepting transportation at less than the duly established rate by receiving an allowance that was referred to in the tariff but was not specified in figures therein, has the defendant a right to offer evidence that the allowance was received under the honest belief that it was lawfully established by the tariff, and under the honest belief that in receiving it he was not disregarding what he believed to be the provisions of the tariff but was complying therewith?

"2. Upon the foregoing facts, and in view of the kind and amount of evidence offered upon the subject of good faith, did the district court err in the present case by refusing to submit the question to the jury?"

The questions asked depend upon the construction of the Elkins Act, as enacted in 1903 (32 Stat. 847) the relevant part of which is as follows: " . . . It shall be unlawful for any person, persons, or corporation to offer, grant, or give or to solicit, accept, or receive any rebate, concession, or discrimination in respect of the transportation of any property in interstate or foreign commerce by any common carrier subject to said Act to regulate commerce and the Acts amendatory thereto whereby any such property shall *by any device whatever be transported at a less rate than that named in the tariffs published and filed by such carrier* [italics ours] . . ." And under an amendment in 1906 (34 Stat. 584) an offender, "whether carrier or shipper who shall, knowingly, offer, grant, or give, or solicit, accept, or receive any such rebate, concession, or discrimination shall be deemed guilty of a misdemeanor."

The way to a correct construction of the act was to an extent cleared by the case of *Armour Packing Co.* v. *United States*, 209 U. S. 56. Its evolution was there detailed. It was said that carrier and shipper are charged with an equal responsibility and liability and that the act "proceeded upon broad lines" to accomplish this equality, and "that the only rate charged to any shipper for the same service under the same conditions should be the one established, published and posted as required by law." And this was declared in various ways to be the test of obligation and liability and the "form by which or the motive for which" its evasion or disregard is accomplished is not of modifying or determining consideration. It was in effect decided that the purpose of the statute took emphasis and meaning from the use of the word "device," and "device" was defined to be "anything which is a plan or contrivance" and is "disassociated" from qualification and "need not be necessarily fraudulent," and by it the act sought "to reach all means and methods by which the unlawful preference of rebate, concession or discrimination is offered, granted, given or received."

It is in effect the contention of the Government that the language of the case exhausts definition and excludes the supposition of the questions of the Circuit Court of Appeals. We are unable to concur. The language of the case is easily explained by the question that was presented for decision. The Armour Packing Company contended that the act was directed only at fraudulent conduct, the obtaining of a rebate by some dishonest or underhand method, concession or discrimination. The language of the court was addressed to this contention and its selection and adequacy are manifest.

No such contention is made in the case at bar and there are other distinguishing elements. It will be observed that by the statute and the decision the test of equality is the tariff rate. It was said in the opinion that it is "the purpose of the act to punish those who give or receive transportation, in the sense of actual carriage, at a concession from the published rates" (*New*

York Central R. R. Co. v. *United States*, 212 U. S. 500, 505). And such was the offense of the Armour Packing Company. There was no evasion of the tariff rate in the case at bar. The filed tariff indicated the existence and obligation of the 10th covenant of the lease from the Company to the Railroad, that is, the fact of the allowance was declared, though it did not have specification in figures. The tariff, of course, would have been more definite and complete with such specification, but its sufficiency was certainly believed in, for between 1906 and the date of the indictment it had 262 repetitions. The Company was given besides the assurance that it had the sanction of the Interstate Commerce Commission.

There was no attempt at deception. The Commission knew by examination of the Company's books of the allowance and the amount of the allowance. Such, then, is the situation, and distinguishes the case from the *Armour Packing Company Case.* There there was an omission to comply with the statute and the omission was attempted to be justified by honesty of motive and purpose; here there was compliance or attempted compliance with the statute — a tariff filed — and if a question could be raised upon its legal sufficiency the belief of the Company in its legality was supported by high authority and those circumstances can bring into action and exculpating effect the provision of the statute which requires the acceptance of a rebate to be "knowingly" done to incur the guilt of a misdemeanor. This conclusion gives no detrimental example against the efficacy of the law.

We think this comment and conclusion enough to dispose of the questions asked and that there is no necessity to review the cases cited by the Company or the Government.

Some of the contentions of the Government we may notice. It is contended that the "lateral allowance" provided for in the 10th covenant and footnote to the tariff was not for transportation services and besides that there was no testimony whatsoever that the meaning of any provision of the tariff was misunderstood. The mistake, if any, it is hence insisted, was a mistake of law, not of fact. Two deductions are hence made by the Government: (1) That the allowances were not made for transportation services; (2) mistake of law is irrelevant to the question of the guilt or innocence of the Company.

To the first we may reply it is not involved as an element in the question asked of this court and if it have any justification, as to which we express no opinion, it no doubt will be considered by the Circuit Court of Appeals upon the return of the case. The other expresses a refinement. Indeed, the contention of the Government is somewhat elusive and we are not sure that we exactly estimate it. It is said "The sole misunderstanding which the excluded testimony tended to show would consist in supposing that the 'allowances' could be justified by the footnote in the tariff and that, as we have seen, would be a misunderstanding of the Elkins Act, not of the tariff." We are unable to concur. There was no misunderstanding of the Elkins Act or what it required. The misunderstanding was induced by practice and the opinion of those in authority that the act was complied with and the word "knowingly" therefore, as we have already indicated, must be considered and given exculpating effect if error there was.

We therefore answer the first question in the affirmative, but as explained by reference to the certificate of facts above. We do not think it is necessary to answer the second question.

MR. JUSTICE MCREYNOLDS took no part in the decision.

APPENDIX

The following very important opinions were rendered by the Supreme Court while this volume was going through the press. The first three opinions should be read after *Illinois Central Railroad* v. *State Public Utilities Commission*, p. 81, *supra*, and the last opinion (*Great Northern Railroad Co.* v. *Merchants Elevator Company*) belongs after *Director General* v. *Viscose Company*, p. 610, *supra*.

RAILROAD COMMISSION OF WISCONSIN, ET AL. *v.* CHICAGO, BURLINGTON & QUINCY RAILROAD CO.

257 U. S. (1922)

The proceeding out of which this case has grown, known as the Wisconsin Passenger Fares, began in an investigation by the Interstate Commerce Commission, under paragraphs 3 and 4 of section 13 of the Interstate Commerce Act as amended by section 416 of the Transportation Act of 1920 (42 Stat. 484), into alleged undue and unreasonable discrimination against interstate commerce arising out of intrastate railroad rates in Wisconsin. The interstate carriers by steam railroad of the State were made respondents, and the Governor and State Railroad Commission were duly notified. The Interstate Commerce Commission made its report and order November 27, 1920. *Wisconsin Passenger Fares*, 59 I. C. C. 391.

The Commission had investigated the interstate rates of carriers in the United States, in a proceeding known as *Ex parte 74, Increased Rates*, 58 I. C. C. 220, for the purpose of complying with section 15a of the Interstate Commerce Act as amended by section 422 of the Transportation Act of 1920 (41 Stat. 488). That section requires that the Commission so adjust rates that the revenues of the carriers shall enable them as a whole or by groups to earn a fixed net income on their railway property. The Commission ordered an increase for the carriers in the group of which the Wisconsin carriers were a part, of thirty-five per cent. in interstate freight rates, and twenty per cent. in interstate passenger fares and excess baggage charges, and a surcharge upon passengers in sleeping cars amounting to fifty per cent. of the charge for space in such cars to accrue to the rail carriers. Thereupon the carriers applied to the Wisconsin Railroad Commission for corresponding increases in intrastate rates. The state commission granted increases in intrastate freight rates of thirty-five per cent., but denied any in intrastate passenger fares and charges on the sole ground that a state statute prescribed a maximum for passengers of 2 cents a mile.

In the *Wisconsin Passenger Fares,* the Interstate Commerce Commission found that all of the respondent carriers of Wisconsin transported both intrastate and interstate passengers on the same train, with the same service and accommodations; that the state passenger paying the lower rate rode on the same train, in the same car, and perhaps in the same seat with the interstate passenger who paid the higher rate; that the circumstances and conditions were substantially similar for interstate as for intrastate passenger service in Wisconsin; that travelers destined to, or coming from, points outside the State found it cheaper to pay the intrastate fare within Wisconsin and the interstate fare beyond the border than to pay the through interstate fare; that undue preference and prejudice were shown by the falling off of sales of tickets from border line points in Minnesota and Michigan to stations in Wisconsin, and by a marked increase in sales of local tickets from corresponding border line points in Wisconsin to stations in Wisconsin; that the evidence as to the practice with respect to passenger fares applied in like manner to the surcharge upon passengers in sleeping and parlor cars and to excess baggage charges.

The Commission further found that the fare necessary to fulfill the requirement as to net income of this interstate railroad group under section 15a was 3.6 cents per mile, and that this was reasonable, that the direct revenue loss to the Wisconsin carriers, due to their failure to secure the 20 per cent. increase in intrastate fares, would approximate $2,400,000 per year if the 3-cent fare fixed by the President under federal war control, were continued and $6,000,000 per year if the 2-cent fare named in the state statute, should become effective.

The Commission found that there was undue, unreasonable and unjust discrimination against persons traveling in interstate commerce and against interstate commerce as a whole; and ordered that the undue discrimination should be removed by increases in all intrastate passenger fares and excess baggage charges and by surcharges corresponding with the increases and surcharges ordered in interstate business.

The order was made without prejudice to the right of the authorities of the State or of any other party in interest to apply in the proper manner for a modification of the order as to any specified intrastate fares or charges if the latter were not related to the interstate fares or charges in such a way as to contravene the provisions of the Interstate Commerce Act.

The carriers filed bills in equity, of which the present is one, in the District Court to enjoin the State Railroad Commission and other state officials from interfering with the maintenance of the fares thus ordered and published.

Application for interlocutory injunction was made to the District Court under section 266 of the Judicial Code. After a hearing before three judges, they granted an interlocutory injunction from which this appeal was taken.

Mr. Chief Justice Taft, after stating the case, delivered the opinion of the Court.

The Commission's order, interference with which was enjoined by the District Court, effects the removal of the unjust discrimination found to exist against persons in interstate commerce, and against interstate commerce by fixing a minimum for intrastate passenger fares in Wisconsin at 3.6 cents per mile per passenger. This is done under paragraph 4 of section 13 of the Interstate Commerce Act, as amended by the Transportation Act of 1920, which authorizes the Interstate Commerce Commission, after a prescribed investigation, to remove

"Any undue or unreasonable advantage, preference or prejudice as between persons or localities in intrastate commerce, on the one hand, and interstate or foreign commerce, on the other hand, or any undue, unreasonable or unjust discrimination against interstate commerce."

We have two questions to decide.

First. Do the intrastate passenger fares work undue prejudice against persons in interstate commerce, such as to justify a horizontal increase of them all?

Second. Are these intrastate fares an undue discrimination against interstate commerce as a whole which it is the duty of the Commission to remove?

We shall consider these in their order.

First. The report and findings of the Commission undoubtedly show that the intrastate fares work an undue discrimination against travelers in interstate commerce and against localities (*Houston & Texas Ry.* v. *United States,* 234 U. S. 342) in typical instances numerous enough to justify a general finding against a large class of fares. In a general order thus supported, possible injustice can be avoided by a saving clause allowing any one to except himself from the order by proper showing. This practice is fully sustained by precedent in what was done as a sequence of the *Shreveport* case (*Houston & Texas Ry. Co.* v. *United States, supra*). Sec. 34, I. C. C. 472; 41 I. C. C. 83; *East Texas R. R. Co.* v. *R. R. Commission,* 242 Fed. Rep. 300; *Looney* v. *R. R. Co.,* 247 U. S. 214. In *Illinois C. R. R. Co.* v. *Public Utilities Commission,* 245 U. S. 493, 508, this Court indicated its approval of such practice which was adopted by the Commission. 49 I. C. C. 713. Any rule which would require specific proof of discrimination as to each fare or rate and its effect would completely block the remedial purpose of the statute.

The order in this case, however, is much wider than the orders made in the proceedings following the *Shreveport* and *Illinois Central* cases. There, as here, the report of the Commission showed discrimination against persons and localities at border points, and the orders were extended to include all rates or fares from all points in the State to border points. But this order is not so restricted. It includes fares between all interior points although neither may be near the border and the fares between them may not work a discrimination against interstate travelers at all. Nothing in the precedents cited justifies an order affecting all rates of a general description when it is clear that this would include many rates not within the proper class or the reason of the order. In such a case, the saving clause by which exceptions are permitted, can not give the order validity. As said by this Court in the *Illinois Central R. R.* case, " it is obvious that an order of a subordinate agency, such as the Commission, should not be given precedence over a state rate statute, otherwise valid, unless, and except so far as, it conforms to a high standard of certainty." See also *American Express Co.* v. *Caldwell,* 244 U. S. 617, 627.

If, in view of the changes, made by federal authority, in a large class of discriminating state rates, it is necessary from a state point of view to change non-discriminating state rates to harmonize with them, only the state authorities can produce such harmony. We cannot sustain the sweep of the order in this case on the showing of discrimination against persons or places alone.

Second. The report of the Commission shows that if the intrastate passenger fares in Wisconsin are to be limited by the statute of that State to 2 cents per mile, and charges for extra baggage and sleeping car accommodations are to be reduced in a corresponding degree, the net income of the interstate carriers of the State will be cut six millions of dollars below what it would be under intrastate rates on the same level with interstate rates. Under paragraphs 3 and 4 of section 13 and section 15a as enacted in sections 416 and 422 respectively of the Transportation Act of 1920 (which are given in part in the margin [1]), are such reduction and disparity an " undue, unreasonable and unjust discrimination against interstate or foreign commerce " which the Interstate Commerce Commission may remove by raising the intrastate fares? A short reference to the circumstances inducing the legislation and a summary of its relevant provisions will aid the answer to this question.

[1] Paragraphs 3 and 4 of section 13 of section 416 and section 15a of section 422 of the same Act are as follows:

" (3) Whenever in any investigation under the provisions of this Act, or in any investigation instituted upon petition of the carrier concerned, which petition is hereby authorized to be filed, there shall be brought in issue any rate, fare, charge, classification, regulation, or practice, made or imposed by authority of any State, or initiated by the President during the period of Federal control, the Commission, before proceeding to hear and dispose of such issue, shall cause the State or States interested to be notified of the proceeding. The Commission may confer with the authorities of any State having regulatory jurisdiction over the class of persons and corporations subject to this Act with respect to the relationship between rate structures and practices of carriers subject to the jurisdiction of such State bodies and of the Commission; and to that end is authorized and empowered under rules to be prescribed by it, and which may be modified from time to time, to hold joint hearings with any such State regulating bodies on any matters wherein the Commission is empowered to act and where the rate-making authority of a State is or may be affected by the action taken by the Commission. The Commission is also authorized to avail itself of the coöperation, services, records, and facilities of such State authorities in the enforcement of any provision of this Act.

"(4) Whenever in any such investigation the Commission, after full hearing, finds that any such rate, fare, charge, classification, regulation, or practice causes *any undue or unreasonable advantage, preference, or preju-*

The Interstate Commerce Act of 1887, 24 St. 379, was enacted by Congress to prevent interstate railroad carriers from charging unreasonable rates and from unjustly discriminating between persons and localities. The railroads availed themselves of the weakness and cumbrous machinery of the original law to defeat its purpose, and this led to various amendments culminating in the amending Act of 1910, 36 St. L. 539, in which the authority of the Commission in dealing with the carriers was made summary and effectively complete. Whatever the causes, the fact was that the carrying capacity of the railroads did not thereafter develop proportionately with the growth of the country, and it became difficult for them to secure additional investment of capital on feasible terms. When the extraordinary demand for transportation arose in 1917, the Congress and the President concluded to take over all the railroads into the management of the Federal Government, and by joint use of facilities, which the Anti Trust Law was thought to forbid under private management and by use of Government credit, to increase their effectiveness. This

---

dice as between persons or localities in intrastate commerce on the one hand and interstate or foreign commerce on the other hand, or any undue, unreasonable, or unjust discrimination against interstate or foreign commerce, which is hereby forbidden and declared to be unlawful it shall prescribe the rate, fare, or charge, or the maximum or minimum, thereafter to be charged, and the classification, regulation, or practice thereafter to be observed, in such manner as, in its judgment, will remove such advantage, preference, prejudice, or discrimination. Such rates, fares, charges, classifications, regulations, and practices shall be observed while in effect by the carriers parties to such proceeding affected thereby, the law of any State or the decision or order of any State authority to the contrary notwithstanding."

Section 422 of the Transportation Act, 1920, 41 Stat. L. 488.

The Interstate Commerce Act is further amended by inserting, after section 15, a new section to be known as section 15a and to read as follows:

"Section 15a (1) . . . .

"(2) In the exercise of its power to prescribe just and reasonable rates, the Commission shall initiate, modify, establish, or adjust such rates so that carriers as a whole (or as a whole in each of such rate groups or territories as the Commission may from time to time designate) will, under honest, efficient, and economical management and reasonable expenditures for maintenance of way, structures and equipment, earn an aggregate annual net railway operating income equal, as nearly as may be, to fair return upon the aggregate value of the railway property of such carriers held for and used in the service of transportation. . . .

"(3) The Commission shall from time to time determine and make public what percentage of such aggregate property value constitutes a

was done by appropriate legislation and executive action under the war power. From January 1, 1918, until March 1, 1920, when the Transportation Act went into effect, the common carriers by steam railroad of the country were operated by the Federal Government. Due to the rapid rise in the prices of material and labor in 1918 and 1919, the expense of their operation had enormously increased by the time it was proposed to return the railroads to their owners. The owners insisted that their properties could not be turned back to them by the Government for useful operation without provision to aid them to meet a situation in which they were likely to face a demoralizing lack of credit and income. Congress acquiesced in this view. The Transportation Act of 1920 was the result. It was adopted after elaborate investigations by the Interstate Commerce Committees of the two Houses.

Under Title II it made provision for the termination of federal control March 1, 1920, for the refunding of the carriers' indebtedness to the United States, and for a guaranty for six months to

---

fair return thereon and such percentage shall be uniform for all rate groups or territories which may be designated by the Commission. In making such determination, it shall give due consideration, among other things, to the transportation needs of the country and the necessity (under honest, efficient, and economical management of existing transportation facilities) of enlarging such facilities in order to provide the people of the United States with adequate transportation. Provided that during two years beginning March 1st, 1920, the Commission shall take as such fair return a sum equal to 5½ per centum of such aggregate value, but may in its discretion, add thereto a sum not exceeding one-half of one per centum of such aggregate value to make provision in whole or in part for improvements, betterments or equipment, which according to the accounting system prescribed by the Commission are chargeable to capital account.

"(4) For the purposes of this section, such aggregate value of the property of the carriers shall be determined by the Commission from time to time and as often as may be necessary. The Commission may utilize the results of its investigation under section 19a of this Act in so far as deemed by it available and shall give due consideration to all the elements of value recognized by the law of the land for rate making purposes, and shall give to the property investment account of the carriers only that consideration which under such law it is entitled to in establishing values for rate making purposes. Whenever pursuant to section 19a of this Act, the value of the railway property of any carrier held for and used in the service of transportation has been finally ascertained, the value so ascertained shall be deemed by the Commission to be the value thereof for the purpose of determining such aggregate value."

the carriers of an income equal to the war-time rental for their properties, and directed that for two years following the termination of federal control, the Secretary of the Treasury, upon certificate of the Commission might make loans to the carriers not exceeding the maximum amount recommended in the certificate, out of a revolving fund of $300,000,000.

Under Title IV, amendments were made to the Interstate Commerce Act which included section 13, paragraphs 3 and 4, and section 15a, already quoted in the margin. The former for the first time authorizes the Commission to deal directly with intrastate rates where they are unduly discriminating against interstate commerce — a power already indirectly exercised as to persons and localities, with approval of this Court in the *Shreveport* and other cases. The latter, the most novel and most important feature of the act, requires the Commission so to prescribe rates as to enable the carriers as a whole or in groups selected by the Commission, to earn an aggregate annual net railway operating income equal to a fair return on the aggregate value of the railway property used in transportation. For two years, the return is to be 5½ per cent., with ½ per cent. for improvements, and thereafter is to be fixed by the Commission.

The act sought to avoid excessive incomes accruing, under the operation of section 15a, to the carriers better circumstanced by using the excess for loans to the others and for other purposes. The act further put under the control of the Interstate Commerce Commission, 1st, the issuing of future railroad securities by the interstate carriers; 2nd, the regulation of their car supply and distribution and the joint use of terminals; and, 3rd, their construction of new lines, and their abandonment of old lines. The validity of some of these provisions has been questioned. Upon that we express no opinion. We only refer to them to show the scope of the congressional purpose in the act.

It is manifest from this very condensed recital that the act made a new departure. Therefore the control which Congress through the Interstate Commerce Commission exercised was primarily for the purpose of preventing injustice by unreasonable or discriminatory rates against persons and localities, and the only provisions of the law that inured to the benefit of the carriers were the requirement that the rates should be reasonable in the sense of furnishing an adequate compensation for the particular service rendered and the abolition of rebates. The new measure imposed an affirmative duty on the Interstate Commerce

Commission to fix rates and to take other important steps to maintain an adequate railway service for the people of the United States. This is expressly declared in section 15a to be one of the purposes of the bill.

Intrastate rates and the income from them must play a most important part in maintaining an adequate national railway system. Twenty per cent. of the gross freight receipts of the railroads of the country are from intrastate traffic, and fifty per cent. of the passenger receipts. The ratio of the gross intrastate revenue to the interstate revenue is a little less than one to three. If the rates, on which such receipts are based, are to be fixed at a substantially lower level than in interstate traffic, the share which the intrastate traffic will contribute will be proportionately less. If the railways are to earn a fixed net percentage of income, the lower the intrastate rates, the higher the interstate rates may have to be. The effective operation of the act will reasonably and justly require that intrastate traffic should pay a fair proportionate share of the cost of maintaining an adequate railway system. Section 15a confers no power on the Commission to deal with intrastate rates. What is done under that section is to be done by the Commission "in the exercise of its powers to prescribe just and reasonable rates," *i.e.*, powers derived from previous amendments to the Interstate Commerce Act, which have never been construed or used to embrace the prescribing of intrastate rates. When we turn to par. 4, section 13, however, and find the Commission for the first time vested with a direct power to remove "any undue, unreasonable, or unjust discrimination against interstate or foreign commerce," it is impossible to escape the dovetail relation between that provision and the purpose of section 15a. If that purpose is interfered with by a disparity of intrastate rates, the Commission is authorized to end the disparity by directly removing it, because it is plainly an "undue, unreasonable, and unjust discrimination against interstate or foreign commerce," within the ordinary meaning of those words.

Counsel for appellants, not able to satisfy their meaning by the suggestion of any other discrimination to which they apply, are forced to the position that the words are tautological and a mere repetition of "any undue or unreasonable advantage, preference or prejudice as between persons and localities in intrastate commerce on the one hand and interstate or foreign commerce on the other hand," which precede them. In view of their apt application to the most important purpose of the legislation, we are not at liberty to take such a view. If " undue, unreasonable and unjust discrimination against interstate or foreign commerce " are tautological, why are they followed by the phrase " which is hereby prohibited and declared to be unlawful? " To accompany a meaningless phrase with words of such special emphasis would be unusual.

It is urged that in previous decisions, notably the *Minnesota Rate Cases,* 230 U. S. 352, the *Shreveport* case, *supra,* and the *Illinois Central* case, *supra,* the expression " unjust discrimination against interstate commerce " was often used when, as the law then was, it could only mean discrimination as between persons and localities, and therefore that it is to be given the same limited meaning here. But, here, the general words are used after discrimination against persons and localities have been specifically mentioned. The natural inference is that even if they include what has gone before, they mean something more. When we find that they aptly include a kind of discrimination against interstate commerce which the operation of the new act for the first time makes important and which would seriously obstruct its chief purpose, we cannot ignore their necessary effect.

Counsel for appellants are driven by the logic of their position to maintain that the valuation required for the purposes of section 15a to be ascertained pursuant to section 19a of the Interstate Commerce Act (37 Stat. L. 701; amended 41 Stat. L. 493), is to be only of that part of the property and equipment of the interstate carriers which is used in commerce among the States and must be segregated from that used in intrastate commerce. This is contrary to the construction which since the enactment of section 19a, March 1, 1913, the Commission has put upon that section in carrying out its injunction. It is inadmissible. The language of section 15a refutes such interpretation. The percentage is to be calculated on " the aggregate value of the railway property of such carriers held for and used in the service of transportation." To impose on the Commission the duty of separating property used in the two services when so much of it is used in both, and to do this in a reasonably short time for practical use, as contemplated by the statute, would be to assign it a well-nigh impossible task. This, of itself, prevents our giving the words such a construction unless they clearly require it. They certainly do not.

It is objected here as it was in the *Shreveport* case that orders of the Commission which raise the intrastate rates to a level of the interstate structure, violate the specific proviso of the original Interstate Commerce Act repeated in the amending acts, that the Commission is not to regulate traffic wholly within a State. To this, the same answer must be made as was made in the *Shreveport* case (234 U. S. 342, 358), that such orders as to intrastate traffic are merely incidental to the regulation of interstate commerce and necessary to its efficiency. Effective control of the one must embrace some control over the other in view of the blending of both in actual operation. The same rails and the same cars carry both. The same men conduct them. Commerce is a unit and does not regard state lines, and while under the Constitution, interstate and intrastate commerce are ordinarily subject to regulation by different sovereignties, yet when they are so mingled together that the supreme authority, the Nation, cannot exercise complete effective control over interstate commerce without incidental regulation of intrastate commerce, such incidental regulation is not an invasion of state authority or a violation of the proviso.

Great stress is put on the legislative history of the Transportation Act to show that the bill was not intended to confer on the Commission power to remove any discrimination against interstate commerce involved in a general disparity between interstate and intrastate rates. Committee reports and explanatory statements of members in charge made in presenting a bill for passage have been held to be a legitimate aid to the interpretation of a statute where its language is doubtful or obscure. *Duplex Co.* v. *Deering*, 254 U. S. 443, 475. But when taking the act as a whole, the effect of the language used is clear to the Court, extraneous aid like this can not control the interpretation. *Pennsylvania R. R. Co.* v. *International Coal Co.*, 230 U. S. 184, 198. *Caminetti* v. *United States*, 242 U. S. 480, 490. Such aids are only admissible to solve doubt and not to create it. For the reasons given, we have no doubt in this case.

Counsel for the appellants have not contested the constitutional validity of the statute construed as we have construed it, although the counsel for the state commissions whom we permitted to file briefs as *amici curiae* have done so. The principles laid down by this court in the *Minnesota Rate Cases*, 230 U. S. 352, 432, 433, the *Shreveport* case, 234 U. S. 342, 351, and the *Illinois Central* case, 245 U. S. 493, 506, which are rate cases, and in the analogous cases of *Baltimore & Ohio R. R. Co.* v.

Interstate Commerce Commission, 221 U. S. 612, 618; *Southern Ry. Co.* v. *United States,* 222 U. S. 20, 26, 27; *Second Employers' Liability Cases,* 223 U. S. 1, 48, 51, we think, leave no room for discussion on this point. Congress in its control of its interstate commerce system is seeking in the Transportation Act to make the system adequate to the needs of the country by securing for it a reasonable compensatory return for all the work it does. The States are seeking to use that same system for intrastate traffic. That entails large duties and expenditures on the interstate commerce system which may burden it unless conpensation is received for the intrastate business reasonably proportionate to that for the interstate business. Congress as the dominant controller of interstate commerce may, therefore, restrain undue limitation of the earning power of the interstate commerce system in doing state work. The affirmative power of Congress in developing interstate commerce agencies is clear. *Wilson* v. *Shaw,* 204 U. S. 24; *Luxton* v. *North River Bridge Co.,* 153 U. S. 525; *California* v. *Pacific Railroad Company,* 127 U. S. 1, 39. In such development, it can impose any reasonable condition on a State's use of interstate carriers for intrastate commerce, it deems necessary or desirable. This is because of the supremacy of the national power in this field.

In *Minnesota Rate Cases,* 230 U. S., where relevant cases were carefully reviewed, it was said, p. 399: "The authority of Congress extends to every part of interstate commerce, and to every instrumentality or agency by which it is carried on; and the full control by Congress of the subjects committed to its regulation is not to be denied or thwarted by the commingling of interstate and intrastate operations. This is not to say that the Nation may deal with the internal concerns of the State, as such, but that the execution by Congress of its constitutional power to regulate interstate commerce is not limited by the fact that intrastate transactions may have become so interwoven therewith that the effective government of the former incidentally controls the latter. This conclusion necessarily results from the supremacy of the national power within its appointed sphere."

It is said that our conclusion gives the Commission unified control of interstate and intrastate commerce. It is only unified to the extent of maintaining efficient regulation of interstate commerce under the paramount power of Congress. It does not involve general regulation of intrastate commerce. Action of the Interstate Commerce Commission in this regard should be directed to substantial disparity which operates as a real discrimination against, and obstruction to, interstate commerce, and must leave appropriate discretion to the state authorities to deal with intrastate rates as between themselves on the general level which the Interstate Commerce Commission has found to be fair to interstate commerce.

It may well turn out that the effect of a general order in increasing all rates, like the one at bar, will, in particular localities, reduce income instead of increasing it, by discouraging patronage. Such cases would be within the saving clause of the order herein, and make proper, an application to the Interstate Commerce Commission for appropriate exception. So, too, in practice when the state commissions shall recognize their obligation to maintain a proportionate and equitable share of the income of the carriers from intrastate rates, conference between the Interstate Commerce Commission and the state commissions may dispense with the necessity for any rigid federal order as to the intrastate rates, and leave to the state commissions power to deal with them and increase them or reduce them in their discretion.

The order of the District Court granting the interlocutory injunction is

Affirmed.

STATE OF NEW YORK AND CHARLES D. NEWTON, PERSONALLY AND AS ATTORNEY GENERAL OF THE STATE OF NEW YORK, APPELLANTS, *v.* THE UNITED STATES AND EDGAR E. CLARK, ET AL., CONSTITUTING THE INTERSTATE COMMERCE COMMISSION, AND INTERVENERS LEHIGH VALLEY RAILROAD COMPANY ET AL., RAILWAYS IN THE STATE OF NEW YORK.

257 U. S. (1922)

Mr. Chief Justice Taft delivered the opinion of the court.

This was a bill in equity against the United States and the Interstate Commerce Commission and others brought by the State of New York and its Attorney General to annul and enjoin the enforcement of an order of the Interstate Commerce Commission requiring the interstate railroads operating in intrastate commerce in the State of New York to charge in such commerce 3.6 cents a mile for all passengers, twenty per cent. increase over the then excess baggage rates to intrastate passengers, a surcharge of fifty per cent. of the charges for space in sleeping cars to such passengers, and 20 per cent. increase in intrastate rates on milk, all for the purpose of bringing the intrastate rates to the level of the interstate rates previously fixed by the Commission. The bill was filed under, and by virtue of, the statute repealing the Commerce Court Act and conferring jurisdiction on the District Court. 38 Stat. 219. The application for an interlocutory injunction was heard by a Circuit Judge and two District Judges. Then a final hearing was had, and the court entered a final decree dismissing the complaint from which this appeal has been taken. The Railroad Companies affected by the order were on their petition permitted to intervene, and are here as appellees.

It appears from the record that in the proceeding by the Interstate Commerce Commission to fix interstate commerce rates to comply with the requirements of section 15a of the Transportation Act of 1920, 41 Stat. 488 — a proceeding known as *Ex parte 74,* Increased Rates, 68 I. C. C. 220 — the Commission, after conference with a committee representing all the state commerce commissions and authorities, directed the group of interstate railroads, of which the railroads operating in New York were a part, to raise their freight rates thirty-five per cent., their passenger rates and excess baggage charges twenty per cent., and to add a surcharge of fifty per cent. for passengers on sleeping cars. As soon as the order in *Ex parte 74* was made, the railroads concerned applied to the Public Service Commission of the State of New York for similar increases in intrastate rates. That Commission granted the increase in freight rates, but denied it as to milk rates and passenger fares. The passenger intrastate fares were 3 cents a mile under the order of the President during the war control, but when that should become ineffective, a statute of New York fixing passenger fares on the New York Central Railroad from Albany to Buffalo at two cents a mile would come into force and operation. As soon as the state commission made its ruling, the railroads applied to the Interstate Commerce Commission for an order under section 13 of which proceeding notice was given to the State of New York, the Attorney General and the Public Service Commission, all of whom appeared, for an order directing the railroads to put intrastate passenger fares, excess baggage charges, sleeping car surtaxes and milk rates on the same level with interstate rates. Proof was offered by the railways to show that conditions of operation in state and interstate passenger traffic were alike and there was no showing otherwise. The record in *Ex parte 74* was put in evidence. There was evidence also to show that at Buffalo and other border points the difference between the interstate and intrastate fares would divert business from the interstate lines between New York City and Buffalo to the New York Central lines, and that the same difference would break up interstate journeys to the west into intrastate journeys to Buffalo from New York and an interstate journey beyond, thus reducing interstate travel and discriminating against passengers carried therein. Evidence was adduced to show the injury to interstate business in the transportation of milk from the country to New York City from points outside of the State in competition with intrastate traffic in this necessity of life. No investigation was made into suburban commuter travel and it is excluded by the Commission from the scope of the order which it made. The order was state wide in its effect and required all interstate carriers to bring their intrastate milk rates, their intrastate passenger fares except commuters' rates, excess baggage charges and sleeping car surcharges to a level with interstate fares and rates as ordered in *Ex parte 74*. The Commission introduced a saving clause in its findings by which the New York authorities or any other interested parties were given leave to apply for modification of its order or findings as to any intrastate fares, charges or rates included therein on the ground that the latter were not related to interstate fares, charges or rates in such a way as to contravene the provisions of the Interstate Commerce Act. Under this clause, at least one petition has been filed by a railroad and the railroad excepted from the order.

The District Court dismissed the bill.

This case differs from the *Wisconsin Rate* case just decided, in that it is a direct proceeding to annul or set aside the order of the Interstate Commerce Commission complained of, brought against the United States and the Commission under the statute. *Skinner & Eddy Corporation* v. *United States,* 249 U. S. 557. The *Wisconsin* case was a suit by a railroad against the state authorities to prevent the latter from penalizing the railroad for complying with the order of the Commission. To this suit the United States and the Commission were not parties. The defense of the state authorities was a collateral attack upon the order, to prevail in which, they were obliged to show that the order was void on the face of the findings without regard to the evidence or the absence of it. In the case before us, the complainants are entitled to rely on the absence of any substantial evidence to sustain a material finding as a basis for attacking the order.

The first objection of the appellants is that there was no sufficient evidence of discrimination against persons and localities under section 13, par. 4, section 416 of the Transportation Act of 1920, to justify a state-wide order of the kind here made. We have considered this objection in the *Wisconsin* case on a similar showing on the findings. Here we consider it on the evidence. We reach the same conclusion here and sustain the objection.

The next objection is that the State has a charter contract with the New York Central Railway Company by which the latter is bound not to charge more than two cents a mile for passenger carriage between Albany and Buffalo, and that if the Transportation Act permits the Interstate Commerce Commission by such an order to enable the railroad company to violate its contract, it impairs the obligation of a contract in violation of section 10, Article 1 of the Federal Constitution. That section provides that "no *state* shall . . . pass a law . . . impairing the obligation of contracts" and does not in terms restrict Congress or the United States. But it is said that it deprives New York and her people of property without due process of law. We said in *Addystone Pipe and Steel Company* v. *United States,* 175 U. S. 211, 229, "Anything which directly obstructs and thus regulates commerce which is carried on among the States, whether it is state legislation or private contracts between individuals or corporations should be subject to the power of Congress in the regulation of that commerce." *Louisville & Nashville R. R.* v. *Mottley,* 219 U. S. 467. See also *Scranton* v. *Wheeler,* 179 U. S. 141, 162, 163; *Union Bridge Co.* v. *United States,* 204 U. S. 364, 400.

The main objections to the order are the same as those presented, considered and overruled in the *Wisconsin Rate* case just decided. The evidence in this case shows that if the passenger and other rates here in controversy were to continue in force as ruled by the Public Service Commission of New York, the annual gross revenues of the interstate railroads operating in the State of New York from both interstate and intrastate passenger and milk business would be less by nearly twelve millions of dollars than those revenues if the intrastate fares and rates were on the same level as the interstate rates as fixed by the Interstate Commerce Commission. If the lower level of intrastate fares and rates is to be maintained, it will discriminate against interstate commerce, in that it will require higher fares and rates in the interstate commerce of the State to secure the income for which the Interstate Commerce Commission must attempt to provide by fixing rates under section 15a of the Interstate Commerce Act as amended by section 422 of the Transportation Act of 1920, 41 Stat. 456, 488, in carrying out the declared congressional purpose "to provide the people of the United States with adequate transportation." As we have just held in the *Wisconsin* case, this constitutes "undue, unreasonable and unjust discrimination against interstate, commerce," which is declared to be unlawful and prohibited by section 13, par. 4 of the Interstate Commerce Act as amended by section 416 of the Transportation Act of 1920, 41 Stat. 456, 484, and which the Interstate Commerce Commission is authorized therein to remove by fixing intrastate rates for the purpose. We need not repeat our reasons for our ruling. Nor need we consider and give again the grounds upon which we hold section 13, par. 4 as thus construed to be valid under the Constitution of the United States.

The decree of the District Court dismissing the bill of complaint is

Affirmed.

THE STATE OF TEXAS, APPELLANT, *v.* EASTERN TEXAS RAILROAD COMPANY, ET AL.

THE STATE OF TEXAS, ET AL., APPELLANTS, *v.* THE UNITED STATES, ET AL.

258 U. S. (1922)

Mr. Justice Van Devanter delivered the opinion of the Court.

By § 402 of the Transportation Act of 1920, c. 91, 41 Stat. 456, 477, several new paragraphs were added to § 1 of the Act to Regulate Commerce as theretofore amended. Paragraphs 18, 19 and 20 are copied in the margin.[1] By them Congress has undertaken to regulate the construction and acquisition of new or additional lines of railroad and the extension and abandonment of old lines, and to invest the Interstate Commerce Commission with important administrative powers in that connection. Like the act of which they are amendatory, these paragraphs are ex-

[1] (18) After ninety days after this paragraph takes effect no carrier by railroad subject to this Act shall undertake the extension of its line of railroad, or the construction of a new line of railroad, or shall acquire or operate any line of railroad, or extension thereof, or shall engage in transportation under this Act over or by means of such additional or extended line of railroad, unless and until there shall first have been obtained from the Commission a certificate that the present or future public convenience and necessity require or will require the construction, or operation, or construction and operation, of such additional or extended line of railroad, and no carrier by railroad subject to this Act shall abandon all or any portion of a line of railroad, or the operation thereof, unless and until there shall first have been obtained from the Commission a certificate that the present or future public convenience and necessity permit of such abandonment.

(19) The application for and issuance of any such certificate shall be under such rules and regulations as to hearings and other matters as the Commission may from time to time prescribe, and the provisions of this Act shall apply to all such proceedings. Upon receipt of any application for such certificate the Commission shall cause notice thereof to be given to and a copy filed with the governor of each State in which such additional or extended line of railroad is proposed to be constructed or operated, or all or any portion of a line of railroad, or the operation thereof, is proposed to be abandoned, with the right to be heard as hereinafter provided with respect to the hearing of complaints or the issuance of securities; and said notice shall also be published for three consecutive weeks in some newspaper of general circulation in each county in or through which said line of railroad is constructed or operated.

(20) The Commission shall have power to issue such certificate as prayed for, or to refuse to issue it, or to issue it for a portion or portions of a line of railroad, or extension thereof, described in the application, or for the partial exercise only of such right or privilege, and may attach to the issuance of the certificate such terms and conditions as in its judgment the public convenience and necessity may require. From and after issuance of such certificate, and not before, the carrier by railroad may, without securing approval other than such certificate, comply with the terms and conditions contained in or attached to the issuance of such certificate and proceed with the construction, operation, or abandonment covered thereby. Any construction, operation, or abandonment contrary to the provisions of this paragraph or of paragraph (18) or (19) of this section may be enjoined by any court of competent jurisdiction at the suit of the United States, the Commission, any commission or regulating body of the State or States affected, or any party in interest; and any carrier which, or any director, officer, receiver, operating trustee, lessee, agent, or person.

pressly restricted to carriers engaged in transporting persons or property in interstate and foreign commerce.[2]

Our present concern is with the provisions relating to the abandonment of existing lines. They declare that "no carrier by railroad subject to this act shall abandon all or any portion of a line of railroad, or the operation thereof, unless and until there shall first have been obtained from the Commission a certificate that the present or future public convenience and necessity permit of such abandonment" (par. 18); that when application for such a certificate is received the Commission shall cause notice thereof to be given to the Governor of the State wherein the line lies and published in newpapers of general circulation in each county along the line, and shall accord a hearing to the State and all parties in interest (par. 19); that the Commission may grant or refuse the certificate in whole or in part and impose such terms and conditions as in its judgment the public convenience and necessity require; and that when the certificate is issued, and not before, the carrier may, "without securing approval other than such certificate," comply with the terms and conditions imposed and proceed with the abandonment covered by the certificate (par. 20).

The Eastern Texas Railroad Company, a Texas corporation, owns and operates in that State a line of railroad 30.3 miles in length. Approximately three-fourths of the traffic over the road is in interstate and foreign commerce and the rest is in intrastate commerce. The company neither owns nor operates any other line. The road was constructed in 1902 to serve extensive lumber industries, but in subsequent years the adjacent timber was removed and the mills dismantled. The company claims that since 1917 the road has been operated at a loss.

On June 3, 1920, the company filed with the Commission an application for a certificate authorizing it to abandon and cease operating its road, full notice of the application being regularly given. The State declined to appear before the Commission, but others, who were being served by the road, appeared and

---

acting for or employed by such carrier, who knowingly authorizes, consents to, or permits any violation of the provisions of this paragraph or of paragraph (18) of this section, shall upon conviction thereof be punished by a fine of not more than $5,000 or by imprisonment for not more than three years, or both.

[2] See amended paragraphs (1) and (2) of the Act to Regulate Commerce as set forth in § 400 of the Transportation Act of 1920.

opposed the application. A full hearing was had and, on December 2, 1920, the Commission made and filed a report concluding as follows: "Upon consideration of the record we find that the present public convenience and necessity permit the abandonment of the applicant's line, and we further find that permission to abandon the line should be made subject to the right of interested persons in the community served to purchase the property at a figure not in excess of $50,000. A certificate and order to that effect will be issued." The certificate and order were issued and the railroad company indicated its assent to the condition imposed, but, so far as appears, no one sought to purchase under the condition.

While the application was pending before the Commission and before the certificate was issued, the State brought a suit in one of its courts against the railroad company and some of its officers to enjoin them from ceasing to operate the road in intrastate commerce. The bill was brought on the theory that under the laws of the State the company was obliged to continue the operation of the road in intrastate commerce; that the provisions of the Transportation Act were unconstitutional and void, if and in so far as they authorized the abandonment of such a road as respects intrastate commerce, and that the company in asking the Commission to sanction such an abandonment was proceeding in disregard of its obligations to the State. At the instance of the defendants the suit was removed to the District Court of the United States for the Western District of Texas. During the pendency of the suit the Commission issued the certificate and the defendants then sought the benefit of it by a supplemental answer. The court held that the certificate constituted a complete defense, and without a hearing on other issues dismissed the suit. The State appealed directly to this court. That appeal is No. 298.

After the Commission granted the certificate the State brought a suit in the District Court of the United States for the Eastern District of Texas against the United States, the railroad company and others to set aside and annul the Commission's order and certificate on the grounds, first, that the provisions of the Transportation Act, rightly interpreted, did not afford any basis for granting a certificate sanctioning the abandonment of the company's road as respects intrastate commerce, and, secondly, if those provisions purported to authorize such a certificate, they were to that extent in excess of the power of Congress and an encroachment on the reserved powers of the State. The defendants moved to dismiss the bill as ill founded in point of merits, and the court sustained the motions and entered a decree of dismissal. The State appealed directly to this court. That appeal is No. 563.

Counsel attribute to these cases a breadth which they do not have; and for obvious reasons we shall deal with them as they are, not as they might be.

Up to the time the Commission made the order granting the certificate a part of the commerce passing over the road was interstate and foreign, that is, was bound to or from other States and foreign countries. It is not questioned that Congress could, nor that it did, authorize the Commission to sanction a discontinuance of this interstate and foreign business. Neither is it questioned that the Commission's certificate was adequate for that purpose. The only matters in controversy are whether, by paragraphs 18, 19 and 20, Congress has assumed to clothe the Commission with authority to sanction the entire abandonment of a road such as this, and, if so, whether the power of Congress extends so far.

The road lies entirely within a single State, is owned and operated by a corporation of that State, and is not a part of another line. Its continued operation solely in intrastate commerce cannot be of more than local concern. Interstate and foreign commerce will not be burdened or affected by any shortage in the earnings, nor will any carrier in such commerce have to bear or make good the shortage. It is not as if the road were a branch or extension whose unremunerative operation would or might burden or cripple the main line and thereby affect its utility or service as an artery of interstate and foreign commerce.

If paragraphs 18, 19 and 20 be construed as authorizing the Commission to deal with the abandonment of such a road as to intrastate as well as interstate and foreign commerce, a serious question of their constitutional validity will be unavoidable. If they be given a more restricted construction, their validity will be undoubted. Of such a situation this court has said, "where a statute is susceptible of two constructions, by one of which grave and doubtful constitutional questions arise and by the other of which such questions are avoided, our duty is to adopt the latter." *United States* v. *Delaware & Hudson Company,* 213 U. S. 366, 407–408.

Although found in the Transportation Act, these paragraphs

are amendments of the Interstate Commerce Act and are so styled. They contain some broad language, but do not plainly or certainly show that they are intended to provide for the complete abandonment of a road like the one we have described. Only by putting a liberal interpretation on general terms can they be said to go so far. Being amendments of the Interstate Commerce Act they are to be read in connection with it and with other amendments of it. As a whole these acts show that what is intended is to regulate interstate and foreign commerce and to affect intrastate commerce only as that may be incidental to the effective regulation and protection of commerce of the other class. They contain many manifestations of a continuing purpose to refrain from any regulation of intrastate commerce, save such as is involved in the rightful exertion of the power of Congress over interstate and foreign commerce. *Minnesota Rate Case,* 230 U. S. 352, 418; *Railroad Commission of Wisconsin* v. *Chicago, Burlington & Quincy R. R. Co., ante,* p. 761. And had there been a purpose here to depart from the accustomed path and to deal with intrastate commerce as such independently of any effect on interstate and foreign commerce, it is but reasonable to believe that that purpose would have been very plainly declared. This was not done.

These considerations persuade us that the paragraphs in question should be interpreted and read as not clothing the Commission with any authority over the discontinuance of the purely intrastate business of a road whose situation and ownership, as here, are such that interstate and foreign commerce will not be burdened or affected by a continuance of that business.

Whether, apart from the Commission's certificate, the railroad company is entitled to abandon its intrastate business is not before us, so we have no occasion for considering to what extent the decisions in *Brooks-Scanlon Co.* v. *Railroad Commission of Louisiana,* 251 U. S. 396, and *Bullock* v. *Railroad Commission of Florida,* 254 U. S. 513, may be applicable to this road.

As the District Courts both accorded to the Commission's certificate a wider operation and effect than can be given to it consistently with the provisions of paragraphs 18, 19 and 20 as we interpret them, the decrees must be reversed and the causes remanded for further proceedings in conformity to this opinion.

Decrees reversed.

GREAT NORTHERN RAILROAD COMPANY *v.* MERCHANTS ELEVATOR COMPANY.

259 U. S. (1922)

Mr. Justice Brandeis delivered the opinion of the Court.

This action was brought by the Merchants Elevator Company in a state court of Minnesota against the Great Northern Railway Company and the Director General to recover $80 alleged to have been exacted in violation of the carrier's tariff. That sum had been demanded by the carrier, under Rule 10 of its tariff, as a reconsignment charge, at the rate of $5 a car, for sixteen cars of corn shipped from points in Iowa and Nebraska to Willmar, Minnesota, and after inspection there rebilled to Anoka, a station beyond. The tariff rate from the points of origin via Willmar to Anoka was the same as to Willmar. Willmar had been named as destination in the original bill of lading, only because it is the place at which grain coming into the State by this route is inspected and graded under the laws of Minnesota and of the United States; and the carrier knew, or should have known, that fact. Immediately after inspection disposition orders were given and the original bills of lading were surrendered in exchange for billing to Anoka. Rule 10 read:

" Diversion or reconsignment to points outside switching limits before placement: If a car is diverted, reconsigned or reforwarded on orders placed with the local freight agent or other designated officer after arrival of car at original destination, but before placement for unloading, . . . a charge of $5.00 per car will be made if car is diverted, reconsigned or reforwarded to a point outside of switching limits of original destination."

The shipper contended that the case was within the exception known as Exception (a), as amended by Supplement One, which provided that rules (including Rule 10) shall not apply to:

" (a) Grain, seed (field), seed (grass), hay or straw, carloads, held in cars on track for inspection and disposition orders incident thereto at billed destination or at point intermediate thereto."

Whether the charge was payable depended solely upon a question of construction; that is, whether the body of the rule or the exception to it applied. On this question there was room for reasonable difference of opinion. The carrier, relying particularly upon *Texas & Pacific Co.* v. *American Tie and Timber Co.,*

234 U. S. 138, and *Loomis v. Lehigh Valley R. R. Co.*, 240 U. S. 43, claimed seasonably that until the true construction of the tariff had been determined by the Interstate Commerce Commission, the trial court was without jurisdiction. That court overruled the objection; construed the exception to mean that cars of grain are exempted from Rule 10 if held on track at billed destination for inspection and for "disposition orders" incident to such inspection; held that the disposition order may be an order to make disposition by way of reconsignment to another destination and that forwarding to Anoka was such disposition; and entered judgment for the shippers. That judgment was affirmed by the Supreme Court of the State on the authority of *Reliance Elevator Co.* v. *Chicago, Milwaukee & St. Paul Ry. Co.*, 139 Minn. 69. The case is here on writ of certiorari, 255 U. S. 567. The tariff containing the rule under which the $5 charge was made was the only governing tariff. It had been duly filed with the Interstate Commerce Commission. The validity of the tariff, including the rule and exception, was admitted. And there was no dispute concerning the facts. The question argued before us is not whether the state courts erred in construing or applying the tariff, but whether any court had jurisdiction of the controversy, in view of the fact that the Interstate Commerce Commission had not passed upon the disputed question of construction.

The contention that courts are without jurisdiction of cases involving a disputed question of construction of an interstate tariff, unless there has been a preliminary resort to the Commission for its decision, rests, in the main, upon the following argument: The purpose of the Act to Regulate Commerce is to secure and preserve uniformity. Hence, the carrier is required to file tariffs establishing uniform rates and charges, and is prohibited from exacting or accepting any payment not set forth in the tariff. Uniformity is impossible, if the several courts, state or federal, are permitted, in case of disputed construction, to determine what the rate or charge is which the tariff prescribes. To ensure uniformity the true construction must, in case of dispute, be determined by the Commission.

This argument is unsound. It is true that uniformity is the paramount purpose of the Commerce Act. But it is not true that uniformity in construction of a tariff can be attained only through a preliminary resort to the Commission to settle the construction in dispute. Every question of the construction of a tariff is deemed a question of law; and where the question concerns an interstate tariff it is one of federal law. If the parties properly preserve their rights, a construction given by any court, whether it be federal or state, may ultimately be reviewed by this Court either on writ of error or on writ of certiorari; and thereby uniformity in construction may be secured. Hence, the attainment of uniformity does not require that in every case where the construction of a tariff is in dispute, there shall be a preliminary resort to the Commission.

Whenever a rate, rule or practice is attacked as unreasonable or as unjustly discriminatory, there must be preliminary resort to the Commission. Sometimes this is required because the function being exercised is in its nature administrative in contradistinction to judicial. But ordinarily the determining factor is not the character of the function, but the character of the controverted question and the nature of the enquiry necessary for its solution. To determine what rate, rule or practice shall be deemed reasonable for the future is a legislative or administrative function. To determine whether a shipper has in the past been wronged by the exaction of an unreasonable or discriminatory rate is a judicial function. Preliminary resort to the Commission is required alike in the two classes of cases. It is required because the enquiry is essentially one of fact and of discretion in technical matters; and uniformity can be secured only if its determination is left to the Commission. Moreover, that determination is reached ordinarily upon voluminous and conflicting evidence, for the adequate appreciation of which acquaintance with many intricate facts of transportation is indispensable; and such acquaintance is commonly to be found only in a body of experts. But what construction shall be given to a railroad tariff presents ordinarily a question of law which does not differ in character from those presented when the construction of any other document is in dispute.

When the words of a written instrument are used in their ordinary meaning, their construction presents a question solely of law. But words are used sometimes in a peculiar meaning. Then extrinsic evidence may be necessary to determine the meaning of words appearing in the document. This is true where technical words or phrases not commonly understood are employed. Or extrinsic evidence may be necessary to establish a usage of trade or locality which attaches provisions not expressed in the language of the instrument. Where such a situation arises, and the peculiar meaning of words, or the existence of a usage, is proved by evidence, the function of construction is necessarily preceded by the determination of the matter of fact. Where the controversy over the writing arises in a case which is being tried before a jury, the decision of the question of fact is left to the jury, with instructions from the Court as to how the document shall be construed, if the jury finds that the alleged peculiar meaning or usage is established.[1] But where the document to be construed is a tariff of an interstate carrier, and before it can be construed it is necessary to determine upon evidence the peculiar meaning of words or the existence of incidents alleged to be attached by usage to the transaction, the preliminary determination must be made by the Commission; and not until this determination has been made, can a court take jurisdiction of the controversy. If this were not so, that uniformity which it is the purpose of the Commerce Act to secure could not be attained. For the effect to be given the tariff might depend, not upon construction of the language — a question of law — but upon whether or not a particular judge or jury had found, as a fact, that the words of the document were used in the peculiar sense attributed to them or that a particular usage existed.

It may happen that there is a dispute concerning the meaning of a tariff which does not involve, properly speaking, any question of construction. The dispute may be merely whether words in the tariff were used in their ordinary meaning, or in a peculiar meaning. This was the situation in the *American Tie and Timber Co.* case, *supra.* The legal issue was whether the carrier did or did not have in effect a rate covering oak ties. The only matter really in issue was whether the word "lumber" which was in the tariff, had been used in a peculiar sense. The trial judge charged the jury: "If you believe from the evidence that oak railway cross ties are lumber within the meaning and usage of the lumber and railroad business, then you are charged the defendant had in effect a rate applying on the ties offered for shipment." This question was obviously not one of construction; and there is not to be found in the opinion of this

[1] Goddard *v.* Foster, 17 Wall. 123, 142; Hutchinson *v.* Bowker, 5 M. & W. 535, 542; Tubbs *v.* Mechanics' Insurance Co., 131 Ia. 217; Aetna Indemnity Co. *v.* Waters, 110 Md. 673; A. J. Tower Co. *v.* Southern Pacific Co., 184 Mass. 472. See Ogden *v.* Parsons, 23 How. 167, 170; Fuller *v.* Metropolitan Life Insurance Co., 70 Conn. 647, 677; Thayer, Preliminary Treatise on Evidence, 203–207, 215, 259.

Court, or in the proceedings in either of the lower courts, a suggestion that the case involved any disputed question of construction. The only real question in the case was one of fact; and upon this question of fact "the views of men engaged in the lumber and railroad business as developed in the testimony" were in "irreconcilable conflict," p. 146. As that question, unlike one of construction, could not be settled ultimately by this Court, preliminary resort to the Commission was necessary to ensure uniformity. The situation in *Loomis* v. *Lehigh Valley R. R. supra,* was similar. There the question to be decided did not require the consideration of voluminous conflicting evidence; but it involved the exercise of administrative judgment. The carrier had been requested by a shipper of grain, fruits and vegetables to supply cars for loading. In order to load ordinary box cars to the minimum capacity on which the freight rates are based and to the maximum to which the shipper is entitled, it is necessary that they should be equipped with grain doors or transverse bulkheads, so that they may safely contain the load and enable unloading to be done without waste and inconvenience. Those sent lacked the inside doors and bulkheads. The carrier having refused to furnish these, the shipper was obliged to do so and sought reimbursement. The tariff was silent on the subject. The controverted question was not how the tariff should be construed, but what character of equipment should be deemed reasonable. To determine this enquiry the Court held that preliminary resort to the Commission must be had, because "an adequate consideration of the ... controversy would require acquaintance with many intricate facts of transportation and a consequent appreciation of the practical effect of any attempt to define services covered by a carrier's published tariffs, or character of equipment which it must provide, or allowances which it may make to shippers for instrumentalities supplied and services rendered."

In the case at bar the situation is entirely different from that presented in the *American Tie and Timber Co.* case, or in the *Loomis* case. Here no fact, evidential or ultimate, is in controversy; and there is no occasion for the exercise of administrative discretion. The task to be performed is to determine the meaning of words of the tariff which were used in their ordinary sense and to apply that meaning to the undisputed facts. That operation was solely one of construction; and preliminary resort to the Commission was, therefore, unnecessary. The petition for certiorari was asked for on the ground that the decision of the Supreme Court of Minnesota in this case was in conflict with the above decisions of this Court and also that the decisions in several state courts and in the lower federal courts were in serious conflict on the question involved. In the brief and argument on the merits, it was also asserted that some recent decisions of this Court are in conflict with the rule declared and applied in the *American Tie and Timber Co.* case, *supra,* and the *Loomis* case, *supra.* If in examining the cases referred to[2] there is borne in mind the distinction above discussed between

[2] In the following cases in which the jurisdiction of the court was sustained without preliminary resort to the Commission, the question involved was solely one of construction of a tariff, or otherwise a question of law, and not one of administrative discretion. (1) Louisville & Nashville R. R. Co. *v.* Cook Brewing Co., 223 U. S. 70, 84; Pennsylvania R. R. Co. *v.* International Coal Co., 230 U. S. 184, 196; Pennsylvania R. R. Co. *v.* Puritan Coal Co., 237 U. S. 121, 134; Eastern Ry. Co. *v.* Littlefield, 237 U. S. 140; Illinois Central R. R. Co. *v.* Mulberry Coal Co., 238 U. S. 275; Pennsylvania R. R. Co. *v.* Sonman Coal Co., 242 U. S. 120; Pennsylvania R. R. Co. *v.* Kittanning Iron & Steel Mfg. Co., 253 U. S. 319. See also Swift & Co. *v.* Hocking Valley Ry. Co., 243 U. S. 281; St. Louis, Iron Mountain & Southern Ry. Co. *v.* Hasty, 255 U. S. 252, 256. (2) Hite *v.* Central R. R. of N. J., 171 Fed. 370, 372; Gimble Bros., Inc., *v.* Barrett, 215 Fed. 1004; 218 Fed. 880; 226 Fed. 623; National Elevator Co. *v.* Chicago, M. & St. P. Ry. Co., 246 Fed. 588; J. C. Francesconi & Co. *v.* Baltimore & Ohio R R. Co., 274 Fed. 687, 691. Compare Empire Refineries *v.* Guaranty Trust Co., 271 Fed. 668. (3) Kansas City Southern Ry. Co. *v.* Tonn, 102 Ark. 20, 26; Western & Atlantic R. R. Co. *v.* White Provision Co., 142 Ga. 246; Gustafson *v.* Michigan Central R. R. Co., 296 Ill. 41; Wolverine Brass Works *v.* Southern Pacific Co., 187 Mich. 393, 396; Reliance Elevator Co. *v.* Chicago, M. & St. P. Ry. Co., 139 Minn. 69; St. Louis, San Francisco & Texas Ry. Co. *v.* Röff Oil & Cotton Co., 61 Tex. Civ. App. 190, 192; Southern Pacific Co. *v.* Frye, 82 Wash. 9. Compare Hardaway *v.* Southern Ry. Co., 90 S. C. 475. See *contra* Cheney *v.* Boston & Maine R. R. 227 Mass. 336. Compare Poor *v.* Western Union Tel. Co., 196 Mo. App. 557, 564.

In the following cases where the court refused to take jurisdiction because there had not been preliminary resort to the Commission, the question presented either was one of fact or called for the exercise of administrative discretion. Texas & Pacific Ry. Co. *v.* Abilene Cotton Oil Co., 204 U. S. 426; Baltimore & Ohio R. R. Co. *v.* Pitcairn Coal Co., 215 U. S. 481; Mitchell Coal Co. *v.* Pennsylvania R. R. Co., 230 U. S. 247; Morrisdale Coal Co. *v.* Pennsylvania R. R. Co., 230 U. S. 304; Northern Pacific Ry. Co. *v.* Solum, 247 U. S. 477, 483; Director General *v.* Viscose Co.. 254 U. S. 498. See also United States *v.* Pacific & Arctic Co., 228 U. S. 87.

oontroversies which involve only questions of law and those which involve issues essentially of fact or call for the exercise of administrative discretion, it will be found that the conflict described does not exist and that the decisions referred to are in harmony also with reason.

Affirmed.

Bei Fragen zur Produktsicherheit wenden Sie sich bitte an:
If you have any questions regarding product safety,
please contact:

Walter de Gruyter GmbH
Genthiner Straße 13
10785 Berlin
productsafety@degruyterbrill.com